MW01015209

The Life and Struggles of Our Mother Walatta Petros

The Life and Struggles of Our Mother Walatta Petros

A Seventeenth-Century African Biography of an Ethiopian Woman

TRANSLATED AND EDITED BY
WENDY LAURA BELCHER AND MICHAEL KLEINER

WRITTEN BY GALAWDEWOS

PRINCETON UNIVERSITY PRESS
PRINCETON AND OXFORD

Published by Princeton University Press, 41 William Street, Princeton, New Jersey 08540
In the United Kingdom: Princeton University Press, 6 Oxford Street,
Woodstock, Oxfordshire OX20 1TW

press.princeton.edu
Jacket image reprinted by kind permission of the photographer, Claire Bosc-Tiessé.
Portrait of Walatta Petros from a manuscript at Walatta Petros's monastery
on Lake Tana; MS D, folio 134v; photographed in 1997.

Library of Congress Cataloging-in-Publication Data

Gadla 'Emna Walata Pétros. English
The life and struggles of our mother Walatta Petros : a seventeenth-century African
biography of an Ethiopian woman / written by Gälawdewos ;
translated and edited by Wendy Laura Belcher and Michael Kleiner.
pages cm
English, translated from Ethiopic (Geez).
A "gädl" or hagiography, originally written by Gälawdewos thirty years after the
subject's death, in 1672-1673. Translated from multiple manuscripts and versions.
Includes bibliographical references and index.
ISBN 978-0-691-16421-2 (hardcover : alk. paper) 1. Walata Pétros, Saint, 1592-1642. 2. Walata Pétros,
Saint, 1592-1642—Miracles. 3. Women saints—Biography. 4. Nuns—Ethiopia—Biography.
5. Ya'Ityopya 'ortodoks tawahedo béta kerestiyan—Biography. 6. Monasticism and religious orders
for women—Ethiopia—History—17th century. I. Belcher, Wendy Laura, translator, editor. II. Kleiner,
Michael, 1962- translator, editor. III. Gälawdewos, author. IV. Title.
BR1725.N42G33 2015
281.75092—dc23
2014038410

British Library Cataloging-in-Publication Data is available

This publication is made possible in part from the Barr Ferree Foundation Fund for
Publications, Department of Art and Archaeology, Princeton University. This fund and the US
Fulbright Scholar Program in large part funded this publication, including its images and the
field research on which it is based. Additional vital funding came from the Princeton Center for
African American Studies, Princeton Department of Comparative Literature, Princeton
University Committee on Research in the Humanities and Social Science, Princeton Council of
the Humanities, Princeton Center for the Study of Religion, and Princeton Program in Gender
and Sexuality Studies. The inception of the translation was a grant from the University of
California at Irvine International Center for Writing and Translation.

Parts of the introduction sections "The Text's Seventeenth-Century Historical Context" and "Ḥabäša
Royal Women's Anticolonial Role" were previously published in a much-extended form in Wendy
Laura Belcher, "Sisters Debating the Jesuits: The Role of African Women in Defeating Portuguese
Proto-Colonialism in Seventeenth-Century Abyssinia," *Northeast African Studies* 12 (Spring 2013).

This book has been composed in Linux Libertine O

Printed on acid-free paper. ∞

Printed in Canada

1 3 5 7 9 10 8 6 4 2

CONTENTS

ABBREVIATIONS

Abb. 88	A manuscript in Antoine d'Abbadie's collection in Paris on which the Carlo Conti Rossini print edition is based
acc.	accusative
adj.	adjective
CR	The Carlo Conti Rossini print edition of the *Gädlä Wälättä Ṗeṭros*
CSCO	Corpus Scriptorum Christianorum Orientalium book series
emph.	emphatic
EMIP	Ethiopian Manuscript Imaging Project
EMML	Ethiopian Manuscript Micofilm Library
EC	Ethiopian Calendar
Ethio-SPaRe	Cultural Heritage of Christian Ethiopia: Salvation, Preservation, Research Project
f.	folio (leaf) of manuscript
fem.	feminine
gen.	genitive
HMML	Hill Museum and Manuscript Library
imper.	imperative
ind.	indicative
LatLon	latitude and longitude
lit.	literally (word for word translation)
masc.	masculine
MS	manuscript
MSS	manuscripts
neg.	negative
nom.	nominative
pl.	plural
ps.	person
sg.	singular
subj.	subjunctive
WP	Wälättä Ṗeṭros
WP gädl	Wälättä Ṗeṭros's whole hagiobiography (including miracles and poems)

CHRONOLOGY

Note: Based on the *Gädlä Wälättä Peṭros*, the *Short History of Walatta Petros's Community*, Susənyos's royal chronicle, and the seventeenth-century Jesuits' accounts. Dates in **bold** represent dates confirmed by these other seventeenth-century sources or stated directly in the *Gädlä Wälättä Peṭros*. See "Calendar" in the glossary regarding issues of dating in the Ethiopian calendar.

1557 Jesuits arrive in Ethiopia.

1591 A monk predicts Walatta Petros's parents will have a holy daughter.

1592 Walatta Petros is born.

1601 Əḫətä Krəstos is born no later than this year; probably five to ten years earlier.

1603 Jesuit missionary Pedro Páez arrives.

1606 Walatta Petros's previous husband, if he existed, is killed by King Yaʿqob (r. 1597–1603, 1604–6) by this date.

1607 Susənyos becomes king.

1608 Walatta Petros is sixteen; at approximately this age she marries Mälkəʾa Krəstos.

1609 Mälkəʾa Krəstos accompanies King Susənyos on a military campaign for the first time, according to Susənyos's royal chronicle.

1612 Páez privately converts King Susənyos and his brother, *Ras* Śəʿəlä Krəstos to Catholicism.

1615 Walatta Petros is twenty-three; at approximately this age, after having three children die in infancy, she first tries to leave her husband and take up the religious life.

1617 Əḫətä Krəstos leaves her husband and becomes a nun.

1617 Mälkəʾa Krəstos takes part in the battle against Yolyos, an anti-Catholic rebel, on 11 May, and returns home with the garments of the murdered *Abunä* Səmʿon.

1617 Walatta Petros successfully leaves her husband, meets Əḫətä Krəstos, and becomes a nun at the age of twenty-five.

1621 King Susənyos forbids the teaching of Ethiopian Orthodoxy and publicly professes Roman Catholicism.

1622 Pedro Páez dies.

1622 Walatta Petros is first called up before King Susənyos and his court.

1622 *Ras* Śəʿəlä Krəstos, the king's brother, persecutes Walatta Petros.

1622 Walatta Petros goes to Waldəbba where she receives her holy commission from Christ and begins preaching.

1622 Walatta Petros leaves Waldəbba and goes to Ṣällämt to preach for approximately three years.

1623 Mälkəʾa Krəstos refuses to assist *Ras* Śəʿəlä Krəstos, Walatta Petros's nemesis, and thus angers King Susənyos, according to his chronicle.

1625 Walatta Petros is again called up before the court in May.

1625 Jesuit missionary Afonso Mendes arrives in Ethiopia and Roman Catholicism becomes stricter.

1626 Afonso Mendes is assigned to convert Walatta Petros; he is unsuccessful.

1627 King Susənyos sends Walatta Petros into exile in the hot lowland region of Žäbäy in November and she stays there three years, while gathering her first community.

1630 Walatta Petros starts her second community, at Č̣anqʷa, where they stay until illness breaks out.

1630 Walatta Petros stays about six months at Ṣana Island, when women were still allowed there.

1630 Walatta Petros starts her third community, at Məṣəlle, and stays there two years.

1631 Walatta Petros's menstruation stops; the text says she is thirty-nine.

1632 Mälkəʾa Krəstos supports the anti-Catholic rebel also named Mälkəʾa Krəstos, according to the royal chronicle.

1632 The anti-Catholic rebel Bihono is killed in battle in June and Walatta Petros's husband Mälkəʾa Krəstos is arrested and sentenced to death for supporting the rebels. His sentence is reduced to exile, according to the royal chronicle.

1632 King Susənyos rescinds the edict forcing conversion to Roman Catholicism, and Walatta Petros honors her vow to stay another year at Məṣəlle if he should renounce Roman Catholicism.

1632 King Susənyos dies on 10 Mäskäräm (17 September) and his son Fasilädäs becomes king.

1632 Ǝḫətä Krəstos becomes a leader in Walatta Petros's community.

1632 Walatta Petros starts her fourth community, at Zäge.

1633 Fasilädäs banishes the Jesuits.

1633 Mälkəʾa Krəstos dies on 4 Taḫśaś (10 December) of the second year of Fasilädäs's reign, according to the *Short Chronicles*.

1636 *Abunä* Marqos is installed as patriarch of the Ethiopian Orthodox Täwaḥədo Church. He praises and encourages Walatta Petros, most likely in this year.

1637 Walatta Petros starts her fifth community, at Dämboza.

1638 Walatta Petros starts her sixth community, at Afär Färäs.

1639 Famine occurs in the year of the locusts.

1640 King Fasilädäs is a patron of Walatta Petros's work.

1641 Walatta Petros starts her seventh community, at Zämbol.

1642 Walatta Petros appoints *Abba* Zä-Ḥawaryat abbot in the month of Miyazya (April–May).

1642 Walatta Petros falls ill on 24 Näḥase (27 August) and dies on Sunday, 17 Ḫədar (23 November), in the tenth year of Fasilädäs's reign at the age of fifty, twenty-six years after becoming a nun.

1642 Ǝḫətä Krəstos becomes abbess of the community upon Walatta Petros's death and is abbess for six years while the community is at Afär Färäs.

1643 The *sälamta* and *mälkəʾ* poems in honor of Walatta Petros may have been composed this year, for the anniversary of her death.

1649 *Ǝmmahoy* Ǝḫətä Krəstos dies on 27 Mäggabit (2 April) in the sixteenth year of Fasilädäs's reign, seven years after becoming abbess and thirty-two years after becoming a nun. She is no younger than fifty-two and probably ten years older than that.

1649 *Ǝmmahoy* Amätä Dəngəl (Anǧäto) is appointed the second abbess of the community after Walatta Petros's death.

1649 Walatta Petros's community moves to Qʷäraṣa.

1650 Walatta Petros's community becomes fully established at Qʷäraṣa in the seventeenth year of Fasilädäs's reign, when Fasilädäs grants land to Walatta Petros's monastery.

1672 Gälawdewos writes the *Gädlä Wälättä Peṭros* thirty years after Walatta Petros dies, in the Year of Mercy 7165, the fifth year of the reign of King Yoḥannəs I (1672–73 CE). This autograph manuscript is most likely MS J.

1681 The abbot Abba Zä-Ḫawaryat dies on 30 August in the fourteenth year of the reign of Yoḥannəs I (1680–81) after forty-one years in office as abbot.

1681 *Abba* Zä-Maryam Ǝsat Bä-Afu becomes abbot.

1681 The abbess *Ǝmmahoy* Amätä Dəngəl may have died the same year, on 22 May.

1681 *Ǝmmahoy* Nazrawit is appointed the third abbess after Walatta Petros.

1693 King Yoḥannəs consults the leaders of Qʷäraṣa about the suitability of the new patriarch, according to his royal chronicle.

1700 The abbess of Qʷäraṣa, *Ǝmmahoy* Tälawitä Krəstos, is cited as an important cleric in King Yoḥannəs's royal chronicle.

1713 The *Gädlä Wälättä Peṭros* manuscript Abb. 88, the basis for the Conti Rossini print edition, is copied from November 1713 through February 1714.

1735 The *Short History of Walatta Petros's Community* is written by Ḫaylä Maryam in the fifth year of the reign of King Iyasu II.

1735 The leadership of Qʷäraṣa is Abbot Haykäləyä Mammo, Prior Iyoʾel, Archpriest Mäzmurä Dəngəl, Abbess ʿAynəyä Mammit, and Prioress Haymanotawit, in the fifth year of King Iyasu II.

1769 A series of miracles that Walatta Petros performed in regard to kings Bäkaffa, Iyasu II, Iyoʾas I, and *Ras* Mikaʾel Səḥul (reigned consecutively 1721–67) is written down.

1790s King Täklä Giyorgis banishes his father-in-law, *Däǧǧazmač* Wäldä Gäbrəʾel, who went to Qʷäraṣa for ten months in the late 1790s hoping for the saint's protection, according to his royal chronicle.

1813 The leadership of Qʷäraṣa includes Gäbrä Amlak, who is appointed abbot on 10 October 1813.

1845 Dr. Constantin von Tischendorf, the biblical scholar, donates a copy of the *Gädlä Wälättä Peṭros* to a library in Germany (MS A).

1848 Antoine d'Abbadie donates a copy of the *Gädlä Wälättä Peṭros* (MS Abb. 88) to a library in France, later used by Carlo Conti Rossini for the first print edition.

1870 A series of miracles that Walatta Petros performed in regard to kings Yoḥannəs II and Täklä Giyorgis I (reigned consecutively 1769–1800) and Tewodros (r. 1855–68) is written down.

1912 The *Gädlä Wälättä Ṗeṭros* is published in print for the first time, by Carlo Conti Rossini.

1970 The *Gädlä Wälättä Ṗeṭros* is translated into Italian by Lanfranco Ricci.

2004 The *Gädlä Wälättä Ṗeṭros* is translated into Amharic by Mälʾakä Gännät Mənasse Zälläqä.

2015 The *Gädlä Wälättä Ṗeṭros* is translated into English by Kleiner and Belcher.

PREFACE

Wendy Laura Belcher

When I was four years old, my American family moved from rainy Seattle, Washington, to the highland city of Gondär, Ethiopia, so that my physician father could teach at a small medical college there. It was the late 1960s, and over the next three years, I learned many facts about this African country that are essential to understanding the book you hold in your hands.

On drives we would admire the round thatched churches of the green Ethiopian countryside (fig. 1). Later, we visited a stone cathedral carved three stories down into the ground (fig. 2). Thus, I learned that the Ḥabäša peoples of highland Ethiopia were Christians and had been Christians for approximately seventeen hundred years. Their devotion was such that many joined monasteries, and more than two hundred Ḥabäša monks and nuns had been elevated to sainthood in the Ethiopian Orthodox Täwaḥədo Church.

When the college gatekeeper in Gondär patiently taught me how to write hundreds of characters that looked nothing like the Latin or Roman alphabet I was studying in school, I learned that the Ḥabäša had been writing in the ancient African script and language of Gəʿəz for longer than they had been Christians. The Ḥabäša used this language for many centuries to conduct worship in their church services and to write original texts of theology, poetry, biography, and history.

Hiking one day from our home in Gondär up the steep mountainside to the ruins of a stone castle, I arrived to see men bent over their laps writing with cane pens on parchment (fig. 3). I learned that these monks were scribes who lived in one of Ethiopia's thousand monasteries, at the eighteenth-century castle of Queen Məntəwwab's at Qʷəsqʷam. Ethiopian monastic scriptoriums such as theirs had been producing bound manuscripts since at least the sixth century, many with lavish illuminations (figs. 4, 5, and 6). These scribes were ensuring that their monastic library was rich in the most important texts, whether translations from other languages or original compositions in Gəʿəz. A huge part of their work involved copying important manuscripts from other monasteries, preserving them without printing presses or cameras.

In other words, I learned at an early age that Ethiopian Christianity, its Gəʿəz language, its devout scribes, and its many books had nothing to do with Europe. The book you hold in your hands will make sense if you, too, remember all this.

It was with these memories of Ethiopian monks, monasteries, and manuscripts that thirty years later I began my dissertation at the University of California at Los Angeles. It was focused on the eighteenth-century British author Samuel Johnson and argued that his experience of translating one of the Jesuits' accounts of Ethio-

Figure 1. Church of the monastery called Azwa Maryam Gädam on Lake Ṭana. Photo by Wendy Laura Belcher, January 2011.

Figure 2. A thirteenth-century church named Betä Giyorgis, carved down into the bedrock at Lalibäla, Ethiopia. Photo by Donald W. Belcher, 1968.

Figure 3. *Qäsis* Fänte writing a parchment manuscript on his knee at home in the town of Gälawdewos, Ethiopia, near Baḥər Dar (July 2009). Reprinted by kind permission of the photographer, Sean Michael Winslow.

pia had had a profound effect on his writing. The Portuguese priest Jerónimo Lobo had written the account in the 1650s, two decades after the failure of the Jesuits' peculiar mission to convert the Ḥabäša from African Christianity to Roman Catholic Christianity. What struck me as I was conducting research about this ill-fated mission is that the Jesuits repeatedly attributed their failure, one of the few failures

Figure 4. Monk's huts at Q^{w}əsq^{w}am monastery outside Gondär. Photo by Wendy Laura Belcher, June 2011.

Figure 5. A monk's cell today at the theological school attached to the Däbrä Bərhan Śəllase church in Gondär. Photo by Wendy Laura Belcher, December 2010.

the Jesuits ever experienced, to the Ḥabäša noblewomen. Although many men of the court converted, their mothers, wives, and daughters mostly did not. Eventually, disheartened by these domestic desertions, the king abandoned Roman Catholicism and reinstated the Täwaḥədo Church. When I first read of this early African-European encounter, I thought that the Jesuits blaming their failure on women was simple misogyny, but the more I read, the more I began to wonder if

Figure 6. An example of a Gəʿəz manuscript page, with an illumination of the Virgin Mary and her son Christ, from an eighteenth-century prayer book made in the Ethiopian royal scriptorium. The Gəʿəz text on the page says "All of creation rejoices together with her [the Virgin Mary], exclaiming and saying: 'Rejoice, O you full of grace, rejoice because you have found favor! Rejoice, God is with you! We proclaim blessed your glory, O revered one.'" Vellum, tempera, and leather binding; h. 32.0 cm., w. 22.0, d. 6.0 cm. (12 5/8 × 8 11/16 × 2 3/8 in.). Reproduced by kind permission of the Princeton Museum of Art, Gift of Frank Jewett Mather Jr., y1951-28.

they had only been stating a plain fact. Could it be that a European incursion in Africa failed due to African women armed with nothing more than words?

Then, in 2005, I met the young Ethiopian scholar of Gəʿəz *Qäsis* (reverend) Melaku Terefe. This happened when Elias Wondimu, the founder of the important Ethiopian diasporic press Tsehai Publishers, arranged for five Täwaḥədo Church priests to make a historic visit to see the outstanding collection of Gəʿəz materials in the UCLA Young Research Library (Belcher 2005). Upon asking *Qäsis* Melaku how I might find out more about these women who had refused to convert, he recommended that I read the saints' lives (also called hagiographies or hagiobiographies) written by seventeenth-century Ḥabäša authors about the Ḥabäša female saints from this period, who had been elevated to sainthood in the Täwaḥədo Church for this very reason: for refusing to convert to the "filthy faith of the foreigners."

I was thrilled to discover that early European texts about an encounter with Africans could be matched with early African texts about that same encounter. At first I could find virtually nothing about these texts, but in 2006, the scholar Selamawit Mecca of Addis Ababa University (fig. 7) made a significant contribution to Ethiopian studies by publishing the first scholarly work on Ḥabäša female saints' hagiobiographies. From her research, I found out that none of these women's hagiobiographies had been translated into English, and only one had been translated into any European language. That one was the *Gädlä Wälättä Ṗeṭros* (Life-Struggles of Walatta Petros), which had been translated into Italian. I then read the French scholar Claire Bosc-Tiessé's (2003) wonderful article about Walatta Petros, which addressed the illustrations in a royal manuscript of the *Gädlä Wälättä Ṗeṭros* (fig. 8). Now I really wanted to read the book! Unfortunately, I did not read Italian, so I asked *Qäsis* Melaku, who came from a distinguished line of Ethiopian scholars of Gəʿəz, to assist me in learning more about the text. Thus began sessions in which he held the Gəʿəz text in one hand while gesturing with the other as he translated and interpreted introductory passages aloud to me in English.

It quickly became clear to me that this amazing text demanded a wider audience. It was about so much more than Europeans in Ethiopia. It was an extraordinary true story about early modern African women's lives, leadership, and passions—two hundred pages of vivid dialogue, heartbreak, and triumph. And it seemed pretty clear, the more research I did, that it was the first true biography of an African woman.

Although *Qäsis* Melaku had full-time preaching and pastoring responsibilities at Virgin Mary Täwaḥədo Church in Los Angeles, and had begun cataloging for Stephen Delamarter's Ethiopian Manuscript Imaging Project (EMIP), we decided to embark on an English translation of the *Gädlä Wälättä Ṗeṭros.* We applied for a grant from Ngũgĩ wa Thiong'o's University of California at Irvine International Center for Writing and Translation (ICWT), and were grateful to receive $5,000 in 2007. We were able to get a little way into the translation, but, unfortunately, it was impossible for *Qäsis* Melaku to continue, given his commitments to the immigrant Ethiopians at his church. Likewise, I was finishing my dissertation and did not have much time to devote to the project either.

Upon completing my dissertation, I was fortunate to receive a position at Princeton University as an assistant professor. At Princeton, I was able to use the ICWT grant and my research fund to hire a fellow alumna of Mount Holyoke College, Julia Gabrick, to make a rough English translation of the Italian translation of the *Gädlä Wälättä Ṗeṭros* so that I could get a better sense of what was in the origi-

Figure 7. Selamawit Mecca (*left*) reading from a Gəʿəz psalter to Wendy Laura Belcher (*right*) at Institute of Ethiopian Studies Library, Addis Ababa University (November 2012).

Figure 8. Claire Bosc-Tiessé at the Däbrä Ṣəyon Church in the Gärʿalta District of Təgray Province examining a fifteenth-century liturgical fan in parchment (technically, a leporello) (31 December 2008). Photo by Philippe Sidot.

nal and write more deeply about it. Reading that rough translation, I learned more about this exceptional female leader and her lifelong female companion, and a certain line in her hagiobiography began to haunt me: "Word of her deeds has spread throughout the world and has been proclaimed from one end to the other." How could word about the deeds of this amazing woman spread if I did not get this text translated into English?

I was on tenure-track, working on my book about Samuel Johnson, but I decided that I needed to learn Gəˁəz so that I could translate the *Gädlä Wälättä Ṗeṭros* myself. I arranged for Princeton to offer its first course in Gəˁəz, taught by Loren Stuckenbruck, professor of the New Testament and Enoch literature at Princeton Theological Seminary at the time. I learned a great deal in the class, but it quickly became apparent that my aim was hubristic: one needed much more time to learn enough Gəˁəz to translate whole books in the language. Once again I began thinking about finding a collaborator to work with me on translating the book.

Unfortunately, only a handful of people in the world have the expertise to translate Gəˁəz into English, especially a book-length work. The first two people I contacted did not have the time to embark on what would turn out to be a five-year project. One was the world's foremost translator of Gəˁəz into English, Getatchew Haile, the MacArthur award–winning authority on Gəˁəz language and literature and Regents Professor Emeritus of Medieval Studies at Saint John's University (fig. 9). The other was Denis Nosnitsin of Hamburg University, a specialist in Gəˁəz literature and hagiobiography, as well as the principal investigator for the Ethio-SPaRe (Cultural Heritage of Christian Ethiopia: Salvation, Preservation, Research) project (fig. 10).

However, Denis then recommended that I ask Dr. Michael Kleiner, who had excellent knowledge of Gəˁəz and English (as well as many other languages) and a doctorate in Ethiopian studies from the University of Hamburg, one of the three leading centers of Ethiopian studies outside of Ethiopia (fig. 11). His scholarly focus was on sixteenth- and seventeenth-century Ethiopia, the precise period of the *Gädlä Wälättä Ṗeṭros.* Among other things, he had produced an edition of the Gəˁəz text *Mäṣḥafä fäws mänfäsawi* (Book of Spiritual Medicine), translated the Gəˁəz episodes transmitted about the Coptic saint Daniel of Scetis (Kleiner 2008), and written many entries for the magisterial *Encyclopaedia Aethiopica.* This was a very fortuitous recommendation.

Michael and I first met in November 2009 at the International Ethiopian Studies Conference in Addis Ababa, having our initial conversation across the aisle in a jouncing bus full of academics traveling from the conference site into town as evening fell. After hammering out the details of our collaboration over the next couple of months, we began working in January 2010, with significant funding from Princeton University.

Our process was as follows. Michael and I started our translation using a print Gəˁəz edition of the *Gädlä Wälättä Ṗeṭros* made by one of the most prominent Ethiopianists of the twentieth century, the Italian scholar Carlo Conti Rossini, from a single parchment manuscript in the Bibliothèque nationale de France in Paris. Mi-

Figure 9. The scholar of Gəʿəz literature Getatchew Haile reading a fifteenth-century Ethiopic Gospel at the J. Paul Getty Museum in Los Angeles (March 2014). Gospel Book, about 1480–1520. Tempera on parchment bound between wood boards. Ms. 105. Los Angeles, J. Paul Getty Museum. Photo by Annelisa Stephan.

Figure 10. Denis Nosnitsin conducting manuscript research in churches in Təgray. Photo by Wendy Laura Belcher, December 2010.

Figure 11. Michael Kleiner in his study at work on Gəʿəz manuscripts (August 2014). Photo by Stanislau Paulau.

chael would regularly send me five to ten pages of translation, which I would then edit with an eye for clarity and smooth English. We would then meet on Skype to go through the translation word by word, doing as much as we could to make it faithful to the Gəʿəz but felicitous. I also wanted to ensure that we did everything we could to avoid orientalist or antifeminist bias, which I perceived as a problem of previous work in Ethiopian studies. Meanwhile, I worked on framing an introduction and writing the cultural, biographical, religious, and geographical notes, which we added to a massive glossary and Michael's extensive philological notes.

As we proceeded, however, we became concerned about the quality of the print edition. We knew that there were other manuscript copies of the *Gädlä Wälättä Ṗeṭros* out there, knowledge based on the never-surpassed catalog of Ḥabäša saints' lives compiled by Kinefe-Rigb Zelleke (1975). To produce the best translation, we decided that we would need to have as many manuscripts of the *Gädlä Wälättä Ṗeṭros* as we could find in order to reconstruct the most authentic version possible.

Fortunately, I then received the Fulbright US Scholar Award to spend a year in Ethiopia, in part to search for manuscripts. I had met Selamawit Mecca, the primary scholar of Ethiopian female saints, at the same 2009 conference, so we decided to team up and spend part of the year looking for female saint hagiobiographies in Ethiopia's monasteries. Perhaps only a quarter of the manuscripts in Ethiopian monastic libraries have been cataloged in European publications, much less digitized, so fieldwork was needed. Selamawit and I decided that the best place to find good-quality parchment manuscripts of Walatta Petros's hagiobiography would be at the monastery devoted to her. Since it had been founded in her time, it was likely to have the earliest copies, and thus those closest to the original.

Figure 12. Kəbran Island on Lake Ṭana (from Ənṭonəs Island), which has several dozen monasteries, many on small islands like this. Photo by Wendy Laura Belcher, January 2011.

Reaching her monastery meant traveling by plane from the capital Addis Ababa to the beautiful city of Baḥər Dar on Lake Ṭana, which has more than forty historical monasteries, many located on tiny islands (fig. 12). We then took an early-morning two-hour boat ride to Qʷäraṭa (called Qʷäraṣa in the hagiobiography), on the lower east side of Lake Ṭana, where Walatta Petros's monastery has been located since 1649. (One must leave in the early morning, when there is no wind, because strong winds that can swamp a small boat strike up in the afternoon.) We arrived at a quiet and sunny hamlet, and hiked up a short hill to the monastery. The monastic leaders welcomed us: the abbess *Əmmahoy* Ağabuš, the prioress Wälättä Bərhan, and the abbot *Mämhər* Kidanä Maryam Śahlu (figs. 13 and 14). On approaching Walatta Petros's church, we found that the building was in quite poor condition, nothing like the lavish churches at other places on Lake Ṭana (figs. 15 and 16). Nevertheless, her monastery was in possession of some of the lake's greatest riches.

For Walatta Petros's monastery at Qʷäraṭa had not just one *Gädlä Wälättä Ṗeṭros* but three. One of these, which we later labeled MS J, was previously unrecorded, definitively written before 1682, and quite possibly the original manuscript written by Gälawdewos. Another, which we labeled MS I, was also invaluable, since it included a number of never-before-recorded miracles regarding eighteenth- and nineteenth-century Ethiopian kings. Both manuscripts included a precious original document found nowhere else, which we call the *Short History of Walatta Petros's Community*. We were able to digitize these three manuscripts at Qʷäraṭa with a

Figure 13. The women leaders of Walatta Petros's Monastery at Qʷäraṣa, the nuns *Ǝmmähoy* Ağabuš (*left*) and Wälättä Bərhan (*right*). Photo by Wendy Laura Belcher, January 2011.

Canon Powershot camera. The manuscripts enabled us not only to make a better translation into English but also to produce a much more accurate history of the events of Walatta Petros's life and monastery.

We spent two days working at Qʷäraṭa and then went to visit Walatta Petros's grave at nearby Rema Island's monastery (fig. 17). There we met two nuns living in very simple circumstances, perhaps much like Walatta Petros did (fig. 18).

The process of translating the text was very collaborative. A story of one instance illustrates this point. When Michael and I were still translating from the Conti Rossini print edition alone, we came across a perplexing anecdote about a number of community members dying because some nuns had pushed each other around. One word in the passage was a bit off, something that the previous translator and editor had not noticed, but it led Michael to suspect that Conti Rossini's manuscript had been miscopied, perhaps deliberately, in order to censor the original, or merely by accident. In a terrific intuitive leap based on the phrase's philology, Michael speculated that the nuns were not fighting but flirting with each other. We planned to check our newly digitized manuscripts later to see if the word in the other copies matched Conti Rossini's, but in the meantime, I decided to ask various experts what they thought of the passage while I was in Ethiopia.

Before we got started, however, Selamawit warned me that if I told traditional Ethiopian scholars what I thought the anecdote actually said, they would just politely agree with me, telling me what I wanted to hear. Or, given the sensitivity of

Figure 14. The abbot *Mämhər* Kidanä Maryam Śahlu of Walatta Petros's monastery at Qʷäraṣa reading her hagiobiography. Photo by Wendy Laura Belcher, January 2011.

Figure 15. The outer circle of the Lake Ṭana church Ura Kidanä Məḥrät. Photo by Wendy Laura Belcher, January 2011.

Figure 16. The entrance to Walatta Petros's monastery at Qʷäraṣa. Photo by Wendy Laura Belcher, January 2011.

the issue of same-sex desire in Ethiopia, my mere presence as an American might skew the answer. I was grateful for her impeccable field methodology. So she and I parted and asked Ethiopian scholars about the passage without hinting at our own thoughts. We separately showed the Conti Rossini print edition passage to several older Ethiopian male scholars. They all said that the two nuns were not pushing each other around but following each other in a game, being frivolous. Sound philological principles backed their understanding of the passage, but playing tag hardly seemed to warrant a deadly disease. Selamawit recommended we approach a different type of scholar, a young former monk for whom she had tremendous respect. Ḫaylä Ṣəyon had grown up in the Täwaḥədo Church but had left it, so he had the scholarly background necessary to read the anecdote with skill but also the distance to read it openly.

Ḫaylä Ṣəyon took one look at the anecdote and immediately said that it was about same-sex desire. Additionally, he interpreted differently than we had Walatta Petros's statement that "my heart caught fire" when she looked at the lustful nuns. He saw it as an example of a line that can be understood in two ways: on the surface, the phrase said that Walatta Petros was angry at the nuns' sin, but on a deeper, hidden level, it said that she felt desire when looking at the nuns. When Selamawit and I then consulted the manuscripts we had digitized, we found that, indeed, the uncensored manuscripts stated clearly what Michael had suspected. Correcting just one character (Conti Rossini's manuscript had mistakenly or censoriously changed a ዓ into a ሐ), the garbled line could now be properly translated: Walatta Petros saw "some young nuns pressing against each other and being lustful with each other, each with a female companion." In this case, Michael's finely tuned

Figure 17. The grave at Rema Island Monastery where Walatta Petros is buried. Photo by Wendy Laura Belcher, January 2011.

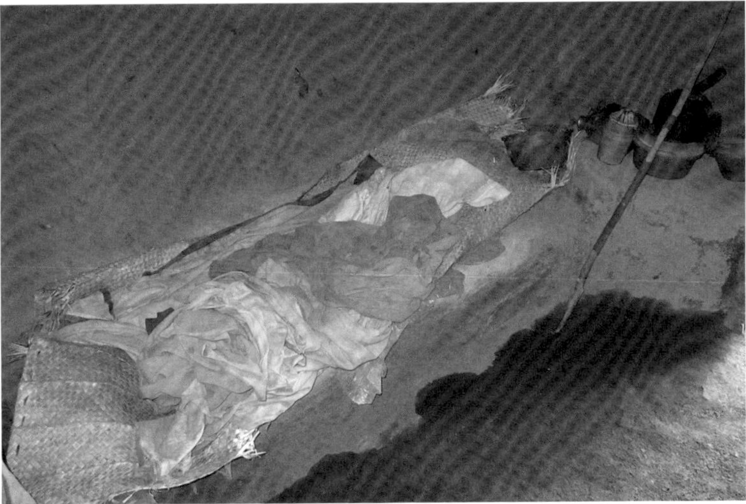

Figure 18. Nun's bed at Rema Monastery. Photo by Wendy Laura Belcher, January 2011.

philological instincts, Selamawit Mecca's rigorous research methods, and Ḫaylä Ṣəyon's interpretative gifts yielded a real discovery. This is the earliest anecdote we know of in which African women express desire for other women.

I hope that this preface illustrates how collaborative the process of translating Walatta Petros's hagiobiography has been. It required the dozens of people named in the acknowledgments but also the Ḥabäša monks and nuns who wrote the text almost 350 years ago, those who copied it and preserved it until today, and my parents, who took our family to Gondär all those years ago and inspired my lifelong interest in African literature. Ethiopians, Americans, and Europeans have all worked together to realize the author's prophecy of spreading the story of the extraordinary Walatta Petros around the world.

ACKNOWLEDGMENTS

Although many aided us in our work, we are solely responsible for all aspects of this volume, including any errors and interpretations. The people mentioned in this volume should not be assumed to accept or agree with any of its findings or interpretations.

We owe our first thanks to *Qäsis* Melaku Terefe, Selamawit Mecca, and Julia Gabrick, without whom this volume would never have seen the light of day, as the preface makes clear. We also owe special thanks to Denis Nosnitsin of Hamburg University, who not only suggested Michael Kleiner as a translator but encouraged us throughout this translation process and answered hundreds of questions in person, by e-mail, and, for a few short days, in the monasteries of Təgray. He also provided access to relevant manuscripts through his project Ethio-SPaRe. We owe similar thanks to Dr. Getatchew Haile, who also answered dozens of e-mails about translating the text into English and access to manuscripts through his leadership of the Ethiopian Manuscript Microfilm Library (EMML) at HMML, Saint John's University.

We are deeply grateful to a scholar of Gəʿəz language and literature who spent a week with us answering philological and cultural questions; to Alessandro Bausi, professor of Ethiopian studies at the University of Hamburg, whose scholarship and advice has been invaluable; and to a lecturer at Addis Ababa University, who also answered questions in person and by e-mail.

For assistance in collecting manuscripts, we are especially thankful to the members of Walatta Petros's monastery at Qʷärața, including the two nuns *Əmmahoy* Ağabuš and Wälättä Bərhan and the abbot *Mämhər* Kidanä Maryam Śahlu. Others have played an important role in the collection process, including Stephen Delamarter of George Fox University and founder of the Ethiopian Manuscript Imaging Project (EMIP), who provided us with digital copies of several of the *Gädlä Wälättä Peṭros* manuscripts, prepared our digital images of manuscripts into files to be held at HMML, and digitized slides of the images in MS D, taken by Claire Bosc-Tiessé in 1997. Loren Stuckenbruck, professor of the New Testament and Enoch literature (now at Ludwig Maximilian University, Munich, Germany), assisted in the field in locating manuscripts and answered questions by e-mail. Many members of the US Embassy in Ethiopia were essential to our work in Ethiopia, including Yohannes Birhanu, Eyerusalem M. Mandefro, Semira J. Alhadi, Alyson L. Grunder, and Jason R. Martin.

For assistance regarding medical situations in the book, we thank my father, Donald W. Belcher; for assistance regarding Latin, we thank Janet Downie and Jessica Wright; for making the maps, we thank Princeton map librarian Tsering Wangyal Shawa; and for assistance in interpreting parts of the text, we thank many members of the Princeton community, including Gayle Salamon, Michael Wood, Judith Weisenfeld, Brian Herrera, Tey Meadow, and Eric Glover. For answering other questions, we thank Elias Wondimu of Tsehai Publishers; the historians Andrew J. Carlson of Capital University, James McCann of Boston University, Samantha Kelly of Rutgers University; the linguist Stefan Weninger at Marburg University, Germany; the art historian Marilyn Heldman; and the Ethiopianist Evgenia Sokolinskaia of the *Encyclopedia Aethiopica*, as well as Nardos Fissha. The poets Derek Gideon and Kristin Fogdall helped by beautifully translating the poems, with assistance from Michael Kleiner. The staff at Princeton University Press was terrific, from the acquisitions editor Alison MacKeen, who immediately expressed her delight at the prospect of publishing something so "extraordinary"; and Press board member Joshua Katz, who urged us to keep going with further projects and translate "all of them"; to expert staff members executive editor Anne Savarese, senior production editor Sara Lerner, copyeditor extraordinaire Cathy Slovensky, indexer Maria DenBoer, illustration manager Dimitri Karetnikov, senior designer Lorraine Doneker, editorial associate Juliana K. Fidler, publicists Colleen Boyle and Katie Lewis, and compositor Lori Holland of Bytheway Publishing Services, who shepherded to publication this volume of immense complexity with skill, dedication, and endless reserves of patience.

Belcher would like to thank her writing group for ten years of encouragement on this project: Mary Bucci Bush, Ellen Krout-Hasegawa, Kathleen McHugh, Harryette Mullen, and Alice Wexler.

We are grateful to the US Fulbright Scholar Program for Belcher's year in Ethiopia. For three years of substantial funding, we thank Eddie Glaude of the Princeton Center for African American Studies, Leonard Barkan of the Princeton Department of Comparative Literature, and David Dobkin, Princeton Dean of Faculty, as well as the Princeton University Committee on Research in the Humanities and Social Science. For additional funding to complete the project, we thank Carole Rigolot, director of the Princeton Council of the Humanities; Robert Wuthnow, director of the Princeton Center for the Study of Religion; and Jill Dolan, director of the Program in Gender and Sexuality Studies. The inception of the translation was a grant from Ngũgĩ wa Thiong'o's University of California at Irvine International Center for Writing and Translation.

The Life and Struggles of Our Mother Walatta Petros

Map 1. Seventeenth-century regions in highland Ethiopia that Walatta Petros visited. Map by Tsering Wangyal Shawa.

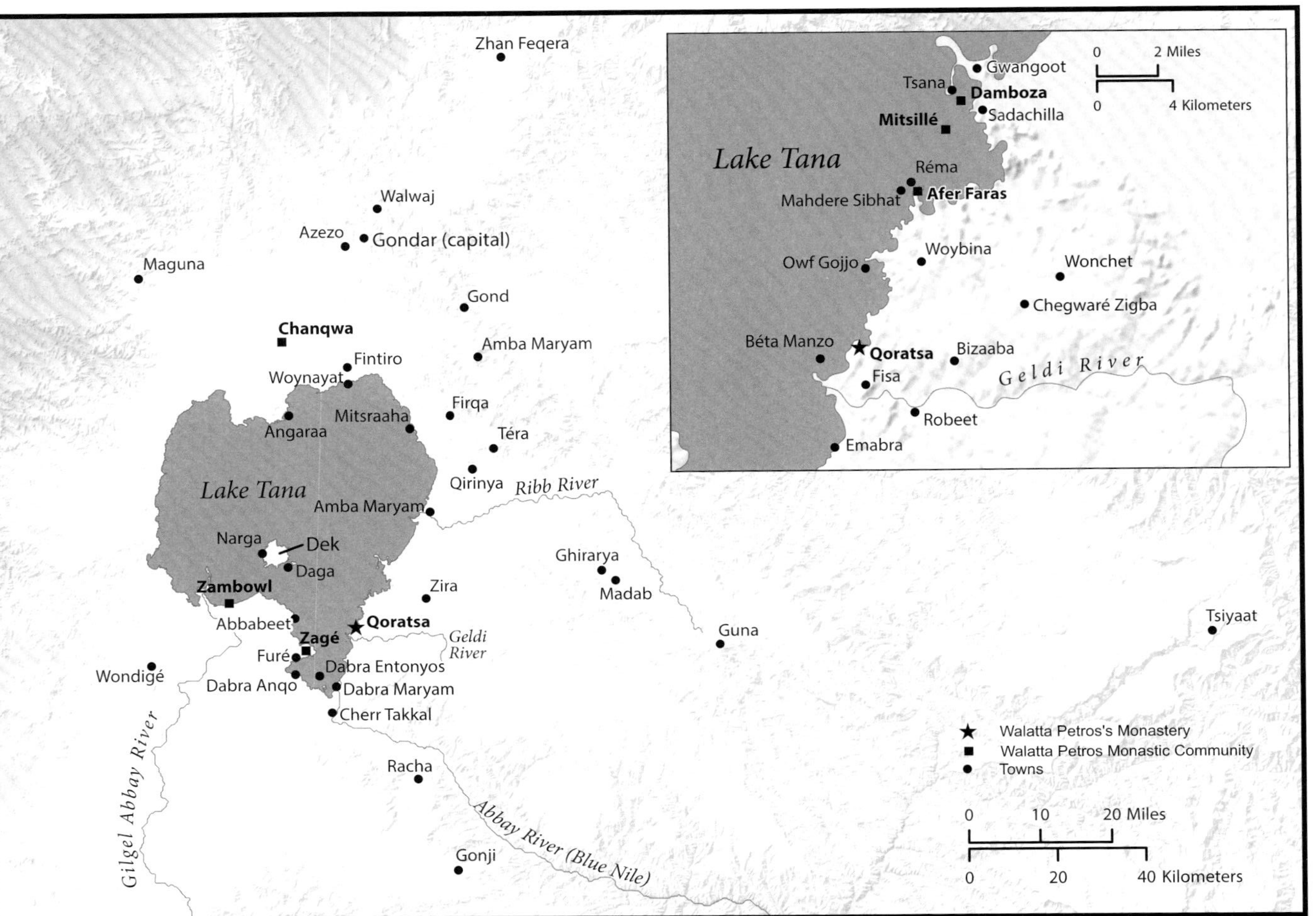

Map 2. Seventeenth-century towns in highland Ethiopia that Walatta Petros visited. Map by Tsering Wangyal Shawa.

Introduction to the Text

Wendy Laura Belcher

This volume introduces and translates the earliest known book-length biography about the life of an African woman: the *Gädlä Wälättä Ṗeṭros*. It was written in 1672 in an African language by Africans for Africans about Africans—in particular, about a revered African religious leader who led a successful nonviolent movement against European protocolonialism in Ethiopia. This is the first time this remarkable text has appeared in English.

When the Jesuits tried to convert the Ḥabäša peoples of highland Ethiopia from their ancient form of Christianity to Roman Catholicism,[1] the seventeenth-century Ḥabäša woman Walatta Petros was among those who fought to retain African Christian beliefs, for which she was elevated to sainthood in the Ethiopian Orthodox Täwaḥədo Church. Thirty years after her death, her Ḥabäša disciples (many of whom were women) wrote a vivid and lively book in Gəʿəz (a classical African language) praising her as an adored daughter, the loving friend of women, a devoted reader, an itinerant preacher, and a radical leader. Walatta Petros must be considered one of the earliest activists against European protocolonialism and the subject of one of the earliest African biographies.

The original text is in a distinctive genre called a *gädl*, which is used to tell the inspirational story of a saint's life, often called a hagiography or hagiobiography (de Porcellet and Garay 2001, 19). This genre represents a vital archive of African literature that has gone almost entirely unexplored, even though it contains fascinating narratives about folk heroes and is a rich repository of indigenous thought. More than two hundred Ethiopian saints have a gädl, including at least six women. One of them was Walatta Petros, a noblewoman who lived from 1592 to 1642, and whose composite name means Spiritual Daughter of Saint Peter (and should never be shortened to Petros). The ገድለ፡ወለተ፡ጴጥሮስ (*Gädlä Wälättä Ṗeṭros* [*Life-Struggles of Walatta Petros*]) is the extraordinary story of her life and her fierce determination to do what was right. Despite the importance of these hagiobiographies, only four other Ethiopian saints have had their gädl translated into English (Anonymous 1898; Täklä Ṣəyon 1906; Täwäldä Mädḫən 2006). The Gəʿəz scholar and translator Getatchew Haile recently translated one of the most important: the *Gädlä Ǝsṭifanos*. The three other translations, done more than one hundred years ago by Sir E. A. Wallis Budge, are available only to the wealthy, as there are no electronic versions

[1] For an explanation of the term *Ḥabäša*, see Müller (2005). For an explanation of the choice to use it sometimes rather than "Ethiopians," see Belcher (2012).

on the Internet: they exist only in art books that cost thousands of dollars each. Two of these four translations are short, and all of them are about men. Furthermore, there has been only one translation into English of the life of any black female saint (whether African or of African descent), the as yet unpublished but carefully researched work on Teresa Chicaba (Houchins and Fra-Molinero 2009), and that was written by Europeans, not Africans. Our translation represents the first accessible translation into English of an early modern African woman's life. And it is one of only a handful of authentic African accounts of early modern African thought.

Our aim in translating has been to produce a rigorous scholarly publication with a wide-ranging introduction; rich substantive notes; a comprehensive glossary of people, places, and concepts; and vivid illustrations from the original manuscripts. Since both literary scholars and historians will use the text, our translation does not take liberties with the text (variations from the original are noted). At the same time, we have translated with a careful eye for the needs of undergraduates and scholars who have no knowledge of Ethiopia or Gəʿəz (see Kleiner's "Introduction to the Translation of the Text" for information on all aspects of the translation). In this way, we hope to bring the *Gädlä Wälättä Ṗeṭros* into the global conversation, aiding its usefulness to religious, historical, literary, gender, and African studies. We believe that the publication of this translation should electrify medieval and early modern studies and meet the demand for early African-authored texts. Not only is the *Gädlä Wälättä Ṗeṭros* the earliest known biography of an African woman, and an early account of resistance to European protocolonialism from an African perspective, it also features a rare look at African women's domestic lives and relationships with other women.

An Exemplary Woman, Not an Exception

Walatta Petros might seem to be unique. She was, after all, a literate seventeenth-century African noblewoman. She was an important leader, directing a successful movement against Europeans and overcoming local male leadership. Her Ethiopian disciples wrote a book about her. Yet closer examination reveals that Walatta Petros is not unique but rather an exemplary case.

Many are surprised to hear that Africans were writing any books several hundred years ago, much less books in an African language about an individual woman. The general public assumes that ancient, medieval, and early modern Africans did not create written texts, and even scholars may assume that the publication of Chinua Achebe's novel *Things Fall Apart* in 1958 represents the genesis of written African literature. Yet, Ethiopia and Eritrea are nations in East Africa whose African peoples the Ḥabäša have been reading and writing bound manuscripts in their literary language of Gəʿəz since the fourth century CE. (To learn more, visit Sean Winslow's online exhibit "Ethiopic Manuscript Production" at larkvi.com/mss/eth/production.) Like Latin (whose vernacular form, so-called Vulgar Latin, evolved into the Romance languages Italian, French, Spanish, and so on), vernacular Gəʿəz evolved into the modern language Təgrəñña, while written Gəʿəz became a fossilized language that changed little from then on (Weninger 2011). The written form, dating to the first millennium, has been and still is the sacred language for liturgy and literature in the church. Ḥabäša boys and some Ḥabäša girls learned how to read in this language from the age of seven onward, therefore some Ḥabäša were literate and are depicted as reading and loving books in the *Gädlä Wälättä Ṗeṭros.*

Many North Americans are also surprised to hear that Africans were Christians well before the 1600s, assuming that Christianity in Africa is always the result of Western missionary activity. Yet the Ḥabäša are among the oldest Christians in the world—King ʿEzana and his court converted in the 330s CE. The Ḥabäša practice a form of African Christianity that predates most forms of European Christianity and is variously called non-Chalcedonian, monophysite, Coptic, Oriental Orthodox, or Ethiopian Orthodox. Members themselves prefer the term Täwaḥədo Church, which we use. Their ancient form of African Christianity is distinctive, holding some beliefs dear that are considered heretical by the Roman Catholic Church, Protestant churches, and Eastern Orthodoxy.

Thousands of churches and hundreds of monasteries have maintained these traditions for the past fourteen hundred years, while their monks and learned men have translated Greek and Arabic texts into Gəʿəz and also created an original literature of theological treatises, royal chronicles, and indigenous hagiobiographies. The hagiobiographies were a particularly important form because there is no formal process of canonization to become a saint in the Täwaḥədo Church; rather, the main requirements are posthumous miracles and that the saint's community write his or her hagiobiography. A marker of the strength of Western constructions of the world is that the scholar must explain that some black peoples were both literate and Christian before some Europeans.

Finally, many assume that Africa is the continent where women have perennially been the most abused and repressed. Yet, parts of Northeast Africa have long traditions of strong ruling queens, of legally independent and literate noblewomen, and of national reverence for female deities and saints. The Ḥabäša claim that their royal line has had women of such distinction that they are known worldwide, including the Queen of Sheba of the Old Testament and Queen Candace of the New Testament. During the early modern period, Ḥabäša queens and princesses were very powerful politically—acting independently of kings, ruling for young kings, owning vast lands, and being undeposable while alive (Lobo and Le Grand 1985, 92, 128, 212, 229; Barradas 1996, 96). For instance, Queen Ǝleni indirectly ruled the country for so long and so competently that when she died, people mourned her as both "father and mother of all," according to a sixteenth-century Portuguese visitor (Alvarez 1961, 434). In the eighteenth century, the powerful Queen Məntəwwab ruled as regent for her husband, her son, and her grandson (Bruce 1813b, 94–104). Säblä Wängel, wife of the sixteenth-century monarch Ləbnä Dəngəl, was also a leader of the nation after the death of her husband (Kleiner 2010). Evidence from multiple sources in multiple languages demonstrates that early modern African women were present in the histories of their nations (Thornton 1998, 1991; Nast 2005), not absent, as the modern public tends to assume.

To summarize, Walatta Petros is not sui generis but an exemplar of the Ḥabäša's long tradition of powerful noblewomen, indigenous literature, and independent Christianity. Unfortunately, scholars of early modern African women continue to write against an absence—not that of the women themselves but the absence of readers' knowledge about Africa and the scarcity of scholarship about these women, which creates assumptions about the scarcity of the women themselves. This book does much to undermine those unfortunate assumptions.

The Text's Seventeenth-Century Historical Context

The *Gädlä Wälättä Peṭros* is written without a Western audience in mind. Its Ḥabäša authors assume a contemporary Ḥabäša readership; that is, those as knowledgeable about its events, people, places, books, time, and rituals as the authors are. For instance, it proceeds without explaining where places are or how far they are from one another. The name of the king appears with little more announcement than those of the humble maids, fishermen, and boat owners of Walatta Petros's community. Thus, it is essential to give a substantial historical background for the twenty-first-century reader.

The seventeenth-century encounter between the Portuguese and the Ḥabäša that forms the backdrop of the *Gädlä Wälättä Peṭros* is a fascinating moment in the history of colonial encounter.[2] As mentioned, the highland Ethiopian kingdom of Abyssinia, of the Ḥabäša people, had become Christian starting in the fourth century. In the 1520s and 1530s, they became concerned about Islamic incursions. A Muslim of the Afar people called Aḥmad b. Ibrāhīm al-Ġāzī (nicknamed "Grañ" by the Ḥabäša, meaning "left-handed" in Amharic) started a war against the Christian kingdoms of the Ethiopian highlands (Morin 2004, 41–43), beginning with the provinces of Fäṭägar and Däwaro, from which Walatta Petros's family came. This military leader led a campaign—burning down churches and monasteries, killing monks and priests, and cutting a swath through the Ḥabäša army—that nearly eradicated the Ḥabäša Empire. The Ḥabäša king Ləbnä Dəngəl sent ambassadors to Europe to ask for help in defending the Ḥabäša, and in 1541 they arrived. Cristóvão da Gama, the son of the Portuguese explorer Vasco da Gama, led an expedition from Goa, India, of four hundred Portuguese with muskets to repel the conquest. After the Ḥabäša and Portuguese successfully repelled the incursion, many of the Portuguese returned home, but some stayed to form a small community, intermarrying with the Ḥabäša.

Then, missionaries from the new Roman Catholic order of the Jesuits, founded just twenty years earlier to combat emergent Protestantism, arrived in Ethiopia in

[2] Much of this section was previously published in an extended form in Belcher (2013).

1557 to endeavor to convert the Ḥabäša from their ancient form of Christianity to Roman Catholicism. The Jesuits' early methods were neither sophisticated nor successful—they declared the Ḥabäša heretics, demanded that they submit to Rome, and did little to persuade them (Pennec 2003, 373). The missionaries were barely tolerated by successive kings and did little beyond ministering to the tiny Catholic community descended from the intermarried families of the Portuguese soldiers.

Then, after fifty years of failure, the Portuguese sent a new group of Jesuits to the Ethiopian highlands in 1603, among whom was a Spanish priest named Pedro Páez. This man was a new sort of missionary, someone who learned the local language, engaged others in conversation, and was sympathetic to many of the tenets of the Täwaḥədo Church. His extraordinary diplomacy, intellectual curiosity, and kind manner enabled him to gain influence among a range of nobles and high-ranking priests. Páez privately converted King Zä-Dəngəl within a few years of arriving. When that king was excommunicated from the Täwaḥədo Church and killed for these actions, a new king seized the throne in 1607, Susənyos (regnal name Mälak Säggäd). Páez converted him and the new king's powerful brother Śəʿəlä Krəstos (who had the title of *Ras*, meaning "duke") as well, in 1612, reassuring them that conversion was only a matter of consolidating Christianity against the threat of Islam, not of abandoning the faith of their fathers.

King Susənyos may not have been much concerned about such an abandonment anyway. He was the extramarital son of a previous king (Täklä Śəllase [Ṭinno] 1892, ix) and had grown up among another ethnic group, the Oromo, life experiences that may have made him more open to a foreign faith (Marcus 2002, 39–40). Certainly, he converted with an eye toward controlling the powerful Täwaḥədo Church and gaining European military assistance (Crummey 2000, 68, 72; Cohen 2009a, 29; Henze 2000, 96). After violently repressing his people's anti-Catholic uprising in 1617 and 1618, Susənyos forced the matter in 1621 by publicly professing Roman Catholicism and rejecting the Täwaḥədo Church, and inviting more Portuguese Jesuits into the country. Over the following decade, the Jesuits established nine churches, translated the Latin liturgy and theological texts into Gəʿəz, and engaged in open debates with local religious leaders over doctrine. Many of the male members of the royal court and high-ranking priests followed Susənyos in converting.

Nevertheless, a significant portion of the population, including many lower-level ecclesiastics, the people in the countryside, and women of the court, did not (Lobo 1971, 189). They rightly suspected that, despite promises to the contrary, they would soon be asked to abandon their most cherished rituals to embrace the Jesuitical version of Christianity. Unlike the high-ranking men, these women and peasants were more involved in the distinctive beliefs and practices of the Ḥabäša church—which touched every part of their daily lives. A few of the practices that the Jesuits later decried included the Ḥabäša's refusal to eat pork or rabbit (as proscribed in the Old Testament) and their celebration of the Sabbath on Saturday and Sunday. The people were horrified at the prospect of eating foods that disgusted them and losing their days of worship. And, to the Ḥabäša mind, the Portuguese priests were clearly barbarians, thinking nothing, for instance, of spitting in church (Castanhoso, Bermudez, and Correa 1902, 90). Many Ḥabäša refused to follow the king in converting to Roman Catholicism—which some called the "filthy faith of the Europeans."

Then a fateful event occurred: Páez died. His successor, Afonso Mendes, was more aggressive, and the fears of the people were realized.[3] In 1626, Mendes had the king issue an edict condemning many cherished Täwaḥədo Church religious practices. For instance, the Ḥabäša baptize sons on the fortieth day after their birth and daughters on the eightieth day. Given infant mortality rates, many children died without baptism. The Jesuits insisted that all such children were in hell (Paez 1903, 63–64).

The king immediately began to face wholesale insurrection, with many taking up their weapons. In the countryside, some priests engaged the armed Portuguese military with nothing more than a portable sacred altar on their heads (Lobo and Le Grand 1985, 91). In his own immediate household, none of the women converted. His mother rebuked him (Páez 2011, 1:333–34), his wife left him due to his conversion (Mendes 1908, 333–34), his beloved niece gave land to shelter anti-Catholic resistors (Täklä Śəllase [Ṭinno] 1900, 78, 374n), and two of his daughters participated in anti-Catholic rebellions against him (Crummey 2000, 69). It seems he was dismayed at having to kill so many of his own people and disheartened by these domestic desertions: "it visibly appear'd that he broke his Heart with Grief, and Trouble, being in perpetual Anguish" (Tellez 1710, 243). Susənyos abandoned the effort to convert the country by force, rescinded his edict of conversion in 1632, and died three months later. His son Fasilädäs came to power and eradicated Roman Catholicism. By 1636, he was executing priests who had converted to Roman Catholicism (Beccari 1913, 110). By 1653, not a single Jesuit was left in Ethiopia: all had been banished or lynched (ibid., 102; Tellez 1710, 264). Three hundred years later, the twentieth-century king Haile Selassie still prevented the Roman Catholic Church from establishing churches or congregations in highland Ethiopia.

Oddly, few scholars have commented on this annihilation of a European protocolonial effort, its absolute failure. And a protocolonial effort it was. Although the Portuguese Jesuits did not engage in international trade, own private property in Ethiopia, or extract tribute, they traveled in and out of the country with soldiers, established a settlement, and lived in Ethiopia for almost a century. They were there due to Portuguese geopolitical interests in curtailing the Ottoman Empire, demanding that the Ḥabäša king submit himself to the European authority of the pope, and using superior military equipment to aid the king in forcing thousands to embrace a European system of very different beliefs and rituals from 1621 to 1632. After a decade of bloody conflict, however, the Portuguese were routed and Europeans did not attempt to colonize Ethiopia for the next two hundred and fifty years. In fact, Europeans never successfully colonized most of the nation afterward. This is the

[3] Some have debated the painting of Mendes as a hard-liner, including Merid Wolde Aregay (1998); Pennec (2003). For a discussion of this point, see Salvadore (2010, 194).

backdrop of Walatta Petros's movement against the Jesuits and Roman Catholicism in Ethiopia.

The Text and Ḥabäša Noblewomen's Anticolonial Role

Two explanations have been offered for the Ḥabäša defeating the Portuguese effort in highland Ethiopia in the 1600s.[4] European scholars tend to say that the Portuguese were culturally insensitive and enraged the populace. Ḥabäša scholars tend to say that rebellions among the Ḥabäša military ranks turned the tide. Both of these explanations are accurate. But the defeat must also be attributed in part to a group many assume had no power: women. Comparing the Portuguese and Ḥabäša sources from the seventeenth century (including the *Gädlä Wälättä Peṭros*) reveals that Ḥabäša noblewomen were partly, and perhaps largely, responsible for evicting the Portuguese and Roman Catholicism from Ethiopia. Comparing the primary sources from two earlier traditions enables us to recover the role of African women in resisting European colonial efforts and shaping their nation's history.

In the seventeenth century, about a dozen now relatively unknown texts were written about the encounter in the first half of the century between the Portuguese and the Ḥabäša. Writing from the European perspective, five of the Portuguese Jesuits who lived in Ethiopia in the early 1600s—Manoel de Almeida (often Manuel de Almeida), Manoel Barradas, Jerónimo Lobo, Afonso Mendes, and Pedro Páez—wrote accounts of their experiences in Ethiopia. Perhaps because of the mission's failure, none of the Portuguese Jesuits' accounts were published in full in Portuguese until the twentieth century, in Camillo Beccari's fifteen-volume series Rerum aethiopicarum scriptores occidentales inediti a saeculo XVI ad XIX (Lobo 1983, xxix). Only some of these texts have appeared in English. Some of the Jesuits also wrote letters and reports that have been preserved (Beccari 1910, 1911, 1912, 1913, 1914). Writing from the African perspective, various seventeenth-century Ḥabäša scholars also documented the encounter, writing royal chronicles that detail the lives of Ḥabäša kings who ruled during this period, and some hagiobiographies that detail the lives of Ḥabäša saints. None of these Gəʿəz texts are currently available in English. There are also the letters of the Roman Catholic Ḥabäša monk *Abba* Gorgoryos, who reported what he saw to the seventeenth-century German scholar Hiob Ludolf.[5]

The texts from this period display quite different perspectives on some of the Ḥabäša noblewomen—the Portuguese texts portray one of them negatively as *diabólica mulher* (diabolical woman), while the Gəʿəz texts portray them positively as *qəddusat* (female saints)—but they concur that these African women participated in defeating this European incursion. The Portuguese texts disparage Ḥabäša noble-

[4] Much of this section was previously published in an extended form in Belcher (2013).

[5] Some of his Gəʿəz letters to Ludolf were translated into German (Flemming 1890–91), and Michael Kleiner is working on translating them into English.

women for obstructing the Jesuits' efforts to convert the Ḥabäša to Roman Catholicism. The Gəʿəz texts praise them for doing so. Comparing the two traditions reveals that the negative Portuguese representations of these Ḥabäša noblewomen were not just the result of misogyny, but were a vanquished foe's bitter depiction of a victorious enemy. Indeed, these early modern African women must be acknowledged as some of the earliest pioneers against European incursions in Africa.

Women appear rarely in the Portuguese accounts, but when they do, they are almost always resisting conversion to Roman Catholicism. Lobo and Mendes claim outright that the noblewomen surrounding the Ḥabäša king—in particular his senior wife, eldest daughter, a daughter-in-law, and a niece—are the reason for the failure of Roman Catholicism in Abyssinia (Lobo and Le Grand 1985, 73–74; Beccari 1903, 147). Part of the reason that Ḥabäša noblewomen were so powerful was that strict exogamous cultural laws meant that noblewomen (*wäyzazər* in Gəʿəz) married outside the royal family; that is, they married men who were beneath them socially: "The *wäyzazər* are not submissive to anyone, not even to their husbands. Given that they do not marry and cannot marry men who are noble like them, only to those who are not, no matter how honored the men may be, their wives will always become their masters. And behind closed doors the men are treated as servants" (our translation) (Barradas 1906, 151–52; 1996, 64).

This asymmetrical power relationship probably contributed to noblewomen's strong sense of their own value and rights. Their literacy, unusual for any seventeenth-century person, would also have contributed to this confidence. Indeed, the Ḥabäša king expressed surprise that the noblewomen were not more interested in the foreign faith, given their literacy, saying, "he was amazed, that they, rising from such a noble lineage, gifted with clear minds and versed in books to such a degree, would endure themselves being inflicted upon by monks from the countryside and from the woods" (our translation) (Mendes 1908, 302).

In my article on the topic, "Sisters Debating the Jesuits" (Belcher 2013), I look more closely at the Portuguese texts' vivid portraits of six individual Ḥabäša noblewomen, five who resisted the Portuguese and one who appears to have supported them. Space does not allow that examination here, but the interested reader is urged to read the article for fascinating anecdotes about the Ḥabäša noblewomen of this period, whom nobody (including their fathers and husbands) could prevent from doing exactly as they liked.

One figure is worth spending a little time on, however: the king's niece. She is a discursively resistant figure in the Portuguese texts who has experiences quite similar to Walatta Petros. While remaining nameless in their texts, she takes up more space than perhaps any other woman, with the Portuguese describing her as well educated and the greatest heretic in the land (Beccari 1912, 185). Lobo wrote, years later, that they were never successful in converting this woman, but Thomas Barneto stated in 1627 that they were (1912, 185–89). They interpreted the encounter differently, as suggested by what Barneto himself recounts of the rhetorical indirection she used to avoid conversion.

In Lobo's account, the Jesuits met her husband when he asked them to come as Roman Catholic missionaries to his region (1983, 186). Unfortunately for the Portuguese, the king's niece was set against them: "a confirmed heretic, so blind and obstinate in her errors that she was unwilling to listen to any discussion of the Catholic faith or any true information concerning her heresies" (ibid.). Although "the greater part of our labours were expended with the king's niece," she heard their preaching with "ill will and worse predisposition" (ibid., 187). In a brilliant rhetorical move, she horrified the locals by telling them that the Jesuits had mixed the blood of unclean animals (camels, dogs, and hares) into the bread of the Eucharist host, polluting the sacred ritual (Lobo and Le Grand 1985, 57). This constituted a dire problem for the Portuguese, because the local women in the entire region refused to convert on the grounds that the king's niece had not converted (Lobo 1971, 386n2). Soon the entire region was "infected with the same prejudices as she" and "they fled from us whenever we approach'd" (Lobo and Le Grand 1985, 57). Whole towns would go into mourning when the Portuguese drew near (Lobo 1983, 188–89).

Given her tremendous influence, the Portuguese made repeated attempts to change her mind (Lobo 1983, 187–89, 197; Lobo and Le Grand 1985, 57–58, 61). At first they hoped that she would "yield" to her husband and convert, but she did not. Then they spent three days attempting to gain an audience with her, but she would not grant it. Eventually, the Portuguese abandoned the effort and returned home: "We again attempted the conversion of the aforementioned lord's wife, whom we found as blind and stubborn as before. And since she refused to give up the battle in any of the many bouts we had with her, we had to return again to Fremona [the Jesuit base, in northern Ethiopia]" (Lobo 1983, 197). Not long after, the entire Portuguese effort in Abyssinia unraveled.

The Portuguese did not record their "battles" with this woman at length, but the original Lobo draft contains a fascinating scene, deleted from the later manuscript, in which the woman debates with the Portuguese priests, employing rhetoric in resisting them (1971, 387). Perhaps Lobo deleted the scene because it demonstrated a mere woman defeating a team of men from the most famous educational European institution of its time, the Society of Jesus. Although the king's niece appears in Lobo's text as a shadow, without a direct voice, there is no doubting her extraordinary role in the text. She resists conversion, convinces other women to resist conversion, and remains true to her faith despite the best efforts of the Portuguese. Indeed, her repression in Lobo's later text makes her stand out all the more because she is the only individual conversion attempt Lobo records. As the reader, one immediately wonders why the Portuguese are spending so much time with one person, and with a woman. Clearly, this woman is a symbol of much more.

Interestingly, several events in Walatta Petros's life parallel those of the king's niece. Both women were noblewomen and the wives of high-ranking officials who had converted to Roman Catholicism. Both women were subjected to intense, one-on-one efforts by the Portuguese to convert them. Like the king's niece, "our holy mother Walatta Petros argued with them, defeated them and embarrassed them." It is tempting to speculate that the hagiobiography and Lobo and Barneto's accounts are about the same woman. The names of their husbands are somewhat similar, appearing as "Miserat Christos" and "Melcha Christos" in the Portuguese sources (Beccari 1912, 185). But the king's niece lived in Šire, Təgray, and Walatta Petros never did. If they are not the same woman, the overlap in their stories suggests that the Portuguese accounts and the Ḥabäša hagiobiographies are both reporting on a much larger movement among Ḥabäša noblewomen during this period.

Despite the different valences of the Portuguese and Ḥabäša texts—the first condemning, the second praising noblewomen—the parallels between them are striking. In both, women are rhetorical warriors, striking at imperial and foreign power with the weapons of language. In the Portuguese texts this resistance is often depicted as sly sarcasm or sullen silence; in the Ḥabäša texts it is depicted as dialogic utterance. Indeed, in one of the other Ethiopian female saint hagiobiographies, the *Gädlä Fəqərtä Krəstos*, women perform a theater of abusive speech and violent physical response that ends not even with the speaker's death, but with a command that the living eat the bodies of the condemnatory and all-powerful dead.

By reading early modern European and African written texts through each other, we come to a better understanding of this period and, in particular, the role of women in the failure of an early modern European protocolonial effort. The Ḥabäša texts suggest that women played an essential role in defeating Roman Catholicism in Ethiopia, but do not say so outright. The Portuguese texts do. The Ḥabäša texts communicate the scale of the rebellion against the Roman Catholics, and the tremendous cost to the Ḥabäša both at the national and familial level. The Portuguese texts are necessarily more focused on the costs to Europeans. Read together, both sets of texts suggest some important historical truths.

The Text's Religious Context

The *Gädlä Wälättä Ṗeṭros* was written within the Täwaḥədo Church tradition, which is both similar to and very different from other forms of Christianity. In this section, I describe the religious differences between Roman Catholicism and the Täwaḥədo Church, particularly their views of human and divine nature; the religious controversies that arose within the Täwaḥədo Church during this period, including Walatta Petros's monastery's affiliation with adherents of Qəbat teaching; the vital place that the Virgin Mary holds in the Täwaḥədo Church; the practices of monasticism in the Täwaḥədo Church, including female leadership; and the deployment of biblical passages in the text, including their alteration.

Täwaḥədo Church Doctrine

Readers familiar with Roman Catholicism or Protestantism will notice that the Christianity of the text is markedly different. Walatta Petros and other Ḥabäša refused to convert to Roman Catholicism for a number of reasons, but one of the most often stated is Christological. That is, the Ḥabäša viewed the nature of Christ differently. The Roman Catholics agreed with the Council of Chalcedon of 451 that Christ had "two natures," fully human and fully divine; the Täwaḥədo Church disagreed with that council and insisted that Christ had "one nature," melding the human and the divine. Along with the Roman Catholics, the Eastern Orthodox, and, later, the Protestant churches, agreed with the two-nature doctrine; it is only the so-called Oriental Orthodox churches, or non-Chalcedonian churches of Egypt, Syria, Armenia, India, Ethiopia, and Eritrea, that disagreed. While this difference may seem small or even nonexistent—neither claimed that Christ was only divine or only human—the theological and political implications were significant. More recently, the non-Chalcedonian churches have decided that the difference is merely semantic, based in a misunderstanding of the Greek terms for "nature" (Ayele Takla Haymanot 1982). Language is powerful, however, and has shaped some distinctive aspects of the Täwaḥədo Church, particularly its emphasis on indivisibility, which seems to have shaped, or emerged from, its view of human nature.

The Täwaḥədo Church does not have a doctrine of original sin, and thus does not posit that all human beings are born in a state of sin. Rather, it has a doctrine of theosis, the transformation of human beings by grace. When saved, people are restored into Christ's image. Thus, all children are types of angels, and Ḥabäša and Africans who do bad things are rarely evil but are led to do evil acts by something outside of themselves: Satan. Walatta Petros's pagan jailor makes advances toward her not due to his own bad character but because "Satan entered into [his] heart." (The Europeans in the text are allowed no such excuse, however.) The text talks about the divinity of human beings, saying that the members of Walatta Petros's flock are "without any blemish." This doctrine means that human beings are not inevitably and wholly sinful but actually have the potential of becoming divine, like Mary (Wright 2002, 30). As a result, the ultimate goal of monks and nuns is to leave the human behind, in part by reducing the body's desires to nothing. This has partly to do with another doctrine that the body as well as the soul will be resurrected on Judgment Day, therefore "both the body and the soul have to be purified and saved" (ibid., 34).

At the same time, if humans are more divine, the divine is more human. When Jesus Christ appears to commission Walatta Petros to guide the community, she does not agree in awe. She fights him tooth and nail, insisting that she is nothing but "mud." Christ deigns to argue back, saying that mud mixed with straw is a strong building block. So, she comes to her main point. She knows her Bible well—she "was anxious that what had happened to Eve not happen to her." She does not want to be tricked, but perhaps she also does not want to be mistakenly held responsible, as a woman, if harm comes to her flock. Only then, having been defeated in argument, does Christ give her his solemn promise that no one in her community, nor anyone who ever calls upon her name, will perish—that is, be condemned to eternal damnation. Only then, having extracted a promise from the all-powerful, does she agree to do as God says. Similarly, an earlier Ḥabäša female saint, Krəstos Śämra, also argues with God, trying to reconcile him with Satan so that human beings will stop suffering due to the war between the two (Filəp̣p̣os 1956).

Although many Ḥabäša, like Walatta Petros, refused to convert to Roman Catholicism, and eventually the country followed suit and abandoned Catholicism, the Ḥabäša's debates with the Jesuits set the stage for divisive theological debates in Ethiopia in the seventeenth century. This internal conflict, starting right after the expulsion of the Jesuits, centered on whether Christ needed the Holy Spirit to anoint him. One side, called Unctionist (adherents of Qəbat teaching, whose followers were called Unctionists, Qəbatočč, əllä Ewosṭatewos, or Goǧǧamewočč), believed that he did need the Holy Spirit: "the Father is the anointer, the Son the anointed, and the Holy Spirit the ointment." The other side, called Unionist (adherents of Karra teaching, whose followers were called Unionists or Täwaḥədowočč), believed that he did not: "the Son is the anointer, the anointed, and the ointment" (Tedros Abraha 2010; Getatchew Haile 2007a). The Unctionists were associated with the monastic house of the fifteenth-century *Abunä* Ewosṭatewos and the monasteries of Goǧǧam (south of Lake Ṭana); the Unionists were associated with the monastic house of thirteenth-century *Abunä* Täklä Haymanot and the monasteries of Azäzo (near Gondär) and Däbrä Libanos. That is, although the Täwaḥədo Church had no orders, it did have "houses," loosely connected networks of monasteries (Kaplan 2014a).

The second half of the *Gädlä Wälättä Ṗeṭros*, which relates what happened after the Jesuits were expelled, will be helpful to scholars trying to understand some of those shifts. In particular, the Ḥabäša monks and monasteries in the text suggest that Walatta Petros's community leaned toward Qəbat teaching. For instance, the high-ranking monk *Abba* Fätlä Śəllase appears in both Susənyos's chronicle and Walatta Petros's hagiobiography. In the hagiobiography, Fätlä Śəllase is a special mentor to Walatta Petros, as well as the "teacher of the entire world." He is the one who enables her to leave her husband's home to become a nun, who twice brokers peace between her and her husband, and who, much later, supports her when male priests attack her leadership on the grounds that she is a woman. Since Fätlä Śəllase is regularly associated in the hagiobiography with a pro-Catholic member of the court, Wälättä Giyorgis (whom Walatta Petros later converts back to Orthodoxy), we might assume that he was one of the priests who initially embraced Roman Catholicism. The hagiobiography speaks approvingly of him, however, so he must have abandoned any pro-Catholic position, if he had espoused any. Meanwhile, this same monk appears in Susənyos's royal chronicle, participating near southeastern Lake Ṭana in a famous debate about Christ's anointing, held before King Susənyos in 1622–23 CE. Fätlä Śəllase is the first of many monks arguing for the Qəbat side, which Susənyos then chose to support (also suggesting that Qəbat was aligned with Roman Catholicism). In the June 1655 public debate, held after Walatta Petros died, King Fasilädäs also chose the Qəbat side, but in the 1667 debate, Fasilädäs chose the opposing side. Likewise, his successor, King Yoḥannəs I, held public debates on the issue in 1668. The Qəbat side again lost, and did so permanently. It seems that Walatta Petros's monastery still had its sympathies with the Qəbat side as of the 1672 writing of the hagiobiography, however. Further evidence is that an entry on Ǝḫətä Krəstos in the *Sənkəssar* (Synaxarium), the thirteenth-century compilation of saints' lives, states that she excommunicated two monks for being Unionist (Nollet 1930).

The Täwaḥədo Church is also distinctive in having great reverence for the Virgin Mary, Christ's mother, the "mother of salvation." Christ saved all humanity by dying on the cross, but Mary is present day to day, providing basic needs, comfort, and forgiveness. The pious recite the prayers in her honor, *Wəddase Maryam*, every day. In the *Täʾamərä Maryam* (Miracles of Mary), read during many church services and the subject of many sermons, Mary is so powerful that she is called "redeemer":

> O Mother of God, our Lady and redeemer, pray for us! Thou hast become the habitation of glory. . . . O Mother of God, our Lady and our redeemer, pray thou for us, and lay peace and safety upon those who are in this thy house! O Mother of God, Bearer of Life, glorious one ... O our Lady and deliverer, pray thou and make supplication on behalf of all the world; thou wast an earthly being and hast become a heavenly being through carrying the One. . . . O Mother of God . . . who existed before everything. . . . O Mother of God, . . .thou shalt fashion completely Him Who is set over everything, Who appointeth king[s], Who establisheth him that putteth his trust in Him, and giveth glory and grace. (Budge 1933b, 104–7)

Indeed, those Christians who do not believe in her power are thought to not attain heaven (Wright 2001, 47). The Jesuits thought that their own reverence for Mary was one reason they were at first successful in converting many Ḥabäša. This reverence opens up a space for female leadership. Mary is seen as having paid Eve's debt and thus having erased the sin of all women (Wright 2001, 42). Walatta Petros also has redeeming power; those who pray directly to her are delivered.

Täwaḥədo Church Monasticism

Those unfamiliar with monastic practices, or familiar with only European monastic traditions, will need some explanation of the life Walatta Petros sought to live as a nun. Since the beginning, the Täwaḥədo Church has been deeply connected to the Egyptian Orthodox Church and to its practices of monasticism and asceticism. Over the centuries, many praised the Ḥabäša for the depth of their commitment to such practices, in particular, to a life of abstaining from worldly pleasures. The Täwaḥədo Church believed (and still does today) that weakening the body reduced desire and thus led to purity. Even ordinary Christians in the Täwaḥədo Church abstained from animal products at least half of the days of the year, and monks and nuns ate once a day or every other day. They often engaged in other rigors, such as praying while standing in cold water, staying up all night in prayer, or living in caves. The body was as nothing to them.

Täwaḥədo Church monasticism had no orders and each monastery had its own rules and procedures. A monastery was not something inextricably tied to a particular monastic building or church edifice but something marked more by its practices of austerity, celibacy, education, and preaching the Gospel. Monks and nuns were not cloistered but lived near the monastery, at home, or as wanderers (Barradas 1996, 141; Alvares 1881). Some monks and nuns lived entirely on their own, as hermits in cells in the mountains or the wilderness, called *anchorite* (Greek, from "to go out") monasticism. Others lived individually but in the same general area, called *idiorythmic* (Greek, from "each according to his rhythm") monasticism. Others lived fully together, sharing meals and work, called *cenobitic* or *coenobitic* (Greek for "communal") monasticism. Nuns moved among these forms, as did Walatta Petros, and the boundaries of the forms were themselves porous. Monks and nuns could live together in monasteries but the double monastery or dual community of monks and nuns living side by side was more typical of Ḥabäša monasticism. As the hagiobiography also explains, it was believed that in the original monasteries, men and women existed without desire for each other, even sleeping in the same bed and wearing each other's clothes (Wright 2001, 10). Thus, the monastery was not a building behind a wall under lock and key, but more like a village surrounding a church in which each monk or nun had a thatched house of stone or wood and clay (figs. 4–5). They maintained themselves through charity and sometimes by farming the land.

Monks and nuns would join one of three types of holy institutions in the Täwaḥədo Church: *gädam*, *däbr*, or *maḫbär*. The term *gädam* was not used for a church or a wealthy, established monastery but for a more autonomous or less settled community of monks, and we have translated it throughout as "monastic settlement." By contrast, a *däbr* was a substantial, established church that had at least three priests and, often, royal patronage, and that served as a center of education. It might or might not have a monastery attached, but since it is the most formal institution, we have always translated it as "monastery." A *maḫbär*, which we always translate as "community," was the type of institution that Walatta Petros established. People who devoted themselves to a life of spirituality in a *mənet*, or monastery, were sometimes called a *maḫbär*. But lay organizations with such a name also have a long history in Ethiopia and were often established by those who revered a particular saint (Marcus 2001). One did not need to be a monk or nun to belong to such an association or even start one. They often provided mutual assistance to members (such as rebuilding houses or caring for orphans) and met regularly at members' homes. In the troubled times of Walatta Petros, when many local churches and monasteries had become tainted by the foreign faith, Walatta Petros may have borrowed from this particular form of maḫbär to establish communities for the Christians who followed her and wanted to live near her to worship in the true faith. Such a use was without precedent, but, as a woman, Walatta Petros could not set up churches (*betä krəstiyan*) or monasteries (gädam or däbr). Later, it seems Walatta Petros worked to establish her maḫbär as a gädam with formal monastic rules.

In Europe, few became monks or nuns, but in Ethiopia, it was a common way of life. Indeed, almost every elderly widow or widower took up the monastic life, as did quite a few boys and girls. Many did not live in monasteries, but continued to live at home. Still, it was highly unusual for Walatta Petros, as a young, married woman, to want to become a nun and live in a monastery.

The positions and titles for nuns in the monastery were generally as follows: Ḥabäša nuns called each other *əḫət* (sister), but ordinary people called them *əmmahoy* (mother), and the nun in charge of the other nuns, the abbess, was called *əmmä mənet* (mother of the monastery). The *əmmä mənet* distributed work and made sure every nun did no more and no less than she should. The *Rules for the Monks* advised that younger nuns should serve older nuns (Wright 2001, 26); younger nuns were called *dəngəl* (virgin) while older nuns were called *mänäkosayt* (female monk). The daily work was done mostly by the young and able-bodied: planting, weeding, harvesting, collecting firewood, fetching water, grinding grain, baking bread, cooking stews, brewing beer, and so on. Class distinctions were not erased; nuns from well-off families had more possessions and sometimes played a larger role in monastic decision making (ibid., 85).

Female leadership of men was rare. The title that Walatta Petros receives in the text suggests that her role as a female leader was uncommon enough to allow some confusion in terms. In the gädl, Christ gives Walatta Petros the title *liqä diyaqonawit* ([male] head [female] deaconess), probably based on the common title *liqä kahənat* ([male] head of the [male] priests). It is grammatically peculiar, however, so Conti Rossini amended it to *liqä diyaqonat* ([male] head of the [male] deacons). In the caption of the relevant image in MS D, her title is *liqtä diyaqonawit* ([female] head [female] deaconess). Meanwhile, in a *Sənkəssar* entry, her role as the leader over men is clearly and unambiguously stated: *wä-astägabəʾat maḫbärä wä-konät liqtä laʿlehomu* (she gathered a community and became the head over them [collective masculine]). This helps explain why the text also says that the people "surrounded her like bees gather around their king."

Christ appointing the saint to a position in the church hierarchy is a common hagiobiographical topos; for instance, Täklä Haymanot was appointed *liqä kahənat* (head of the priests). The grammatically problematic *liqä diyaqonawit* that appears in all the manuscripts may be Gälawdewos's neologism for the feminine equivalent of liqä kahənat, since there was no such thing as a female head of the priests or deacons in the Täwaḥədo Church, and since the word for a female religious leader, *liqt*, is rare. Several commentators have remarked on this sentence in the gädl, pointing out that Walatta Petros is the only female saint known to be given this position, either on her deathbed or otherwise. The term *liqä diyaqonawit* or *liqtä diyaqonawitä* means that Walatta Petros was the head of all the female deaconesses but also perhaps of the male deacons. Just as the word "archdeaconess" in English does not make it clear whom the woman is in charge of, the Gəʿəz is also not clear. Since Walatta Petros was the head of her community, it is not clear why Christ would need to give her a special dispensation to be in charge of only the female deaconesses. Traditionally, there were women who were head deaconesses of the women and there were men who were head deacons of the men and women. Finally, the text makes explicit the claim that Walatta Petros was the head of all, whether men or women: "She truly was worthy of this name [Walatta Petros, meaning Daughter-of-Saint-Peter] since the son of a king becomes a king and the son of a priest becomes a priest; and just as Peter became the head of the apostles, she likewise became the head of all [religious] teachers."

When an individual decided to become a nun or monk, she or he marked this by shaving the head (being tonsured) and putting on the *qobʿ* (monastic cap) as a signal of intention. The abbot who gave the qobʿ to the individual had a special role in his or her spiritual life. During the novitiate, which lasted from a few weeks to several years (Chaillot 2002, 154; Wright 2001, 59), the main task was learning to deal with the difficulties of frequent fasting, prayer, and labor. In this *rädʾ* (or first) level, the nun received the qobʿ and tried out the life. She abstained from all sexual activity, attended church daily, and followed strict fasting laws. When the woman felt ready, she was initiated, a ceremony that gave her special power to resist temptation. This ceremony marked her passing from the things of this world, and thus the funeral rite was read over her. She received the mantle, sash, and belt, and became a full member of the community, passing into the *ardəʾt* (or second) level. For forty days after this powerful ceremony, she was believed to be free from sin. Then began her life of gädl (struggle) to resist temptation, the most dangerous of which was thought to be the desire for sex, but also for sleep, food, and ease.

There were ten steps in the spiritual life, as described in the *Mäṣaḥəftä Mänäkosat* (Books of the Monks), each of which focused on a different set of spiritual practices, including the first step of "silence, understanding, and praise" and the second of "tears, subjection, and love" (Wright 2001, 96, 135–38). To achieve these qualities, a typical day for a nun would be to get up before 4:00 AM to pray alone, attend group morning prayer from 6:00 to 8:00 AM, spend another hour in prayer, do group work from 9:00 AM until 1:00 to 3:00 PM, do private work for an hour or two (while stopping to pray for ten to fifteen minutes at noon, 3:00 PM, and 5:00 PM), eat around 5:00 PM, visit with others in the evening, and sleep around 8:00 or 9:00 PM (Wright 2001, 101–2). Prayer usually included prostration (bowing, kneeling, or lying down). This routine was broken on the Sabbaths and feast days, or during illness.

The most important scholarly work done to date on Täwaḥədo Church nuns is Marta Camilla Wright's master's thesis, *The Holy Gender, Becoming Male: The Life of Ethiopian Orthodox Nuns*, based on field research, and her related article (2001, 2002). These works provide detail on the life of contemporary Ethiopian nuns, as well as useful appendixes that translate the prayers and processes for consecrating nuns. Wright argues that the Täwaḥədo Church, like the early Christian church, considers the female body impure and, therefore, that Ḥabäša nuns "abandon female characteristics in their search for a holy life," becoming a third, sexless gender (2001, 9, 110). Nuns did so by rejecting the role of wife and mother, praying for the end of their menses, shaving their heads, wearing many layers of dirty clothes, and purifying their bodies of its desires and pollutants. Wright asserts that many women became nuns in order to escape gender role norms, in particular to avoid marriage (ibid., 22, 32). Some of these constraints followed them into the monastery, however, as women were considered impure during their menses. For seven days, they stayed sixty feet away from any holy site and were not allowed to pray certain prayers (ibid., 66), which interrupted their spiritual progress. Wright's informants felt that women were more likely to have become nuns before the eighteenth century, because after that "men started interfering and overtook the power of the women" (ibid., 21).

The Täwaḥədo Church Bible

The *Gädlä Wälättä Ṗeṭros* is lush with quotations from the Bible, inserted by Gälawdewos and his interlocutors from memory. Although some of these quotes may seem to have been corrupted, almost all are direct from the Gəʿəz Bible, which is based on the ancient Greek translation, or Septuagint, and thus is unlike the Bibles that modern Jews and Western Christians are used to reading. For example, in the anecdote about Samson in Judges 14, some may be startled to read that Samson found bees in the lion's mouth, not its carcass, and that it is the jawbone of the ass that springs forth with water, not the ground. Yet this is the story as it appears in the Gəʿəz Bible.

At the same time, Gälawdewos does not have a fundamentalist approach to scripture. He deliberately adapts biblical quotes for his purposes, a practice that a Gəʿəz scholar calls "localizing the text." In recounting the Samson anecdote, Gälawdewos inserts a second riddle, not found in the Bible and perhaps of his own invention, about the jawbone: "A drink in the time of thirst and a weapon for warfare." In citing the famous story of sibling rivalry between Jacob and Esau, the sons of Isaac, in Genesis 25:28, Gälawdewos interprets the passage rather than reciting it. He writes, "Esau was beautiful in his appearance and Isaac loved him, while Jacob was ugly in his appearance and God loved him." While the Bible passage indeed says that Isaac preferred Esau, it attributes this not to Esau's good looks but to the animals he hunted and cooked for his father. Moreover, the verse does not contrast the preferences of Isaac and God, but of Isaac and his wife Rebecca: she is the one said to prefer Jacob, who stayed by her side. However, the Gəʿəz Bible does mention that Jacob was a "plain" man and that he had to put on an animal skin to fool his father into thinking he had Esau's more masculine frame. The two men undoubtedly looked quite different, with Esau living his life outdoors hunting and Jacob staying indoors with his mother. Gälawdewos thus interprets the passage here, suggesting that God was not fooled by Esau's beautiful masculinity. Since other parts of the Bible speak of how God looks at the pure heart, not the beautiful face, this interpretation is an example of Gälawdewos's learnedness and skill. In another instance, after praising Walatta Petros's willingness to do physical labor, he cites the first part of 1 Timothy 4:8, which mentions the benefits of physical labor. For rhetorical effect, he omits that the verse goes on to say that the benefits of spiritual labor are far greater. But he has not distorted the quote, only included the part that is useful to his story.

We took advantage of Ricci's notes in the Italian translation, which identified many of the biblical references in the text. We checked all of them, however, sometimes changing them where we thought Ricci's attribution was incorrect; moreover, we added attributions he had missed. Ricci's translation does include a chart of biblical citations (Gälawdewos 1970, 145–46).

The Text's Authorship

Gəʿəz manuscripts rarely identify a named scribe, much less an author. The *Gädlä Wälättä Peṭros* is an exception, however. We learn on the first page that the person writing the story down is a monk named Gälawdewos: "I, the sinner and transgressor Galawdewos, will write a small part of the story . . . of our holy mother Saint Walatta Petros."[6] We learn nothing of his personal history, although he describes himself as a *ḥaddis täkl* (a new plant) in the monastic life and thus was probably a young man when he wrote down the *Gädlä Wälättä Peṭros* in 1672–73. He also seems to suggest that he is not well liked, comparing himself to a caustic but productive bee: "I am cruel in my deeds, stinging people with my tongue and causing much pain," but ultimately producing "a story that is sweeter than honeycomb." Since he wrote the text thirty years after Walatta Petros's death, and had only recently become a monk, it is safe to assume that he did not know her personally but is relating stories told to him by others. Indeed, he regularly says as much in the text.

So, is Gälawdewos merely the scribe (merely a transcriber of the story) or an author (the inventor of the text)? The answer is—both.

On the one hand, Gälawdewos is an author. Manuscripts were always written down or copied by *däbtära*, who are highly educated but nonordained clergy responsible for the creative processes of the church (Kaplan 2003c). Some are dancers or musicians, others are painters, still others are poets or authors. Ordained priests are required to study religious texts and learn to read Gəʿəz, but däbtära further undertake a long course of study in the creative arts, including poetry (*qəne*), dance (*aqqʷaqʷam*), hymns (*dəggʷa*), liturgical music (*zema*), and written charms (*asmat*), as well as learning to write Gəʿəz and prepare plants for healing medicines. Such a long and complicated text as the *Gädlä Wälättä Peṭros*, with its profusion of biblical references, had to have been written by a trained däbtära who had memorized vast swaths of the Bible. Certainly, the obsessions of the "I" of the text are those of a däbtära: not only the effort to make appropriate mentions of scriptures along the way but the inclusion of so many miracles that involve books, either their being written or saved from thieves. Gälawdewos is definitely not a mere copyist but likely is the sole crafter of the elegant introduction and the inventor of much of its biblical intertextuality.

On the other hand, Gälawdewos is an amanuensis. That is, he did not invent the stories of the text but rather was assigned or commissioned by those in Walatta

[6] Unfortunately, the Conti Rossini print edition (Gälawdewos 1912) and the Ricci translation (Gälawdewos 1970) did not have the author's name, since it had been erased from Abb. 88. The author's name does appear in all eleven of the other manuscripts.

Petros's community to write down the oral histories of others. (This oral quality makes the *Gädlä Wälättä Peṭros* atypical of Ḥabäša literature, a communal text, a kind of *testimonio*—defined as a literary historical genre in which an eyewitness narrates a collectivity's experience—based on eyewitness accounts but using literary techniques [Reyes and Curry Rodríguez 2012]). First and foremost among these community members was Qəddəstä Krəstos, a young nun who "burned with love for Walatta Petros" and who urged Gälawdewos, saying, "Write, so that Walatta Petros's story may be known." The story would never have been written down, Gälawdewos says, unless this "rejected" and "lowly" woman had not insisted that he "reveal this treasure that lay hidden in the field of the hearts of the older people." Gälawdewos notes that while some of those who had known Walatta Petros personally were still living, it was Qəddəstä Krəstos, "who is younger than them all," who made the book come about.

Although Qəddəstä Krəstos is mentioned first in the text, and alone, Gälawdewos writes at the end of the text, in the miracles part of the translation, that a bedridden monk named Mäzgäbä Haymanot had first urged him to write. The monk, who had grown up in Walatta Petros's community, told Gälawdewos that he saw in a vision that Gälawdewos would write down the story of Walatta Petros: "You write to the end an important book, elegantly worded and in beautiful handwriting." Gälawdewos humbly responds that the elders of the community would have to request such. Apparently they did not, since seven years passed—during which Mäzgäbä Haymanot died and the matter was forgotten, Gälawdewos writes—before Qəddəstä Krəstos went to the abbess of the community to demand that the task be undertaken. Thus, a woman was the subject of the text, a woman was the prompter of the text, and a woman authorized the writing of the text.

But Qəddəstä Krəstos was also too young to have known Walatta Petros, and Mäzgäbä Haymanot had died by the time the text was written, so whose stories do we read about in the text? Given the detailed nature of the stories—in particular the use of specific proper names for dozens of people and places, and the historical facts corroborated by other accounts—it is impossible that most of the stories were created by those who had not lived through the events. In many places, the text actually states who the author of a particular story is: "Eheta Kristos and Ghirmana were witnesses and have told us." After another story, the text states, "That man is still alive now. He has told us, and we have written it down." After still another, the text reports that Läbasitä Krəstos told Əḫ̮ətä Krəstos what she saw in a vision, suggesting that we know of it through Əḫ̮ətä Krəstos. In another place, a long section of text is reported as direct speech from the monk Śəʿəlä Krəstos, and after the story the text adds: "Silla Kristos told us all these things ... He is alive right up to now, and his testimony is trustworthy; he does not lie." In another case, authorship is inferred. After telling the story of a disciple traveling alone who escapes a snake, the text asks, "Who would have told us, and how would we have written down this miracle" if God had not protected the disciple, its author? Further, these are not the only places where the text switches from "I" to "we." The text also has "we certainly have not written lies, nor have we used ingenious fables to acquaint you with the story of our holy mother Walatta Petros's glory." These comments, as well as others like them, clarify that the text was a collection of eyewitness accounts rather than solely Gälawdewos's invention.

Finally, the illustrations in some manuscripts of the *Gädlä Wälättä Ṗeṭros* confirm that the text was a community oral history. One in MS D depicts Gälawdewos in every part of the process: being told that he should write the gädl by a man (Mäzgäbä Haymanot) and then a woman (the nun Qəddəstä Krəstos), and then sitting with pen to parchment facing three men and two women (perhaps including the abbess Amätä Dəngəl) who are talking to him (plate 55). Another image in the same text "could be the nun Qəddəstä Krəstos who supported the *Gädl*'s writing, or one of the community's abbesses" (Bosc-Tiessé 2003, 413), or possibly Ǝḫətä Krəstos (plate 63). MS A has a similar image, with Gälawdewos writing while listening to Mäzgäbä Haymanot.

The *Gädlä Wälättä Ṗeṭros* is, then, a written text that is a record of oral testimony. One question remains: If Gälawdewos is the author of many of the biblical allusions in the text, while individuals in the community are the authors of the anecdotes in the text, who is responsible for the arc of it, for suturing it into order? During this period, when scratch paper did not exist, an original text would have been composed orally and then written down. Did Gälawdewos collect all the tales and then write them down from memory? It seems unlikely that Gälawdewos, a relative newcomer, would somehow figure out the correct order since the text is organized largely chronologically. Or did one eyewitness tell most of the stories from beginning to end, with insertions by others? Someone took the time to organize the stories of multiple authors into a particular order.

The most likely such organizer would have been Walatta Petros's partner Ǝḫətä Krəstos, who became a nun with her and traveled everywhere with her in the early days, spent twenty-five years with her (1617–42), was appointed her successor, and lived six years after her. Most of the stories in the *Gädlä Wälättä Ṗeṭros* are those that Ǝḫətä Krəstos would have witnessed herself; many of the early stories only she could have witnessed. The name that appears most often in the text, after the saint's name, is Ǝḫətä Krəstos, which appears twice as often as the name of Walatta Petros's husband Mälkəʾa Krəstos. In two of the *Gädlä Wälättä Ṗeṭros* manuscripts, poems to Ǝḫətä Krəstos appear at the end, indicating how closely aligned the two women were in life and death. Finally, many of the preoccupations of the text are not those of a male author. The concerns, themes, and characters of the text itself suggest the possibility of a female authorial organizer: the long, loving exchanges among female friends, the aggravation of lazy female servants, and the preparation rather than the growing of food. Near the beginning, the text claims that Walatta Petros was very beautiful, but then argues at length that physical beauty is unimportant, with a long disquisition on the biblical Rachel's barren beauty and Leah's fecund ugliness. It seems that Ǝḫətä Krəstos would be the most likely author of many of the tales and the arc of the text.

Indeed, without the male name Gälawdewos, we might have speculated that the literate Ǝḫətä Krəstos actually sat down and wrote out this tale. While women could never be priests, they could sometimes be däbtära. Literacy was relatively high in highland Ethiopia due to the Täwaḥədo Church: all boys went to the first stage of church school, in which they learned to read and write Gəʿəz characters. Girls from Ḥabäša noble families during this period went to school as well, as both the Portuguese accounts and the gädl itself confirm. One of the Jesuits wrote that nobles had live-in monks who taught their daughters "not just to read but also to understand Saint Paul and the Gospel" (Páez 2011, 1:222). While the *Gädlä Wälättä Ṗeṭros* does not depict women writing, it does have multiple scenes of such women reading. Ǝḫətä Krəstos reads the Gospels to Walatta Petros when her friend is sick. Fälasitä Krəstos reads the Psalms of David to her at night and the Gospels during the day on her deathbed. When the king rescinds his conversion, Walatta Petros reads the message he sends her. Walatta Petros is in the habit of reading the Gospel of John every day and is depicted reading the *Täʾamərä Maryam* (Miracles of Mary) and *Mäṣḥafä Ḥawi* (Comprehensive Book). The *Gädlä Wälättä Ṗeṭros* is not the first text at least coauthored by a Ḥabäša woman. According to some, Queen Ǝleni (1450s–1522) wrote two hymn collections in Gəʿəz, the *Ḫoḫtä Bərhan* (Gate of Light) and the *ʿƎnzira Səbḥat* (Lyre of Praise) (Chernetsov 2005a).[7]

Ǝḫətä Krəstos could not have physically written the text: she died two decades before it was written down. Yet, the collecting and organizing of stories might have happened before they were written down in a manuscript. Although the text was written in 1672–73, its stories date much earlier. Since a gädl is essential to establishing a community and saint—and independence from neighboring monasteries—writing one would have been the desire of early members of Walatta Petros's communities, which dated to the mid-1620s.[8] Additionally, as the scholar and Roman Catholic nun Sue Houchins (2007) points out, those in religious orders are usually on the lookout for and acutely aware of exemplary sisters among them and may begin to collect anecdotes and evidence long before any hagiobiography is written down. When considering the joint authorship of the gädl, such early collection must be kept in mind. No doubt, members of the community often told stories to one another, as well as to new members and children, about the exploits of their founder. Ǝḫətä Krəstos was there from the beginning, and constituted an important archive of information about Walatta Petros.

Whether Ǝḫətä Krəstos organized the tales in the text or her tales were organized by others after her death, the *Gädlä Wälättä Ṗeṭros* was at least partially authored by Ǝḫətä Krəstos and the women who surrounded Walatta Petros. Although some men play important roles later in the text, in the early days of Walatta Petros's monastic life, it is mostly women who are named. Thus, the *Gädlä Wälättä Ṗeṭros* represents an early modern written African text orally co-

[7] For a dissenting view on their authorship, see Habtemichael Kidane (2005) and Pankhurst (2009).

[8] As Kaplan points out, "The life of a saint was usually written by a monk from the saint's own monastery, who sought by writing the work to glorify the saint as well as his monastery" (1981, 110).

constructed by African women and can be considered an early example of African female authorship.

The Text's Genres

The text translated here, which we call the *Gädlä Wälättä Ṗeṭros*, is actually a composite text including four different subgenres: *gädl* (the saint's life, or vita), *tä'amər* (the saint's miracles), *mälkə'* (a long poem praising the saint from head to toe), and *sälamta* (a short hymn praising the saint's virtues). The first two, *gädl* and *tä'amər*, almost always appear, and in this order, in a hagiobiography of an indigenous saint. The word *gädl* is used for the first part of the text, but also as an umbrella term for the composite text. The entire *gädl*, then, is a distinctive genre of indigenous Ḥabäša literature, which flourished from the fourteenth century through the next five centuries. It is the most common Gəʿəz original genre.

A direct translation of the Gəʿəz word *gädl* would be "[spiritual] struggle" or, as earlier scholars translated it, "contending." It might also be translated as "acts" (as in the biblical book of the Acts of the Apostles) or "vita" (as in biography). In all cases, a gädl was a biography of a holy person, something the Greeks called a "hagiography" (literally, writing about saints). Since the term hagiography has developed so many pejorative associations, however, scholars of the genre have begun to argue for the term *hagiobiography*, defined as "biographies written with the intention of representing life as 'more exemplary than real' " (de Porcellet and Garay 2001, 19). Since the gädl is its own distinctive genre, we have often used the term hagiography, but also use hagiobiography.

A full-length scholarly study of the gädl genre remains to be published, but the genre was inspired by the many hagiobiographies created in the early Christian Church, quite a few of which were translated into Gəʿəz and with which Ḥabäša authors would have been very familiar (such as that of third-century Desert Father Saint Anthony) (Kaplan 2005c). For instance, parts of the *Sənkəssar*, the tales of other saints, are read during every liturgy in the Täwaḥədo Church, perhaps inspiring authors.

The *gädlat* (the plural form of *gädl*) about the lives of Ḥabäša saints appear in a variety of lengths—some are short and some are lengthy (more than 150 pages in a print edition). Many gädlat were composed long after the death of their subjects, some of whom may have even been mythical. Contrary to Greek hagiobiographies, Gəʿəz hagiobiographies almost never feature martyrs; their saints are rarely victims, but almost always victorious. The gädlat are more generally the stories of monastic leaders, often evangelizers, who struggle with worldly authorities. This different emphasis may be because the Ḥabäša have so long been Christians and lived in a region where they were dominant and not persecuted.

A gädl follows a strict order. It tends to begin with a stylistically elevated introduction and then tells the story of the saint's life in chronological order. It almost always includes the miraculous circumstances of the saint's birth to pious parents, a precocious childhood, the suffering he or she endured in pursuing a holy life, the saint's ordination and/or becoming a monk or nun, the miracles the saint performed while alive, the abandonment or avoidance of a traditional family life, and a description of the moment when Christ gives the saint a *kidan*, a covenant in which Christ promises to honor the prayers of anyone who calls upon the saint's name and to grant eternal life to all Christians who dedicate themselves to the saint, listen to the saint's gädl, and observe the commemoration of the saint's holy day. It ends with the saint's death and a call for blessings on those who wrote the text and paid for its costs. Nosnitsin (2013) argues that the gädl changed in the fifteenth century, becoming more story-driven, more likely to use fictional techniques.

The miracles, *täʾamər* (literally, "signs"), make up the next part of a saint's life. These are not the miracles that were performed while the saint was alive, but those that happened after the saint's death, when followers called upon the saint to intervene with God and grant their prayers. These posthumous miracles follow a typical arc: they start with a blessing formula, then someone has a problem and calls upon the saint, which results in divine intervention and a sudden improvement in the problem (Nosnitsin 2010e). These problems generally have to do with physical danger (whether from illness, animals, or attackers) or everyday life. The number of miracles in hagiobiographies varies widely. Indeed, the number of miracles in a particular saint's life can increase over time, as people continue to pray to the saint. Thus, Saint Täklä Haymanot has three cycles of twenty-two miracles each, and some manuscripts include additional miracles that he performed in a specific area (Nosnitsin 2010f). Some hagiobiographies do not have the section at all: Saint Kaleb, for instance, has no täʾamər section. The genre grew in popularity, probably due to the arrival of the *Täʾamərä Maryam* (Miracles of Mary) in the fourteenth century.

The *Täʾamərä Wälättä Ṗeṭros* consists of the miracles that happened after the saint's death (mostly between 1642 and 1672). Walatta Petros's posthumous miracles often consist of food that multiplies; people saved from death by disease, storm, or wild animals; and the finding of lost objects. The main *Täʾamərä Wälättä Ṗeṭros*, the miracles that appear in almost all the texts, has eleven subsections, each devoted to the miracles that happened to one person. While most of them experienced only one miracle, some experienced more than one, and thus some of the eleven subsections describe more than one miracle. This organization again suggests an oral component to the text, in which individuals reported what happened to them. The miracles are probably not in chronological order; none appears with any date. The *Täʾamərä Wälättä Ṗeṭros* is perhaps distinctive in featuring several miracles about books: one about the writing of the gädl and two others about recovering lost books of the *Mälkəʾa Wälättä Ṗeṭros* poems.

A second set of the *Täʾamərä Wälättä Ṗeṭros* exists in two of the manuscripts, but they are dated later and relate to miracles that took place later, during the consecutive reigns of Bäkaffa (r. 1721–30), Iyasu II (r. 1730–55), Iyoʾas I (r. 1755–69), and Yoḥannəs II (r. 1769), and then later, Täklä Giyorgis I (r. 1779–1800) and King Tewodros II (r. 1855–68). In these miracles, Walatta Petros protects her monastery from the persecution of kings and aids critics of the king who seek asylum at her monastery. We have not translated them in full but have provided summaries.

There then appear, in some of the manuscripts, the *Mälkəʾa Wälättä Ṗeṭros* and the *Sälamta Wälättä Ṗeṭros*: two hymns or spiritual poems, part of a vast African tradition of praise poems, "one of the most developed and elaborate poetic genres in Africa" (Finnegan 1970, 111). The poems both appear in five of the manuscripts (Abb. 88, A, C, E, F) but are missing entirely from six of the manuscripts (B, D, G, H, I, and K). In MS J only one of the poems appears, the sälamta.

The first poem is of the type called *mälkəʾ* (meaning "image," "icon," or "portrait" in Gəʿəz), a unique Gəʿəz genre consisting of praise of a saint's body from head to toe. The beauty, strength, and potency of the body are presented as mirrors of the saint's perfect soul, both having been purified by monkish asceticism. Such a poem also alludes to episodes in the saint's virtuous life. For instance, in the *Mälkəʾa Wälättä Ṗeṭros,* stanza 6 appears to allude to the angels drizzling perfume from paradise into Walatta Petros's nose, and stanza 8 alludes to Walatta Petros's miraculous escape from her jailor in Žäbäy who made advances toward her. The *Mälkəʾa Wälättä Ṗeṭros* does not always match the content of the *Gädlä Wälättä Ṗeṭros* exactly because the poem was likely written by a different author than Gälawdewos and before the life (as discussed below).

According to Habtemichael Kidane (2007a), *mälkəʾat* (the plural form of *mälkəʾ*) have between twenty and fifty stanzas, each composed of five rhyming verses. The rhyme scheme is AAAAA, BBBBB, and so on. Generally, the lines rhyme only the last syllable of the line (i.e., the last character of the line), which always ends in a vowel. Even if it looks like the rhyme is slant (i.e., sharing just a consonant sound), in traditional recitation the singer adds a schwa sound to any sixth-form syllable at the end of a line (e.g., singing *amlak* as *amlakə*). Each stanza starts with the words *sälam lä-*, meaning "peace upon" or "hail to," and the saint's name is frequently mentioned in the third line. In praising the saint's body, the poem moves from the head (including eyelashes, nostrils, lips, and breath), to the torso (including shoulders, breasts, fingers, and nails), to the organs (including womb and heart), and to the lower body (including knees and toes). Honorary parts of the body include the saint's monastic garments of the tunic, belt, mantle, and cap. Often, the first two lines of any stanza will praise the body and the last three lines will invoke events in the saint's life, including his or her birth, death, and burial. It is possible that certain parts of the body are associated with certain saintly abilities. For instance, it seems arms are associated with active spiritual labor in the world, while internal organs are associated with spiritual thought. Stanzas at the beginning and end of the poem may break the formula by invoking God's help or blessings upon the author of the poem. The separate lines of the poem are not set separately in the manuscripts but run continuously with special punctuation marks at the end of lines.

Those who revere a particular saint will often, even daily, recite that saint's mälkəʾ, and students in the traditional Täwaḥədo Church schools must learn to recite many of them from memory (Habtemichael Kidane 1998). Saints' mälkəʾat would also have been sung or recited in church on their feast days. The most famous mälkəʾ is that for the Virgin Mary, the *Mälkəʾa Maryam*, which is sung in monasteries every morning and evening, often said at home before meals, and used by schoolchildren to memorize the alphabet (Böll 2007). There are also mälkəʾat for Christ, the Holy Spirit, God the Father, the Eucharist, the Crucifixion, and some kings and queens. Unfortunately, as the scholar Habtemichael Kidane (2007a) points out, a preoccupation with mälkəʾat origins rather than its literary features has dominated the scholarship.

The second poem is of the type called *sälam* or *sälamta*, meaning "greetings," a shorter genre. Sälamat generally have between six and twelve stanzas, each beginning with the words *sälam lä-* (peace upon, or hail to). Sälamat have only three lines per stanza, with the first line quite long, the second line midlength, and the third line even shorter, often with no more than three words. The last stanza varies by having four lines. Sälamat poems in praise of saints are also found in the *Sənkəssar*, following the commemoration of the saint, but those usually have only one stanza of five lines (Nosnitsin 2010b). The interested reader can read the sälamat poems for Mary and God the Father for comparison with the *Sälamta Wälättä Ṗeṭros* (Dillmann 1866, 147–49). Sälamat poems do not praise the body of the saint but summarize the saint's deeds, often focusing on the more distinctive ones.

These four parts of the hagiobiography—gädl, täʾamər, mälkəʾ, and sälamta—were not written in the order they appear in the Conti Rossini print edition. The main part of the original manuscript, the gädl, was written down in 1672–73, according to Gälawdewos's comment at its beginning. The täʾamər seem to have been written down next, right away, in the same manuscript, because they appear exactly the same in eleven manuscripts and always in the same handwriting within each manuscript. It is extremely unlikely that so many manuscripts would match if the miracles had only been written down in another manuscript at a later date. The poems were likely written before the gädl and täʾamər, in 1643, for the anniversary of Walatta Petros's death.

Although the poems are missing from six of the manuscripts, the evidence suggests that the poems predate the writing of the täʾamər, both as oral compositions and written ones. In MS J, the earliest manuscript extant, the sälamta appears before the täʾamər, perhaps evidence that it was written before it. More important, it is impossible for any text to cite a text written *after* it. Therefore, since the *Täʾamərä Wälättä Ṗeṭros* cites the *Sälamta Wälättä Ṗeṭros* and the *Mälkəʾa Wälättä Ṗeṭros*, the poems must have been written *before* the miracles. Specifically, in the *Täʾamərä Wälättä Ṗeṭros*, a priest sings the first three lines of the *Sälamta Wälättä Ṗeṭros* exactly as they appear in the poem. Thus, the priest and/or the author Gälawdewos had to have access to this poem. Likewise, books of the *Mälkəʾa Wälättä Ṗeṭros* are twice stolen and recovered in the *Täʾamərä Wälättä Ṗeṭros*. Therefore, the sälamta existed as at least an oral composition and the mälkəʾ existed as a written composition before the täʾamər.

The order in which the poems and the gädl were written is less clear. The sälamta starts with a reference to Walatta Petros as a shelter for "doves," which seems to be an allusion to the kidan (covenant) episode of the gädl, in which Christ entrusts Walatta Petros with followers, who are depicted as "pure white doves" who descend all around her. This might suggest the sälamta was written after the gädl but before the täʾamər, just as it appears in MS J. But it seems to me most likely that the mälkəʾ and sälamta were oral compositions predating the written composition of the gädl as well. Some evidence for this order is that Ǝḫətä Krəstos has a mälkəʾ, a sälamta, and a *Sənkəssar* entry, but no gädl or täʾamər. Based on his study of Täklä Haymanot, Nosnitsin (2007a) suspects that a community would write something about the saint within a year of his or her death, to be read at the annual commemoration. In some cases, this might be a *Sənkəssar* narrative and a sälamta to the saint, but sometimes it might be only the sälamta, without a narrative. Mälkeʾ were less necessary for the saint's reverence, while sälamta had to appear with the *Sənkəssar* narrative.

A member of the community, often a less skilled writer than an author of a hagiobiography, would write these short texts. (Since a new saint's monastery was often not yet well funded, the community might take the time to seek out skilled writers, often available only in important monasteries, meaning the hagiobiography would be written by someone from outside the saint's monastery.) Such *Sənkəssar* entries and poems could be added in the margin under the necessary date (since all *Sənkəssar* are organized chronologically by saints' days), at the end of the text, or on separate leaves attached somehow to the volume. Then, through copying, the narrative would enter the local tradition of the *Sənkəssar*, which is part of the reason why *Sənkəssar* manuscripts can vary so much. Research is still needed to ascertain whether the singing or reciting of these poem hymns was common in nonliturgical contexts, and thus transmitted as much orally as in written form. It was not until the eighteenth century that scribes started copying a saint's entire hagiobiographical dossier into one manuscript. Before then, as the mention of separate books of mälkəʾ in the *Gädlä Wälättä Ṗeṭros* makes clear, manuscripts would often have only one or two parts, most often the gädl and the täʾamər. The absence of the mälkəʾ from six of the twelve manuscripts of the *Gädlä Wälättä Ṗeṭros* suggests that it was not until quite late that someone collected all four texts into one manuscript. So far, no manuscript with just the mälkəʾ alone for Walatta Petros has been cataloged or digitized.

Therefore, the most likely sequence of the elements of the hagiobiography being written down was, first the poems (sälamta and mälkəʾ), then the life (gädl), and last the miracles (täʾamər). Meanwhile, the events in Walatta Petros's life must have been told among community members' from almost the moment they happened, then preserved in the oral tradition until they could be written down. So the stories about her would have been oral compositions first.

The Text's Genres and Its Historical Value

One reason that so few Ḥabäša gädlat have appeared in English is that few people can read Gəʿəz and write English well enough to translate the former into the latter. The other reason is that early African literature has been the subject of study by historians, not literary critics. (Unfortunately, scholars of literature have been slow to acknowledge, much less work on, the vast body of written texts created on the continent before the twentieth century.) For the seeker of historical facts, the genre of hagiobiography is a problematic source, as it seldom behaves as a good "native informant."

That is, the gädl is a literary genre, often more devoted to celebrating the subject's extraordinary accomplishments than adhering narrowly to the real. For instance, the authors of a gädl often use consistent biographical tropes that may be more spiritually than physically true. For instance, a surprisingly high number of Ḥabäša saints' parents are said to have been of noble lineage and previously childless due to the mother's barrenness. On the one hand, this seems unlikely to have been true of all of them. On the other hand, nobles would have had more resources to take up contemplative lives or start monastic communities, which may be why most saints worldwide are said to be from elite families. Furthermore, in Ethiopia, childless couples who prayed to be blessed with a child often vowed to hand any such child over to the church to become a monk or nun (following the example of some previously childless couples in the Bible who dedicate their children to the temple). Thus, children conceived after a long period of childlessness were often dedicated by their parents to God, returning the miracle to its maker, as it were. Growing up with this knowledge, such children may have been more inclined to spiritual lives. Then, as a child, the saint is usually precocious, and as an adult, the saint rarely marries but often lives on the margins of familial society, an ascetic who performs feats of endurance and works to convert hearts to God. Again, the presence of so many precocious ascetics may reflect a reality of human outliers—men and women who were unusual enough and dedicated enough to be elevated to sainthood. Finally, many Ḥabäša saints are said to have made a pilgrimage to Jerusalem. While this may seem to strain credulity, it was actually not unheard of for Ḥabäša monks and nuns to do so—a matter of a six-month journey down from the Ethiopian highlands into Egypt and across the isthmus to Palestine. Thus, life and literature may serve to reinforce each other—becoming the real.

Some tropes more conventional than true, however, are not connected to biographical details but miraculous ones. Saints often encounter and defeat magicians and demons. In every gädl, Christ himself visits the saint to establish the kidan. Finally, saints regularly raise people from the dead (including themselves), heal the incurably ill, predict the future, and fly. Because of such tropes, texts in this genre are often dismissed as credulous and antihistorical.

The *Gädlä Wälättä Ṗeṭros* is an unusual hagiobiography, however. First, Walatta Petros and her husband, Mälkəʾa Krəstos, were prominent historical figures mentioned in both the Portuguese accounts and the Gəʿəz royal chronicles of the period. In the royal chronicle of Susənyos, Mälkəʾa Krəstos is mentioned on forty of just over four hundred pages (Täklä Śəllase [Ṭinno] 1900, 309). In the so-called *Short Chronicles*, which does not specify wives unless they are well known, his wife Walatta Petros is mentioned by appositive upon his death (Basset 1882, 29): "In the second year [of King Fasilädäs' reign], on the fourth of [the month of] Taḫśaś, Mälkəʾa Krəstos died, who formerly had been *bəḥtwäddäd* [that is, chief minister];

he was the husband of that righteous daughter, [she] of the monastery of Qʷärasa."[9] One Jesuit account also mentions her while discussing the monasteries of Waldəbba, where many men and women went to take up a religious life. Barradas reports that, "The women who normally become nuns are those whom the world has seen as old . . . or they are those who have separated from their husbands." He adds that such "nuns go into retreat . . . into the desert, . . . where they live as beggars" and "we saw the wife of Belatina Goitâ Melcha Christôs do [this] when he abandoned her" (Barradas 1996, 141; 1906, 258). Although many men are named Mälkəʾa Krəstos—nearly a dozen appear in the Portuguese texts—only two of the men with this name were leading officials, and only one had the title *Blattengeta* (lit., Lord of the Pages, but meaning head councillor): Walatta Petros's husband. In addition, the hagiobiography states that her husband was the commander of the Śəlṭan Märʿəd regiment, and the Portuguese texts also state that *Blattengeta* Mälkəʾa Krəstos was the commander. The other official with this name was Susənyos's brother, who cannot be Walatta Petros's husband (not only would such a close connection to the king have been mentioned in the hagiobiography, but also this man died before Susənyos was king). Thus, *Blattengeta* Mälkəʾa Krəstos must be Walatta Petros's husband.

The second reason the *Gädlä Wälättä Ṗeṭros* is historically valuable is that it is remarkably detailed—filled with specific names of historical people and places, and the dates when historical events occurred. Further, certain details leap off the page as connected to actual lived experience. In one monastery, the nuns' teeth become green because they are reduced to eating so many plants. On another occasion, Walatta Petros reluctantly agrees to return to her angry husband on one condition: that she not be made to "see the face of his mother." Third, many common gädl tropes do not appear. Walatta Petros is not an only child, but the youngest of four siblings, and she performs no miracles as an infant or teen. She never goes to Jerusalem and encounters no magicians. When Christ speaks to her, no effort is made to establish that he is there in the flesh rather than in a vision.

Third, most of the text proceeds without any supernatural miracles but rather the infusion of God's hand into everyday life. For instance, God is responsible, the text tells us, for Walatta Petros falling on a soft landing spot when her mule throws her, and for her failing to burn at the stake because a fire fizzles. To attribute such to God rather than chance will always be the act of the faithful—but the event itself is not supernatural. Other relatively normal occurrences that the text describes as miracles are Walatta Petros's displays of great fortitude in the face of dangerous animals, wild seas, deadly illnesses, and immense thirst. Walatta Petros suddenly understands the foreign language of the people among whom she finds herself—an impressive feat but not unheard of among gifted language learners. A fisherman catches exactly thirteen fish, not twelve or fourteen, because the number of the apostles with Christ is thirteen. These are the "miracles" of the *Gädlä Wälättä*

[9] Lit., *Wä-bä-2 ʿamät amä 4 lä-taḫśaś motä Mälkəʾa Krəstos zä-näbärä qädami bəḥtwäddäd wä-wəʾətu məta lä-wälättä* [*sic* for *wälätt*] *Dadəqt* [*sic* for *ṣadəqt*, "righteous"] *zä-gädämä* [*sic* for *gädamä*] *Qʷäraṣa*. See also the French translation of the sentence: "Il avait épousé la fille de Dâdëqt de Gadama-Quarâtsâ" (Basset 1882, 133).

Peṭros. Indeed, sometimes they are so subtle that they must be highlighted or defended. After a disciple slept under a tree unharmed, God ordered the serpent above to make a noise, the text states, so that the man would know he had experienced a miracle. At the age of thirty-nine, Walatta Petros prays to the Virgin Mary to be cured of suddenly heavy menstrual periods. When her periods permanently stop, the text explains that this was a miracle, for Walatta Petros was "still young" and had not reached the age of menopause.

Some events defying the laws of nature, or probability, do happen, but most of these occur later in Walatta Petros's life, after Roman Catholicism is defeated: Walatta Petros's boat flies over the water, a follower flies as if he has wings, an icon of the Virgin Mary moves its finger, and a man dies and comes back to life a few hours later. Walatta Petros regularly has visions and speaks to angels and the Virgin Mary. But, anytime there is an unbelievable event, the text does something most telling—it defends its likelihood: "we know and are certain that the testimony of two or three people is trustworthy" or "this testimony is trustworthy and no lie." Stories that are nothing but myth proffer no such defenses of the illogical. Most hagiobiographies have no such claims. Only stories that are a mix of fact and fiction, where the unbelievable fits uneasily into the actual, must be defended.

Fourth, the vividness of Walatta Petros's gädl stands in contrast to some of those written later about other women saints from this period. For instance, the *Gädlä Fəqərtä Krəstos* is about another seventeenth-century noblewoman, Fəqərtä Krəstos (also called Ǝmmä Məʿuz), who was married to an officer of the king, like Walatta Petros, and who also refused to obey the king's religious edicts (Anonymous 2002). The *Gädlä Fəqərtä Krəstos* is more conventional, however, in that Fəqərtä Krəstos is not a lone woman leader but her husband's follower. After standing in Lake Ṭana for forty days to protest the king's religious policies, Fəqərtä Krəstos and her husband are tortured and killed, along with thousands of other Ḥabäša martyrs. She rises from the dead, however, to threaten the king with the relics of her own dead body, and he repents. She then travels, after her death, to Jerusalem and Armenia to found a monastic community. She is believed to be the founder of the Ǝmmä Məʿuz Monastery in Mäqet, Wällo, about two hundred miles east of Robit. Her birth name was Maryam Ṣädala (Saint Mary Is Her Halo), her ordinary name was Muzit, and after she became a nun, she was also called Fəqərtä Krəstos and Ǝmmä Məʿuz. Some research has been conducted on this text (Nosnitsin 2005a). According to modern oral traditions about her, she was brought before the king and condemned him for his conversion, upon which he was struck dumb and his tongue leaped from his mouth onto the ground.[10] The fanciful nature of some parts of the *Gädlä Fəqərtä Krəstos* may suggest it was written long after she lived.

This brings us to a significant point about the *Gädlä Wälättä Peṭros*—it was written down close to the events, not long after them. According to the *Gädlä Wälättä*

[10] Selamawit Mecca heard this anecdote while conducting research on Ḥabäša female saints at Šänkorä Giyorgis's monastery in Anbäsami, South Gondär, Ethiopia, in February 2010.

Peṭros, it was written down "thirty years" after Walatta Petros's death, in the "Year of Mercy 7165," or 1672–73 CE.[11] The *Gädlä Wälättä Peṭros* repeatedly states that the men and women who knew Walatta Petros personally were the engine behind the creation and completion of the text. The liveliness of the *Gädlä Wälättä Peṭros* is due to being an eyewitness account of those who lived the events as members of Walatta Petros's community.

Aside from being an important literary text, then, the *Gädlä Wälättä Peṭros* provides insight into various historical questions. For those scholars who argue that King Susənyos did not abdicate to his son Fasilädäs (Berry 2009), the *Gädlä Wälättä Peṭros* provides support. For those interested in understanding early modern Ḥabäša monastic conventions, cultural patterns, and gendered leadership, the *Gädlä Wälättä Peṭros* is vital. It is widely agreed that the *Gädlä Wälättä Peṭros* is not only the richest of the women's gädlat but may also be the most historically valuable gädl ever written.

Finally, the *Gädlä Wälättä Peṭros* is currently the oldest book-length biography written by Africans about an African woman. We hope that earlier biographies are found, but, as of now, the extant texts do not seem to qualify for this honor. They are too short (in the form of letters, eulogies, or sermons), too apocryphal (written long after the saint's life), or written by non-Africans. One of the more intriguing possibilities is the hagiobiography of Perpetua and Felicity, a Roman woman and her North African slave who were martyred in the early third century. Although their hagiobiography is short, a fifth of the length of the *Gädlä Wälättä Peṭros*, it was most likely written by Perpetua (Heffernan 2012). The three earlier Gəʿəz hagiobiographies about women are fascinating, but perhaps do not qualify as biographies of women: the *Gädlä Mäsqäl Kəbra* is really about her famous husband Lalibäla, and the *Gädlä Zena Maryam* and the *Gädlä Krəstos Śämra* were likely written long after they lived. Further research is needed, however, as very little is known about these texts, and they would all be worthwhile to translate into English.

Other Gəʿəz Texts about Walatta Petros

Walatta Petros is mentioned in other Gəʿəz texts written in the centuries after her death. Until more work is done on Gəʿəz collections of saints' lives, it will remain unknown how many *Sənkəssar* manuscripts have entries on Walatta Petros and whether those entries have substantial variations.

She and her monastery appear more than once in the royal chronicles. For instance, the king twice consulted the leaders of her monastery at Qʷäraṣa: in 1693 about the suitability of the new patriarch and later about theological questions (Anonymous 1903a, 174–75, 214). In 1700, the abbess of Qʷäraṣa, Tälawitä Krəstos, was cited as an important cleric (Anonymous 1983, 232).

[11] Due to its reliance on MS Abb. 88 only, CR was incorrect in stating it was twenty-nine years later. All the other manuscripts state it was thirty years later.

Walatta Petros features prominently in the early pages of the royal chronicle of King Iyasu II (r. 1730–55), son of King Bäkaffa and Queen Məntəwwab (Anonymous 1912, 13–16). Walatta Petros is heralded as a prophet of his reign with a four-page story. After praising her as a champion of the faith who rebuked the heretical king, it depicts her on her way into exile to Žäbäy. According to the chronicle, she then happened to be present at the birth of Damo, Iyasu's great-grandfather. In a dream, she then saw cattle dancing in front of Iyasu's great-grandmother and Məntəwwab's grandmother, who was named Yolyana, thus predicting that their line would yield a son who would lead the nation. Walatta Petros seems to have received significant attention during Iyasu's reign, as MSS H and I of the *Gädlä Wälättä Ṗeṭros* contain a different set of miracles that happened during the fifth year of his own reign and during the reign of his father Bäkaffa.

Soon Qʷäraṣa became famous as a place of asylum for those nobles who, like Walatta Petros, sought to escape punishment by the king. When King Täklä Giyorgis (1751–1817) banished his father-in-law, Wäldä Gäbrəʾel, who was a *däğğazmač* (general), the man went to Qʷäraṣa for ten months in the late 1790s hoping for the saint's protection. He and some of his men "all lived there at Quaratsa together, and at work, they spent the time listening to the voice of the books (reading aloud) and conversing with the monks, and the nights they passed in the Church which was a house of prayer, . . . and he prayed always for Walatta Petros, for the monks, the refuge from oppression and oppressors," according to the royal chronicle (Blundell 1922, 340). Not long before, another däğğazmač had taken refuge there and escaped seizure "by help of the prayer of Waleta Petros, holy among the holy persons; monks and nuns had prayed much [for him]" (ibid., 334). Later, Qʷäraṣa became the place where monks negotiated reconciliations between warring nobles (ibid., 436). As Bosc-Tiessé notes, Qʷäraṣa probably became a place of refuge because it was closely associated with Walatta Petros, who herself had succeeded in escaping the wrath of the king.

Walatta Petros also appears in other saints' stories. An eighteenth-century *Sənkəssar* tells the story of an abbot of Leba Mäṭaya Śəllase Monastery near Däbrä Tabor who knew Walatta Petros and also went into exile "when the Roman faith happened in our country, and the Christian faith was lost" (Getatchew Haile 2007b). *Abunä* Śärṣ̌ä Maryam was also told that martyrdom was not his path. After the faith was restored, one day he traveled by *tankʷa*, a papyrus boat in use on Lake Ṭana for many centuries, with Walatta Petros, here called the "Abbess of Rema Monastery." The historicity of the anecdote is unclear: perhaps they actually met, or perhaps the story was invented later. According to the *Sənkəssar*, while the two saints were

> talking with each other about the glory given to them from God, his hand cross fell in the depth of the lake. Pilots, who knew swimming, came and searched for the cross; [but] they did not find it. At that time, he was very saddened over [the loss of] his hand [cross]. Three years later, a fisherman found it when he was fishing. He brought it out, with its appearance [intact], as it was before. He handed it over to Walatta

> Petros, who was present when it fell. She recognized it, that it was the hand cross of Abunä Śärṣä Maryam. She sent it [to his monastery] with honor, saying, "Place it gracefully, having written its miracles." Then they received it with pleasure and joy. He worked miracles and wonders with it. (Getatchew Haile 2007b, 40)

Walatta Petros continued to live on in the minds of the people as the finder of lost objects of faith and a visionary with power over kings' futures.

The Text's Genre and Female Saints

In 1975, the scholar Kinefe-Rigb Zelleke identified about two hundred Ḥabäša saints, including eight female saints.[12] Quite a few saints have been identified since, and the preeminent scholar of Ethiopian female saints, Selamawit Mecca (2006), puts the total of female Ḥabäša saints at approximately thirty (the known female Ḥabäša saints appear in table 1). However, scholars have seen, cataloged, or digitized the gädlat for only six of these female saints. Since it is estimated that only a fraction of the manuscripts in Ethiopia and Eritrea have been digitized and/or cataloged, more gädlat are likely to emerge. Interestingly, nine of the thirty identified female saints are seventeenth-century women who resisted conversion to Roman Catholicism, including Walatta Petros and Fəqərtä Krəstos, both of whom have gädlat (table 1).

It is not surprising, as the early twentieth-century scholar J. M. Harden noted, that this period of religious struggle in the Ethiopian highlands would yield many saints (1926, chap. 7). Thousands of Ḥabäša died defending their beliefs, and those remaining were eager to honor the heroism of those who had died. What is striking, however, is that so many of the Ḥabäša hagiobiographies from this period are about women, and that the hagiobiographies devoted to women cluster in this period specifically, suggesting that women played a special role in defending Ḥabäša beliefs against European incursions in the 1600s, as I have argued in previous sections. Others have remarked on the historical prevalence of African female saints: "A statistical analysis of all known pre-Constantinian martyrs reveals that, compared to general Mediterranean trends, African women represented a markedly higher proportion of all female saints" (Shaw 1993, 13).

Scholarship on the Text

Most people outside of Ethiopia have never heard of Walatta Petros. Garbled information about her appears on some Roman Catholic websites in Europe, which often incorrectly celebrate her as a Roman Catholic saint. Such misinformation re-

[12] After forty years, this groundbreaking work is in dire need of updating, although it may take a team of scholars to equal the work that Kinefe-Rigb Zelleke did on his own without computers.

TABLE 1
Some Täwaḥədo Church Female Saints

Female Saint	*Era*	*Region*	*Gädl?*	*Print Gəʿəz Edition?*	*Translation?*	*Kinefe-Rigb*
Ṣäbälä Maryam	500s	Gondär	Uncertain		No	
Mäsqäl Kəbra, wife of King Lalibäla	1100s–1200s	Lalibäla	Yes		Uncertain	No. 98
Zena Maryam, founder of a monastery	1300s	Addis Zämän, South Gondär	Yes		Italian	No. 201
Krəstos Śämra, most famous female saint	1300s–1400s	Šäwa, Lake Ṭana	Yes	CSCO	Italian	No. 88
Wälättä Ṗeṭros, resisted Catholicism	1600s	Šäwa, Lake Ṭana	Yes	CSCO	Italian Amharic	No. 163
Fəqərtä Krəstos (Ǝmmämuz, Ǝmmä Məʿuz) resisted Catholicism	1600s	Lake Ṭana, South Gondär	Yes		Amharic	No. 52
Wälättä Maryam	1600s	Däbra Wärq, East Goǧǧam	Yes		No	No. 162
Ǝḫətä Krəstos, resisted Catholicism	1600s	Lake Ṭana, South Gondär	*Sənkəssar* only?		French	No. 40
Ǝḫətä Ṗeṭros, resisted Catholicism	1600s	Lake Ṭana, South Gondär	Uncertain		No	No. 41
Wälättä Ṗawlos, resisted Catholicism	1600s	Lake Ṭana, South Gondär	Uncertain		No	
Wälättä Ṣəyon, resisted Catholicism	1600s	Wällo, Amhara	Uncertain		No	No. 164
Ǝmmä Wätät, resisted Catholicism	1600s	Maḫdärä Maryam, S. Gondär	Uncertain		No	
Ǝmmä Šänkora Giyorgis, resisted Catholicism	1600s	Anbäsami, South Gondär	Uncertain		No	
Salome		Wäräb and Däbrä Libanos	*Sənkəssar* only			

verses the purpose of her life, which was to repulse Roman Catholicism. On a site hosted by Spanish Catholics, for instance, Walatta Petros is incorrectly described as a pagan who converted to Christianity due to the Jesuits, who attempted to tie the Täwaḥədo Church to Rome, and who left her husband because he refused to convert.

> Conviene conocer la vida de esta mujer santa aunque con un nombre raro. Había nacido y muerto en Etiopía en los años 1594–1643. Se llevaba muy bien con su marido, que era ministro. Se convirtió al cristianismo gracias al padre jesuita español Paez. Ella intentó entonces unir a toda la Iglesia de Etiopía con la de Roma, pero la tentativa fracasó. . . . Su marido no quería convertirse y, por esta razón, dejó su lecho conyugal. . . . Walatta era una mujer muy guapa. Contaba 35 años. Se alejó de la corte y se fue a un convento que ella había construido en un campo abisinio.
>
> [It is useful to know the life of this holy woman with a rare name. She was born and died in Ethiopia in the years 1594–1643. She was getting along very well with her husband, who was an official. She converted to Christianity due to the Spanish Jesuit Father Paez. She then tried to unite the Ethiopian Church with Rome, but the attempt failed. Her husband did not want to convert and, for this reason, she left their conjugal bed. . . . Walatta was an attractive woman, 35 years old. She moved away from the court and took refuge in a convent that she had constructed in a remote place in Abyssinia.] (our translation)[13]

Similarly, on a site hosted by the Roman Catholic Church of France, she is praised merely as a beautiful woman who moved to the countryside to create communes. No mention is made of the Täwaḥədo Church.

> Cette femme très belle et très bonne était l'épouse d'un ministre du négus d'Ethiopie. Elle quitta son mari consentant pour se retirer parmi les serfs de la campagne abyssine où elle créa un village dans lequel l'on menait la vie communautaire. . . . Sept de ces villages existaient quand elle mourut.
>
> [This very beautiful and very good woman was the wife of an official of the Ethiopian king. She left her consenting husband and withdrew to live among the lowly peasants of the Ethiopian countryside, where she created a village in which people lived a communal life. . . . Seven such villages existed when she died.] (our translation)[14]

More scholarly entries on Walatta Petros started to appear after 1970 in encyclopedias on Africa or saints, probably due to the publication of the Italian translation of her gädl in 1970 (Appiah and Gates 2005; Belaynesh Michael 1975, 1977a, 1977b; Cohen 2010b). She also was mentioned in histories of Africa (Ogot 1992; Crummey 2000), although they did little more than summarize the text and sometimes short-

[13] Padre Felipe Santos Campaña SDB, "Santa Walatta Petros, Noviembre 24," Autores Catolicos, http://www.autorescatolicos.org/felipesantosantawalattapetros.htm. Now at http://churchforum.butacas-cine.com/santa-walatta-petros.htm.

[14] "Sainte Walatta [*sic*]." Nomínis, Eglise catholique en France, http://nominis.cef.fr/contenus/saint/9372/Sainte-Walatta.html.

ened her name incorrectly to "Walatta." Only once does a historian rise to a real discussion of her case. In his book on the church in Africa, Adrian Hastings describes the text as "perhaps the first biography of an African woman," adding that she seems more of a "witch than a saint," and concluding direly that she was "something of an ecclesiastical feminist" (1994, 159–60). The first mention in English of the *Gädlä Wälättä Ṗeṭros* appeared in 1936, when Robert Cheesman provided a one-paragraph summary of its contents after visiting monasteries on Lake Ṭana (1936, 168–70).

Aside from these mentions, few scholars have studied the *Gädlä Wälättä Ṗeṭros.* In Indo-European languages other than English, four scholars have written about the work. The first was the Russian scholar Boris Turaev, an expert on Gəˁəz texts, who wrote an article on the *Gädlä Wälättä Ṗeṭros* ten years before any print edition of it was published and, perhaps for that reason, got so many of the basic details about her wrong that his analysis cannot be considered useful (Turaev 1902, 278–79). For instance, he incorrectly states that the text depicts Walatta Petros in a struggle against the Täwaḥədo Church only, not Roman Catholicism.[15] In 1943, Maria Rosaria Papi published an Italian précis of the text, several decades before the full Italian translation was available. In the last two paragraphs, she praises Gälawdewos, author of the *Gädlä Wälättä Ṗeṭros,* as "un uomo di notevole cultura per un Abissino" (a man of considerable culture for an Abyssinian), listing many of the books discussed in the text and adding that he has "uno stile quanto mai vivo e forma chiara" (a particularly lively style and clear structure). She concludes that it possesses "intrinseco valore letterario" (intrinsic literary value) and "un posto d'onore nella letteratura etiopica" (a place of honor in Ethiopian literature). Conti Rossini included in Latin (then still the language of much European scholarship on so-called oriental texts) a four-page preface (describing its composition, contents, and importance) in his Gəˁəz print edition of the *Gädlä Wälättä Ṗeṭros* (Conti Rossini and Jaeger 1912).

Ricci was the first to do more than summarize, providing an eight-page Italian preface to his 1970 translation.[16] He rightly notes that there seems to be no basis for Conti Rossini's attribution of the composition of the text to a place called Afär Färäs. This attribution has spread widely, even though the *Gädlä Wälättä Ṗeṭros* states that it was composed in Qʷäraṣa. (Of course, the two places were very near each other, about seven miles apart on the southeast shore of Lake Ṭana.) None of these four pieces represents a substantial contribution to the study of Walatta Petros.

In English, only two articles dedicated to Walatta Petros have appeared. One is an outstanding contribution by the art historian Claire Bosc-Tiessé, who conducted field research at monasteries on Lake Ṭana about the creation of the manuscript of

[15] Turaev states that "In the entire lengthy story of her sufferings we never even find the name of Rome or of the Pope; the entire matter deals with 'the Orthodox faith of Dioscorus' and 'the impure faith of Leo', as if this happened not in the seventeenth, but in the fifth century. . . . Thus, Walatta Petros' struggle against the Propaganda is at its core a struggle against Orthodoxy," according to the translation by Chernetsov (2005b).

[16] Although Conti Rossini sometimes mentioned the text in his other published work.

Walatta Petros's gädl. Her article is a model for scholarship on Gəʿəz manuscripts, providing many original insights. Among other points, Bosc-Tiessé argues that the text, in depicting Christ conferring the rank of archdeaconess on her, gives Walatta Petros "an unequalled hierarchical rank for a woman in the Ethiopian Church" (2003, 412).[17] Bosc-Tiessé analyzes a number of historical sources written after Walatta Petros's death that mention Qʷärasa, revealing that her monastery was a center of Orthodoxy, a home for powerful abbesses, and an asylum for those seeking mercy from the king. Finally, she argues that Walatta Petros's gädl is unusual in that it represents "as far as we know today, the first life of an Ethiopian saint for which a narrative iconographic cycle has been made" (ibid., 411). That is, Walatta Petros's community was established enough to create sometime between 1716 and 1721 an expensive version of her gädl with twenty-three images depicting her posthumous miracles (ibid., 409). With her kind permission, we have reproduced these images from photographs that Bosc-Tiessé took in the field from the now lost manuscript. She carefully studies this cycle, offering a number of useful observations; for instance, noting that it portrays Walatta Petros in nun's clothes before her death but in the Virgin Mary's clothes after her death, when she is performing her miracles.

The late Russian scholar Sevir Chernetsov (2005d) wrote the second article in English, pointing out that Walatta Petros was a trailblazer not only in defending the faith but in transgressing the norms for women's behavior by becoming an outspoken female leader. Most of the article is a summary of the plot of the hagiobiography, with his translations of important phrases. However, the later part of the article is an inimical interpretation of the text's claims. For instance, Chernetsov argues that Walatta Petros was able to become such an important leader not because of her persuasive skills or spirituality but because of her noble birth and softhearted husband, who more than once delivered her from a death sentence for treason. Chernetsov likewise argues that the reason Walatta Petros asked the monks to forbid women from entering Məṣəlle Monastery is that she wanted to avoid being under male leadership and wanted to return to Zäge with just the women, who were reluctant to leave Məṣəlle (2005d, 62). Nowhere does the text say that the women were reluctant to move, however, and it was impossible for her to escape some aspects of male leadership, as only men could celebrate the Liturgy. Indeed, men participated in her community in Zäge, as the next pages reveal. Chernetsov is also suspicious of Gälawdewos, asserting about one passage that his "reference to St. Paul is fictitious; [the quote] is absent in his epistles," when, in fact, it is there, just altered (2005d, 70). Although Chernetsov's suggestion that Walatta Petros had initially hoped to set up a monastery for women only is intriguing, there is no evidence for this in the text. Like so many of the publications on Walatta Petros, Chernetsov's consists of summaries and assertions unsupported by the text.

The scholar Leonardo Cohen (2010b) wrote a solid encyclopedic article about her, although marred by the previous scholarship's errors. Pace his article, the *Gädlä*

[17] See also her related work in 2000, 2004, and 2008.

Wälättä Peṭros was not written in Afär Färäs; it does not say that all three of her children were sons; she was not born in 1594; she did not die in 1644; and she never went to Aksum. While a few other articles or chapters in English mention Walatta Petros in passing, or summarize her story in a paragraph, none discuss her at length (Gundani 2004; Cohen 2009b, 2009a; Andrzejewski, Piłaszewicz, and Tyloch 1985, 282). As this review of previous scholarship on the text makes clear, the *Gädlä Wälättä Peṭros* is in need of more and deeper research.

New Directions for Scholarship on the Text

The *Gädlä Wälättä Peṭros* is a significant historical text in need of better scholarship, but, just as importantly, it offers much to scholars in a variety of fields, including undergraduates writing about this for the classroom. The way that this text thinks, to use Stathis Gourgouris's formulation, challenges us to theorize more richly (2003). How the text theorizes "the conditions of the world from which it emerges and to which it addresses itself" forces scholars to rethink their own habits of thought regarding literature and the world. Below, I briefly discuss six of these opportunities for rethinking. The following interpretations about sexuality are those of myself, Belcher, and should not be assumed to represent the opinions of anyone else involved in this translation.

First, the text theorizes female agency in a radical way. For instance, in Ethiopian hagiobiographies of female saints, female sainthood represents the ascent of a woman who is not sweetly kind but brutally powerful. She will not fit Protestant or Roman Catholic ideas of how a saint should behave. In a word, she is not "nice." When Christ comes to her in person, Walatta Petros refuses to do as he commands, repeatedly rejecting his advice. In other instances, she lies.[18] She is quick to judge and punish. Faced with others' natural emotions of fear or sadness, she rebukes rather than comforts. She forbids a mother to weep over her dead son. We might forgive such "sins" in a male saint, but other acts are harder for modern readers to stomach from a woman or a man. Walatta Petros slaps servants who disobey her. When her followers are particularly wicked or particularly good, she calls on God to kill them and they do, indeed, die. In one case, she deliberately causes the death of a disobedient disciple through what one can only call a potion. This has led one critic to call her more witch than saint (Hastings 1997). Another argues that such incidents demonstrate female nuns' aim to attain a "holy gender," one of masculine distance (Wright 2001).

While Walatta Petros's actions may seem cruel, the seventeenth century was a crueler time. She was abused by her husband and hunted down by European soldiers. All her children died, and death was a daily possibility for her as well. In such

[18] The "monastic lie" is common because nuns and monks avoid boasting about the extent of their asceticism and thus spiritual attainments; therefore, they lie to disguise their suffering (Wright 2001, 93).

a context, her followers wanted power, not sweetness. At the beginning of her religious life, the text says, she was soft, a noblewoman who had led a life of luxury. Her tender, noble feet bled easily when she had to walk long distances, and her delicate hands were not used to the difficult work. Faced with the brute strength of her husband, the king, and the military, she engaged in evasion: playing dead and lying. But she was soon eating little other than leaves and building churches of stone with her own hands. The text notes that she stopped menstruating when she was thirty-nine, perhaps because she weighed so little due to fasting. She became a tough woman who led a tough life and was tough with her followers. And yet, she could be tender as well. In one long passage, she and a woman friend reach a destination where they are supposed to part, but Walatta Petros begs her friend to go a little farther with her, and a little farther again, and then a little farther. Walatta Petros provided a home and food for those whom the new religion had made homeless and hungry. She gave up her own food and medicine so that others might be restored. Despite the regular decimation of her community and her own longing to take up a solitary religious life, she stayed with her followers and ministered to them. And when she died, the entire community was distraught.

Unlike saints in the European tradition, perhaps, Walatta Petros is not merely a good woman with a special connection to the divine. She is not superhuman either; for instance, while she does perform domestic miracles (replenishing ale and flour), she does not endure torture and martyrdom, and she is not a model of ecstatic and masochistic endurance as so many women saints are. She is, actually, a human goddess. The text states this hybrid status directly: "while she was a human being like us, to her it was given to be a god." This means that Walatta Petros is not a mere intermediary with the divine but a direct redeemer. While the text sometimes states that Walatta Petros can save her followers because God has accepted her intercession, it also often states that she is their savior ("many souls will be saved through [her]") or has her say it directly ("those . . . who invoke my name will be saved and not damned"). She works miracles, the text exclaims, "which had never been before and shall never be again." In the text, Walatta Petros may start off as a lady whose actions are regulated by gendered social norms, but she steadily moves toward being a protective and avenging Old Testament god who lives outside the rules of polite society.

The text's conception of female agency suggests that perhaps current literary scholars' theorizing of it arises too much from masochistic frameworks that reinscribe women as weak. Walatta Petros is never weak. In leadership, she is direct, all-powerful. She is not the self-annihilating saint who would rather die than be raped, or rather cut out her own tongue than disagree with male authority. She acts with impunity. Yet, nowhere does the *Gädlä Wälättä Ṗeṭros* suggest that Walatta Petros's strength is anything other than feminine: in almost every sentence, she is called "our mother," "our holy mother," or "our holy and blessed mother," who leads through muscular fierceness. Thus, this text challenges our views of gender.

Second, the text offers a unique opportunity to view how a text written by Africans for Africans before the modern period theorizes animal agency. In the bestiary that is the *Gädlä Wälättä Ṗeṭros*—with dogs, bees, and donkeys appearing in the extended metaphor of the first pages, and thereafter leopards, lions, wolves, hyenas, snakes, doves, partridges, eagles, vultures, gazelles, stags, antelopes, hippopotamuses, fish, mice, locusts, and so on—animals are simultaneously their own agents and God's agents. As one of my undergraduate students argued, the wild animals are neither romantic allies of African peoples living in nature, nor are they perpetual enemies of human beings (Gideon 2012). Animals and human beings live in a state of reciprocal recognition, with animals having an agency little different from that of human beings.

Third, the *Gädlä Wälättä Ṗeṭros* challenges facile ideas about the traditional African family and sexuality. In her early twenties, without sadness or regret, Walatta Petros left her husband to become a nun and the mother of an alternative family: she is the *əmmä maḫbär* (the mother of the community) of hundreds of followers. No "father" is mentioned; she commands her followers in every aspect of their lives as she sees fit. At the same time, she does have a lifelong partner who leads with her: a woman (Belcher forthcoming).

When Walatta Petros first became a nun, she was introduced to another woman who also had recently become a nun, Əḫətä Krəstos, and the description of their first encounter is rapturous. As soon as Walatta Petros and Əḫətä Krəstos saw each other, the text states, "love was infused into both their hearts, love for one another, and . . . they were like people who had known each other" their whole lives. Later, the text says, they "lived together in mutual love, like soul and body. From that day onward the two did not separate, neither in times of tribulation and persecution, nor in those of tranquillity, but only in death." They became lifelong companions, a holy and celibate couple, leading the community together, part of a new family. Upon her deathbed, Walatta Petros's last thoughts and words were about her friend, worrying about how Əḫətä Krəstos would fare without her, saying three times, "She will be disconsolate; she has no other hope than me!" There is no doubt that the two women were involved in a lifelong partnership of deep, romantic friendship.

To identify them as lesbians would be anachronistic, however, using a twentieth-century Anglo-American term and identity for a very different seventeenth-century African reality. For one thing, Walatta Petros was deeply committed to celibacy, as were all sincere monks and nuns in Ethiopia. Once, upon seeing a monk and nun flirting, she angrily asserted that she wished she had a spear so that she could drive it through them together, as did a priest of the Old Testament who witnessed fornication near the temple. Later, near the time of her death, Walatta Petros claimed that a plague that had killed more than one hundred people was a "mercy" because she had witnessed nuns being lustful with each other. Nevertheless, abstaining from or condemning sexual activity does not change the nature of one's desire. Indeed, some interpret the anecdote about same-sex desire as suggesting that Walatta Petros struggled with it (see the notes to chapter 86 in the translation). Her husband and the king discussed her loving relationship with Əḫətä Krəstos as abnormal, that is, as disruptive of familial norms. Furthermore, the very presence in the text of an anecdote about same-sex desire and sexual activity is telling. Under conditions of disavowal, the only way to bring up same-sex desire is in negation. Finally, the way that same-sex desire is presented in the text suggests that the sin was not monstrous, not inhuman, but known, an ordinary sign of the human frailty of monks and nuns committed to avoiding the temptations of the flesh. Little distinction is made between expressions of heterosexual desire and homosexual desire: both are seen as wrong. When asked whether any of her followers, including the lustful nuns, were condemned to hell, Walatta Petros asserts that all were saved. The text's theorizing of what constitutes proper family and human sexuality challenges, at the very least, problematic assertions that same-sex desire was unknown in Ethiopia before the arrival of Europeans. While the nature of the saint's own relationships with women is unclear in the text, a matter of interpretation, the fact of women's desire for other women is not unclear in the text and is not a matter of interpretation. Rather, the text clearly and unequivocally describes desire between women and states that women-desiring women, if they are faithful believers, go to heaven.

Fourth, the *Gädlä Wälättä Ṗeṭros* celebrates the power of language and books. It is massively intertextual (quoting from forty books of the Bible alone) and regularly focuses on books as books. When a flash flood surprises Walatta Petros's group, the water "did not damage the books at all; not even a single letter of them was wiped out." The written word is stronger than the elements, particularly when it is about Walatta Petros. Integral to the text are two poems rich in allusions and double meanings. A priest near death on a stormy Lake Ṭana sings the words of one and is saved. His friends urge him to tell the wonderful story again and again, begging him to sing the hymn for them, which he does in a sweet voice. They part in awe, marveling at the power of our mother to save through the word. Two of the miracles feature beloved books of poems to Walatta Petros. A nun wears the book of the *Mälkəʾa Wälättä Ṗeṭros* poems around her neck. When a fisherman steals the book and tries to sell it, he is unable to find a buyer—it has a sign of her community's ownership that everyone recognizes—and, chastened, he returns it to its rightful owner. A recent convert steals another nun's copy of the same book but is also thwarted in trying to gain value from what can only live in community. Another miracle involves the making of the *Gädlä Wälättä Ṗeṭros*, when a monk tells Gälawdewos that he has had a vision of how Gälawdewos will start and complete a beautiful book about Walatta Petros. Would that all authors should have such! The *Gädlä Wälättä Ṗeṭros* insists on its own power in the world.

Fifth, the text's theology is fascinating and deserves real thought in the context of the Täwaḥədo Church. For instance, prayer is often not so much a polite request, but a wrenching of favors from reluctant deities. Christ, Mary, and Walatta Petros herself are often in need of persuasion. When a woman on her way to honor Walatta Petros loses the candle necessary for the process, the text says that the woman "began to argue with our holy mother Walatta Petros," even exclaiming, "Why are you treating me like this and humiliating me?" In another case, Walatta

Petros rebukes the Virgin Mary for misunderstanding her demand that she chasten a monk, not kill him.

A final challenge to our thinking arises from how the *Gädlä Wälättä Ṗeṭros* presents authorship, as laid out in "The Text's Authorship" section in this volume. The complicated authorship of the *Gädlä Wälättä Ṗeṭros* aids those seeking to problematize ideas of authorship, both supporting and challenging Saussurean ideas about language, not authors, speaking and Barthesian ideas about authors as facilitators not originators.

The Text's Images

We have reproduced images from four manuscripts in this volume: thirty-three illustrations from MS A (three of which are divided into separate images), twenty-five illustrations from MS D, and one illustration each from MSS F and J. These images illustrate many moments in Walatta Petros's life, making it more vivid, as well as providing rich cultural detail and historical information, as Claire Bosc-Tiessé and Donald Crummey have both laid out (Bosc-Tiessé 2003; Crummey 2000, 137–43). For instance, the images depict the behavior of servants around kings (plate 7), monks and nuns preparing and eating Ethiopian food (plates 24 and 25), and the size and shape of such everyday objects as jars, pots, bowls, stirrers, razors, tables, boats, saddles, shirts, gowns, candles, books, bookstands, pens, inkwells, and swords (plates 16, 19, 25, 26, 47, and 54).

The manuscripts date from different centuries and thus the images in them represent different periods in Ethiopian painting aesthetics. It's not possible to explore these styles richly here; we hope others will use this volume to research these images. Briefly, however, MS J is the oldest manuscript, most likely dating to 1672, and its pale purple, green, and gold colors are from natural dyes. The purple is likely from indigo dye (from the plant *Indigofera tinctoria*), the green from terre verte, and the gold from the mineral orpiment or yellow flowers. By contrast, MS F was most likely made sometime in the twentieth century, and its vivid, bright, and multiple colors (blue, purple, yellow, green, and black) are from nonnatural dyes. John Mellors and Anne Parsons, experts on Ethiopian icon and manuscript painting methods (2002), suggest that the colors in the MS F image were made from a child's watercolor paint set. Blue is a difficult color to produce, while reds and yellows are easily made from ochres found locally.

The images must be read with care and without assuming Western conventions, however. First, many of the images have more than one panel and are meant to be read in sequence. By Western convention, one reads images the same way one reads texts: from top left to top right and then bottom left to bottom right. However, the images in MS D with four or more panels are generally read counterclockwise from the top left image. Moreover, if there are two panels with one on top and one below, the bottom one is sometimes the first in the sequence. This does not seem to be the case with MS A, so variations in reading direction may be due to when the manuscript was written. Work on line directions in Gəʿəz texts has been done by Stephen Delamarter (2010), but not on image order in Gəʿəz texts so far.

Second, the size of people in the images does not always indicate whether someone is a child or an adult, short or tall, but rather their rank and status. Walatta Petros generally appears larger than those around her, therefore, and servants are almost always depicted as small and childlike (plate 5).

Third, the two vertical marks on characters' cheeks in many of the images are not physical scars on their bodies but the sign of strong emotions—in particular, distress, fear, and grief (plate 9). In a moving image on the positive end of the affect spectrum, a healed child clasps his mother around her neck, hiding his face behind hers (plate 34).

Fourth, hand gestures and body postures constitute entire symbolic systems. While research has been done on such in Byzantine and medieval art (Bremmer and Roodenburg 1993; Kendon 2004), and some of these gestures appear in Ethiopian paintings as well, more research is needed. One ancient sign—in images from many regions and in some of the images in this translation—is a person depicted with one hand's index finger and middle finger extended, which is a gesture of enunciation signaling that the person is speaking (plate 1). Other hand gestures are religious. For instance, holding both hands palm open with arms extended and the eyes turned skyward is a posture of worship, called *orans* (in Latin, praying) in medieval European art (plates 1 and 2). Priests confer benediction by holding the right hand up with the first two fingers extended and the other two fingers folded down, sometimes with the thumb touching (plate 1). Forming the thumb, index, and middle finger into a point symbolizes the Trinity (plate 2). The arms crossed across the chest over the heart is not a sign of aggression or coldness, but a sign of one's Christian devotion by making the sign of the cross. In these illustrations, hand gesture rather than facial expression most often conveys emotion. Holding an index finger to one's chin is a sign of sorrow (plate 46). Cupping one's cheek with a hand is a sign that the person is feeling amazed or bewildered (plate 18). Holding the left hand to the forehead is a traditional Ethiopian gesture of pity and sorrow (plate 38). Two hands clasped to the cheek with the head tilted is a sign that the person is sleeping, even if they are standing up (plate 37). Other gestures clearly have meanings, although to us now uncertain: one hand clasping the shoulder perhaps means fear (plates 18 and 38).

Fifth, to distinguish gender, one must examine the face, not the clothing. Both men and women wear long gowns, but only men have facial hair and only women have neck rings (creased skin indicating a beautiful chubbiness) (plate 2).

Sixth, only the dead have halos. Thus, Walatta Petros has no halo when alive, but wears a halo when dead (plates 12 and 48).

Seventh, figures depicted lying down under portraits of Walatta Petros are not angels but the patrons of the manuscript, who are depicted as prostrate with devotion (plate 13).

Eighth, evil characters are depicted in profile with only one eye showing, while good people are never depicted in profile (plate 15). Many other images similarly depict symbolic meanings rather than simple realities—the sun is shown with a face (plate 57) and Walatta Petros sits on a cloud (plate 58).

Finally, note that the images were painted by scribes other than Gälawdewos and do not always exactly match the text. For instance, the captions in some manuscripts do not call ale *säwa*, as the manuscript does, but *ṭälla*. In one case, the woman beside Walatta Petros is identified as Ǝḫətä Krəstos, whereas the manuscript says it is Fälasitä Krəstos (plate 21).

Claire Bosc-Tiessé's articles address many other interesting aspects of the images in MS D.

The Biography of Walatta Petros

A summary of Walatta Petros's life story may give the reader a better sense of its arc. Below I have interwoven what we know about her life from her hagiobiography as well as other historical sources, which sometimes differ in their details.

According to multiple parts of her hagiobiography, Walatta Petros died in 1642 at the age of fifty, and thus was born in 1592. Her brothers were leading officials mentioned regularly in the royal chronicle of King Susənyos, part of a noble and powerful family with hereditary rights to vast lands to the south but outside the control of the Christian kingdom during her lifetime. At approximately the age of sixteen, Walatta Petros was married to a powerful man named Mälkəʾa Krəstos, one of the king's most important counselors and military commanders. As a member of the court, her husband decided to convert to Roman Catholicism. Walatta Petros did not wish to convert to Roman Catholicism, however, and because all three of her children had died in infancy, leaving married life without its fruits, she decided to take up the life of a nun. When Mälkəʾa Krəstos left home to repress the anti-Catholic rebellion started in 1617, Täwaḥədo Church bishops in the powerful monasteries on Lake Ṭana helped the twenty-three-year-old Walatta Petros to leave her husband and join them. After arriving at one of the monasteries on Lake Ṭana, she took a vow of celibacy and shaved her head. Walatta Petros then was persuaded to return to her husband, but when she learned that he had supported the killing of the head of the Täwaḥədo Church, she withdrew from him in disgust, abandoning his bed, all forms of adornment, and eating. Finally, her husband allowed her to leave him for good and fulfill her dream of entering the religious life.

Regarding her marriage, the hagiobiography lacks information that appears in other sources. Some *Sənkəssar* manuscripts have an entry about Walatta Petros for the day of her death, 17 Ḫədar. Most do not have it—the manuscripts Budge used for his English translation of the *Sənkəssar* mention Walatta Petros's name but do not include her story. However, the *Sənkəssar* entry about Walatta Petros in the two manuscripts we consulted (both from Təgray) state that Mälkəʾa Krəstos was her second husband, even though the hagiobiography makes no mention of a first husband. That is, the entry states, "when she reached the capacity of women, one man took her as a wife, but he was killed unjustly by King Yaʿqob [r. 1597–1603, 1604–6]. Then, Mälkəʾa Krəstos took her as a wife and he had three children with her" (Anonymous 1800s, 1900s). Since she was born in 1592, and was only fourteen by the time King Yaʿqob died, she could not have been married to this unnamed man for long. As the *Sənkəssar* entry was likely written within a year of her death, to be read upon her annual commemoration, and Gälawdewos wrote the gädl several decades later, it would seem Gälawdewos deliberately omitted this information. Since the first marriage did not result in children, perhaps Gälawdewos did not consider it important enough to mention.

The hagiobiography presents her second marriage in a different light than the European sources as well. While the Ethiopian sources state that Walatta Petros left her husband, the Jesuits claimed that it was the other way around, that her husband had "abandoned" her (Barradas 1996, 141). Since she was unable to give Mälkəʾa Krəstos heirs, all three children having died, it may be that her husband left her and she therefore became a nun. One of the Jesuits noted that divorces were readily allowed for various reasons, including "want of children" (Tellez 1710, 43). But perhaps the Portuguese author got the story wrong. Susənyos's wife also left him because of his conversion to Roman Catholicism, so Walatta Petros would not have been alone. Either way, all the sources—one Portuguese text and two Ḥabäša texts—record that Walatta Petros, the wife of Mälkəʾa Krəstos, became a nun, moving to Zäge Monastery on Lake Ṭana.

On leaving her husband's home, Walatta Petros met another noblewoman who was resisting Roman Catholic conversion, Əḫətä Krəstos, who became her lifelong partner and companion, the subject of many long anecdotes. At this point, Walatta Petros began her life as a radical itinerant preacher. Despising the king's abandonment of Ethiopia's faith to embrace foreign beliefs and rituals, Walatta Petros decided to speak up. She publicly rebuked all those who had converted—including the king, his counselors, and the high priests. She preached that the people should reject the faith of the foreigners and that priests should not call down blessings on the king during the Divine Liturgy. The latter was a direct attack on Susənyos's authority, implying that he was no longer the legitimate head of state. She became an enemy of the state and regularly had to flee persecution, with such high-ranking figures as the king's brother and second-in-command *Ras* Śəʿəlä Krəstos hunting her down. Enraged by her behavior, the king ordered that she appear before the entire court—all its princes, governors, officials, and scholars—a sign of what a threat she was considered. Walatta Petros stood before the court with "a determined heart and a strong faith" and was not terrified by their status, great number, or empty words. She was so fearless that her husband, Mälkəʾa Krəstos, had to beg the king to spare her life. He made this plea, the text states, because he still loved her.

Is it likely that her twice-abandoned husband defended her? Reading between the lines of the Portuguese texts suggests that Mälkəʾa Krəstos was conflicted about his role in fighting the faithful. Several of the Portuguese texts denigrate Mälkəʾa Krəstos for strategic rather than deeply felt beliefs. One calls him "homem fraco, mas muito astuto e prudente" (a weak, but very cunning and prudent man [our translation]) (Täklä Śəllase [Ṭinno] 1900, 2:420n). They also complain that the king forgave him too many times; the reason is left unclear but likely was the failure to fulfill the king's wishes. Perhaps Mälkəʾa Krəstos was caught between a king and a wife, trying to please both and pleasing neither. One of the Jesuits noted that "the Emperor's own Brother Raz Sela Christos . . . [and] his own cousin Melca Christos, Lord Steward to the Emperor," enjoyed the traditional church service and were glad to participate in dancing and the playing of instruments (Tellez 1710, 109). Men who thought nothing of swearing obedience to a foreign pope may have been more hesitant about forcing their wives to give up the practices that they themselves cherished. Even if the hagiobiography does not represent what really happened between two historical figures, it beautifully dramatizes the domestic conflicts that the king's conversion engendered.

Walatta Petros's fame skyrocketed after her confrontation with the king, and many of the faithful came long distances to join her religious community. Walatta Petros's community kept moving, just one step ahead of the king's spies and the "European soldiers." Although it seems as if Walatta Petros was a nomad by nature, preferring to move frequently from place to place, perhaps this nature was fashioned by the years she spent escaping her husband and fleeing persecution. Between the king's conversion to Roman Catholicism in 1621, and his rescinding that conversion in 1632, Walatta Petros traveled constantly in an area approximately 150 miles by 100 miles, from her husband's home south of Lake Ṭana all the way north to Waldəbba and all the way west to the modern border with Sudan (map 2). While she was at Waldəbba, a monk prophesied that she would establish and lead seven religious communities.

Soon Walatta Petros was hauled before the court again to be killed, but Mälkəʾa Krəstos saved her life by suggesting that the king subject her to thought reform. The king agreed, and a team of Jesuits and Afonso Mendes himself, the leader of the Roman Catholic mission in Ethiopia, spent every Saturday with her, from the morning into the evening, working to convert her to Roman Catholicism. They were not successful. Every week the king would ask Mendes whether he had succeeded, and every week the Jesuit leader had to report that he had not. She resisted the blandishments of one of the most persuasive educational institutions ever invented. When all these efforts failed, the king made up his mind to kill her, but yet again Mälkəʾa Krəstos saved her life by suggesting another compromise: exile. So the king sent her to Žäbäy, a place on the edge of the known world, more than one hundred miles to the west, where she was kept in chains among the "pagans." But her people eventually followed her there, and this foreign land became the first of the seven foretold communities. Her jailer tried to seduce and then kill her, but she prevailed. Eventually, struck by the force of her convictions, he became a devotee. By special dispensation, the king allowed her to return then, after three years in the wilderness.

When Walatta Petros returned to the Ethiopian highlands, she established her second and third communities. She encountered strong resistance from local male leaders, many of whom had converted to Roman Catholicism and challenged her authority, asking by what right she led and preached. She had been in conflict with male leadership throughout her life—with her husband, her brother, the king, the Jesuit patriarch, her jailer, the king's main advisors, and so on. The only male in her life with whom she did not have a conflict appears to have been her father, who doted on her. Later, the hagiobiography states that the male leaders were jealous "when they saw that all the world followed her." They began saying, "Is there a verse in scripture that [states that] a woman, even though she is a woman, can become a religious leader and teacher? This is something that scripture forbids to a woman." Nothing good, they argued, could come from women trying to be superior to men. As before, with her husband, a man came to Walatta Petros's defense. The great monk and scholar Fätlä Śəllase replied to her antagonists, "Did God not raise her up for our chastisement because we have become corrupt, so that God appointed her and gave our leadership role to her, while dismissing us? For this reason, you will not be able to make her quit."

Not long after, in 1632, the king rescinded his edict commanding conversion to Roman Catholicism, and Walatta Petros was elevated by her people as a heroine. She spent the remaining twelve years of her life traveling and setting up her fourth through seventh communities. The events of this later part of her life take up more than half the book. She performs many miracles and saves her community from repeated threats, only growing in reputation. At one point, "many women of high rank, daughters of princesses, concubines of the king, wives of great lords" all worked with her on restoring a church, and she spent time visiting with the new king, Fasilädäs, an admirer of her dedication. When she became sick, she went to Rema Island and died there at the age of fifty, having spent twenty-six years as a nun. Upon her deathbed, Christ arrived to affirm his covenant with her and to establish her as archdeaconess. Finally, after her death, her community set up a monastery devoted to her at Qʷäraṣa, on the eastern shore of Lake Ṭana. There, Ǝḫətä Krəstos became the abbess of her community until her death. Walatta Petros resisted converting to European forms of Christianity, and she and her sisters inspired a nation to do the same.

The Biography of Ǝḫətä Krəstos

Ǝḫətä Krəstos was Walatta Petros's lifelong companion, a noblewoman who left her husband and daughter to become a nun, and someone the community also considered elevating to sainthood. Such elevation required the writing of a gädl, and rumors of one devoted to Ǝḫətä Krəstos have long existed, with Kinefe-Rigb Zelleke saying a copy exists at Kämkäm (1975). Selamawit Mecca did not find such a gädl there in March 2010, however, and one scholar commented long ago, "Quant au *gadl*, on ignore s'il existe" (As for [her] *gädl*, it is unclear if it exists) (Nollet 1930).

Some scholars continue to think it must exist somewhere, since her mälkəʾ appears in some manuscripts of Walatta Petros's hagiobiography, and some think it is unusual for such poems to exist without a gädl (although my research shows that Walatta Petros's mälkəʾ likely existed before the gädl and did not appear with the earliest gädl, which suggests it is quite possible for Ǝḫ̮ətä Krəstos to have a mälkəʾ but not a gädl). At least one *Sənkəssar*, Vatican Eth. No. 112, gives a short (one-thousand-word) biography of Ǝḫ̮ətä Krəstos's life, however, which includes some information corroborated by the *Gädlä Wälättä Peṭros*, along with other details that do not appear in it. We did not translate Ǝḫ̮ətä Krəstos's mälkəʾ nor the *Sənkəssar* entry about her, but summarize some of the entry's information here.

Ǝḫ̮ətä Krəstos was born sometime before 1601, became a nun in 1617, and died on 2 April 1649. Walatta Petros, while on her deathbed, had named Ǝḫ̮ətä Krəstos her successor in November 1642, and Ǝḫ̮ətä Krəstos led the community for six-and-a-half years after the death of her partner. According to the *Gädlä Wälättä Peṭros*, Ǝḫ̮ətä Krəstos met Walatta Petros in 1617 while living with her sister because her spiritual leader *Abba* Ṣəge Haymanot recommended that she meet and think about living with Walatta Petros.

According to the *Sənkəssar* entry,[19] Ǝḫ̮ətä Krəstos came from an illustrious and noble family. She was married, gave birth to a daughter called Tərasya,[20] and later became a nun at the church in Fure called Däbrä Sina. The *Sənkəssar* states that she lived thirty-two years as a nun and twenty-seven years as a leader in the monastery,[21] information the *Gädlä Wälättä Peṭros* does not contain. The two texts agree that the two women met in nearby Robit, then went to Däbrä ʿAnqo, Ṣəyat, Zäge, Waldəbba, and Žäbäy. The *Sənkəssar*'s entry also has language very similar to that in the *Gädlä Wälättä Peṭros*, likewise saying that after they met, the two women "remained together, loving each other as soul and body and they parted never, not in times of trial and persecution, neither in times of rest, but only in death, as Our Lady Mary and Salome. There was no suspicion between them, nor cunning." It agrees that Ǝḫ̮ətä Krəstos pleaded with Queen Amätä Krəstos and Mälkəʾa Krəstos to be reunited with Walatta Petros in exile, "weeping and lamenting as a small child whose mother has abandoned it."

There are some slight differences or additions. The Ǝḫ̮ətä Krəstos entry says that Ǝḫ̮ətä Krəstos helped a monk in Žäbäy who fell ill with fever, cleaned his bedclothes without repugnance (even though they stank of fever), washed his dead body with her own hands, and buried him. Her faithfulness was such that Satan "made war" against her and even threw her out of a church window during her prayers. Upon Walatta Petros's death, Ǝḫ̮ətä Krəstos was instituted the leader in her place, enduring many trials and even kicking out two heretics, Zä-Maryam and Akalä Krəstos, who asserted that Christ had not anointed the Holy Spirit (that is,

[19] Unfortunately, Nollet consistently confused sixes with sevens in her translation, so we have checked it against a digital copy of Vatican Eth. No. 112 and corrected where necessary.

[20] Pace Zanetti (2005), who has "son."

[21] Nollet mistakenly translated ፳፯ as twenty-six.

they were Unionists, adherents of Karra teaching, and not adherents of Qəbat teaching). Then, when God wished her to rest from the labors of this world, he gave her three crowns: the crown of the persecuted, the crown of the disciples, and the crown of teachers. She then became violently ill and died on Wednesday Mäggabit 27,[22] in the evening. All this is lacking in the *Gädlä Wälättä Ṗeṭros.*

Conclusion

This volume contributes not only to the study of Ethiopian literature and women but also to the study of the history of resistance to European expansion. A vital task of the twenty-first century is to make earlier African texts available and understood, since their contents will revolutionize thinking in a number of disciplines, including history and literature. Bringing attention to these early texts will also do much to dismantle stereotypes of Africa as a continent without written literature before European contact, and to build representations of Africa as a continent of extraordinary intellectual effervescence.

[22] Nollet again mistakenly translated ፳፯ as twenty-six.

Manuscripts of the Text and Earlier Translations

Wendy Laura Belcher

The renowned scholar Lanfranco Ricci published an Italian translation of the *Gädlä Wälättä Ṗeṭros* in 1970 in the renowned Corpus Scriptorum Christianorum Orientalium (CSCO) series of edited and translated Eastern Christian texts (Gälawdewos 1970). He based his translation on the Gəʿəz print edition of 1912 in the same series, prepared by one of the most prominent Ethiopianists of the twentieth century, Carlo Conti Rossini (Gälawdewos 1912). Both books were based on a single manuscript from the Antoine d'Abbadie manuscript collection at the Bibliothèque nationale de France (hereafter called MS Abb. 88), which Conti Rossini had cataloged. Conti Rossini had prepared a Latin translation but, due to World War I, it was never published (Papi 1943; Conti Rossini 1946, 69n). Over the next two decades of his life, Conti Rossini did not return to this work, perhaps because Latin became less viable as a scholarly language over those years. The Täwaḥədo Church also published a nonacademic but solid translation into Amharic in 2004 (Gälawdewos 2004). These three books are the extent of the print versions.

Unfortunately, the Conti Rossini print edition and the Italian translation are problematic, largely because they are based on a single manuscript that was quite flawed. When Conti Rossini embarked on his print edition, three manuscripts of the *Gädlä Wälättä Ṗeṭros* were available in Europe—in the national libraries of Paris and London, and the state libraries of Dresden, Germany. Conti Rossini did check a few folios of MS Abb. 88 against the manuscript at the British Library (our MS E) (Conti Rossini and Jaeger 1912, viii), concluding that MS Abb. 88 was a reliable and representative text. However, both were of comparatively low textual quality. Furthermore, inevitably, errors crept into the Conti Rossini print edition (which we always abbreviate as CR in the notes and sometimes elsewhere) that were not in MS Abb. 88.

While Ricci was aware of the limitations of the print edition, he understandably considered it important to provide a translation of this vital text. His translation is valuable—for instance, in identifying the hundreds of biblical sources for the text's many quotes and allusions, which we have included in the notes of our translation—but was seriously undercut by the flawed print edition. Moreover, the volume was published in the academic series CSCO and was translated into academic Italian, both of which factors greatly limited the translation's audience. Finally, Ricci made the disastrous decision to transform all of the text's rich and lively dialogue into deadened indirect speech (e.g., "she said 'I beg you now, my lady, . . . have mercy on me!' " became "she begged her to have mercy on her").

Therefore, we have sought to do better service to the text and its readers by translating the *Gädlä Wälättä Ṗeṭros* from more than one manuscript, with a critical approach, and into the global lingua franca, English, for a general audience. Some of the most important steps in this process of producing a better, more authoritative translation involved identifying the *Gädlä Wälättä Ṗeṭros* manuscripts, collecting digital versions of them, establishing which were closest to the original creation, and then documenting the variations. For more about this process, see Kleiner's "Introduction to the Translation of the Text" and "Manuscript Comparison" in this volume.

The original text was written between 11 September 1672 and 10 September 1673, at Qʷäraṣa (not Afär Färäs), the monastery devoted to Walatta Petros on the eastern shore of Lake Ṭana. We know this because the text states that Walatta Petros once "hid at the monastic settlement of Qoraatsa, where we currently find ourselves." Like other manuscripts produced in the Ethiopian highlands, it was written on parchment, also called vellum, laboriously created from stretching, drying, and scraping cow, sheep, or goat skin. After impressing the page with lines, the author Gälawedewos wrote the text with a reed pen and red and black ink. Experts then bound the vellum folio together with thread in an open chain stitch and wooden boards, probably covered in tooled leather. Such manuscripts were expensive to prepare, requiring dozens of animal skins and three to six months of work.

After this first manuscript was written, scribes transmitted it to other monasteries and churches by copying it. Since many monasteries would want the hagiobiography of an important saint, monks would borrow someone else's original, or a copy of the original, to copy by hand. Copying by hand, rather than reproducing by computer or printing press, has implications. The more copies there are, the more versions there are, with each a little different from the original text, sometimes deliberately but mostly accidentally. Each time it was copied, the text changed slightly: lettering or spelling errors were introduced, words were omitted or added. Since the original manuscript was written, Täwaḥədo Church scribes have made more than a dozen copies of the original manuscript, perhaps up to twenty. Table 2 summarizes the information about and variations among these manuscripts.

Four manuscripts of the *Gädlä Wälättä Ṗeṭros* are known to exist outside of Ethiopia and Eritrea: at the British Library (MS E),[1] at the Bibliothèque nationale de France (National Library of France, MS Abb. 88),[2] at the Staatsbibliothek zu Berlin (State Library of Berlin, MS C),[3] and at the Sächsische Landesbibliothek Staats- und Universitätsbibliothek Dresden (Saxony State and University Library Dresden [SLUB], Germany, MS A).[4] Since the famous German collector Lobegott Friedrich Constantin von Tischendorf found the manuscript now in the Dresden library in

[1] British Library Orient. MS No. 730; Wright (1877, 197–98).

[2] MS Abb. 88; Abbadie (1859); Conti Rossini (1912, 57).

[3] MS Orient. Quart. No. 1014; Hammerschmidt and Six (1983), No. 134, 249–51. See also Wion (2012).

[4] Mscr. Dresd. Eb. No. 415e; Hammerschmidt and Jäger (1968, 70–85). See also Six (1994, 213–15).

the 1840s at Saint Catherine's of Sinai (1845, 19), it seems possible that other copies exist in Egyptian monasteries. Approximately ten manuscripts are known in Eritrea and Ethiopia, most held in Lake Ṭana monastic libraries. The monastery on Lake Ṭana devoted to Walatta Petros, Qʷäraṭa, possesses three manuscripts and used to have four (D, F, I, and J).

Twelve of these manuscripts are available in digital form. Five copies were microfilmed in Ethiopia in the 1960s and 1970s by the Ethiopian Manuscript Microfilm Library (EMML), which is now housed in the Hill Museum and Manuscript Library (HMML) at Saint John's University in Collegeville, Minnesota. Three of the manuscripts microfilmed by HMML were digitized by others, but two were unique (G and K). The Austrian scholar Ernst Hammerschmidt also microfilmed manuscripts, but with a focus around Lake Ṭana, and he published some facsimiles from one of the two *Gädlä Wälättä Ṗeṭros* he microfilmed (MS B).[5] The other of these manuscripts (MS D) was later microfilmed by EMML, and both are available digitally through the Ethiopian Manuscript Imaging Project (EMIP) at HMML. The original of this very old and image-rich MS D, which was the source of Claire Bosc-Tiessé's article on Walatta Petros iconography, was stolen in approximately 2007, according to monks at the Qʷäraṭa Monastery interviewed by Selamawit Mecca and me in 2011. Thus, the Hammerschmidt low-resolution black-and-white microfilm is the only full record of this manuscript, which is now available digitally through EMIP at HMML or wendybelcher.com.[6]

In January 2011, Selamawit Mecca and I digitized four manuscripts, three at Qʷäraṭa (F, I, J) and one at Bäträ Maryam Monastery (MS H), both on Lake Ṭana.[7] One of these manuscripts, at Qʷäraṭa, had been previously microfilmed by EMML (MS F). We digitized them informally—we did not foliate the manuscripts, measure the manuscripts, or photograph the flyleaves and spine. Therefore, we do not have folio numbers for them, and instead refer to image numbers, according to the PDF created by Delamarter's EMIP from our photographs. The PDFs of these images are available in the EMIP collection at HMML or wendybelcher.com.

MS I turned out to be spectacularly valuable to scholars, as it included a number of extra miracles regarding eighteenth- and nineteenth-century kings, as well as a history of the community, giving the names and dates of the community's abbots and abbesses, which are all summarized in the translation.

[5] Tanasee MS 179; Six (1999, 239–42).

[6] Note that, over the years, this particular manuscript, *Gädlä Wälättä Ṗeṭros* EMML MS No. 8438, has sometimes mistakenly been called EMML MS No. 8448 in publications, including in Grierson (1993) and Bosc-Tiessé (2003). EMML MS No. 8448 is a *Tä'amərä Maryam* manuscript at Ṭana Qirqos, according to an HMML handlist, but since Ṭana Qirqos is reported to have a *Gädlä Wälättä Ṗeṭros*, perhaps EMML MS No. 8448 is actually that.

[7] MSS I and J have what appear to be previous cataloging marks, perhaps from the UNESCO Mobile Microfilm Unit that microfilmed 368 manuscripts in monasteries and churches in and around Lake Ṭana from September 1969 to January 1970 (Addis Ababa University Library 1970, 21, 30); or perhaps from the Ethiopian Ministry of Culture, which did some registration work in the area in the 1970s–80s.

Table 2
Gädlä Wälättä Ṗeṭros Manuscripts Worldwide

Catalog No.	*Code*	*Where/When Acquired or Digitized*	*Provenance*	*Date*	*Digital Available?*
1. Abbadie MS No. 88	Abb. 88	Acquired by Antoine d'Abbadie in Ethiopia between 1837 and 1849 and now in Bibliothèque nationale de France	Unknown	1713–14	In print
2. Mscr. Dresd. Eb. 415e	MS A	Acquired in the 1840s in Egypt and now in SLUB Dresden	Unknown	1800s	From Dresden
3. Ṭānāsee 97; Rema 8, EMIP 0202	MS B	Microfilmed in Rema Monastery on Lake Ṭana in 1970s	Rema Island	Late 1600s–early 1700s	From EMIP
4. Prussian Cultural Heritage, Berlin, MS orient. quart. 1014	MS C	Acquired in Lake Ṭana by Johannes Flemming in 1905 and now in State Library of Berlin	Lake Ṭana	1672–82	From Berlin
5. EMML MS No. 8438 Ṭānāsee 179 EMIP 0284	MS D	Microfilmed in Walatta Petros's monastery of Qʷäraṭa on Lake Ṭana in 1970s; Probably photographed by Otto Jäger as well, MS No. 25	Qʷäraṣa	1716–21	From EMIP not HMML
6. BL Orient No. 730	MS E	Taken at the fall of Mäqdäla in Ethiopia in 1868 and now in British Library; most likely originally of Rema Monastery	Rema Island	1800s?	From British Library
7. EMML MS No. 8471 EMIP 2140 Belcher & Selamawit 03	MS F	Microfilmed in WP's monastery of Qʷäraṭa on Lake Ṭana in April 1986; digitized there in 2011	Qʷäraṣa	1900s	From HMML and EMIP
8. EMML MS No. 8132	MS G	Microfilmed in Kidanä Məḥrät monastery on Zäge Island in Lake Ṭana in 1970s	Kidanä Məḥrät	1700s	From HMML

Poems	*Additional Material*	*Missing Material*	*Images?*	*Commissioners/ Scribes/ Owners*	*Note*
Mälkəʾ and sälamta for WP; mälkəʾ for Ǝḫətä Krəstos	Expanded ends of gädl and of miracles; colophon	Omits about one folio of the content	3 images (not inc. in this volume)		Source of the Conti Rossini print edition and Ricci translation
Mälkəʾ and sälamta for WP; none for Ǝḫətä Krəstos			33 images (17 for gädl, 14 for miracles)	Very faded; names in red unreadable	Pace catalog, not made in 1672–73 but in 1800s
No poems			None	Commissioner: *Abba* Agnaṭəyos of Däga. Scribe: Ḥawarya Mäsqäl	Gädl text marked for daily readings
Mälkəʾ and sälamta for WP; mälkəʾ and sälamta for Ǝḫətä Krəstos			None	Commissioner: [Princess] Wälättä Ǝsraʾel. Scribe: Gʷəndä Haymanot	Comprehensive set of poems. Abbot Zä-Ḥawaryat (d. 1682) blessed
No poems	Land scale contract mentions *Ras* Gugsa [of Yäǧǧu, ca. 1775–1825] and Qʷäraṭa officeholders		27 images for the miracles	Commissioner: Ḫirutä Śəllase?	Source of Claire Bosc-Tiessé's article; stolen in the mid-2000s; mentions King Dawit III as the sitting monarch
Mälkəʾ and sälamta for WP; none for Ǝḫətä Krəstos			None	Commissioners: priest Täwäldä Mädḫən and his brother Gäbrä Krəstos; Scribe: Zä-Wängel	Title given as *The Life of WP, of Holy Mädḫane ʿAläm [Church]*, the church on Rema Island
Mälkəʾ and sälamta for WP; none for Ǝḫətä Krəstos			1 image	Commissioner: Gälawdewos	Gädl text marked for daily readings
No poems			No images	Names erased	Microfilm missing first and last folios; starts with animal parables; ends at first line of last miracle

TABLE 2. *(continued)*

Catalog No.	*Code*	*Where/When Acquired or Digitized*	*Provenance*	*Date*	*Digital Available?*
9. EMIP 2138 Belcher & Selamawit 01	MS H	Digitized in Bäträ Maryam Monastery on Zäge Peninsula on Lake Ṭana in 2011	Bäträ Maryam	After 1770	From EMIP
10. EMIP 2139 Belcher & Selamawit 02	MS I	Microfilmed in Walatta Petros's monastery of Qʷäraṭa on Lake Tana in 1970s; digitized there in 2011	Qʷäraṣa	After 1770, after 1860	From EMIP
11. EMIP 2141 Belcher & Selamawit 04	MS J	Microfilmed in Walatta Petros's monastery of Qʷäraṭa on Lake Tana in 1970s; digitized there in 2011	Qʷäraṣa	1672?; definitely before 1681	From EMIP
12. EMML MS No. 6842	MS K	Microfilmed in Lasta, Wällo in 1970s	Lasta	1800s	From HMML
Partial manuscripts					
13. EMML MS No. 659		Microfilmed in Church of Saint George in Addis Ababa in the 1970s	Addis Ababa	1800s	From HMML (not consulted)
Uncataloged, undigitized manuscripts					
14. Ḥabru MS			Church Ǝroge Giyorgis in Yäǧǧu, Ḥabru, Wällo		No digital

Poems	*Additional Material*	*Missing Material*	*Images?*	*Commissioners/ Scribes/ Owners*	*Note*
No poems	Entirely different set of miracles, eight miracles about eighteenth-century figures Bäkaffa, Iyasu II, Iyoʾas I, and *Ras* Mikaʾel Səḥul, same as in MS I (and not those in other MSS)		16 outlined drawings, figural and ornamental	Commissioners: Yaʿqob and [his wife?] Melkol	Gädl and täʾamər text marked for monthly readings, short external texts between sections
No poems	Same miracles as in other manuscripts; plus entirely different set of miracles in a different hand (same as MS H) plus three additional miracles about nineteenth-century figures like Tewodros; plus additional short history of the community (same as in MS J) dated 1735		No images	Commissioners: Aśaʾənä Maryam (for gädl), Gäbrä Maryam and his wife Wälättä Maryam; scribes: Gälawdewos and ʿAṣqä Maryam (for gädl), and Kidanä Maryam	
Sälamta for WP (same as in other MSS, but after gädl), no other poems	Additional short (four pages) history of the community (same as in MS I) in a different hand, dated 1681		1 image	Blessings invoked upon abbess Amätä Dəngəl, abbot Zä-Ḫawaryat, and scribe Gälawdewos	Marked for monthly reading. Urtext?
No poems	Chanting instructions for carrying the gädl		No images	Owner: Zämädä Maryam; scribe: Wärädä Qal; commissioner: Zärʾa Krəstos	No numbering of the miracles
Mälkəʾ for WP only			No images for mälkəʾ		A collection of more than 75 mälkəʾ to various saints (on folios 130b–132b)
					Inventory penned in EMML 5909 margin says this church has a WP MS

TABLE 2. *(continued)*

Catalog No.	*Code*	*Where/When Acquired or Digitized*	*Provenance*	*Date*	*Digital Available?*
15. Ṭana Qirqos M			Ṭana Qirqos, Lake Ṭana		No digital
16. Gälila MS			Gälila monastery, Lake Ṭana		No digital
17. Rema MS			Rema Mädḫane ʿAläm on Rema Island		Wouldn't allow digitizing in 2010
18. Waldəbba MS			Waldəbba, Sämen		No digital
19. Däbrä Tabor MS			Däbrä Tabor, Bägemdər	1800s	No digital
20. Zapa MS			Zapa, Ǝste, Bägemdər		No digital
21. Wäybəla MS			Maryam church, Wäybəla, Lake Ṭana	1700s	No digital
22. Däbrä Məṭmaq Maryam MS			Däbrä Məṭmaq Maryam, Gondär	1780s	No digital
Sənkəssar Entries					
23. Ethio-SPaRe MKL-019		Digitized in Läqay Kidanä Məḥrät Church in Təgray in 2010s	Wäräda Ganta Afäšum, Qušät Läqay,Təgray	1800s	From Ethio-SPaRe
24. Ethio-SPaRe MR-003		Digitized in Mədrä Ruba Däbrä Gännät Qəddəst Śəllase Church in Təgray in 2010s	Wäräda Gulo Mäkäda, Qušät Däbrä Gännät, Təgray	Late 1800s, early 1900s	From Ethio-SPaRe

Poems	*Additional Material*	*Missing Material*	*Images?*	*Commissioners/ Scribes/ Owners*	*Note*
					According to priests there, Loren Stuckenbruck
					According to priests there, Loren Stuckenbruck
					This may be Ṭānāsee No. 97.
					Attested in Kinefe-Rigb Zelleke
					Attested in Kinefe-Rigb Zelleke; site of Tewodros's earlier capital
					Attested in Kinefe-Rigb Zelleke
					Existence mentioned in MS. I's 12th miracle
					Existence mentioned in MS. I's 27th miracle
One stanza, five-line sälamta			No images		F. 64v
			No images		F. 91vc–92vb.

MS J at Qʷäraṭa was also extremely valuable as the most accurate and earliest extant manuscript. Based on provenance, commissioners or honorees, age, poems, textual correspondence, corrections, and illustration, Belcher speculates that MS J may be the urtext—the original manuscript written by Gälawdewos. MS J is found today in Walatta Petros's monastery at Qʷäraṭa, where the original was written and thus where one would most expect to find it. The blessings and invocations of MS J name three people who do not appear in any other manuscript, including "the scribe Gälawdewos," that is, the author, whose name would appear only in the original manuscript or any he copied. Blessings are also invoked on the abbess and abbot of Qʷäraṣa when Gälawdewos was writing—Amätä Dəngəl and Zä-Ḥawaryat. Since blessings are always invoked on the living, and Zä-Ḥawaryat died in 1681, this marks the latest possible date of MS J's copying to 1681, within ten years of the original's composition in 1672–73. A short section added in a different hand at the end of MS J confirms this, as it states that the addition was written in 1687–88 (in the fifth year of King Iyasu's reign). Thus, the earlier part of the manuscript must have been written before 1687. MS J does not have the mälkəʾ poem for Walatta Petros. If MS J was the original, it would explain why the *Mälkəʾa Wälättä Ṗeṭros* was omitted from nine of our twelve manuscripts. As mentioned, mälkəʾ were often written before the gädl and kept separately in cheaper small volumes, only later being compiled into one volume with the gädl, täʾamər, and mälkəʾ.

Textual correspondence and corrections also suggest it could be the original. MS J almost never has a variation that appears in no other manuscript, suggesting that the other manuscripts resemble it most closely. Indeed, in only one substantive case does MS J stand alone in varying from MSS Abb. 88, B, and D (the latter have "they the resentful theologians" but MS J has "you the resentful theologians"). This reflects the reality that successive iterations of handwritten copies of a text will vary most from one another, not the original.

Moreover, MS J has interesting patterns of erasure and interlinear corrections, made in the same hand as the original text. On almost every page are examples of one or two letters in a row that the scribe has erased and rewritten before writing further. The character spacing on the line remains even, however, demonstrating that these erasures were made immediately, not at the end of the line or page. This pattern, combined with the uneven lettering and varying sizes of the script, suggests that the person writing is composing. As anyone who has written by hand can attest, one's letters are more uniform when copying than when composing. On every tenth page or so are interlinear corrections, entire words added between lines, one line erased and replaced by two more tightly lettered lines, or lines added below the standard bottom line of the page. These squeezed-in types of corrections reveal that the scribe made them after completing the entire page, or perhaps the entire manuscript. This type might mean that the scribe proofread his copy against the original text at the very end of the process and only then corrected it, but this is not common. The type seems more likely to be the corrections an author would make on rereading his own composition or having others read it. For instance, an example of a correction made in the text is the erasure of a line and reinsertion of two lines of a biblical passage (MS J, image 26). Perhaps the scribe managed to garble an entire biblical passage while copying, but it seems more likely that the author made a mistake in rendering the biblical passage from memory. Then, when someone else read the original, they informed him and he corrected it. In addition, in three cases, MS J has single words or phrases added in between two lines, words that appear in the other manuscripts: *mäkära* (tribulation, MS J image 71; CR, p. 66), *motä* (had died, MS J image 72; CR, p. 67), and *əntä* (she who, MS J image 87; CR, p. 81). Only one other *Gädlä Wälättä Ṗeṭros* has interlinear corrections: MS I.

Finally, it seems unlikely that the monastery would commission and keep a second manuscript within ten years of the original. If MS J is not the original manuscript, it is almost undoubtedly a copy made directly from the original by the original author, Gälawdewos.

Some seven other manuscripts are attested but have been neither cataloged nor digitized. According to Kinefe-Rigb Zelleke's bibliography of saints' lives in Ethiopia (1975), there are four other manuscripts of the *Gädlä Wälättä Ṗeṭros*: one at the monastery on Rema Island on Lake Ṭana where Walatta Petros is buried, one at a Waldəbba monastery north of Gondär where she spent time, and two at monasteries east of Lake Ṭana. Monks at the Rema Monastery told Belcher and Mecca in January 2011 that there was a manuscript there, but due to construction, it was not then available for digitizing. However, there is a good chance that this manuscript is the one already microfilmed by Hammerschmidt and available from HMML (MS B).[8] An inventory in another manuscript (EMML 5909) suggests that there is one at Ḥabru Monastery (about 160 miles east of Lake Ṭana). According to oral reports received by Loren Stuckenbruck, there are *Gädlä Wälättä Ṗeṭros* manuscripts at Ṭana Qirqos Monastery and Gälila Monastery on Lake Ṭana (which only men can enter and thus which we could not check). It seems quite possible that most monasteries around Lake Ṭana would have this important text.

Recent preservation projects had not come across any *Gädlä Wälättä Ṗeṭros* manuscripts by fall 2013, including the EMIP launched in 2005 by Delamarter to study manuscripts in Addis Ababa, the Ethio-SPaRe project launched in 2009 by Nosnitsin to study manuscripts in Təgray, and the Ethiopian Manuscript Digital Library (EMDL) project launched in 2010 by Meley Mulugetta to study manuscripts in Goǧǧam and the Əndärta and Säḥarti regions of Təgray.

There are also quite a few *Sənkəssar* entries about Walatta Petros that are shortened versions of her life. Most *Sənkəssar* do not appear to have entries on her; for instance, Budge's English translation of the *Sənkəssar* includes her name on her saint's day, but not her story. It will be a wonderful day when optical character recognition is invented for Gəˁəz manuscripts and we can quickly collate information on the content of composite texts like the *Sənkəssar*.

Finally, there are oral texts about Walatta Petros based in a living tradition about her. A twenty-first-century religious text published in Gondär about the monastery at Ṭana Qirqos lists stories about Walatta Petros that do not appear in any of the

[8] Ṭānāsee No. 97; Hammerschmidt (1977a, 134–36).

manuscripts. These include anecdotes about the other Ḥabäša female saint Krəstos Śämra helping Walatta Petros to build a church, and about Walatta Petros being carried on the wings of the archangels Michael and Gabriel to a monastery. The book would seem to be based on an oral tradition at Ṭana Qirqos about the saint (Anonymous n.d. [2000s]).

Introduction to the Translation of the Text

Michael Kleiner

In working on the *Gädlä Wälättä Peṭros*, we sought to do justice to this major text of Ethiopian literature by producing an accessible and fluid English translation while also remaining faithful to the Gəˁəz original. Our goal was a translation that would be of use to a wide range of potential readers, students and scholars alike, coming from a variety of disciplines and with different regional interests.

But what exactly is the Gəˁəz original of the *Gädlä Wälättä Peṭros*? The answer to this seemingly simple question involves a number of philological issues that we had to address in the course of our work, and that affected our translation procedure. In the following, I describe those philological issues and explain how we addressed them. Then I present our translation approach, outlining the techniques and procedures we adopted in rendering the Gəˁəz original into English.

Manuscript Comparison

The obvious starting point for our translation was the Gəˁəz text of the 1912 Conti Rossini print edition. That edition was not a critical one, however, but based on only one manuscript from the Bibliothèque nationale de France (Paris), as discussed by Belcher in this volume in "Manuscripts of the Text and Earlier Translations." While never intending to prepare a traditional edition of the *Gädlä Wälättä Peṭros*—the time and funding were not available to closely compare all the manuscripts and produce a separate Gəˁəz volume that would present an editorially established best text and document all the manuscript variants—we were thus aware, from the project's inception, that at some point we would have to consult other manuscripts so as to put our translation on a more solid footing. To work exclusively from the Conti Rossini print edition, as Ricci had done for his 1970 Italian translation, was not the way forward.

Yet, we decided that we could embark on our translation without integrating manuscript comparisons right away, deferring them until later. One reason we felt safe with this approach was that Conti Rossini's Parisian manuscript base, MS Abb. 88, was dated to 1713–14. The *Gädlä Wälättä Peṭros* itself was composed in 1672–73, so MS Abb. 88 had been written down little more than forty years later. In an era of exclusively manual text reproduction—the printing press was not yet known in seventeenth- and eighteenth-century Ethiopia—this is a comparatively short time span, giving us confidence that MS Abb. 88, and hence the Conti Rossini print edition, would be close to the original and little corrupted.

Another reason was that it seemed ineffective to burden ourselves with manuscript comparisons at the very beginning of the translation process. Belcher hoped to conduct field research in the Lake Ṭana area, the center of Walatta Petros's activity, with the goal of searching for hitherto unknown *Gädlä Wälättä Ṗeṭros* manuscripts. Therefore, it did not seem advisable to collate and compare the already known *Gädlä Wälättä Ṗeṭros* manuscripts from the beginning of the translation process: If new ones were unearthed in the course of Belcher's field research, we would have to cover the same ground again. Hence, it seemed better to defer manuscript comparisons until we had more specimens and thus a fuller picture. In the meantime, as we worked on the translation, I noted all those instances where the Conti Rossini print edition called for later targeted manuscript comparisons because it came across as not fully grammatical or as unidiomatic.

When Belcher received Fulbright funding to go to the Lake Ṭana area in search of *Gädlä Wälättä Ṗeṭros* manuscripts, the results of her January 2011 mission were impressive. She and Selamawit Mecca found, and digitized for the first time, one manuscript of very high textual quality (MS J) and two of considerable philological merit (MSS H and I). In addition, Belcher and Mecca digitized a manuscript from the area that had been microfilmed before (MS F).

With these new finds at our disposal, it now made sense to collate the complete available range of manuscripts with the Conti Rossini print edition. The results of our initial sampling were surprising, however. Contrary to our expectations, the Conti Rossini print edition (and by implication the text of MS Abb. 88, on which Conti Rossini had exclusively relied) turned out to be of comparatively low quality. This manifested itself in numerous inferior variants vis-à-vis what may loosely be termed the consensus text, as well as in quite a few short omissions. Even if most of the Abb. 88/CR variants and omissions only slightly affect the text's shape and meaning, in the aggregate they make it distinctively different. In addition, on some occasions even small differences can carry substantial weight and dramatically affect the text's value. For instance, on the very first folio, all eleven manuscripts now collated provide the name of the text's author, Gälawdewos; by contrast, Abb. 88/CR deleteriously omits it. Similarly, all eleven collated manuscripts state that Walatta Petros had died thirty years before the composition of her gädl; it is exclusively in Abb. 88/CR that this number appears as twenty-nine instead. In addition, Abb. 88/CR has one large gap, comprising two full manuscript pages.

In light of this discovery, we knew it would not suffice to conduct targeted comparisons of suspicious Abb. 88/CR words or phrases against the other manuscripts, as we had envisaged earlier. Rather, we would have to compare the entire Conti Rossini print edition against the manuscript evidence, so as to reconstruct from the complete material the most authentic *Gädlä Wälättä Ṗeṭros* version possible. The text thus established would then serve as the basis for our translation.

How was this text to be established? The instinctive response of most philologists would be to say: through a traditional edition. However, we wondered whether that was in fact required. Were there not perhaps other, more effective ways to cope creatively with a situation such as ours? While we frankly acknowledge that time and funding constraints urged such questions upon us, it remains true that traditional editions document much textual chaff: obviously inferior and late variants that neither have much intrinsic semantic value nor contribute to the reconstruction of the original text. In many cases, the traditional format even buries the most important differences in meaning among numerous variants with little to no significance.

Bearing in mind our original goal—producing a fluid English translation that would do justice to the original Gəʿəz text—we conceived a different way forward, one that stopped short of a full traditional edition but that nonetheless established a new and sound philological basis from which our translation could then flow. In working toward that goal, we developed an innovative type of apparatus to document our philological findings.

How, then, did we proceed? For the introduction to the *Gädlä Wälättä Ṗeṭros* (chapters 1 and 2 in our translation), I meticulously compared the Conti Rossini print edition against all eleven manuscripts at our disposal. This was done not only to establish the variants but also to assess the textual quality of each of those eleven manuscripts, as well as group them based on their variants. In addition to being of philological interest, the findings of this step would allow us to reduce the number of manuscripts that henceforth would have to be compared against the Conti Rossini print edition. We would be able to drop manuscripts whose inferior textual quality had been established, as well as individual manuscripts from larger sets transmitting an essentially identical text. As a beneficial side effect, a substantive reduction in the number of collated manuscripts would reduce the time required for philological comparison, without a loss of quality to the basis for our translation.

Fortunately, the initial complete manuscript collation yielded the results for which we had hoped. It allowed us to put aside eight manuscripts, either because their low textual value had been established or because they were redundant members of textual families better represented by other copies. Therefore, from our chapter 3 onward—but excluding the two poems in honor of Walatta Petros, for which a different attestation situation obtains (see below)—we limited our collation to MSS B, D, and J.

The following can be said regarding the eight manuscripts that we dropped. MS A from a library in Dresden, Germany, was so fragile that the library staff initially were uncertain whether they could even digitize it for us. More important, its script had faded over large stretches, destroying its readability in many passages. Furthermore, manuscript comparison revealed that MS A repeatedly had inferior variants, sometimes shared by a Qʷäraṭa manuscript, MS I.

Next to the AI group, MSS E, H, and K could be established as a second subset. MSS H and K displayed many identical inferior variants; frequently these were shared by MS E, housed in the British Library. In addition, the inferior EHK text often aligned with that of Abb. 88/CR—although the latter has quite a few more instances of inferior text than are found in the EHK text. Finally, the AI and EHK texts did not display variants superior to other manuscripts to counterbalance their defects. So, we excluded them.

This left us with MSS B, C, D, F, G, and J as candidates for further collation. They were in almost complete agreement among themselves in chapters 1 and 2. Hence, their number could be reduced with the reasonable expectation of no loss of valuable variants. This broad selection of six quality manuscripts allowed us to take into account another factor, namely, easy legibility due to clear handwriting and proper digitizing or microfilming. MS G was problematic in this respect. At the same time, it shared a small number of interesting variants with MS B. In view of this, it made sense to drop MS G but retain MS B. Since MSS C, D, F, and J all had similar profiles and sound texts, we picked MS J from among them, it being most representative of the mainstream. We further selected MS D, which was comparable to MS B insofar as it sometimes had unique but interesting—and potentially superior—variants. Furthermore, as the MS D variants rarely coincided with those of MS B, we chose to retain them both so as not to miss out on any of their small but interesting variations. The interested reader can trace the process of manuscript comparison and selection described here by studying the textual notes to chapters 1 and 2.

From then on, wherever MSS B, D, and J uniformly provided a text superior to the Conti Rossini print edition, we translated that better text and documented it in a note. Simultaneously, we there also documented and translated the variant of the Conti Rossini print edition for easy comparison. Through the better *Gädlä Wälättä Ṗeṭros* text thus established, we were able to arrive at a clearer, richer, and more accurate translation than the Italian one published by Ricci. In addition to their usefulness for our translation, the new manuscript variants that we established and then documented for the first time also represent a major advance in *Gädlä Wälättä Ṗeṭros* philology. Not only their quality but also their large number demonstrate that Conti Rossini's choice of MS Abb. 88 as the basis for his print edition was a particularly unfortunate one. In light of our findings, MS Abb. 88 today appears as a highly unrepresentative *Gädlä Wälättä Ṗeṭros* manuscript of low textual quality, marked by many small corruptions and omissions.

Only a minority of the manuscripts included the two poems in honor of Walatta Petros that appear in the Conti Rossini print edition. For those poems, we therefore compared all the manuscripts in which they were extant. For the mälkəʾ, these were three (C, E, and F); for the sälamta, four (C, E, F, and J).

The only part of the Conti Rossini print edition that we did not include in our translation was its third poem, a mälkəʾ in honor of Walatta Petros's companion Ǝḫ̮ətä Krəstos. Among our manuscripts, this poem only appeared in MS C. Neither did we translate a sälamta to Ǝḫ̮ətä Krəstos that appears also in MS C, but not in the Conti Rossini print edition. The fact that the Ǝḫ̮ətä Krəstos poems are found in, at best, two of the twelve *Gädlä Wälättä Ṗeṭros* manuscripts (namely, Abb. 88 and C) shows that they were not generally regarded as constituent parts of the Walatta Petros text group. This justifies our choice to exclude them from the translation.

Finally, textual comparison revealed one large omission and two large additions that further make MS Abb. 88 stand out among *Gädlä Wälättä Peṭros* manuscripts. Toward the end of the biographical core gädl of the comprehensive *Gädlä Wälättä Peṭros* text, when it is related how the saint is preparing to die, one entire folium apparently went missing from MS Abb. 88. In the Conti Rossini print edition, this material, had it not been lost in the manuscript base, would have stood between lines thirty-one and thirty-two on page 107. By chance, the loose textual ends created by this large gap still fit together reasonably well, so that the narrative retained some plausible continuity despite the loss. Therefore, this major omission could go undetected by Conti Rossini: MS Abb. 88 still read sufficiently smoothly at the concerned spot. Our translation integrates this hitherto missing material at the appropriate location. As to its original Gəʿəz text, due to its quantity we do not transcribe it in a note but provide it separately in the manuscript facsimile in the appendix.

In terms of substantive textual additions, MS Abb. 88 stands out by its extension and alteration of the final lines of the biographical core gädl, as well as of the colophons at the ends of both the biographical and miracle sections of the *Gädlä Wälättä Peṭros*. These MS Abb. 88 features do not have parallels in any other of the eleven available manuscripts. On all these occasions, we based our translation on the majority text, providing translations of the extended MS Abb. 88 variants as separate units.

Philological Annotation

In the notes to the translation, we documented those shared variants from the collated manuscripts that deviate in substantive ways from the Conti Rossini print edition. By contrast, purely orthographic variants were not considered, only differences that were important philologically or semantically. Equally, from chapter 3 onward—when we markedly narrowed down the number of collated manuscripts—we did not document minority variants from among the three selected manuscripts any longer, so long as these variants were clearly inferior as well as stand-alone, that is, diverging not only from an unproblematic Abb. 88/CR text but also from the two other collated manuscripts. Thus, from chapter 3 onward we only documented high-quality stand-alone variants from among MSS BDJ, which were rare. In the vast majority of cases where the collated manuscripts differ from the Conti Rossini print edition, their superior variants are in agreement among themselves. This high level of cohesion among the selected collated manuscripts, in combination with the generally high quality of their variants, further vindicates our choice of them. Overall, we are confident that the variants we documented from our selection of manuscripts already comprise a near totality of all superior and majoritarian—and hence presumably original—*Gädlä Wälättä Peṭros* variants that would come to light in a complete collation of all available manuscripts.

In our documentation of variants in the notes, the variant we considered best always appears first and is the one we translate in the main text. However, our philological notes throughout not only provide the text we translate in the given instance, by default coming from the collated manuscripts, but also the inferior variant(s), by default coming from Abb. 88/CR, for quick comparison and so as to make our judgment transparent.

In the notes, we standardized the Gəʿəz orthography. In Gəʿəz manuscripts, scribes almost freely exchange one symbol for another within four sets of symbols. These sets are: ሀ ሐ ኀ (transcriptions: h ḥ ḫ); ሰ ሠ (s ś); አ ዐ (ʾ ʿ); and, finally, ጸ ፀ (ṣ ṣ́). The scribes felt free to do so for two reasons. First, by the second millennium, Gəʿəz was no longer a vernacular, and the written form had fossilized as a classical language; second, the interchangeable symbols represent old sound differences of Gəʿəz that had disappeared completely or partially in the scribes' native languages, mostly Amharic and, to a lesser extent, Tigrinya. In our transcriptions in the notes, as well as in the complete transcriptions of the two poems, we standardized these spelling variations, adopting the etymologically correct forms as provided by the reference dictionaries of August Dillmann and Wolf Leslau (Dillmann 1865; Leslau 1987). For the poems, we also applied this orthographic standardization to their *fidäl* reproductions. *Fidäl* is the indigenous name for the Ethiopian script, which is explained in detail in the next section, "The Ethiopian Script and Its Transcription."

The Gəʿəz manuscripts we consulted display two other typical and widespread orthographic variations. One, the prefix conjugation vowel regularly appears as *ä* instead of the grammatically correct *a* in *a*-prefixed verbs from roots in which the first root consonant is a so-called guttural (i.e., *ʾ ʿ; h ḥ ḫ*). For instance, *aḫdägä* in the present tense thus appears vocalized as *yäḫaddəg* instead of required *yaḫaddəg*. Two, in second-person feminine singular verb forms, the *-i* of the conjugation suffixes is frequently reduced to *-ə* when a further suffix is attached. This latter vowel reduction is near-universal in all collated manuscripts if the concerned verb form appears in the present tense, or in the subjunctive or imperative modes; it is not infrequent when the verb form is a past-tense second-person feminine singular. Examples are *nəgərini* (tell [fem. sg. imper.] me!) being reduced to *nəgərəni*, or *gäśśäṣkinä* (you [fem. sg.] have scolded us) appearing as *gäśśäṣkənä*. Whenever we quoted such forms in our notes, we did not standardize their spellings but provided them as we found them. We indicated, however, that they are substandard forms.

Translation Principles and Procedures

Our translation is not a free literary rendition; it does not take liberties with the Gəʿəz text but follows it closely. Yet, while fidelity to the original ranked high on our agenda, we also aspired to produce a fluid English version. Given the linguistic distance between the source and target languages on the one hand and the cultural distance between seventeenth-century Ethiopia and the twenty-first-century modern world on the other, doing equal justice to both goals was not always easy. Despite our best efforts, it is inevitable that sometimes we have fallen short of this ideal. We are well aware of the old Italian adage *Traduttore, traditore* (a translator is a traitor), which is why we have tried all the harder to limit its applicability to our work.

In order to meet the twin goals of accuracy and readability as much as possible, we adopted a number of procedures and translation techniques that we make transparent in the following.

Added words. Gəˁəz texts can be quite elliptic and condensed in narrative style. To keep the story easily comprehensible throughout, in particular, for readers unfamiliar with Ethiopian history and culture, we sometimes have inserted words or short phrases into the English that have no direct counterpart in the Gəˁəz. We have indicated these with square brackets.

Where we felt that our translation somewhat pushed the envelope of the underlying Gəˁəz expression's semantic range, or where we saw ourselves compelled to resort to a rather free rendering, we did not use brackets but provided a literal translation of the underlying Gəˁəz word or phrase in a note (beginning with "Lit."). Regarding places, throughout we have added the word "island" to the names of the various Lake Ṭana islands that frequently occur in the text. Thereby, the reader unfamiliar with the region's topography will immediately know that the concerned place is not on the mainland. Similarly, we have added, where appropriate, designations such as "monastery" after plain toponyms to provide immediate clarity for the nonspecialist reader.

Pronouns. Gəˁəz has several focus particles that assist the reader in keeping track of who is acting or speaking in long narrative passages or extended direct speech scenes, even if only pronouns—but no nouns, names, or titles—are used to refer to the various persons involved. English does not have equivalent particles, so a literal translation of such passages could easily cause the reader to become confused by, for instance, a long chain of *she*s that refer to different women. Therefore, we have often substituted a full English noun for a pronoun or pronominal suffix of the Gəˁəz original (e.g., translating a sentence as "Walatta Petros replied to Malkiya Kristos" instead of the more literal "she replied to him"), wherever we felt this was required for an effortless understanding. Conversely, if the Gəˁəz unnecessarily (according to English usage) repeated a noun where a pronoun sufficed in English, we have not hesitated to substitute the pronoun in our translation.

Direct objects. Gəˁəz transitive verbs often come without the nominal or pronominal direct objects that are required in English. In such cases, we tacitly inserted them in our translation, without indicating them with brackets. Examples would be an expansion of a literal Gəˁəz "The woman lost her book, but the monk found again" to "The woman lost her book, but the monk found it again," or of literal Gəˁəz "She prayed to God, and God accepted" to "She prayed to God, and God accepted her prayer."

Infinitive verb complements. Analogously, we sometimes have expanded adjectival constructions with English infinitive verb complements that have no counterpart in the Gəˁəz. For instance, in our translation we may tacitly expand a literal Gəˁəz "He found it easy" to "He found it easy to do."

Passive voice. Regarding transitive verbs, the *Gädlä Wälättä Ṗeṭros* frequently avoids the use of the passive voice through periphrastic constructions employing third-person masculine plural active verb forms, which, however, come without a clear explicit or implicit subject. In such cases we often, where stylistically appropriate, have opted for a translation in the passive voice. For instance, a literal Gəʿəz "They revered and loved Walatta Petros" (with a *they* of unspecific reference) might thereby become "Walatta Petros was revered and loved" in our text.

Modal verbs. Gəʿəz phraseology often does not require the use of modal verbs (e.g., can/be able to; must/have to) where English does; regularly, they are contextually implied and understood. For instance, Gəʿəz "Will he carry that load?" does not have to mean "Is he willing to carry that load?" Rather, the phrase's intention, depending on the context, may very well be "Will he be able to carry that load?" As the example shows, the English requires the insertion of "be able to," which is not in the original, to express the latter meaning unambiguously. In our translation, we have added such modal verbs where they were contextually required, without indicating their insertion through brackets. For the same reasons, we have often tacitly inserted English "to begin" as a temporal modifier verb, without there being a direct equivalent in the Gəʿəz.

The conjunction *wä*-. We have translated the ubiquitous and semantically rather indeterminate connector element *wä*- in a variety of ways, beyond the customary "and" and "or," as we felt the context required. Consequently, our interpretations of *wä*- may also be causal (leading to translations such as "therefore" or "thus") or temporal (resulting in translations such as "then," "immediately," and occasionally even "meanwhile").

Dialogue. The *Gädlä Wälättä Ṗeṭros* includes much vivacious dialogue. To better capture the spirit of these exchanges, we felt entitled to use more colloquial language and submit slightly freer translations in such passages. This seemed especially justified given that these exchanges originally took place not in Gəʿəz but in Amharic, which at the time was not yet a commonly written tongue. Their codification in Gəʿəz thus amounted to the transposition of plain, everyday speech into a written prestige language, which involved a process of formalization and literalization that inevitably altered the flavor of these conversations. Our more colloquial translations attempt to reverse this process to a degree.

Hendiadyses. The rhetoric of the *Gädlä Wälättä Ṗeṭros* abounds with doublings (technically, hendiadyses, which is Greek for "one through two"). Most frequently, this is the case with verbs, but also, though noticeably less often, with adjectives or nouns. This stylistic device, employed for narrative emphasis and amplification, reflects the written text's embeddedness in a larger cultural context dominated by orality. In fact, the *Gädlä Wälättä Ṗeṭros* was not intended mainly for silent individual reading, but rather primarily for communal reading aloud in Walatta Petros's community, as well as in the churches and monasteries where she was revered and regarded as an inspirational figure. In our text, for stylistic reasons, we have often reduced these Gəʿəz hendiadyses to one verb, adjective, or noun only. For instance, where the Gəʿəz literally has "*Ras* Silla Kristos sent one of his soldiers as a spy to investigate and ascertain our holy mother Walatta Petros's situation," we chose between the two verbs and used only "investigate" in our translation (see chapter 17).

Conversely, on rare occasions we have employed two English terms to translate a single but semantically rich Gəʿəz lexeme. The Gəʿəz verb *aʿräfä*, for instance, literally "to (find) rest," is also a common euphemism for "to die." Therefore, we have sometimes rendered it as "to pass away and find rest."

Singular and plural nouns. Gəʿəz treats number in nouns differently from English. Except when referring to human beings, plural forms are not strictly required to indicate plurality. So long as it is clear from the context that a given noun is to be understood in the plural sense, its singular suffices. (The plural may be used, but then it tends to imply a finite and countable plurality.) Thus, the use of the singular is significantly more widespread in Gəʿəz than in English, and more ambiguous. It can indicate actual singularity, but also plurality (often of a generic or collective character). Hence, context is crucial for a proper understanding, and formally singular Gəʿəz nouns often underlie plurals of our translation. One such case are formulaic expressions, which are numerous in the *Gädlä Wälättä Ṗeṭros*. For instance, requests for Walatta Petros's intercession on behalf of believers frequently recur in the text using grammatical singulars throughout (e.g., *ṣälot, bäräkät*). We normally translate these as plurals (i.e., prayers, blessings) unless the context suggests otherwise.

Punctuation marks. Gəʿəz manuscripts operate with a very limited set of punctuation marks: the equivalents of the comma, the period, and, in very rare instances, the semicolon. As the placement of commas varies by language, our commas reflect the requirements of the English translation. Regarding Gəʿəz period equivalents, their positions frequently vary between different manuscripts of the same text. Therefore, our periods, while regularly coinciding with those of at least some manuscripts or/and the Conti Rossini print edition, do not slavishly bind themselves to these models. Finally, Gəʿəz manuscripts separate each word from the next with an interpunct of two dots ፡, which our translation reflects with the usual interword space of Latin scripts. Gəʿəz manuscripts have no parentheses, hyphens, dashes, exclamation marks, and so on. In the translation, therefore, all these marks are ours, inserted as the English requires.

Gəʿəz texts do communicate the equivalents of some punctuation marks through their grammar, however. For instance, while there is no question mark in traditional fidäl, questions are clearly indicated in Gəʿəz through interrogative pronouns or enclitic interrogative particles. In our translation, we have always put the requisite question marks.

Direct speech is a particularly interesting case. In Gəʿəz, its onset is not indicated with the equivalents of quotation marks or a colon but rather by placing a verb of speech, in a contextually appropriate form, immediately before the utterance. Unsurprisingly, the verb most frequently used in this function is "to say," but similar verbs abound, including "to reply" and "to respond" (often combined with a modal subordinate clause using "to say"; for instance, "She replied while saying").

Where Gəʿəz verbs of speech primarily function as speech-opening signals, we have dealt with them in a variety of ways. We have sometimes translated them literally, but we have also regularly shortened such expressions (e.g., "She replied and said to them" to "She replied"), transformed them (e.g., "He responded saying" to "He responded with the following words"), intensified them if contextually warranted (e.g., "She said" to "She begged"), or left them untranslated.

While verbs of speech thus often serve as the functional equivalents of opening quotation marks, Gəʿəz has no grammatical counterpart to closing quotation marks. Most of the time contextual semantics are sufficient to determine clearly where a given utterance ends. Sometimes an irreducible uncertainty can arise, however. We were confronted with such cases a few times, and in each case signaled the problem in a note.

Line spacing. Gəʿəz manuscripts usually display few if any paragraphs; that is, prose marked off by a line break and an indent. Conti Rossini sparingly introduced paragraphs into his print edition, and Ricci closely adhered to Conti Rossini's model in his Italian translation. By contrast, our translation has many more paragraphs, so as to facilitate its readability and follow standard practices in English dialogue of indicating a change in speaker with a new paragraph.

Chapters and subchapters are often indicated in Gəʿəz manuscripts, either with line breaks with new chapter titles, or with elaborately worked-out series of closing punctuation marks plus line breaks. In our *Gädlä Wälättä Ṗeṭros* manuscripts, however, there were no such chapter divisions in the biographical core gädl, let alone chapter titles. Hence, our chapter breaks and chapter titles are Belcher's creations, inserted with the goal of structuring the text for the contemporary reader. Only the miracle section of the *Gädlä Wälättä Ṗeṭros* manuscripts is clearly subdivided, with each miracle forming a chapter of its own. Finally, the poems are written as continuous text in the few manuscripts where they are extant, optically undistinguished from prose. Not even new stanzas are indicated with line breaks. Line and stanza ends are regularly marked by the period equivalent, however, often enriched with color. In our text, we have set the poems in normal English format, with each verse on a new line, and with stanzas separated from one another by a line break and a line space.

Amharic influence. The Gəʿəz of the *Gädlä Wälättä Ṗeṭros* occasionally has Amharic loanwords. Mostly these are nouns denoting seventeenth-century Ethiopian items or concepts that had no equivalents in the first millennium when Gəʿəz was still an everyday language, and for which, therefore, no Gəʿəz terms existed. We indicate and explain such loans in notes, using the exemplary Amharic-English dictionary of Thomas L. Kane (1990) as our standard reference.

Syntactically, a specific Amharic construction also left its traces in the Gəʿəz of the *Gädlä Wälättä Ṗeṭros*. In Amharic, the suffix *-ll-* can be added to many verbs, to which an object suffix (e.g., me, her, them) then has to be further attached. In its entirety, this Amharic construction usually expresses for whose benefit the action denoted by the verb is carried out (e.g., *färrädä-ll-ən*, lit., "he judged in our favor," thus, "he acquitted us"). Standard Gəʿəz has no equivalent construction. Yet, in the

Gädlä Wälättä Ṗeṭros, we sometimes encountered expressions with a postverbal *lä-* (for, to) plus object suffix (e.g., *länä* [for us]), which are redundant according to the rules of standard Gəʿəz. We have come to regard such Gəʿəz constructions as being modeled unconsciously upon the Amharic *-ll-* plus object suffix construction. Contextually, it was not always required that such Gəʿəz constructions be reflected expressly in our translation. However, where we saw the need for this, our translations typically involve expressions such as "for so-and-so's benefit" or "for so-and-so's sake." To provide an example, in chapter 63 the *Gädlä Wälättä Ṗeṭros* describes how Walatta Petros caused a demon to leave a man, employing the expression *yətʾattät lotu*, literally, "so that it [the demon] would withdraw to him." Obviously, *lotu* ("to him," an irregular form for *lä-* plus the third-person singular masculine suffix) makes no sense here if understood literally; the Christian point of the story would be inverted if the demon withdrew back into the man. Rather, it makes perfect sense to interpret this Gəʿəz phrase as modeled on the Amharic *-ll-* suffix construction, and therefore understand *yətʾattät lotu* as "so that it would withdraw, fortunately for him."

Substantive notes. When people, places, events, and so on first appear in the translation, we have provided the contextually essential information on them in a brief note. This material is complemented, however, by much fuller information in the glossary. Therefore, the reader looking for further background and insight is advised to consult it.

The Ethiopian Script and Its Transcription

Michael Kleiner

The Semitic-language speakers of the northern and central Eritrean and Ethiopian highlands have their own unique script (table 3), which has its roots in pre-Islamic Yemen, the *Arabia felix* of the Romans. Before the ancient South Arabian script became extinct in its country of origin, after the Islamic conquests of the seventh century CE, Ethiopians had long adapted and improved it for their language of Gəʿəz, calling the script *fidäl*. Subsequently, they wrote all of Gəʿəz literature using fidäl—including, of course, the *Gädlä Wälättä Ṗeṭros*. Amharic and Tigrinya, the two dominant Semitic languages of modern-day Ethiopia and Eritrea, are also written exclusively with fidäl and, as carriers of a vibrant and variegated literary culture, ensure the survival of this unique script in the modern world.

The peoples of pre-Islamic Yemen spoke Semitic languages, and their script was also characteristically Semitic in denoting only a given word's consonants, but not its vowels (some rare exceptions notwithstanding), which readers were assumed to fill in correctly. To provide an English parallel, the expectation was that the reader would be able to interpret "Ths prfrmnc ws brllnt" as "This performance was brilliant." While the required filling-in process is certainly doable in this example, one can easily imagine English sentences where the same task would be much more difficult to achieve. The specific morphological structure of Semitic languages, however, ensures that for them, a consonantal script is sufficient to produce unambiguous text virtually all the time.

Among Semitic scripts, Ethiopian fidäl is innovative and stands out for making vowel notation mandatory, starting sometime in the fourth century CE. All preserved Gəʿəz manuscripts are written with full vowel notation, in vocalized fidäl. But even in vocalized fidäl, the vowels do not appear as independent symbols on a par with the consonants. Rather, they are indicated through small modifications on the consonantal symbols, so that a given fidäl character normally represents a consonant-plus-vowel (CV) sequence.

Gəʿəz has seven vowels, which, in combination with their preceding consonants, are represented through a basic fidäl symbol and six modifications of it. Due to ongoing innovation, today's fidäl has about forty basic consonant characters, as well as marks for punctuation and numbers. This means that the complete fidäl set comprises more than three hundred symbols. The vowels represented through fidäl are:

Basic fidäl symbol, called first order by scholars: ä (to be pronounced as in the English word *hat*)

Second order: u (as in *rude* or *goose*)

TABLE 3
Ethiopian Fidäl Script (in the traditional order of consonants and vowels)

	Transcribed Vowels of Fidäl						
Transcribed Consonants of Fidäl	1 *ä (a after h, ḥ, ḫ, hʷ, ʾ, ʿ)*	2 *u*	3 *i*	4 *a*	5 *e*	6 *ə*	7 *o*
h	ሀ	ሁ	ሂ	ሃ	ሄ	ህ	ሆ
l	ለ	ሉ	ሊ	ላ	ሌ	ል	ሎ
ḥ	ሐ	ሑ	ሒ	ሓ	ሔ	ሕ	ሖ
m	መ	ሙ	ሚ	ማ	ሜ	ም	ሞ
ś	ሠ	ሡ	ሢ	ሣ	ሤ	ሥ	ሦ
r	ረ	ሩ	ሪ	ራ	ሬ	ር	ሮ
s	ሰ	ሱ	ሲ	ሳ	ሴ	ስ	ሶ
š	ሸ	ሹ	ሺ	ሻ	ሼ	ሽ	ሾ
q	ቀ	ቁ	ቂ	ቃ	ቄ	ቅ	ቆ
b	በ	ቡ	ቢ	ባ	ቤ	ብ	ቦ
v	ቨ	ቩ	ቪ	ቫ	ቬ	ቭ	ቮ
t	ተ	ቱ	ቲ	ታ	ቴ	ት	ቶ
č	ቸ	ቹ	ቺ	ቻ	ቼ	ች	ቾ
ḫ	ኀ	ኁ	ኂ	ኃ	ኄ	ኅ	ኆ
n	ነ	ኑ	ኒ	ና	ኔ	ን	ኖ
ñ	ኘ	ኙ	ኚ	ኛ	ኜ	ኝ	ኞ
ʾ	አ	ኡ	ኢ	ኣ	ኤ	እ	ኦ
k	ከ	ኩ	ኪ	ካ	ኬ	ክ	ኮ
ḵ	ኸ	ኹ	ኺ	ኻ	ኼ	ኽ	ኾ
w	ወ	ዉ	ዊ	ዋ	ዌ	ው	ዎ
ʿ	ዐ	ዑ	ዒ	ዓ	ዔ	ዕ	ዖ
z	ዘ	ዙ	ዚ	ዛ	ዜ	ዝ	ዞ
ž	ዠ	ዡ	ዢ	ዣ	ዤ	ዥ	ዦ
y	የ	ዩ	ዪ	ያ	ዬ	ይ	ዮ
d	ደ	ዱ	ዲ	ዳ	ዴ	ድ	ዶ
ǧ	ጀ	ጁ	ጂ	ጃ	ጄ	ጅ	ጆ
g	ገ	ጉ	ጊ	ጋ	ጌ	ግ	ጎ
ṭ	ጠ	ጡ	ጢ	ጣ	ጤ	ጥ	ጦ
č̣	ጨ	ጩ	ጪ	ጫ	ጬ	ጭ	ጮ
p̣	ጰ	ጱ	ጲ	ጳ	ጴ	ጵ	ጶ
ṣ	ጸ	ጹ	ጺ	ጻ	ጼ	ጽ	ጾ
ṣ́	ፀ	ፁ	ፂ	ፃ	ፄ	ፅ	ፆ
f	ፈ	ፉ	ፊ	ፋ	ፌ	ፍ	ፎ
p	ፐ	ፑ	ፒ	ፓ	ፔ	ፕ	ፖ
qʷ	ቈ		ቊ	ቋ	ቌ	ቍ	
ḫʷ	ኈ		ኊ	ኋ	ኌ	ኍ	
kʷ	ኰ		ኲ	ኳ	ኴ	ኵ	
gʷ	ጐ		ጒ	ጓ	ጔ	ጕ	

1	፩	7	፯	40	፵	100	፻
2	፪	8	፰	50	፶	200	፪፻
3	፫	9	፱	60	፷	500	፭፻
4	፬	10	፲	70	፸	1,000	፲፻
5	፭	20	፳	80	፹	10,000	፼
6	፮	30	፴	90	፺	90,000	፱፼

Third order: i (as in *meet, sheep*)
Fourth order: a (as in *father, car*)
Fifth order: e (as in *blasé, soufflé*; a clear and undiphthongized *e* that in English is only found in loanwords)
Sixth order: ə (as in *dim, king*; a lax and short *i*, the transcription symbol *ə* is called *schwa*)
Seventh order: o (as in *toga*, an undiphthongized *o*)

Two examples, using *b* and *k* as the consonantal carriers, demonstrate the principle of fidäl vowel notation (table 4):

TABLE 4
Examples of the Principle of Fidäl Vowel Notation.

ä	*u*	*i*	*a*	*e*	*ə*	*o*
በ bä	ቡ bu	ቢ bi	ባ ba	ቤ be	ብ bə	ቦ bo
ከ kä	ኩ ku	ኪ ki	ካ ka	ኬ ke	ክ kə	ኮ ko

As can be seen in this sample, the modifications of the basic symbols are largely regular, with a right mid-stem indicating *u*, a right foot-stem indicating *i*, a short left leg indicating *a*, and so on. Notwithstanding some outliers, the reader looking at the complete fidäl chart (table 3) will find this regularity essentially confirmed for the other symbols.

Yet two questions remain open: How does one write a pure consonant in fidäl, and how, conversely, a pure vowel? For pure consonants, one uses the sixth order symbols. The symbols of this order are thus irreducibly ambiguous, sometimes indicating a pure consonant and sometimes a consonant plus the schwa vowel. Only a knowledge of Gəʿəz morphology and its lexicon can reveal how to read them in a given context. As to pure vowels, they are expressed through modifications of the consonantally "empty" symbol አ (which, strictly speaking, represents the short stop in the airstream before the articulation of a vowel not preceded by a consonant).

The fidäl chart on the preceding page includes a number of consonant characters not in use for the older language Gəʿəz but only needed and employed in more recent Amharic (specifically, š, v, č, ñ, ḵ, ž, ğ, ç̣). The inclusion of these characters was required, however, because the *Gädlä Wälättä Ṗeṭros* has loanwords from Amharic.

In preparing this volume, we have, as a rule, not used fidäl because the overwhelming majority of our target audience is not conversant with this writing system. For instance, most readers would have no idea what ማርያም means. If we represent this word with Latin script, however, they can understand: it spells "Maryam." Therefore, in this volume, we have transcribed fidäl into Latin script. We have done this in two different ways. In the translation itself, we have avoided diacritical marks so as to ease reading, employing our own simplified transcription of Gəʿəz proper names and terms (e.g., Malkiya Kristos for መልክአ:ክርስቶስ). However, in this volume's scholarly parts—the introduction, substantive and text-critical notes, and glossary—we have used a more rigorous system.

In the history of Ethiopian studies, scholars have devised various fidäl transcription systems, and considerable variation is found in scholarship published before 2003. However, the system used by the *Encyclopaedia Aethiopica* has now become dominant in international Ethiopian studies, and it is the one we use in the introduction, substantive and text-critical notes, and glossary. For instance, the man's proper name that appears as "Malkiya Kristos" in the translation appears as "Mälkəʾa Krəstos" in the introduction, the notes, and the glossary following *Encyclopaedia Aethiopica* transcription rules. We deviate from the *Encyclopaedia Aethiopica* model in only three minor points. First, we separate enclitic prefixes from their carrier lexemes by hyphens. For instance, we write *bä-zä-gəbr* (through this deed), instead of *bäzəgəbr*. We believe that our morphologically motivated hyphenation renders our transcriptions more transparent. Second, we have used the symbols ʾ and ʿ, not ʾ and ʿ, to transcribe አ and ዐ. Third, we simplify the constantly recurring name of our text's subject, Wälättä Ṗeṭros, as "Walatta Petros" in the chronology and introduction, and as "WP" in the notes and glossary.

Scholars of Gəʿəz may wonder why we do not use fidäl instead of transcription in the notes, where it would not interfere with the flow of the translation. The reason is that variants given in transcription in the notes can convey a general impression of the sounds and patterns of the Gəʿəz language to the uninitiated. Students just learning the language may find it helpful and, through access, others may be inspired to study Gəʿəz. Moreover, no information is lost for the initiated through *Encyclopaedia Aethiopica*–based transcription, as it allows unambiguous reconversion into fidäl.

A few more words on the *Encyclopaedia Aethiopica* transcription system are in order. Regarding vowels, it has only two symbols not found in the standard English alphabet, namely *ä* and *ə*, whose pronunciations have been explained already. *Encyclopaedia Aethiopica* consonant transcriptions, however, include almost twenty symbols not found in the standard English inventory. These nonstandard symbols (see table 3) typically consist of a familiar letter complemented by a diacritical mark, such as a dot below it (e.g., *ḥ*, *ṭ*), a haček above it (e.g., *č*, *ž*), and so forth. In addition, there are the symbols ʾ (for the "consonantally empty" vowel carrier አ) and ʿ (for the harsh, throaty sound that linguists characterize as a voiced pharyngeal fricative), which are not based on any letters of the Latin alphabet.

In some cases, these special transcription signs represent consonants that have no exact equivalents in English or indeed in any other Western language. For instance, *ḥ* and *ṭ* stand for consonants that sound almost like the English *h* and *t* but are not precisely the same. The existence of these small yet linguistically important differences is the rationale behind many of the diacritical marks and one reason why a scholarly transcription system is required.

Other special transcription signs express sounds that *are* found in European languages, but are expressed differently in various national orthographies. For instance, *č* stands for the sound that English expresses with *ch*, as in *church* or *change*. In Italian, however, the same sound would be expressed through *c* or *ci* (cf. *cento* [one hundred] and *ciao*), while *ch* in German orthography regularly represents a quite different sound, namely, the same as in Scottish *Loch Ness*. These examples demonstrate the need for a transcription system like that of the *Encyclopaedia Aethiopica*, which provides unambiguous clarity, beyond national spelling conventions. The *Encyclopaedia Aethiopica* system further ensures a strict correspondence of exactly one transcription symbol to one fidäl consonant (e.g., single *č* and not double *ch* for single fidäl ቸ).

In the English translation text, however, we employ a radically simplified transcription for Gəʿəz proper names and culturally specific terms, providing the *Encyclopaedia Aethiopica* transcription only in a note on the word's first occurrence. We eliminated diacritical marks from the transcription in the translation (except a French-style *é* to express the clear, plain *e*-vowel of the fifth fidäl order) and otherwise applied the normal spelling conventions of English. Our goal was to produce transcriptions from which English speakers could intuitively arrive at good-enough pronunciations. This means, for instance, that our simplified transcription disregards the distinctions between plain and ejective consonants (e.g., between *s* and *ṣ*). It also means that we were not always fully consistent in the transcription of one and the same Gəʿəz phoneme, as its pronunciation may vary due to allophony. Generally, our simplified transcription, in accordance with its stated goals, is oriented phonetically, not phonemically.

Given this double system of transcription, one in the translation and the other in the scholarly sections, a few last notes are in order. The reader searching for the scholarly transcription of any given Gəʿəz term after its first occurrence in the translation may turn to the glossary. The glossary is arranged according to the simplified transcriptions so that a nonspecialist may easily find them. The specialist searching for a word should adjust accordingly; for instance, by searching for terms beginning with *č* under *ch*.

Names of non-Ethiopian people and places appear in their familiar English forms in our translation, not as transcriptions of their Gəʿəz versions. For instance, we give the name of the fourth evangelist as English *John* and not as Gəʿəz *Yohannes* (simplified from the *Encyclopaedia Aethiopica* transcription *Yoḥannəs*). By contrast, the Ethiopian king named *Yoḥannəs* appears as *Yohannes* in our text.

Over the history of Western scholarship on Ethiopia, researchers and audiences have sometimes confused Gəʿəz honorific titles with names, combining them improperly. To prevent such confusion, we italicize Gəʿəz titles throughout. For instance, the great lord Śəʿəlä Krəstos, who had the title of *ras* (duke), appears as "*Ras* Silla Kristos" whenever the text mentions him with his title.

We also italicize Gəʿəz cultural terms on first appearance, adding a descriptive English equivalent. The distinctive Lake Ṭana *tankʷa* boat thus first appears as "*tankwa* papyrus boat" in our text, but as "tankwa" on later occasions.

Finally, please note that the subject of this hagiobiography, Wälättä Ṗeṭros, has had her name spelled in a variety of ways in the previous scholarship, including the Library of Congress's Walata Péṭros and Walatta Pēṭros, as well as Walata Petros, Wallatta Petros, Wallata Petros, Waleta Petros, Waletta Petros, Walete Petros, Walleta Petros, Welete Petros, Wolata Petros plus Walatta Pétros, Walatta Pietros, Walatta Petrus, and Wälätä Pʾétʾros.

The Translation of the *Life-Struggles of Walatta Petros* (*Gädlä Wälättä P̣eṭros*)

In the name of God, who was before all time and who will be for eternity, who is without beginning and without end![1] He is our Lord by virtue of his divinity and our Father by virtue of his benevolence. Our praise of him comes from him, and our glorification of him emanates from that which belongs to him. He is all-powerful, nothing is impossible for him. For eternity, amen. 1

Introduction

I, the sinner and transgressor Galawdewos,[2] will write a small part of the story of her persecution,[3] as well as of the many struggles and virtuous deeds of our holy mother Walatta Petros,[4] the mother-of-pearl, the mother of a myriad of precious

[1] The chapter breaks and chapter titles throughout the translation are Belcher's inventions, inserted to structure the text for the contemporary reader. The numbers floating in the margin indicate the Gəʿəz print edition page number.

In the margin of the Abb. 88 manuscript (which Conti Rossini used for his Gəʿəz print edition, which in turn became the basis for Ricci's Italian translation) appears the following: *Zə-mäṣḥaf zä-Ǝnṭonyos Wäldä Abbädi fəransawi zä-täśayätä* [*sic*, for *zä-täśayäṭä*] *əm-ḫabä abba Wäldä Giyorgis* (this book belongs to Antoine d'Abbadie, the Frenchman. He bought it from *Abba* Wäldä Giyorgis). The latter might be the same person who, writing his name as Wäldä Geworgis, implores WP's intercession at the end of the miracle section and at the end of the sälamta poem to WP.

[2] CDEFHIJ: *anä ḫaṭəʾ wä-giguy Gälawdewos* (I, the sinner and transgressor Gälawdewos); B omits; G: first folio missing, text begins with the Gospel quote below; AK: the proper name faded or illegible; CR: *anä ḫaṭəʾ gäbra* (I, the sinner, her servant). In Abb. 88, the name of the author is erased, so the *gäbra* (her servant) of CR is a Conti Rossini emendation. Still in Abb. 88, however, the following names have then been inserted: "Finḥas, Minas, Naʿod, Muzu, Ṣota Maryam, Wəbit, Säblä Maryam, Mikaʾel, Ṣəge, Arägawi, Bäkaffa." That is, when this particular manuscript went to a new owner, the author's name was erased and the names of secondary owners were inserted. Although it is common for owners' or commissioners' names to appear in manuscripts, especially at the beginning and end of miracles in hagiobiographies, it is uncommon for the author's name to appear. This is what probably led the scribe to mistakenly erase an author's name to insert owners' names. The first inserted name is likely that of the owner, and the subsequent names are individuals, men and women, in his family.

[3] ABCDEFHIJK: *səddäta* (her persecution *or* her exile); CR: *lədäta* (her birth).

[4] *Wälättä P̣eṭros* (Daughter of [Saint] Peter). The formulation *əmmənä qəddəst* (our holy mother) appears almost always before the name "Wälättä P̣eṭros." Sometimes scribes do vary this formula, however, according to their taste. For instance, MS B almost always expands it to *əmmənä qəddəst wä-burəkt* (our holy and blessed mother), while Abb. 88/CR varies the

stones, she of holy lips and mouth. Word of her deeds[1] has spread throughout the world and has been proclaimed[2] from one end to the other. Truly, this word benefits anyone who hears it, profits anyone who listens to it,[3] and is a path to salvation for anyone who pursues and follows it.

I now write[4] this out of neither presumption nor pride, nor because I seek empty praise or vain accolades. Rather [I write it] because [the young nun] Qiddista Kristos,[5] who burned with love for Walatta Petros, made me do it,[6] saying, "Write, so that Walatta Petros's story may be known, so that it may reach those places which it has not yet reached, that anyone who has not yet heard it may hear it,[7] and that her commemoration may be read by the generations of those who will come after us, in perpetuity!"[8] As Christ says in the Gospel, "What I told you in the dark, proclaim in the light, and what I whispered in your ears, preach on the rooftops. A city built upon a hill cannot be hid. Neither do people light a lamp[9] to then put it under a basket. Instead they will put it on a stand so that it gives light to everyone in the house."[10]

Chapter 1: The Author's Worthiness

Because of Qiddista Kristos's urging,[11] I, too, became eager to follow this story from its beginning to its end. Even though I am not worthy to mention Walatta Petros's

---

əmmənä qəddəst formula, sometimes replacing *qəddəst* (holy) with *burəkt* (blessed), *ḫərit* (chosen), or *bəṣəʿt* (beatified, which Ricci sometimes incorrectly translates as *perfetta*) or adding one of the latter adjectives to the former. We do not again note these variations in praise adjectives for WP throughout the text and simply use *əmmənä qəddəst* from DJ. If WP's name is not preceded by this formula, it means that her name did not appear in the original, just a pronoun, which we have replaced with her name for clarity.

[1] Lit., *səmuʿatiha* (the things heard about her).

[2] Lit., *täsäbkä* (has been preached).

[3] CR omits *wä-bäqʷʿet lä-zä-yaṣämmə'o* (lit., and is a profit for him who listens to it).

[4] Lit., *gäbärku* (I now do).

[5] *Qəddəstä Krəstos* (Saintly woman of Christ).

[6] ADE: *agbärätäni* (lit., made me do); BCFHIJK, CR: *agäbbärätäni* (compelled me).

[7] ABCDEHIJ: *wä-yəsmaʿ zä-i-sämʿa* (that anyone who has not yet heard it may hear it); F: *wä-yessämaʿ zä-i-sämʿa* (that it may be heard who did not yet hear [*sic*]); K, CR: *wä-yəssämaʿ ḫabä zä-i-täsämʿa* (that it may be heard where it has not yet been heard).

[8] The eleventh miracle in the *Tä'amərä Wälättä Ṗeṭros* gives further details about those who urged the writing of the book.

[9] DG: *wä-i-yaḫattəwu maḫtotä* (neither do people light a lamp); A illegible; BCIJ with the substandard orthographic variant *wä-i-yäḫattəwu maḫtotä*; EFHK, Abb. 88/CR with further orthographic deterioration to *wä-i-yäḫattəw maḫtotä.* Conti Rossini, working only from Abb. 88, mistook its *yäḫattəw* as not resulting from progressive orthographic degradation but as the original intransitive verb form (it is being lit). Consequently, he emended the subsequent acc. *maḫtotä* to the nom. *maḫtot* in order to make it tally with the supposedly intransitive verb (neither is a lamp being lit).

[10] Combined from Luke 12:3 and Matthew 5:14–15.

[11] Lit., *bä'əntä-zə* (because of this).

name with my impure mouth or to write[1] her story with my polluted hand, truly,[2]
I know that her pure and holy story will not be defiled by my impurity; that it will
not harm the listener in any way, that my foolishness will not taint it,[3] if he listens 2
to and receives from me this pure, holy, and sweet story that comes from my mouth.

While I am impure in all my deeds and rotten of character inside[4] and out, I am capable of carrying out useful work just like three [other] laborers who live in the world. One of them belongs to the pure and two belong to the impure creatures.[5] Even though they are foul, bad,[6] and impure by nature, they please people with their good works. They are[7] the bee, the donkey, and the dog.

The bee belongs to the pure creatures.[8] [Yet] she is cruel and her poison is bitter.[9] She stings people[10] and causes much pain. However, in her service to human beings, she goes[11] into the wilderness[12] and industriously collects nectar.[13] She also goes down to the stream to draw [water] and brings it to everything that is important to her work. She is not idle in the least, but ever-diligent. She takes the nectar[14] and puts it[15] into a beehive basket, rock crevice, or tree hollow—wherever she lives. When blessings descend on it from heaven above, then it becomes sweet honeycomb. When someone comes near to her, be it her owner or a stranger, the bee will sting without qualms, she will spare no one.

Those who know her ways will create smoke and fan it in her direction, and she will flee for fear of the smoke. When she withdraws and leaves the honey behind, then they will take it from her. The honey is sweet when eaten, fragrant when smelled, and delights the hearts of kings and lords when made into mead. Furthermore, its wax becomes a lamp for the church and the palace. People do not abandon

[1] ABCDEFGHIJK: *wä-əṣḥaf* (lit., or that I write [subj.]); CR: *wä-əṣəḥəf* (or I write [ind.]).

[2] ABCDFGHIJK: *əsmä* (truly *or* because); E, CR: *baḥtu əsmä* (However, because).

[3] Lit., *i-yəttossaḥ botu* (will not be mixed into it).

[4] ABCDEFHIJK: *əntä wəsṭəyä*; G: illegible; CR: *anä wəsṭəyä* (I my inside [*sic*]).

[5] The Eritrean and Ethiopian Orthodox Täwaḥədo Churches follow the laws of Leviticus and Deuteronomy regarding animals that are considered ritually unclean or impure. All canines and equines are impure; that is, their dead bodies should not be eaten or touched; Leviticus 11:27. Strictly, bees are also impure, but their honey is not.

[6] AC omit *əkuyan* (bad).

[7] ABCDFGIJ: *zä-wəʾətomu*; EHK, CR omit.

[8] Bees are often portrayed in Gəʿəz hagiobiographies as a symbol of purity and constancy, for instance, in the *Gädlä Lalibäla* and the *Gädlä Märḥa Krəstos*. Beekeeping is one of Ethiopia's oldest agricultural activities, partially inspired by the need for candle beeswax in monasteries. Many farmers construct cylindrical beehives, sometimes from logs, but also from straw and bark, and hang them from trees or houses. Bees can collect up to a quart of water a day for the smooth running of the hive. See Admasu Addi (2003).

[9] ABCDFGIJ: *märir* [masc. adj.]; EHK, CR: *märar* [fem. adj.].

[10] BCDEFGHIJK: *säbʾa* [acc.]; A: *säbʾ* [nom.].

[11] BCDEFGHIJK, CR: *təwäffər* (lit., she goes to work); A: *täwäkäf* (accept! [imper.]).

[12] *Gädam*, a word that means wilderness or monastic settlement. This word suggests that the author might be thinking also of WP when writing of the bee.

[13] Lit., *aqmaḥa ṣəgeyat* (the produce of the flowers).

[14] Lit., *tənäśśəʾ əmənnehu* (she takes of it).

[15] BCDEFGHIJK: *təgäbbəro* (lit., she does it); A: illegible; CR: *təgäbbər* (she does).

honey just because of the painful poison of the bee. As for the bee, she is not saddened[1] nor resentful nor does she abandon working[2] if people take [her honey] away from her, but rather the next day again goes into the fields as is her habit[3] because she is ordained to be the servant of humanity.[4]

Similarly,[5] I am cruel in my deeds, stinging people with my tongue and causing much pain. However,[6] because I am [also] ordained to serve you[7] I have drawn inspiration[8] from the holy books and from the words of the learned Fathers and now will write the story of our holy mother Walatta Petros, a story which is sweeter than honeycomb and which will delight people's hearts.

3 As for the donkey, it is impure and yet carries the holy vessels of the house of God,[9] as well as food for the people. Such a [holy] vessel is not abandoned because of the donkey's impurity; rather people remove from the donkey[10] what belongs to the house of God and what is needed[11] for sustenance. Similarly, I also[12] carry a chosen vessel and spiritual food: the struggles and virtues of our blessed mother Walatta Petros.

The dog is also impure, and yet he goes into the wilderness with his master to hunt. If the dog sees a gazelle[13] or another wild animal, a partridge or other birds that may be eaten,[14] he runs tirelessly to seize it. Then his master pats him, the dog abandons [the prey] to him, the master takes[15] what had been seized[16] by the dog's mouth, eats it and does not abandon it just because of the dog's impurity. Similarly,

[1] ABCDFGIJ: *i-täḥazzən* (she is not saddened); EHK, CR: *i-täḫaddəg* (she does not leave).

[2] ABCDEFGHIJK: *tägäbbəro* (working); CR: *tägbara* (her work).

[3] ABCDFGHIJK: *kämä ləmada* (as is her habit); E, CR: *zä-kämä ləmada* (according to her habit).

[4] Lit., *əsmä əzzəzt yəʾəti lä-säbʾ* (because she is ordered to humanity).

[5] ACDFHIJK: *kämahu* (similiarly); BEG, CR: *kämaha* (like her [viz., the bee]).

[6] AI: *baḥtu* (however); BCDEFGHIJK, CR omit.

[7] ABCDFGHIJK: *bäʾəntä täʾazzəzotəyä läkəmu* (lit., because of my being ordered to you); E: *bäʾəntä tänazəzotəyä läkəmu* (because I console myself for you [*sic*]); CR: *bäʾəntä-zə nazəzotəyä läkəmu* (because of this, as my consolation for you).

[8] AI: *astägabaʾku* (lit., I collected); BCDEFGHJK, CR: *astägabbəʾ* (I collect *or* I will collect).

[9] BCDEFGHJK, CR: *zä-betä əgziʾabḥer* (of the house of God); AI: *lä-betä əgziʾabḥer* (for the house of God).

[10] ABCDEFGHIJK: *yänäśśəʾəwwo* (lit., they remove from it); CR: *yanäśśəʾəwwo* (they raise it).

[11] ABCDEFGHIJK: *zä-yətfäqqäd* (what is needed); CR: *zä-yəfäqqəd* (what he needs).

[12] ABCDEFHIJK: *anä-hi* (I also); G illegible, CR *anä-ni* [same meaning].

[13] ABCDEFGIJK: *mədaqʷä* (gazelle [acc.]); H: *mədaqʷa* (her gazelle); CR with note "*Sic* ms.": *mədaqʷ* [nom.].

[14] ABCDFGIJ: *kaləʾanä aʿwafä əllä yətbälləʿu* (other birds that may be eaten) HK: *kaləʾanä aʿwafä sämay əllä yətbälləʿu* (other birds of the sky that may be eaten); E: *kaləʾanä əm-aʿwafä sämay əllä yətbälləʿu* (others from among the birds of the sky that may be eaten); CR: *kaləʾanä əm-aʿwafä sämay əllä yətbälləʿa* [final verb in the fem. instead of the masc. pl.].

[15] E, CR omit "Then his master pats him . . . takes" (*Wəʾətä gize yəzäbbəṭo əgziʾu wä-yəḫaddəg lotu wä-yənäśśəʾ*).

[16] BCDEFGHIJK: *wəʾətä zä-täʾəḫzä* (what had been seized); A, CR: *wä-wəʾətu zä-täʾəḫzä* (and he who had been seized [*sic*]).

I also hunt in the holy books for the story of the life and holiness of our chosen and beatified[1] mother Walatta Petros.[2] I write for you, therefore you should receive this story in faith, like the pure sacrifices which are[3] the flesh and blood of the Savior [during the Eucharist] when you say "Amen and amen"; do not reject it because of my impurity.

Does not the Orit[4] say: Samson found honey in the mouth of a dead lion that he himself had killed [earlier]?[5] He then ate [that honey], and as he himself [later] put it in a riddle, "From the mouth of the eater came food, from the strong, sweetness."[6] Moreover, when Samson was parched from thirst and near to death, he prayed to God, and God made sweet water flow forth for him from the jawbone of a donkey. Samson then drank and life returned to him, as he himself [later] put it in a riddle: "A drink in the time of thirst and a weapon for warfare."[7] Also, every day a raven brought food[8] to the prophet Elijah, who took it and ate it and did not consider it impure.[9] If these saints[10] did not deem these impure creatures impure,[11] neither should you deem impure this story[12] that comes from my impure mouth.

[1] Lit., *bəṣeʿt*, which could also be translated as "blessed." We have consistently rendered it as "beatified," however, so as to distinguish it from *burəkt* (masc.: *buruk*), which is the more common term for "blessed." In this text, "beatified" does not mean officially elevated to sainthood as in the Roman Catholic Church but rather in a state of blessedness or heavenly bliss.

[2] It is not clear which holy books the author has in mind here. It may mean the earlier WP poetry, the earlier WP *Sənkəssar* entry, or earlier books about other saints, which would have provided a model of language and anecdote.

[3] ABCDFGHIJK: *kämä mäśwaʿt nəṣuḥ zä-wəʾətu* (lit., like the pure sacrifice which is); E, CR: *kämä mäśwaʿt nəṣuḥ bä-amsalä* (as a pure sacrifice, in the manner of).

[4] Orit (law) generally means the Torah or Old Testament as a whole, but more specifically means the Octateuch, the first eight books of the Bible, including Judges.

[5] BCDEFGHIJK, CR: *zä-qätälo lälihu* (that he himself had killed); A: *wä-qätälo lälihu* (and he himself killed him). See Judges 14:8–9. The Septuagint, in the Satterthwaite translation: "and see, a swarm of bees in the mouth of the lion, and there was honey."

[6] ABCDFGIJ: *wä-əmənnä ṣənuʿ ṭaʿm* (from the strong, sweetness); EHK, CR: *wä-əm-afä gərum wäṣʾa ṭəʿum* (from the mouth of the fearsome came something sweet). The EHK, CR variant has internal rhyme (*gərum/ṭəʿum*). Judges 14:14, adapted. Samson was a powerful Israelite warrior of the Old Testament. Although the Protestant Bible does not specify that Samson actually ate the honey he found in the carcass of the lion he killed, the Septuagint Bible, on which the Gəʿəz Bible is based, does.

[7] See Judges 15:15–19. The Septuagint, in the Satterthwaite translation: "And God opened the wound of the jawbone, and waters came from it." This story appears several times in the *Sənkəssar*: "God made water to flow out from a Jawbone" (Budge 1928). This riddle does not appear in the Protestant Bible, but seems to be part of an Ethiopian oral tradition, or an invention of the author arising from the African riddle tradition, which poses a metaphorical description of nature and expects listeners to guess (or know) its referent.

[8] ADH: *sisayä* (food [acc.]) BCEFGIJK: *sisayo* (his food).

[9] BCDEFGIJK: *wä-i-yaräkkʷəso* (and did not consider it impure); AH: *wä-i-yaräkkʷəs* (and did not consider impure). 1 Kings 17:1–6.

[10] ABCDEFGHIJK: *əllu qəddusan* (these saints); CR: *kʷəllu qəddusan* (all saints).

[11] ABCDFGJ: *i-yarkʷäsəwwomu lä-əmuntu rəkʷəsan* (did not deem these impure creatures impure); EHIK, CR: *i-yaräkkʷəsəwwomu lä-əmuntu rəkʷəsan* (do not deem these impure creatures impure).

[12] ABCDFGIJ: *i-tastärakʷəsəwwo lä-zentu zena* (neither should you deem impure this story); EHK, CR: *i-tarkʷəsəwwo lä-zentu zena* [same meaning, but different verbal stems].

As for me, I am not worthy to write[1] this, for I am a sinner and transgressor[2] and because "holy things should be handled by the holy" and "pure things by the pure."[3] Nevertheless, love for Walatta Petros compelled me[4] to write down[5] for you a few of the many things [about her], insofar as allowed by my poor understanding[6] and weak intellect, as well as by what you are able to hear—just like the *dinbeets* bird[7] dives into the big lake,[8] but can drink only what her tiny stomach[9] allows.

Chapter 2: The Author's Petition

4 And now you people, lovers of God, who have come from distant regions[10] or who live in this monastery,[11] monks and nuns,[12] fling wide the windows of your ears and awaken your hearts so that you can hear this sweet story I have written down for you. As[13] David said, "Hear this, all you peoples, and listen, all who live in the world, in your various lands,[14] [you] children of Eve,[15] rich and poor! My mouth will speak wisdom, and the meditation of my heart [will give] counsel. With my ears I will listen to parables, and I will expound my words with song."[16] He further said,

[1] Lit., *litä-ssä akko dəlwät litä əgbär* (as for me, there is no worthiness that I do).

[2] BG add *Gälawdewos.*

[3] Lit., *qəddəsat lä-qəddusan wä-nəṣuḥ lä-nəṣuḥan* (lit., holy things to the holy ones and the pure things to the pure ones). From the Täwaḥədo Church liturgy for the Eucharist called the Anaphora of the Apostles; see Habtemichael Kidane (2003).

[4] Due to the similarity and imprecise execution of various g's, it is unclear whether the manuscripts have አገበረኒ *agäbbäräni* (compelled me) or አግበረኒ *agbäräni* (made me).

[5] BCDEFGHIJK, CR: *əṣḥaf* [subj.]; A: *əṣəḥəf* [ind.].

[6] BCDEFGHJK: *amṭanä ḥəṣṣätä aʾəmrotəyä* (lit., according to the paucity of my understanding); AI: *mäṭänä ḥəṣṣätä aʾəmrotəyä* [same meaning]; CR: *amṭanä ḫəṣbätä aʾəmrotəyä* (according to the washing [*sic*] of my understanding).

[7] *Dənbiṣ* (Amharic *dənbiṭ* or *dəmbiṭ*), the name for one of two small Ethiopian birds, either the *Sylvia lugens* (Brown warbler) or *Uraeginthus bengalus* (sometimes called the Abyssinian Red-cheeked Cordon-bleu). It appears frequently in proverbs and folklore as an exemplar of smallness. Amharic definitions always come from Kane (1990).

[8] Lit., *təwärrəd ḫabä qälayä baḥər* (goes down to the bottom of the sea *or* the big lake *or* the big river). The author probably has Lake Ṭana in mind.

[9] Lit, *ṣəbbätä kärśa* (the narrowness of her stomach).

[10] A omits *bəḥer* (regions).

[11] ACDEFHIJK, CR: *gädam* (monastic settlement); BG: *däset* (island). It is interesting to note that MSS B and G were microfilmed at island monasteries (Rema and Zäge, respectively). The alteration of *gädam* to *däset* suggests that they were made there and the copyist localized the text.

[12] BG add *aʾrug wä-ḥəṣ́anat* (old and young).

[13] A omits *bä-kämä* (as).

[14] ADEGHIJK: *bä-bä-bäḥawərtikəmu* (in your various lands); BCF, CR: *bä-bäḥawərtikəmu* (in your lands).

[15] Lit., *däqiqä əgʷalä əmmä-ḥəyaw* (children of the offspring of the mother of the living).

[16] Psalm 48[49]:1–4. Throughout, when citing Psalms, the first number represents that used in the Täwaḥədo Church, from the Greek (Septuagint) manuscripts, and the second number, in brackets, that used in the Protestant tradition, from the Hebrew (Masoretic) manuscripts. In many Christian traditions, David was considered the author of Psalms, and in

"My people, listen to my law and incline your ears to the words of my mouth. I will open my mouth[1] with parables and I will speak in proverbs of old, all that we have heard and seen and which our fathers have told us."[2]

Before all else,[3] I thank God who has deemed me worthy of writing this book—I who have neither worthiness nor ability and am a fool, the first among fools.[4] It is just as our Lord says in the Gospel, "I trust in you, O Father, and I praise you, Lord of heaven and earth, who hid this from the wise and the learned and revealed it[5] to children. Yes, Father, for like this it was[6] your will."[7]

Furthermore, I beg and implore the Lord to help me and grant to me the power of the word so that I will be able to tell [Walatta Petros's story] from its beginning to its end, lest people[8] mock me[9] and say,[10] "This man began to build, but then was unable to finish!" For I am weak of heart and many are those who have wanted to write these things down[11] but did not because the time and day[12] that pleased God had not yet come. Indeed, for this reason we [of her community] have been distressed for some time that the story of our holy mother Walatta Petros had not been written down for our benefit,[13] including the virtuous deeds[14] and the miracles that she performed during her lifetime and after her demise.

Therefore, because spiritual ardor for our holy[15] mother Walatta Petros moved us, we wrote down this book of her *Life and Struggles*[16] in the thirtieth year[17] after she

---

Ethiopia, Psalms is often referred to as *Dawit.* Thus, whenever the text has "David says," it means "*Psalms* says."

[1] BF: *afayä* [acc.]; ACDEGHIJK, CR: *afuyä* [nom.]. Ricci tacitly translated the accusative.

[2] Psalm 77[78]:1–3.

[3] ABCDFGHIJK: *mäqdəmä kʷəllu* (before all else); E, CR: *mäqdəmä* (first).

[4] Lit., *rəʾsomu lä-abdan* (the head of the fools).

[5] BCEFGIJK: *zä-säwwärko lä-zəntu . . . wä-käśätko* (who hid this . . . and revealed it); H: *zä-säwwärko lä-zəntu . . . wä-käśätkä* (who hid this . . . and revealed); AD: illegible; CR: *zä-säwwärkä lä-zəntu* [*sic*] *. . . wä-käśätkä* (who hid this . . . and revealed).

[6] ABCDFGIJ: *was* implied; EHK, CR: *konä* (was).

[7] Matthew 11:25; Luke 10:21.

[8] ABCDFGIJ: *säbʾ* (people); EHK, CR omit.

[9] ABCDEFGHIJK: *kämä i-yəssaläquni* (lit., so that they do not mock me); Abb. 88: *kämä yəssaläquni* (so that they mock me). Sensibly, CR emended this to *kämä i-yəssaläquni.*

[10] ABCDEFGHIJK: *wä-i-yəbäluni* (lit., and say not to me [subj.]); Abb. 88: *wä-i-yəbeluni* (and say not to me [ind.]). Sensibly CR emended this to *wä-i-yəbäluni.*

[11] That is, it had long been the wish of her community to write the *Gädlä Wälättä Pəṭros.*

[12] A omits *wä-ʿəlät* (and day).

[13] Lit., *länä* (for us). However, we interpret this language use as modeled upon the Amharic postverbal benefactive infix *-ll-*, which, together with the mandatorily following personal suffix, indicates for whose benefit the action denoted by the preceding verb was performed. This type of structural influence of Amharic on the hagiobiography's Gəʿəz can be observed repeatedly in the text.

[14] ABCDFGIJ: *wä-məgbarä tərufat* (lit., and virtuous deeds); HK: *wä-məgbariha tərufatä* (and her virtuous deeds); E, CR: *wä-məgbaratiha wä-tərufatiha* (and her deeds and virtues).

[15] E, CR omit *qəddəst* (holy).

[16] Lit., *gädl* (spiritual struggle).

[17] ABCDEFGHIJK: *bä-30 ʿamät* (in the thirtieth year); CR: *bä-20 wä-9 ʿamät* (in the twenty-ninth year).

had passed away and found rest, in the Year of Mercy 7165 [i.e., 1672–73 CE],[1] in the eleventh *epact*[2] [and] the nineteenth *matqi*,[3] in the fifth year of the reign of our King Yohannes,[4] lover of God, in a year of Matthew the Evangelist.[5] This book is to be read out aloud on every seventeenth of the month of Hidaar [24 November, the anniversary of Walatta Petros's death].[6] May the blessing of her prayers[7] and the grace of her assistance be with __________[8] for eternity, amen.[9]

[1] According to the Täwaḥədo Church, time started when God created the world 5,500 years before the birth of Christ. Thus, the year 7165 minus 5,500 is the year 1665. However, the Ethiopian calendar is seven years behind the Western or Gregorian calendar, and the new year begins on 11 September. Therefore, the reference is to sometime between 11 September 1672 and 10 September 1673 CE.

[2] Lit., *abäqte*, from the Greek *épaktai hēmérai* (added days). An epact is the number of days into the lunar cycle on the first of the year. The year this text was written had an epact of eleven, meaning that there was an ecclesiastical new moon that fell on the eleventh of the month during this year. An epact is part of a complicated formula for calculating the dates on which certain Christian holidays should fall each year. For instance, Christ is said to have risen from the dead on Sunday, the seventeenth day of the Paschal moon, and so Christians use the Greek Metonic Lunar Cycle to identify a Sunday before that day every year. There are 235 lunar months for every nineteen solar years; thus, after a period of nineteen solar years, the new moons occur again on the same days of the solar year.

[3] Lit., *mäṭqəʿ*, the number of days left in the lunar month on the first of the year. That is, the abäqte and the mäṭqəʿ always add up to thirty. They match the date.

[4] *Yoḥannəs* (John) I (r. 1667–82); thus, the fifth year of his reign was 1672–73.

[5] Ricci silently corrected this to *l'evangelista Luca,* as the evangelist's name for this year is Luke not Matthew. Another Ethiopian way of representing a particular year is using a four-year cycle, with each year named after one of the authors of the Gospels: Matthew, Mark, Luke, and, for the leap year, John.

[6] Ḫədar (the month from 11 November to 10 December). That is, on the anniversary of her death, the priests would read the entire *Gädlä Wälättä Peṭros* out loud, spending the whole day to do it. Reading an entire saint's life out loud was believed to confer special blessings on the community.

[7] "Prayer," "blessing," and "heavens" often appear in the singular or plural in Gəʿəz, where English would have them vice versa. So we have converted them throughout to the number typical in English.

[8] Gəʿəz manuscripts typically invoke blessings by name for the owner or commissioner of the particular manuscript. That person then receives special blessings from being in the saint's text and having his or her name recited when the text is read aloud. In Abb. 88, the original name had been erased here and a secondary list of owners inserted again, almost identical to that on the first page: Minas, Finḥa (which Conti Rossini sensibly emended to Finḥas), Naʿod, Muzu, Ṣəge, Arägawi, Bäkaffa, Ṣ́ota Maryam, Wəbit, Säblä Maryam, Melkol. Other manuscripts inserted other names or phrases, as follows: A: *fəqura* _____ (her beloved [name illegible]); B: *fəqura Agnaṭəyos* (her beloved Ignatius [the abbot of Daga Monastery who commissioned the copying of the manuscript]); C: *ḫaṭəʾt wälätta Wälättä Ǝsraʾel* (her sinful daughter Walatta Israel); D: *nəguśənä Dawit* (our king David [r. 1716–21]); E: *gäbra Täwäldä Mädḫən* (her servant Tewolde Medhin); FJ: [*məsle*]*nä* ([with] us); G: [name illegible]; H: *gäbra Yaʿqob* (her servant Jacob); I: *fəqura Aśaʾənä Maryam wä-məslä kʷəllənä sämaʿəyan* (her beloved Asaina Maryam and with all of us who hear this); K: *gäbra Zärʾa Yaʿqob* (her servant Zera Yaqob).

[9] The CR print edition was checked against manuscripts ABCDEFJK only through this point in the manuscript. After, only three manuscripts, BDJ, were checked against CR. See "Introduction to the Translation of the Text" in this volume.

Chapter 3: Our Mother's Conception and Birth

Let us begin[1] with the help of God to write the story of the conception and birth of our holy mother of exalted memory, Walatta Petros, of a distinguished family and noble lineage, from the house of Dawaro and Fatagar.[2] Her father's name was Bahir Saggad,[3] her mother's Kristos Ebayaa.[4] Both of them were righteous and God-fearing people, as well as very rich in the possessions of this world. People would praise them for all their good deeds, their fasting, prayers, and mercy toward the poor. Her brothers were great lords whose names were Pawlos,[5] Za-Manfas Qidduus,[6] Lisaana Kristos,[7] Za-Dinghil,[8] and Yohannes.

As for her father Bahir Saggad, every year during the fast of Nahaasé,[9] he would go to the island of Réma[10] and [there] fast with a clean heart and a pure mind, out of his love for our Lady Mary. [For additional mortification,] he would stand in the lake during the night, dressed in a garment of iron, praying and supplicating for the salvation of his soul.[11] When the fasting period[12] was over and the feast [of the Assumption] arrived, he would prepare a banquet and [thereby] make the poor and the wretched happy. One day, when he lacked what he needed for the banquet, he

[1] BJ, CR: *nəwäṭṭən* (let us begin); D: *nəweṭṭən* (we begin).

[2] Däwaro and Fäṭägar were two historical Christian provinces located in today's south-central Ethiopia, south and southeast of today's Addis Ababa, but WP's family would have been driven out by Oromo pastoralists migrating north in the second half of the sixteenth century.

[3] *Baḥər Säggäd* (The [regions by the] sea submit[s] [to him]). Unusually, WP's father is not identified by his Christian name, as most others in the text are, but by his secular name. Secular names were more often used in everyday interactions; although everyone had a Christian name as well. Several possible explanations have been forwarded: as a prominent nobleman, Baḥər Säggäd was well known and therefore the author Gälawdewos uses the name by which he was famous; military men were rarely known by their Christian names; and WP's father died when she was so young that her community did not know his Christian name (which was not often used in public).

[4] *Krəstos ʿƎbäya* (In Christ lies her greatness).

[5] *P̣awlos* (Paul).

[6] *Zä-Mänfäs Qəddus* (He of the Holy Spirit).

[7] *Ləsanä Krəstos* (Tongue of Christ).

[8] *Zä-Dəngəl* (He of the Virgin [Mary]).

[9] The fast in honor of Our Lady Mary's Assumption takes place during the first fifteen days of the month of Näḥase (7–21 August). Afterward, there is the feast in honor of her ascent into heaven (or Assumption) on 16 Näḥase. Thus, Baḥər Säggäd either stayed on Rema Island for fifteen days or he went every day to Rema for fifteen days.

[10] *Rema* Island, home of one of Ethiopia's most important monasteries, is about six miles north of Qʷärasa, and is a frequent setting of this text.

[11] BDJ: *ənzä . . . yəṣelli wä-yastäbäqqʷəʿ bäʾəntä mädḫanitä näfsu* (praying and supplicating for the salvation of his soul); CR: *ənzä . . . yəṣelli bäʾəntä mädḫanitä näfs* (praying for the salvation of the soul). "Generally speaking, the People of Ethiopia are much inclin'd to Penance, wherein these Religious Men signaliz'd themselves, going into Water in cold Weather, and continuing in it several Hours" (Tellez 1710, 98).

[12] BDJ: *ṣom* (the fasting period); CR omits.

Plate 1. How our mother's father prayed while standing in Lake Tana (top panel), "how he found [gold] inside the fish's belly" (bottom left), and how he learned from a monk that he had seen a vision that his wife would give birth to an extraordinary daughter (bottom right). Passages between quotation marks are our translations of still readable Gəʿəz captions or caption parts, with square brackets indicating conjectures of ours. (MS A, f. 144v © Saxony State Library–Dresden State and University Library SLUB Mscr.Dresd.Eb.415.e,2).

became extremely sad, and while he prayed in the lake, as was his custom, he found a fish. When he tore open its belly, in it was gold weighing an ounce.[1] He much marveled [at this], rejoicing and praising our Lady Mary. With this gold, he achieved his desire[2] [to hold the banquet].

It was further told about him that while in church during the liturgy, he would see the mystery of Communion, with the host changing from bread to white lamb, and also would see it return to its previous state.

While he was living this kind of life, a righteous monk said to him, "I have seen[3] a great vision, with a bright sun dwelling in the womb of your wife Kristos Ebayaa."[4]

Bahir Saggad replied, "*Abba*,[5] please interpret the meaning of your vision to me." **6**

So, the monk interpreted [the vision] to him and said, "A beautiful daughter who will shine like the sun to the ends of the world will be born to you. She will be a guide for the blind of heart, and the kings of the earth and the bishops will bow to her. From the four corners of the world, many people will assemble around her and become one community—people pleasing God. Through her[6] your names [Bahir Saggad and Kristos Ebayaa] will be called out until the consummation of the world."

Bahir Saggad then also saw a vision like the monk. He told his wife what the righteous monk had imparted to him, and that he himself had seen [the same vision]. He said to her, "Come, let us hold a vigil and pray with great penitence for seven days so that God may reveal to us and make us certain that this thing is true."[7]

She replied, "Very well." Therefore, that is what they did. After completing a week, he said to her, "Let us do another week since nothing has been revealed to me."[8] Again she said to him, "Very well," and that is what they did. After they had completed the two weeks, they too saw what the righteous monk had seen. However, they kept this thing [secret] in their hearts until its time had come.

[1] Similar stories about finding gold in the belly of a fish appear in many cultures, perhaps earliest in Greek, Sanskrit, and Hebrew tales. However, the story probably owes most to a similar tale in the *Sənkəssar*, which relates for 12 Ḫədar (21 November) the story of Dorotheus, a poor man who wanted to make a feast for Saint Michael and similarly found gold in the belly of a fish (Budge 1928, 1:232).

[2] BDJ: *wä-fäṣṣämä botu fäqado* (lit., and through it he accomplished his desire); CR: *wä-fäṣṣämä zäntä fäqado* (and he accomplished this desire of his).

[3] BDJ: *rəʾiku* (I have seen); CR: *raʾayku* [*sic*], from Abb. 88 *rəʾyä* (he has seen).

[4] This is reminiscent of the renowned fourteenth-century Ethiopian text the *Kəbrä Nägäśt*, in which the Queen of Sheba, Makədda, sees a vision that "there was a star in my womb . . . and I saved . . . all the men of my country thereby" (Budge 1922, 154).

[5] *Abba*, meaning "father," is a form of address for monks, priests, and other clerical dignitaries. Among themselves, they usually call each other "brother." Likewise, "mother" is a form of address for nuns, but among themselves they usually call each other "sister."

[6] BDJ: *bati* (through her); CR: *baḥtu* (however; moreover).

[7] In the Bible, the walls of Jericho fell after seven days dedicated to prayer and marching around the city with the Ark of the Covenant. See also Leviticus 8:33 and Exodus 29:35.

[8] BDJ: *əsmä i-täkäśtä litä mənt-ni* (since nothing has been revealed to me); CR omits *litä* (to me).

Plate 2. How Walatta Petros's father and mother prayed after having learned about the vision (top), and how "her father saw a sun [in] his wife's belly" (bottom) (MS A, f. 145r © SLUB Mscr.Dresd.Eb.415.e,2).

After a few days, Kristos Ebayaa conceived by the will of God. When the time arrived for her to give birth, pain gripped her. Hearing this, Bahir Saggad withdrew to a chapel and prayed that she would give birth without pain and suffering. Continuously he sent messengers [to the house], one after another. At the proper time, Kristos Ebayaa gave birth, and a servant[1] who had been sent came carrying the good news and announced to Bahir Saggad that she had given birth.

He asked, "What is the newborn child, boy or girl?"

The servant responded, "It's a girl."

At that moment, Bahir Saggad was amazed and praised God because it was fulfilled for him what the righteous monk had told him and what he himself had seen. Therefore, he went happily and exultantly into the house of childbed, even though he was a great lord and it was not appropriate for him to enter into such a house.[2]

They said to him, "How can you enter the house of childbed before the time for entering has arrived?"

Bahir Saggad responded, "Let me enter, I who already knows! You don't yet know what secret is associated with that girl child." Thus he entered, sat down, and said to the midwife,[3] "Please show me the child! Give her to me to hold her and kiss 7
her."

The midwife said to him, "How can you hold and kiss a newborn who is all covered in blood?"

He responded, "Give her to me! Truly, there is no unclean blood or filth on this daughter of mine."

Therefore, the midwife wrapped her in a garment of fine linen and gave her to him. He received her and carried her in his arms for a while, looking her in the face and kissing her head. He marveled at the beauty of her appearance and said to her, "You are blessed, child that God has chosen and sanctified[4] to be his servant while still in your mother's womb!"[5] Having said this, Bahir Saggad left the room and went away.[6]

On account of [all] this, we consider blessed[7] Walatta Petros's father and mother who brought forth for us this blessed and holy mother through whom we have found salvation. She became our guide toward righteousness and hope, she revealed to us the way of renunciation and of monastic life and taught us the law of

[1] *Gäbr*, which we have translated as "servant" throughout; debates continue in Ethiopian studies, however, over the translation of this term, which some, with good evidence, translate as "slave."

[2] BDJ: *wəstä betä ḫaris* (lit., into the house of childbed); CR: *wəstä ḫaris* (lit., into the childbed). A man was not supposed to enter the room of childbirth. If he did so, he became impure and could not enter a church or other holy place for forty days. See Kaplan (2003b).

[3] BDJ: *wä-yəbela lä-mäwäldit* (and said to the midwife); CR: *wä-yəbela lä-wäladit* (and said to the mother).

[4] BDK: *ḥəṣ́an zä-ḫaräyäki əgziʾabḥer wä-qäddäsäki* (child that God has chosen and sanctified); CR omits *wä-qäddäsäki* (and sanctified [you]).

[5] Compare with Jeremiah 1:4.

[6] This account of practices around childbirth is one of the earliest in Gəʿəz literature.

[7] BJ: *nastäbäṣṣəʿ* (we consider blessed); CR, D: *nastäbṣəʿ* (let us consider blessed).

love and humility. If they had not brought her forth for us, our lives would have been destined for perdition. As the prophet Isaiah says, "If the Lord of Hosts had not left us a seed, we would have become like Sodom and would have resembled Gomorrah."[1] Behold, in her the sign of her parents' righteousness was visible, since the good tree produces good fruit, but the bad tree produces bad fruit. As our Lord says in the Gospel, "No good tree produces bad fruit,[2] and no bad tree produces good fruit. Every tree is known by its fruit."[3] Paul further says, "If the first fruit is holy, the [entire] dough[4] also will be holy, and if the root is holy, the branches also will be holy."[5]

Chapter 4: Our Mother's Baptism and Childhood

When the infant was eighty days old,[6] they baptized her in Christian baptism according to the order of the book[7] and named her Walatta Petros. And truly, she was a daughter of Peter,[8] since the work of the father is found in the one who is born from him.[9] As our Lord said to Peter, "Upon you I will build my church,"[10] and upon her, too, the Lord built a community and made them a house [of God]. As Paul says, "You [all] are the house of the Lord."[11] Just as the Lord gave Peter the keys to the Kingdom of Heaven, so he likewise gave to Walatta Petros that those who follow her will enter into the Kingdom of Heaven. And as the Lord three times said to
8 Peter, "Tend my sheep,"[12] so to her likewise he conferred the tending of his sheep in the pasture of meritorious spiritual struggle.

She truly was worthy of this name [of Walatta Petros] since the son of a king becomes a king and the son of a priest becomes a priest; and just as Peter became the head of the apostles, she likewise became the head of all [religious] teachers.

[1] Isaiah 1:9, Romans 9:29. God destroyed these cities in Canaan with fire and brimstone because its people were wicked sinners, according to Genesis 13:13.

[2] BDJ: *albo ʿəṣ śännay zä-yəfärri fəre əkuyä* (no good tree produces bad fruit); CR omits.

[3] Matthew 7:18; Luke 6:44.

[4] BDJ: *wä-bəḥuʾ-ni* (the dough also). CR: *wä-bəṣəʿtä* (and beatified), from Abb. 88 *wä-bəṣuʿanä* (and the beatified people).

[5] Romans 11:16.

[6] Girls were baptized on the eightieth day, boys on the fortieth (Kaplan 2003b).

[7] The book could be the Bible or perhaps another book that articulates the rituals of baptism.

[8] Saint Peter was one of Christ's Twelve Apostles in the New Testament, the one upon whom Christ said he would found his church. Throughout the *WP gädl*, the author compares WP to her namesake, especially in their founding of communities. Often the author does so without naming Saint Peter, but by telling stories about WP that the well-versed biblical reader will recognize as parallel to Peter's life.

[9] Conti Rossini notes that two lines here are missing in Abb. 88. BDJ, however, have no gap here, nor any sign of erasure and correction.

[10] BDJ: *betä krəstiyanəyä* (my church); CR: *betä krəstiyan* (the church). Matthew 16:18.

[11] 1 Corinthians 3:9.

[12] John 21:15–17.

Just as Peter could kill and resurrect through his authority, she likewise could kill and resurrect.[1] She became a god by grace, as scripture says,[2] "You are gods, all of you are children of the Most High."[3] O glory, glory of such dimensions! O sublimity, sublimity of such greatness! While she was a human being like us, to her it was given to be a god.[4]

But let us return to our story. The young girl was pleasant to look at and had a beautiful figure. The look in her eyes was like a shining star; her teeth were white like milk. As Solomon says in the Song of Songs, "You are wholly beautiful; there is no flaw in you. There is nothing [ugly] upon you."[5] But the outer beauty of her appearance was surpassed by the inner beauty of her mind. Listen, my loved ones: What should make us boastful of the beauty of our appearance, which changes and decays? Is a human being justified [before God] by his beautiful appearance, or damned by his ugly aspect?

About this the Orit says,[6] Rachel had a beautiful appearance and beautiful eyes, and Jacob loved her very much.[7] For seven years he served her father for the sake of her. Yet her father did not give her to him, but stealthily gave him[8] Leah; and Leah, instead, had bleary eyes and Jacob did not love her. As soon as he saw her, he was very[9] distressed. However, Laban, [the girls' father,] said to him, "Do not be in pain. This doesn't happen in our country; people do not first give the younger one while an older [unmarried] one is there. Complete another seven years [of service], and I will give her to you, too." So, Jacob again served Laban for seven years, and Laban then gave Rachel to him, too.[10]

God, by contrast,[11] favored Leah—who was despised because she was ugly in appearance and had bleary eyes—by opening her womb, and so she gave birth to Judah from whose seed Christ was born. As Jacob said, "Kingship will not vanish

[1] Acts 5:1–10; Acts 9:40.

[2] BDJ: *bä-kämä yəbe mäṣḥaf* (as scripture says); CR: *bä-kämä yəbe bä-mäṣḥaf* (as it says in scripture).

[3] Psalm 81[82]:6; John 10:34.

[4] CR adds *bä-ṣagga* (by grace). In calling WP a "god" (*amlak*), the author is relying on biblical precedent. As he notes, in the Old Testament, in Psalm 81[82]:6, the Lord says, "You are gods," and in the New Testament, in John 10:34, Jesus says, "I have said you are gods." Also, in Isaiah 41:23, the Lord says, "That we may know that you are gods"; in Exodus 7:1 and Exodus 4:16, the Lord tells Moses that "I have made you like God to Pharaoh." In the New Testament, in 2 Peter 1:4, Paul says that we "become sharers of the divine nature." Also, the oft-called Father of Orthodoxy, Saint Athanasius, says in *De Incarnatione*, "For the Son of God became man so that we might become God."

[5] Song of Songs 4:7.

[6] See Genesis 29:15–35 for the entire episode that follows.

[7] BDJ: *ṭəqqä* (very much); CR omits.

[8] BDJ: *wähabo* (gave him); CR omits.

[9] BDJ: *ṭəqqä* (very); CR omits.

[10] CR omits the entire sentence (*wä-täqänyä lotu kaʿəbä 7 ʿamätä wä-wähabo kiyaha-ni*; lit., thereupon he again served him for seven years, and he then gave her to him, too).

[11] BDF: *əgziʾabḥer-əssä* (God, by contrast); CR: *əgziʾabḥer-ni* (God, moreover).

from Judah, nor princely power from his member."[1] As for Rachel, who had beautiful eyes and whom Jacob loved, God did not love her and did not give her a child, so ultimately she became jealous of her sister. So she said to Jacob, "Give me a child,
9 or else I will die!"[2] With great difficulty Rachel then gave birth to Joseph and to Benjamin, but from their seed Christ was not born.[3] God for his part does not look at outer beauty, but at inner beauty.[4]

Furthermore, the Orit says: Esau was beautiful in his appearance and Isaac loved him, while Jacob was ugly in his appearance and God loved him.[5] He says, "Jacob I loved, but Esau I hated."[6] Also, Christ was not born from the seed of Esau, but from that of Jacob. David, too, says, "He took me from my father's sheep and anointed me with holy oil. My brothers were handsome and older but God was not pleased with them."[7] Because of this, we should not boast about the beauty of our looks, nor need we be ashamed of the ugliness of [our] appearance, since that which is perishable should clothe itself with that which is imperishable.[8]

Listen further and we will tell you [more of] the story of Bahir Saggad, the father of our holy mother Walatta Petros. He loved her more than all his grown male children, with his whole heart and his entire mind, and he was proud of her. While she was still a child and of a tender age so that she did not yet know her father's and mother's name, he used to put her on a chair and on a bed.[9] He would take his sword and pace in front of her, lifting up his feet and marching for her, just like soldiers march in front of the king. He would sing her name and say to her, "I will die for you, I, your father, blessed child whom God has chosen, blessed and made holy." He would do this every day, not [only] after having had his fill and being

[1] Genesis 49:10.

[2] Genesis 30:1.

[3] See Genesis 30:22–24 and 35:16–18; Matthew 1:17.

[4] 1 Samuel 16:7.

[5] While Genesis 25:28 indeed says that Isaac preferred Esau, the Bible attributes this not to Esau's good looks but to the animals he hunted and cooked for his father. Moreover, the verse does not contrast the preferences of Isaac and God, but of Isaac and his wife Rebecca: it is of her that it says that she preferred Jacob, who stayed by her side. However, the Gəʿəz Bible, like the Vulgate, does mention that Jacob was a "plain" man and that he had to put on an animal skin to fool his father into thinking he had Esau's more masculine frame (Mersha 2011, 532). The two men undoubtedly looked quite different, with Esau living his life outdoors hunting and Jacob his life indoors with his mother. The author thus interprets the passage here, suggesting that God was not fooled by Esau's beautiful masculinity.

[6] Malachi 1:2–3 and Romans 9:13.

[7] Psalm 151:4–5 (this psalm does not appear in the Protestant Bible). But see also 1 Samuel 16:6–13, where it is said that David too was handsome.

[8] BDJ: *halläwo lä-zəntu zä-yəmassən yəlbäs zä-i-yəmassən* (that which is perishable should clothe itself with that which is imperishable); CR omits *yəlbäs zä-i-yəmassən* (clothe itself with that which is imperishable).

[9] In that era, it was considered inappropriate for a child to sit on rare and therefore precious pieces of furniture. Also, the word "bed" in Gəʿəz (*ʿarat*) and Amharic (*alga*) is used metaphorically to mean "throne," so this passage may connote elevating on a pedestal. Also, as royal audiences demonstrate, those who sit are higher in rank than those who stand.

drunk but while he was hungry and thirsty.[1] Truly, he was drunk with love for her and knew the secret of what would happen through her.

[Nevertheless,] he soon died and his joy did not have fulfillment. He desired but did not see, he looked but did not find. As our Lord says in the Gospel,[2] "Truly, many prophets and righteous ones wanted to see what you see but did not see it."[3]

Chapter 5: Our Mother's Marriage and Children

Therefore, her mother and brothers then raised our holy mother Walatta Petros, in wisdom and the fear of God, and taught her the books of the Church. When she grew up and reached the legal age for marriage,[4] they gave her to one of the great lords of the land whose name was Malkiya Kristos[5]—he was the chief adviser of King Susinyos, who sat on the throne having adopted the faith of the Europeans[6]— so that she would become his wife, according to the ritual of matrimony for the **10**
daughters of great lords, in order to procreate.[7] For scripture says, "Be many and multiply and fill the earth."[8] When Malkiya Kristos brought her into his house, he loved her very much; he knew her, and she conceived.

She then, like Martha, prayed to God, using these words, "If this unborn child which is inside my womb shall be born and please you,[9] may it live; but if not, may

[1] That is, it is normal for people to play when they are satiated and have extra energy; it is rare for someone to do so even when they are enervated by lack of sustenance.

[2] D: *bä-kämä yəbe əgziʾənä bä-wängel* (as our Lord says in the Gospel); CR: *bä-kämä yəbe mäṣḥaf* (as scripture says); BJ: *bä-kämä yəbe* (as he [*or*: it] says).

[3] Luke 10:24.

[4] Girls were often legally married at the age of seven, but the marriage would not be consummated until she went to live as a wife with her husband. In the past, girls reached puberty at later ages, so WP may have been around sixteen when she joined her husband. Currently, the average age at menarche in Ethiopia is 15.8 years (Zegeye, Megabiaw, and Mulu 2009).

[5] *Mälkəʾa Krəstos* (Image of Christ).

[6] *Haymanotä Afrənǧ* (faith of the Europeans). Susənyos ruled Ethiopia from 1606 to 1632 and, under the influence of Portuguese Jesuit missionaries, converted from Orthodoxy to Catholicism in 1622. This triggered major internal upheavals—one of the main subjects of this hagiobiography—until 1632, when he rescinded his conversion.

[7] At least two *Sənkəssar* entries on WP (Ethio-SPaRe MKL-019 and MR-003; see table 2) state that she was married to another man before Mälkəʾa Krəstos, an unnamed man who was killed by King Yaʿqob (r. 1597–1603, 1604–6), the king who preceeded Susənyos (a matter discussed in "The Biography of Walatta Petros" in this volume). As the *Sənkəssar* entry was likely written within a year of her death, to be read upon her annual commemoration, and the author Gälawdewos wrote the *WP gädl* several decades later, it would seem Gälawdewos deliberately omits this information. Since WP would have been only nine in 1606, this earlier marriage would not have been consummated and therefore did not result in children; thus, Gälawdewos might not have considered it important enough to mention.

[8] Genesis 1:28.

[9] BDJ: *yətwälläd wä-yaśämməräkä* (shall be born and please you); CR: *zä-yətwälläd əm-yaśämməräkä* (which shall be born, if then it pleases you).

it quickly die."[1] When her pregnancy reached term she gave birth. She had the boy child baptized, but then he immediately died, God having listened to her prayer. Saying the same prayer, she gave birth to three children,[2] and all of them died by the will of God. Nonetheless, Malkiya Kristos, the husband[3] of our holy mother Walatta Petros, was very generous and [still] loved her very much.[4] Yet she[5] did not want to stay with him because she [now] bore in mind the transience of the world.

As the Apostle Peter says, "All flesh is like grass, and all the glory of man is like the flower of the grass."[6] And John further says, "Do not love the world and that which is in the world because everything in the world is the desire of the eye and the desire of the flesh. Life's distress does not come from the Father but from the world. In addition, the world will perish, and its desires will perish."[7] Moreover Paul says, "It is right, O our brothers, that it be like this, because all the things of this world are soon to perish: Those people who have married shall be as if they did not marry, those who live comfortably as if they did not live comfortably, those who cry as if they did not cry, those who rejoice as if they did not rejoice, those who purchase as if they did not purchase, those who have possessions as if they did not have them, those who eat as if they did not eat, and those who drink as if they did not drink, since all the pleasures of this world will pass and perish."[8] Furthermore, our Lord says[9] in the Gospel, "What would it benefit man if he gained the entire world but lost his soul? What can man give as ransom for his soul?"[10]

[1] This would appear to be WP's first prayer for someone's death. This Martha is not that of the New Testament, who has nothing to do with children, but probably a Martha of the *Sənkəssar* or *Täʾamərä Maryam*. There are two childless Marthas in the *Sənkəssar* who pray for children: one is the mother of Saint Vincent, celebrated on 5 Taḫśaś (14 December), the other is the grandmother of *Abba* Simon of the monastery of Antioch, celebrated on 29 Gənbot (6 June). However, this specific prayer is not mentioned in the *Sənkəssar*. A *Täʾamərä Maryam* at Mekane Yesus Seminary, Addis Ababa, includes a miracle about how the Virgin Mary gave a child to a certain woman named Martha from a royal family in the East and how the Virgin Mary raised that child from the dead when the wife of the emperor Diocletian threw the child to the floor out of jealousy (EMIP 601, Mekane Yesus Seminary 1, 190rv).

[2] Lit., *3 wəludä*, which could also mean three sons.

[3] BDJ: *bəʾəsiha-ssä Mälkəʾa Krəstos* (lit., her husband nonetheless, Mälkəʾa Krəstos); CR omits *-ssä* (nonetheless).

[4] BDJ: *baʿəl wəʾətu ṭəqqä wä-yafäqqəra fädfadä* (was very generous [lit., rich] and loved her very much); CR: *yafäqqəra fädfadä wä-baʿəl wəʾətu ṭəqqä* (loved her very much, and was very rich).

[5] BDJ: *wä-yəʾəti-ssä* (yet she); CR: *wä-yəʾəti* (she).

[6] Lit., *fəre śaʿr* (fruit of the grass). 1 Peter 1:24. See also Isaiah 40:6–8.

[7] 1 John 2:15–17.

[8] 1 Corinthians 7:29–31.

[9] BDJ: *yəbe* (says); CR omits.

[10] BDJ: *məntä əm-wähabä säbʾ bezaha lä-näfsu* (What can man give as ransom for his soul); CR: *məntä əmmä i-wähabä säbʾ bezaha lä-näfsu* (What if man did not give the ransom for his soul). Matthew 16:26.

This is why our holy mother Walatta Petros spent all her days in fasting and
prayer, while in the evenings she entered into the church and kept vigil all night
without interruption, [in turns] standing upright and prostrating herself as well as **11**
praying in all manners. Thus she would go into ecstasy[1] and disappear from [the
view of] the women who had followed her.[2] At dawn, she would reappear to them
and return home.

Every Sunday Walatta Petros would sponsor a meal for the clergy of the church. With her was a woman who cooked the *wot* stews[3] and the other various dishes.[4] That woman used to grumble; she did not like to cook for the clergy. When our holy mother Walatta Petros understood what that woman harbored in her mind, she one evening took the woman with her to the church and let her see the vigil and exertions of the clergy.[5]

As a result, the woman repented and said, "I have sinned! Forgive me for causing you distress. Before this, I didn't know what the priests did, but now I have seen it and marveled [at them]. From now on I will certainly do all you desire and will not disobey your orders."

Those who know [Walatta Petros's story] further relate: When our holy mother Walatta Petros celebrated a holiday with a banquet, she provided everything the body needs, all kinds of food and drink,[6] as well as meats. She then assembled the poor and wretched, all the people of the town[7] as well as the priests of the church, and seated them at the table, each one at the seat that was due to them. Then they would eat and drink until they had had enough and were happy. She on the other hand would not taste anything from all this, but would eat cooked bitter *ranch* leaves[8]

[1] Lit., *tətmäśśäṭ* (she would be seized). Alternatively, the author might mean that WP was seized by an external heavenly force.

[2] Many Täwaḥədo Church monasteries have tales of particularly holy monks and nuns who become invisible.

[3] *Wäṭ* is the generic name for the variety of stews that are served with a staple at most meals. On fasting days, it will be a vegetable stew, often with greens. On nonfasting days, if the family is not poor, it may be a meat stew such as *doro wäṭ* (chicken stew), often spiced with red peppers.

[4] BDJ: *zä-tətgebbär . . . gəbrä mäbaləʿt zä-zä-ziʾahu* (who cooked . . . the other various dishes); CR: *zä-tətgebbär . . . gəbrä mälʾəkt zä-zä-ziʾahu* (who performed . . . various other services).

[5] A working servant would not see the clergy performing their ritual duties, partly because she would not have much time to go to church and partly because much of this is done in the church during the night, when no congregation is there.

[6] BDJ: *kʷəllo mäfqədatä śəga mäbaləʿtä wä-səteyatä zä-zä-ziʾahu* (everything the body [lit., flesh] needs, all kinds of food and drink); CR: *kʷəllo mäbaləʿtä mäfqədatä śəga wä-səteyatä zä-zä-ziʾahu* (all foods, what the body [lit., flesh] needs, and all kinds of drinks).

[7] *Hagär*, a capacious term that can mean village, town, district, or region, and that we have most often translated as "town." In the seventeenth century, towns were modest settlements of around a couple hundred people or less. See Pankhurst (1982).

[8] *Ränč* or *renč*, an Amharic loanword, is an indigenous plant of Ethiopia with edible

and drink [only] water,[1] while it appeared to the others that she ate and drank like them. Nobody from among the people [at the banquet] knew [this] about her except for the maidservant who served her. For a long time she maintained this way of life, and desired not at all the pleasures of this ephemeral world.

She lived a regular married life with her husband Malkiya Kristos, but waited and looked for the day on which it would please God for her to leave, escaping and fleeing from her husband, abandoning the world and becoming a nun. She prayed continuously [for this] and implored God, saying, "Show me your way, Lord, and teach me your path. Lead me with your righteousness, and, O Lord, teach me, your servant,[2] your path,[3] the right path."[4] Our holy mother Walatta Petros kept praying
12 like this.[5]

Chapter 6: Our Mother Tries to Take Up the Holy Life

When the time came that it pleased God for her to leave this world[ly life], her husband Malkiya Kristos went on a military campaign with the king.[6] As for her, she stayed in the region of Simaada,[7] on the third story of the [couple's] castle[8] [where] no one could see her. At that time, by the will of God, two monks came to our holy mother Walatta Petros, *Abba* Yamaana Kristos[9] of Réma Monastery and *Abba* Tazkaara Dinghil[10] of [Lake] Tana. They had been sent by *Abba* Fatla Sillasé[11] to bring her stealthily[12] out [of her husband's home] and take her with them to Zagé.[13] When she saw them, she was very happy. In charity, she then gave all her

---

leaves: *Caylusea abyssinica*. Monks and nuns especially devoted to asceticism would eat only leaves; the Ethiopian saint Täklä Haymanot ate bitter leaves during Lent.

1 Alcoholic drinks would have been served at a banquet.

2 CR adds *Wälättä Ṗeṭros*.

3 BDJ: *fənotäkä* (your path); CR omits.

4 Partly based on Psalm 26[27]:11.

5 BDJ: *näbärät ənzä təṣelli kämä-zə* (kept praying like this); CR: *näbärät ənzä təbəl kämä-zə* (kept speaking like this).

6 According to Susənyos's royal chronicle, Mälkəʾa Krəstos often went on military campaign with Susənyos (Täklä Śəllase [Ṭinno] 1900, chapter 53).

7 *Səmada* is a region about seventy miles southeast of Lake Ṭana.

8 Lit., *maḫfäd* (tower *or* fortress).

9 *Yämanä Krəstos* (Right Hand of Christ) is a monk from Rema who also appears in one of the miracles.

10 *Täzkarä Dəngəl* (Commemoration of the Virgin).

11 *Fätlä Śəllase* (Cord of the Trinity) is a famous historical figure and high-ranking monk associated with the royal court. In Susənyos's royal chronicle, Fätlä Śəllase participates near southeastern Lake Ṭana in a famous debate before Emperor Susənyos about the nature of Christ. In this hagiobiography, Fätlä Śəllase is a special defender of WP, protecting her from her husband and church leaders.

12 BDJ: *ṣəmmitä* (stealthily); CR omits.

13 *Zäge* is a small peninsula protruding into Lake Ṭana at its narrow southernmost end, not far from today's regional metropolis Baḥər Dar.

possessions to the poor and the wretched. In addition, she took all her jewelry, eighty ounces weight of gold, in order to distribute it to the needy and to churches on their way. They then came to an agreement[1] about the time when they would leave. When it became evening and after people had fallen asleep, she summoned her three maidservants, Maryamaweet,[2] Eskindiraweet,[3] and Iyopraxia[4] so that they would follow her.

Then our holy mother Walatta Petros left [the castle], and the monks received her, took her with them, and made her mount a mule. They spent the entire night walking and thus in [only] one day reached [the church of] the Abode of Our Lady Mary[5] at Racha;[6] there they rested. Then she began to distribute the gold all along the way. What is truly astonishing and wondrous, though, is that within [just] one day she marched such a long way, even though she was weak and her body tender. If it had not been for the power of God that strengthened her, who would have been able to march like that? Not even a strong young man could have marched like that, let alone a woman like her. For she lacked strength and her feet were delicate because she had never trod the earth before in her entire life.[7] If she got up from her resting couch,[8] she would stand upon a carpet that had been spread out, and if [so much as] fallen dry breadcrumbs found her there, they hurt her feet so that they would bleed. However, the power of God strengthened her and she did not feel any weakness because she was inebriated with love for Him. [She was drawn to her destination] like someone invited to a wedding or like a mighty warrior[9] to a prize.[10]
And indeed our holy mother Walatta Petros marched to a heavenly wedding and to **13**
the groom Jesus Christ; indeed, she marched toward a prize, fighting against the devil[11] and taking from him many souls that he had made his prey.

[1] BDJ: *täsänaʾawu wä-täʿadämu* (lit., they came to and reached an agreement); CR: *täsänaʾawu wä-tämakäru* (they came to an agreement and deliberated).

[2] *Maryamawit* (She of [Saint] Mary).

[3] *Ǝskəndərawit* (She of Alexander). Alexander the Great was considered a saint in Eastern Christianity.

[4] *Iyopäraqsəya* (Eupraxia [good conduct]). This is an elegant Greek name rather than a typical Ḥabäša name, and thus, counterintuitively, the sign of a servant or slave. Just as in ancient Greece, in Ethiopia a recently enslaved person from elsewhere was renamed with a type of name that distinguished him or her from a citizen. In Ethiopia, foreign slaves were often given classical names, just as in the United States, where slaves were often given classical names like "Caesar," "Cato," or "Jupiter."

[5] Lit., *Maḫdärä Ǝgzəʾtənä Maryam* (Abode of Our Lady Mary).

[6] *Räča* is a town about fifteen miles southeast of Lake Ṭana, on the way from Səmada to Zäge. The distance they traveled in one night is about fifty miles. Since mules generally travel between fifteen and twenty miles a day, this is quite far.

[7] BDJ: *bä-kʷəllu mäwaʿəliha* (lit., in all her days); CR omits *kʷəllu* (all).

[8] Lit., *ʿarat* (bed *or* throne).

[9] CR adds *zä-yəräwwəṣ* (who runs).

[10] Lit., *məhərka* (loot).

[11] *Diyabolos.* This is rare; the *WP gädl* usually has *säyṭan* (Satan).

Again they set off from Racha and came to Chegwaré Zigba [town],[1] and then, moving on from there, to Wonchet [town].[2] [There] they hid in the house of an old nun named[3] Amata Petros;[4] she remained there for a few days. Then our holy mother Walatta Petros set off from Wonchet, went to Robeet[5] [town], and [eventually] reached Emabra[6] [town] opposite Zagé [on Lake Tana]. There, at the lakeshore, was a man named Kifla Maryam[7] who owned a *tankwa* papyrus boat[8] and was a good person. Thus, Walatta Petros became his guest: he received her, took her into his house, and gave her shelter.[9] The next day he came with the tankwa and took her to the monastic settlement of Zagé. When she arrived there, she was happy and gave thanks to the Lord. She greeted the saints[10] who lived in that monastic settlement, monks and nuns, and implored them to kindly remember her in their prayers.

Then she remained there, saying, "This is my resting-place[11] forever. Here I will live because[12] I have chosen it." She therefore shaved her head's hair and put on a nun's cap.[13]

[1] *Čäggʷarre Zəgba* (Caterpillar Cedar) is a town in the Dära region along southeastern Lake Ṭana, presumably south of Wänčäṭ.

[2] *Wänčät* is about fifteen miles up from Baḥər Dar on southeastern Lake Ṭana, about five miles southeast of Qʷäraṣa. The distance from Räča up to Wänčäṭ is about thirty miles.

[3] BDJ: *əntä təssämmäy* (lit., who was called [3rd-ps. fem. sg.]); CR: *əntä təssämmäyi* (you [2nd-ps. fem. sg.] who are called).

[4] *Amätä Ṗeṭros* (Maidservant of [Saint] Peter).

[5] *Robit* is a town on the southeastern side of Lake Ṭana, about ten miles south of Qʷäraṣa. The distance from Wänčät down to Robit is about nine miles.

[6] *Əmäbra* is probably directly east of Robit about two miles, on the shore of Lake Ṭana, directly opposite Zäge.

[7] *Kəflä Maryam* (Dedicated to [Saint] Mary).

[8] *Tankʷa*, a long, narrow, shallow boat (canoe) made of bundles of locally grown papyrus, still common on Lake Ṭana (plate 3). Owners propelled them mostly by pole not paddle, so they tended to stay close to shore where it was shallow. It averaged about one mile an hour.

[9] BDJ: *wä-aḫdära* (and gave her shelter); CR: *wä-ḫadärät* (and she found shelter).

[10] In the early Christian church, all Christians were referred to as saints, a usage continued here.

[11] BDJ: *məʿrafəyä* (my resting place); CR omits *-yä* (my).

[12] BDJ: *zəyyä aḫaddər əsmä* (here I will live because); CR: *zəyyä əsmä* (here indeed [*əsmä* = because *or* indeed]).

[13] *Qobʿ*. When an individual decides to become a nun or monk, he or she marks this by shaving the head (being tonsured) and putting on the qobʿ as a signal of intention. The abbot who gives the qobʿ to the individual has a special role in his or her spiritual life, although given the upheaval in the church at the time, and the lack of Orthodox priests, WP might have done it alone. There is then usually a three-year novitiate, although this varies (Chaillot 2002, 154). Two stages characterize the process of becoming a monk or nun. In the *rädʾ* (or first) level, they receive the qobʿ and are trying out the life. They are free to travel, for instance. In the *ardəʾt* (or second) level, they receive the mantle, sash, and belt, and are full members.

Plate 3. How two monks and a boatman took our mother and her servants on Lake Tana to the Zagé monastery (MS A, f. 145v © SLUB Mscr.Dresd.Eb.415.e,2).

Plate 4. How our mother was received and blessed by a monk (top) and "how her [head's] hair was shaved so as to prepare her to become a nun" (bottom) (MS A, f. 146r © SLUB Mscr.Dresd.Eb.415.e,2).

Chapter 7: Our Mother's Husband Hunts Her Down

When her husband, Malkiya Kristos, while he was at the camp with the king, learned that our holy mother Walatta Petros had fled and disappeared, he told the king and asked leave so that he could go[1] tracking her and searching for her. The king gave him permission and dispatched him. Malkiya Kristos set out immediately, in great anger and roaring like a lion.[2]

He called up his regiment,[3] named Siltaan Marid,[4] which he had set up in the region of Wuddo,[5] along with their leader, an *azmach*.[6] He took them with him and crisscrossed the entire region, asking around about where Walatta Petros had gone; and people told him that she had entered Zagé [Monastery].[7] Straightaway, he surrounded the town of Robeet and ordered his regiment Siltaan Marid to destroy it, plunder the inhabitants' possessions, eat up their provisions without restraint, and have no mercy. When they found that man [Kifla Maryam], the owner of the tankwa, they took him prisoner, plundered his goods, and seized his livestock. They acted according to Malkiya Kristos's orders.

The people of the town, men and women, broke out in cries of wailing, and there 14
was great upheaval.

Malkiya Kristos furthermore told the soldiers' leader, "Build a lookout in a treetop at the lakeshore, climb up it, observe the tankwas[8] that come and go, in each direction, and if you discover Walatta Petros, arrest her." That man did as[9] his lord had ordered him, climbing up to the lookout and keeping watch day and night. Whenever he saw a tankwa coming, he went down to look at it, and if she was not in it,[10] he let it go.

[1] Lit., BDJ: *wä-täsänäʾalä əmənnehu kämä yəḥur* (and asked leave from him so he could go); CR: *wä-täsänäʾalä əm-kämä yəḥur* (and asked leave as soon as to go [*sic*]).

[2] It is still common for families to try to prevent women from leaving to become nuns (Wright 2001, 57).

[3] BDJ: *ḥarrahu* (his regiment); CR: *ḥarra* (the regiment).

[4] *Śəlṭan Märʿəd* (It makes the [Muslim] sultan shiver). The exploits of this famous regiment are documented in Susənyos's royal chronicle.

[5] *Wəddo* is a region directly east of Lake Ṭana.

[6] BDJ: *azmač*; CR: *azmači*. An *azmač* is a military campaign leader.

[7] BDJ: *wä-nägärəwwo kämä boʾat Zäge* (and people told him that she had entered Zäge); CR: *wä-nägärəwwo ḫabä bäʾatä Zäge* (and people told him: to a monastic cell at Zäge).

[8] BDJ: *näṣṣər tankʷa* (observe the tankwas); CR: *näṣṣər tankʷaha* (observe her tankwa).

[9] BDJ: *bä-kämä* (as); CR: *wä-kämä* (and like).

[10] Our translation here assumes a feminine subject, *ḫaṭʾat* (lit., she was missing), whereas BDJ and CR all have masc. *ḫaṭʾa* (he was missing).

On his part, Malkiya Kristos had gone to Woynayat [town][1] to *Woyzaro*[2] Walatta Giyorgis,[3] daughter of the [late] King Sartsa Dinghil,[4] and to *Abba* Fatla Sillasé.

They rebuked him, saying to him, "Why did you lay waste to the town [of Robeet] without reason and bring ruin to people who did nothing wrong or unjust? Beware of God's wrath coming down[5] upon you!"

Immediately, he fell at their feet and replied, "I entrust myself to you, pass judgment on me and bring about peace between me and my wife. If I have done anything wrong [against her] in the past, she shall have her compensation.[6] From now on, though, I will not commit any wrongdoing again. [Even] if she tells me, 'Quit being a soldier of the king!,' I will quit it for her sake, as she has chosen." While he spoke these things, he cried and spilled tears.

After they had heard his words, they said to him, "These words of yours are not sincere. Rather, they will change tomorrow." So, he swore before them a strict oath.

Following this, *Abba*[7] Fatla Sillasé went to our holy mother Walatta Petros and told her about the devastation of the town [of Robeet] that had come about because of her, and about all that Malkiya Kristos had spoken, and that he had sworn a strict oath.

After our holy mother Walatta Petros had heard [this], she said, "No! No![8] I will not leave this monastic settlement,[9] and neither will I reconcile with him."

Abba Fatla Sillasé rebuked her, telling her, "If it is you who leave him, and if he marries another woman, his transgression is your fault.[10] As for me, I advise you that reconciling with him is better for you. If he has acted wrongfully against you

[1] *Wäynayät*, somewhere near Lake Ṭana.

[2] *Wäyzäro* is a title for women of royal blood, often translated as "Princess" or "Lady." Following the typical commonalization of aristocratic titles of address, *wäyzäro* means "Mrs." in contemporary Ethiopia.

[3] *Wälättä Giyorgis* (Daughter of [Saint] George). She was the daughter of King Śärṣä Dəngəl (r. 1563–97) and Queen Amätä Krəstos. She was also the wife of a powerful man, *Ras* Atənatewos, and the mother of Wälättä Ṗawlos, who later became a nun with WP.

[4] *Śärṣä Dəngəl* (Scion of the Virgin [Mary]).

[5] BDJ: *ʿuq . . . kämä i-yətmäʿaʿ əgziʾabḥer* (lit., watch out . . . that God does not become enraged); CR without the negation: *ʿuq . . . kämä yətmäʿaʿ əgziʾabḥer* (watch out . . . that God does become enraged [*sic*]).

[6] In traditional customary law, compensation can be paid for an injury or an offense. It is unclear what offense Mälkəʾa Krəstos is offering to pay for, whether those named in the text, such as his killing the bishop, or perhaps something not named in the text, such as an affair. Although he and WP did not have any living children, it seems unlikely that he took up with or married another woman for this reason. Historical records show that he did have three sons, two of whom were governors in the 1620s, which suggests that they were born long before his marriage to WP and were of an age with her. He is not recorded as having married anyone else.

[7] BDJ: *abba*; CR omits.

[8] BDJ: *ənbəyä ənbəyä* (no, no); CR with single, and less emphatic, *ənbəyä*.

[9] Lit., *gädam* (wilderness *or* monastic settlement). Three types of holy institutions exist in the Täwaḥədo Church: *gädam, däbr,* and *maḥbär.* See "The Text's Religious Context" in this volume.

[10] Married women did not usually become nuns until late in life for this reason.

in the past, take your compensation. [Concerning the future], I have made him swear that he will not wrong you again. Furthermore, since[1] the people of the town [of Robeet] wept because of the devastation they suffered, God is displeased with you. He does not love your repudiation of the world and will not accept your prayers."

Our holy mother Walatta Petros responded[2] with these words, "I know Malkiya
Kristos's character, that it is not founded on righteousness. However, I will obey 15
your word, my father and teacher. It shall be as you said so that the people of the town [of Robeet] will not complain about me. You have to swear to me, though, that you will not make me see the face of his mother."[3]

He replied, "Very well," and they agreed on this. *Abba* Fatla Sillasé then left first, in order to send her a mule, while our holy mother Walatta Petros remained there for the night.

Do you see, my loved ones, the noble virtue of our holy mother Walatta Petros, in that she returned herself to Malkiya Kristos, saying, "I prefer that I should perish rather than all the people perish on account of me"? This is reminiscent of what our Lord said to the guards[4] who came to arrest him. As the Gospel says, "The Lord Jesus said to them, 'Who are you looking for?' and they replied, 'Jesus of Nazareth.' He responded, 'I am he. If you want me, let these [disciples] go.' "[5] Our holy mother Walatta Petros did likewise and said, "God's will[6] be done! He can save me; to him nothing is impossible. He who saved Sarah from the hands of Pharaoh, the king of Egypt, and from the hands of Abimelech, king of Gerara, he will also save me.[7] He who saved Susanna from the hands of the old men, he will also save me.[8] He who

[1] Lit., *läʾəmmä* (if).

[2] CR adds *lä-abba Fätlä Śəllase* (to *Abba* Fätlä Śəllase).

[3] BDJ: *lä-əmməyä* (of my mother); CR: *lä-əmmu* (of his mother). Although most WP manuscripts state that she did not wish to see the face of her own mother, other aspects of the text suggest that in fact it is *his* mother's face that she does not wish to see. For instance, her friends revile Mälkəʾa Krəstos's mother later on the same page of the text. His mother was *Wäyzäro* Mäsqäl ʿƎbäya (In the cross lies her greatness), according to Susənyos's royal chronicle. She begged the king to spare her son from execution (Täklä Śəllase [Ṭinno] 1900, 235). She was the second wife of the grandson of King Ləbnä Dəngəl (r. 1508–40), Śärṣä Krəstos, who was King Susənyos's father by his first wife. However, the text might be referring to a woman who appears later in this text helping WP: Mälkəʾa Krəstos's stepmother Amätä Krəstos (Täklä Śəllase [Ṭinno] 1900, 78, 133n).

[4] BDJ: *śägärat* (guards); CR: *śärawit* (soldiers).

[5] John 18:5.

[6] BDJ: *fäqadä əgziʾabḥer* (God's will); CR: *fäqadəkä* (your will).

[7] According to Genesis 20 and 26, Abimelech was the king of the Philistines, of the region Gerar, who tries to take Abraham's wife Sarah when Abraham claims she is his sister.

[8] Daniel 13:1–64. While the Protestant (Masoretic-based) book of Daniel stops at chapter 12, the Orthodox (Septuagint-based) version has two extra chapters. Two older men see Susanna in her bath and attempt to blackmail her into having sex with them by threatening her with the false accusation that she had a young lover. She refuses to sleep with them and is about to be executed for adultery, when Daniel demands that the old men be questioned about their account. She is saved and they are executed.

saved [my countrywoman] Egzi Harayaa[1] from the hands of [King] Motalami,[2] he will also save me."

In addition, she said, "'I do not fear evil[3] because you, [Lord,] are with me.' 'God will shine a light for me and will save me: what then can make me afraid? God is my life's refuge: what then can terrify me'?[4] 'I put my trust in God; I have nothing to fear. What can men do to me?'"[5] Raising this and similar prayers, she spent the entire night.

Chapter 8: Our Mother Returns to Her Husband

The next night they put a tankwa in water and had our mother Walatta Petros and her maidservants get in it. The boatmen were *Abba* Yamaana Kristos and *Abba* Tazkaara Dinghil; they poled it, one at the prow and the other at the stern.

While they were on the open water, the soldiers who were watching for them from on high in the lookout heard their voices and recognized them from their words, since the [clerical] boatmen abused Malkiya Kristos and reviled his mother. Our holy mother Walatta Petros, however, reprimanded them, saying, "Why do you
16 talk so much and heap scorn on a noblewoman? Do your mouths have no locks?"

After the soldiers had climbed down from the lookout and hid themselves from Walatta Petros's party, some of them ran to their lord to tell him the good news.[6] The voyagers, for their part, reached the lakeshore at Emabra and docked their tankwa. Since it was night and morning had not yet come, they did not see the soldiers who had hid themselves from them[7] and lay in wait for them. Walatta Petros and her companions remained on the lakeshore until morning came and until Walatta Petros would be sent[8] a mule.

[1] *Ǝgziʾ Ḫaräya* (The Lord has chosen her). She was the mother of Ethiopia's most famous saint, Täklä Haymanot. According to his hagiobiography, in her youth she was abducted by the wicked heathen king Motälämi, who planned to assault her chastity. Before he could do so, however, she was miraculously saved by the Lord.

[2] *Motälämi* (thus BDJ; CR: *Mätälomi*) may be partially derived from the word *motii* (or a variant thereof), the word for "king" in many Cushitic Ethiopian languages. Also, *lam* is the word for "cow" in Amharic, so perhaps the name indicates that he was the king of a pastoralist community.

[3] Psalm 22[23]:4. In the Gəʿəz text, the grammatically masculine *əkuy* (evil) can refer to evil in the abstract or to an evil male person. Through this ambiguity, the text denounces Mälkəʾa Krəstos.

[4] Psalm 26[27]:1.

[5] Psalm 55[56]:4.

[6] BDJ: *kämä yabsərəwwo* (to tell him the good news); CR: *kämä yəbsərəwwo* [*sic*], editing the *kämä yəsbərəwwo* (to break him) of Abb. 88.

[7] BDJ: *əllä yətḫabbəʾəwwomu* (who had hid themselves from them); CR: *wä-täḫabbʾəwwomu* (they had hid themselves from them).

[8] BDJ: *wä-əskä yəfennəwu lati* (lit., and until they would send her); CR: *wä-əskä yəfennu lati* (and until he [*Abba* Fätlä Śəllase] would send her).

As soon as morning had come, the commander of the soldiers emerged from where he had hidden and wanted to arrest the monks. When they resisted him, he got rough with them and abused them, saying, "You are rascally monks who do violence to a married woman![1] Today, though, God has abandoned you and given you into my hands." He then held his sword sideways, inside its sheath, and struck them in order to frighten them. The commander hit *Abba* Tazkaara Dinghil's legs and wounded him; the scar from the wound remained on his legs until he died.

Immediately, our holy mother Walatta Petros rose up in great anger, slapped the commander on his cheeks, and said to him, "You insolent servant,[2] how dare you disrespect me!"

Those [other] soldiers reached Malkiya Kristos and informed him [about finding Walatta Petros]. When he heard [this news] he rose up with joy, mounted his horse, and hurried to her. He forgot his oath and wanted to seize her and take her away, without *Abba* Fatla Sillasé and *Woyzaro* Walatta Giyorgis knowing.

He knocked her nun's cap off her head, prodded her[3] from behind with his feet, and said to her, "Get going!"

Upon that, our holy mother Walatta Petros immediately let herself fall on the ground and acted as if dead. She kept silent and obstinately[4] stopped moving. It was not possible to put her on a mule. Malkiya Kristos then ordered his soldiers to transport her by grasping her wrists and ankles[5] through her clothes. However, they [almost] were unable to move her.[6] With great difficulty they carried her a short distance. Everywhere on their way there were thorns, and walking was difficult for them. Therefore, they set her on the ground. As for Malkiya Kristos, he became enraged, gnashing his teeth, frightening the soldiers, and scowling at them.

At that time, the soldiers began to implore Walatta Petros with gentle words,
saying, "Our merciful and compassionate lady,[7] have mercy on us and be kind to us,
as is your custom! For if you resist us and we are unable to carry you therefore, our 17
lord will get angry with us and will kill us. Comply with us and show us compas-

[1] *ʿammäśä*, the Gəʿəz verb employed here, means "to do injustice *or* violence to someone" and has been translated accordingly. It can also be employed for rape, however. Overtones of this are present here as becomes clear when the overbearing soldier makes a point of denouncing the monks' alleged injustice against a "married woman" (*bəʾəsitä bəʾəsi*, lit., "a[nother] man's woman"), effectively accusing them of having committed acts of sexual violence against WP, a charge all the more outrageous given their monastic commitment to chastity.

[2] Or "You disobedient servant," if, assuming a common variation of Ethiopic orthography, one chooses to read *ʾəbuy gäbr* instead of the *ʿəbuy gäbr* of BDJ and CR.

[3] Lit., *läkäfa nəstitä* (lightly touched her).

[4] Lit., *bä-əkäy* (with malice).

[5] BDJ: *əḫizomu bä-arbaʿtu ṣənäfihu* (lit., they grasping by the four extremities); CR: *əḫizomu arbaʿtä ṣənäfihu* (they grasping the four extremities).

[6] According to the Jesuits, the women of the court often weighed quite a bit. WP had only just started her journey as a nun, and the text makes clear that she had all the softness of a wealthy woman.

[7] The soldiers address WP in terms normally used only when addressing Saint Mary.

sion." When she heard their words, she had mercy on them and stood up so they could put her on a mule.

While they said these things, there arrived envoys who had been sent by *Abba* Fatla Sillasé and *Woyzaro* Walatta Giyorgis. These envoys said to Malkiya Kristos, "How could you lie to us, deceive us,[1] and secretly, unknown to us, go and seize her on the road like a thief and bandit? You made a childish judgment! This decision of yours is not going to be a good one. Now we are telling you to come here, [to our home at Woynayat,] and she shall come too, so that we can effect a reconciliation between you. If, however, you refuse to come, being contemptuous of us and not heeding our word, we will consider ourselves wronged by you, and together with us God will have been wronged."

When Malkiya Kristos heard this message,[2] he became afraid, changed his mind,[3] and set off toward them. As for our holy mother Walatta Petros, they made her mount a mule and conveyed her to them at Woynayat, too. There *Abba* Fatla Sillasé and *Woyzaro* Walatta Giyorgis adjudicated between them, reconciled them, and dispatched them in peace. Thus our holy mother Walatta Petros and Malkiya Kristos returned to their region of Simaada.

Chapter 9: Our Mother Leaves Her Husband Again

After this, our holy mother Walatta Petros lived looking for a reason to separate from Malkiya Kristos. In those days, the faith of the Europeans had begun [in Ethiopia] and *Abuna* Simeon,[4] the patriarch [of the Orthodox Church],[5] had been killed, along with Yolyos,[6] so that they became martyrs.[7] That man, the patriarch's killer,

[1] BDJ: *əfo . . . ḫeṭkänä* (how could . . . you deceive us); CR: *əfo . . . meṭkä* (how could . . . you change).

[2] BDJ: *wä-sämiʿo zäntä mälʾəktä* (lit., when he heard this message); CR: *wä-sämiʿo zäntä Mälkəʾa Krəstos* (when Mälkəʾa Krəstos heard this).

[3] Lit., *tämäyṭä* (to turn around, turn back), can be interpreted spatially or metaphorically.

[4] *Səmʿon* (Simon) was the Egyptian patriarch of the Täwaḥədo Church under Susənyos, and he refused to convert to Roman Catholicism. He supported the anti-Catholic rebel Yolyos, and after Yolyos was defeated in battle on 11 May 1617, Səmʿon was dragged onto the battlefield, tortured, killed, and left for dead for two days. In a further affront to the faithful, his severed head was delivered to the king.

[5] *Päppas* (patriarch *or* metropolitan), the highest-ranking figure in and head leader of the Täwaḥədo Church (also called the Coptic metropolitan), who always came from Egypt, being assigned by the head church in Alexandria.

[6] *Yolyos* (Julius). Yolyos started off as a lowly lieutenant to Susənyos before the latter was made king. After, Susənyos married him to his daughter Mäläkotawit and made him the governor of Goǧǧam. In 1609, however, Yolyos participated in a plot against Susənyos stopped by *Ras* Śəʿəlä Krəstos. He then died fighting in the anti-Catholic rebellion of 11 May 1617.

[7] BDJ: *wä-konu sämaʿtä* (so that they became martyrs); CR: *wä-konä sämaʿtä* (so that he became a martyr).

then took the patriarch's vestment and gave it to Malkiya Kristos.[1] When our holy mother Walatta Petros learned [about this], her mind shuddered and she was filled with revulsion for Malkiya Kristos. She refused to come close to him and stopped sleeping with him.

She said to him, "How can I live with you when you are not a Christian? You have had the patriarch killed! And look: You have the patriarch's vestment in your possession!"

After this, she ceased[2] eating and drinking, and abandoned beautifying herself in the manner of women. She did not style her hair or put on oils and perfumes, nor perfume herself by burning various fragrant substances, nor paint her fingernails, nor color her eyelids with kohl,[3] nor adorn herself with beautiful clothes.[4] She gave up all these things, as well as other similar ones. She lived like a nun, making herself wretched in every way.

When Malkiya Kristos saw our holy mother Walatta Petros's behavior and the determination of her heart, and when furthermore it pleased God, he said to her on
his own account, without anybody forcing him, "For how long will you live with 18
me like this? Go where you please: I will not hinder you."

She replied, "Swear to me that you will not go back on your word."

So he swore to her. He also asked her likewise.[5] So she swore to him.[6]

The next day she said to him, "Dispatch me according to your word."

He replied, "Very well," and ordered his soldiers to saddle a mule, make her mount it, and accompany her.

[1] BDJ: *näśʾa ləbsä pappas wä-wähabo lä-Mälkəʾa Krəstos* (took the patriarch's vestment and gave it to Mälkəʾa Krəstos); CR: *wä-wähabo ləbsä pappas lä-Mälkəʾa Krəstos* (gave the patriarch's vestment to Mälkəʾa Krəstos). The text makes clear that Mälkəʾa Krəstos did not kill the patriarch. However, he did take part in the battle against Yolyos, and the killer knew Mälkəʾa Krəstos well enough that he gave him the patriarch's garments of office.

[2] Lit., *ḥarrämät* (she anathematized).

[3] BDJ: *wä-täʿaṭno mäʿaza zä-zä-ziʾahu wä-gäbirä ṭəmʿatatä ḥəbr zä-aṣfar wä-täkʷəḥlo aʿyənt* (nor perfume herself by burning various fragrant substances, nor paint her fingernails, nor color her eyelids with kohl); CR instead only *wä-təwzəft* (and jewelry), but Conti Rossini notes that two lines were erased here in Abb. 88.

[4] CR adds: *wä-ḥartämät* (and she became emaciated).

[5] BDJ, Abb. 88: *wəʾətu-ni yəbela kämähu* (lit., he also said to her likewise); CR altered to: *wəʾətu-ni [wä]-yəbela [mäḥali litä] kämähu* (he also [then] said to her, "[Swear to me] likewise").

[6] It is unclear why Mälkəʾa Krəstos needs WP to swear likewise since she has made no promises and he is the one who has reneged on a solemn promise. Perhaps he means that she should not change her mind and return to him since he wants to marry another. Perhaps it is intertextual. This exchange of vows is reminiscent of those exchanged between King Solomon and Makədda, the Queen of Sheba, in the fourteenth-century *Kəbrä Nägäśt* (The Glory of the Kings), when Solomon uses vows to trick and seduce her. Makədda asks him to promise to take nothing of hers "by force" (namely, her virginity) and Solomon makes her promise that she will take nothing of his "by force." When she takes up a glass of water in his house, he claims she broke her vow and has his way with her.

He also sent word to her family, "Take back your daughter. After[1] I reconciled with her, she never made me happy but only gave me displeasure. In addition, she is no longer one body with me as is the decree for husband and wife. From now on, she may do as she wants[2] and pleases."

At that time all the people of his household, men and women, wailed and cried and said to their lord, "Don't let her go!"

He replied, "But I have sworn an oath and therefore it is impossible for me to hold her back." It was not he who let her go, [however,] but rather the will of God that prevented him [from reneging].

Then our holy mother Walatta Petros mounted a mule and went on her way, with crying and wailing men and women seeing her off because she was leaving them. In sadness they returned to their homes. Those others who had been dispatched together with her took her to her brother Za-Dinghil,[3] told him about their mission, and then returned home. Za-Dinghil received her well and accommodated her in his residence.

As for Walatta Petros, she was very happy and glad. She praised God, saying, "I would rather be a castaway in the house of God[4] than live [pleasantly] in the house of sinners."[5]

When our holy mother Walatta Petros had left her home, she had not taken anything with her, neither gold nor silver to sustain her on the way,[6] nor a staff, nor shoes, even though she was the wife of a lord and the daughter of noble parents. As our Lord said to the disciples, "Acquire for yourselves neither gold nor silver."[7] Rather, she had left [her husband's home] with nothing, saying, "Naked did I emerge from my mother's womb, and naked will I return to the womb of the grave."[8]

As David says, "The law from your mouth is better for me than countless amounts of gold and silver."[9] "This is why I have loved your commandment more than gold and topaz."[10] What, then, is God's commandment? Is it not to renounce
19 possessions and to carry the cross? Our Lord further says, "It is easier for a camel to pass through the eye of a needle than for a rich man to enter into the Kingdom

[1] DJ: *əm-dəḫrä* (after); B, CR: *əm-kämä* (as soon as).

[2] BDJ: *təgbär zä-fäqädät* (lit., she may do what she wants); CR: *tənbär zä-fäqädät* (she may live what [*sic*] she wants).

[3] *Zä-Dəngəl* (He of the Virgin [Mary]) is WP's fourth brother, an important lord of the court.

[4] BDJ: *wəstä betä əgziʾabḥer* (in the house of God); CR: *wəstä əgziʾabḥer* (in God).

[5] Psalms 83[84]:10.

[6] BDJ: *i-wärqä wä-i-bərurä sənqä lä-fənot* (lit., neither gold nor silver as provisions for the way); CR: *i-wärqä wä-i-bərurä wä-i-sənqä lä-fənot* (neither gold nor silver nor provisions for the way).

[7] Matthew 10:9.

[8] Job 1:21. The original Hebrew does not have the second "womb," just "return to the grave."

[9] Psalm 118[119]:72.

[10] Psalm 118[119]:127.

of Heaven."[1] In addition, the *Sayings of the Fathers*[2] relate, "Dear ones, what is gold? Is it not an evil shackle and a chain? Iron only destroys the body, while gold is an affliction for the body and a torment for the soul." And again Paul says, "The love of money is the root of all evil" because through it many went astray and deserted their faith.[3] This is why our holy mother Walatta Petros also abhorred worldly wealth and regarded it as nothing.

Chapter 10: Our Mother Leaves Her Brother's House to Become a Nun

A short time thereafter, when our holy mother Walatta Petros had made up her mind to go away and become a nun, she said to her brother Za-Dinghil, "Allow me to go visit my [spiritual] teacher [*Abba* Fatla Sillasé] because he is sick and suffers. It has been a long time since I have seen him. If he dies without me seeing him, he will curse me. Truly, the spiritual father is greater than the corporeal father."

Za-Dinghil replied, "Go ahead," not realizing that she had spoken to him deceptively and with cunning words;[4] she appeared sincere to him.[5] Thus he ordered his retainers to saddle a mule for her, help her to mount it, guard her[6] [on the way], and conduct her to her teacher. They acted on her behalf as her brother had ordered them. Thus she went, while with her were her maidservants who [always] followed her.

When she was close to reaching the town [of Robeet], she told the retainers, "Help me dismount. I will camp here today. I don't want to increase the burden on my teacher since we are many and he cannot host [all of] us. So, you, return on your way. You can collect me again another day because I will remain with my teacher quite a while." With these words, she sent them away, and they went.

She had already premeditated this decision with her teacher. He had devised this ruse craftily[7] so that they would not feel betrayed by or hostile toward him. [Thus] our holy mother Walatta Petros stayed behind, together with her maidservants.

[1] Matthew 19:24; Mark 10:25; Luke 18:25.

[2] *Nägärä Abäw* may be a loose title for *Apophthegmata Patrum Aegyptiorum* (Sayings of the Desert [lit., Egyptian] Fathers) or it may not be a title at all, but simply mean here "a saying of the Fathers is as follows." We have not been able to locate the saying in other sources.

[3] 1 Timothy 6:10.

[4] BDJ: *bä-täṭbabä nägär* (lit., with a ruseful discourse); CR: *bä-ṭəbäbä nägär* (with a prudent discourse).

[5] It is still the case that women steal away from their families to become nuns (Wright 2001, 16–17, 56). Many never communicate with their families again, because they are supposed "to leave one's blood relatives, riches, and worldly pleasure," according to the *Fətḥa Nägäśt* (Ibn al-ʿAssāl 1968, 67).

[6] J: *yəṣäwwənəwwa* (guard her); BD: *yəṣṣäwwänəwwa* (seek refuge with her); CR: *yəṣurəwwa* (carry her).

[7] BDJ: *täṭäbbäbä* (lit., he had acted craftily); CR: *täṭäbbäbät* (she had acted craftily). Since WP engaged in lying in order to escape living under the authority of the men in her family,

Plate 5. How our mother left her brother's house with a maidservant (top) and "how the owner of the house said to her: 'You can spend the night [here]' " (bottom) (MS A, f. 146v © SLUB Mscr.Dresd. Eb.415.e,2).

She proceeded to the house of one of the people of a [nearby] town and spent
the night there.[1] However, when it was deep night and all the maidservants were
asleep, she woke up a young servant girl[2] to guide her[3] [to her teacher's house].
Together with that girl, she then stealthily left, walking on foot, while her blood
flowed like water because the sharp edges of the stones cut into her feet. They were
truly soft, like the feet of an infant just come from its mother's womb. The people
who saw[4] that blood [the next morning] wondered among themselves: 20

"What is this blood? Is it the blood of a goat or a sheep that a leopard has torn apart, or that a thief has slaughtered?"

On her part, our holy mother Walatta Petros, proceeding slowly together with the girl, reached the town of Robeet [the next day,] and [entered] into the Presentation of Our Lady Mary Church,[5] its sanctuary. She sat down in the church courtyard of the people of that place.

They, however, said to her, "Get up! We don't have a lodging place here. Rather, go into the town where you will find lodging."[6]

She replied, "I will not go to the town but will stay in your courtyard." Then, when evening came, they allowed her into a hut that a nun had abandoned. For that week, our holy mother Walatta Petros went and lived there, together with that girl. She came to like that hut very much and wanted to stay there until God's judgment.[7]

Chapter 11: Our Mother Finds a New Servant

That girl gave her much trouble, however, more than that of one hundred people.[8] So Walatta Petros became very distressed and said [to herself], "If I found someone who, for my benefit, would take her [with them], I would send her back. I would

the text allays any concerns about her behavior by explaining that it was not she but her teacher who devised this falsehood.

[1] A home was traditionally several buildings inside a fenced compound, with buildings for people, animals, and storage. Wealthy people often had separate buildings for cooking and receiving guests. Poor people would have only one. Most buildings would be round and windowless with adobe walls, thatched roofs, and only one door. The floor and walls were smooth, with built-in clay benches.

[2] Lit., *ḥəśan* (infant).

[3] Lit., *kämä tətləwa* (so that she [WP] could follow her [the girl]).

[4] BDJ: *wä-əllä rəʾyu säbʾ* (the people who saw); CR: *wä-sobä rəʾyu säbʾ* (when people saw).

[5] Lit., *betä krəstiyanä Ǝgzəʾtənä Maryam Zä-Bäʾata* (lit., the church of Our Lady Mary, of Her Entry). This church is named after the ritual in which as a girl Mary was presented by her parents to serve in the temple, according to the Apocrypha.

[6] The townspeople's unfriendliness may have something to do with her husband's actions in destroying the town previously.

[7] Lit., *əskä tətfättaḥ bä-əgziʾabḥer* (until she would be judged [*or* released] by God).

[8] BDJ: *ʿabiyä hukätä zä-yəbäzzəḫ əm-hukätä 100 säbʾ* (lit., much trouble, more than the trouble of one hundred people); CR omits *100*, resulting in the translation, "much trouble, more than [ordinary] people [would]."

prefer to remain behind on my own in order to find rest from trouble and live in tranquillity."

When God saw the strength of her distress, he brought a woman to Walatta Petros who was going to that town [from which the girl originated]. So, our holy mother Walatta Petros asked that woman to take the girl back to her home and dispatched her with the girl. Our holy mother Walatta Petros then remained behind alone.[1] However,[2] God did not abandon her.

On that very day, a young servant woman[3] came to her who had been sent by Lebaseeta Kristos,[4] who was living in Furé.[5] Because she had heard the news about our holy mother Walatta Petros, Lebaseeta Kristos had sent the young woman in order to pay our holy mother Walatta Petros a visit and investigate her situation. The young woman arrived alone among the [other] passersby, came near to that place [where Walatta Petros stayed,] and inquired, "Where does the lady stranger live?"[6]

She came [to Walatta Petros's hut] without anybody guiding her. She stood at the gate and clapped her hands, as is the custom in monasteries. So, our holy mother Walatta Petros stuck her head out of the door, looked at the young woman, and with her hands beckoned her since she was alone[7] that day, without anybody
21 serving her. The young woman then approached her, and our holy mother Walatta Petros[8] asked her, "Where are you from and for whom have you come?"

The young woman replied, "My mistress Lebaseeta Kristos has sent me to you. She says to you, 'How are you? And, how are you doing? Peace be unto you, and may the peace of God be with you, amen.' "

When our holy mother Walatta Petros heard this salutation, she was amazed and praised God[9] who had not let her live alone for a single day. So the young woman stayed with her for that day.

The next day, however, she said to Walatta Petros, "Allow me to go to my mistress and bring her your return message."

But our holy mother Walatta Petros[10] replied, "Stay with me this week because I am alone."

[1] BDJ: *baḥtita* (alone); CR omits.

[2] BDJ: *wä-baḥtu* (however); Abb. 88: *wä-bati* (in her *or* with her), which CR altered to *wä-lati* (as to her).

[3] Lit., *wälätt* (a daughter).

[4] *Läbasitä Krəstos* (She who wears Christ as her garment) is presumably a wealthy woman, since she can spare a servant.

[5] *Fure* is a town on the southwestern shore of Lake Ṭana, just south of Lake Ṭana's Zäge Peninsula. It is now called Furi Maryam.

[6] BDJ: *ayte täḫaddər zati əngəda* (lit., where does this [fem.] stranger live); CR: *ayte ḥorät zati əngəda* (where has this [fem.] stranger gone).

[7] BDJ: *baḥtita* (alone); CR omits.

[8] CR omits *Wälättä Ṗeṭros.*

[9] BDJ: *ankärät wä-säbbəḥato lä-əgziʾabḥer* (she was amazed and praised God); CR: *ankärätö wä-säbbəḥato lä-əgziʾabḥer* (she marveled at God and praised him).

[10] CR omits *Wälättä Ṗeṭros.*

The young woman answered, "Very well." Truly, she was of good character; she spoke with ease and appropriately and was loved by all. She stayed with Walatta Petros and pleased her doubly since, before, Walatta Petros had been distressed on account of the spiteful deeds of that girl who had gone away.

Do you see the justness of God's understanding? He chased away the young servant girl[1] who had accompanied Walatta Petros into exile but drew close this young servant woman who had been far away, and made her stay with Walatta Petros. He truly is all-powerful. He acts as he pleases and what he decides he carries out. Nobody can argue with him.[2] He removes what is nearby and brings close what is distant.[3] Truly, he scrutinizes the heart and the kidneys.[4]

Chapter 12: Our Mother Meets Her Lifelong Companion Eheta Kristos

In those days, while our holy mother Walatta Petros was living with that young woman, *Abba* Tsigé Haymanot[5] came from Furé to visit her when he heard the news that[6] she was in Robeet. When he arrived there, he met with her and learned that[7] she lived alone. He said to her, "My child,[8] how can you live alone without a companion?[9] This is not good for you."

Our holy mother Walatta Petros replied, "How do I do that? From where can I find a companion who will live with me?[10] Am I not a stranger in this town?"

He responded, "If you want, I myself will bring you one. There is a fine woman named Eheta Kristos[11] who, like you, left her husband and home, became a nun, and now lives with her sister. This would be good for both of you." 22

[1] BDJ: *lä-ḥəṣan . . . sädäda* (lit., he chased away the young girl); CR: *lä-ḥəṣan . . . fännäwa* (he sent away the young girl).

[2] See Job 36:22–23.

[3] See James 4:8; Deuteronomy 30:4.

[4] Lit., *əsmä wəʾətu fätane ləbb wä-kʷələyat* (truly, he is the scrutinizer of the heart and the kidneys). Revelation 2:23. Heart and kidneys (or, in reverse order, *nephroùs kaì kardías* in the Greek original of the Revelation verse) is a metaphor for the innermost feelings.

[5] *Ṣəge Haymanot* (Flower of the faith). This monk from Fure plays an important role in WP's life.

[6] BDJ: *kämä* (that); CR: *ḫabä* (where).

[7] BDJ: *kämä* (that); CR: *ḫabä* (where).

[8] Lit., *anti ḥəṣan* (you, child).

[9] Someone starting off in the spiritual life needs a guard on her virtue, to prevent against temptation.

[10] BDJ: *əntä tənäbbər məsleyä* (who will live with me); CR: *ənzä tənäbbər məsleyä* (while she will live with me).

[11] *Ǝḫətä Krəstos* (Sister of Christ), a noblewoman who left her husband and daughter to become a nun, later became WP's long-term companion. Ǝḫətä Krəstos was born sometime before 1601, became a nun in 1617, and lived thirty-two years as a nun until her death on 2 April 1649. For twenty-six of her monastic years, she was a leader in WP's community, including almost seven years after the death of WP in 1642. She is also revered as a saint, but

Our holy mother Walatta Petros replied, "As for me, I don't want to live with a woman who has left her home."

He responded, "But, I know that woman's character: it is good. If you see her yourself, you will like her."

Having said this, he took leave from her and returned to Furé. [There] he then said to Eheta Kristos, "If you live a pampered life[1] with your sister, and fatten your body with food and drink, how[2] have you repudiated the world? And, which pleasure have you ever abandoned for the sake of God? Truly, it would have been better for you to stay in your home with your husband than to live your current life! However, if you listen to my word and accept my pronouncement, I advise you [as follows]: It would be better for you[3] to live together with Walatta Petros who is at Robeet. She truly is a fine woman." Then he revealed to her all that Walatta Petros had done, from the beginning to the end.

Eheta Kristos replied, "But I don't want to live with a woman who has lived at court![4] If[5] I were to live with her, what might she teach me, and what example might I take from her? Both of us are indeed new plants [in the religious life]."[6]

He replied, "Please go to meet her once to observe her character and examine her conduct. If you like her, you can stay with her, but if you dislike her, nobody will force you [to live with her]."

Eheta Kristos said to him, "Very well. I will do this so that your will may be done. However, I absolutely don't want to live with her."

Then Eheta Kristos secretly went to our holy mother Walatta Petros[7] in a tankwa, without anyone knowing [about it] except the two of them, [namely, Eheta Kristos and *Abba* Tsigé Haymanot]. She arrived at the place, stood at the gate, and clapped her hands. So, our holy mother Walatta Petros said to the young servant woman [who now served her], "Go out, please, and inquire who is clapping."

When the young woman came out, she recognized Eheta Kristos.[8] She returned and told our holy mother Walatta Petros that it was Eheta Kristos because she knew

---

a full-length gädl of her life has yet to be found. See "The Biography of Ǝḫətä Krəstos" in this volume.

[1] BDJ: *bä-ḥənqaqe* (lit., in pamperedness); CR: *bä-ḥəbqʷaqʷe* (in impurity). Like many nuns, Ǝḫətä Krəstos was living at home with family rather than in a monastery. As the monk points out, it is difficult to repudiate the world when living with those who have not.

[2] Lit., *maʾze* (when).

[3] BDJ: *yəḫeyyəsäki* (it would be better for you); CR omits.

[4] Lit., *kätäma*, which originally designated the royal itinerant military encampment but also came to mean, more generally, the royal court. Until Gondär was founded by Fasilädäs in the seventeenth century, Ethiopia's court was itinerant, a mobile royal military camp in tents, moving frequently to places in need of closer rule. See Stylianoudi and Nosnitsin (2007).

[5] BDJ: *əmmä* (if); CR: *ama* (when).

[6] *Ḥaddis täkl* (new plant) is the exact equivalent of the Greek word "neophyte."

[7] BDJ: *wä-əmzə ḥorät ḫabä əmmənä qəddəst Wälättä Ṗeṭros ṣəmmitä* (lit., then she secretly went to our holy mother Wälättä Ṗeṭros); CR: *wä-əmze ḥorät Ǝḫətä Krəstos ṣəmmitä* (then Ǝḫətä Krəstos secretly went).

[8] BDJ: *Ǝḫətä Krəstos*; CR omits.

her from before, when she had been at Furé. Our holy mother Walatta Petros said to her, "Tell her 'Come in!' " So the maidservant went and brought Eheta Kristos in.

As soon as our holy mother Walatta Petros and Eheta Kristos saw each other from afar, love was infused into both their hearts, love for one another, and [approaching,] they exchanged the kiss of greeting. Then they sat down and told each
other stories [about the workings] of God. There was no fear or mistrust between 23
them. They were like people who had known each other beforehand because the Holy Spirit united them.

Chapter 13: Our Mother and Eheta Kristos Decide to Live Together and Become Nuns

They then deliberated together and decided that they would live together. So,[1] Eheta Kristos said to Walatta Petros, "I will now return [to Furé] and send you a tankwa, so you can come there. Then we will meet to ponder the plan that God has revealed to us." Immediately, Eheta Kristos went and sent her the tankwa. Our holy mother Walatta Petros received it and arrived at Furé. There she greeted *Abba* Tsigé Haymanot and all the [devout] sisters who were there.[2] Then Eheta Kristos came and greeted her like a stranger whom she had not known before.

Thereafter *Abba* Tsigé Haymanot said to the two of them, when they were alone, "My daughters, how have you fared? Did you take a liking to each other or not?"

They replied, "We love each other very much indeed. However, we do not know how to flee and escape [our families]."

He responded, "Indeed, this is also a challenge for me." He then said to Eheta Kristos, "You tell your sister, 'I do not enjoy living with you in comfort and abundance. It doesn't seem a righteous thing to me. Therefore, with your permission, allow me to become a disciple of Ersinna.[3] If not, I will run away from you and go to where you will never see me again.' "

They said to him, "What you say is good. However, you yourself should go [to Eheta Kristos's sister] and get this done."

So, he went and told this to Eheta Kristos's sister. In response, she said to him, "Very well. Let it be as you said. I herewith give her permission to leave."[4]

[1] Lit., *baḥtu* (nevertheless).

[2] "Sisters" is the word used for women in WP's community. It is unclear whether the word "sisters" in the texts means any woman in WP's community or just nuns.

[3] *Ersənna* apparently was a contemporary local female religious leader, now unknown. Her name might be a variant of Arsima, Gəʿəz for Armenian "Hripsime" or "Rhipsime." Hripsime was a third-century female Armenian martyr popular in Ethiopia; the Arsima Sämaʿtat Church on nearby Däq Island is dedicated to her.

[4] BDJ: *baḥtu ḥur antä lälikä wä-gəbär kämä-zə. Wä-ḥorä wä-nägära. Wä-təbelo oho yəkun bä-kämä təbe abaḥkəwwa təḥur* (However, you yourself should go . . . I herewith give her permission to leave); CR with feminine forms throughout, as if Ǝḫ̮ətä Krəstos or Wälättä Ṗeṭros were addressing Ǝḫ̮ətä Krəstos's sister: *baḥtu ḥuri anti läliki wä-gəbäri kämä-zə. Wä-ḥorät wä-nägärat zäntä* [Abb. 88: *Wä-ḥora wä-nägära*]. *Wä-təbela oho yəkun bä-kämä təbeli*

Abba Tsigé Haymanot then took Walatta Petros[1] to Ersinna and revealed his secret plan to the latter, adding, "Don't reveal this secret to anyone." He then got a tankwa[2] ready for Walatta Petros and Eheta Kristos and by night dispatched them, telling them, "Today go back to Zagé and stay [there] for three days[3] so that those who are after you will not find you." They did as he had instructed them.

Three days later, Walatta Petros and Eheta Kristos climbed aboard that same tankwa[4] and went to Robeet, where our holy mother Walatta Petros had lived before, and [there] lived together in mutual love, like soul and body.[5] From that day onward, the two did not separate, neither in times of tribulation and persecution nor in those of tranquillity, but only in death.

After some days, they went to [the monastery of] Dabra Anqo,[6] and there our
24 holy mother Walatta Petros took on the habit[7] and dedicated herself[8] devotedly to the service of God, with fasts and prayers and all kinds of virtuous deeds. She also began the labor of humility and took up menial work like a maidservant. Thus, in a single day[9] she would grind five *éf* measures[10] of barley or of wheat, even though her hands were delicate and not used to grinding or to any work at all.

With her were Eheta Kristos and Walatta Pawlos,[11] daughter of [*Ras*] Atinatewos.[12] Their meeting and living together there was a fine thing, just as David says,[13]

---

abaḥkuki ḥuri (However, you yourself [fem.] should go and do [fem.] this. So she went and told this [Abb. 88: So he went to her and told her]. She thereupon said to her, Very well. Let it be as you [fem.] said. I herewith give you [fem.] permission to leave).

[1] BDJ: *Wälättä P̣eṭros*; CR: *Ǝḫətä Krəstos.*

[2] BDJ: *tankʷa* (a papyrus boat); CR: *tankʷaha* (her papyrus boat *or* the papyrus boat).

[3] BDJ: *wä-nəbära əskä śälus ʿəlät* (and stay [there] for three days); CR omits.

[4] BDJ: *ʿarga bä-wəʾətu tankʷa* (lit., they climbed aboard that tankwa); CR: *ʿarga bä-wəstä tankʷa* (they climbed inside the tankwa).

[5] This metaphor is used repeatedly in the text to suggest intimate complementarity; here, it shows that the two women together form a symbiotic whole.

[6] *Däbrä ʿAnqo* (Monastery of [the Jewel?]). An unidentified place probably on the southwest side of Lake Ṭana near Zäge.

[7] Lit., *albasä mənkʷəsənna* (the garments of monasticism).

[8] BDJ: *wä-näbärät ənzä tətqännäy* (lit., and lived dedicating herself); CR omits grammatically required *ənzä.*

[9] BDJ: *lelit* (lit., night); CR: *ʿəlät* (day).

[10] An *ef* is a dry measure that frequently appears in the Old Testament (Hebrew *ʿephah*), most often used for grain. The Amharic Bible notes that an ef is about 40 liters (approximately 10.5 gallons). A main task of nuns was grinding grain for the Communion bread, as well as for their own sustenance, and it is an extremely arduous task.

[11] *Wälättä P̣äwlos* (Daughter of [Saint] Paul). She is the daughter of *Ras* Atənatewos and *Wäyzäro* Wälättä Giyorgis. Since Wälättä Giyorgis was a daughter of King Śärṣä Dəngəl (r. 1563–97), her daughter Wälättä P̣äwlos was a noblewoman too, the granddaughter of a king. Wälättä P̣äwlos also became a nun around the time that WP and Ǝḫətä Krəstos did, in 1617, perhaps partly because her father and mother had just been exiled from the court.

[12] *Atənatewos* (Athanasius) helped Susənyos come to power and was one of the highest members of his court, a *ras*, but was then sidelined until Susənyos put him on trial and exiled him to Amhara in 1617.

[13] B: *bä-kämä yəbe Dawit* (just as David says); DJ, Abb. 88 omit *Dawit* (David), therefore CR inserts *mäzmur* (the Psalter) in brackets.

Plate 6. "How she [ground] fifty [*sic*] measures" of grain (top), and "how she drew [and fetched] water" (bottom) (MS A, f. 147r © SLUB Mscr.Dresd.Eb.415.e,2).

"Mercy and justice have met, righteousness and peace have kissed."[1] "It is good and pleasant indeed when sisters are together."[2]

As for our holy mother Walatta Petros, nobody resembled or equaled her in all kinds of work.[3] If she occupied herself with the preparation of the *wot* stew, it turned out tasty and delicious smelling, and so abundant that it exceeded the measure. Or if she went out into the countryside in order to collect [fire]wood, a large load immediately[4] came together for her. In all she did, God gave her success. Furthermore, she used to go to a faraway river carrying a jar.[5] There she would draw water and carry [it back].[6] [To do so,] she had to climb up a steep ascent on all fours.[7] On that path, there was a large stone where she used to sit down and rest a bit, catching her breath, because her body was exhausted. People call this stone "Walatta Petros's Resting Place," and even today everybody who goes up or down [this ascent] kisses and salutes it. It will remain[8] a monument to the memory of her name[9] until the consummation of the world. From there, she would then rise up [again], carrying that jar and returning to their home. Everybody who saw her marveled. [Walking] the length of the path to that river took from dawn to the third hour[10] [i.e., 9:00 AM].

The sisters who were with her did likewise because she was their example and she taught them the works of humility. As our Lord says, "He who among you wants to be a leader should be a servant to the others."[11] Similarly, [the Apostle] Peter says, "Be examples for his flock, so that when the Lord of the shepherds appears, you may obtain the crown of glory that does not wither."[12]

In the monastery there also were idle and lazy nuns who did no work at all and
25 lived in sloth. They let their fingernails grow and did *hatsanaa* beautifying.[13] Yet

1 Psalm 84[85]:10.

2 Psalm 132[133]:1. The author has changed the biblical "brothers" to "sisters."

3 BDJ: *bä-ṣota kʷəllu tägbar* (in all kinds of work); CR: *bä-ṣota kʷəllu tägbar zä-zä-ziʾahu* (in all the various kinds of work).

4 BDJ: *fəṭunä wä-bä-gizeha* (lit., quickly and immediately); CR *fəṭunä* (quickly).

5 BDJ, Abb. 88: *kora* (a jar). CR mistakenly altered this to *korä,* the accusative of *kor* (saddle).

6 BDJ: *wä-təqäddəḥ mayä wä-təṣäwwər* (lit., she would draw water and carry); CR omits.

7 Walking long distances, drawing water, and then carrying it home on one's back was the daily and extremely laborious task of most women in Ethiopia. As a woman from a noble family, WP would not have been used to such tasks.

8 Lit., *wä-konä* (it has become).

9 BDJ: *lä-täzkarä səma* (to the memory of her name); CR: *lä-täzkarä ziʾaha* (to her memory).

10 Ethiopians count the hours as they do in the Bible, from sunrise, with the first hour of the day ending at 7:00 AM. Thus, the third hour of the day is 9:00 AM.

11 BDJ: *yəkunkəmu gäbrä* (lit., should be a servant to you [masc. pl.]); CR: *yəkun gäbrä* (should be a servant). Mark 10:44; Matthew 20:27.

12 1 Peter 5:2, 4.

13 The term *ḥaṣäna* (BDJ, CR) is very uncommon and does not appear in any of the standard dictionaries. The Italian translator Ricci squarely admitted that he was at a loss (Gälawdewos 1970, 23n6), and other Gəʿəz scholars we consulted did not know the word

when they saw the humility and toil of our holy mother Walatta Petros, they began to scold and rebuke themselves, saying, "Woe and doubly woe are we who have spent our days in laziness and indolence, even though we are poor people's daughters and the wives of Walatta Petros's servants and retainers.[1] Normally we would be grinding [grain] and fetching water. We have not been mindful[2] of the day of our death and have ignored that there will be a retribution for the lazy. Yet, Walatta Petros—a lady, a daughter of nobles, and the wife of a lord—has made herself poor and entered through the narrow gate that leads to eternal life. By contrast, we are in the broad gate that leads to perdition."[3] Having considered this, they repented of their past behavior, emulated our holy mother Walatta Petros, and began to work like her.

Of how many virtuous deeds of our holy mother Walatta Petros could we tell? They are oh so many! Moreover, the prayers, prostrations, and virtuous deeds that she performed secretly remain unknown: the works of the righteous are concealed.

Chapter 14: King Susinyos Establishes the Filthy Faith of the Europeans

After this,[4] King Susinyos began to make changes and established the filthy faith of the Europeans [i.e., Roman Catholicism], which says: Christ has two natures, [even] after He, [in his divine and human natures,] became one[5] and he became the perfect human being. [Thereby,] Susinyos repudiated the holy faith of Alexandria,[6]

---

either. The root *ḥ-ṣ-n* denotes the semantic field of caretaking, derived from a basic meaning of womb/lap. In Tigrinya, *ḥəṣənot* means what the bride does to prepare to welcome the bridegroom, which includes putting oil in one's hair, brightening one's face, putting on woody perfumes, and making one's palms black. Thus, it seems that the nuns were doing some kind of grooming or beautifying, perhaps even manicures or hennaing the hands, which would not be appropriate for women withdrawn from the world.

[1] BDJ: *anəstiya agbərtiha wä-wäʿaləyaniha* (lit., the wives of her servants and retainers); CR: *wä-i-nəkäwwən əm-aʾmatiha wä-wäʿaləyaniha* (and we would not be among her maid-servants and retainers). Previously married women could remain married (but celibate) even after they became nuns.

[2] BDJ: *i-täzäkkärnä* (we have not been mindful); CR: *əsmä i-täzäkkärnä* (truly, we have not been mindful).

[3] Matthew 7:13.

[4] BDJ, Abb. 88 here all add a *sobä* (when), which does not make sense syntactically. Therefore, our translation here follows CR, who ignored this *sobä* in his print edition.

[5] B, CR: *täwäḥadä* (became one); DJ: *täwaḥadä* (became one). The English translation is identical; however, the verb in DJ here is of a different stem, which more strongly suggests a reciprocal union of the two natures *with each other.*

[6] The Egyptian metropolis of Alexandria is invoked because it was the seat of the patriarch of the Coptic Church, whom the Täwaḥədo Church recognized at the time as their supreme spiritual authority.

which says as follows: Christ became the perfect human being; he is not split or divided in anything he does;[1] [he is] one Son. [In him] there is [only] one aspect, one essence, and one divine nature,[2] namely, that of God the logos.[3]

When our holy mother Walatta Petros heard this, she could not bear it but withdrew[4] and fled from place to place, exiling herself until she reached Tsiyaat[5] together with her female companions, whom we mentioned before.

As the Gospel says, "Blessed are those who are persecuted for the sake of righteousness because they will have the Kingdom of Heaven."[6] It further says, "Turn away from the lying prophets who come to you in sheep's clothing while inside they are ravenous wolves.[7] By their fruits you shall know them."[8] In addition, Paul says, "Our brothers, I implore you to beware of those[9] who create turmoil and bring quarrels against the doctrine you have learned.[10] Truly, they serve their belly
26 and not God, and with artful language and pleasant manners lead astray many simple people."[11] Do not waver and "do not place yourselves under the yoke of the unbelievers."[12] Therefore, leave their midst and separate from them. God says, "Do not come close to the impure. I will receive you and be your father, and you will be my sons and daughters."[13] [Thus] says God who has power over everything. Fur-

[1] BDJ: *bä-k^{w}əllu gəbru* (lit., in all his deeds/conduct/activity); CR: *bä-k^{w}əllu* (in anything [lit., in everything]).

[2] *1-ra*ʾ*y wä-1-həllawe wä-1-mäläkot.* Lit., *ra*ʾ*y* (vision), but in this context we take it to mean what is seen, hence "aspect."

[3] These same words are found in the sixth line of the hymn of praise for Monday in the *Wəddase Maryam* (Praise for Mary), which Budge translates as "He was a perfect man, without division and without separation, in all His work the Only-begotten, but with one form, one being, and one divinity (or Godhead)—God the Word" (1933a, 282). See "The Text's Religious Context" in this volume.

[4] The Gəʿəz equivalents of English "to bear" and "to withdraw" are closely similar: ተዓገሠ *täʿaggäśä* and ተገሕሠ *tägəḥśä*. By using them in proximity to each other, the author displays literary skill.

[5] BDJ: *hagärä Ṣəyat* (lit., the town *or* district of Ṣəyat); CR: *hagärä Ṣəyan.* This town or district is around one hundred miles due east of Lake Ṭana. The error in CR, spelling the name with a final "n," and thus Ricci's translation "Ṣyān," lead some scholars to say that WP went to the home of Zion (the Ark of the Covenant), which is Aksum, but nothing in the text says she went there.

[6] Matthew 5:10.

[7] DJ: *täk^{w}əlat mäśäṭṭ* (ravenous wolves); B, CR: *täk^{w}əlat wä-mäśäṭṭ* (wolves and predators).

[8] Matthew 7:15–16.

[9] BDJ: *täʿaqäbəwwomu* (beware of those); CR: *täʿaqqəbəwwomu* (you will guard those [*sic*]).

[10] Based on the original Greek, our translation assumes a Gəʿəz original of *zä-täməhərkəmu* (that you [masc. pl.] have learned). By contrast, BDJ have: *təgbäru* (lit., so that you [masc. pl.] do/perform); CR: *tənbäru* (so that you [masc. pl.] endure).

[11] Romans 16:17–18.

[12] 2 Corinthians 6:14.

[13] 2 Corinthians 6:17–18.

thermore, the *Rules for the Monks*[1] says, "Do not pray[2] together with *arseesaan*,[3] that is to say, heretics."[4]

This is why our holy mother Walatta Petros kept away [from them] and fled, going to the faraway region [of Tsiyaat] so as not to hear the blasphemy of the Europeans and not to have company with anyone who had joined that creed.

There she lived, dedicating herself devotedly to the service of God with fasts and prayers. She also rendered service with the same works as before, by grinding [cereals], drawing water, and gathering wood in the countryside, while her feet were being injured by the pricking of thorns, by sharp splinters of wood, and by small stones,[5] until they bled abundantly. Those who saw that blood on the way said to one another, "This blood[6] is from Walatta Petros."

She and her companions also used to go to the harvested fields in order to glean [leftover] grain; they would collect it for their sustenance. When she started to glean, after a little while her basket would suddenly fill up for her.[7] Even though she would pour [its contents] into a leather sack or another basket, they would not harmfully diminish because God's blessing was in her hands. Those [other] sisters would glean [only] a small quantity, however.

[One time,] when the owner of the field came and saw her gleanings as opposed to theirs, he reviled her and said about her, "She has stolen from my sheaves, that was how she so quickly filled it!" Then, injuriously,[8] he scattered all that she had gathered on the ground. She was not sad, however, and did not grumble at all when he reviled her and harmed her by pouring it out,[9] but was patient and accepted with praise [for God] all that happened to her.

[1] *Ḥənṣa mänäkosat* is a section of the *Haymanotä Abäw*, the most important expression of the Täwaḥədo Church creed during this period.

[2] BDJ: *i-təṣälləyu* (do not pray [neg. imper. pl.]); CR: *i-təṣelləyu* (you [pl.] will not pray).

[3] From Greek *haíresis* (heresy), which in Gəʿəz came to be understood to refer not to a false doctrine but to its adherents.

[4] A modern Ethiopian print edition of the *Haymanotä Abäw* gives this sentence as follows: *i-təṣälli məslä arsisan zä-wəʾətomu ʿalawəyan* (Do not pray [neg. imper. sg.] together with *arseesaan*, that is to say, heretics) (Anonymous 1994, chap. 20, sec. 3; p. 56, l. 17). In the *WP gädl*, by contrast, the text is: *i-təṣälləyu məslä arsisan zä-wəʾətomu mänafəqan* (Do not pray [neg. imper. pl.] with *arseesaan*, that is to say, heretics). In addition to the singular versus plural contrast in the imperative, both versions also differ with regard to the term they use for heretics, namely, *ʿalawəyan* versus *mänafəqan*. The first one has a strong connotation of rebellion, whereas the second one carries overtones of a lack of conviction.

[5] BDJ: *wä-bä-aʾban däqqaq* (and by small stones); CR: *wä-baʿədan däqiq* (and other small objects).

[6] BDJ: *däm* (blood); CR omits.

[7] *Yəmälləʾ lati*, which can be transitive or intransitive, and thus can also be translated as "he [i.e., God] filled [it] for her."

[8] Lit., *bati* (on her), a syntactic structure modeled on Amharic, the negative equivalent to more frequent *lati* (to her benefit), on which we had a note when this pattern first appeared. See also our explanation in "Translation Principles and Procedures."

[9] BDJ: *yəkəʿu bati* (lit., poured out to her detriment); CR: *yəkəʿu lati* (poured out for her benefit [*sic*]).

Chapter 15: Our Mother Preaches and Incurs the King's Wrath

While our holy mother Walatta Petros lived like this in that region[1] [of Tsiyaat], she
became animated by religious zeal and could not contain it. She exhorted the peo-
27 ple of the town not to accept the filthy faith of Leo[2] and not to mention the name
of the apostate king during the Liturgy since he was outside the true faith and accursed. As Paul says, "If an angel from above taught you something different from
that which we have taught you, let him be accursed."[3]

When King Susinyos heard about this talk, he became extremely angry and exceedingly furious. He roared like a lion and threatened Walatta Petros's brothers and [other] relatives. He proclaimed against them, "I call the sky and the earth as witnesses against you! I swear by my mighty kingdom[4] that I will punish you, that you will die a terrible death, and that I will purge your memory from the earth if you don't quickly bring in Walatta Petros. Behold, [with her words] she has stripped me of my kingship, rebelled against me, betrayed me, and insulted me as well as my faith. She has subverted the hearts of that town's people so that they don't accept my faith and don't mention my name in the Liturgy. Before, there was no enmity between you and me. From now on, though, I have a feud with you!"

When Walatta Petros's relatives heard the threats that the king spoke against them, they became very afraid and were shaken because that king was fierce. He did not show clemency to anyone; as he said he would do, he would do.

So, they sent her these words, "Behold, all of us will perish on account of you! None of us will be spared,[5] neither young nor old, because the king is angry indeed and has proclaimed against us and promised us death. He has said to us, 'Walatta Petros has stripped me of my kingship and rebelled against me. If you don't bring her in quickly, you will die a terrible death.' Now we say to you: Come quickly, don't tarry, and don't determine our death, because you are flesh from our flesh and bone from our bone: your mother and your brothers."[6]

When she heard this message, our holy mother Walatta Petros became very sad and took counsel with her companions. All of them together, unanimously,[7] said, "We prefer to go and die for our faith than that our relatives die on our account. Do

[1] BDJ: *bä-wəʾətu hagär* (in that region); CR: *bä-wəstä hagär* (in the region).

[2] *Ləyon.* Pope Leo I was a fifth-century head of the Roman Catholic Church. He wrote a theological treatise important to the Council of Chalcedon, which approved the doctrine of the dual nature of Christ. The Täwaḥədo Church rejected this council and saw Leo as emblematic of the heresy.

[3] Galatians 1:8.

[4] *Mängəśt* can mean "kingdom," "rule," or "kingship."

[5] BDJ: *i-yətärrəfʿa aḥaduʾa əmənnenäʾa* (lit., not one of us will be spared); CR: *i-nətärrəfʿa aḥadäʾa* [*sic*] *əmənnenäʾa* (we will not be spared, not one of us).

[6] BDJ: *əmməki wä-aḫawki* (your mother and your brothers); CR: *əmməki wä-aḫawki nəḥnä* (we are your mother and your brothers).

[7] Lit.: *bä-1 qal* (with one voice).

we not hope and wait for this [anyway]?[1] Our faith[2] is with us in our hearts; no one can rob us [of it]. As the Gospel says,[3] 'As for Mary, she has chosen the good part, which will not be taken away from her.' "[4]

Having said these things, they set out from there and returned [to her familial **28**
home]. [There] our holy mother Walatta Petros met with her mother and her brothers. They implored her, "Do not violate the word of the king, so that he will not kill you and us because of your rebelling."

What is more, her mother lifted her breasts and said to her, "Am I not your mother who nurtured you with these breasts of mine? Do you have no regard for me?"[5]

However, our holy mother Walatta Petros did not listen to their words and did not bend her mind to their advice. As the apostles say, "Is it right that we should listen to you and not to God? We prefer to please God than to please men."[6]

Chapter 16: Our Mother Appears Before King Susinyos

At that time, the king was in his castle. He ordered that her relatives bring her to him, so they took her in. She went hoping to die for the true faith. With her went her mother and her brothers: they followed her in tears, as if they were seeing her off to death, like a corpse that is taken away to be buried.

Our holy mother Walatta Petros did not lift her face and did not look at them, however, but rather said to them, "Why do you cry and break my heart? Why do you place an obstacle in my way? Do not cry for me but rather cry over yourselves. Truly, from now on nothing bothers me. Truly, I carry the suffering of Christ in my flesh.

" 'Who can make me abandon my love for Christ? Suffering? Tribulation? Exile, hunger, nakedness, the sword, anguish?'[7] As scripture says, 'Because of you, [Lord,] they will kill us every day.[8] We have become like sheep that will be slaughtered.'[9]

[1] BDJ: *akko-nu zäntä nəseffo wä-nəṣännəḥ* (do we not hope and wait for this?); CR with an emphatic construction: *akko-nu zäntä zä-nəseffo wä-nəṣännəḥ* (is it not this that we hope and wait for?).

[2] CR adds *nəḥnä* (we).

[3] BDJ: *bä-kämä yəbe* (lit., as it [or: He] says); CR: *bä-kämä yəbe əgziʾənä* (as our Lord says).

[4] Luke 10:42. This is not the Virgin Mary, the mother of Christ, but Mary of Bethany, the sister of Lazarus and Martha. She chose to sit at the feet of Jesus and listen to his words rather than assist her sister Martha in the domestic chores necessary to care for the guests. Jesus praised her choice.

[5] A mother lifting her breasts or pointing to them to remind a child of her sacrifices was a common gesture in Ethiopia.

[6] Acts 4:19–20; 1 Thessalonians 2:4.

[7] Romans 8:35. While one would expect "what" as the initial interrogative, the Greek original also has "who" (*tís*). In addition, for rhetorical effect, the Ethiopian author has changed the pronoun from "us" to "me" and the verb from "separate" to "abandon."

[8] BDJ: *ʿəlätä* (day); CR: *amirä* (day).

[9] Psalm 43[44]:22; Romans 8:36.

'I am confident, however, that nothing can make me abandon the love for God through Jesus Christ: neither death, nor life; neither angels,[1] nor nobles;[2] neither what is, nor what will come; neither someone powerful, nor anything above nor the abyss,'[3] not even being born again in hell.[4] There is nothing that can make me abandon the love of Christ. As for me, I will always be faithful and will never renege. Nobody whosoever can persuade my heart that I should renounce my faith, whether they frighten me with banishment to remote places, put me into the fire, throw me to the lions, drown me in the great lake, cut up my body and my limbs,
29 or punish me with each and every sort of torture.[5] Still, I will never renounce my
faith. Rather I am strong of heart through the word of our Lord Jesus Christ,[6] who says, 'Do not fear those who kill your flesh. Your soul nobody can kill. Rather, fear him who has permission, after having killed,[7] to put soul and body together into the fire of hell.' "[8]

Continuing [on her way], our holy mother Walatta Petros then arrived at the king's castle. The king ordered all the great lords, nobles, learned men, and judges to assemble, and they did as the king had commanded. They all assembled, richly adorned, in great magnificence, and sat down in a circle, according to their ranks and orders.[9] Then the king commanded that they bring in our holy mother Walatta Petros. She came and stood in front of them with a determined heart and a strong faith. She did not tremble[10] due to their magnificence, the great number of their assembly, or their empty talk. As David said, "Why are the gentiles in uproar, and why do the people make empty talk? The kings of the earth have risen up, and the rulers have conspired with them against God and against his Anointed One."[11]

[1] *Mäla'əkt* can also mean "captains" or "lords."

[2] *Qäddämt* can also mean "forefathers" or "ancestors."

[3] Romans 8:38–39. As in the earlier quote from Romans 8:35, the verb is changed from "separate" to "abandon."

[4] BDJ: *wä-i-dagəm lədät zä-mäthət* (lit., and not the second birth of below); Abb. 88: *wä-i-gädam səddät zä-mäthət* (and not the wilderness exile of below), which CR altered to *wä-i-gädam* [*wä-i-*]*səddät zä-mäthət* (and not the wilderness, and not exile of below).

[5] WP or the author may be thinking of the suffering of various martyrs in the *Sənkəssar*, but perhaps just the future events of WP's own life, since she was banished to a remote place, her guard attempted to burn her to death, her community was attacked by a lion, she almost drowned in Lake Ṭana, and her feet were cut by sharp stones.

[6] BDJ: *bä-qalä əgzi'ənä Iyäsus Krəstos* (through the word of our Lord Jesus Christ); CR: *bä-qalä əgzi'abḥer əgzi'ənä Iyäsus Krəstos* (through the Word of God, our Lord Jesus Christ).

[7] BDJ: *əm-dəḫrä qätälä* (lit., after he killed); CR: *əm-dəḫrä yəqättəl* (after he kills).

[8] Matthew 10:28.

[9] BDJ: *wä-näbäru ʿawdä bä-bä-mänabərtihomu wä-bä-bä-śərʿatomu* (and sat down in a circle, according to their ranks and orders); CR: *wä-näbäru ʿawdä mänabərtihomu wä-bä-bä-śərʿatomu* (and sat down in a circle of their chairs, according to their orders).

[10] BDJ: *wä-i-gäggäṣät* (she did not tremble); CR: *wä-i-dängäśät* (she was not terrified).

[11] Psalm 2:1–2. The author thus compares WP to Christ, the Anointed One.

Walatta Petros, by contrast, stood alone,[1] according to the procedure for a rebel against the king.[2] Then those charged with speaking for the king[3]—[while he stayed in another room]—said to her, "You have rebelled against the king, you have rebelled against God. You have resisted his order, you have transgressed against his word, and you have blasphemed against his faith.[4] You have subverted the hearts of the people of the land so that they don't accept his faith and don't mention his name in the Liturgy!"

However, our holy mother Walatta Petros did not respond or reply at all. Rather she listened with her head bowed and a critical smile, but humbly said, "I have not reviled the king. Rather, I will never renounce my faith."

On his part, the king regularly sent servants to inquire, "What does she say?"[5]

They told him, "She does not respond at all. Rather she keeps silent and expresses amusement."

Upon that, the king became enraged and said, "She despises me,[6] laughs at me, and mocks me," and ordered that she be killed or [at least] her breasts cut off.

At that point [Walatta Petros's husband] Malkiya Kristos stood up before the 30
king and said to him soothingly, "My lord, do not lose your temper. It is not due to contempt for you that she is laughing. Rather, an [evil] spirit that has been residing in her since her childhood makes her laugh."

With these words, Malkiya Kristos calmed the king's rage. Truly, Malkiya Kristos [still] loved Walatta Petros very much. As for our holy mother Walatta Petros, she did not fear death and was not terrified by the king's majesty.[7] As Peter says, "Do not fear that which strikes you with awe, and do not be terrified by it. Rather

[1] BDJ: *wä-yəʾəti-ssä təqäwwəm baḥtita* (lit., she by contrast stood alone); Abb. 88: *wä-yəḥtətəwwa* (let them interrogate her), which CR altered to *wä-yäḥattətəwwa* (they interrogated her).

[2] Other women underwent this type of court trial during this period. The Jesuit Pedro Páez excerpted and translated a section from Susənyos's royal chronicle about the court trial of Wälättä Giyorgis, the daughter of the former king Śärṣä Dəngəl (r. 1563–97), because she refused to convert to Catholicism (2011, 2:252).

[3] BDJ: *ʿaqabəyanä näbib zä-nəguś* (lit., the guardians of speech for the king); CR: *ʿaqabəyanä nəguś* (the officials of the king).

[4] At this point the multiple masc. possessive pronouns in the sentence are ambiguous. Whose order has WP allegedly resisted and against whose word has she allegedly transgressed: God's or the king's? Only subsequently does it become clear that the officials' reference is to the king. This ambiguity may be their way of ascribing almost divine authority to the king.

[5] BDJ: *məntä təbəl wä-məntä tawäśśəʾ* (lit., what does she say and respond); CR: *məntä tawäśśəʾ* (what does she respond). According to Ethiopian court protocol, the king would not have been present at the inquiry.

[6] BDJ, CR: *sobä tastäḥäqqəräni* (lit., when she despises me). But *sobä* (when) does not make sense here, so we do not consider it in our translation.

[7] Lit., *gərmahu* (his *or* its [namely, death's] majesty). Gəʿəz does not have a neuter in the third-person singular, therefore the masculine possessive suffix *-hu* could potentially also refer to nongendered death.

Plate 7. "How King Susinyos questioned her about her faith and looked at her in anger" and how "the great lords" watched her being questioned. It seems that her husband stands next to her, advising the king not to kill her (MS A, f. 147v © SLUB Mscr.Dresd.Eb.415.e,2).

Plate 8. Mural prepped for restoration at Réma Monastery Church of our mother confronting King Susinyos. Photo by Wendy Laura Belcher, January 2011.

sanctify God with all your heart."[1] So, Walatta Petros prayed,[2] "You who have strengthened the prophets, strengthen me! You who have strengthened the apostles, strengthen me! You who have strengthened the martyrs, strengthen me so that I die for the sake of your name and receive the crown of martyrdom."

The king's counselors then advised him, "Hear us, O King! It is better for you to abandon [the idea of] killing a woman than to have her entire lineage, [the house of] Dawaro and Fatagar, as your enemies."[3]

The king replied, "If she leaves me alone[4] and keeps quiet, leave her alone."

[1] 1 Peter 3:14–15.

[2] Lit., *təbəl* ([she] says).

[3] DJ: *aṣrarăkä* (as your enemies); CR: *aṣrarä* (as enemies); B illegible.

[4] Abb. 88 adds *zä-konä* (that which happened), which makes no sense in the context (thus already CR 30n2; nonetheless, he did not edit here). Obviously, it is a copying error due to *zä-konä* of the next sentence in Abb. 88/CR.

All of this happened, however,[1] because it did not please God for her to walk down this path [of martyrdom].[2] Rather, he had prepared another path for her, namely, the path of Anthony and Macarius,[3] just as the monk before her conception had said that she would guard his flocks. Truly, our Lord says, "My Father has many dwelling places."[4]

They let her go then, but told her, "Don't go to a faraway region, and don't teach again. Rather, stay with your family." So, her family took her and made her live with them.

Chapter 17: Our Mother Escapes *Ras* Silla Kristos

Then many theological teachers who were of the true faith came there. They found comfort in Walatta Petros's presence, and encouragement through each other.

Soon thereafter, she fled [again] and entered the monastic settlement of Zagé. With her were Walatta Pawlos, Eheta Kristos, and many others, as well as her maidservants Iyopraxia, Maryamaweet, and Eskindiraweet. *Abba* Tsigé Haymanot was also there with them. He used to comfort and encourage them.[5] They lived together in peace.

Then a wily man came there deceitfully, under the guise of a friend wanting to
31 visit them, just like that man who had visited *Abba* Babnooda.[6] They did not understand that he had come in bad faith, however, and offered him good food,[7] which he

[1] BDJ: *zə-ni konä* (lit., this however happened); CR: *zə-ni zä-konä* (this thing however which happened).

[2] The text frequently addresses the fact that WP was not a martyr. Such was not strictly required of a saint, but she sometimes struggled with this fate, as did Saint Paul himself in Phillipians 1:21–25, "For to me, to live is Christ and to die is gain. . . . But I am hard-pressed from both directions, having the desire to depart and be with Christ, for that is very much better; yet to remain on in the flesh is more necessary for your sake. Convinced of this, I know that I will remain and continue with you all for your progress."

[3] Name forms in DJ: *Ǝnṭonəyos, Mäqarəyos*; in CR: *Ǝnṭonəs, Mäqarəyos*; in B: *Ǝnṭos* [*sic*], *Mäqarəs*. These are two of the Desert Fathers, ascetics who lived in fourth-century Egypt and founded Christian monasticism. Saint Anthony is frequently invoked in Gəʿəz hagiobiographies, usually with his disciple, Saint Macarius.

[4] John 14:2.

[5] Gəʿəz distinguishes between masculine and feminine third-person plural object pronouns (English "them"). The Gəʿəz text here, as well as at the end of the preceding sentence, has the masculine form, which is also used for mixed-gender groups. The use of this form suggests that the monastic settlement of the Zäge Peninsula comprised both men and women.

[6] BDJ: *bä-kämä ḥawwäṣo lä-abba Bäbnuda* (lit., just as he had visited *Abba* Bäbnuda); Abb. 88: *lä-abba Ṣəge* (namely, *Abba* Ṣəge), which CR altered to *lä-abba Ṣəge* [*Haymanot*] (namely, *Abba* Ṣəge [Haymanot]). According to certain versions of the *Sənkəssar*, *Abba* Bäbnuda was a third-century Egyptian monk condemned by God to be devoured by a lion for sharing his "heavenly food" with a deceitful monk.

[7] CR adds *wä-ṭəḥnä* (and *təḥn*). *Təḥn* is an uncooked food made of mixing water with ground, roasted barley, good for travelers and soldiers.

ate. Then, he took a little of that food and wrapped it up in his clothes to take home and show to others. Now he left immediately.

When he came home, he took that food out of his clothes to show to his wife. However, while he held it in his hand, an angel of God snatched the food away from him. He was shocked and bewildered and therefore told his wife what he had done. She became irritated with him and said to him, "Why did you act like that and seek out [divine] punishment for yourself?"

Also, *Ras* Silla Kristos[1] sent one of his soldiers as a spy to investigate our holy mother Walatta Petros's situation [at Zagé]. The solider arrived and met with them. They gave him food to eat also, which he ate.[2] Now, imagine, that soldier was a son of Eheta Kristos's husband![3]

Then the soldier left[4] and reported back to Silla Kristos what he had seen and that he had eaten fine, delicious, and good-smelling food. He added, "My lord, you worry needlessly. Walatta Petros's situation is better than even yours!"[5]

When Silla Kristos heard this, he gnashed his teeth and longed to mount a surprise attack against them. At that time, he was at Dabra Entonyos.[6]

When our holy mother Walatta Petros heard about this, she hurriedly left [Zagé] and headed toward Abbabeet[7] in a tankwa. In that part of the lake, there were three large hippopotamuses.[8] One of them broke away [from the group] and, snorting, approached with the intention of overturning [their tankwa] and drowning them.

The boatmen as well as the sisters who were with Walatta Petros were afraid and exclaimed, "Let us throw ourselves overboard, of our own volition, so that this hippo will not drown us!"[9]

Our holy mother Walatta Petros, however, scolded them, "Do not be afraid, O you of little faith! What makes you fear? Do you think that you will never die?

[1] *Śəʿəlä Krəstos* (Image of Christ) was the Roman Catholic counselor of King Susənyos who persecuted WP for her beliefs and later was executed by Fasilädäs.

[2] BDJ: *wä-bälʿa* (lit., and he ate); CR omits.

[3] That is, a son by a woman other than Ǝḫətä Krəstos.

[4] BDJ: *wä-ḥorä* (lit., then he left); CR omits.

[5] BDJ: *əm-halləwotä ziʾakä-ssä* (lit., than your situation even); CR: *əm-halləwotä ziʾakä* (than your situation). This fact is noteworthy to the spy, and Śəʿəlä Krəstos subsequently becomes angry, because they expect monasteries to be poor and have little and bad food. The monks may have eaten simply, but have prepared good food for visitors. Before, the angel had snatched the food from the soldier to protect WP against such accusations.

[6] *Däbrä Ǝnṭonyos* must be a place near Zäge on southern Lake Ṭana. Since it can also mean "the monastery at Ǝnṭonyos," it most likely is Ǝnṭonəs, an island with a famous monastery (and once a convent) about three miles from Zäge.

[7] *Abbabit* is a town on the southwestern side of Lake Ṭana above the Zäge Peninsula.

[8] Hippopotamuses are common in Ethiopian lakes and rivers. Christians considered them unclean, according to Old Testament law, thus adding an extra element of terror to the incident.

[9] BDJ: *kämä i-yasṭəmänä* (lit., so that it does not drown us); Abb. 88: *kämä i-yasṭəmäni* (so that it does not drown me), which CR correctly edited to *kämä i-yasṭəmänä*.

Plate 9. "How she counted the hippo's teeth" on Lake Tana (MS A, f. 148r © SLUB Mscr.Dresd. Eb.415.e,2).

Whether you throw yourselves overboard or whether that hippopotamus overturns you, you will die one and the same death. Take heart and don't be afraid."[1]

When fear completely gripped them, however, Walatta Petros covered them
with her *atsf* vestment[2] while she prayed in her heart the *Salama Malaak.*[3] Meanwhile, that hippopotamus came ever closer, [eventually] setting its [front] feet on
the tankwa and yawning open its mouth. Our holy mother Walatta Petros, how- 32
ever, was not afraid at all but counted its teeth: their number was nine.

After the hippopotamus had hung on for a while, it pulled down[4] its feet and turned back, fleeing as though someone was following and chasing it from behind, until it disappeared from view. It did not reunite with its companions; it remained unknown where it went.[5]

Do you see, my loved ones, what wonders God worked for our holy mother Walatta Petros because of the strength of her faith? As scripture[6] says, "God works wonders for his saints."[7] And, "Blessed is the man who puts his trust in the name of God."[8]

On that day, Walatta Petros emerged from the lake safe and sound and reached the place she wanted, [Abbabeet]. [There] she remained for a few days and then returned to Zagé.

[1] Matthew 14:22–31; Mark 6:45–50; John 6:16–21. The scene is reminiscent of Jesus calming the fearful disciples (whom he also accuses of having too little faith) when a strong storm begins to shake the little vessel on which they try to cross the Sea of Galilee.

[2] *ʿAṣf* is a yellowish, knee-length leather tunic of fine and durable quality worn by nuns and monks or students of traditional (religious) schools.

[3] *Sälamä Mälʾak* (Hail of the Angel) is a prayer that WP prays in situations of extreme physical distress on Lake Ṭana. It may be the *Hail Mary* or *Ave Maria,* based on the words in Luke 1:28 with which the Archangel Gabriel praised the Virgin Mary when telling her that she would give birth to the savior. Or it may be from the *Arganonä Maryam* (Lyre of [Saint] Mary; it is also known as the *Arganonä Wəddase* [Lyre of Praise]), one of the great works of original Gəʿəz literature, which praises Mary. Relevant passages that suggest it may be in use here include "the ark that is not shaken by a wave of flood" and "I have found thee a refuge from" many beasts, including lions, wolves, and panthers, and that "the flooding of the rivers cannot overwhelm him [who prays to Mary], and the violence of the winds cannot cast him down." Perhaps completely silent prayer was still unusual in WP's time since the text specifies that she prayed silently.

[4] BDJ: *awrädä* (lit., it took down); Abb. 88 omits; CR inserted *anśəʾa* (it removed).

[5] The *Gädlä Yafqərännä Əgziʾ*, about a male Lake Ṭana saint, also recounts a frightening encounter with a hippopotamus, but that saint escapes in miraculous fashion by walking on his coat. The *Gädlä Mäbaʾa Ṣəyon* also includes an inserted story about the miraculous saving of a Rema monk from a hippopotamus. See Störk and Pankhurst (2007).

[6] B: *mäṣḥaf* (scripture); DJ, CR omit.

[7] See Psalm 65[66]:5; Psalm 76[77]:14; Psalm 39[40]:5.

[8] Jeremiah 17:7; Psalm 39[40]:5; Psalm 83[84]:12.

Chapter 18: Our Mother Moves from the Zagé Monastic Settlement to a Waldeba Monastery

Then, when the European soldiers searching and lying in wait for her became many, our holy mother Walatta Petros fled from Zagé together with the sisters she was in charge of; she wanted to go to Waldeba.[1] She left *Abba* Tsigé Haymanot behind, hiding her secret plan from him. She did not reveal it to him so that he would not stand in her way nor prevent her from going.

Later though, when he found out [that she had left], he followed her and tracked her, asking around and inquiring about where she had gone. Eventually he found her on the road and took a stand against her to prevent her from going; he entreated and condemned her. She did not obey him, however. She did not accept his words but instead continued on her way. Nevertheless, he did not stop following her.

So, our holy mother Walatta Petros said to him, with words of reprimand, "Why won't you return home?[2] What business do you have with me, and what do you want from me? Have you not heard what the book says,[3] 'First of all, righteous men and monks should stay away[4] from women'?"[5]

When she said this to him, he was pained in his heart, but also angry. So, he left her and returned home.

As for our holy mother Walatta Petros, she kept on walking, ever so slowly, on her delicate feet, ascending steep passes and descending steep slopes, [sometimes] crawling like children do, with blood flowing from her delicate feet. They were all numb from walking on rough and rugged roads. When she was no longer able to walk, she wrapped her feet in pieces of cloth.

33 Progressing in this manner, around the sixth hour [i.e., at noon], she arrived at a place[6] where there was no water. She rested in the shade of a tree and wanted to stay there. [Meanwhile], the disciples who were with her were looking for water but did not find any. So they became agitated and desperate and said to our holy mother Walatta Petros, "Let us leave this place so that we do not perish from thirst!"

[1] *Waldəbba* is a historical region more than 150 miles north of Lake Ṭana in a rugged lowland area. It is famous for its three monasteries and the extreme asceticism of its monks. During this period, it was a hotbed of anti-Catholic sentiment and especially popular with women seeking to take up the religious life.

[2] BDJ: *i-təgäbbəʾ-nu bəḥeräkä* (lit., will you not return to your region); CR with a statement instead of a question: *i-təgäbbəʾ bəḥeräkä* (you will not return to your region).

[3] This may be from one of the three constituent parts, or books, of the *Mäṣaḥəftä Mänäkosat* (Books of the Monks), which gives rules for living as a monk or nun, including warnings that monks should avoid women. Or it might be from *Fətḥa Nägäśt*, Ethiopia's book of law, which gives similar warnings. The reference is definitely not to the Bible, which predates monasticism and monks.

[4] BDJ: *yərḥaqu* (should stay away); CR: *yərəḥəqu* (will stay away).

[5] According to the Jesuits, priests could have ulterior motives for befriending women. Barradas claimed that the priests "began to fall into debauchery, particularly with the women of the noblemen when the latter went to war" (1996, 140). Mendes claimed that Susənyos chastised the women for taking the part of the priests and "bearing their children" (1908, 302).

[6] BDJ: *ḫabä mäkan* (at a place); CR omits.

Plate 10. "How she [made spring forth] water while on her way to the wilderness of Waldeba" (MS A, f. 148v © SLUB Mscr.Dresd.Eb.415.e,2).

She, however, replied, "O you of little faith! Why are you agitated and desperate?" Then she turned her head and pointed with her fingers, "I say to you, 'Go and search over there, and water will not be found wanting.' "

Having gone to that nearby place she had pointed out to them, her disciples found [a spring of] clear water that was surrounded by high cacti[1] on all sides. They drank from that water and were happy. Through the prayers of our holy mother Walatta Petros, the water had gushed out at a place where none had been before.

Then Walatta Petros entered Waldeba. There she lived, dedicating herself devotedly to the service of God with fasts and prayers, while strenuously exerting herself spiritually and through many virtuous deeds, through toil and labor. As scripture says, "He who has toiled in this world will live forever. Truly, he will not see decay."[2]

Chapter 19: Our Mother Assists the Wicked Old Woman

Meanwhile, an extremely ill-tempered old woman [also] lived there: she would constantly be angry. No one could bear her wicked character. She did not express thanks when the sisters attended to her and never blessed them when they worked [for her]. They could never satisfy her. Rather, she insulted and reviled them. So all the sisters of the monastic settlement kept away from her, and she lived alone in great misery. None of the sisters would [go to] see her.

When our holy mother Walatta Petros then saw the old woman's entire disposition and all the misery she suffered, she girded herself with the belt of faith, wrapped herself in the cloth of humility, and began to serve her like a maidservant, with a determined heart. She became the old woman's helper and placed herself under her feet: she ground flour, baked bread, and drew water. When she lacked grain, she went gleaning, returning with it to sustain the old woman. She fulfilled the old woman's every wish.

The old woman showed no gratitude for Walatta Petros's work, however, but rather was [always] angry, reviling[3] and insulting her, "You, girl, are a thief! Although you outwardly pose as a righteous woman,[4] inside you are a wicked serpent."

When Walatta Petros baked bread, she would use her hands,[5] burning them on
34 the red-hot, flaming oven[6] until they peeled. Then the old woman would reprimand

[1] *Qʷəlqʷas* (Amharic: *qʷəlqʷal*) is a treelike cactus endemic to the Horn of Africa. Its scientific name is *Euphorbia candelabrum*, due to its distinctive upright branches.

[2] Psalm 48[49]:8–9. The author seems to have altered the verse for rhetorical purposes.

[3] BDJ: *wä-təṣärrəf laʿleha* (lit., and reviled her); CR omits.

[4] BDJ: *wä-tətmessäli ṣadəqtä bä-afʿa* (although you outwardly pose as a righteous woman); CR: *wä-təmessəli ṣadəqtä bä-afʿa* (although you outwardly imitate a righteous woman).

[5] BDJ: *təʾəḫəz ədeha* (lit., she takes her hand); CR: *təʾəḫəz bä-ədäwiha* (she takes [the bread] with her hands).

[6] BDJ: *bä-ətonä əssat zä-räsnä* (lit., in the red-hot oven of fire); CR: *bä-ətonä aṣḥərt zä-räsnä* (in the red-hot oven pit).

her, "How did your mother raise you? How did she teach you and train you in this terrible way of doing things?"

Every day, the old woman would speak many insulting and derisive words like this against Walatta Petros. Our holy mother would not be distressed, however, and would not grumble because of all this, but would bear it happily and patiently, emulating John the Short.[1]

When Eheta Kristos one day overheard the old woman heaping insults on Walatta Petros, she wept copiously and said to Walatta Petros, "What is your business with this old woman so that you serve her even though she abuses and insults you? Is there no other work than this that pleases God?"

Our holy mother Walatta Petros replied, "Don't weep on my behalf. [All] that abuse does not come[2] from her but from Satan. As for me, it does not distress me. Rather, I consider it[3] a benefit and a blessing. Truly, the Gospel says, 'Woe are you when[4] people say[5] nice things about you'[6] and praise you."

Then, when Walatta Petros had completed a year serving her, the old woman passed away. Our holy mother Walatta Petros shrouded her [corpse] with her own hands and buried her.

See then, my loved ones, the extraordinary gifts Walatta Petros had been given! O what humility! O what goodness! O what patience! Being a noblewoman, of her own free will[7] she made herself into a servant of one who was inferior to her and[8] reviled her, so as to attain[9] through her the crown of the long-suffering martyrs. Truly, he who loves the [stinging] bee will taste the honey. Conversely, he who does not love her and flees from her will not taste the honey.

Likewise, our holy mother Walatta Petros loved this old woman and subjected herself to her, because by virtue of her she could taste the sweetness of the Kingdom of Heaven. Moreover, if she had not subjugated herself to this old woman,[10] the kings and great lords [later] would not have submitted to her, and the demons[11] would not have conceded defeat before her.

[1] *Yoḥannəs Ḫaṣir* was an Egyptian Coptic saint, much venerated in the Täwaḥədo Church, who was treated abusively by his mentor, a strong old man named *Abba* Bamoy, which aided him greatly on his way to sainthood.

[2] BDJ: *akko zä-ziʾaha* (lit., [is] *not* [emph.] of her); CR: *i-konä zä-ziʾaha* (is not of her).

[3] BDJ: *əḫʷelləqo* (lit., I count it); CR: *əḫʷelləqomu* (I count them).

[4] D: *sobä* (when); BJ: *əsmä* (because); CR omits.

[5] BDJ, Abb. 88: *yəbəl* (lit., says), the subject "people" (*säbʾ*) is thus treated as a singular according to the rules of Gəʿəz grammar; CR altered to *yəbəlu* (say [3rd-ps. pl.]).

[6] Luke 6:26.

[7] DJ: *bä-fäqada* (of her own free will); Abb. 88: *wä-fäqäda* (and he cared for her), which CR altered to *wä-fäqädäta* (and she cared for her); B illegible.

[8] DJ: *wä-əntä* (lit., and who); CR: *wä-lä-əmmä* (even though); B illegible.

[9] BDJ: *kämä tərkäb* (so as to attain [subj.]); Abb. 88: *kämä təräkkəb* (*sic*: ind.), which CR left unedited, but marked with "*sic*."

[10] BD: *lä-zati arägit* (to this old woman); CR, J: *lä-arägit* (to the old woman).

[11] Lit., *säyṭanat* (devils). The ordinary term for demons is *aganənt*, connected with Arabic *ǧinn* and Latin *genius*, but throughout we translate *säyṭan* and *säyṭanat* as "demon" and "demons," unless it is clear the text means the fallen angel Satan.

As the Spiritual Elder[1] says, "If Joseph had not first subjected himself to slavery,[2]
he would not have become lord over the land of Egypt."[3] Also, Paul says, "Working
35 in the flesh brings benefit for a short time, but righteousness[4] gives power in every-
thing, and in it lies hope for life in this world and in the one to come."[5] Woe and doubly woe are we who do not act likewise and do not subjugate ourselves. Let alone those who abuse and curse us, not even those who praise and bless us do we serve properly. Even though we are in good health we say that we are sick [to avoid serving], and even though we have strength we say that we are weak, and we make many excuses.

Chapter 20: Our Mother Receives Food and a Message from Her Mother

Listen up:[6] We again want to tell you the story of our holy mother Walatta Petros, how for six months she lived in that monastic settlement [in Waldeba] sustaining herself on green leaves [only], together with Eheta Kristos and with all the women who were with her, until their teeth changed from being white[7] to resembling those greens.

One day, when our holy mother[8] Walatta Petros saw Eheta Kristos's teeth, she asked her, "My sister, what has happened to your teeth?"

Eheta Kristos retorted, "The same as to yours!"

[1] *Arägawi Mänfäsawi* (Spiritual Elder) is John Saba, a Christian ascetic from eighth-century Syria whose writings were translated into Gəʿəz in the early sixteenth century. He wrote more than two dozen homilies and more than fifty letters, which are included in the eponymous book that is one of the three parts of the *Mäṣaḥəftä Mänäkosat* (Books of the Monks).

[2] BDJ: *gəbrənnat* (slavery); CR: *gəbrat* (works).

[3] This quote is from *Arägawi Mänfäsawi*, which provides commentary on Genesis chapters 37–50.

[4] BDJ: *wä-ṣədqə-ssä* (but righteousness); CR: *wä-taṣäddəq* (and confers righteousness *or* and confirms).

[5] BJ: *wä-bati täsfa ḥəywät bä-zə-ʿaläm wä-bä-zä-yəmäṣṣəʾ* (and in it lies hope for life in this world and in the one to come); D: *bä-zə-ʿaläm wä-bä-zä-yəmäṣṣəʾ* (in this world and in the one to come); CR: *wä-bati täsfa ḥəywät bä-zə-mäwaʿəl* (and in it lies hope for life in these [earthly] days). 1 Timothy 4:8. This is one of the biblical passages from which the word for hagiobiography, *gädl* (spiritual struggle), was taken.

[6] These calls by the author for the audience to "listen" may mark where, traditionally, a priest would begin again to read aloud after a break.

[7] BDJ: *əskä täwälläṭä asnanihon əm-ṣəʿdawehu* (lit., until their teeth changed from whiteness); CR: *əsmä täwälläṭä asnaniha əm-ṣəʿdawihon* [*sic*] (truly, her teeth changed from their whiteness).

[8] DJ: *əmmənä qəddəst* (our holy mother); B: *əmmənä qəddəst wä-burəkt* (our holy and blessed mother); CR omits.

As scripture says, "They lived in misery and hardship and suffering. They experienced what one should never experience and roamed the mountains, the wildernesses, caves, and pits of the earth."[1]

Then Walatta Petros's mother Kristos Ebayaa dispatched [to them] many donkeys loaded with flour and every sort of necessary provision. The dispatched servants arrived at Waldeba, and all the sisters were happy when they saw this because they had gone hungry[2] for a period of six months; it appeared to them that now they would eat. They told our holy mother Walatta Petros [about the food].

Upon hearing [this], however, she became very sad and said, "What have I done to anger God so that he has brought upon me that which I have run away from?"

The sisters said to her, "We are happy and eager to eat. Why are you distressed?"[3]

She replied, "Me? I am distressed because it looks to me like something that Satan has brought upon us to tempt us because he is deceitful. He tempted our Lord likewise, as the Gospel reports, 'He fasted forty days and forty nights. Then he was hungry, and the Tempter approached him.'[4] He wants to put us to the test[5] as well with this temptation."

The sisters then said to her, "Shall the dispatched servants come and tell you the message they bring?"

Our holy mother Walatta Petros replied, "No, today they shall spend the night
outside [our compound]. For dinner, they can eat from the flour they have brought. 36
[Today] I will not listen to their message nor receive anyone of them."

So, the servants spent the night outside; they kept on waiting for three days. As for Walatta Petros, she locked her hut and kept praying to God that he reveal to her the reason for their coming. God answered her prayers, and she understood that their coming was God's will because he is compassionate toward the afflicted and the hungry. As we have already mentioned before, when Samson was hungry he prayed to God, obtained honey from the mouth of a lion, and ate it.[6] God furthermore fed Elijah through the beak of a raven,[7] and, when they had thrown Daniel into a pit, God sent Habakkuk with bread to Daniel because hunger tormented him.[8]

[1] Hebrews 11:37–38. Note the difference of the Gəʿəz from the original Greek: *zä-i-yədälləwo lä-ʿaläm räkäbu* (lit., that which it is not appropriate ever [or: for the world] they found).

[2] BDJ: *rəḫubat* [fem. pl.]; CR: *rəḫuban* [masc. pl.].

[3] BDJ: *ənbäynä mənt-nu täḥazzəni anti* (lit., why are *you* [emph.] distressed); CR: *ənbäynä mənt-nu täḥazzəni* (why are you distressed).

[4] Matthew 4:2–3.

[5] BDJ: *fäqädä yamäkkəränä* (he wants to put us to the test [subj.]); CR: *fäqäda yamekkəränä* [*sic*: ind.].

[6] Judges 14:5–9.

[7] 1 Kings 17:4. Elijah was a Jewish prophet of the Old Testament who preached against foreign idols. To escape persecution, Elijah fled into the wilderness, where God kept him alive by commanding ravens to feed him.

[8] Daniel 14:31–42. While the Protestant (Masoretic) book of Daniel stops at chapter 12, the Orthodox and Catholic (Septuagint) version has two extra chapters. Daniel is a young

Therefore, on the third day,[1] our holy mother Walatta Petros said to Eheta Kristos, "Summon the dispatched servants and accept the provisions they have brought." Eheta Kristos went and summoned them.

They entered [the compound] and told Walatta Petros the following message from her mother, "Come immediately because I long to see you! Also, I have something that I want to talk with you face to face about.[2] What makes you so stubborn?[3] Am I not your mother who carried you in my womb and who nurtured you with my breasts? Do I happen to have another daughter than you, either older or younger than you? May the peace of God be with us, amen!"[4]

After having listened, our holy mother Walatta Petros remained silent and did not respond to them. The sisters then urged her, "Give them a return message so they can go home."

So she replied to the dispatched servants, "Say the following to my mother, 'It would not be right for me to abandon the monastic settlement and return to the world, which I left. Rather, it would be right for you to follow[5] your daughter to where she has gone.' " With these words she dispatched the messengers, and they returned home.

Eheta Kristos then asked her, "How come you at first refused[6] [the sent food], and why did you later accept it?"

Our holy mother Walatta Petros replied, "I first refused it because it seemed to me that it came from Satan. Later, however, I accepted it since I understood that it had come by the will of God."

So then, understand and comprehend, my loved ones! For whom would it be possible to show such endurance while being hungry, after not having tasted any
37 [proper] food for six months? Which hungry person would not be eager to eat when seeing food? Leave aside someone whose mother sent [provisions] to him: I believe any hungry person would have gone even to strangers in order to beg or steal.[7] Our holy mother Walatta Petros, however, was capable [of rejecting food]

Jewish nobleman of the Old Testament who remains faithful in foreign lands and about whom many stories are told. One of these is that an angry Persian king threw him into the lion's den, where he was not eaten. Indeed, he was there long enough that, according to the Apocrypha, he became hungry and an angel magically transported the prophet Habakkuk from Israel to Babylon to feed Daniel.

[1] BDJ: *bä-śaləst ʿəlät* (on the third day); CR omits *ʿəlät* (day).

[2] Lit., *afä bä-af* (mouth to mouth).

[3] BDJ, CR: *mənt-nu yaṣännəʿaki* (lit., what makes you strong). Conti Rossini hypothesized this might result from corruption of the original *mənt-nu yaṣännəḥaki* (what makes you wait).

[4] This conclusion has the formality of a written letter, even though it appears to be oral.

[5] BDJ: *dəlwät-əssä läki tətləwi* (rather, it would be right for you to follow [subj.]); CR: *dəlwät-əssä läki tətälləwi* [*sic*: ind.].

[6] BDJ: *mənt-nu zä-abäyki qädimu* (lit., why did you first refuse); CR: *mənt-nu* [*sic*] *abäyki qädimu* (what did you first refuse).

[7] The wording here is condensed. The author Gälawdewos's idea seems to be the following: Any normal person suffering from severe hunger (of whom many contemporary readers and listeners would count themselves) will easily discard moral rules. Against this back-

through the power of God. As Paul says, "I can master[1] everything, destitution as well as luxury. I am accustomed to everything:[2] to hunger as well as to abundance, to suffering[3] as well as to joy. I can master everything because God has enabled me to do this."[4]

Chapter 21: A Righteous Monk Predicts Our Mother Will Found Communities

In that monastic settlement [of Waldeba], there lived a righteous monk whose name was Malkiya Kristos.[5] When he realized that the time of his passing away was near, he came to our holy mother Walatta Petros to tell her the day of his death and to take his leave of her. Truly, he knew what was hidden and what would happen before it happened.

As soon as he had informed her about the day of his death, our holy mother Walatta Petros became very distressed and said in her heart, "I wish God would let me die before this righteous man. How can he die [and not me]?" This thought was not right before God, however. Therefore, she immediately began to suffer a piercing pain[6] and almost died, just like Hezekiah had suffered and said, "Like a pelican I croak and like a dove I speak."[7]

The monk was aware of what went through Walatta Petros's mind and reprimanded her, "Why do you desire death and oppose God's judgment? Truly, it is he who multiplies or diminishes a person's time [on earth]. It is he who dispenses death and life[8] according to his will; it does not happen due to human will. This is why such strong suffering has befallen you: in order to test you. However, you will not die. From now on, do not think such a thought again.

"Listen up, I will tell you the word that God has put into my mouth, 'Through your stewardship, communities will be formed seven times in seven places, and

---

ground, it is all the more astounding that WP could dominate her natural impulse to eat, especially acceptable food sent to her by her mother.

[1] BDJ: *kähali anə-ssä* (lit., as for me, I am capable); CR: *kəhilä anə-ssä* (as for me, I the capability [acc.] [*sic*]).

[2] BDJ: *wä-wəstä kʷəllu lämädku* (I am accustomed to everything); CR: *wä-wəʾətä lämädku* (and to that I am accustomed).

[3] BDJ: *ḥamimä-hi* (to suffering); CR omits.

[4] BDJ: *bä-zä-wəʾətu akhaläni əgziʾabḥer* (lit., through the fact that God has enabled me); CR omits *zä-*: *bä-wəʾətu akhaläni əgziʾabḥer* (God has empowered me with that). Philippians 4:12–13, although the quote here would seem to be more of a paraphrase.

[5] *Mälkəʾa Krəstos* (Image of Christ). This monk has the same name as WP's husband and plays a powerful role in her life.

[6] Lit., *ḥəmamä wəgʿat* (suffering of piercing).

[7] Isaiah 38:[1–]14. In the Old Testament, this righteous king of Judah fell ill and was close to dying, but when he repented of his sins and prayed to God for healing, it was granted. Upon his recovery, he composed a poem. See also 2 Kings 20:1; 2 Chronicles 32:24; Psalm 101[102]:6.

[8] BDJ: *yaḥayyu* (dispenses . . . life); CR: *yäḥayyu* (lives).

many souls will be saved through you. The first community will be that of Zhebey,
the second that of Chanqwa, the third that of Mitsillé,[1] the fourth that of Zagé
(whose members will be killed by an epidemic),[2] the fifth that of Damboza, the sixth
that of Afer Faras, and the seventh that of Zambowl.[3] [Only] after that will be your
death.' And I further tell you: Constantly read the Gospel of John,[4] since I have had
38 a true vision that he who constantly reads it[5] will be greatly honored.[6] For him,[7] a
canopy of light will be erected above him, and an ornamented golden throne[8] covered with carpets will be placed below him for his sake. That's why I tell you: Read
this gospel all the days of your life!"[9]

After the monk had told Walatta Petros these and other similar things from among the secrets of God, he took his leave of her. He returned to his cell, parted from this world, and went to God who loved him.[10] May his prayers and blessing forever be with us,[11] amen.

Chapter 22: Our Mother Commands the Animals

It was customary for the monks of Waldeba to hold *mihillaa* supplications:[12] they would beseech [the Lord in prayer] from the second until the eighth of the month

[1] BDJ: *Məṣəlle*; CR: *Məṣraḥ*.

[2] BDJ: *əllä qätälomu bədbəd* (lit., those whom an epidemic will have killed); CR: *ḫabä qätälomu bədbəd* (where an epidemic will have killed them).

[3] BDJ: *Zämbol*; CR: *Zäbol*.

[4] BDJ: *anbəbi wäträ wängelä zä-Yoḥannəs* (constantly read the Gospel of John); CR: *anbəbi wängelä Yoḥannəs* (read the Gospel of John).

[5] BDJ: *zä-yanäbbəb kiyahu wäträ* (he who constantly reads it); CR: *zä-yanäbbəb kämahu wäträ* (he who constantly reads likewise).

[6] In general, the reading of the Gospel of John is favored by Ḥabäša monks and is a feature of monastic life. According to Denis Nosnitsin, it was the only Gospel copied separately in pocket format, which indicates that it was often used for private devotion and meditation, not just in church services. Some priests say Christ's words come through most clearly in this Gospel. It is also the Gospel in which WP's namesake, Saint Peter, is mentioned most. However, now, Täwaḥədo Church nuns are not allowed to touch this Gospel (Wright 2001, 67).

[7] BDJ: *lotu* (for him); CR omits.

[8] BDJ: *ʿarat* (throne); CR omits.

[9] D: *anbəbi kʷəllo mäwaʿəlä ḥəywätəki zäntä wängelä* (read this Gospel all the days of your life); BJ, CR: *zäntä anbəbi kʷəllo mäwaʿəlä ḥəywätəki* (read this all the days of your life).

[10] *Zä-afqäro* can also mean, because Gəʿəz relative particles are case-neutral, "to God whom he loved."

[11] CR: *məslenä* (with us); B: *məslä fəquru Agnaṭəyos* (with his beloved Ignatius); D: *məslä fəquru nəguśənä Dawit* (with his beloved, our king David); J: *məslä fəqərtu Amätä Dəngəl* (with his beloved [fem.] Amätä Dəngəl).

[12] *Məḥəlla* is a day of entreaty held on ten fixed dates throughout the year, but they are also held as the need arises, when priests pray intensely for guidance on a particular matter, such as the election of a patriarch, to end a drought, or to gain victory in war. Since this is Waldəbba, where most practices are done more intensely, it seems this supplication lasted

of Hamlé.[1] Thereafter they would receive blessings from the elders [among them], take leave of each other, and [again] go about their occupations in order to gain their daily bread. For that period, our holy mother Walatta Petros withdrew and separated herself from the sisters who were with her. She stayed near the monks' place in order to listen to the recitation of their supplications—without constructing a shelter for herself against either the rain or the sun until those months[2] were completed, keeping vigil all night and day, all alone.

There was one disciple named Takla Maryam[3] who looked after her, ministered to her, and brought her *qwarf* roots[4] as her food. Now he is the one about whom it has been said that[5] he once found a large serpent in the shelter where he slept. When he saw it, he was terrified and afraid, and trembling went to our holy mother Walatta Petros.

When she saw him, she knew what was on his mind [before he had spoken]. She said to him, "What scares you? Go and lie down on top of the serpent. If it is God's will, it will be given power over you[6] and you will not escape it. However, if it is not God's will, nothing will hurt you."

Obediently, he turned back, strew grass on the serpent, and lay down there. At the time, the serpent was underneath [him], but did not attack him.

---

for much longer than a day. In just such ways did the monks of Waldəbba, inspired by the example of the Ethiopian saint *Abba* Samuʾel, differentiate themselves from other monks of the Täwaḥədo Church.

[1] BJ: *əm-2 lä-wärḫa ḥamle əskä 8 lä-wärḫa ḥamle* (lit., from the second of the month of Ḥamle to the eighth of the month of Ḥamle); D: *əm-2 lä-wärḫa ḥamle əskä 8 lä-wärḫa ṭəqəmt* (lit., from the second of the month of Ḥamle to the eighth of the month of Ṭəqəmt), with *ṭəqəmt* having been filled in for an erased earlier name; CR: *əm-2 lä-wärḫa ḥamle əskä 8 lä-wärḫa ḫədar* (lit., from the second of the month of Ḥamle to the eighth of the month of Ḫədar). That is, BJ have that the supplication lasts for six days, from 10 to 16 July; D has that it lasts for more than three months, from 10 July to 19 October; CR has that it lasts for more than four months, from 10 July to 18 November. This divergence among the manuscripts is very unusual. Perhaps this progression to ever-increasingly longer periods of time from the earliest to the later manuscripts reflects a natural process of exaggerating how long the holy saints of Waldəbba spent in arduous prayer. Or perhaps later scribes are trying to align the text with the comment two sentences later that WP spent "months" listening to the supplications. Regardless of length, all these periods fell during the rainy season, *kərämt*, which normally begins in mid-June and lasts to mid- or late September.

[2] Above, it said the supplication lasted one week, but here it suggests it lasted months. This may be a reference to her staying outside during the entire cold and rainy season of *kərämt*.

[3] *Täklä Maryam* (Plant of [the Virgin] Mary). This was a faithful male disciple of WP's who followed her into the wilderness, witnessed her kidan, and was saved from a serpent.

[4] *Qʷarf* is a dish of bitter roots eaten by monks and nuns at Waldəbba only. Eating grains such as wheat, barley, or corn is forbidden in Waldəbba, and qʷarf is a sign of the extreme asceticism of the place.

[5] BDJ: *kämä* (that); CR: *amä* (when).

[6] BDJ: *yətbäwwaḥ laʿlekä* (it will be given power over you); Abb. 88 *i-täbäwḥa laʿlekä* (it has not been given power over you), which CR altered to *täbäwḥo* [*sic*] *laʿlekä* (to it has been given power over you).

Plate 11. "How she kept the snake in check while she was in the wilderness with the wild animals" (top) and how Christ appeared to her while she was there in the wilderness of Waldeba (bottom) (MS A, f. 149r © SLUB Mscr.Dresd.Eb.415.e,2).

While our holy mother Walatta Petros lived in [wilderness] seclusion, two wild animals of different species, a stag and an antelope, used to guard her [at night], one at her head and the other at her feet. Each morning that disciple Takla Maryam would come and find their tracks in the places where each of them had slept. **39**

Chapter 23: Our Mother Debates with Jesus Christ and Receives His Promise

On one day during that period, while our holy mother Walatta Petros was praying with her arms stretched out,[1] our Lord Jesus Christ—he be praised—came to her and greeted her, "Peace be with you."

He then took her hands in his and said to her, "You have no role in this monastic settlement [of Waldeba], which is why you stay by yourself. Instead, you will leave it, and then many people will gather around you, from east and west. They will be pure doves, and they will benefit [from you] for the salvation of their souls. Not a single soul among them will be lost."

Our holy mother Walatta Petros replied, "How will this be possible for me [to do]?[2] How will I be able to save others, I who cannot save myself? Am I not mud, and a pit of filthy sludge?"[3]

Our Lord responded, "Even mud, when it is mixed with straw, becomes strong and enduring and can hold grain.[4] You, too, I will make likewise strong."

Walatta Petros did not accept our Lord's words, however, and did not believe what he said. So, he now made pure white doves come to her and descend all over her. They surrounded her completely, from her head to her feet. Some [even] entered into her tunic while others wanted to alight on her head,[5] but she turned them away with her hands and collected them into her lap. He then said to her, "They are the ones whom I entrust to you so that you will take care of them."

Our holy mother Walatta Petros replied, "But I cannot take care of them! They will fly away and escape me." When she opposed him [like this], he left her and ascended into heaven.

However, our Lord came again the next day and spoke to Walatta Petros in the same way, and she too replied to him as before. Then, in a golden basket, he brought shining glass and crystal vessels[6] and said to her, "These are chosen vessels, which

[1] WP's likely praying posture may have been standing, facing east, with her arms raised; kneeling and bowing with her forehead to the ground and her arms stretched out in front of her; or bending at the waist until the tips of her extended hands touched the ground (which the subjects of feudal lords did).

[2] BDJ: *əfo yəkäwwənäni zəntu* (how will this be possible for me); CR omits.

[3] BDJ: *wä-ʿazäqtä ʿamʿam ṣəyyəʾt* (and a pit of filthy sludge); CR omits.

[4] Christ's poignant response is an allusion to adobe, the straw and mud building material of the granaries in which life-giving grain is stored and protected.

[5] CR: *laʿlä rəʾsa* (on her head); BDJ omit.

[6] Lit., *maḫwatä wä-birälleyatä ṣəʿdəwatä* (white glass and crystal vessels). To understand the flask shape of these vessels, see the illustration of WP receiving them from Christ in plate 13.

Plate 12. "How he [i.e., Christ] gave her souls in the likeness of doves" (top) and "how he gave her souls in the likeness of crystal vessels" (bottom) (MS A, f. 149v © SLUB Mscr.Dresd.Eb.415.e,2).

Plate 13. How our mother received her kidaan from Christ. The two figures prostrated below may be two of the three community members upon whom blessings are called in MS J: the abbot Za-Hawaryaat, the author Galawdeos, and the abbess Amata Dinghil (MS J, photo 120).

I hereby entrust to you to take care of on my behalf until I request them back from you and take them back to me."

She replied, "I cannot take care of them: they will break, and I will be held responsible!"[1]

Our Lord responded, "Not even one of them will perish, because I will be in your midst."[2] In this way, he spoke to her once, twice, thrice. Our holy mother Walatta Petros did not accept[3] his words, however, and did not believe what he said. She was anxious that what had happened to Eve not happen to her.[4]

Our Lord then gave Walatta Petros a *kidaan* promise:[5] "Heaven and earth will pass
40 away but my word will not pass away.[6] Not only those on the inside (who are in your
care [already]), but also those on the outside (who will come from east and west[7] to
invoke your name): they will all be saved and will not perish! If you don't believe
what I tell you, behold, I will send a lion[8] and he will kill one of your disciples."

Having said this, our Lord left her, but things happened as he had proclaimed: A lion came, terrified and dispersed her disciples, and killed one of them. The others came running and rushing and amassed around her, falling over her and squeezing her so that she almost died.

She scolded them, saying, "What scares you? Do you really believe you will never die?" Then she rose and prayed together with them. Immediately the lion grew quiet and returned to his lair.[9] Then the sisters also turned back and went to their huts, and our holy mother Walatta Petros remained behind alone.

[1] *Yəssäbbäru bəyä* (they will break, and I will be held responsible) can also be understood to mean "they will break through me." The two different translations are contingent upon the interpretation of the particle *bə-*. It can be understood as introducing either the agent (leading to the translation of *bəyä* as "through me") or, as the result of interference from Amharic morphology, the person to whose detriment the action denoted in the verb takes place ("they will be broken to my detriment," leading to "I will be held responsible").

[2] Lit., *maʾkäleki wä-maʾkälehomu* (between you and between them).

[3] BDJ: *i-tətwekkäf* (did not accept); CR: *i-tətwäkkäf* [same meaning, but incorrect verbal stem].

[4] BDJ: *kämä i-yərkäba* (lit., that not happen to her [subj.]); CR: *kämä i-yəräkkəba* [*sic*: ind.]. WP is concerned that she will be misled like Eve was by Satan or that she will be blamed for the fall (or brokenness) of these vessels in the same way that Eve was blamed for the fall (or brokenness) of human beings.

[5] *Kidan* (promise) is an important concept in the Täwaḥədo Church and a vital part of any of its hagiobiographies. It is a pact or covenant made by Christ with a particularly holy person during a visitation. Christ promises that anyone who follows that saint will find favor with God. Saints typically receive their kidan toward the end of their lives, even on their deathbeds, but Christ grants a kidan to WP as a young woman here.

[6] Mark 13:31; Matthew 24:35; Luke 21:33.

[7] BDJ: *əllä halläwu əm-məśraq wä-əm-məʿrab* (lit., who are from east and west); CR: *əsmä halläwu wəstä məśraq wä-məʿrab* (because [or: indeed] they are in the east and in the west).

[8] Lions were common in Ethiopia until the twentieth century, including the distinctive black lion (*Panthera leo roosevelti*), which has a black mane. The kings of Ethiopia, with the title of the Lion of Judah, kept lions in captivity as symbols of their power, and thus, sending a lion after her here may have metaphorical meaning.

[9] BDJ: *ḫabä ḥəzʾatu* (to his lair); Abb. 88; *ḥəzʾatu* (his lair), which CR altered to *ḥəzʾato* (to his lair).

Plate 14. When Christ appeared to our mother in the wilderness, he told her about the souls he would send her and admonished her to believe or else he would send a wild beast as a frightful sign (top). Christ fulfilled his promise: this is "how the lion killed one of her disciples" (bottom) (MS A, f. 150r © SLUB Mscr.Dresd.Eb.415.e,2).

Chapter 24: Our Mother Agrees to Found Seven Communities

Then our Lord came to her again and said to her, "Didn't I tell you, 'Leave this monastic settlement so that you can gather souls'? Saving only yourself won't help you. I have given you a kidaan: I will be with you and will help you to take care[1] [of all your followers]. As I myself say in the Gospel,[2] 'Where two or three are gathered in my name, there I am[3] among them.'[4] And if one day you [so] ask me, and you want someone who entered [your community] to die, I will do that for you[5] and I will fulfill your wish."[6]

He then again, as he had before, brought her those white doves and those glass and crystal vessels, saying to her, "Take care of them for me, for they are chosen vessels without any blemish. They are the souls of your sons and your daughters: whosoever enters into your house[7] will not perish, and neither will your house disappear until the end of the world. This is the sign of the kidaan that is between me and you."

[Finally,] she then said to Him, "Your will be done, O my Lord."

This is the behavior of the wise: they do not immediately believe [someone] when they are told what is going to happen. As Luke the Evangelist reports, "The angel said to him, 'Don't be afraid, Zacharias![8] Behold, your prayers have been heard and your wife Elizabeth[9] will conceive and bear you a son, whom you will

[1] BDJ: *wä-aʿaqqəb läki* (lit., and I will take care for you); CR: *wä-aʿaqqəbäki* (and I will take care of you).

[2] BDJ: *bä-wängel* (in the Gospel); CR: *bä-wängeləyä* (in my Gospel).

[3] BDJ: *halläwku* (I am); CR: *əhellu* (I will be).

[4] Matthew 18:20.

[5] BDJ: *wä-fäqädki yəmut bä-ʿəlät zä-boʾa əgäbbər läki* (lit., and want that he might die, one day, who entered, I will do [that] for you); Abb. 88: *wä-fäqädki yəmut bä-ʿəlät zä-anä əgäbbər läki* (and want that he might die one day, I indeed will do [that] for you), which CR altered to *wä-fäqädki təmut bä-ʿəlät zä-anä əgäbbər läki* (and want that she might die one day, I indeed will do [that] for you). Ricci translates CR incorrectly: *che muoiano* (that they die).

[6] We are unaware of Christ promising any other saint that he would kill disciples for that saint. WP later repeatedly prays to the Lord to let members of her community die and is regularly granted her wish. Usually, she asks for those who are in danger of committing sins that could jeopardize their eternal salvation to die. In Genesis 12:3, God promises Abraham that he will curse whom Abraham curses.

[7] *Bet.* A monastery might be referred to as the "house" of its founder, as in "the house of *Abba* Mäṭṭa," meaning Däbrä Libanos of Šəmäzana. Also, there were two main monastic "houses" in Ethiopia, that of Saint Täklä Haymanot and that of Saint Ewosṭatewos. By using the word "house" here, the author may be suggesting that WP was founding a monastic line or house.

[8] *Zäkarəyas* was a Jewish priest in the New Testament and the father of John the Baptist.

[9] *Elsabeṭ* was a cousin of the Virgin Mary in the New Testament and the mother of John the Baptist.

name John.[1] He will be a joy unto you, and many will rejoice about his birth. For[2] 41
he will be great before God.'[3] Zacharias said to the angel, 'How do I know that all this will happen? After all, I am old, and also my wife's [fertile] days have passed.' The angel replied to him, 'I am Gabriel[4] who stands before God! I have been sent to speak to you and announce this [good news] to you. Behold, now you will become mute and will be unable to speak because you have not believed my words, which will come true at the set time.'"[5] And so it happened.

Luke further reports, regarding our Lady Mary, when the angel made the announcement to her, "he said to her, 'Don't be afraid, O Mary, for you have found favor with God.[6] Behold, you will conceive and give birth to a son whom you will name Jesus. He will be great, and will be called the Son of God Most High.'" Then "Mary said to the angel, 'How can this happen to me since I have not known a man?' The angel responded, 'God's Holy Spirit will come over you, and the power of the Most High will overshadow you.'" He who will be born from you[7] will be holy, "'and will be called the Son of God Most High. Behold, even your relative Elizabeth has conceived and become pregnant with a child, despite her mature years;[8] and behold, this is the sixth month for her, who had been called barren. For there is nothing which is impossible for God.' Now Mary said to the angel, 'Here I am, a maidservant of God. May it happen to me as you have told me.'"[9] And so it happened.

Also, our holy mother Walatta Petros first resisted Christ because she thought he might be Satan. As Paul says, "For Satan disguises himself as an angel of light."[10] Afterward, however, she accepted Christ when she saw a reliable sign from him.[11] By contrast, when Eve immediately believed the word of the serpent—who promised her that she would become God by eating from the tree which[12] enables one to discern good and evil—she became opposed to God.[13] She therefore had to leave

[1] *Yoḥannəs* was John the Baptist, the prophet in the New Testament who foretold the coming of the Messiah, Jesus Christ.

[2] BDJ: *wä-bəzuḫan yətfeśśəḥu bä-lədätu. Əsmä* (and many will rejoice about his birth. For); CR omits.

[3] Luke 1:13–15.

[4] *Gäbrəʾel* is an angel of the New Testament, one of the nine archangels who are God's messengers. He and Michael are the most important and venerated angels in the Täwaḥədo Church.

[5] Luke 1:18–20. In comparison with the Greek original, the author seems to have made some slight omissions.

[6] BDJ: *bä-ḫabä əgziʾabḥer* (with God); CR: *bä-əgziʾabḥer* (through God).

[7] BDJ: *wä-zä-ni yətwälläd əmənneki* (he who will be born from you); CR: *wä-zə-ni yətwälläd əmənneki* (this one will be born from you).

[8] B, CR add *wä-bä-rəśʾatiha* (lit., and in her advanced age).

[9] Luke 1:30–32a; 34–38.

[10] 2 Corinthians 11:14.

[11] The sign is Christ's action of sending the king of beasts, the lion, to kill a disciple; only the Almighty has such power.

[12] BDJ: *əntä* (which); CR: *ənzä* (while).

[13] Genesis 3:5. The entire story can be found in Genesis 2 and 3.

paradise and live in the land of[1] thorns and thistles. She brought down death upon herself because God had told them before, "Do not eat from the tree that stands in the middle of paradise![2] For on the day on which you eat from it, you will become subject to death."[3] Eve did not [even] get that which she had wanted, [to become
42 like God]. All this has been written for our protection and benefit.

Christ further told Walatta Petros that she would go to the region of Zhebey[4] where she would be imprisoned and guarded by a Black man,[5] remaining [there] for three years; that she would become sick from the *maqwé* illness,[6] and that after this she would leave [Zhebey].[7]

See then, my loved ones, how God lets the saints know beforehand that they will encounter imprisonment, exile, and every type of tribulation from infidel kings on account of the true faith. As the Gospel says, "Behold, I send you as sheep among wolves."[8] Furthermore, the Gospel says, after this,[9] "They will seize you and take you to the tribunals, before the kings and great lords.[10] This[11] will happen to you for the sake of my name."[12] Paul too says in the Acts of the Apostles, "Yet in various cities the Holy Spirit let me know, 'Suffering and shackles await you.' "[13] And the Apostle Peter says in his letter, "However, for now, for a little while, you will have

[1] BDJ: *wəstä mədrä* (in the land of); CR: *wəstä kärśä* (in the belly of).

[2] BDJ: *zä-maʾkälä gännät* (lit., that is in the middle of paradise); CR: *bä-maʾkälä gännät* (in the middle of paradise).

[3] Genesis 2:17.

[4] *Žäbäy* was a hot lowland region on the border with Sudan. It was at least one hundred miles west of Lake Ṭana. BDJ consistently have *Žäbäy*, but CR sometimes has *Žäbäl.*

[5] Lit., *šanqəlla,* which is a pejorative ethnic term used by highland Ethiopians for the populations living west of the Ethiopian kingdom's border. Such peoples were held in contempt by highland Ethiopians, Christians and Muslims alike, on account of their traditional religion, different cultures, Nilo-Saharan rather than Semitic languages, and physical appearance, including a darker skin complexion. Traditionally, highland Ethiopians would describe the šanqəlla (and similar groups) as "black," while they characterized their own skin tone as "red." Ricci describes this man as Muslim, but the text does not say this.

[6] *Maqʷe* is an illness, probably with a fever, that a person was likely to catch in lowland areas, so perhaps malaria.

[7] This is indeed what happened to her.

[8] Matthew 10:16.

[9] BDJ, CR: *əm-qədmä zəntu kʷəllu* (before all this), which we assume to be a mistake in the original or a corruption of its opposite, *əm-dəḫrä zəntu kʷəllu* (lit., after all this), because what follows is a paraphrase of Matthew 10:17. Extant *əm-qədmä zəntu kʷəllu* may have been made plausible by the fact that WP actually was brought before a royal court before she was exiled to Žäbäy. Ricci interprets "before all this" as the initial words of the biblical quote even though it does not begin with such words.

[10] BDJ: *yəwässədukəmu aʿwadatä ḫabä nägäśt wä-makʷanənt* (lit., they will take you to the tribunals, to the kings and great lords); CR: *yəwässədukəmu ḫabä aʿwadat wä-ḫabä nägäśt wä-makʷanənt* (they will take you to the tribunals and to the kings and great lords).

[11] BDJ: *wä-zə* (this); CR: *wä-zə-kʷəllu* (all this).

[12] Matthew 10:17. For rhetorical effect, the author appears to have omitted from and expanded upon the original biblical quote.

[13] Acts 20:23. The author altered the biblical quote to include direct speech.

to suffer grief due to various tribulations, which will meet you as a test of your faith."[1] Tribulations do not happen unexpectedly to the saints. Rather, they are told about them beforehand so that they can be steadfast with hope and understanding, protect themselves with the shield of faith, don[2] the armor of righteousness, and shod themselves with the shoes of the Gospel.[3]

In just this way,[4] in advance, God also informed our holy mother Walatta Petros about what would happen before it happened. By contrast, tribulations befall sinners unexpectedly. As Paul says, "You know very well that the Day of our Lord will arrive like the coming of a thief, at a time when those who deny him[5] think that they are in safety and peace. Then, suddenly, destruction will come upon them, like labor pains upon a pregnant woman, and they will be unable to escape."[6]

Chapter 25: Our Mother Discusses Christ's Promise

After the supplications ritual of Waldeba was finished, our holy mother Walatta Petros returned from seclusion and [again] joined her companions. Eheta Kristos and Ghirmana[7] asked her, "What did you experience, and what kind of visions have you seen since[8] you withdrew from us, over those months?"

She kept it hidden from them, however, and said, "As for me, I[9] did not experience or see[10] anything because the veil of sin covered me and the curtain of transgression screened me [from any vision]."[11]

The two women kept asking her individually, however. Walatta Petros became 43
exasperated with them and did not tell them anything because she was afraid of empty praise. But they did not stop asking her; they implored and pressured her. So, she lifted her mind up to God and spent many hours in silence. Then she obtained permission from God, and now she told them how our Lord had come to her and taken her hand; how he had told her everything that would happen, from the beginning to the end; how she had said to him, "I am mud. How can I do this?"; and how he had given her the kidaan.

Eheta Kristos and Ghirmana were witnesses and have told us [what Walatta Petros said]. Likewise, the disciple Takla Maryam was her witness as well, and the testimony of all three agrees. We know that their testimony is true. We certainly

[1] 1 Peter 1:6–7.

[2] BDJ: *yəlbəsu* (so that they can . . . don [subj.]); CR: *yəläbbəsu* [*sic*: ind.].

[3] Based on Ephesians 6:14–15.

[4] BDJ: *kämahu* (lit., in this way); CR: *kämahomu* (like them).

[5] BDJ: *əllä yəkəḥədu kiyahu* (those who deny him); CR: *əllä kəḥdu kiyahu* (those who denied him).

[6] 1 Thessalonians 5:2–3. The author has altered the biblical quote slightly.

[7] *Gərmana* is one of WP's companions and a nun.

[8] BDJ: *əm-amä* (since); CR: *əm-kämä* (as soon as).

[9] BDJ: *anə-ssä* (lit., I for one); CR omits.

[10] BDJ: *wä-i-rəʾiku* (lit., and I did not see); CR omits.

[11] Modesty and humility are so important that they justify this deception.

have not written lies, nor have we used ingenious fables[1] to acquaint you with the story of our holy mother Walatta Petros's glory. Rather, we know and are certain that the testimony of two or three people is trustworthy.[2] We ourselves, too, have seen as we have heard.[3]

Chapter 26: Our Mother Preaches and Works Miracles

Thus, our holy mother Walatta Petros lived, teaching the people of Waldeba the true faith and exhorting them not to accept the filthy faith of the Europeans.[4] When King Susinyos heard this news about her, he secretly sent out spies to keep an eye on her. However, people told our holy mother Walatta Petros that spies sent by the king were approaching. [Therefore,] she, together with her companions, withdrew from that place where she had lived until then and set up camp in a dry riverbed, since it was the dry season.

She had the *Faith of the Fathers*[5] with her, as well as other books. One day it then rained very hard, so much so that[6] the riverbed was filled [with water] instantly. It streamed down and overflowed the people and the books. Yet it did not damage the books at all; not even a single letter of them[7] was wiped out. They remained intact thanks to the powerful help of our holy mother Walatta Petros; they remained unaffected.[8] Thereafter, she returned to her previous abode [in Waldeba].

[1] Lit., *wä-i-konnä mähaddämtä ṭəbäb zä-tälonä* (nor is it not ingenious fables that we have followed).

[2] See 2 Corinthians 13:1, which cites Deuteronomy 19:15, that "Every matter must be established by the testimony of two or three witnesses."

[3] That is, those in the community have seen her miracles, whether because they are old enough to have known WP, or because they have seen the miracles done in her name after her death.

[4] It was extremely unusual for a woman to teach or preach, especially in a monastic region famous for its many teachers. Although she had not spent years in the church education system, as did learned priests, even scholars might listen to a particularly holy person, like her, preaching from the heart so that they might learn the will of God.

[5] The *Haymanotä Abäw* is a collection of the writings of the early Church Fathers and non-Chalcedonian patriarchs of Egypt. In the anti-Catholic struggles of WP's time, the *Haymanotä Abäw* became the preferred doctrinal reference work of the Orthodox.

[6] BDJ: *əskä* (so much so that); CR: *əsmä* (truly).

[7] Lit., *wä-i-näkäyo* (it did not damage it) and *1-ni fidäl əmənnehu* (not even a single letter of it). Our translation twice regards singular "it" (in *näkäyo, əmənnehu*), as well as the next sentence's singular verb forms *dəḫnä, täwälläṭä* (to remain intact *and* to remain unaffected), as semantically collective, referring to the books that were with the group in their entirety. Alternatively, all these singulars could be taken to refer exclusively to the *Haymanotä Abäw*, but that seems contextually ill suited.

[8] BDJ: *i-täwälläṭä* (lit., it was unchanged); Abb. 88. with meaningless *i-täṭṭäṭä*, which CR altered to *i-täsäṭṭäṭä* (for etymologically correct *i-täśäṭṭäṭä*, it was torn apart). This insistence that the *Haymanotä Abäw* remained unchanged may be a reference to the Jesuits' efforts to amend the *Haymanotä Abäw* to be less favorable to the non-Chalcedonian view.

Listen up! Again we will tell you about our holy mother Walatta Petros's perfect
virtue and how God worked miracles and wonders for her. When a tapeworm had 44
appeared in her belly, the sisters prepared a medicine for her to drink so that she would expel the tapeworm.[1] While they were carefully treating her, a man came by who [also] was plagued by tapeworm, and had been for quite a while because he lacked the medicine to drink. He asked that they give him [that medicine] and told them[2] how tapeworm had plagued him. When she heard this, our holy mother Walatta Petros felt compassion for him, abstained from drinking the medicine,[3] gave it to him, and he drank it.[4] However, she also recovered, [even] before him, without drinking, and the tapeworm never again appeared [in her].

Have you ever seen such a love of one's neighbor and such a surrendering of one's own [means of] deliverance to another soul? As Christ says,[5] "Blessed is he who surrenders himself in redemption of his neighbor."[6] This is a great gift of charity, greater than all others.[7]

Thereafter, God sent a scourge to Waldeba, a wild beast called a *shilhoolhoot*.[8] It would come at night to where people slept, pierce their heads, and eat their brains.

Because of this frightful development, terror and tumult gripped all the sisters, and they said to our holy mother Walatta Petros, "It's impossible for us to remain here due to that dumb beast's great, awe-inspiring power![9] [Even] a locked door

[1] Tapeworm infestations were extremely common and most undertook an exhausting purge every other month, using the dried flowers of a local tree called *koso* (*Hagenia abyssinica*) as a taenicide. The cheap and widely available powder was mixed with water, drunk on an empty stomach, and the worms expelled in the stool. See Zemede Asfaw (2007).

[2] In contrast to the previous sentence, "they" and "them" here are not in the feminine plural but in the masculine plural, as if the suffering man was not addressing only women.

[3] BDJ: *wä-ḫadägät sätəyä* (lit., she desisted from drinking); CR omits.

[4] BDJ: *wä-sätyä* (lit., and he drank); CR omits.

[5] Lit., *bä-kämä yəbe* (as he says *or* as it [the Gospel] says). Gəʿəz does not distinguish between masculine and neuter in the third-person singular.

[6] John 15:13, although Ricci gives 1 Timothy 2:6.

[7] See 1 Corinthians 13:3.

[8] *Šəlḫʷəlḫʷət* is not a Gəʿəz term, and not an established Amharic noun either. However, due to several broadly similar vocabulary items in Amharic, *Šəlḫʷəlḫʷət* evokes slime and filth, crawling and creeping, and pointedness. See such terms as *šäläl* (excrement, filth), *šälala* (lame, crippled), *tänšallälä* (to crawl), *šəl* (embryo, fetus; together with related *šəla bäll* [barbaric person who eats the unborn or newborn of cows and sheep]), and finally, *šul*, with its reduplicative variant *šulašul*, "pointed, sharp." If real, the animal may be related to the Amharic *wäbbo šämmane*, a cheetah (*Acinonyx jubatus*) that came by night to dig up human graves and feed on the cadavers, and that plagued the monks of Däbrä Zämäddo until they finally hunted it. Alternately, it may be related to the animal described by the Amharic word *šuluwliwit*, which Kane (1990) translates with "marmoset-like animal" or "kind of bird."

[9] Lit., *gərma*, a word associated with the great and powerful, like kings and lions, which means something that both inspires fear and that is majestic. We have usually translated this as "awe-inspiring power" or "great majesty."

does not prevent it from entering because it comes through the roof of the house. Not even lions or snakes scare us like this beast does! Let us leave and go to another place. If you refuse, we will scatter on our own and leave you behind alone!"

When they spoke to her like this, [together with them] she left that place and went to the region of Tsellemt.[1] There, too, she lived teaching the inhabitants the true faith and exhorting them not to adopt the filthy faith of the Europeans.

Chapter 27: Our Mother Again Incurs the King's Wrath

Then, when King Susinyos heard that our holy mother Walatta Petros was in the district of Tsellemt and that she was teaching the [Orthodox] faith, he became angry and enraged, roaring like a lion.

He said, "Even though I left her alone, she doesn't leave me alone! Even though I was lenient toward her, she's not lenient toward me. From now on, however, I will decide on my own what to do [with her]."

So, he summoned one of his military men, whose name was *Amba-Ras*[2] Filaatawos[3] and who was in charge of that district of Tsellemt. He said to him, "Go and bring Walatta Petros to me quickly!"[4]

Filaatawos went as the king had commanded him,[5] arrived at where she stayed,
45 and said to her, "The king has ordered me to you. He says to you, 'Come immediately, and don't say, "Tomorrow!" ' "

Our holy mother Walatta Petros replied, "Behold, I am in your hands. Do with me as the king has ordered. I am ready for it and prepared to die. I'm not afraid of anything."

Immediately then, our holy mother Walatta Petros set off from there and went with him. With her were [the sisters] Eheta Kristos and Kristos Sinnaa,[6] [as well as her maidservants] Maryamaweet and Eskindiraweet.

[1] *Ṣällämt* is a historical province around 150 miles north of Lake Ṭana in what was Bägemdər and is now Təgray. It is east of Waldəbba, stretching from the Səmen Mountains north to the Täkkäze River. It was largely populated by Betä Ǝsraʾel, who were Jewish, and in 1623–24, Susənyos suppressed a rebellion there.

[2] *Amba-Ras* is a mid-rank military title originally meaning "Commander of an *amba*," that is, of one of the Ethiopian flat-topped table mountains that were often used as natural fortresses. In the mountainous region of Ṣällämt, this person was in charge of the local population.

[3] BDJ, CR: *Filatawos* (commonly: Filatewos), from the Greek *Philotheos* (He who loves God).

[4] BDJ: *Wälättä Ṗeṭros-ha* [acc.]; CR: *lä-Wälättä Ṗeṭros-ha* [*sic*: dative and acc.].

[5] BDJ: *bä-kämä yəbelo* (lit., as he had said to him); CR: *bä-kämä yəbe* (as he had said).

[6] BDJ: *Krəstos Śənna* (In Christ lies her beauty); CR: *Maryam Śənna* (In [Saint] Mary lies her beauty).

Chapter 28: The Europeans Try to Convert Our Mother

Walatta Petros arrived at and entered the king's castle in the month of Ginbowt.[1] They lodged her in[2] the house of *Dejjazmatch*[3] Billa Kristos.[4] Then they began to [try to] persuade her with many clever tricks to abandon the true faith of Dioscoros[5] and adopt the filthy faith of Leo.

Three renowned European false teachers[6] came to her[7] and debated with her about their filthy faith, which says, "Christ [still] has two natures after the ineffable union [of his humanity and divinity]."

She argued with them, defeated them, and embarrassed them. Each morning, other Europeans came to her, reading to her and explaining their filthy book to her.[8] Our holy mother Walatta Petros, however, did not listen to their talk and did not accept[9] their faith. Rather, she laughed and made fun of them.

As the Gospel says, "Therefore, you all should not call yourselves teachers on this earth because your teacher is one, Christ."[10] Also, the Apostle John in his letter says, "Our brothers, do not believe every spirit, but test the spirit, whether it is from God, because many false prophets have come into the world" who do not believe in

[1] *Gənbot* is the ninth month of the year in the Ethiopian calendar, extending from 9 May to 7 June. Holy Week and Easter often fall during this month.

[2] BDJ: *anbärəwwa ḫabä* (they lodged her in); CR: *agbəʾəwwa ḫabä* (they entered her into).

[3] *Däǧǧazmač* (lit., He who leads the center column into battle) is one of the highest, sometimes the highest, traditional military rank, generally below a *ras*. The leader with this title had the duties of being a regional governor, a regional judge, or a regional military commander, depending on the period.

[4] *Bəʿlä Krəstos* (Wealth of Christ) was the king's cousin and confidant, a great lord who helped to bring Susənyos to power and who was a friend of the Jesuits. He had become Roman Catholic and even wrote scholarship attempting to show that the Täwaḥədo Church had not always been anti-Chalcedonian.

[5] *Diyosqoros* was a pope of the Alexandrian Church in the fifth century and remained so even after he had been deposed as a heretic in 451 by the Council of Chalcedon for refusing to agree with its doctrine. He is thus a hero in the Täwaḥədo Church, which rejects the Council of Chalcedon. One of the fourteen Täwaḥədo Church liturgies is the Anaphora of Saint Dioscorus.

[6] In May 1625, when this likely happened, about sixteen Jesuit priests lived in Ethiopia, including Jerónimo Lobo, Manoel de Almeida, and Manoel Barradas, all of whom later wrote about their experiences in Ethiopia. The three who initially visited WP would not have included Páez, who had died, nor Mendes, who was brought in to talk to WP later, as a last resort. Regarding the Jesuits' attempts to convert Ḫabäša women, see Belcher (2013).

[7] BDJ: *ḫabeha* (to her); CR omits.

[8] It is unclear to which book the author alludes. Susənyos encouraged the Jesuits to translate many works into Gəʿəz (Cohen 2005). It may be the Catholic catechism, which was translated into Amharic around 1619 (Páez 2011, 39).

[9] BDJ: *i-tətwekkäf* (did not accept); CR: *təwekkäf* [nonexistent form].

[10] Matthew 23:8. The original biblical text does not have the word "Christ." In Matthew, it is Christ himself who speaks this verse, and the teacher he alludes to is God.

Jesus Christ, that he has come in the flesh.[1] "By this you will know the Spirit of God: each spirit which believes[2] in Jesus Christ, that he came in the flesh of a man, is from God,[3] but each spirit which does not believe in Jesus Christ, that he came in the flesh, is not from God. Rather it is from the false messiah of whom you have heard that he would come."[4] John further says, "Anyone who wavers and does not remain in the teaching of Christ is not with God. But he who remains in the teaching of Christ is in the Father and the Son.[5] He who comes to you and does not
46 bring[6] this teaching, do not let him enter your houses and do not even greet him because he who greets him has fellowship with him in his evil deeds."[7] This is why our holy mother Walatta Petros treated these European false teachers with contempt and repudiated them.

The king then inquired about her, "What does she say?"

The Europeans replied to him,[8] "She does not listen and does not accept what we say. Instead, she insults us. Can water penetrate a heart of stone?"

Because of this, the king became enraged and wanted to kill her.

His counselors prevented him, however, saying, "Do not do something like that! If you kill her here,[9] everyone[10] will follow her and join her in death. And once the people have perished, over whom will you rule? Instead, order that she remain a captive."

So the king ordered that she be taken to the region of Zhebey and handed over to the Black man so that she would live [there] as a captive.

Following this [decision], Malkiya Kristos entered into the king's chamber, stood before him, and implored him, "My lord king, I beseech you, if I find grace before you, hand Walatta Petros over to me until the months of the rainy season are over.[11] During that time, I will admonish and advise her. In addition, the spiritual

[1] 1 John 4:1.

[2] BDJ: *əntä tä'ammən* (which believes); Abb. 88 *əntä i-tä'ammən* (which does not believe), which CR sensibly edited to *əntä tä'ammən*.

[3] BDJ: *əmənnä əgzi'abḥer yə'əti* (is from God); Abb. 88 omits *əmənnä* (from), but CR aptly inserted *əm-* (from [enclitic variant of *əmənnä*]).

[4] 1 John 4:2–3.

[5] BDJ: *wä-i-yənäbbər bä-təmhərtu lä-Krəstos i-hallo məslä əgzi'abḥer. Wä-zä-ssä yənäbbər bä-təmhərtu lä-Krəstos bä-ab wä-bä-wäld hallo* (and does not remain in the teaching of Christ is not with God. But he who remains in the teaching of Christ is in the Father and the Son); CR: *wä-i-yənäbbər bä-təmhərtu lä-Krəstos bä-ab wä-bä-wäld i-hallo* (and he who does not remain in the teaching of Christ is not in the Father and in the Son).

[6] BDJ: *i-yamäṣṣə'* (does not bring); CR: *yamäṣṣə'* (brings).

[7] 2 John 1:9–11.

[8] BDJ: *awśə'əwwo wä-yəbeləwwo* (lit., replied to him and said to him); CR omits *wä-yəbeləwwo* (and said to him).

[9] BDJ: *bä-zəyyä* (here); CR omits.

[10] BDJ: *kʷəllu ʿaläm* (lit., the entire world); CR: *zə-kʷəllu ʿaläm* (this entire world).

[11] BDJ: *əskä yäḫalləf wärḫa kərämt* (lit., until the month [*sic*] of the rainy season is over); CR omits *wärḫa* (the month of). Most people stayed in one place during the rainy season (*kərämt*), since traveling during this period was difficult and even posed serious health risks due to the cold, wet, swollen rivers and lack of adequate shelter along the road. Furthermore,

leader[1] of the Europeans, Afonsu,[2] shall read his book to her[3] and have her listen [to it] every day. If then she still refuses to convert, we will send her away."

The king replied, "Yes, I agree to your proposal."

Our holy mother Walatta Petros was then handed over to Malkiya Kristos. He took her to Azezo,[4] lodged her in his house, and provided her with food. With her were Eheta Kristos and Walatta Kristos.[5] Throughout their entire lives, Walatta Petros and Eheta Kristos were like our Lady Mary and Salome.[6]

Afonsu went to Walatta Petros each Saturday morning, without breaking for lunch,[7] in a clever move to make her fast likewise,[8] and read his book to her. How-

---

the people of the court traditionally spent the rainy season in their ancestral homes rather than at court. WP had arrived at the court in May; kərämt ends in mid- to late September.

[1] *Mämhər*, which can mean "teacher" or "master," but is also regularly used to designate an abbot, and sometimes in the sense of "theologian"; for instance, when the Jesuit theologians (*mämhəran*) at Susənyos's court argue with WP. The words "abbot," "teacher," "theologian," and "spiritual leader" in the text are always a translation of this same word.

[2] The Portuguese Jesuit Afonso Mendes (1579–1656) was appointed Catholic patriarch of Ethiopia in 1622 by the pope and served in Ethiopia as a missionary from 1625 to 1634. He was important in increasing the king's pro-Catholic policies and officially establishing Roman Catholicism as the state religion. Because Mendes was stricter than Páez, many scholars attribute the failure of Roman Catholicism in Ethiopia to him. Mendes worked one-on-one to convert the women of the royal court, as the Jesuit accounts attest.

[3] This may have been Mendes's *Bran-Haymanot Id Est Lux Fidei In Epithalamium Aethiopissae, Sive In Nuptias Uerbiet Ecclesiae* (1692), which Mendes composed in Latin and later translated into Gəʿəz with Wäldä Krəstos, a relative of *Ras* Śəʿəlä Krəstos, who admired it and recommended that it be called *Light of Faith* rather than *Doctrine of Faith* (Cohen 2009a, 11).

[4] *Azäzo* is an important town, north of Lake Ṭana but about eight miles southwest of Gondär, that served as the de facto capital during the Susənyos period. Susənyos and his court, and therefore the Jesuits, lived there from 1607 until 1632, building castles, palaces, and churches, and otherwise supporting the arts. It was from this town's church that the Jesuits announced Catholicism the official state religion and where Susənyos was buried. It was an important religious center, as thousands of monks came to debate the religious issues inspired by the presence of the Jesuits. It is not surprising, then, that WP's husband Mälkəʾa Krəstos had a home in this town and brought her there to be converted by Mendes. Gondär only became the capital after Fasilädäs came to power.

[5] *Wälättä Krəstos* (Daughter of Christ) is a nun who was with WP at Mälkəʾa Krəstos's house in Azäzo, but fled when WP was banished to Žäbäy. She is probably not the same woman as *Wäyzäro* Wälättä Krəstos, a noblewoman who appears later in the text and always with her title *Wäyzäro.*

[6] *Sälome* is not the salacious Salome but Mary Salome, who was Mary's sister and Jesus's aunt. According to the *Sənkəssar*, she was midwife at the birth of Christ, fled with the Holy Family into Egypt, and was a second mother to Christ throughout his life. Although the *Sənkəssar* does not specify the closeness of Mary and Salome, the author extrapolates this from Salome's closeness to the Holy Family.

[7] CR: *ənzä i-yemässəḥ* (lit., without him having lunch); BDJ: *ənzä i-temässəḥ* (without her having lunch). In view of the continuation of the text, this appears to be one of the rare occasions where the Abb. 88/CR variant is superior to BDJ.

[8] Orthodox Christians are required to break the fast after the Sabbath services on Saturdays.

ever, he would return embarrassed because she treated him with contempt, repudiated him, and did not listen to his teaching.[1]

Each time, the king asked, "Has Walatta Petros converted and embraced our faith?"

47 But they responded, "No."

Chapter 29: King Susinyos Banishes Our Mother to Zhebey

Then, when the months of the rainy season had passed and the month of Hidaar had begun, and the time was near that our Lord had predicted to her, "You will go down to Zhebey,"[2] the king summoned one of his military men and said to him, "Go and take Walatta Petros, her alone, to the region of Zhebey. Do not let anyone follow her, neither men nor women."

Having received the king's order, the soldier went, arrived at where our holy mother Walatta Petros was [at Azezo] and told her, "The king has ordered me to take you to the region of Zhebey."

Our holy mother Walatta Petros replied to him, "Here I am, in your hands. Do as the king has ordered."

At this time, Walatta Kristos became afraid and fled, carrying a water container[3] and wearing the clothes of a maidservant, like one who is going to draw water. Eheta Kristos, on the other hand, remained behind[4] at that place, [Azezo]. So, our holy mother Walatta Petros went away alone, just as our Lord Jesus Christ had gone to Calvary alone, carrying his cross; she was like him. As Paul says, "Let us follow Christ's example in order to proceed from glory to glory."[5]

Now, that soldier was very rough[6] and of bad character, without mercy and fear of God. He took Walatta Petros, made her mount a recalcitrant mule, and did not hold the reins for her but rather drove the mule from behind, poking at its anus[7] with a stick so that it would become angry and throw her down,[8] and she would die. He did not feel any compassion for her at all because Satan had rendered him hard-hearted. Acting thus, he took her down a rough and rugged road and beat that mule so hard that it fell and tumbled down a precipice. Immediately, though, an

[1] BDJ: *təmhərto* (his teaching); CR: *təmhərtä* (the teaching).

[2] Since Žäbäy was a hot, lowland region, "going down" evokes associations of a descent into hell, climatically as well as culturally.

[3] BDJ: *qäśutä* (a water container); CR: *qäśuta* (her water container).

[4] BDJ: *tärfät* ([she] remained behind); Abb. 88 omits, CR then filled the obvious gap by inserting *näbärät* ([she] stayed).

[5] 2 Corinthians 3:18. The author has reversed the order of the original biblical quote.

[6] Lit., *gəzufä kəsad* (thick-necked).

[7] BDJ: *məkʷsaḥu* (its anus); Abb. 88/CR: *säkʷänahu* (its heels). Perhaps this later manuscript was conciously sanitized.

[8] BDJ: *kämä . . . yawdəqa* (so that it would . . . throw her down [subj.]); Abb. 88: *kämä . . . yawäddəqa* [*sic*: ind.], which CR sensibly altered to the required subjunctive.

Plate 15. "How he [i.e., Susinyos's soldier] put her on a mule and it threw her into an abyss" (top) and "how an angel saved her" (bottom) (MS A, f. 150v © SLUB Mscr.Dresd.Eb.415.e,2).

angel caught our holy mother Walatta Petros, laying her down on good land in soft grass so that she stood up alive and unharmed.

As the book says, "Having taken three names, I lean on a staff. Even if I fall, I stand up again."[1] Likewise, David says, "Many are the sufferings of the righteous. However, God delivers them from everything. God protects all their bones, not one of them will be shattered inside them."[2] He furthermore says, "Truly, for your sake
48 God has ordered his angels to guard you in all your ways. They will lift you up with their hands[3] so that your feet will not trip over a stone."[4] In addition, Paul says, "We have a treasure in an earthen vessel, [which shows] that the great power is from God, not from us. While we suffer from everything, we are not distressed; while we are despised, we do not feel disgraced; while we are persecuted, we do not feel cast out; while we are tormented, we do not perish. We always carry the death of Christ in our flesh, so that the life of Christ may be known through this mortal body of ours."[5] The same also happened to our holy mother Walatta Petros.

Chapter 30: Our Mother in Exile Earns the Fear of Her Guard

After this, the soldier made Walatta Petros mount the mule again and brought her to the region of Zhebey. He handed her over[6] to the Black man, whom he told all the king's orders.[7] The soldier said to him, "Guard her until the time when the king orders either [her] death or [her] life."

So, she was alone. When her mother Kristos Ebayaa heard that Walatta Petros had gone away alone,[8] she became very distressed. Then she sent her maidservant Ilarya[9] to her so that she would stay with Walatta Petros and serve her.

[1] This is a lyric from a hymn by Saint Yared in the *Ṣomä Dəggʷa*, an original literary work and the liturgical text for the Lenten services of the Täwaḥədo Church. This quote has the double meaning (*säm-ənna wärq*, lit., wax and gold, but a metaphor for surface and deeper meaning) characteristic of much of Ethiopian poetry, or *qəne*. The three names are Christ, the Father, and the Holy Spirit, who are one in the Trinity, thus providing the support of faith that allows the priest to stand strong, who leans on a staff during the long hours of the service. Ricci says this line is from Micah 7:8, and perhaps the hymn lyric was inspired by it, but the biblical verse does not mention three names or a staff, but only standing up again.

[2] Psalm 33[34]:19–20.

[3] BD: *bä-ədäwihomu* (with their hands); J, CR: *bä-ədäw* (with hands).

[4] B: *əgrəkä* [nom.] (lit., your foot); DJ, CR: *əgräkä* [acc.] (your foot). Psalm 90[91]:11–12.

[5] 2 Corinthians 4:7–10.

[6] BDJ: *wähabä kiyaha* (he handed her over); CR: *wähaba kiyaha* [*sic*] (he handed her over, her).

[7] Although the highland peoples despised the peoples they called Šanqəlla, frequently raiding them and trading them as slaves, this man seems to have an official status in Susənyos's kingdom. He takes the king's orders and may be a kind of partner in a clientele state.

[8] BDJ: *baḥtita* (alone); CR omits.

[9] *Ilarya* (Hillary) is an elegant Greek name and thus typical for a servant or slave. WP's

The Black man then took charge of Walatta Petros, did as the king had ordered him, and cast our holy mother Walatta Petros into prison.[1] She spent three days without eating or drinking because the Black man was an impure heathen who had nothing in common with her, be it in way of life or in faith.[2] She did not understand his words when he spoke with her, whether they were kind or cruel.

How terrible was this day and how difficult this hour[3] in which our holy mother Walatta Petros suffered tribulation and banishment! It was much worse and much more difficult than any tribulation and banishment that met the [other Orthodox] Christians in those years. Where is she among women who is equal to Walatta Petros? Who could have patiently born all this like her? Not only a weak woman, but even men who possess strength—they would not have been able to endure like Walatta Petros. However, the power of God that was upon her enabled her to endure and gave her strength. As the Apostle Peter says, "After you have suffered for a little while, God will perfect you, strengthen you,[4] and make you understand."[5] If, by contrast, Walatta Petros had been made to stay in a region of Christians whose language she would have understood, whose way of life she would have known, and with whom she could have participated in eating and drinking, her endurance
would not have been extraordinary and difficult, but easy. 49

When the Black man saw her [abstaining], he said to her in his language, "What's the matter with you? What is this you're doing, that you don't eat and drink? How will you stay alive?"

Unfortunately, there was no one who could translate between them. Suddenly, however, God opened Walatta Petros's ears and she understood his language. As scripture says, "The Lord granted Joseph a sign as he went to the land of Egypt, and he understood a language that he had not known [before]."[6] The same happened to her.

Therefore, our holy mother Walatta Petros replied to the Black man, "How can I, a Christian woman, eat food that you have prepared? How can I drink water from a cup that you drink from, you, an impure heathen who does not share my faith? You don't have any sacred prohibitions: you eat mice and serpents and all the im-

---

mother's servant woman was likely a slave from what is modern southern or western Ethiopia. This woman served WP for many years and is called "saintly" in the text. Indeed, later, she successfully stops the sun.

[1] BDJ: *wəstä betä moqəḥ* (into prison); CR: *wəstä moqəḥ* (into chains).

[2] Ethiopian highland culture—Jewish, Christian, and Muslim alike—is characterized by strict restrictions on commensality, especially with regard to meat. Normally, adherents will only eat meat from an animal slaughtered by someone of their own faith. Furthermore, those of different classes or stations do not eat together.

[3] BDJ: *mi-mäṭän gərəmt zati ʿəlät wä-ʿəṣəbt zati säʿat* (how terrible was this day and how difficult this hour); CR: *mi-mäṭän gərəmt wä-ʿəṣəbt zati säʿat* (how terrible and difficult was this hour).

[4] BDJ: *wä-yaṣännəʿakəmu* (he will strengthen you [pl.]); CR omits.

[5] 1 Peter 5:10.

[6] Psalm 80[81]:5.

pure animals that the Law has forbidden people to touch and eat. So bring me[1] raw food, an unused pot for cooking, and an unused gourd for drawing water!"

He, too, understood her language [now]. So, he did accordingly and brought Walatta Petros what she had requested. Ilarya then cooked that food and served it to her but Walatta Petros tasted [only] a little of it and then left the rest. Ilarya cried bitterly because our holy mother Walatta Petros had refrained from eating.[2] The two of them lived[3] for a month in this way, all by themselves.

Then Satan entered into the heart of the Black man so that he laid his eyes on Walatta Petros: he began to make advances toward her, as men do with women. When she rejected him, he used a cord to tie her back to the house post and secured her in that position. He then gathered wood and brought fire to light the wood near her feet and torment her[4] with the smoke. That fire went out, however: it did not burn and did not smoke. Therefore, when he failed, he let her go, untying the ropes from around her.

He did not stop making advances toward Walatta Petros, however, and one day he went to see her at the prompting of Satan, thinking that he would be able to fulfill his desire [to have her]. But when he entered the hut where our holy and chosen mother Walatta Petros lived, he saw her standing in prayer, with her face resplendent like the sun. With her, by her side, stood an angel of God, holding a drawn sword in his hand near her ear.

50 Instantly, the Black man was shocked[5] and scared. He retreated, falling on his back. From that day onward, he was chastened and did not make advances toward Walatta Petros again. Rather, he treated her with respect and was afraid of her. Satan, too, was humiliated and defeated. How could that Black man aspire to what he aspired to? An act that was not [even] granted to [Walatta Petros's husband] Malkiya Kristos[6]—did he imagine that it would be granted to him, a foul servant?[7] However, that idea was not his own but Satan's, because in his insolence he wanted to become Lord.[8]

[1] BDJ: *wä-baḥtu amṣəʾ litä* (lit., but bring to me); CR omits *litä* (to me).

[2] It is unclear why she did not eat more; perhaps it was for the usual ascetic reasons.

[3] BDJ: *näbära kəlʾehon* (the two of them lived [fem. pl.]); Abb. 88: *näbäru kəlʾehon* (the two of them [fem. pl.] lived [masc. pl.]); CR pointed out the gender error in the verb form (49n1), but did not correct it.

[4] DJ: *kämä . . . yamändəba* (to . . . torment her [subj.]); B, CR: *kämä . . . yamänäddəba* [*sic*: ind.].

[5] BDJ: *dängäṣä* (was shocked); CR omits.

[6] BDJ: *əfo ḫalläyä ḫabä ḫalläyä. Zä-i-konä gəbr lä-Mälkəʾa Krəstos* (lit., how could he think of what he thought of? An act that was not granted to Mälkəʾa Krəstos); CR omits the second *ḫalläyä*, leading to a different syntactic division: *əfo ḫalläyä ḫabä zä-i-konä gəbr lä-Mälkəʾa Krəstos* (how could he aspire to an act that was not granted to Mälkəʾa Krəstos). That is, she had not slept with her husband since she had renounced the world for good after learning about his involvement in the death of *Abunä* Səmʿon.

[7] The disgust here is triple: that he was not a Christian, that he was from a despised ethnic group, and that he was of a much lower class. As noted before, the word *gäbr*, here translated as "servant," can sometimes mean "slave."

[8] The sentence's "his" refers to Satan's not the Black man's insolence (because the term

Plate 16. How the heathen Black man tied our holy mother to a post and lit a fire at her feet, and "how an angel chastised him" when he tried to rape her (MS A, f. 151r © SLUB Mscr.Dresd.Eb.415.e,2).

Chapter 31: The Queen Helps Eheta Kristos to Rejoin Our Mother

As for Eheta Kristos, as soon as she was separated from Walatta Petros, she cried and wailed day and night because she had remained behind alone and because her mother, holy and blessed Walatta Petros, had left her. She was like an infant whom they had made leave its mother's breast. So she went to her majesty *Ité* Amata Kristos[1] and stood before her, crying and weeping bitterly.

Therefore, Amata Kristos asked her, "What[2] makes you weep, my woman?"[3]

Eheta Kristos replied, "I weep because I have been separated from my mother Walatta Petros and made to remain behind alone. So, I beg you now, my lady, if I find grace before you, have mercy on me. Look upon my sorrow, and on my behalf request Malkiya Kristos to dispatch me so that I can go to my mother [Walatta Petros]."

Amata Kristos felt compassion for Eheta Kristos.[4] She summoned Malkiya Kristos and, as Eheta Kristos had requested, asked him[5] and got him to agree.[6]

Malkiya Kristos then went to the king, stood before him, and said to him, "[Long] may you live, my lord king! I have seen something amazing and witnessed something extraordinary that happened in your kingdom today."

The king inquired, "What have you seen and witnessed?"

---

amlak, "Lord," is reserved for God), but the underlying suggestion is that both share the sinful feature of aspiring to reach beyond their station in the divinely ordained order of the world. The despised black "servant" here aspires to have intercourse with a superior and forbidden woman—and thereby symbolically to become "lord" of her, as Mälkəʾa Krəstos had been.

[1] *Amätä Krəstos* (Maidservant of Christ). Amätä Krəstos was King Susənyos's cousin, being the daughter of his mother Ḥamälmal Wärq's brother. She was also the stepmother of Mälkəʾa Krəstos, WP's husband, and the mother of Wälättä Giyorgis, whom WP later worked so hard to convert back from the faith of the Europeans. Amätä Krəstos was a great favorite of the king and was addressed with the honorific *Ǝte* (Her Majesty) but was not an official queen. According to the Jesuits, she only appeared to convert to Roman Catholicism but was in fact against it and gave her land to monks to shelter anti-Catholic resisters. In the hagiobiography, Amätä Krəstos helps Ǝḫətä Krəstos and WP.

[2] BDJ: *mənt* [nom.] (what); CR: *məntä* [*sic*: acc.] (what).

[3] *O-bəʾəsito,* a rare construction in which the hailing "o" is put at both the beginning and the end of the word. This question is similar to the question that angels ask Mary Magdalene at Christ's tomb in John 20:13, "Woman, why are you weeping?" She replies, "They have taken my Lord away." This is one of the subtle ways that the text aligns WP with Christ.

[4] BDJ: *täraḫrəḫat laʿleha* (lit., she felt compassion for her); Abb. 88 with ungrammatical *täraḫaraḫa* [*sic*] *ləbba laʿleha,* which CR altered to *täraḫrəḫa ləbba laʿleha* (her heart felt compassion for her).

[5] BDJ: *wä-säʾaläto* (and asked him); CR omits.

[6] Lit., *abäläto oho* (lit., made him say "yes"). This expression, and our translation of it, recurs in the text, but we only note it here.

Malkiya Kristos replied, "Most people, when[1] oppressed,[2] exiled, and separated from their family, cry and grieve. That woman, though, who used to live with Walatta Petros, cries and wails when we tell her, 'Live with your family in your own land.'"

The king said to him, "So then,[3] what do *you* suggest we do with her?"

Malkiya Kristos responded, "I suggest that we send her to that region [Zhebey] so that the *maqwé* illness may kill her and so that she will not perpetually cause us trouble and annoy us."

The king was pleased with this proposal and said to Malkiya Kristos, "Let it be
as you have said." 51

So Malkiya Kristos emerged [from the king's hall] and told Eheta Kristos, "Hereby, we give you permission:[4] Go!"

When Eheta Kristos heard this, she sank down, kissed Malkiya Kristos's feet, rejoiced and was so[5] happy, thanking God. Then, she arose, went forth, and reached the region where our holy and chosen mother Walatta Petros was. Eheta Kristos found her and kissed her in greeting. But when she noticed how Walatta Petros's appearance had darkened[6] and her body had become emaciated, Eheta Kristos hugged her and cried over her.

Our holy mother Walatta Petros consoled her, however, "What makes you cry, now that you have found me? Was it not me that you were looking for? From now on, rather, we should rejoice and thank God who has arranged for us to live together in one place[7] and has not let you and me be separated." By saying this, she made Eheta Kristos stop crying.[8]

Thereafter, Eheta Kristos and Ilarya spent their days serving Walatta Petros and preparing what she would eat and drink. Our holy mother Walatta Petros for her part spent her time applying herself devotedly to the service of God.

Chapter 32: Our Mother and the Miracle of the Serpent

Thereafter, Walatta Petros's two disciples Takla Maryam and Atsqa Hawaryaat[9] arrived. [From then on,] they would go regularly to Walatta Petros's mother, broth-

[1] BDJ: *sobä* (when); CR: *ḫabä* (where).

[2] BDJ: [*sobä*] *gäfʿəwwo* [past tense] (lit., [when] they oppress him); CR: [*sobä*] *yəgäffəʿəwwo* [present tense].

[3] BDJ: *antä-ssä-ke* (lit., so *you*, then); CR: *antä-ke* (*you*, then).

[4] BDJ: *abaḥnaki* (hereby we give you [fem. sg.] permission); CR: *abaḥnakä* (hereby we give you [masc. sg.] permission). Ricci noted this deficiency.

[5] BDJ: *fädfadä* (lit., very); CR omits.

[6] This may mean she is darker because of tanning in the hot lowlands, but more likely that her face showed her physical or emotional ill health, in the same way that one might say a sick white person looked pale or wan.

[7] BDJ: *aḥattäne* (in one place); CR: *aḥattä-ni* (as one indeed).

[8] DJ: *bəkayä* (crying); B, CR: *bəkäya* (her crying).

[9] *ʿAṣqä Ḥawaryat* (Branch of the Apostles).

ers, and [other] relatives to collect various belongings and fine garments[1] and bring[2] them to her.[3] One day Takla Maryam went to Walatta Petros's mother, collected many things, loaded them onto a donkey, and turned back [toward Zhebey].

While he was walking on a path in the wilderness, evening overtook him and he found no house in which he could stay as a guest. So he took shelter[4] under a tree that had grown above [the lair of] a serpent. He took the load from the donkey and then tied him to the tree, which stood on top of the serpent['s lair]. Takla Maryam then lay down there[5] without noticing the serpent and fell asleep. At the break of dawn, that serpent[6] then hissed, crawled about, and shook the tree.

When the disciple saw the serpent,[7] he was shocked and afraid. He quickly untied the donkey, loaded him with the valuables, and left, running. He believed that[8] the serpent would pursue him. If that serpent had wanted to get that disciple, however, it would have devoured him during the night while he was asleep; and it
52 would not have spared the donkey either.[9] However, when God wanted to reveal the power of our holy mother Walatta Petros, he ordered the serpent to hiss and crawl about. For if the serpent had kept quiet, that disciple would not have noticed it. And if the disciple had not noticed it,[10] who would have told us, and how would we have written down this miracle?

The disciple then traveled on in amazement and reached that settlement [in Zhebey where Walatta Petros lived in exile]. He took the load from the donkey, went to our holy mother Walatta Petros, and, in front of her, put down the things that he had brought. Then, standing before her, he relayed a message from her mother and her brothers, reporting [their] greetings and warm wishes. [Meanwhile,] she looked him up and down, since she knew, before he revealed it to her, about the scare that he had received[11] in the wilderness.

[1] DJ: *nəwayä zä-zä-zi'ahu wä-albasatä śännayatä zä-zä-zi'ahu* (lit., various belongings and various fine garments); B: *nəwayä zä-zi'aha wä-albasatä śännayatä zä-zi'ahu* (her belongings and his [*sic*] fine garments); CR: *nəwayä zä-zi'ahu wä-albasatä śännayatä zä-zä-zi'ahu* (his [*sic*] belongings, and various fine garments).

[2] BDJ: *wä-yəbäṣṣəḥu* (and [they] bring); CR: *wä-yəbäṣṣəḥu* (and [they] arrive).

[3] The seven religious communities WP started would have needed resources to survive. Although WP had only four disciples with her at this point, her family sending goods suggests that WP's wealthy family may have financially supported all of her religious communities.

[4] BDJ: *aṣlälä* (he took shelter); CR: *täṣällälä* (shelter was found).

[5] BDJ: *həyyä* (there); CR omits.

[6] BDJ: *wə'ətu tämän* (that serpent); CR: *tämän* (the serpent).

[7] BDJ: *wä-sobä rə'yo* (lit., when he saw it); CR: *wä-sobä rə'yä* (when he saw).

[8] BDJ: *zä-* (that); CR: *ənzä* (while).

[9] This was probably an African rock python (*Python sebae*). Found in lowland Ethiopia, it can grow to twenty feet long and two hundred pounds, and eats mammals by wrapping around them and strangling them. Such snakes have been known, in rare cases, to eat human beings.

[10] DJ: *wä-əmmä i-rə'yo wə'ətu räd'* (lit., and if the disciple had not seen it); B, CR omit.

[11] BDJ: *dəngaṣe zä-räkäbo* (lit., the scare that had found him); CR: *dəngaṣe zä-räkäbä* (the scare that he had found).

Therefore, she asked him, "Where did you spend last night, and what was the scare that you received?" She asked him as if she did not know.

He then told her everything that had happened.

She said, "Why were you afraid? Why were you terrified? Was not God with you? Does not scripture say, 'If God our Lord is with us, nobody can overcome us'?[1] And does it not further say, 'Righteousness will surround you with a shield, and you will not be afraid[2] of the dreadfulness of night. You will ride on the wolf and the serpent'?[3] Therefore, do not be afraid of anything: Nothing will be able to harm you."[4]

Chapter 33: More Disciples Join Our Mother in Zhebey

Then Walatta Petros took the things—the garments and the gold [that Takla Maryam had brought]—and gave some to the Black man every day, giving away [her gifts] in this way.[5] When he then realized her supreme virtue, as well as the great grace and favor [from God] that rested on her, he honored and cherished her very much and in the language of his region called her *Sitti*, which means "My Lady."[6]

Indeed, God was with our holy mother Walatta Petros, just as the Orit says, "They threw Joseph into prison, the place where the prisoners live. He stayed there in prison,[7] but God's help was with Joseph, and he poured out mercy[8] and his love onto him. God gave Joseph favor and put clemency and compassion for him into the heart of the chief jailer. Therefore, the chief jailer appointed Joseph above all the prisoners because God was with Joseph and gave him success[9] in everything he did."[10] In addition, David says, "I was with him in the time of his trouble."[11] Furthermore, our Lord says, "I will be with you every day until the end of days."[12]

[1] Romans 8:13. Ricci suggests 2 Chronicles 14:11 and 32:8, which do not seem apt.

[2] BDJ: *i-təfärrəh* (you will not be afraid); CR: *i-təfrah* (do not be afraid).

[3] Psalm 90[91]:4–5, 13. The original Hebrew has "tread upon" not "ride on."

[4] BDJ: *bäʾəntä-zə i-təfrah məntä-ni. Albo zä-yənäkkəyäkä* (therefore do not be afraid of anything. Nothing will be able to harm you); CR: *bäʾəntä-zə təbe lä-mənt təfärrəh zä-yənäkkəyäkä* (this is why she said: Why were you afraid of what could harm you?).

[5] BDJ: *kämä-zə* (lit., like this); CR: *əmzə* (then).

[6] *Sətti* goes back to Sudan Arabic *sittī*. WP was exiled to the border region of today's Ethiopia and Sudan, where the local people were in close contact with their Arabic-speaking neighbors. Thus, her guard could use a loanword from a Muslim prestige language to designate his high-ranking Christian Ethiopian prisoner.

[7] BDJ: *ḫabä yənäbbəru muquḥan. Wä-näbärä həyyä wəstä betä muqəḥ* (the place where the prisoners live. He stayed there in prison); CR omits.

[8] BDJ: *məḥrätä* (mercy); CR: *məḥräto* (his mercy).

[9] BDJ: *yəśerrəḥo* (gave him success); CR: *yəśärrəḥo* [*sic*: subj.].

[10] Genesis 39:20–23. In the Bible, Joseph is the son of Jacob and Rachel, but since Joseph was his father's favorite, his half brothers sold him into slavery in Egypt. But Joseph rose to second-in-command there and later saved his brothers during a famine.

[11] Psalm 90[91]:15.

[12] Matthew 28:20.

Likewise, God was with our holy mother Walatta Petros and showed her favor in front of the heathen Black man. At that time, the Black man said to her, of his
53 own volition and without anybody forcing him, "Everybody who wants to may come and live with you. Even if there are many of them, even one hundred, I will not be distressed and will not hinder them." Before this time, though, when he had seen two or three people [approaching], he would chase them and want to kill them; but God would conceal them from his eyes so that when he searched for them he would not find them.

Now, however, when he witnessed Walatta Petros's supreme virtue, as well as the great glory and favor [from God] that rested on her, he turned from evil toward goodness and allowed Walatta Petros's followers to stay. Thus, many persecuted [Orthodox Christians] came from all directions and gathered around her. They surrounded her like bees gather around their king and surround him.[1] Many were the men and women who formed a community with her [in Zhebey]. This was the first community.

Our holy mother Walatta Petros remained in Zhebey for three years, overseeing them.

A captive also lived in Zhebey whose name was Ba-Haila Maryam.[2] He was a monk whose feet had been put in heavy chains because of his true faith—he was a truly righteous monk. He had lived in that place before Walatta Petros, but no one would visit him. When our holy mother Walatta Petros noticed him, however, she became very distressed and from then on assisted him and provided him with food.

He then prophesied to her, "You will leave this place, but I will die here.[3] Yet, if I die while you are [still] here and if you bury me, I know that God will have mercy on me on Judgment Day when he will come to judge the world. Otherwise, though, it will not be: He will not have mercy on me then."

Chapter 34: Our Mother Disobeys the King

After our holy mother had lived in Zhebey for three years, her brother Yohannes went to Fasiladas,[4] son of the king [and the future king], and beseeched him to

[1] In the past, people thought the queen bee was the king bee; in Europe it was only after WP's time, in the late 1660s, that they realized otherwise, when a Dutch scientist dissecting the biggest bee found ovaries. Perhaps the author intends us to understand WP as some kind of competitive court to Susənyos. Bees were closely connected to the king (even the recent Ethiopia leader Meles Zenawi represented a vote for him as a bee) and treated as oracles in the selection of kings.

[2] *Bä-Ḫaylä Maryam* (Through the power of [Saint] Mary).

[3] BDJ: *wä-əmäwwət anä bä-zəyyä* (but I will die here); CR: *wä-anä-ssä əmäwwət bä-zəyyä* (but I for my part will die here).

[4] *Fasilädäs*, regnal names Səlṭan Säggäd and ʿAläm Säggäd, reigned from 1632 to 1667 and is the Ethiopian king who restored Orthodoxy after his father, King Susənyos, had converted the country to Roman Catholicism. Although he officially converted to Roman Catholicism on 11 February 1626, along with most of the rest of the court, he did not long remain a sup-

speak to the king so that he would release our holy mother Walatta Petros from captivity.

Yohannes said to Fasiladas, "Would it be right if she died in the land of pagans? She has been sick already, and death has just barely[1] spared her. But such a thing must not be allowed to happen: mourning must not come between our two families."

So, Fasiladas went to the king and spoke to him, "Order that Walatta Petros be
released from Zhebey so that she won't die there and so that her brothers won't **54**
[one day] become embittered against you. Truly, they love you and zealously support your rule."

The king replied, "Yes, I agree to your proposal. Let it be as you said."

Now the king dispatched one of his troops[2] to the Black man to say to him, "Dismiss Walatta Petros, whom I had ordered you to guard."

When the messenger arrived, he told the Black man the king's message, and he also told Walatta Petros that the king said to her, "Depart!"

When the captive [monk] whom we mentioned before, [Ba-Haila Maryam,] heard this, he became very sad and lost all hope. He said [to himself], "Now I know that God will not have mercy on me." God was gracious toward him, however,[3] and showed [him] his salvation and, before the multitudes,[4] revealed his covenant with the righteous monk. Then the captive [monk] fell sick and said to our holy mother Walatta Petros, "How can you leave without burying me?"

She replied, "I will not leave without burying you!" So he rejoiced and kissed her hands.

Our holy mother Walatta Petros[5] then asked the Black man to come up with an excuse and say [to the king's messenger], "No [written] document of the king has reached me. You have lied to me—I will not dismiss her."[6] The Black man said, "Very well," and did as she had told him.

Therefore, the messenger went away, returned to the king, and told him the response. The king instantly became enraged. Yet, he then wrote[7] [the document,] the sign that was [established] between them, and dispatched that messenger again.

Meanwhile, the captive [monk] had died from his illness on the seventh day [after the messenger's departure] and thus found what he had desired. They buried him with chants and prayers, laying him in the tomb with his chains because they were so strong that they could not be unfastened. In this way, he consummated his

---

porter and worked in 1631 and 1632 to restore Orthodoxy. In the hagiobiography, Fasilädäs is a great friend to WP, persuading his father the king to allow WP to return from exile and later granting her lands for a monastery.

[1] BDJ: *ḥəqqä kəmmä* (lit., merely by a little); CR: *ḥəqqä kämä* ([it was] by a little that).

[2] *Ḥarrahu* (lit., his troops). However, what follows shows that normally collective *ḥarra* is used as a singular here.

[3] BDJ: *wä-baḥtu täśahalä əgziʾabḥer laʿlehu* (God was gracious toward him, however); CR: *wä-baḥtu täśahalo* [*sic*] *əgziʾabḥer laʿlehu* [ungrammatical, but no translation difference].

[4] Lit., *aḥzab* (multitudes *or* nations *or* gentiles *or* heathens).

[5] CR omits *Wälättä P̣eṭros.*

[6] This is just one more instance where the text hails the power of the written word.

[7] BDJ: *wä-ṣäḥafä* (yet he then wrote); CR: *wä-ṣäḥafä nəguś* (yet the king then wrote).

good[1] struggle and rested in peace, inheriting eternal life. May his prayers and blessing be with ________[2] for eternity, amen.

Chapter 35: Our Mother Is Freed and Returns from Exile

After this, the king's messenger arrived [again] and gave the Black man the king's written message. The Black man received it and said, "The king's word is good."

Do you see, my loved ones, how an earthly king has no power and authority to kill anyone without the consent of God? Rather, God is[3] the heavenly king, king of all flesh and spirit![4]

Many times King Susinyos had wanted to kill our holy mother Walatta Petros.
55 Once [for instance] with the sword, when she stood before him and heaped abuse on him. But his counselors made him spare her, saying, "If you kill her, all her kin will be your enemies, [the house of] Dawaro and Fatagar."

Furthermore, Susinyos cleverly contrived a devilish stratagem to hide his wickedness, when[5] he sent her to Zhebey. He ordered[6] the Black man, "Build a hut for her as her dwelling place amidst the grass of the wilderness, and then set the grass ablaze when the wind blows so that the fire will consume her and she will die. If you do this, I will reward you greatly."

So the Black man did as the king had ordered him and made our holy mother Walatta Petros live in a hut amidst the grass—very high grass that he set ablaze at a distance. The fire burned down the grass, and its thundering sound could be heard from afar.[7] Eventually, the fire reached the hut, rumbling like the thunder of the rainy season, and surrounded our holy mother Walatta Petros on every side, like a fence. Immediately, she prayed the prayer of the three [biblical] youths [Shadrach, Meshach, and Abednego]—"The fire and the flame praise God! He is glorified and exalted for eternity"[8]—from its beginning to its end. She was not afraid, nor terrified at all, but rather eager to achieve death and collect the crown of martyrdom.

[1] BDJ: *śännayä* (good); CR omits.

[2] B: *fəquru Agnaṭəyos* (his beloved Ignatius); D: *nəguśənä Dawit* (our king David); J: [*məsle*]*nä* ([with] us); Abb. 88: *fəquru* [name erased] (his beloved [name erased]), which CR edited to [*məsle*]*nä* ([with] us).

[3] D: *wəʾətu-ssä* (lit., rather, he is); BJ: *wä-wəʾətu* (and he is); CR: *lä-wəʾətu-ssä* (as for him, by contrast).

[4] CR adds: *kʷəllu zä-yətkähalo kämä yəqtəl wä-yaḥyu* (to whom everything is possible, so that he may kill and let live).

[5] BDJ: *amä* (when); Abb. 88 omits, CR inserted *wä-* (and).

[6] Lit., *yəbelo* (he said to).

[7] BDJ: *wä-awʿayo lä-wəʾətu śaʿr wä-yəssämmaʿ dəmṣä nägʷädgʷadu əm-rəḥuq* (lit., it burned down the grass, and its thundering sound could be heard from afar); CR omits.

[8] Daniel 3:66. While the Protestant (Masoretic) book of Daniel stops at verse 30, the third chapter of the book of Daniel in the Orthodox and Catholic (Septuagint) version has one hundred verses, including a song of praise sung by the three Jewish youths Shadrach, Meshach, and Abednego, whom God saved from the fiery furnace (verses 51–90).

Yet right away that fire went out; it was as if rain had fallen down on it.[1] Thus, God demonstrated his power for her and saved her as he had saved the three youths.

She was not happy about her salvation, however, but instead sad because she desired death more than life, in keeping with what Paul says, "I desire to depart and separate from the world so that[2] I can be with Christ. That would be much better and much more appropriate for me." However, God did not want our holy mother Walatta Petros to die,[3] but rather to live and tend his flock.

Therefore, when the king was incapable of killing her, he ordered that she be set free. Thus the Black man said to her, "Depart and go forth, according to what the king has ordered."

So, she departed and went forth, rejoicing in God, the father of mercy and Lord
of all[4] happiness. As the survivors of Babylon said, "When God revoked Zion's **56**
exile, we were overjoyed. Our mouths were filled with happiness and our tongues exulted."[5]

Chapter 36: Our Mother Starts Her Second Community, at Chanqwa

With Walatta Petros were Eheta Kristos and Ilarya as well as the disciples Takla Maryam and Atsqa Hawaryaat. Also, other exiled monks and nuns departed together with her. On her [return] journey, our holy mother Walatta Petros arrived at Chanqwa,[6] in the region of Dembiya.[7] There[8] she stayed for a while because the king had allowed her to live where she wanted.[9] Many of the persecuted—[Orthodox] men and women who had taken off their monastic caps, [thereby] posing as

[1] BDJ: *wä-konä kämä zä-wärädä laʿlehu zənam* (it was as if rain had fallen down on it); CR: *wä-konä zä-wärädä laʿlehu zənam* (and it so happened that rain fell down on it). Ricci correctly speculated that Abb. 88/CR was corrupt here.

[2] BDJ: *kämä* (so that); CR: *bä-kämä* (according to). Ricci correctly speculated that Abb. 88/CR was corrupt here as well, noting that the copyist may have mistakenly copied the *bä-kämä* that appeared shortly before, in the introduction of the Paul quote.

[3] BDJ: *kämä təmut* (lit., that she should die [subj.]); Abb. 88: *kämä təmäwwət* [*sic*: ind.]. CR drew attention to this indicative, but he did not emend it.

[4] BDJ, Abb. 88: *kʷəllu* [masc.] (all), which CR needlessly altered to its fem. equivalent *kʷəlla*.

[5] Psalm 125[126]:1–2.

[6] *Č̣anqʷa* was a town in the region of Dämbəya. It was north of Gorgora on Lake Ṭana but south of Gondär, on the left bank of the Gälikora River.

[7] *Dämbəya* is the fertile region bordering north Lake Ṭana, which since the mid-sixteenth century increasingly had become the political center of gravity of the Ethiopian kingdom. Its main historical towns are Gorgora, Azäzo, and Gondär.

[8] BDJ: *həyyä* (there); CR omits.

[9] BDJ: *əsmä abəḥa nəguś ḫabä zä-fäqädät tənbär* (because the king had allowed her to live where she wanted); CR: *əsmä abṣəḥa ḫabä zä-fäqädät tənbär* (because he [viz., God] had brought her to where she wanted to stay). Later copyists appear to have rewritten this phrase to foreground divine rather than worldly authority. Changing texts to attribute events to

secular people, and who had been scattered throughout the regions—gathered around her. They became like sons and daughters to her so that the words of the psalm might be fulfilled that say, "In the place of your fathers, children have been born unto you, and you will establish them as messengers to all the world.[1] They will remember your name for all eternity."[2] Their number increased with each day.[3]

They became a single community. This was the second community.

Chapter 37: Our Mother's Community Suffers a Violent Illness

While our holy mother Walatta Petros was there, a violent illness broke out and many of her community contracted it.[4] For this reason, the people of the region [of Chanqwa] became afraid and began to grumble against them, saying, "These wandering strangers brought a violent illness upon us." Therefore, the local people refrained from approaching them and rather kept their distance.

As a result, our holy mother Walatta Petros said, "If we remain here, [soon] there will be not one person [left] to bury those who have died. The hyenas will tear our dead bodies to pieces. It would be better for us to seek refuge on the island of Angaraa."[5] That island was close to the region where they were.

Immediately, therefore, they set out and, carrying their sick, went to that island and lived [there].

There was a young nun, a servant girl of Lebaseeta Kristos.[6] She was of good

God rather than man may be a typical copyists' habit and perhaps even a distinguishing mark of a copy.

[1] There is a change of the addressee's gender from male to female that diverges from the biblical original. The psalmist addresses his words to a male, namely, the king. On the occasion of his wedding, the psalmist predicts that he will have many sons who one day will continue the line of rulers that began with his own forefathers. Also, the author has taken a biblical quote about worldly authority to speak of WP's spiritual authority. Thus, we have translated polysemic Gəʿəz *mälaʾəkt* as "messengers" rather than as "governors" or "rulers."

[2] Lit., *bä-kʷəllu təwlədda təwlədd* (until the generation of generations). Psalm 44[45]: 16–17.

[3] BDJ: *əntä ṣäbḥat* [fem.] (lit., when it became morning); CR: *əntä ṣäbḥa* [masc.; no translation difference].

[4] WP seemed to be setting up not a "celliotic" community in Čanqʷa, in which monks and nuns lived in separate cells and met perhaps only once a week, but a "coenobitic" community, where everyone lived, ate, and prayed together under one authority. This close living may be why her communities so often contracted deadly illnesses that decimated their populations (Chernetsov 2005d, 61).

[5] *Angära* is a small island in northern Lake Ṭana just south of Gorgora and east of Susənyos's palace, close to shore. Its church is called Angära Täklä Haymanot.

[6] *Dəngəl ḥəṣan zä-Läbasitä Krəstos* (lit., a virgin, an infant of Läbasitä Krəstos). This wording does not mean that she was the biological child of Läbasitä Krəstos; such a daughter would be called *wälättä Läbasitä Krəstos* and likely would not be left unnamed. Moreover, the text always points out biological relationships. Thus, we interpret *ḥəṣan zä-* here to have the same meaning as in the American South, where a female servant was called her

character:[1] she served everyone without ever growing weary and without grumbling in the least, neither against those of low rank nor against those of high rank.
Rather, she served everyone equally, without partiality. One day, while the girl recited the *Praise of Our Lady Mary*[2] for the day of Thursday, Eheta Kristos summoned her and sent her on an errand. The girl embarked upon the task as ordered,
carrying out her commission, and returned. The prayer was on her lips[3] without
ceasing. Eheta Kristos then sent her on another errand. Again, she went with the 57
prayer[4] on her lips.

Then our Lady Mary appeared to the girl and said, "Are you weary and exhausted?[5] Quickly finish this prayer that is on your lips, then I will relieve you of this wearying and exhausting labor and take you to eternal rest."

As soon as the girl had completed her prayer, she began to feel a little unwell, as if exhausted. She told [Eheta Kristos] what our Lady Mary had said to her. Then, she instantly passed away, and another girl from among the sick community members passed away together with her.[6]

At that time, there was no man around who could dig [the needed] graves except *Abba* Zikra Maryam.[7]

So, our holy and chosen mother Walatta Petros became distressed and, addressing him politely, asked, "My brother, what shall we do? Who will dig the graves for us?"

---

mistress's "girl." It is unclear whether this is the previous unnamed servant whom Läbasitä Krəstos sent to help WP earlier in the text. While Läbasitä Krəstos apparently did not have any royal blood (she is not called *wäyzäro*), she seems to have been a wealthy and influential woman, interacting with WP as if coming from a similar noble background. She could easily have had several domestic servants, and perhaps she spared two for WP. In addition, that earlier woman sent by her was not called *ḥəṣan* (young girl) but *walätt* (young woman). That these particular servants go unnamed, unlike the servant Ilarya, for instance, may indicate that they are slaves. That this girl has her own story indicates some of the truth of the author Gälawdewos's later claim that servants became equals with their masters in WP's communities.

[1] Lit., *śännayt* (of good character *or* pretty).

[2] The *Wəddase Maryam* is an extremely important lectionary containing prayers in praise of the Holy Virgin for each day of the week. The Thursday prayer begins "The bush which Moses saw in flaming fire in the desert, the wood of which was not consumed, is a similitude of Mary, the Virgin who was spotless" (Budge 1933a, 289–92). The pious pray the *Wəddase Maryam* every day.

[3] Lit., *wəstä afuha* (in her mouth), here and twice more in this and the next paragraph.

[4] BDJ: *ənzä tə'əḫəz ṣälotä* [acc.] (lit., having taken the prayer); CR: *ənzä tə'əḫəz ṣälot* [*sic*: nom.; no translation difference].

[5] Lit., *mənt-nu taṣamməwäki wä-mənt-nu tasärrəḥaki* (what wearies you and what exhausts you).

[6] BDJ: *wä-aʿräfät fəṭunä bä-gizeha. Kalə't-ni wälätt aʿräfät məsleha əm-əllu ḥəmuman* (lit., then she quickly and immediately passed away. Also another girl passed away with her from among the sick ones [masc./mixed gender]); CR: *wä-aʿräfät məslehon əm-əllu ḥəmuman* (she passed away with them [fem.] from among the sick [masc./mixed gender]).

[7] *Zəkrä Maryam* (Commemoration of [Saint] Mary).

He replied indignantly, however, "What do you want from me? What are you saying to me? Do you expect *me* to dig[1] them even though I don't know[2] [how] and can't? You yourself get up, gird your loins, and dig! Was it not you who gathered and assembled all the people and brought this illness? Yet, who will now enter into your service? But you go and finish what you have begun!"

She politely implored him again, however. This time he got up, indignant and grumbling, and our holy mother Walatta Petros pointed out to him the place where he should dig. So, he took a spade and shoved it into the ground with one angry thrust. Right away, a deep and spacious pit[3] fell open, one that could hold many people![4] Nobody had known of that pit before, rather it was revealed thanks to the prayers of our holy mother Walatta Petros. Then, into that pit, they put all those nuns, all together, who had passed away. After them, many [other] sisters passed away and were also put into that pit. They entered into the Kingdom of Heaven. May their prayers and blessings be with __________[5] for eternity, amen.[6]

Chapter 38: Our Mother Looks for a New Place to Live

While our blessed mother Walatta Petros was there [on Angaraa Island in Lake Tana], her brother Za-Dinghil sent her these words, "Live on my land which lies
58 near Enfraaz.[7] It is really beautiful, with trees and water. It will be better for you to live there."

Upon hearing this, Walatta Petros said "May God's will be done" and she began exploring many places—monastic settlements as well as islands such as Daga[8] and Tsana[9]—for the best location for her to live. At that time, she placed crosses on the

[1] BDJ: *kämä anä əkärri* (lit., that *I* [emph.] dig); CR: *kämä əkärri* (that I dig).

[2] BDJ: *i-yäʾammər* [*sic*, for *i-yaʾammər*] (I don't know); CR: *i-yäʾamməro* [*sic*, for *i-yaʾamməro*] (I don't know it).

[3] BDJ: *afä ʿazäqt ʿəmuq wä-rəḥib* (lit., the mouth of a deep and spacious pit); CR: *afä mäqabər wä-konä ʿazäqt ʿəmuq wä-rəḥib* [*sic*: nom.] (the mouth of a grave: it was a deep and spacious pit).

[4] BDJ: *mäṭänä bəzuḫ säbʾ* [nom.] (lit., of the measure of many people); CR: *mäṭänä bəzuḫa säbʾa* [*sic*: acc.; no translation difference].

[5] B: *fəquron Agnaṭəyos* (their beloved Ignatius); D: *fəquron nəguśənä Dawit* (their beloved king David); J: *fəqərton Amätä Dəngəl* (their beloved Amätä Dəngəl [fem.]); Abb. 88: *fəquru* [name erased] (his beloved [name erased]), which CR edited to *məslenä* (with us). That is, the author calls for the prayers and blessings of the ancestors, those who have died, upon the living, not vice versa. This might reflect African traditional religions rather than Christianity.

[6] CR adds: *wä-amen. Lä-yəkun lä-yəkun* (and amen. May it be, may it be).

[7] *Ǝnfraz* is a fertile plain that goes down the east side of Lake Ṭana, around what is the modern town of Addis Zämän. It was the seat of Orthodoxy and the kingdom in the sixteenth century, and the Jesuits heavily proselytized therein during the seventeenth century.

[8] *Daga* is an island located near the middle of Lake Ṭana, next to the largest island, Däq. It is home to the monastery of Daga Ǝsṭifanos, one of the most important and ancient monasteries on Lake Ṭana.

[9] *Ṣana* is an island near the shore in southwestern Lake Ṭana. Often called Ṭana Qirqos

tabot[1] and with great devotion prayed for three weeks so that God would reveal to her the place where she should live. She cast lots,[2] and by the will of God, three times, each week, the lots came out in favor of the region of Dera.[3]

After this, she sent these words to [her husband] Malkiya Kristos, "On which of the islands [near Dera] will the king allow me to live? And may the king command that people [there] not argue with me about the faith and the Eucharist."

Malkiya Kristos went to King [Susinyos] and asked him as requested.[4]

The king replied, "Hereby, I grant her permission to live on Tsana Island, and no one shall harm her [there]!"

After this [news], she broke camp, departed from the island [of Angaraa], and moved to Tsana Island. [There] she began to live in the [deserted] hut of a monk.

Chapter 39: Our Mother Sees the Icon of Saint Mary

At that time, she saw the church[5] [of Miraafa Egzitina Maryam] of Tsana Island. Indeed, in the time of the Europeans, women could enter there![6] In addition, she

---

or Ṣana Qirqos Island, it is home to the monastery of Ṣana Qirqos, another of the most important and ancient monasteries on Lake Ṭana. Locals claim that the Ark of the Covenant first stayed on this island for six hundred years before being moved to Aksum, that the Holy Family stayed here when fleeing Herod, and that the first abbot was the son of a Jewish high priest from Jerusalem. It was a center for missionary activity in the region for several centuries. It had the status of a royal church with significant funding from both Susənyos and, later, Fasilädäs.

[1] A *tabot* can mean "altar" (as Ricci here translated) but is also a specific object sacred to the Täwaḥədo Church. Copies of the tablets of the Ten Commandments are kept in every Täwaḥədo Church, as well as their container, a replica of the original Ark of the Covenant, both of which are called tabot. Their presence renders a church a consecrated place. Churches often have more than one tabot, each dedicated to a different saint.

[2] BDJ: *mäkanä zä-wə'ətu fäqädä. Wä-gäbrät ʿəṣa* (lit., the place that he wanted. She did lots); CR: *mäkanä zä-tənäbbər* (the place where she would live).

[3] *Dära* is a region on the southeast side of Lake Ṭana, immediately south of Ǝnfraz and near her brother's land. It stretches from where the Blue Nile flows out of the lake up north to Ṣana Qirqos. Casting lots is a biblical way of determining God's will. In Ethiopia, one places three objects (such as crosses) on the altar (each representing different decisions), a priest prays for guidance, and then one waits for someone unknown to come into the church and randomly pick one.

[4] BDJ: *kämä-zə* (lit., like this); CR: *zä-kämä-zə* (that which is like this).

[5] Lit., *mäqdäs* (the holy place). This word can refer to the "holy of holies," the inner sanctum of the Täwaḥədo Church where only priests can go, or, more loosely, the entire church building. Women were never allowed into the inner sanctum unless the tabot had been removed, when they might go in to collect some dust to use in healing medicines. See Fritsch (2007).

[6] It is unclear what place women were excluded from here: the inner sanctum, the church, or the island. Women had always been excluded from the inner sanctum of the church, but the verb *bo'a* (to enter) suggests WP entered a building or a room, not just the island, and perhaps the author means to suggest that, under the "filthy faith" of Catholicism, women could do the

was shown its icon of our Lady Mary, one that was of the Egyptians,[1] painted in gold.[2] [In it], the Holy Virgin was neither too light nor too dark but of medium complexion,[3] like the people of the Ethiopia.[4]

Immediately, our holy and chosen mother Walatta Petros exclaimed, "This painting truly resembles our Lady Mary!"[5]

So the women who were with her inquired, "When have you seen our Lady Mary?!"

Immediately she altered[6] her story and kept them in the dark, replying [modestly], "I have not seen her. What I said was, 'Does this icon of our Lady Mary resemble her?' No, I didn't say, 'I have seen her.' "

Our holy mother Walatta Petros then observed three fasts on Tsana Island; namely, those of Qusqwaam, of Advent, and of Lent.[7]

Chapter 40: Our Mother Founds Her Third Community, on Mitsillé Island

[Over time,] our holy mother Walatta Petros made Tsana Island resemble a capital city owing to the great number of people [assembling around her]. Therefore, she

most extreme things. Today, women are not allowed on Ṣana Island at all, much less into the church, although Queen Məntəwwab went to this island in the eighteenth century.

[1] Lit., *əntä yəʾəti śəʿəlä Gəbṣawəyan* (lit., that was a picture of the Egyptians). This was a famous painting at Ṣana Qirqos, sometimes called *The Egyptian* (fem. sg., hence, in effect, *The Egyptian* [*Madonna*]), given to the monastery by King Śärṣä Dəngəl in 1597 and probably one of the post-Byzantine icons brought into Ethiopia by King Ləbnä Dəngəl before 1531 (Heldman 2005b, 141). *Gəbṣawəyan* (Egyptians) is often used in Ethiopia for foreigners of the Orthodox faith, including Greeks and Armenians. Thus, the author is probably not saying it is a painting done by Egyptians, but rather one done in a foreign style.

[2] Byzantine icons were painted on a gold ground, so "painted in gold" along with "Gəbṣawəyan" may mean "in a Byzantine style."

[3] Lit., *wä-i-konät qäyyəḥtä wä-i-ṣällamä* [fem.; thus D, CR; BJ with masc. *ṣällimä*] *alla maʾkälawit yəʾəti* (lit., she was not red, nor black, but in the middle).

[4] BDJ: *kämä säbʾa Ityopəya* (like the people of Ethiopia); CR: *kämä säbʾa ʿalämä Ityopəya* (like the people of the Ethiopian sphere).

[5] BDJ: *bä-aman təmässəla zati śəʿəl lä-əgzəʾtənä Maryam* (this painting truly resembles our Lady Mary); CR: *bä-aman təmässəl zati śəʿəl zä-əgzəʾtənä Maryam* (this painting of our Lady Mary truly resembles [*sic*]). Interestingly, WP claims that the Virgin Mary looks like an Ethiopian. WP interacts with five icons of the Virgin Mary: at Ṣana Island, Məṣəlle, Rema, Amba Maryam, and Fure.

[6] BDJ: *meṭät* (altered); CR: *walläṭät* (changed).

[7] This means that she stayed there about six months, from mid-November through late March or early April. The feast of Qʷəsqʷam, celebrating the successful flight of the Holy Family from Herod, is preceded by a ten-day fast, from 26 Ṭəqəmt until 6 Ḫədar. The Advent fast, anticipating the birth of Christ, is from 15 Ḫədar until 29 Taḫśaś, a forty-day fast. The Lenten fast, anticipating the resurrection of Christ, begins on a Monday in Yäkkatit and lasts fifty-six days. These are the three longest fasts. (See "Calendar" in the glossary for comparable months in English.)

did not want to remain there. So she prayed to God to reveal a place to her where she could live in solitude.

Thereupon, an angel of God appeared to her and said, "Go to Mitsillé Island![1] 59
Truly, that is your destined place."

Now our holy mother Walatta Petros sent these words to Malkiya Kristos, "Intercede for me before the king so that he will allow me to live on Mitsillé Island: it is a place of tranquillity and I prefer to live there."

So Malkiya Kristos asked King [Susinyos] as requested, and the king replied, "Hereby, I allow her to live [there]."

As a result, our holy mother Walatta Petros went forth and proceeded to Mitsillé Island. As soon as she saw that island, she loved it very much. The people there selected a house for her to live in. They found her one whose owner had abandoned it:[2] he had been sent into exile. Walatta Petros took possession [of it] and lived there.

Then, the abbot of the [Mitsillé] Monastery came to her, accompanied by monks who were of the faith of the Europeans,[3] and said to her, "Who admitted you to our place?[4] You who have rebelled against the king? If the king hears [of this],[5] he will flare up in anger against us and take vengeance upon us. Leave us, in peace! Otherwise we will have to use force against you."

Our holy mother Walatta Petros replied to them politely, "But the king[6] told me 'Live where you wish'! If you regard me as your enemy, however, I will leave you and abandon your monastery to you. But if I remain here, it will cause you no harm whatsoever."

As a result they left her alone and went away, since she had vanquished them by speaking politely, just as scripture[7] says, "Do not vanquish evil with evil but vanquish evil through doing good."[8] Furthermore, the Apostle Peter says, "For such is the will of God, that with your good deeds you tie the tongues[9] of foolish men who do not know God."[10]

[1] *Məṣəlle* Island, with a monastery called Məṣəlle Fasilädäs. It is about half a mile south of Ṣana Qirqos Island in Lake Ṭana and maybe two miles north of Rema Island. In former centuries, it was the residence of the famous saint Afqärännä Ǝgziʾ.

[2] BDJ: *zä-ḫadägo əgziʾu* (whose owner had abandoned it); CR: *zä-ḫadägä əgziʾu* (whose owner had abandoned).

[3] All three of the islands that WP thought about living on—Məṣəlle, Ṣana, and Daga—were small islands (no more than fifteen hundred feet long) that had long-established monasteries. So, it was not surprising that the priests there would be concerned about newcomers. Likewise, it seems both Məṣəlle and Ṣana were run by priests who had converted to Roman Catholicism or were sympathetic to it.

[4] Lit., *däbrənä* (our monastery).

[5] BDJ: *wä-lä-əmmä sämʿa nəguś* (if the king hears); CR omits.

[6] BJ: *nəguś-əssä* (but the king); D: *nəguś-ni* [same translation]; CR: *daʾəmu nəguś* (yet the king).

[7] BDJ: *mäṣḥaf* (scripture); CR: *P̣awlos* (Paul).

[8] Romans 12:21.

[9] BDJ, CR all with nominative *afuhomu* (their mouth), where accusative *afahomu* is clearly required.

[10] 1 Peter 2:15.

Afterward, our holy mother Walatta Petros lived [on Mitsillé Island] in perfect tranquillity. Many people, men and women, gathered around her and lived with her. Also Tsegga Kristos[1] of Amba Maryam[2] was there. They became a community:[3] it was[4] the third community.

Chapter 41: Our Mother is Persecuted by *Ras* Silla Kristos

At that time, [*Ras*] Silla Kristos, who [ultimately] died in the faith of the Europeans, heard that our mother Walatta Petros was on Mitsillé Island together with many people, and that she had refused the Eucharist [when administered by its Catholic priests]. He became enraged, roaring like a lion,[5] and ranted against her. He de-
60 manded: "Can it be that a woman defeats me? I will go to her, chastise her with the whip, and strike her on her cheeks! I will make her profess the faith of the Europeans[6] and take [their] Eucharist!"

When our holy mother Walatta Petros heard this, she left Mitsillé Island by night and, fleeing, arrived and hid at the monastic settlement of Qoratsa,[7] where we currently find ourselves.[8] From there, she stealthily[9] went to the Saint Michael church[10]

[1] *Ṣägga Krəstos* (The Grace of Christ) appears to be a learned monk. He later helps them interpret the holy book *Mäṣḥafä Ḥawi.*

[2] *Amba Maryam* may be in Ǝnfraz, just south of Qorada, about ten miles due east of the top northern part of Lake Ṭana, or it may be what is now known as Ṭeza Amba Maryam, about twenty miles north of Qʷäraṣa on the eastern shore of Lake Ṭana.

[3] BJ: *wä-konu l-maḫbärä* (they became a community); D: *wä-konä aḥadä maḫbärä* (it became a community); CR: *wä-konä aḥadä maḫdärä* (it became a dwelling place). We assume that *maḫbär* became corrupted to *maḫdär* due to the great acoustic similarity of the two words. Since their appearance in writing differs more, this is an indication that oral transmission played a role in the manuscript reproduction process.

[4] BDJ: *zə-wəʾətu* (it was); CR: *zä-wəʾətu* (that was).

[5] BDJ: *kämä ʿanbäsa* (like a lion); CR omits.

[6] BDJ: *əressəya təʾmän haymanotä afrənǧ* (I will make her profess the faith of the Europeans); CR: *əressəya təʾmän bä-haymanotä afrənǧ* (I will make her believe in the faith of the Europeans).

[7] *Qʷäraṣa,* but today *Qʷäraṭa,* is a town and monastery on the eastern shore of Lake Ṭana, within five miles of Məṣəlle and Ṣana islands, and in the region of Dära. Although Qʷäraṣa is mentioned only twice in the main text and not as one of WP's seven communities, the history appended to the text in 1735 stated that her community moved to Qʷäraṣa in 1649, six years after her death. The monastery there is dedicated to her. Perhaps partly because WP fled from *Ras* Śəʿəlä Krəstos to Qʷäraṣa, it became famous in the seventeenth and eighteenth century as a place of asylum.

[8] That is, where the author resides while writing this very text, or at least this portion of it.

[9] BDJ: *dəbutä* (stealthily); CR omits.

[10] *Qəddus Mikaʾel* may have been the name of the church at Qʷäraṣa at that time, as suggested by Bosc-Tiessé (2003, 414). Or, this may be a reference to any one of five Saint Michael's churches within one mile inland from Qʷäraṣa. Many churches were dedicated to Saint Michael.

and concealed herself in the vestry[1] [outside the church], staying there for a number of days. Meanwhile, [*Ras*] Silla Kristos sallied forth but passed by in a tankwa [without noticing her] because God did not allow him to do her harm: thus, his plan failed abjectly. For the Psalter rightly says, "The Lord frustrates the plans of the princes."[2] It was not for fear of flagellation or death that our holy mother Walatta Petros fled [from Mitsillé Island] but rather on account of the verse that says, "Do not put God your Lord to the test!"[3]

Thereafter, our holy mother Walatta Petros returned to Mitsillé Island. Then people told her,[4] "Mezraata Kristos[5] has come with a written authorization from the king to take captive the Christians in the entire region of Dera who have not embraced the faith of the Europeans, and he is also looking for you specifically. In fact, he is already here!"

When our holy mother Walatta Petros heard this, she again departed, fleeing to Sadachilla,[6] which was safe. Later, she again returned to Mitsillé.

Furthermore, people relate,[7] "She [once] was sent out[8] [onto Lake Tana] all alone on a tankwa without a pole and without anyone [accompanying her], while a violent wind was blowing, so that the waves would capsize her and make her drown, and she would die. Immediately though, the tankwa was lifted up from the lake and flew like an arrow flies, taking her to a port. Flying once again, it then took her back to her place of departure." Many from among the monastic brothers and sisters were witnesses to this miracle, and their testimonies agree.

After this, our holy mother Walatta Petros lived on Mitsillé Island in peace. With her were about fifty people in number. They lived in a single house, blessing the meal together and eating their food joyfully. The men and the women were not
separated except for sleeping because there was no thought of sin in their hearts.[9] 61
They were all pure, as Walatta Petros herself testified when she said, "The demon of fornication and the demon of desire are not permitted in my house!"

[1] Lit., *bä-betä mäzagəbt* (in the storehouse), a small building outside the church itself, but in the church compound, where the religious implements needed for the Liturgy are kept.

[2] Psalm 32[33]:10.

[3] Deuteronomy 6:16; Matthew 4:7; Luke 4:12. This is another example of where the text defends why WP did not always seek martyrdom.

[4] BDJ, CR: *wä-kaʿəbä sobä yəbeləwwa* (lit., when people then again told her). However, *sobä* (when) does not fit in here syntactically and therefore has been omitted in our translation.

[5] *Mäzraʿtä Krəstos* (Strong arm of/for Christ) appears to be a functionary of the royal court.

[6] *Sädäç̣əlla* is a town on the shore of southeastern Lake Ṭana directly opposite Məṣəlle Island, less than a mile away.

[7] BDJ: *yəbelu* (lit., said); CR: *yəbəlu* (say). That this story starts off abruptly and unclearly, a digression in a miraculous vein unlike little else said about WP, is suggestive about the drafting process of the book.

[8] J: *fännäwəwwa* (lit., they sent her out); BD, CR: *fännəwəwwa* (send her out! [imper. masc. pl.). Ricci assumed CR was erroneous and translated *la inviarono* (they sent her out). It remains unclear who here dispatched WP onto the troubled lake.

[9] Her *maḫbär* was not set up in a formal monastic way at this point. The *Gädlä Täklä Haymanot* also speaks of nuns and monks living together without sin (Guidi 1906, 378–83).

It is said of one of them, whose name was Marqoréwos,[1] that he used to leap up into the air on wings and go to Zagé.

Chapter 42: King Susinyos Renounces the Filthy Faith of the Europeans

While our holy mother Walatta Petros lived on Mitsillé Island, there rose up a pretender to the throne[2] whose name was Malkiya Kristos;[3] he declared himself king in Lasta.[4] Then Bihono[5] and his army, who had been sent by Malkiya Kristos, came and besieged King [Susinyos]. Malkiya Kristos wanted to kill the king and seize his kingdom.

As a result, King Susinyos became frightened and terrified and made a vow, "If God[6] gives me power and victory, and if he delivers this rebel into my hand, I will profess the faith of Dioscoros[7] and renounce the faith of filthy Leo."[8]

[1] *Märqorewos* (Mercurius).

[2] *Wäräñña* (pretender to the throne) is not Gəʿəz but an Amharic loanword.

[3] *Mälkəʾa Krəstos* was a nobleman (but not WP's husband) who claimed to be the rightful king between 1629 and 1635, partly because he remained Orthodox and Susənyos had converted to Roman Catholicism. In 1632, Susənyos defeated Mälkəʾa Krəstos in battle, but he escaped. Fasilädäs killed him in battle in 1635.

[4] *Lasta* is a historical province in a rugged region about one hundred miles due east of Lake Ṭana, in what is now known as Wällo. Its population long retained its separate Agäw identity even after having converted to Christianity and having been incorporated politically into the Amhara-dominated Ethiopian Christian kingdom. Inaccessibility and a separate ethnocultural identity made Lasta a breeding ground and refuge for rebels against the central authority and the monarch.

[5] *Bihono* commanded the anti-Catholic rebel forces (for a man who had the same name as WP's husband) fighting to depose Susənyos. He was a brilliant military strategist; among other victories he defeated *Ras* Śəʿəlä Krəstos. Although these forces were successful in almost reaching the royal court, in June 1632 Susənyos defeated Bihono, who died on the battlefield.

[6] BDJ: *əgziʾabḥer* (God); CR omits.

[7] D, CR: *Diyosqoros*; BJ: *Diyosqoros qəddus* (holy Dioscoros).

[8] BDJ: *haymanotä Ləyon rəkus* [masc.] (the faith of filthy Leo); CR: *haymanotä Ləyon rəkʷəst* [fem.] (the filthy faith of Leo). Since the adjective appears in the feminine in CR, it refers to the faith, not the person, and thus follows the usual formula "filthy faith" not "filthy Leo." BDJ has the reverse, the masculine form *rəkus*, and thus in BJ this phrase rhymes with the earlier *qəddus* (holy) after Dioscoros. As for historical context, within months of defeating Bihono, Susənyos had restored Orthodoxy. The closeness of these events may be why the *WP gädl* and that monarch's royal chronicle state that Susənyos vowed that, should he be successful in defeating Bihono, he would abandon Roman Catholicism. According to Susənyos's royal chronicle, Fasilädäs says to his father, "Lord King, see how everything is laid waste and agitated by the belief of the Franks, which we do not know and which we never heard of and which is not in the books of our fathers. We fear you and we love your face: we are united with you mouth and heart. Vow to the Lord to return to the faith of Alexandria if he gives you the victory over your enemies" (Basset 1882, 132).

Luckily for King Susinyos, things went as he had asked: he beat and killed Bihono and returned [to his court] in tranquillity. After this, he sent around a herald who proclaimed, "Whosoever, after he has heard my word, disobeys my order, and professes the faith of the Europeans—may his house be pillaged and may he himself be punished with death. Those Christians who have been sent into exile, however, may each return to their provinces and private lands."

This was a great joy for the Christians:[1] they returned to their homes praising God and thanking Him. Then the king sent a message with the good news[2] to our holy mother Walatta Petros, "Behold, I have reestablished the faith of the Christians and abolished the faith of the Europeans! Rejoice and exult! May there be peace between you and me from now on."

Chapter 43: Our Mother Celebrates the Return of the True Faith

When the king's messenger[3] arrived at our holy mother Walatta Petros['s home on Mitsillé Island], he gave her the written message that said this. She received it, read it, and was happy,[4] shouting with joy, just as the Psalter says, "You peoples all clap your hands and celebrate before God with joyful voices!"[5] Also, the priests who were with her sang, "We praise God the praiseworthy to whom praise is due!"[6] That day was[7] the third of the month of Hamlé.[8]

The next day the king's messenger[9] said to our holy mother Walatta Petros, 62
"Grant me leave to go to Tsana Island because the king has ordered me to take the good news there, too."

[1] Throughout the text, the author refers to the Orthodox faith as "the faith" and the Orthodox Christians as "the Christians," thus excluding the Roman Catholics from the realm of Christendom.

[2] *Bəśrat* does not refer to just any "good news" but is a religiously charged term, most often used specifically for the good news of the Gospel.

[3] BDJ: *laʾəkä nəguś* (the king's messenger); CR: *laʾək zä-nəguś* [different construction, but identical translation].

[4] BJ: *täfäśśəḥat* ([she] was happy); D: *täfäśśəḥat wä-täḥaśyät* ([she] was happy and joyful); CR omits.

[5] Psalm 46[47]:1.

[6] Exodus 15:2, as it appears in the first biblical canticle of the prophets in the Gəʿəz Psalter. See also Psalm 68[69]:30–31.

[7] BDJ: *wä-konä wəʾətu ʿəlät* (that day was); CR: *wä-konä zə-nägär* (this thing happened on).

[8] *Ḥamle* is the eleventh of Ethiopia's thirteen months, running that year from early July to early August. The text states that the return to the Orthodox faith happened officially on this date, 3 Ḥamle, which was 7 July (in 1632).

[9] BDJ: *laʾəkä nəguś* (the king's messenger); CR: *laʾək zä-nəguś* [different construction, but identical translation].

Accordingly, our holy mother Walatta Petros instructed *Abba* Za-Sillasé,[1] "Take this messenger to Tsana Island. Also, catch some fish for me there so that I can serve them in a *wot* stew[2] for the Feast of Peter and Paul."[3]

He responded, "Very well."

So, she blessed *Abba* Za-Sillasé and dismissed him. He left with the king's messenger and took him to Tsana Island. Right after this, *Abba* Za-Sillasé dropped his nets, throwing them into the lake, and was lucky enough to catch fish.[4] He spent the entire day fishing and then returned to Mitsillé Island, coming with a catch of thirteen fish.

These he presented to our holy mother Walatta Petros, saying, "Look, now I bring you what God has given me through your blessing."

Our holy mother Walatta Petros responded, "These twelve fish are[5] like the apostles, but this one is like their master, Christ. May the blessings of the apostles and the blessing of their master, Christ, rest upon you!"

"Amen!" *Abba* Za-Sillasé replied.

This thing that happened was truly miraculous, that the quantity of fish neither exceeded[6] nor fell short of this number.[7] On the next day was the Feast of Paul and Peter. Walatta Petros had a stew prepared from those fish and fed her entire community and all the people of the monastery.[8]

Chapter 44: King Susinyos Dies and Our Mother Remains at Mitsillé

After this had happened in the month of Hamlé, King Susinyos died on the tenth [day] of the month of Maskaram,[9] on the Feast of Tsédénya.[10] In his stead, his son

[1] *Zä-Śəllase* (He of the Trinity).

[2] Lit., *kämä yəkunäni ṣäbḫa* (so that they can be stew for me).

[3] The Feast of Peter and Paul happens on 5 Ḥamle, in honor of the two most important apostles of Christ. It is at the end of the *Ṣomä Ḥawaryat* (Fast of the Apostles), which lasts from the Monday after Pentecost to this feast.

[4] Eighteen fish are endemic to Lake Ṭana; most are cyprinids, and Nile tilapia (*Oreochromis niloticus*) is common.

[5] BDJ: *əmuntu* (are); CR omits.

[6] BDJ: *i-yətwessäk* (lit., does not exceed); CR: *yətwessäk* (exceeds).

[7] That is, catching thirteen fish that matched the apostles plus Christ was miraculous because it happened for the Feast of Peter and Paul, and the Apostle Peter was a fisherman, the one who caught no fish one day until Christ blessed him.

[8] Since Məṣəlle Monastery had been Catholic, and its monks had protested when WP had arrived on the island, fearing reprisals from Susənyos, WP shows exemplary Christian magnanimity in providing a feast for them.

[9] *Mäskäräm* is the first month of the Ethiopian solar year calendar, extending in 1632 from 8 September to 7 October. Thus, this would have been 17 September. The year of King Susənyos's death was 1632.

[10] *Ṣedenya* is the Feast of the Holy Virgin of Ṣaydnāyā (thus in Arabic), a place in Syria

Fasiladas became king;[1] he [fully] restored the [Orthodox] faith. *Abba* Atsfa Kristos,[2] the [rightful] abbot of [the monastery of] Mitsillé Island,[3] who had been a captive in the town of Téra,[4] returned in those days, and also other monks who had been exiled or who had fled from[5] the religion of the Europeans.[6]

After this our holy mother Walatta Petros remained [on Mitsillé Island] for a full year[7] because she had made a vow to Saint Fasiladas[8] with the following words, "If the [Orthodox] faith is reestablished, I will remain for [another] year, and I will receive[9] the Eucharist in this church of yours."[10]

Thus, she remained on Mitsillé Island, receiving[11] the Eucharist from the hands of [formerly] exiled priests. Every time [during Communion that] a priest said, "Send the grace of the Holy Spirit,"[12] she would plainly see the descent of the Holy Spirit. Also, when evening fell [each day] she would enter the church and stand like a fixed pillar before the icon of our Lady Mary, without leaning against a wall
or a column. She would pray and plead for the salvation of her soul and the deliv- 63
erance of all the people. She would spend the entire night praying, without rest. Then, when morning came and the sun rose, when the *Lives of the Saints*[13] was

---

with an icon of Mary that performed miracles. There are thirty-three feast days for Saint Mary in the Täwaḥədo Church; this is one of them and it is on 10 Mäskäräm.

[1] Fasilädäs ruled Ethiopia from 1632 to 1667. Regarding the scholarly debate on whether Susənyos abdicated, it is worthwhile to note that the *WP gädl* says nothing of Fasilädäs becoming king *before* his father died.

[2] *ʿAṣfä Krəstos* (The Mantle of Christ).

[3] As the text related earlier, the monks of Məṣəlle Island had converted to Catholicism when it was the state religion, and had installed a new abbot who wanted to chase away the known Orthodox stalwart WP when she had first arrived on the island.

[4] *Tera* is the name of several places. This may be what is now a monastery ten miles east of mid–Lake Ṭana or what was a region one hundred miles northeast of Lake Ṭana in the Səmen Mountains.

[5] BDJ: *əm-* (from); CR: *bä-* (due to).

[6] The previous Orthodox leadership of the Məṣəlle Island Monastery returned to take up leadership again.

[7] BDJ: *ʿamätä fəṣṣəmtä* (for a full year); CR: *ʿamätä fəṣṣəmənna* (for a year of completion).

[8] *Fasilädäs* was a second-century Greek Christian martyr celebrated on 11 Mäskäräm. He is a popular Ethiopian saint (the new king was named after him) and, as one of the equestrian or military saints commonly believed to possess apotropaic power, was often painted near the entrance of churches. The church on Məṣəlle Island was dedicated to Saint Fasilädäs in the early fifteenth century, and in the *WP gädl* the saint plays a special role in the text for those who stay on the island.

[9] D: *ətmeṭṭo* (I will receive), in parallel with the earlier indicative *ənäbber* (I will remain); BJ, CR: *ətmäṭṭo* [*sic*: subj.].

[10] Previously, she had refused to receive the Eucharist there (and elsewhere) because it was administered by priests converted to Catholicism. Now, with the right faith restored, she could, with a clear conscience, do so.

[11] BDJ, Abb. 88: *ənzä tətmeṭṭo* (receiving); CR altered this to *ənzä tətmeṭṭomu* [*sic*, probably intended for *ənzä tətmeṭṭäwwomu* (receiving them)].

[12] BD: *mänfäs qəddus* (the Holy Spirit); J omits *qəddus* (holy); CR: *mänfäs qəddəs* [*sic*; *qəddəs* is a nonexistent form, clearly a corruption from *qəddus* (holy)].

[13] The *Sənkəssar*, from Greek *synaxárion* (collection), called *Synaxarium* in Latin, and

read, and when the closing prayer was finished, she would leave the church and go to her home. There she would read the Gospel of John.[1] She would do this every day, becoming like *Abba* Arsenius.[2] The number of her years in that year was thirty-nine.[3]

Chapter 45: Our Mother Is Healed of an Abundant Flow of Blood

[At that time,] an abundant flow of [menstrual] blood used to torment Walatta Petros, and she suffered greatly.[4] During her standing [at night in the church], she would implore the icon of our Lady Mary, saying to her, "I beg you, my Lady, for my sake, implore [the Lord] that this blood may dry up![5] I am truly tormented."

[One night,] the icon then spoke to her[6] and said, "Why do you constantly importune me?[7] Behold, I have heard your prayers[8] and have seen your suffering! For your sake, I now dry up[9] your period. From now on, therefore, blood will never again flow from you."

Right away, then, her period dried up, even though she was still young and had not yet reached the age at which menstruation ceases. She resembled the woman who had touched the hem of the Lord Jesus's clothes, in keeping with what Jesus

---

Lives of the Saints in English, is a large collection of short accounts of foreign and indigenous saints' lives in Gəʿəz. The readings for any given day are for the saints who died that day, and it is traditionally read right before the closing words of the service.

[1] The monk Mälkəʾa Krəstos had commanded her to read the Gospel of John constantly.

[2] *Arsanyos* was one of the Desert Fathers, a fifth-century learned Roman deacon and solitary monk (sometimes called Arsenius the Deacon or Arsenius of Scetis). According to the *Sayings of the Fathers*, he frequently stayed up all night praying.

[3] BDJ: *39*; CR: *49*. A year after Susənyos died, in 1633, WP would have been forty-one by our calculations. If she was thirty-nine, her birth year would have been 1594, but most other dating in the *WP gädl* suggests that she was born in 1592.

[4] She may have had uterine fibroids, a common condition associated with extremely heavy menstrual bleeding and prolonged menses.

[5] Lit., *kämä yənṣəf litä zəntu däm bä-səʾlätəki* (so that this blood may dry up for me through your entreaty). At least two other Ethiopian female saints' hagiobiographies depict them praying to be relieved of their menstrual periods, those of Zena Maryam and Wälättä Maryam. Christian women were not secluded during menstruation, so they could still participate in the life of the community then, but they could not enter the church during menstruation.

[6] BDJ: *wä-tänagäräta zati śəʿəl* (the icon then spoke to her); Abb. 88: *wä-tanägäräta* [*sic*: an nonexistent form] *zati śəʿəl*, which CR inadequately altered to *wä-tänägäräta zati śəʿəl* (the icon then it was spoken to her [*sic*]).

[7] BDJ: *mənt-nu tanäṭṭəyəni* [*sic*, substandard for *tanäṭṭəyini*] *zälfä* (why do you constantly importune me); CR: *i-tanṭəyəni* [*sic*, substandard for *i-tanṭəyini*] *zälfä* (do not constantly importune me).

[8] CR adds: *wä-səʾlätäki* (and your entreaties).

[9] BDJ: *wä-aybäsku* (I now dry up); CR: *wä-anṣäfku* [synonymous verb, hence, same meaning].

had said to her, "Your faith has healed you."[1] Likewise, full of faith, our holy mother Walatta Petros had stood before the icon of our Lady Mary and was healed from this illness.

As for the [former] exiles, they used to visit our holy mother Walatta Petros every day and exchange stories of all the tribulations and hardships that each had encountered in exile. But they also rejoiced over their return and spoke among themselves just as Paul had spoken, "Now indeed that life of ours for which we had hoped is near. The night has passed and the day has come."[2]

Furthermore, they said, "Blessed be our Lord God who did not deliver us into the treacherous net of the Europeans![3] Indeed, our souls fled like birds from a hunting net. Now, the net has been torn asunder, and we are safe."[4]

Chapter 46: Our Mother Is Challenged by a Monk

In those days, our holy mother Walatta Petros celebrated the *tazkaar* commemoration[5] of our father *Abba* Zara Yohannes[6] because he had died on Amba Maryam
(from which he [previously] had been exiled). She generously gave much to eat and 64
drink to the people of the [Mitsillé Island] Monastery and to the entire community.
She exhausted everything she had and did not save anything for the next day, according to what the Gospel says, "Do not say: '[This is] for the next day,' because
the next day will itself take care of itself."[7]

[1] BDJ: *aḥyäwätäki* (has healed you); Abb. 88 with ungrammatical *aḥyäwätəki*, which CR altered to correct *aḥyäwätäki*. Matthew 9:22. The story of Mark 5:25–34; Matthew 9:20–22; and Luke 8:42–48 is of a woman whose period had not ceased in twelve years. Desperate, she decides that if she can merely touch the hem of Jesus's cloak, she will be healed. She does so and is healed, with Jesus responding kindly to her even though she is in an impure state.

[2] Romans 13:11–12.

[3] BDJ: *wəstä mäśgärtä maʿgätomu lä-Afrənǧ* (lit., into the net of the Europeans' snares); CR: *wəstä mäśgärtomu lä-Afrənǧ* (into the net of the Europeans).

[4] Based on Psalms 123[124]:6–7.

[5] *Täzkar* is a feast held on a set of days after a person dies (the thirtieth, fortieth, and ninetieth days) including the anniversary. Daily prayers are held every day for forty days after a person's death while God judges where his or her soul shall spend the time until the Second Coming of Christ. On the fortieth day is God's final decision. Some commemorate the death of a loved one on every anniversary of the death.

[6] BDJ: *abunä abba Zärʾa Yoḥannəs* (our father *Abba* Seed of [Saint] John); CR: *abunä abba Yoḥannəs* (our father *Abba* John). He may have been a leading member of WP's community, but since *abunä* can mean patriarch, perhaps he was treated as the Orthodox patriarch for the ten years that Mendes was the official patriarch during the period of Roman Catholicism.

[7] Matthew 6:34. In this case and many others, the biblical quote appears slightly different than in the original Greek or Hebrew. We did not check each quote against the Gəʿəz Bible to identify whether these differences reflect those of the Ethiopic Bible itself or are merely the alterations of the hagiobiography's author Gälawdewos.

Yet one monk grumbled when he saw this, "What is this giving without restraint while we don't have our daily bread? Is this not being done for empty praise? But what will *we* eat tomorrow!"[1]

Eheta Kristos rebuked him, however, "O you of poor understanding and lacking in hope! Do you imagine God is as poor as yourself? Is he not so rich that he can satisfy whoever calls out to him, today just as much as tomorrow?"

At that very moment, messengers arrived with food about which no one had had any prior knowledge, nine donkey loads[2] here and four donkey loads there. Those who witnessed it[3] marveled and praised God.

Chapter 47: Our Mother Establishes Her Fourth Community, at Zagé

One full year after the days of persecution were over, Walatta Petros again prayed for three weeks with great devotion, standing before that icon [of Saint Mary], which previously had spoken to her.[4] Walatta Petros said to Saint Mary, "My Lady, I implore you to reveal to me the place where I should live and to enlighten me[5] as to your will and the will of your son."

So the icon once again spoke to our holy mother Walatta Petros and said to her, "Go to Zagé! Truly, this is my wish, and the wish of my beloved son."

After Walatta Petros had heard this pronouncement[6] from the icon of our Lady Mary, she assembled *Abba* Atsfa Kristos, abbot of the Mitsillé Island [Monastery], and the monks. She bid them farewell and told them that she would go to Zagé. In addition, she implored them not to bring anything female onto Mitsillé Island because in the hagiography of our father Afqaranna Egzee[7] she had found the prohibition that no female creature should set foot on the island.[8]

[1] BDJ: *wä-nəḥnä məntä nəbälləʿ gesämä* (but what will we [emph.] eat tomorrow); CR: *wä-albənä zä-nəbälləʿ gesämä* (but we will have nothing we can eat tomorrow).

[2] *Č̣an* (lit., load) is an Amharic word for a particular measurement of grain, the amount of grain one donkey can carry.

[3] BDJ: *wä-əllä rəʾyu zäntä* (lit., those who saw this); CR: *wä-sobä rəʾyu zäntä* (when they saw this).

[4] BDJ: *zä-tänagäräta qädimu* (which previously had spoken to her); CR: *zä-nägäräta qädimu* (which previously had told her).

[5] BDJ: *wä-təśärrəḫani* (and to enlighten me); CR: *wä-təśrəḫani* (and be bright me [*sic*: intransitive verb combined with the object suffix *-ni*]). Ricci suggests an error here by reproducing the CR verb in a note and by translating it as *secondare* (to assist *or* to favor). We fail to see the justification for such a translation.

[6] BDJ: *zäntä qalä* (this pronouncement); CR: *zäntä* (this).

[7] BDJ, CR: *Afqärännä Ǝgziʾ* (the Lord has loved us). He is a venerated fourteenth-century saint, said to be the founder of the monasteries at Məṣəlle Island and Gʷəgʷəben on Lake Ṭana. The hagiobiography of his life, *Gädla Yafqərännä Ǝgziʾ*, is an important source on Christianity and monasticism around Lake Ṭana. The first element of the saint's name, Afqärännä, here differs from that in most texts, which have *Yafqərännä Ǝgziʾ*, meaning "May the Lord love us."

[8] BDJ: *kämä i-yəbaʾ fəṭrätä anəst wəstä yəʾəti däset* (that no female creature should set

They replied, "So be it!" and on that very day they expelled the female creatures who were on Mitsillé Island. *Abba* Atsfa Kristos furthermore forbade female creatures from ever being readmitted [to Mitsillé Island].[1]

Our holy mother Walatta Petros took her leave from them after she had established this rule. She left that day and spent the night at Owf Gojjo.[2] From there, she departed and arrived at the monastic settlement of Zagé. **65**

There she remained, and many people gathered around her, grown men as well as grown women, old folks as well as children, young men as well as young women. They came from east and west, with their number increasing by the day. This was the fourth community.

Chapter 48: Zagé Male Leaders Work Against Our Mother

Then Satan entered into the hearts of important men[3] [of the previously established Zagé community] and roused them against Walatta Petros. They went to her with their spiritual leader and said to her, "Who brought you here, and who has given this monastic settlement to you? Is it not ours?[4] So, now we say to you, 'Leave, in peace!' or else we will use force with you and set your hut on fire."

Our holy mother Walatta Petros received them with love and courtesy, however, and served them food and drink. They ate their fill and came to their senses. They returned to goodness, left her in peace, and went away. Truly, scripture says likewise, "If your enemy is hungry, feed him, if he is thirsty, give him something to drink. If you do this, you will heap burning coals upon his head."[5]

At that time, after having heard of this, *Abba* Tsawaaré Masqal,[6] the abbot of Tsana Island [Monastery], and *Abba* Mankir[7] of Wonchet [Monastery] came to

---

foot on the island); CR: *kämä i-yəgbaʾ fəṭrätä anəst wəstä yəʾəti däset* (that no female creature should enter the island). All females, human and animal, are forbidden from some monasteries, including some of those on Lake Ṭana. The Jesuits tried to abolish this prohibition, and queens did sometimes go to such monasteries for refuge, but most strongly held to the tradition. The editor of *Gädlä Yafqərännä Əgziʾ* notes, however, that the saint's text does not contain this prohibition on female creatures (although Yafqərännä Əgziʾ had many conflicts with nuns) (Wajnberg 1917, 11). Thus, this prohibition may be from an oral tradition about the saint or from a variant manuscript.

1 The *Kəbrä Nägäśt* also features a scene in which a powerful woman in authority forbids other women from having authority: Makədda forbids any women being queen in future.

2 *ʿOf goǧǧo* (bird's nest) is an island on Lake Ṭana. WP uses it to go from Məṣəlle (in the southeast of the lake) to Zäge (on the southwest of the lake), so it may be in southern Lake Ṭana.

3 Lit., *kəburan säbʾ* (honored men).

4 BDJ: *akko-nu ziʾanä wəʾətu* (is it not ours); CR: *akko-nu zä-ziʾaki wəʾətu* (is it not by your own [whim that you have come here]).

5 Romans 12:20; Proverbs 25:21–22.

6 *Ṣäware Mäsqäl* (He who carries the cross).

7 *Mänkər* (The miraculous one).

visit our holy mother Walatta Petros. She told them what the important men had said to her.

Upon hearing [this], *Abba* Tsawaaré Masqal replied, "Don't be distressed. If you want to live at Zagé, no one can hinder you. Let us send [a message] to the king, and he will announce this monastic settlement as your place of residence.[1] Or else, live in the monastic settlement of Qoratsa; I myself will grant it to you.[2] However, [first,] give us your okay.

"[For now,] we would like to suggest one [other] thing: Come and let us go to Béta Manzo.[3] We would like to spend some time there with you so that Tsegga Kristos[4] might interpret the *Comprehensive Book*[5] for us."

Chapter 49: Our Mother Escapes an Epidemic

With difficulty, they managed to get her to consent [to leave Zagé]. But this [departure] was due to God's wise foresight[6] because he wanted to protect her from an epidemic.[7] Also, other religious people[8] who possessed foreknowledge informed her, "Behold, an epidemic will come and kill many of your followers.[9] You should depart so that you may survive and [later again] be an example for everyone."

[1] Lit., *läki* (for you).

[2] Although the leader of Ṣana Island and its Ṣana Qirqos Monastery only suggests that he will give Qʷäraṣa to her here, it seems he later in fact did, since it became the monastery most closely associated with her, as attested in the *Short History of Walatta Petros's Community*.

[3] *Betä Mänzo* is a very small island right in front of Qʷäraṣa.

[4] *Ṣägga Krəstos* (Grace of Christ) was probably not the well-known seventeenth-century church leader and *əčč̣äge* (head monk) of Däbrä Libanos Monastery. The latter was active in the 1670s through the 1690s, while this anecdote took place in the 1630s. However, since the author was writing in the 1680s, perhaps he retroactively inserted the then-famous leader.

[5] *Mäṣḥäfä Ḥawi* (The Ḥawi Book). This is a collection of rules of moral theology used to teach church dogma and history, translated in 1582 from the Arabic, which was itself translated from an eleventh-century Greek original. It includes detailed instructions regarding monks and nuns. The Arabic title, *Al-kitāb al-ḥāwī*, means "The Comprehensive Book" (with *ḥāwī* [comprehensive] just being transcribed in Gəʿəz, but not translated).

[6] Lit., *zə-ni ṭəbäbä əgziʾabḥer wəʾətu* (this however was God's wisdom).

[7] This unspecified "epidemic" (*bədbəd)* was probably typhus. The contagious diseases in Ethiopia that could have caused an epidemic were typhus (*nədad*), cholera (*fängəl*), smallpox (*bädädo, kufañ*), dysentery (*ḥəmamä fänṣänt, ḥəmamä aṭraqi*), influenza, and the plague (*däwe qʷəsl*). The plague is attested for this region of Ethiopia in the mid-1630s and cholera specifically for 1634–35. In the *WP gädl*, the first victim dies three days after developing symptoms, however, which is more typical of typhus and plague than cholera, which killed more quickly. Typhus was most likely to happen in crowded environments, such as WP's constantly growing communities.

[8] Lit., *qəddusan* (saints).

[9] Lit., *däqiq* (children). The *WP gädl* often refers to her followers as her "children." To avoid readers' confusing her followers with biological children, we have always translated *däqiq* as "followers" when it has this contextual meaning.

Some people [even] say, "The epidemic revealed itself to her[1] while bending its bow." So they urged her, "Depart!"

So our holy mother Walatta Petros went with *Abba* Tsawaaré Masqal and *Abba*
Mankir, came to Béta Manzo, and stayed there. After this a man, the father of Kris- 66
tos Sinnaa,[2] came to Zagé, where Walatta Petros's community welcomed him. But on that same day, he began to suffer from the epidemic's illness, and died on the third day. In those days, many monks and nuns fell ill due to that epidemic.

When our holy mother Walatta Petros heard of this, she said, "I, too, will go and die together with my disciples. I want to share in their illness and in every tribulation that befalls them."

But they implored her and forbade her to go; they said to her, "If you went and died together with them, that would not benefit them in any way. Rather, we will send people who can carry [away] the sick and bury the dead."

With difficulty, they made Walatta Petros give up [the idea of] returning [to Zagé]. Then they dispatched people [there], as they had promised. During that period, fifty-seven[3] souls died from the epidemic. They completed their earthly struggle and entered the Kingdom of Heaven, gaining what[4] God had [also] solemnly promised to our father Takla Haymanot,[5] saying to him, "If your followers die of an epidemic, I will count them among the martyrs and I will entrust them to you in the Kingdom of Heaven."[6] May their prayers and blessings be with ___________[7] for eternity, amen.

Chapter 50: The Mother of Our Mother Dies

So, our holy mother Walatta Petros remained in Béta Manzo. [There] she began to restore the church, which had gone to ruin. At that time, her mother Kristos Ebayaa arrived because she wanted to visit our holy mother Walatta Petros. At Béta Manzo, Kristos Ebayaa fell ill by the will of God. When the illness violently seized her and she was close to death, Walatta Petros ordered her to be taken to Réma Monastery,

[1] BDJ: *lati* (to her); CR: *bati* (against her), also implying a different syntactic division: bending its bow against her.

[2] *Krəstos Śənna* (In Christ lies her beauty).

[3] BDJ: *57*; CR: *56*.

[4] Lit., *bä-kämä* (as).

[5] *Täklä Haymanot* (Plant of the faith) is the most venerated indigenous saint in the Täwaḥədo Church. This monk lived in the fourteenth century, founded the Däbrä Libanos Monastery, and was an evangelist in much of central and southern Ethiopia.

[6] The quote is from the *Gädlä Täklä Haymanot* (Täklä Ṣəyon 1906, 227). The point that those who follow saints and die of epidemics are automatically saved is essential to understanding the later anecodote about lustful nuns.

[7] B: *fəquromu Agnaṭəyos* (their beloved Ignatius); D: *nəguśənä Dawit* (our king David); J: *fəqərtomu Mälkəʾa Maryam* (their beloved Mälkəʾa Maryam [Image of Mary (fem. name)]); Abb. 88: *fəquru* [name erased] (his beloved [name erased]), which CR edited to [*məsle*]*nä* ([with] us).

but she died while she was [still] on the tankwa, before arriving on the island. Then she was buried on Réma Island. Meanwhile, our holy mother Walatta Petros was at Béta Manzo, where she heard [the news] and wept for her mother.[1]

As for the church [of Béta Manzo], it was [re]built through the will of God, with Walatta Petros drawing water and carrying stones [for the construction]. Afterward, she sent people with tankwas to pick up the surviving sick [from Zagé]. They [went and] took them to[2] a little island that was close to Gwangoot[3] until they had fully recovered. After this, our holy mother Walatta Petros went to Réma Monastery to hold the tazkaar for her mother. There she performed the tazkaars of the thirtieth and the fortieth day. After this, the months of the rainy season began.

Chapter 51: Our Mother Raises the Monk Silla Kristos from the Dead

Walatta Petros spent the rainy season on Réma Island and while there worked a
67 miracle: She resuscitated Silla Kristos[4] after he had died, as he himself has testified.

One day, while Réma Monastery lacked a deacon who could celebrate the Liturgy—because the Europeans had contaminated the deacons [with Catholicism] and a patriarch[5] [who could ordain deacons] had not yet arrived[6]—our holy mother Walatta Petros ordered Silla Kristos to celebrate the Liturgy, but he replied,[7] "No!"

So she ordered him again, but he again replied, "No!" [Thereby,] he aggrieved her.

Furthermore, he disdained her and held her in contempt, saying in his heart, but not with his mouth, "What is it with this woman who gives me orders, acting as if she were a spiritual leader or a monastic superior? Does not scripture say to her, 'We do not allow a woman to teach, nor may she exercise authority over a man'?"[8]

[1] BDJ: *wä-bäkäyäta lä-əmma* (and wept for her mother); CR: *wä-bäkäyät lä-əmma* [different construction, but identical translation].

[2] BDJ: *wä-amṣəʾəwwomu wä-anbärəwwomu wəstä* (lit., they brought them and put them on); CR: *wä-anbärəwwomu wä-amṣəʾəwwomu wəstä* (they put them [in the tankwas] and brought them to).

[3] *Gʷangʷət* is a place on southeastern Lake Ṭana, north of Ṣana Qirqos, that is now most closely associated with fifteenth-century Krəstos Śämra, Ethiopia's most venerated indigenous female saint. The island may be what is now called Č̣əqla Mänzo.

[4] *Śəʿəlä Krəstos* was a priest and monk, not the Roman Catholic counselor of former emperor Susənyos who persecuted WP for her beliefs and was executed by Fasilädäs.

[5] *P̣appas* (patriarch).

[6] Since the head of the Täwaḥədo Church was the only one authorized to ordain new priests, none had been authorized since the Roman Catholic Jesuit Afonso Mendes had acted as the patriarch of Ethiopia from 1622 to 1632.

[7] BDJ: *yəbela* (lit., said to her); CR: *yəbe* (said).

[8] BDJ: *bəʾəsit-əssä təmhar i-nabäwwəḥa wä-i-təmäbbəl laʿlä bəʾəsi* (lit., as for a woman, we do not allow her to teach, nor may she exercise authority over a man); CR: *zə-*[*sic*]*bəʾəsit təmhar i-nabäwwəḥa wä-təmäbbəl laʿlä bəʾəsi* (this [*sic*: masc.] woman, we do not allow her to teach or to exercise authority over a man). 1 Timothy 2:12.

Our holy mother Walatta Petros was aware of his concealed thoughts, but did not reveal anything to him. In that month, on the eleventh of the month of Maskaram,[1] was the Feast of Saint Fasiladas. For this reason, Silla Kristos went to Mitsillé Island. But when God wanted to reveal the power of our holy mother Walatta Petros, he brought down a severe disease on Silla Kristos, who fell sick on the very day that he had left [Réma Island].

When the disease began to affect him badly,[2] he said, "Take me to Réma," and right away, he was picked up and taken there.[3] He was laid down in Tabota Kristos's house.[4] He [already] was like a corpse. He did not eat, he did not drink, he did not move, and he did not speak. Rather, the whole day he groaned, "Elohé, elohé."[5] His entire body swelled: he was afflicted with dropsy.[6]

On the eighth day after he had fallen sick, Silla Kristos died on the Feast of *Abba* Ewostatéwos,[7] on the eighteenth of the month of Maskaram.[8] Then water was heated to wash him, a cloth was brought to shroud him, and his dead body was wrapped in it. The threads of the shrouding cloth were carefully tied together,[9] and everything one does for a dead body was properly performed.[10] Then messengers went and told our holy mother Walatta Petros [about Silla Kristos' passing]. They found her reading the book of the *Miracles of Our Lady Mary*,[11] and told her that he had died.

[1] That is, on 18 or 19 September of that year.

[2] Lit., *wä-sobä ṣänʿa laʿlehu* (when it grew strong against him).

[3] It seems that Rema Island was believed to have healing properties, because WP's mother had been sent there when she was sick as well.

[4] *Tabotä Krəstos* (Altar of Christ). Perhaps people were mentioned in passing like this because they were still alive when the author was writing the *WP gädl.*

[5] *Elohe, Elohe* (my God, my God) is a hybrid of Hebrew *elohim* and the Amharic first singular possessive suffix *-e.*

[6] BDJ: *wä-konä qəbəwä* (he was afflicted with dropsy); CR: *wä-konä bəqəwä* (his mouth stood open). This would not have been an infectious disease but organ failure related to an underlying heart, kidney, or liver disease, which leads to generalized swelling, such as acute or chronic viral hepatitis.

[7] DJ: *abba Ewosṭatewos*; B: *abunä abba Ewosṭatewos* (our father *Abba* Ewostatewos); CR: *Ewosṭatewos.* This *Ewosṭatewos* (Eustathios) was a medieval monastic reform leader, perhaps the second most important indigenous saint after Täklä Haymanot.

[8] That is, on 25 or 26 September of that year.

[9] Lit., *aśännäyu fätlä gənzät* (they carefully executed the threads of the shrouding).

[10] According to the specifications of the *Mäṣḥafä Gənzät* (Book of the Funeral Ritual), people were buried the day they died, and an older person of the same sex would wash them with water, seal all body openings, tie thumbs together and first toes together, and wrap the whole body in a white shroud. Monks and nuns would be buried slightly differently than others: only another monk or nun could prepare the body, and they placed crosses made of thread on the body.

[11] *Täʾamməriha lä-Əgzəʾtənä Maryam* (more often simply called *Täʾamərä Maryam* [Miracles of Mary]) is a collection of stories about the miracles that the Virgin Mary performed for the faithful. Perhaps two dozen of the tales were originally written down in twelfth-century France (although they often appear substantially altered in the *Täʾamərä Maryam*)

Plate 17. "How she [i.e., our mother] told the icon of our Lady Mary about her distress" (top) and "how she killed Silla Kristos through her prayer and how she resurrected him" (bottom) (MS A, f. 151v © SLUB Mscr.Dresd.Eb.415.e,2).

Instantly, she went to the church, taking that book with her. Then she stood before the icon of our Lady Mary and implored her, "My Lady, it shouldn't be like this! Truly, I didn't ask you to kill him but to chasten him. The chastening that he received through his disease suffices [as punishment] for him. Merciful One, have mercy for my sake!"

Now fingers emerged from the *Miracles*[1] and tapped on Walatta Petros's mouth.[2] In addition, a voice emanated from inside the icon and said to her, "You of two tongues, go away![3] I hereby grant you [the] mercy [you have asked for]."

Immediately[4] our holy mother Walatta Petros left the church, returned to her **68**
home, summoned Eheta Kristos, and said to her, "Has Silla Kristos died before turning himself into a monk? I beg you, go to him, call out his name three times, and say to him, 'Silla Kristos, turn yourself into a monk!' "

Eheta Kristos went to him, called out his name three times, and said to him, "Silla Kristos, turn yourself into a monk!"

Instantly, he woke up, opened his eyes, looked at her, and heard the words that she had addressed to him. With his eyes, he then made a sign to her as if saying "Yes!"

Now they brought a monk's cap, blessed it for him, and put it on his head. At that moment, he rose up and was alive again, like before.[5] Then they brought him food, and he ate.

Chapter 52: The Monk Silla Kristos Sees a Vision

Listen further: We will tell you about the vision that Silla Kristos saw on the day that his soul separated from his body. He recounted, "A man of light with the appearance of a monk came to me. It seemed to me that he was *Abba* Ewostatéwos; the day, in fact, was that of his feast. This man took me with him, making me ascend up high and showing me a luminous and bright town whose colors are unknown [in this world] and whose shapes are inexpressible in earthly terms.[6] Beyond that town, he furthermore showed me another one that was called Paradise. In that town were big trees[7] without fruit, but also small trees with fruit. So, I asked

---

and translated from Arabic into Gəʿəz in the fourteenth century. Hundreds of original stories were added in Egypt or Ethiopia afterward.

[1] BDJ: *əmənnä täʾamər* (from the *Miracles*); CR: *əmənnä śəʿəl* (from the icon). This is an example of a significant difference in manuscripts, with most once again emphasizing the power of the written word.

[2] BDJ: *wä-dägʷäṣa afaha* (lit., and they tapped on her mouth); CR: *wä-dägʷäṣäta afuha* [*sic*: nom.] (and it tapped her [on] her mouth).

[3] The Virgin Mary often speaks sternly to WP, like a mother to a straying child.

[4] BDJ: *wä-sobeha* (immediately); CR: *wä-* (then).

[5] BDJ: *kämä qädami* (like before); CR: *kämä zä-qädami* (the same one as before).

[6] Lit., *bä-dibä mədr* (on earth).

[7] As part of the extended metaphor here, *big* appears in the masculine personal plural *ʿabiyan*, for which there is no justification in its immediate referent trees (*aʿwam*). Rather,

the man, 'What are these big trees that bear no fruit?' The man responded, 'They are monks who thought highly of themselves. They went by the name of monks, wore the clothes of monks, and wanted to be called *abba* here and *abba* there, but they did not do the work of monks. Rather, they spent their days in laziness and sloth, constantly wandering from town to town. Therefore, they did not bring forth any fruitful works.' I then further asked him, 'So, those small trees that bear fruit, what are they?,' and he further replied, 'They are monks who humbled themselves, who were not famous and whom nobody knew except God. They stayed awake day
69 and night in prayer and in prostration, wandering to minister for the relief of others. Therefore, they brought forth abundant fruit, as the Gospel says in the Parable of the Seed, "There is some seed that falls between the thorns, and the thorns suffocate and choke it so that it does not bear fruit. But there is also some seed that falls on good soil and yields fruit, some hundredfold, some sixtyfold, and some thirtyfold." ' "[1]

Silla Kristos told us all these things: that Walatta Petros had killed him, that she had resuscitated him, and that he had seen this [vision].[2] He is alive right up to now, and his testimony is trustworthy; he does not lie.

Do you see the great power of our holy mother Walatta Petros, how she made him who covertly had spoken ill of her and abused her, fall ill and die? She, too, covertly killed him and covertly resuscitated him. [That is,] she did not say to him, "Rise up!" but rather said to him, "Turn yourself into a monk!" because she feared vain praise.[3] Saying "Turn yourself into a monk," however, amounts to saying, "Rise up!" She herself told him this, saying, "I killed you and I resuscitated you through the power of my Lord. For you had treated me with contempt and abused me."

So, it is not acceptable for people to speak ill of and abuse those whom God has set up as leaders and appointed, in keeping with what scripture says: "Do not speak ill of your people's leader."[4] In the past, when Miriam and Aaron had secretly spoken ill of and abused Moses, leprosy [sores] had appeared on Miriam and she had

---

this masculine personal plural foreshadows the monks symbolized by the trees, but expressly only mentioned later. The same is true of small trees, *ʿəṣ́äwat nəʾusan*, in the next sentence.

[1] D: *bo-ḫabä 100 wä-bo ḫabä 60 wä-bo ḫabä 30* (some hundredfold, some sixtyfold, and some thirtyfold); J: *bo 100 wä-bo 60 wä-bo 30* (some one hundred, some sixty, and some thirty); B: *bo zä-100 wä-bo zä-60 wä-bo zä-30* (some hundredfold, some sixtyfold, and some thirtyfold); CR: *bo zä-40 wä-bo zä-60 wä-bo zä-100* (some fortyfold, some sixtyfold, and some hundredfold). See Matthew 13:8, which in the Greek is *hò mèn hekatón hò dè hexḗkonta hò dè triákonta* (some indeed a hundredfold, some moreover sixty, some moreover thirty). See also Mark 4:7 and Luke 8:7.

[2] BDJ: *kämä-hi qätäläto wä-kämä-hi anśəʾato wä-kämä-hi rəʾyä zäntä* (lit., that she killed him, that she resuscitated him, and that he saw this); CR: *əmmä-hi qätäläto wä-əmmä-hi anśəʾato wä-əmmä-hi rəʾyä zäntä* (be it she killed him, be it she resuscitated him, or be it he saw this).

[3] In other words, she did not command him to rise from the dead, she commanded him to raise himself from the dead, in order to conceal her wonder-working powers from the community.

[4] Exodus 22:28.

been expelled from the camp [of the Israelites] for seven days until they had confessed with their mouths and openly declared their sins, with Aaron saying to Moses,[1] "We have sinned because we have spoken ill of God. Please, pray for her so that this leprosy disappears from her."[2] So, Moses prayed for Miriam, and she was healed. This [story of Silla Kristos] is similar.

Chapter 53: Our Mother Saves Her Followers from an Epidemic

After this incident, our holy mother Walatta Petros went forth and proceeded to the island of Damboza.[3] She remained there for some time. But on Damboza, too, a grave disease broke out from which the entire community fell sick. Twelve souls from among them who had survived the [earlier] epidemic died. They completed their [earthly] struggle[4] and passed away in peace, inheriting eternal life. May their prayers and blessings be with ____________,[5] for eternity, amen.

Those who survived suffered great torment, such that their bodies were covered with scabs and their [entire] appearance changed by the ferocity of the disease and 70
by hunger.[6]

In those days, the [new Ethiopian Orthodox] patriarch, *Abuna* Marqos,[7] arrived [from Egypt]; he had reached the district of Walwaj.[8] Therefore, the leaders of the [local] church[9] sent [a message] to Walatta Petros and informed her about the

[1] BDJ: *wä-yəbelo Aron* (lit., and Aaron said to him); Abb. 88: *wä-yəbelu Aron* (and they said, [viz.,] Aaron), which CR emended to *wä-yəbelu Aron wä-Maryam* (and Aaron and Miriam said). Through Conti Rossini's emendation, however, the text is made to deviate from the biblical original, which here has only Aaron speaking. This was already pointed out by Ricci. BDJ now provide a better and fully coherent text.

[2] Numbers 12:10–11. The author has altered the quote; the second sentence here is a paraphrase. In addition, Aaron and Miriam had spoken ill not of God but of Moses.

[3] *Dämboza* is an island adjacent to Ṣana Island in southeastern Lake Ṭana. It no longer has a monastery.

[4] BDJ: *gädlomu* (their [earthly] struggle); CR: *bädromu* (their [earthly] course).

[5] B: *fəquromu Agnaṭəyos* (their beloved Ignatius); D: *fəquromu nəguśənä Dawit* (their beloved, our king David); J: *fəqərtomu Amätä Dəngəl* (their beloved Amätä Dəngəl [fem. name]); Abb. 88: *fəquromu* [name erased] *wä-ṣäḥafihu-ni nəʾusä məgbar wä-ḫəṭuʾa ṣäwän* [name erased] (their beloved [name erased], and also with its [= the manuscript's] modest and helpless scribe [name erased]), which CR shortened to [*məsle*]*nä* ([with] us).

[6] This epidemic appears to be smallpox, which has a pink rash that turns into scabs and then permanently alters the appearance through deep scarring of the face and body. Because it is attended by vomiting and diarrhea, it may be associated with hunger. It spreads easily through saliva.

[7] *Marqos* III (Mark) was the Egyptian patriarch of the Täwaḥədo Church assigned by the head church in Alexandria. He was the first to fill the office after *Abunä* Səmʿon was killed in 1617 under Susənyos, arriving in 1636 and dying in 1647–48.

[8] BDJ: *Walwağ*(*ə*), CR: *Walwaği*. It is a place in the Dämbəya region, north of Lake Ṭana and northeast of Gondar, at least one hundred miles from where WP was, in Dämboza.

[9] Lit., *mämhəranä betä krəstiyan* (teachers of the church), which can refer to the learned clerics as well as the abbots.

patriarch's arrival. They said to her, "Come and let us go to the patriarch in order to welcome him, ask to be blessed by him, and then receive his blessing."

When our holy mother[1] Walatta Petros heard this, she felt greatly distressed and said [to herself], "If I go forth alone and leave these sick disciples behind [on Damboza], they will die of hunger. I will then have nobody to follow me [as my disciples].[2] But, if I make them follow me [now], they will not be able to walk. Then again, if[3] I desist from going, I will be deprived of the patriarch's blessing." She was at a loss about what to do. This took place in the month of Tirr.[4] While our holy mother Walatta Petros found herself thus between two thoughts, she prayed to God so that he might reveal to her which of the two courses of action[5] he wanted and would be pleased with.

Now a word came from heaven, "Order all the sick ones to go down to the lake on Timqat festival:[6] the Holy Spirit will then descend on them and they will be cured of their illness."

So when the day of Timqat[7] came, Walatta Petros took her sick followers down to the lake, and they all performed the ritual immersion.[8] The Holy Spirit then descended upon them, just as[9] it had once descended at the fortress of Zion[10] in the guise of fire. Directly, all the sick were cured that day, becoming as though the illness had never touched them at all. All those present at the Timqat site saw this and marveled at it.

Chapter 54: Our Mother Is Blessed by the Egyptian Patriarch

Now our holy mother Walatta Petros set out and joyfully traveled to [see] the patriarch.[11] As for him, he had been informed about her entire story before she met

[1] DJ: *əmmənä qəddəst* (our holy mother); B: *əmmənä qəddəst wä-burəkt* (our holy and blessed mother); CR: *əmmənä* (our mother). For once, CR omits instead of adding.

[2] Lit., *litä-hi albo zä-yətälləwäni* (as for me, there will be nobody who will follow me).

[3] BDJ: *wä-kaʿəbä lä-əmmä* (then again, if); CR: *wä-lä-əmmä* (if).

[4] *Ṭərr* is the fifth month of the Ethiopian calendar, from early January to early February.

[5] BDJ: *gəbr* (lit., deeds); CR: *nägär* (things).

[6] *Ṭəmqät* (baptism) is one of the most important festivals of the Täwaḥədo Church, celebrated each year on 11 Ṭərr in commemoration of Christ's baptism in the river Jordan by John the Baptist (see Mark 1:9–13; Luke 3:21–24).

[7] BDJ: *ʿəlätä ṭəmqät* (the day of Ṭəmqät); Abb. 88 omits *ṭəmqät*, but CR sensibly inserted it.

[8] Lit., *täṭämqu* (were baptized). We have avoided a literal translation to avoid fueling the old Western misunderstanding of Ṭəmqät as an annual rebaptism. *Täṭämqu* here must be seen as metaphoric language use, and not as an indication that the Täwaḥədo Church in fact officially understood the annual Ṭəmqät ceremony as a rebaptism, even if some of its adherents vaguely may have regarded it as such.

[9] BDJ: *kämä* (just as); CR: *kämä zä-* [different syntax, but identical translation].

[10] The fortress of Zion is the City of David, the oldest part of Jerusalem, where, tradition has it, Pentecost occurred.

[11] This must have been in early 1636, not long after January's Ṭəmqät.

him—how, [for instance,] she had separated from her husband Malkiya Kristos because [he had] the garments of *Abuna* Simeon. He further had been told, "Behold,[1] Walatta Petros is on her way." He then waited until she arrived.[2] When our holy mother Walatta Petros arrived, she greeted the patriarch respectfully.[3]

When the patriarch saw her, he inquired [of his retinue], "Is this the one whose fame has reached our land, the land of Egypt?"

They replied, "Yes, that's her."

So he blessed her with a blessing appropriate for [a person of] her [spiritual achievements] and loved her very much. She now told him what was foremost on her mind, saying to him,[4] "What am I to do? Behold, people assemble around me
even though I don't want that.[5] Do I have to accept it[6] or not?" 71
The patriarch replied, "Don't be afraid of anything! Nothing happens but by the will of God. May he now therefore strengthen you, and may he let his Spirit rest upon you."[7] He then conferred the priesthood upon the men who were with her.[8] Thereafter, they took their leave of each other: the patriarch proceeded [on his way] to the king, while Walatta Petros returned the way she had come.

Chapter 55: Our Mother's Community Flees a Leopard at Zagé

In the meantime, many people, men and women with their sons[9] and daughters, had joined Walatta Petros's community[10] [at Damboza]; they had become very numerous indeed. Shortly afterward, Walatta Petros arrived back at Damboza. When[11]

[1] BDJ: *näya* (behold); CR omits.

[2] Waiting is a sign of respect, even deference.

[3] Lit., *täʾamməḫato,* which could mean that she kissed him in greeting, that she kissed his cross, or that she greeted him with words. Traditionally, Christians upon meeting a priest upon the road would bow and kiss the cross he would hold out.

[4] BDJ: *wä-təbelo* (lit., and said to him); CR: *wä-təbe* (and said).

[5] BDJ: *ənzä anä i-yəfäqqəd* (lit., even though I myself don't want); CR: *ənzä i-yəfäqqəd* (even though I don't want).

[6] BDJ: *yədälləwäni-nu zəntu* (lit., is this incumbent upon me); CR: *yədälləwäni-nu* (is it incumbent upon me).

[7] BJ: *wä-yaḫdər mänfäso laʿleki* (and may he let his Spirit rest upon you); D: *wä-yəḫdər mänfäs qəddus laʿleki* (and may the Holy Spirit rest upon you); CR: *wä-yəḫdər mänfäs laʿleki* (and may the Spirit rest upon you). See Isaiah 41:10; Ephesians 3:16.

[8] This blanket conferral of priesthood was not uncommon in Ethiopia, although European visitors found it scandalous. However, only the patriarch could consecrate priests. Since the post had been vacant since at least 1632, when the Roman Catholic patriarch Afonso Mendes left, but really since 1617, when the last Orthodox patriarch had been killed, this was probably the first opportunity that members of WP's community had to become priests.

[9] BDJ: *däqiqomu* (their sons); CR: *däqqomu* [lexical variant (or corruption?), but identical meaning].

[10] Lit., *täläwəwwa* (had followed her).

[11] BDJ: *wä-sobä* (when); CR: *wä-sobeha* (now).

she saw how numerous the people [there] had become, she realized that no place other than Zagé would be able to hold them. Therefore, she [again] wanted to live at Zagé.[1]

However, she [first] went to Béta Manzo, where she began a fast. She continued it until [the Feast of] the Mount of Olives.[2] She also completed the [re]construction of the church [at Béta Manzo] that she had previously begun.

After that, she moved to Zagé. Then the feast of Easter[3] came, the feast of our Lord's resurrection. On that very night, while our holy mother Walatta Petros kept praying after all the others had fallen asleep—while her eyes remained open[4]—she was struck by a drowsiness, as in a vision. Then she heard a voice tell her, "Say 'Deliver me from blood, God, Lord of my Salvation!' "[5]

She regarded this as a dream, however,[6] and returned to her earlier prayer. But again, a drowsiness struck her, like before, and again she heard [something], as if a voice were saying the same thing to her. Then again, for a third time, it said to her, "Say 'Deliver me from blood, God, Lord of my Salvation!' "

Now our holy mother Walatta Petros pondered, asking [herself], "What does this vision mean?" At that moment, she perceived the shadow of a leopard,[7] creeping along, outside in the moonlight. Sometimes it would pause, wanting to surge forth, sometimes it would crouch on the ground,[8] lying in wait and ready to attack. She did not realize, however, that it was a [real] leopard. Then, while our holy mother Walatta Petros marveled at the vision, the leopard surged forth and snatched a little boy who was sleeping [in the compound]. Now our holy mother Walatta Petros saw the leopard as it went away.[9]

[1] BDJ: *wä-fäqädät tənbär Zäge* (therefore she wanted to live at Zäge); CR omits.

[2] *Däbrä Zäyt* honors the prophecies about the Second Coming that Christ delivered to his disciples on the Mount of Olives. It is celebrated on the Sunday midway through the Lenten fast. The Mount of Olives is associated with four biblical events: Christ's triumphal entry into Jerusalem on Palm Sunday, Christ foretelling his Second Coming, Christ praying with his disciples the night before he was arrested, and Christ ascending into heaven.

[3] BDJ: *bäʿalä fasika* (the feast of Easter); CR: *fasika* (Easter).

[4] BDJ: *ənzä kəśutat aʿyəntiha* (while her eyes remained open); CR: *zä-ənbälä kəśutat aʿyəntiha* (without her eyes remaining open).

[5] Psalm 50[51]:14.

[6] BDJ: *wä-yəʾəti-ssä amsäläto ḥəlmä* (she regarded this as a dream, however); CR: *wä-yəʾəti-ssä amsäläto kämä säyṭan* (she regarded this as [if coming from] Satan, however).

[7] The Abyssinian leopard is a subspecies of *Panthera pardus pardus* and indigenous to the Ethiopian highlands.

[8] BDJ: *ṣəlalotä nämr ənzä yətḥawwäs bä-afʿa bä-bərhanä wärḫ. Bo-gize ənzä yəqäwwəm wä-yəfäqqəd yəbaʾ wä-bo gize ənzä yasämmək dibä mədr* (the shadow of a leopard, creeping along, outside in the moonlight. Sometimes it would pause, wanting to surge forth, sometimes it would crouch on the ground); CR: *ṣəlalotä nämr ənzä yasämmək dibä mədr* (the shadow of a leopard crouching on the ground).

[9] Lit., *wä-ḥorä* (and it went away). It is unclear whether WP believes that she is still dreaming or has realized that the leopard is real. Either way, she never says aloud what she was commanded to say, "Deliver me from blood," and she does not warn others about what she saw.

At that time, none of the sisters except for her had perceived the leopard,[1]
which had taken the child away and hid him. Then the leopard came again and
snatched a little girl who was sleeping. It seized her by the sole of her foot and,
dragging her, pulled her outside. The little girl screamed while the leopard dragged
her, and all the sisters who had been sleeping immediately woke up and saw the
leopard dragging the little girl, tossing her around on the ground and amusing 72
himself with her.

Afraid and terrified, they all fled toward our holy mother Walatta Petros, seeking refuge with her, falling all over her and squeezing against her[2] until she almost died. Meanwhile, the leopard kept amusing itself with the screaming little girl outside. Truly, the leopard had been ordered [by God] to scare and terrify them. After this, it went away. As for the boy child the leopard had snatched first, it had eaten into his body and then buried him in the ground, left him and then gone back [to snatch the girl].

The sisters spent the entire night agitated and terrified. When morning came, they remembered the little boy.[3] They searched for him, but did not find him, and realized that the leopard had snatched him at night. Now all the monks gathered and searched for those children's dead bodies. With difficulty, they found the boy, and they buried him. But the girl remained missing.

On that day, great terror and tumult reigned in the entire community. They unanimously said to our holy mother Walatta Petros, "Let's leave! Fear and terror of that leopard's great, awe-inspiring power have us in their grip. We don't have it in us to remain in this wild place." Others said to her, "Leave and don't oppose God! Don't be like someone who fights with God."[4]

She agreed and went along with them in this decision.[5] She allowed the healthy to leave on foot and the sick by tankwa. On that very day, they left [Zagé] and went to Furé.[6] Our holy mother Walatta Petros left with the sick ones.[7] Then, the healthy ones departed on foot, whereas she had left by tankwa together with the ill and weak ones. They all met again at Damboza.

My loved ones, please do not think that our holy mother Walatta Petros fled for fear of that leopard or because she was horrified by death. Rather [it was] because

[1] Lit., *i-yaʾmäro* (knew about it).

[2] BDJ: *wä-aṣʿaqaha* (lit., and they squeezed her); Abb. 88 with meaningless *wä-aṣqaha*, which CR altered to *wä-aṣhaqaha* (and they importuned her).

[3] This makes clear that WP still had not told the sisters about seeing the leopard snatch the boy, perhaps still assuming that it was a dream.

[4] BDJ: *wä-kämä zä-yətbäʾas məslehu i-təkuni* (lit., don't be like someone who fights with him); CR: *wä-zä-kämä yətbäʾas məslehu i-təkuni* ([*sic*: not meaningful]).

[5] Although WP often rebukes members of her community for fearfulness, in this case and that of the Šəlḫ^{w}əlḫ^{w}ət, she allowed the majority to dictate fleeing from life-threatening circumstances.

[6] *Fure* is about one mile south of Lake Ṭana's Zäge Peninsula. It is home to the Fure Maryam church.

[7] Lit., *əm-dəḫrehomu* (after them).

of the fear of the sisters, her daughters. As scripture says, "Truly, if one member
suffers, our entire body suffers with it."[1] As for her, she understood perfectly well
that she could not escape God's will[2] by running away. As David says, "Where can
73 I go from your Spirit, and where can I flee from your face? If I ascended into the sky,
you would be there too, and if I descended into the abyss, you would be there also.
If I took wings like an eagle[3] and flew to the end of the ocean, there also your hand
would guide me, and your right hand would hold me."[4]

Now, regarding those children whom the leopard had snatched, God authorized and allowed it [to take them], according to what David says, "The flesh of your righteous ones is for the animals of the wilderness."[5]

Chapter 56: Our Mother Founds Her Fifth Community, at Damboza

After that, our holy and blessed mother Walatta Petros[6] had people construct a large *saqalaa* building[7] in Damboza. She lived there with her daughters, the nuns. As for the monks, they lived on Tsana Island [nearby]. In Damboza, too, many people, men and women, gathered around her, like vultures gather around carcasses.[8] They grew numerous; their number increased with each day,[9] just as it says

[1] 1 Corinthians 12:26.

[2] Lit., *tə'zaz* (command).

[3] BDJ: *kənfä kämä nəsr* (wings like an eagle); CR: *kənfä nəsr* (the wings of an eagle). In the original Hebrew, and most translations, the phrase is "on the wings of dawn." Only the Aramaic Bible also has "wings of an eagle."

[4] Psalm 138[139]:7–10.

[5] B, CR: *wä-śəgahomu-ni lä-ṣadəqanikä lä-aräwitä gädam* (the flesh of your righteous ones is for the animals of the wilderness); DJ: *wä-śəgahomu-ni lä-aräwitä gädam* (their flesh is for the animals of the wilderness). Psalm 78[79]:2. The Hebrew biblical text has something slightly different, "the [pagan] nations have . . . given . . . the flesh of your saints to the wild animals."

[6] BDJ: *əmmənä qəddəst wä-burəkt Wälättä Ṗeṭros* (our holy and blessed mother WP); CR: *əmmənä qəddəst* (our holy mother).

[7] *Säqäla*, a large rectangular building with a pitched roof. Some monasteries on Lake Ṭana still have them, with some divided into single room apartments for nuns or monks to live in.

[8] In the bestiary that is the *Gädlä Wälättä Ṗeṭros*, it is not surprising that vultures should appear at least once. Although the analogy is startling, comparing WP to the food of her community is apt. It is probably related to the puzzling passage in Matthew 24:28 and Luke 17:37, where Christ compares the Messiah to a dead body: "Wherever there is a carcass, there the vultures will gather." That is, someone important cannot be hidden but will be obvious due to all those who gather around.

[9] BDJ: *wä-əntä ṣäbḥat yətwessäku* (lit., and when it became morning, they increased); CR: *wä-ənzä ṣəbaḥ yətwessäku* (and while it was morning, they increased).

in the Acts of the Apostles.[1] At that time, *Abba* Za-Hawaryaat[2] and *Abba* Eda Kristos[3] arrived [at her community]. This was the fifth community.

Then a severe disease broke out, and many monks and nuns fell ill. During that period, eighty-seven souls died. They completed their earthly course, passed away in peace, and inherited eternal life.[4] May their prayers and blessings be with ___________[5] for eternity, amen.

Chapter 57: Why Our Mother Prayed for the Faithful to Die

But there were also those who recovered from that illness. They are alive today and witnesses regarding Walatta Petros. They report, "When our holy mother Walatta Petros said to us, 'If at this moment I so desired, you would be shot with guns,[6] or pierced with spears,' we immediately fell sick and almost died. Furthermore, when she watched over us and sent us the following message, 'May God have mercy on you and heal you!', we responded, 'If *you* have mercy on us, God too will be willing to show us mercy.' So then she asked us,[7] 'Do you really want to live?' We replied,[8] 'Yes indeed, we want to live!' She responded, 'Don't be afraid, you will not die.' Then she swore the customary oath.[9] Now we were happy because[10] she had let us know [our fate] in no uncertain terms. Immediately then, we recovered and could stand up [again]."

[1] Acts 5:14; 6:7.

[2] *Zä-Ḥawaryat* (He of the Apostles). This monk plays an important role in WP's life. *Abba* Zä-Ḥawaryat was WP's first abbot (appointed in 1642) and her confidant, leading her community for over forty years until his death on 30 August 1681.

[3] *Ǝdä Krəstos* (Hand of Christ).

[4] BDJ: *wä-wäräsu ḥəywätä zä-lä-ʿaläm* (and inherited eternal life); CR omits.

[5] B: *fəquromu Agnaṭəyos* (their beloved Ignatius); D: *fəquromu nəguśənä Dawit* (their beloved, our king David); J: *fəqərtomu Mälkəʾa Maryam* (their beloved Mälkəʾa Maryam [fem. name]); Abb. 88: [name erased], which CR altered to [*məsle*]*nä* ([with] us).

[6] BDJ: *əm-fäqädku yəʾəze yəndəfukəmu bä-näfṭ* (lit., if at this moment I desired, they would shoot you with guns); CR: *əm-fäqädku yəʾəze yəndəfukəmu bä-ḥaṣṣ wä-bä-näfṭ* (if at this moment I desired, they would shoot you with arrows and with guns). Firearms first arrived in Ethiopia in the fifteenth century and by the 1620s, according to Almeida, there were fifteen hundred muskets in the country. It would seem that, by the time of these events in 1630s, or later when the story was written down in the 1670s, guns were common enough to be mentioned. See Pankhurst (2005b).

[7] BDJ: *wä-yəʾəti-ni təbelänä* (lit., she then said to us); CR: *wä-yəʾəze-ni təbelänä* (now she said to us).

[8] BDJ: *wä-nəbela* (lit., thereupon we said to her); Abb. 88 omits, which led CR to fill the obvious gap with *wä-awśəʾnä wä-nəbela* (thereupon we replied and said to her).

[9] It is unclear what the customary oath is, but it may simply mean that she asks Christ to honor his kidan with her.

[10] BDJ, Abb. 88 all have *əmmä* (if), which makes no sense in the context. Therefore, in our translation we follow Conti Rossini's emendation of *əmmä* to *əsmä* (because).

This testimony is trustworthy and no lie. It is just as the Apostle James[1] says, "The prayer of a righteous one helps greatly. It is powerful, and it confers power. Elijah was a man like us, and like we suffer, he suffered. Yet, he prayed that it might
74 not rain, and for three years and six months it did not rain on the earth. Then, he prayed again that it might rain,[2] and accordingly the sky released its rain and the earth let sprout its fruits."[3] In this manner, God obeys his saints,[4] listens to their prayers, and does for them all they desire.

When our holy mother Walatta Petros came to understand her disciples' thinking but also realized what awaited them on Judgment Day, she asked God in prayer that the sick might immediately die in their flesh but live with their souls in eternal life, which never ceases.[5] As David says [about the Lord], "Truly, your mercy is better than living,"[6] and Paul furthermore says, "As you [believers] have assembled in the name of our Lord Jesus Christ, hand that man over to Satan so that his flesh be destroyed but his spirit saved on the Day of our Lord Jesus Christ."[7]

For this reason, our holy mother Walatta Petros would not spare anybody[8] regarding death in the flesh, since the secrets of everyone lay open to her, and she had insight into each person's character.[9] As Paul says, "He who has the Holy Spirit

[1] Lit., *Yaʿqob* (Jacob). Following the original Greek, the Gəʿəz text refers to the Apostle James as Jacob.

[2] BDJ: *kämä yəznəm zənam* (lit., that it might rain rain [emph.]); CR: *kämä yəznəm* (that it might rain).

[3] James 5:16–18. The Aramaic Bible is closer to this version. See also 1 Kings 17:1; 18:1; 18:42–45.

[4] BJ, CR: *yətʾezzäz lomu əgziʾabḥer lä-qəddusanihu* (God obeys his saints); D: *yətʾezzäz lomu əgziʾabḥer lä-fəquranihu* (God obeys his beloved ones). Although this may seem to border on the scandalous theologically, there can be no doubt that in this text the saints command God. This follows Isaiah 45:11, which in some versions suggests that we command God to do what he wants to do, "Thus says the Lord . . . 'concerning the work of my hands, you command me.' "

[5] WP wants her followers to die while they do not have many sins, so that they will not face a damning verdict on Judgment Day. Since WP, as a saint, can see the future and knows what people will do next, she prays for people to die before they sin. The Täwaḥədo Church does not have a "saved by grace" doctrine but believes in works. Absolution exists, it is offered twice during the Liturgy, but it is better for believers to avoid sin. The scholars we consulted did not know of any other saint who prayed for the death of good people. However, in the *Täʾamərä Maryam,* the Virgin Mary frequently appears to good young people, promising to take them to heaven, and they die in three days. Given the number of people who died in WP's life before she was twenty (three infants and her father), as well as, later, her mother, her brother, and hundreds of her followers, the text may reflect an attempt on her part to control these experiences.

[6] Psalm 62[63]: 3. *Əm-ḥayəw* (than living) is unusual; it would be more common to find *əm-ḥəywät* (than life), which is what the original Hebrew has.

[7] 1 Corinthians 5:4–5. Paul, in the original reference, is discussing a man who was sleeping with his stepmother (1 Cor. 5:1). The Bible makes clear that the apostles could inflict diseases upon sinners through Satan, who was seen as the author of physical diseases.

[8] BDJ: *männä-hi* [acc.] (anybody); Abb. 88: *männu-hi* [*sic*: nom.], which CR altered to *lä-männu-hi* [a legitimate prepositional variant to BDJ's *männä-hi*].

[9] BJ: *wä-täʾammər* [*sic*, substandard for *taʾammər*] *gəʿzomu lä-lä-1-1* (lit., and knew their

scrutinizes everything.[1] Him, however, nobody can scrutinize."[2] And truly, the Holy Spirit[3] rested on our holy mother Walatta Petros: She knew what would happen before it happened, be it good or bad; she examined [everyone's] heart and innermost feelings,[4] had insight into people's thoughts, and told them[5] [those thoughts] before they expressed them to her. Therefore, nobody would approach her without examining and scrutinizing themselves. Just as that which is poured into a glass cup, be it scant or abundant,[6] is visible, so the thoughts that were in the hearts of men were visible to her.

Because of this [ability], she did not desire that anyone should perish [forever], but rather implored God, and he would do for her everything she desired. He would bring illness and [thereby] kill, according to what she had asked from him because he had promised her [to do so] when he had granted her the kidaan in Waldeba. Our holy mother Walatta Petros always did as follows:[7] When she saw people [from her community] producing numerous and abundant good works,[8] she implored God for [their] death[9] and dispatched them to God as a gift, just as a farmer watches and looks at his field, how it ripens[10] and becomes ready for the harvest, and then assembles the harvesters, dispatches them to harvest for him, and collects
his grain into his granaries.[11] 75

character, of each one); D, CR: *wä-tä'ammər* [*sic*, substandard for *ta'ammər*] *gə'zo lä-lä-1-1* (lit., and knew his character, of each one).

[1] BDJ: *k^{w}əllo* [acc.] (everything); CR: *k^{w}əllu* [nom.] (everything). This corruption likely happened because the fidäl symbols for ሎ *lo* and ሉ *lu* are very similar.

[2] BJ: *lotu-ssä albo zä-yəthaśśäśo* (him, however, nobody can scrutinize); D, CR: *lotu-ssä albo zä-yəthaśśäś* [identical meaning, but grammatically substandard]. The two variants point to silent, reading-based copying because the fidäl symbols for ሦ *śo* and ሥ *ś* look very similar, but the sounds they stand for are quite different. As, by contrast, other variants point to the role of dictation in the manuscript reproduction process, this mixed evidence suggests a mixed copying procedure, partly based on dictation and partly on silent reading. 1 Corinthians 2:10, 11.

[3] BDJ: *mänfäs qəddus* (the Holy Spirit); CR: *mänfäs* (the spirit).

[4] Psalm 7:9; Revelation 2:23, "I am he who searches hearts and kidneys." In the Bible, it is God who scrutinizes and knows man down to his innermost parts, so WP is being likened to God.

[5] BDJ: *wä-tənäggəromu läliha* (lit., and told them herself); CR: *wä-tənäggəromu lä-həllinna* (and told them regarding the thoughts).

[6] BDJ: *əmmä-hi həṣuṣ* [nom.] *wä-əmmä-hi məlu'* [nom.] (be it scant or abundant); CR: *əmmä-hi həṣuṣä* [acc.] *wä-əmmä-hi məlu'* [acc.; no translation difference].

[7] BDJ: *kämä-zə* (lit., like this); CR: *əm-zə* (then [*sic*]).

[8] D: *sobä təre'əyomu lä-säb' ənzä yabäzzəhu wä-yafädäffədu fəre məgbarat* (when she saw people producing numerous and abundant good works); BJ, CR: *sobä təre'əyomu lä-säb' ənzä yəbäzzəhu wä-yafädäffədu fəre məgbarat* (when she saw people becoming numerous, and producing abundant good works).

[9] BDJ: *təsə'əl motä habä əgzi'abher* (she implored God for [their] death); CR: *təsə'əl habä əgzi'abher* (she implored God).

[10] Lit., *kämä ṣä'däwä* (how it yellows), as the grain *ṭef* (*eragrostis tef*), perhaps the most important Ethiopian staple, turns golden when it ripens.

[11] Here the text suggests that WP does not dispatch the faithful for their own good merely

Chapter 58: Our Mother Orders the Separation of Monks and Nuns

Furthermore, when the monks and the nuns had become numerous,[1] Walatta Petros established among them a rule: that they should not talk and flirt with each other, neither while walking nor standing nor sitting, so that Satan would not assault them, nor sow *hintsiwaal*[2] and weeds in their hearts, thereby spoiling the seeds of righteousness which had been sown into their hearts, just as the Gospel relates in the Parable of the Seed.[3]

My loved ones, please do not think that our holy mother Walatta Petros established a peculiar rule. Rather the 318 Bishops[4] had already established it, saying, "More than anything else, the righteous ones and the monks must stay away from women. They must not respond to them, and definitely must not actively engage them in conversation."[5] Therefore, for us it is also righteous and proper to follow[6] this rule and place it like a ring on[7] our heart or like a *maateb* seal[8] on our arm. As Paul says, "If our fathers who have begotten us in the flesh discipline us[9] and we

---

but as a beautiful gift to God, a pure and holy sacrifice. This might be inspired by John 12:24, which states that only through death does the kernel of wheat yield a good harvest.

[1] BDJ: *bäzḫu* (had become numerous); CR: *yəbäzzəḫu* (became numerous).

[2] *Ḫənṣəwal* is a type of oat (*Avena abyssinica*) used as horse fodder. It was not cultivated on purpose but allowed to grow wild in barley fields and therefore was seen as a weed.

[3] Matthew 13:24–30; Mark 4:13–20; Luke 8:11–15. That is, it is only upon setting up her fifth community—when she also appoints a male religious leader, *Abba* Zä-Ḥawaryat, for the first time—that she institutes laws separating men and women.

[4] The number of bishops said to have attended the Council of Nicea in 325, which rejected the Arian heresy that denied the presence of a fully divine nature in Christ.

[5] According to Canon 4 of a document ascribed to the Council of Nicea bishops (i.e., the 318 Bishops), "We decree that bishops shall not live with women; nor shall a presbyter who is a widower; neither shall they escort them; nor be familiar with them, nor gaze upon them persistently. . . . For the devil with such arms slays religious, bishops, presbyters, and deacons, and incites them to the fires of desire." On this text in Ethiopia, which is called *Nägär zä-qəddusan abäw 318 zä-yəkäwwən ḥənṣa lä-mänäkosat* (Discourse of the 318 Holy Fathers which Will Be a Rule for the Monks), see Leonessa (1942) and Bausi (2007).

[6] BDJ: *nətlu* (lit., that we follow); CR: *natlu* (that we make follow).

[7] Lit., *wəstä* (in).

[8] *Maʿtäb* (seal) is a sign of the wearer's adherence to Täwaḥədo Christianity. The term most often refers to the silk cord tied around a child's neck during baptism and that most adult Christians also wear. But it can also include tattoos, such as a blue cross tattooed on the hand, arm, or forehead. These were called seals partly because they precluded the wearer from giving in to the temptation to deny Christianity in times of persecution (mostly from Muslims).

[9] D, CR: *əmmä-ssä abäwinä əllä wälädunä bä-śəga yəgeśśəṣunä* (if our fathers who have begotten us in the flesh disicpline us); BJ: *halläwu abäwinä əllä wälädunä bä-śəga yəgeśśəṣunä* (our fathers who have begotten us in the flesh used to discipline us).

respect them, how much more should we not then humble ourselves before the Father of our spirit and obey him, so that we may live? They [our fathers in the flesh] for [our] benefit disciplined us for a short time as they thought best, whereas he, [God, disciplines us] for our sake so that we may obtain his sanctification."[1] In the moment when it is meted out[2] each reprimand does not feel like a pleasure but like an affliction. Later though, its fruit is peace for those who have been reprimanded, and it earns them[3] righteousness.

This is why our holy mother Walatta Petros said, "If with my own eyes I should see a monk and a nun talking and flirting with each other, I would want to jointly pierce them through, both of them, with a spear. I would not be worried that my doing this would be considered a crime, for just like the [biblical] priest Phinehas killed Zimri and the Midianite woman,[4] and just like Samuel killed Agag[5]—even though Phinehas and Samuel were priests who were not allowed to kill—they were moved by great zeal for God, so it was not a crime for them. Rather God said to them, 'You have given my heart relief.' "[6]

Furthermore, if our holy mother Walatta Petros was informed that a monk and a nun had violated this [rule],[7] she would suffer exceedingly. She would moan and roll around on the ground, until she was vomiting, as well as urinating blood and pus.[8]

[1] Hebrews 12:9–10.

[2] BDJ: *bä-gizehu* (lit., at its time); CR: *baḥtu . . . lä-gizehu* (however, at its time).

[3] BDJ: *wä-tä*ʿ*assəyomu* [fem. verb form] (and it earns them); CR: *wä-yä*ʿ*assəyomu* [masc. verb form; no translation difference].

[4] BDJ write *mädinawit*, CR *madonawit* for "Midianite woman." Numbers 25:6–8, 14. In this passage, Phinehas (Finḥas in the Gəʿəz), the Jewish high priest, stopped the plague that God had brought upon the Israelites for worshipping idols, by going in search of the Israelite Zimri (Zänbäri in the Gəʿəz) and a Midanite woman, who were having coitus in view of the temple, and driving a spear through both of them with righteous zeal. Murdering the sinful to save the community was considered justified.

[5] 1 Samuel 15:33. Saul defeated and then spared the life of this king of the Amalekites. Samuel rebuked Saul for this unsanctioned mercy and then killed Agag himself.

[6] BDJ: *astänfäskəməwwa lä-ləbbəyä* (you have given my heart relief); CR: *astäfśaḥkəməwwo* [*sic*, for correct *astäfäśśaḥkəməwwo*] *lä-ləbbəyä* (you have made my heart rejoice). Also note the different genders of *ləbb* (heart) in BDJ on the one hand and CR on the other, as indicated by the differing object suffixes on the verbs. In BDJ, God's heart is regarded as feminine (object suffix -*wa*), whereas in CR it is treated as masculine (object suffix -*wo*). Psalm 4:1; 1 Samuel 2:1; Psalm 85[86]:11.

[7] BDJ: *zäntä* (this); CR: *zäntä śərʿatä* (this rule).

[8] We can only speculate about the physical and/or spiritual nature of this response. It may be some kind of intestinal problem (gastroenteritis, a peptic ulcer) that causes similar symptoms and can be provoked by such stressors as receiving upsetting news. Urinating blood and pus suggests a urinary or vaginal infection, common disorders. Among these are sexually transmitted diseases, which WP may have contracted long ago from her husband, or which may be WP psychically taking on the consequences of the inappropriate sexual behavior of her flock.

Chapter 59: Our Mother Suffers a Secret Affliction

76 Walatta Petros also suffered continuously from a subtle affliction that was invisible to the eyes of others.[1] Due to this condition, she can be counted among the martyrs,[2] according to what she herself testified when the sisters asked her, "Our Mother, everything that the prophets, apostles, and saints have spoken has been fulfilled in due time. Can it be that the words of the saints regarding you should be false? Namely, we have heard that you are destined to become a martyr."

Our holy mother Walatta Petros replied to them, "I have no idea. I don't know if God, for my sake, would consider the suffering that, hidden from you, I endure[3] on a daily basis to be like the suffering of the martyrs." This is why our holy mother Walatta Petros spent many days afflicted by that [kind of] suffering, or by a similar one, when she saw or heard that members of her community had transgressed the spiritual statute that she had imposed on them. She did not leave them to be tormented by the afflictions they brought upon themselves;[4] rather, she would suffer on their behalf and would offer herself up as a ransom for their souls, just as Paul says, "Who is it who suffers even though he is not sick?[5] Me. And who is it who laughs and is not scared?"[6] He furthermore[7] says, "In truth I say to you, in Christ—I do not lie and my witness is the Holy Spirit who is in my heart—that my heart constantly grieves and suffers [for them], such that I desire to be separated from Christ[8] for the sake of my brothers and my kin."[9]

[1] Given the previous symptoms, this chronic "affliction" might be endometriosis, in which the lining of the uterus grows outside of the uterus. It causes severe pain, sometimes debilitating, as well as vomiting and diarrhea (sometimes bloody), and bloody urine during menses. In 2 Corinthians 12:7, Paul also complained of a chronic affliction. Through this lofty precedent, WP's affliction also becomes spiritually honorable.

[2] BDJ: *tətḫʷälläqʷ kämä sämaʿtat* (lit., she may be counted like [one of] the martyrs); CR: *täḫʷälläqʷät məslä sämaʿtat* (she was counted with the martyrs).

[3] BDJ: *śəqay zä-yəräkkəbäni* (lit., the suffering . . . that befalls me); CR: *śəqay zä-räkäbäni* (the suffering . . . that has befallen me).

[4] BDJ: *bä-zä-amṣəʾu mäkära lälihomu* (lit., by the afflictions which they themselves had brought); CR: *bä-zä-amṣəʾu mäkära laʿlehomu* (by the afflictions which they brought over themselves).

[5] BDJ: *männu zä-yədäwwi wä-i-yäḥamməm* (who is it who suffers even though he is not sick); CR: *männu zä-yədäwwi wä-yäḥamməm* (who is it who suffers and is sick).

[6] CR adds: *anä* (I). 2 Corinthians 11:29, except with radical changes here. The original Greek is more similar to "Who is weak, and I do not feel weak? Who is led into sin, and I do not inwardly burn?"

[7] CR adds a nonsensical *anä* (I).

[8] BDJ: *wä-əfättu kämä anä ətʿalläl əm-Krəstos* (such that I desire to be separated from Christ); CR: *wä-əfättu kämä anä ətläʿal əm-Krəstos* (such that I desire to be elevated higher than Christ [*sic*]). Ricci suspected that Abb. 88's blasphemous *täläʿalä əm-Krəstos* (to be higher than Christ) resulted from corruption of an original *täʿallälä əm-Krəstos* (to be separated from Christ)—but went on to translate *e desidero estollermi al di sopra di Cristo* (I would like to elevate myself above Christ) nonetheless.

[9] Romans 9:1–3. That is, Paul would prefer to be under God's curse and separated from Christ himself than to see his fellow Christians suffer.

Our holy mother Walatta Petros emulated Paul and [always] was worried that she would be held responsible for the souls of her disciples,[1] according to what the Gospel says, "Truly, to whom great authority has been given, of him much will be asked; and to whom much has been entrusted, he will be thoroughly scrutinized."[2] Therefore, if our holy mother Walatta Petros was sick and suffered for our sake[3] to this extent, it is then necessary that we scrupulously observe her rules, as well as carry out her commandments carefully and diligently, and not eat from the [forbidden] tree like Adam and Eve, so as not to be chased from paradise.[4] Let us not, like Achan,[5] steal what God has forbidden,[6] so as not to bring death on ourselves—not [only] the death of the body but the death of the soul.

Chapter 60: Our Mother Repairs the Church on Réma Island

But let us return to our previous narration. Our holy mother Walatta Petros was
living in a similar way [to Paul] in Damboza, in the *saqalaa* building[7] that she had
ordered to be built, near the church whose tabot was dedicated to [Saint Mary of]
Qusqwaam. There, each day, she would spend much of the night and the early 77
morning hours imploring and supplicating our Lady Mary and her beloved Son for
the salvation of her soul, and particularly for the souls of all the members of her
community.

Then *Abba* Za-Maryam,[8] the abbot of Réma Monastery, arrived at Damboza with many monks. They implored Walatta Petros to renovate[9] their church for them,

[1] BDJ: *wä-təfärrəh kämä i-yətḫaśäś näfsomu əmənneha* (lit., and was afraid that their souls should not be sought from her); CR: *wä-təfärrəh kämä yəḫaśśəś* [*sic*: ind.] *näfsomu əmənneha* (was afraid that he [i.e., the Lord] would request their souls from her).

[2] BDJ: *əsmä lä-zä-bəzuḫ* [D: *lä-zä-bəzuḫa* (*sic*)] *amäggäbəwwo bəzuḫa yətḫaśśäśəwwo wä-lä-zä-hi fädfadä amaḥṣänəwwo fädfadä yäḥattətəwwo* (lit., truly, from him to whom they have given great authority much will be asked, and he to whom they have entrusted much, they will scrutinize him thoroughly); CR: *əsmä bəzuḫa* [altered from Abb. 88: *lä-bəzuḫa* (*sic*)] *amändäbəwwo bəzuḫa yətḫaśśäśəwwo wä-lä-zä-hi fädfadä yäḥattətəwwo* (truly, he whom they much afflicted [and] much asked [*sic*], and he whom they will much scrutinize [*sic*]). Luke 12:48, except the original does not have "thoroughly scrutinized" but "required more of."

[3] 1 Peter 2:1, 3:18, "Christ suffered for our sins." In addition to emulating Paul, WP is also shown as Christlike in enduring vicarious suffering for the redemption of others.

[4] Genesis 3 tells the story of the first human beings, Adam and Eve, who were commanded in Genesis 2:17 not to eat of the fruit of the Tree of the Knowledge of Good and Evil. When they did, they became aware of their nakedness and were cast out of paradise.

[5] *Akan* is a biblical person in the book of Joshua who steals a block of gold, which results in the Israelites being punished.

[6] BDJ: *i-nəsrəq ḥərumä kämä Akan* (lit., let us not, like Achan, steal what is sacrosanct); CR: *i-nəsärrəq ḥərumä kämä Akan* (we must not, like Achan, steal what is sacrosanct).

[7] BDJ: *bä-wəʾətu säqäla* (in the *säqäla*-building); CR: *bä-wəstä säqäla* (inside the *säqäla*-building).

[8] *Zä-Maryam* (He of [Saint] Mary).

[9] Lit., *kämä təḥnəṣ* (that she build). Rema Island had been the site of a monastery since the

which was dedicated to the Savior of the World,[1] and in which Walatta Petros's father and mother lay buried.

She replied to them, "How could I, of all people, be capable of carrying out such a great task? However, let us pray[2] to God, you and me, and then what he wills may happen." With these words, she granted them their leave. Thus, the monks turned back, returning to their monastery.

So our holy mother Walatta Petros prayed with great devotion for seven days in the church of Damboza, and our Lord[3] revealed to her, "Go and build![4] I will be with you and assist you, and I will see to it that you complete the task."

After this, our blessed mother Walatta Petros left Damboza and went to Réma Island, accompanied by all the monks and nuns. She tore down the roof of the earlier large saqalaa-like church[5] and began [building] a beautiful structure, herself [contributing by] drawing water[6] from Lake Tana and carrying it [in a vessel] on her back.[7]

Many women of high rank—daughters of princesses, concubines of the king, and the wives of great lords—were with Walatta Petros and took part in this work together with her, following her.[8] On one occasion, they would draw water, on another carry mud and stones. There also were many monks.

Chapter 61: Our Mother Founds Her Sixth Community, at Afer Faras

Furthermore, [in her community,] there were those who had left father and mother, or wife and children, or all their possessions and fields, while others had sacrificed

---

thirteenth century, and WP's parents and brother lay buried in the church under discussion, suggesting that the church was in need of renovation only. Later, WP tore down the roof of the church building (*säqäla*) that was already there.

[1] *Mädḫane ʿAläm* (Savior of the World, i.e., the Messiah). Many churches are dedicated to Christ in this role.

[2] D, CR: *nəṣälli* (let us pray); BJ: *nəṣelli* (we will pray).

[3] J, CR: *əgziʾənä* (our Lord); BD: *əgziʾabḥer* (God).

[4] BJ: *ḥuri ḥənəṣi* (lit., go, build); D: *ḥənəṣi ḥuri* (build, go); CR: *nəkura ḥənəṣi* (as a marvelous thing build her).

[5] Lit., *säqäla* (large rectangular building). This word suggests that this particular church was rectangular rather than round. The circular churches so commonly seen now in Ethiopia are a relatively late innovation of the last six hundred years; rectangular stone buildings have been built in northern Ethiopia since the first millennium BCE. While almost all of the churches in the Lake Ṭana region are round with a conical roof, rectangular church foundations do exist at Ṣana Qirqos and Daga Ǝsṭifanos, two of the earliest monasteries on Lake Ṭana. Rema no longer has a rectangular church, however.

[6] BDJ: *ənzä yəʾəti təqäddəḥ mayä* (lit., while she herself was drawing water); CR: *ənzä təqäddəḥ mayä* (while she was drawing water).

[7] This arduous manual labor of carrying water was typically done by women, but normally by poor rural women or the female domestic servants or slaves of wealthy families. That WP, of a noble family, takes on such work is a sign of her spiritually motivated humility.

[8] WP clearly kept her court contacts and was a leader among royal women.

their youth and all their carnal desires. There also were women who had left their
husbands, and teenage girls[1] who had preserved their virginity and betrothed
themselves to their groom Christ. They loved him dearly and followed him every
day of their lives, just as Solomon says, "The maidens have loved you and have followed you."[2] There further were children, boys and girls, who had followed their
fathers and mothers. There were manservants and maidservants who had followed
their masters, thereby liberating themselves from servitude, freeing themselves **78**
from subjection and becoming equal with their masters.[3] In this way, they found
rest from their difficult toil and labor, just as the Gospel says, "Come to me, you
who are weary and carry a heavy load,[4] and I will give you rest."[5]

There were sinners and fornicators who had turned toward repentance, abandoning their former conduct and becoming chaste[6] for Christ. And, finally, there were poor and wretched folks, the blind and the lame: they had entrusted themselves to Walatta Petros, and found refuge with her.

She opened the door to her house to anyone who wanted to enter, just as the Gospel says, "I will not chase away or expel anyone[7] who comes to me."[8] And as Paul says, "There is neither Jew nor heathen,[9] and there is neither slave nor free."[10] In those days, peace and love reigned. Nobody sought his own advantage, but rather that of his neighbor.[11] There were no strangers there and no kin; rather, all were equal,[12] of a single heart and of a single soul while[13] Christ was in their midst.[14]

When the community became very numerous, however, Réma Island became too small for them and could not hold them anymore. Truly, their number increased

[1] Lit., *dänagəl* (virgins). We translate this term variously depending on context, sometimes as "maidens," sometimes as "teenage girls," and most often as "nuns" or "young nuns." A monstery of women only was called *beta dänagəl* (house of virgins).

[2] Song of Solomon 1:2–4.

[3] WP's communities had some utopian elements and the leveling of status was one of them.

[4] BDJ: *wä-kəbudanä ṣor* (lit., and are burdened with a heavy load); CR omits.

[5] Matthew 11:28.

[6] Lit., *dänagəlä* [acc.] (virgins).

[7] BDJ: *i-yawäṣṣəʾo afʾa* (lit., I will not expel him to the outside); CR: *i-yawäṣṣəʾo* (I will not expel him).

[8] John 6:37.

[9] *Arämawi* (heathen). In the Greek New Testament, the term is *héllēn* (Greek), but metaphorically "gentile" or "heathen." We translated with the latter term because Gəʿəz *arämawi* has strong connotations of uncouthness and barbarity.

[10] Galatians 3:28.

[11] BDJ: *albo zä-yadällu lä-rəʾso zä-ənbälä lä-biṣu* (lit., nobody favored himself, but rather his neighbor); CR: *albo zä-yədällu lä-rəʾso zä-ənbälä lä-biṣu* (nothing was for oneself, but rather for one's neighbor).

[12] BDJ: *ʿəruyan* (equal); CR omits.

[13] Lit., *ənzä*. Perhaps corrupted from an original *əsmä* (because), which seems to fit better semantically.

[14] BDJ adds: *zə-wəʾətu sadəs maḫbär* (this was the sixth community); CR has this sentence at the end of the next paragraph. In this rare case, we have followed CR since Rema was not WP's sixth community; according to the prophecy given earlier in the text, Afär Färäs was.

with each day! Walatta Petros then received a plot of land on the lakeshore that was called Afer Faras.[1] This was the sixth community.[2]

At Afer Faras, she built a house for herself and the sisters, while the brothers lived in the compound of the [Afer Faras] Church of Saint John. Our holy mother Walatta Petros herself would take turns: sometimes she would stay on Réma Island, other times she would stay at Afer Faras. But each morning she would go to Réma Island and supervise[3] the construction of the church. In the evening, she would then leave and return to Afer Faras, spending the night [there] together with the sisters.

One day, while our holy mother Walatta Petros was in a tankwa, leaving [Réma Island] and returning to Afer Faras, a strong wind called *lagooni*[4] suddenly arose. It propelled the tankwa and in an instant took it to Mahdere Sibhat.[5] Those in the tankwa with her despaired of surviving, while those on the mainland, as well as those who stood on [Réma] Island, all loudly wailed out in unison for it appeared to them that she would perish.

Our blessed mother Walatta Petros was not afraid or terrified, however, because she put her trust in God, the Lord of deliverance who can do everything: nothing is
79 impossible for God. Rather she prayed in her heart the *Salama Malaak*. In addition, she sternly admonished those who were with her not to be afraid. At that very moment, the wind felt sternly admonished [too],[6] so the waves quieted down, and calm reigned.[7] Thus, she could return [to Afer Faras] safe and sound and go home.

Our holy mother Walatta Petros continued to toil every day until the reconstruction of the church [on Réma Island] was complete. [For instance,] one day she went to fetch wood from Wondigé.[8] Everything went as she had planned, and she returned safely.

[1] *Afär Färäs* (Horse's soil) was a place on the southeastern shore of Lake Ṭana, just opposite Rema Island and near a cliff, and about seven miles north of Q^{w}äraṣa. It had a church dedicated to Saint John. The text does not make clear who gave WP this land, whether local landowners, the Täwaḥədo Church, or the king.

[2] CR: *zə-wəʾətu sadəs maḫbär* (this was the sixth community); BDJ omit, but have this sentence at the end of the preceding paragraph. Factually, and according to the prophecy given earlier in the text, however, it is CR that is correct here.

[3] Lit., *tastägebbər* (drive forward the work on).

[4] *Lag^{w}əni* has no discernible meaning in Amharic or Gəʿəz and might be a term from a local language such as Agäw.

[5] *Maḫdärä Səbḥat* (Residence of Praise [for God]) is a tiny island about one thousand feet from Rema Island in Lake Ṭana.

[6] BDJ: *tägäššäṣä näfas* (lit., the wind was sternly admonished); Abb. 88 with incongruent *tägäššäṣä näfasä* [*sic*: acc.], as if the verb were transitive. CR altered this to still incongruent *tägäššäṣät näfasä*: now the verb is third-person singular feminine, but still intransitive, and hence, there is still no justification for accusative *näfasä*.

[7] Compare with Matthew 8:23–27; Mark 4:35–41; Luke 8:22–25. WP is depicted as like Christ, who calmed the Sea of Galilee when the disciples were frightened and feared for their lives.

[8] *Wändəge* (Men's land) is a place near the southwestern shore of Lake Ṭana, perhaps five to ten miles west of the Gəlgäl Abbay River. It briefly served as an imperial capital for King

Chapter 62: Our Mother Establishes an Order of Communal Life

Meanwhile, her community[1] had grown immensely and reached the number of eight hundred. So, Walatta Petros established an order of communal life[2] for them, compiling it from the holy books,[3] from the *History of the Holy Fathers*,[4] and from the *Canons of the Apostles*.[5]

As the Acts[6] [of the Apostles] says, "All those who believe shall live together, and all their possessions they shall have in common. They shall sell their assets and donate [the proceeds] to the poor.[7] Every day they shall eagerly bind themselves to the house of worship[8] as one in spirit. At home they shall bless the meal[9] together, and eat their food joyfully and with a meek heart. They shall praise God,"[10] and no one among them shall say, "But this here belongs to me"; rather it shall belong to all together.

Zä-Dəngəl (He of the Virgin [Mary]) in 1603–4. Since some palace building had gone on at Wändəge, perhaps building materials were available there.

[1] Lit., *əllu-ssä maḫbär* (these community), an *ad sensum* construction.

[2] Lit., *śərʿatä maḫbär* (order of the community). Monasteries have their own individualized *śərʿat,* the collection of rules that regulate communal life. This may mark the moment when WP's community becomes a formal gadäm. No written document like this has been found, but this section of the *WP gädl* may preserve essential parts of it. *Śərʿatä Maḫbär* is also the title of the *Rules of Pachomius* in the Täwaḥədo Church. WP "was the first Ethiopian to try and systematically organize the monastic life of nuns" and to advocate "running monasteries for women along the same lines as men" (Cohen 2010b).

[3] BDJ: *ənzä tastäwaṣṣəʾ əmənnä mäṣaḥəft qeddusat* (lit., compiling from the holy books); CR: *ənzä tawäṣṣəʾo əmənnä qeddusat mäṣaḥəft* (bringing it out from the holy books).

[4] *Zenatä Abäw Kəburan* (lit., Stories of the Venerated Fathers) is a collection of anecdotes about and sayings by the Desert Fathers who founded monasticism in the fourth and fifth century. Part of the patristic literature, it is the *Apophthegmata Patrum Aegyptiorum* (Sayings of the Desert [lit., Egyptian] Fathers), but with hagiobiographical accounts added.

[5] BDJ: *Śərʿatä Ḥawaryat* (Canons of the Apostles); CR: *Śərʿatä Ḥawaryat Ḫəruyan* (Canons of the Elect Apostles). This is the last chapter of the eighth book of the *Apostolic Constitutions,* a pseudo-apostolic collection of ecclesiastical decrees of the early Christian Church, part of the genre of Ancient Church Orders. It includes eighty-five canons approved in the Eastern Church in 692. Descriptions of assembling the law from such texts are a topos of the hagiobiographical literature (Bausi 1992).

[6] Lit., *Abrəksis,* a rough transcription of the original Greek term *práxeis* (deeds, acts). Using the one word "acts" as a shorthand for the New Testament book Acts of the Apostles is common in many languages, but using Greek-based *abrəksis* (here and later in the manuscript) instead of the more indigenous and typical *Gəbr[ä ḥawaryat]* underscores the author Gälawdewos's credentials as a learned man.

[7] BDJ: *lä-nädday* [sg., but with generic meaning] (to the poor); CR: *lä-näddayan* [pl.] (to the poor).

[8] Lit., *betä mäqdäs* (house of holiness).

[9] Lit., *maʾədd* (the table).

[10] Acts 2:44–47. This is another case where the author Gälawdewos has amended the biblical text to better suit the context. While the original text in Greek is descriptive, the Gəʿəz here is prescriptive.

The same circumstances prevailed in the time of our holy mother Walatta Petros. Everybody esteemed her highly, and she was feared and respected. Therefore, nobody would disobey her statutes. The members of her community embraced one another in love, like soul and body, brother with brother and sister with sister.

Nobody among them would say, "Only I eat, or only I drink, or clothe myself." Rather, they shared everything; even if it was only a single fruit, nobody would eat it alone. When they relaxed in the drinking place, if one of them received the cup, he gave it to his neighbor, saying, "You are thirstier than me,[1] and I am in better shape than you are."[2] While one passed it on to the next [like this], the cup went around and would return to the first brother[3] [untouched]. When, furthermore, community members went out on errands or to the market, be it brothers or sisters,[4] those remaining behind in the morning bade them farewell in tears and in the evening received them back laughing joyfully.

Furthermore, our blessed mother Walatta Petros imposed a rule on the brothers
80 and sisters that they should not go out one with one alone, but rather in pairs of
twos,[5] be it [to a place] near or far, be it to the church or to the people of the town.[6]
And in the case that members of her community traveled to another town, she established that [while on the road] a monk should not eat at the same table with women, nor the nuns with men; and that a monk should not spend the night in a house where there was a woman, nor a nun spend the night in a house in which there was a man. She said to them, "It is better for you if the wild animals devour your flesh than that demons devour your souls and your bodies."

Her remaining orders were the following:[7] that the members of her community should not speak loudly but softly;[8] that they should not absent themselves as they pleased—be it [even] to [receive] the Eucharist or to the clothes' washing place—without [properly] taking their leave; and that they should not drink any medical

[1] BDJ: *antä təṣämmə' əmənneyä* (you are thirstier than me); CR: *antä taṣämmə' əmənneyä* (you make thirstier [*sic*] than me).

[2] Lit., *əḫeyyəs əmənnekä* (I am better than you are). Ricci pointed out that the contextually required translation for *ḫayyäsä əmənnä* is not in the dictionaries.

[3] BDJ: *ḫabä qädamawi əḫ*^{w} (to the first brother); CR: *ḫabä qädami əḫ*^{w} (to the original brother).

[4] BDJ: *əmmä-ni aḫaw wä-əmmä-ni aḫat* (be it brothers or sisters); CR: *əmmä-ni aḫaw wä-aḫat* [same translation, but grammatically substandard].

[5] Lit., *kämä i-yəḫuru 1-wä-1 əntä baḥtitomu, alla bä-bä-2* (lit., that they should not go out one and one alone, but in pairs of twos). Here our translation differs substantively from Ricci's, who takes the first part of this phrase to mean that they should not go out singly alone (*non . . . ognuno a solo, ma a due a due*), thereby obscuring the sexual point of the rule.

[6] Only now, in her sixth community, does WP establish strict rules regarding the interaction of the sexes.

[7] Lit., *wä-əllä-hi tärfu əm-tə'zazat* (lit., and those that remained from among the orders). Here our translation differs substantively from Ricci's, who has *quelli poi esenti da incombenze* (those however free from chores).

[8] Lit., *kämä i-yətnagäru qalä bä-kəlaḥ alla bä-läḥosas* (lit., that they should not speak words with shouting, but with whispers).

potion.[1] If they went to town, they should not eat [there] if they did not spend the night [there]. If they went to [receive] the Eucharist, they should not speak on their way, neither going nor coming. A healthy community member should not receive the Eucharist during the week, only on holy days.[2] They should not shave their heads.[3] Finally, they had to assemble for the prayer at meals, for the prayer upon retiring to sleep, and at any time at which the bell rang.[4]

If anyone transgressed these orders, be it someone low or someone high [in her community], she established forty whiplashes as the standard disciplinary measure against them.[5] Eheta Kristos functioned as head [of the community], second to Walatta Petros;[6] Eheta Kristos had authority over everything.

Regarding the community members, monks and nuns, they were assiduously devoted to God. They had no other concern than him, and submitted themselves under the feet of our holy mother Walatta Petros. As for her, she guarded them like the pupils of her eyes and watched [over them] like the ostrich watches over her eggs. Walatta Petros watched over their souls in the same way, day and night. But every day she had to swallow ashes and dung[7] on account of them, just as our Lord had to drink bile and myrrh when he tasted death for the redemption of the entire world.[8]

[1] BDJ: *fäwsä zä-zä-ziʾahu* (lit., a medicine of any type); CR: *fäwsä bä-zä-zä-ziʾhomu fäqad* (a medicine according to their own arbitrary decision).

[2] BDJ: *wä-i-yəqräb* [*sic*: substandard for *yəqʷräb*] *ṭəʿuy bä-sämun zä-ənbälä bä-bäʿalat* (lit., a healthy one should not receive the Eucharist during the week, only on feast days); CR: *wä-i-yəqräb ṭəʿuy bä-musun zä-ənbälä bä-bäʿalat* (a healthy one should not come near a sick one except on feast days). That is, they should not take the Eucharist except on Sundays and religious holidays.

[3] Since shaving the head was part of being initiated into the religious life or of mourning someone's death, perhaps she thought monks or nuns should not repeat or perform such rituals. Or, perhaps *wä-i-yətlaṣäyu rəʾsomu* means, in imperfect and unidiomatic Gəʿəz, that they should not shave each other's heads, since Abba Shenoute warned against such.

[4] Lit., *gize yənäqqu däwäl* (at a time at which the *däwäl* sounded). A *däwäl* is not a western-type metal bell—those were rare in Ethiopia even after the Jesuits brought them—but a church lithophone or phonolith. It was a large stone hung from a wooden post and struck with another stone to make a sound, a very ancient type of bell that remains common in Täwaḥədo Church churches and monasteries. See Mersha Alehegne and Nosnitsin (2005).

[5] BDJ: *anbärät laʿlehomu ḥəggä tägśaṣ bä-bä-40 ṭəbṭabe* (lit., she established against them a disciplinary law of forty whiplashes on each occasion); CR: *anbärät laʿlehomu ḥəggä tägśaṣ bä-40 ṭəbṭabe* (she established against them a disciplinary law of forty whiplashes). For an account of the *abunä* assigning forty whiplashes for serious sins, see Páez (2011, 213).

[6] Lit., *əm-taḥteha* (under her).

[7] As Ricci put in his note, *kos* is not a proper Gəʿəz term but a variant of Amharic *kʷəs* or *kus* (excrements, animal manure, bird droppings, dung). Ostriches, scientific name *Struthio camelus*, are a species of East Africa known to swallow sand and pebbles to aid digestion.

[8] On the way to the cross, the soldiers served Christ wine or vinegar (bile) mixed with myrrh, but after tasting it, he refused to drink it. Mark 15:23; Matthew 27:34.

Listen further, my loved ones! Lead weighs heavier than any other load, but heavier still weighs[1] putting up with the temperament of [even] one person! Our holy mother Walatta Petros said, "If the community grew in number from its cur-
81 rent size and increased twofold, my heart would be able to carry it fully through the power of God, my Lord, because I have been given[2] the gift of patient endurance." Indeed, patient endurance is the first of all virtues,[3] and the Kingdom of Heaven is obtained through it, just as the Gospel says, "Through your patient endurance you will acquire your souls."[4]

Chapter 63: Praise for the Nun Qiddista Kristos and Our Mother

How beautiful and sweet is the story of our holy mother Walatta Petros! Neither honey nor sugar[5] are as sweet as it is.[6] For this reason, it behooves us to love Qiddista Kristos,[7] who was rejected by [our] people and regarded as lowly by all the sisters. Truly, Qiddista Kristos eagerly devoted herself [to it] and, burning with love for Walatta Petros, compelled me to write down this story and to reveal this treasure that lay hidden in the field of the old people's hearts.[8] So it is fitting that we remember her, [Qiddista Kristos,] and that we read the story[9] of our holy mother Walatta Petros. As our Lord in the Gospel says about the woman who anointed him with fragrant oil, "Truly,[10] I say to you, wherever this gospel is preached in the entire world, may they proclaim what this woman has done, and may they remember

[1] BDJ: *wä-əmənnehu-ni yəkäbbəd* (but heavier still weighs); CR: *wä-əmənnehu yəkäbbəd* (but heavier weighs).

[2] BDJ: *täwəhbä litä* (I have been given); CR: *täwəhbäni litä* (I have been given [emph.]).

[3] Lit., *reʾsä məgbarat yəʿəti* (is the head of deeds).

[4] Luke 21:19.

[5] Sugarcane, from which most sugar is made, originated in South Asia and was being refined by the Persians and Greeks before the birth of Christ. India and China were producing sugar for trade by the sixth century CE. Sugarcane spread from the Middle East along with Islam and was being cultivated in Ethiopia by the thirteenth century at the latest.

[6] Lit., *zä-kämaha* (as it *or* as her). Since the pronoun *-ha* is feminine, it is unclear whether it refers to WP (natural gender) or to WP's story (grammatical gender).

[7] BDJ: *yədälləwänä nafqəra lä-zati Qəddəstä Krəstos* (lit., it behooves us to love this Qəddəstä Krəstos); CR: *yədälləwänä nafqəra lä-zati əḫətä* (it behooves us to love this sister). However, erasures suggest MS J also once had "this sister."

[8] The author Gälawdewos makes clear that the stories told in the *WP gädl* came not from himself but from those who knew WP.

[9] BDJ, Abb. 88 all with ungrammatical *lä-lä-nanäbbəb zenaha* (for for [*sic*] we read her story). CR sensibly altered initial *lä-lä-* to *wä-* (and), which is what we translate. In fidäl script, it is not inconceivable that deficient ለለ (*lä-lä-*) came about through corruption of an original ወ (*wä-*). In addition, indicative *nanäbbəb* (we read) of all four manuscripts seems questionable, as preceding *mäftəw* (it is fitting) normally requires the subjunctive in the dependent verb (which in this case would be *nanbəb*).

[10] BDJ: *aman* (truly); CR reduplicates: *aman aman* (truly, truly).

her!"[1] O profound richness of God's wisdom, hidden to us! While many [of our] older ones were among Walatta Petros's followers,[2] God stirred up Qiddista Kristos,[3] who is younger than them all, and put his praises in her mouth. As scripture says, "Out of the mouth of children and infants you have made praise come forth."[4]

Now it likewise behooves us to remember the virtues of our holy mother Walatta Petros, the sweet taste of her words and the fine speech of her lips.[5] Truly, she spoke consolingly and persuasively,[6] and did not impose herself with force. It was just as Peter says, "When you guard them, do not exercise control over them by force but rather through righteousness for the sake of God, without oppressing his people."[7]

If, [for instance,] an angry brother came to Walatta Petros in arrogance, the demon of anger and arrogance would leave him as soon as she put her hands on his shoulders and admonished him. Instantly, he would become gentle and humble, falling at her feet and saying, "I have sinned, forgive me!" Also, if a brother was possessed by the demon of fornication and lust, and revealed it to her, if she exhorted him and spoke consolingly to that brother,[8] the demon would withdraw[9] instantly, fortunately for the brother, and not assail him[10] again.

Furthermore, if nobles came to her who wanted to renounce their worldly status, whether they were men or women, she did not impose great [ascetic] burdens **82**
on them, neither in terms of food nor drink, which they would have been unable to bear.[11] Rather, she let them have what they required so that they would not run away and turn back [to their old lives], for in their hearts they were infants. It was just as Paul says, "As is done for infants in the faith of Christ, I have fed you milk and have not given you solid food to eat because you are not strong enough yet.

[1] Matthew 26:13. When the disciples protest the woman's wasteful display of costly perfume on Christ, claiming the money had been better spent on the poor, Christ responds that the woman should not be attacked for doing something generous but remembered for preparing his body for burial. Likewise, the costly process of producing a gädl is necessary for the appropriate commemoration of WP.

[2] Lit., *wəluda* (her children).

[3] BDJ: *astänaśəʾa kiyaha lä-Qəddəstä Krəstos* (lit., he stirred up Qəddəstä Krəstos); CR: *astänaśəʾa kiyaha lä-zati əḫət* (he stirred up this sister).

[4] Psalm 8:2; Matthew 21:16.

[5] Lit., *afuha* ([of] her mouth).

[6] Lit., *əsmä yəʾəti tənazzəz wä-təyäwwəh* (truly, she consoled and persuaded).

[7] 1 Peter 5:2–3.

[8] Lit., *wä-nazäzäto* (and consoled him).

[9] BDJ: *yətʾattät lotu sobeha* (lit., it would, fortunately for him, instantly withdraw); CR: *yətʾattät lotu ḫabehu* (it would, fortunately for him, withdraw toward him [*sic*]). Note the use of *lä-* plus personal suffix (*lotu*; lit., for him) in the manner of the Amharic postverbal *-ll-* infix plus personal suffixes, which together indicate for whose benefit the action denoted in the verb is being carried out.

[10] BDJ: *wä-i-yətqattälo* (and not assail him); CR: *wä-i-yətqattälu* (and they would not fight with each other).

[11] BDJ: *zä-i-yəkəlu ṣäwiroto* (lit., the carrying of which they cannot); CR: *zä-i-yəkəlu ṣäwirotä* (the carrying they cannot).

You are still living under the law of flesh and blood [not spirit]."[1] Our holy mother Walatta Petros acted in the same manner: She did not deprive them of anything, rather, of their own free will, they quickly abandoned [luxuries] and adopted the ways of the community.[2]

As for our holy mother Walatta Petros, when she sat down at table with the sisters, she would hold her nose when the various finely seasoned foods were served so that their aroma would not affect her: she despised it[3] like the stench of excrement. For her a dish prepared with ash would be placed underneath the table,[4] and she would eat it as if eating a proper dish together with the sisters.[5]

Chapter 64: Our Mother Has a Vision of *Abba* Absaadi

Furthermore, it behooves us to recall the vision that God revealed to our holy mother Walatta Petros when she was at Afer Faras and, standing [in the church], recited the midnight prayers.[6] In this vision,[7] an angel of God seized *Abba* Absaadi[8] from Maguna.[9] Guiding him, the angel ascended with him and took him all the way to the gate of the Seventh Heaven.[10] There the angel of God stopped and said to

[1] 1 Corinthians 3:1–3.

[2] BDJ: *wä-yəssattäfu bä-kämä ləmadä maḫbär* (lit., and participated according to the custom of the community); CR: *wä-yəssattäfu zä-kämä ləmadä maḫbär* (and participated how it was the custom of the community).

[3] BDJ: *wä-tastämassəlo* [with masc. obj. suffix *-o*] (lit., she considered it); CR: *wä-tastämassəla* [with fem. obj. suffix *-a*; no translation difference].

[4] BDJ: *əm-taḥtä maʾədd* (underneath the table); Abb. 88 with substandard orthography: *əm-təḥtä* [*sic*] *maʾədd.* CR altered this to *əm-dəḫrä maʾədd* (after the meal), but Ricci rejected Conti Rossini's emendation. Alternatively, as tables for eating were not that common in monasteries, the phrase under discussion might also mean "under the [real] meal."

[5] This is an ancient ascetic practice, mentioned several times in the *Sənkəssar.* For instance, the seventh-century *Abba* Isaac of Syria, celebrated on 19 Gənbot, mixed ashes from the censer into his food to prevent himself from enjoying it.

[6] In the Täwaḥədo Church, one is expected to pray seven times a day. The midnight prayer—said at the hour Christ was born, baptized, arose from the dead, and will come again—consists of set prayers, ending with saying, "Lord have mercy upon us" forty-one times. Monasteries have slightly different prayer and liturgical schedules than regular churches.

[7] Lit., *ameha* (at that time).

[8] BDJ: *mäśäṭo lä-abba Absadi* (seized *Abba* Absadi); CR: *mäśäṭä lä-abba Absadi* [ungrammatical, but no translation difference]. Little is known about Absadi, although he has a gädl.

[9] *Mägʷəna* Monastery near Gondär is associated with Absadi.

[10] The Seventh Heaven is the highest of the heavens, where the curtained throne of God is. According to various religious traditions, the task of the saint is to move to the highest level possible, which is difficult because angels guard each level, preventing the unworthy from progressing higher by testing them. The *Gädlä Mäbaʾa Ṣəyon, Gädlä Gäbrä Mänfäs Qəddus,* and *Gädlä Lalibäla* depict their respective saints being shown their future dwelling

Abba Absaadi, "Enter on your own, salute your Lord's throne, stand before him, and hear from him the words he will say to you! Truly, he has granted you permission [to enter]! But he does not allow me [in], and [thus] it is not appropriate for me to pass through this gate."

At that moment, our holy mother Walatta Petros was seized as well, and she saw and heard this mystery through the words of the angel, that[1] *Abba* Absaadi's rank was higher than the angel's. Absaadi went to enter into the curtained chamber, while the angel stood outside.

She marveled at this and said, "Walatta Maryam,[2] have you heard[3] this amazing
and stunning thing that the angel has said to *Abba* Absaadi, 'You enter on your
own. But for me it is not appropriate to pass through this gate'?" Our blessed
mother Walatta Petros said this while all alone; yet it appeared to her as if she was 83
constantly speaking with Walatta Maryam.

Meanwhile, there was a young woman[4] who stood [undetected] near Walatta Petros because the dark of night concealed her. Therefore, she could overhear this conversation through the words of our holy mother Walatta Petros, and later told it to us, so we have written it down. Since God wanted to make this vision known, he awakened the young woman so that she overheard this vision. It resembles the one written down in the letter of the Apostle Paul, who says,[5] "I know a man who believes in Christ. Fourteen years ago, whether in the flesh or not in the flesh I don't know—only God knows—he was snatched[6] up to the Third Heaven. I know this man. Whether [he was snatched up] in the flesh or not in the flesh, I don't know; only God knows. He was transported to paradise[7] and there heard words that cannot be translated, and which mortal men cannot utter."[8] Do you see the greatness of our blessed mother Walatta Petros, that she was granted[9] this gift of hearing the mysteries of heaven while she was present in the flesh?

---

place in the Seventh Heaven. Saint Paul had a similar vision of ascending to the Third Heaven, as noted in the next paragraphs.

[1] BDJ: *kämä* (that); CR: *zä-kämä* [emph.; no translation difference].

[2] *Wälättä Maryam* (Daughter of [Saint] Mary) was a member of the Afär Färäs community and a close companion of WP.

[3] Lit., *tәreʾәyi-nu* (have you seen).

[4] Lit., *wälätt* (daughter).

[5] *Zä-yәbәl* can also mean "which says." Since Gәʿәz does not have a neuter gender, the masculine relative particle *zä-* can refer to Paul or to his letter.

[6] BDJ: *mäśäṭәwwo lä-wәʾәtu* (lit., they snatched him); CR: *mäśäṭәwwo lä-wәʾәtu bәʾәsi* (they snatched this man).

[7] BDJ: *wä-mäśäṭәwwo wәstä gännät* (lit., they snatched him into paradise); CR: *wä-boʾa wәstä wәsaṭe mänṭolaʿt* (he proceeded to enter into the [Lord's] curtained-off hall).

[8] 2 Corinthians 12:2–4.

[9] BDJ: *kämä täwәhbä lati* (lit., that she was given); CR: *kämä täwәhba lati* (that she was given [emph.]).

Chapter 65: Our Mother Drives Demons Away from a Royal Woman

Now we will further tell you about our holy mother Walatta Petros's great, awe-inspiring power: how the demons feared and fled her.[1] One day, a great lady[2] from among those of royal blood[3] came to our holy mother Walatta Petros to pay her a visit. The princess met with Walatta Petros, sat down in front of her, and the two of them conversed with each other for some time. Then our blessed mother Walatta Petros raised her eyes and saw demons amusing themselves with the princess and surrounding her entire body, like flies and mosquitoes surround a rotting carcass. When our holy mother Walatta Petros looked straight at the demons, they became terrified and took flight. Yet when she lowered [her eyes] to the ground again, they instantly swarmed back and surrounded the princess as before. But when Walatta Petros again looked at them, they [again] took flight.

After the woman had left, Ghirmana asked Walatta Petros about this matter because she had been with them.[4] Ghirmana said to Walatta Petros, "Please tell me what you have seen over that woman, because I saw you raising your eyes once and looking toward her, but then casting them down to the ground in embarrass-
84 ment.[5] Therefore, I have come to suspect that you noticed something."

Our blessed mother Walatta Petros indignantly replied to her,[6] "What type of thought rises in your heart? I have seen nothing whatsoever over her!" Yet, Ghirmana again implored her. So Walatta Petros then told her that she had seen demons, as we described earlier.

My loved ones, do you see how the demons feared our holy mother Walatta Petros and took flight from her? Truly, this recalls the saying of the Spiritual Elder, "Just as jackals become scared and hide at the roar of the lion, so the word of the sage frightens[7] the evil spirits[8] and puts them to flight."

[1] BDJ: *zä-kämä färhu säyṭanat wä-gʷäyyu əmənneha* (lit., how the devils feared [her] and fled from her); CR: *zä-kämä yəfrəhu* [*sic*; Abb. 88: *yəfärrəhu*] *säyṭanat wä-yəgʷyəyu* [*sic*] *əmənneha* (how the devils fear [her] and flee from her [CR twice, Abb. 88 once with unwarranted subj.]).

[2] BDJ: *bəʾəsit ʿabbay* (lit., a great woman); Abb. 88: *bəʾəsit akkayt* [fem.] (a wicked woman), which CR altered to *bəʾəsit akkay* [no translation difference, but CR incorrectly presumed a different adjectival type, and hence a different formation of the fem. form].

[3] Lit., *əmənnä wäyzazər* (from among the female members of the extended royal family).

[4] BDJ: *məslehon* (with them); CR: *məsleha* (with her).

[5] BDJ: *əsmä anä rəʾiki aḥadä gize ənzä tanäśśəʾi aʿyəntiki wä-təneṣṣəri mängäleha wä-aḥadä gize ənzä tədännəni wəstä mədr bä-ḫafrät* (because I once saw you raising your eyes and looking toward her, but then casting them down to the ground in embarrassment); CR: *əsmä anä rəʾiki aḥadä gize ənzä tədännəni wəstä mədr bä-ḫafrät* (because I once saw you casting your eyes down to the ground in embarrassment).

[6] BDJ: *awśəʾata* (replied to her); CR; *awśəʾat* (replied).

[7] BDJ: *yafärrəh* (frightens); CR: *yəfärrəh* (becomes frightened [*sic*]).

[8] Lit., *aganənt* (demons).

Chapter 66: Our Mother Cripples the Disobedient Nuns

In accordance with this saying, we would like to reveal to you the gift of spiritual power[1] that our holy mother Walatta Petros had been given.[2] Among the young nuns, there was one named Amata Kristos.[3] She was charmingly beautiful and marvelously pretty; nobody in the world compared to her. One day our holy mother Walatta Petros saw her bragging and arguing with a companion.[4] Instantly, Walatta Petros summoned her and made her stand before her.

With an angry eye, Walatta Petros looked her up and down and said to her, "What is it with this curviness [of yours]?[5] What about [attaining spiritual] beauty [instead] through eating little food and drinking cold water? So far as I am concerned, I would like to pierce you with a spear and kill you!"[6]

Walatta Petros scolded her severely and then sent Amata Kristos back to her house. Soon, then, Amata Kristos fell ill with the piercing sickness.[7] She remained ill for a long time,[8] until her appearance had changed [completely], with her flesh adhering tightly to her bones. She became paralyzed and never got up again.[9]

Then there was another young nun like Amata Kristos, named Eheta Kristos.[10] She became agitated as well and got it into her mind to go home to visit her relatives. Our holy mother Walatta Petros was then informed that Eheta Kristos had become agitated. Walatta Petros now summoned and questioned her. However, Eheta Kristos concealed [her thoughts] from Walatta Petros; she did not tell her.[11] In addition, due to her great agitation, she refused to eat. So, Walatta Petros ordered that ashes be brought and mixed into bread, which Eheta Kristos forcibly was made

[1] *Ṣägga asot* (lit., grace of healing). However, given that the two stories that follow are about crippling and not healing, such a literal translation seems inadequate here.

[2] BDJ: *zä-täwəhbä lati lä-əmmənä qəddəst Wälättä Ṗeṭros* (lit., that had been given to our holy mother Wälättä Ṗeṭros); CR: *zä-täwəhba lati lä-əmmənä qəddəst Wälättä Ṗeṭros* (that had been given to her, to our holy mother Wälättä Ṗeṭros).

[3] *Amätä Krəstos* (Maidservant of Christ).

[4] BDJ: *ənzä . . . tətlakkʷäy məslä kaləʾta* (lit., arguing with a companion of hers); CR: *ənzä . . . tətläḥay məslä kaləʾta* (adorning herself together with a companion of hers).

[5] Lit., *gəzäf* (density, stoutness, obesity). Ricci translates *gəzäf* as *floridezza* (flowering, blossoming).

[6] A second instance where devotion to the flesh causes WP to call for a spear.

[7] Lit., *ḥəmamä wəgʿat* (the sickness of piercing). It is unlikely she had a stroke (since they are rarely painful). Rheumatism is a somewhat more likely possibility, even if it only rarely sets in at a young age. Alternatively, Amätä Krəstos's symptoms might have resulted from severe depression. Condemned for pride, perhaps the vivacious girl took to her bed and stayed there, losing muscle mass and becoming incapacitated. Not wanting to eat or move around due to chronic pain, she further deteriorated, becoming paralyzed and wasted.

[8] BDJ: *gʷənduyä mäwaʿəlä* (for a long time); CR: *gʷənduyä ʿamätä* (for many years).

[9] Lit., *wä-i-tänśəʾat əskä amä motät* (she did not get up until she died).

[10] *Əḫətä Krəstos* (Sister of Christ), but not the same woman as WP's close friend, who was in her forties by this time.

[11] BDJ: *i-nägäräta* (she did not tell her); CR: *i-tänägäräta* [*sic*] (she was not told her [*sic*]).

to eat.[1] Then, she too fell sick and became paralyzed. For a long time, she lived
85 crawling like an infant, due to the power of our blessed mother Walatta Petros.
Eheta Kristos never walked again.[2]

Chapter 67: Our Mother and the Miracle of the Righteous Nun Ilarya

Through this door[3] we have also found a path that leads us to the story of the saintly Ilarya. Recall that she[4] is the one who had gone down to Zhebey with our holy mother Walatta Petros. There she had served her and done the cooking. Now, Ilarya had developed a strong affection for Saint Fasiladas the Martyr[5] while[6] living on Mitsillé Island with our holy mother Walatta Petros.[7] Since that time, love for Saint Fasiladas had been instilled in her heart, and the chanting of his name[8] had been written on her tongue so that she continually said, "Fasiladas!" As for Saint Fasiladas, he never parted from Ilarya and gave her success in her work so that her dishes turned out delicious-smelling and tasty. All day long, Ilarya would stand [on the shore] opposite Mitsillé, tapping her feet and chanting [her song] out loud, "O Fasiladas the saint, Fasiladas the martyr, Fasiladas the strong,[9] help me, come to

[1] It is due to passages like this that some call WP a "witch" (Gundani 2004; Chernetsov 2005d). This is the only case, however, where WP directly causes an illness though physical means rather than calling on God to punish the sinner or cursing him or her. Since WP herself ate food with ashes without coming to any harm, perhaps this act was meant only to reveal that the woman was not suited to the ascetic life.

[2] Lit., *wä-i-ḥorät bä-əgäriha əskä amä motät* (she did not walk on her feet until she died). Despite the proximity of two women with paralysis, they probably did not have the same illness. The syndromes of sickness, paralysis, and inability to walk in a young adult had two common causes: polio, which tends to affect the young, and hip muscle contractures that prevent walking. A sick person confined to bed for ten days or longer, lying in a fetal position, may develop severe hip muscle contractures and then cannot straighten their legs or walk.

[3] Lit., *anqäṣ*, which can also mean "chapter" or "section." The phrase therefore can also be understood as "In this chapter." The author here likely deliberately plays with this ambiguity, as Ricci suggested.

[4] BDJ: *wä-yəʾəti-ke* (lit., she, in fact); CR: *wä-yəʾəti-ssä* (as for her, she).

[5] This is not the reigning seventeenth-century king Fasilädäs, but the fourth-century saint, although perhaps this particular saint was especially regarded during this period, and by Ilarya, because the king of the same name had restored the true faith.

[6] BDJ, CR all with *əsmä* (because *or* truly). However, since neither meaning makes sense in the context, we regard the manuscripts' *əsmä* as the corruption of an original *ənzä* (while).

[7] DJ: [*ənzä*] *näbärät wəstä Məṣəlle məslä əmmənä qəddəst Wälättä Ṗeṭros* (lit., [while] living on Mitsillé together with our holy mother WP); B: [*ənzä*] *näbärät wəstä Məṣəlle məslä əmmənä qəddəst wä-burəkt Wälättä Ṗeṭros* ([while] living on Mitsillé together with our holy and blessed mother WP); CR: [*ənzä*] *näbärät wəstä Məṣəlle əmmənä burəkt* ([while] our holy mother lived on Mitsillé).

[8] Lit., *zəkrä səmu* (the saying *or* the commemoration of his name).

[9] Abb. 88 here adds *täbbaʿ* (valorous), which CR altered to *täbaʿt* (male, masculine),

him who is in need!"[1] Straightaway, Saint Fasiladas then would come to her, and she would be so happy when she saw him, frolicking like a child who sees the faces of his father and mother. While alone, Ilarya would laugh as though she were with other people. She behaved like this every day. The place where she would stand was [generally] known, next to the cliff on the lakeshore of Afer Faras.

Whenever the sisters looked for her, they would find Ilarya engaged in such activity. They would marvel at her and ask her, "What are you saying, and with whom are you speaking?" But Ilarya[2] would then change the topic[3] and with her words would artfully and cleverly deceive them.

[Meanwhile,] our holy mother Walatta Petros always said to Ilarya, when the latter did the kitchen work, "Ask Walatta Maryam whether she would like some stew, and do what she orders you to do!"

Every day Ilarya carried out Walatta Maryam's wishes. One day she was charged as usual by her, and so she prepared the stew that Walatta Maryam had ordered her to prepare. Then, when it had become evening, she presented the stew and placed it before Walatta Maryam. But when God wanted to reveal Ilarya's great power, he instilled depression into Walatta Maryam's heart so that she was disgusted by the stew and refused to eat it.[4]

When our blessed mother Walatta Petros learned that Walatta Maryam had refused to eat [the stew], she said to Ilarya, "Why have you not cooked today as 86
Walatta Maryam wishes? Look, she refuses to eat!"

Ilarya responded, "Perhaps I should hurry and bring her [something else]." She then left, went to her house, and said to the women who were with her in the kitchen, "You women, prepare [some fresh stew] right away, and liberally add[5] salt and all the spices appropriate for fish![6] Meanwhile I will go to a fisherman[7] and buy a fish."

Then she took some grain, got a young servant girl to accompany her, and left in a hurry.

---

thereby accentuating the latent erotic aspect of Ilarya's longing. This extra adjective would change the segmentation, and translation, of the entire sentence (to "O holy Fasilädäs the martyr, Fasilädäs the strong, Fasilädäs the valorous").

[1] Lit., *lä-ṣənnus* (the needy one). Gəʿəz distinguishes gender in adjectives, and *ṣənnus* (needy) is masculine, making it clear that Ilarya is not thinking of herself only. Our translation was chosen so as to make this immediately clear.

[2] BDJ: *wä-yəʾəti-ni* (lit., she however); CR: *wä-yəʾəti* (she).

[3] Lit., *təwelləṭ kaləʾa nägärä* (change to a different discourse).

[4] This is the second time that Ilarya has had one of the women refuse her food; WP had also done so in Žäbäy.

[5] BDJ: *wä-aśännəya* [imper. fem. pl.] (and liberally add); CR: *wä-aśännäya* [past tense fem. pl.] (and they liberally added).

[6] The stew was probably *ʿaśa dulät*, a fish dish common around Lake Ṭana but not elsewhere in Ethiopia. Those fasting were permitted to eat fish, although extreme ascetics would not do so.

[7] BDJ: *mäśäggər* (fisherman); CR here and throughout with the variant *mäśagər*, which is undocumented in the major dictionaries.

Plate 18. "How she [i.e., Ilarya] made the sun stand still" and "how she [i.e., a kitchen servant] cooked a stew" (MS A, f. 152r © SLUB Mscr.Dresd.Eb.415.e,2).

Now she saw that the sun had begun to sink and was about to set. Therefore, she said to it, "You, Sun, I implore you by the Lord of Saint Fasiladas to stand still and wait for me until I return,[1] having carried out what I wanted to do."[2]

The servant girl said to Ilarya, "What are you saying? Are you really talking with the sun today?" However, she did not [really] comprehend what was going on because she was just a girl then.

Ilarya came to a fisherman then, bought a fish, and turned back in a hurry. Meanwhile the sun stood still as she had ordered it. After Ilarya had arrived at her house, she cooked that fish with great care, and taking it to the table, she put it before Walatta Maryam, who happily ate it.

Meanwhile, Ilarya had forgotten about the sun;[3] she just did not think about it. Thus, it kept standing still for quite a long time. The sisters marveled [at this] and said among themselves, "What has happened to the sun today?"[4]

Then Ilarya remembered, went outside, and saw the sun standing still. Now she said to it, "Be blessed, Sun, because you have waited for me! Now, however, you have done enough: continue on your way." Right away, then, the sun set and complete darkness reigned.[5]

The servant girl heard this, as well as the sisters who were with Ilarya. At that time, however, they did not understand what it meant, but only after Ilarya's death. The servant girl [later] told this episode to a priest, and he then told it to everybody.

Chapter 68: Our Mother Lives in Austerity

Now, though, it is appropriate for us [to continue] to reveal to you the story of our holy mother Walatta Petros. Truly, she spent all the days of her life wearing[6] a dress of cowhide[7] sewn together with sinew.[8] [At night,] she spread out a palm-leaf mat

[1] BDJ: *əskä əgäbbə*ʾ (until I return); CR: *əskä əgäbbər* (until I have done).

[2] Stopping the sun is a common theme of Gəʿəz hagiobiographies' miracles, including another female saint hagiobiography titled *Gädlä Wälättä Maryam*. For a biblical instance, see Joshua 10:13. It was the perception of Christian Ethiopians that their ancestors and those of other cultures were sun worshippers; for instance, the *Kəbrä Nägäśt* depicts the Queen of Sheba as a sun worshipper. Since, as noted previously, Ilarya's name suggests that she is an outsider, this anecdote may play on this perception. In the eleventh miracle, another woman successfully pleads with WP to stop the sun.

[3] BDJ: *wä-Ilarya-ssä räsʿata lä-ṣ̌äḥay* (lit., as for Ilarya, she had forgotten about the sun); CR: *wä-Ilarya-ssä räsʿat* [*sic*] *lä-ṣ̌äḥay* [not fully grammatical, but no difference in meaning].

[4] Without watches or timepieces, perceived time could be quite elastic.

[5] BDJ: *wä-konä fəṣṣumä ṣəlmätä* (and complete darkness reigned); Abb. 88: *wä-konä fəssumu* [*sic*] (and it was complete), which CR altered to *wä-konä fəṣmu* (and that was its completion).

[6] Lit., *ənzä təgäbbər* (doing). This use of *gäbrä* (to do; *təgäbbər* is a conjugated form) in the sense of "to wear, to don" is an Amharism. The proper Gəʿəz verb would be *läbsä*.

[7] Lit., *qämisä anäda zä-əgʷlä alhəmt* (a dress of the hide of the young of cows).

[8] BDJ: *bä-amtənt* (with sinew); CR: *bä-mənt* (with what [*sic*]). Thick threads made from animal sinew were often used in sewing leather.

and a sheepskin. She always slept [like this],[1] and never slept on a bed, nor did she
87 ever put shoes on her feet.[2] Furthermore, she had devices of sharpened iron[3] manu-
factured [for her] that resembled bracelets with points and teeth like a saw, and she
wore them[4] on her arms and ankles.[5] Finally, she covered her loins with sackcloth
and always swept the ashes from the oven.[6]

Chapter 69: Our Mother Speaks with Our Lady Mary at Amba Maryam

In addition, it is appropriate for us to recall[7] what happened to our blessed mother Walatta Petros at Amba Maryam.[8] One year,[9] our holy mother Walatta Petros went to Amba Maryam together with a few of her community. Some of the rest of the community went to Bizaaba[10] with Eheta Kristos and spent the rainy season there. The others stayed at Afer Faras and were afflicted by great tribulation and distress because they had become orphans [since Walatta Petros and Eheta Kristos were elsewhere]. But our holy mother Walatta Petros spent the [entire] rainy season at Amba Maryam, by the will of our Lady Mary.

People knowledgeable about this matter have informed us accordingly, relating, "When our holy mother Walatta Petros wanted to return to Afer Faras, she went to the church [at Amba Maryam], stood before the icon of our Lady Mary, and prayed,

[1] BDJ: *wä-təsäkkəb zälfä* (she always slept); CR omits. Even in BDJ the phrase comes across as incomplete and requiring the addition of [like this].

[2] At the time, raised beds on bed frames, as well as shoes, were rare luxury items and hence aristocratic status markers. By renouncing both, WP renounced the privileges of the class she had been born into in the name of Christian humility and material equality with her followers.

[3] BDJ: *ḫaṣawəntä bäliḫatä* (lit., sharp irons); CR: *ḥaṣ́antä bäliḫatä* [not meaningful: a lexeme *ḥaṣ́ant*—or, alternatively, *ḥaṣant*—is not documented].

[4] Lit., *wä-təgäbberon* (and she did them). This use of *gäbrä* (to do, with *təgäbbər* being the conjugated form) in the sense of "to wear, to don" again is an Amharism.

[5] BDJ: *wä-əgäriha* (lit., and her feet); CR omits.

[6] Ascetics use sackcloth for undergarments because it is made of animal hair and thus very irritating next to the skin. Sweeping the hearth was a particularly distasteful and lowly job, but also ashes are associated with humiliation of the flesh in ascetic practice.

[7] BDJ: *yədälləwänä nəzzäkär* (it is appropriate for us to recall); CR: *yədälləwänä nəzkər* [different verbal stem, but identical meaning].

[8] *Amba Maryam* is what is now known as Ṭeza Amba Maryam, about twenty miles north of Qʷäraṣa on the eastern shore of Lake Ṭana. Its church was famous as one of the places where the Virgin Mary stopped on her way to Ṣana Qirqos by tankwa. This may be a different Amba Maryam than that previously mentioned in the text, where one priest came from and another died.

[9] BDJ: *wä-bä-1 ʿamät əm-əllon ʿamätat* (lit., in one year from among these years); CR: *wä-bä-1 ʿamät əm-kʷəllon ʿamätat* (in one year from among all years).

[10] *Bizaba* may be what is now known as *Bizäb*, a town about four miles directly east and inland from Qʷäraṣa. Often, Ethiopians would move due to seasons.

'My Lady, I ask my leave from you, so allow me[1] to return to my followers at Afer Faras.' But the icon stretched out a hand, seized Walatta Petros by her gown,[2] and spoke to her with these words, 'I won't allow you to leave me! Rather, I want you to spend the rainy season here with me.' This is why Walatta Petros spent the rainy season at Amba Maryam. This did not please those who were with her, however. Instead,[3] they grumbled because they did not know what the icon of our Lady Mary had said to Walatta Petros.

"Our holy mother Walatta Petros addressed the icon in prayer again, asking Saint Mary to reveal the place where she should live. She said, 'My Lady, I beg you to reveal the place of my future home to me, the place that would please you as well as your beloved Son.' Now the icon took her by her hand and replied as follows, 'I implore you to not ever become restless[4] and move from your [assigned] place! Don't say, "Here! There!" [Go] neither to the right nor to the left. For your assigned lot is Afer Faras.' After having heard these words of our Lady Mary, Walatta Petros became calm and ceased to be restless.

"In those days, a brother was with her, and he asked our holy mother Walatta Petros, 'Some of the community have gone to Bizaaba while we stay here. Why
don't we join them?' She replied, 'No, we won't go—instead, they will come to us. **88**
You see, a man said to me, "Don't go!" ' So the brother asked her, 'Who is that man[5] who said this to you?' Our holy mother Walatta Petros replied, 'I won't tell you his name. And if you disclose this matter and tell somebody else, that man will be very disappointed with me.' In reaction, the brother reassured her, 'I certainly won't tell anybody!' Now she made him swear that he would only disclose this matter after her death, and [then] told him that, as we have said before, it had been our Lady Mary who said this to her and who had implored her [to stay]."

That very brother[6] is still alive now. He has told us [about this encounter], and we have written it down.

Chapter 70: Our Mother's Brother Yohannes Dies

While our holy mother Walatta Petros[7] was at that monastery, [Amba Maryam], [through a vision] she learned about the death of [her brother] Yohannes on the day he died in Tigré,[8] before she was told about it.

[1] BDJ: *kämä tabəḥəni* [substandard orthography for *tabəḥini*] (lit., so that you allow me); CR: *kämä tabṣəḥəni* [substandard orthography for *tabṣəḥini*] (so that you take me).

[2] Lit., *aḫazät ləbsa* (seized her gown).

[3] BJ: *daʾəmu* (instead); D, CR omit.

[4] Lit., *kämä i-təthawäki lä-ʿaläm* (to not ever become restless). Ricci interpreted this phrase's idiomatic *lä-ʿaläm* (ever) according to its constituent parts ("for" and "the world"), and thus translated *di non lasciarsi prendere da agitazione per il mondo esterno* (to not let herself be moved to restlessness by the external world).

[5] BDJ: *männu wəʾətu bəʾəsi* (who is that man); CR: *männu wəʾətu bəʾəsihu* (who is he, the man).

[6] BDJ: *wä-wəʾətu-hi* (lit., he specifically); CR: *wä-wəʾətu* (he).

[7] CR omits *Wälättä Ṗeṭros.*

[8] *Təgre* is a northern region of highland Ethiopia, at least 150 miles north of where WP

Thereupon she sighed, "Woe, Yohannes, what has happened today!"[1]

A few days later, Walatta Petros was then informed that her brother Yohannes had died. She wept over him and mourned him greatly.[2] Thus, the vision that she had seen turned out to have been true.

Meanwhile, Eheta Kristos was in Bizaaba. From the time she had separated from Walatta Petros, she wept and lamented continuously until she fell ill from depression.

After our holy mother Walatta Petros had heard about Yohannes's death,[3] she descended from the monastery [at Amba Maryam] in the month of Maskaram, [after the end of the rainy season,] since the day of Yohannes's death had been the first of that month. She arrived at Afer Faras and reunited with those from her community who had remained there. Together with them, she mourned [her brother] and celebrated his tazkaar on Réma Island. Afterward, she lived in Afer Faras.

A few days later, Eheta Kristos also arrived [from Bizaaba], together with those from the community who had been with her. She reunited with our holy mother Walatta Petros and wept with her[4] over her brother Yohannes. Thereafter the entire community lived together [again] in Afer Faras, in one place.[5]

Chapter 71: Our Mother Converts Walatta Giyorgis Back to the True Faith

At that time King Fasiladas sent Walatta Giyorgis,[6] daughter of *Ité* Amata Kristos, to our holy mother Walatta Petros so that she might convert her back[7] from the

was. In its indigenous Təgrəñña language, the name of the region is Təgray, whereas the *WP gädl*'s "Təgre" is the Amharic form.

[1] BDJ: *ah məntä konä yom Yoḥannəs* (woe, Yoḥannəs, what has happened today); CR: *əḫʷəyä məntä konä Yoḥannəs* (my brother, Yoḥannəs, what has happened).

[2] Lit., *wä-läḥawäto ʿabiyä laḥwä* (and lamented him greatly). The spelling *läḥawäto* is substandard for *laḥawäto.*

[3] BDJ: *sämʿat moto lä-Yoḥannəs* (had heard about Yoḥannəs's death); CR: *sämʿat motä* [*sic*] *lä-Yoḥannəs* [ungrammatical, but identical translation].

[4] BJ, CR: *wä-bäkäyäta* [*sic*] (lit., and wept her); D: *wä-bäkäyät* (and wept).

[5] BDJ: *aḥattäne* (in one place); CR: *bä-aḥattäne* [substandard construction, but identical translation].

[6] This is not the same Wälättä Giyorgis who appeared previously in the text, the daughter of the former king Śärṣä Dəngəl. Rather, this is Wälättä Giyorgis, the daughter of "Queen" Amätä Krəstos, the cousin of Fasilädäs, and the wife of *Abeto* [Prince] Zä-Iyäsus. According to the hagiobiography, it was not until after the death of Susənyos that this Wälättä Giyorgis was converted back to the Täwaḥədo Church. Meanwhile, according to Mendes and Almeida, as Ricci pointed out, Wälättä Giyorgis never reconverted to Orthodoxy but rather died a Catholic martyr. Mendes reports that, after he left the country, he heard that she was sent to Däq Island to be converted by nuns and, because she refused, was tortured until she died in 1652 (1909, 335–41).

[7] BDJ: *kämä təmiṭa* (so that she might convert her back); CR: *kämä təmiṭ* (so that she might convert back).

faith of the Europeans and teach her the true faith. All the [Orthodox] theologians
had been unable to convert her [back]: the faith of the Europeans had burgeoned in
her heart. When Walatta Giyorgis arrived at our holy mother Walatta Petros's, the
latter welcomed her, lodged her with herself, and taught her the [true] faith. How- 89
ever, even she was unable to convert her [back at first].

Also, at that time, a sister named Fihirta Kristos[1] became restless and wanted to return to her region. Therefore, she said to our holy mother Walatta Petros, "Allow me to return home."

But our holy mother Walatta Petros implored her, "Just wait for a week. After that, I will let you go."

The sister replied, "Very well," and refrained from leaving.

When Walatta Giyorgis refused to convert back from the faith of the Europeans, Walatta Petros's entire community rose up against Walatta Giyorgis and wanted to stone her. So our holy mother Walatta Petros took her and fled with her to Sadachilla, where Walatta Petros went to the house of a nun[2] and stayed [there with Walatta Giyorgis].

On that very day, the sister named Fihirta Kristos fell ill; she then died the same week.[3] Therefore, some sisters [from Afer Faras] went to Sadachilla to tell our holy mother Walatta Petros. Having arrived there, they stood at the gate. One [Sadachilla] sister who was there went outside, greeted them, and asked why they had come. They told her that Fihirta Kristos had died. Having heard this, the sister went back into the house and told our holy mother Walatta Petros that those sisters had arrived.

Walatta Petros replied, "Summon them." When they came to her, she asked them, "When did Fihirta Kristos die?"

They replied [politely], "She is alive and well, and not dead!"[4]

But Walatta Petros responded, "And yet I know she died yesterday!"[5]

So then they admitted to her, "Yes, she has died."[6]

Walatta Petros gave praise to God then, and the sisters marveled that she had known [about the death] before they had told her.

Later, Walatta Maryam came in, for she had been outside. Our holy mother Walatta Petros said to her, "Did you hear that Fihirta Kristos has died?"

Walatta Maryam was shocked and asked, "When did she fall ill? When did she die?"

[1] *Fəḫərtä Krəstos* (Betrothed of Christ). BDJ, CR do not have Fəqərtä Krəstos, the name of a contemporaneous female saint who also has a hagiobiography.

[2] BDJ: *ḫabä betä aḥatti mänäkosayt* (to the house of a nun); CR: *ḫabä aḥatti mänäkosayt* (to a nun).

[3] BDJ: *bä-yəʾəti sämun* (lit., in that week); CR: *bä-yəʾəti ʿəlät* (on that day).

[4] It is not culturally polite to announce someone's death directly; further, to allow proper mourning, it must be at a particular time of day and with particular people.

[5] BDJ: *təmaləm* (yesterday); CR omits.

[6] BDJ: *wä-yəbelaha əwwä motät* (lit., so they said to her: Yes, she has died); CR omits.

But our holy mother Walatta Petros said to her, “Don’t be distressed! Through the power of God my Lord, it was I who[1] killed her.”

Do you see the power of our holy mother Walatta Petros, how she kills when she so desires, and how she knew before she was told?

Then, one day, while the two of them, our holy mother Walatta Petros and
90 Walatta Giyorgis, were alone in the house,[2] a sister was cooking vegetables next to
them because Walatta Giyorgis liked to eat vegetable stew.[3] That [servant] sister put the pot on the stove, lit the fire, and then left to go outside. Soon the liquid in the pot of vegetables boiled and spilled over. Immediately, our holy mother Walatta Petros got up, stirred the vegetables,[4] and [re]lit the fire that had gone out [due to the spill].

When Walatta Giyorgis saw Walatta Petros’s humility, she said to her, “You did this for my sake, didn’t you? Now, due to your humility, I hereby convert from the filthy faith of the Europeans and enter your holy faith.[5] Rejoice[6] and be happy!”

When our holy mother Walatta Petros heard this good news, she fell to the ground and kissed Walatta Giyorgis’s feet. Then she rose up and ululated[7] at the top of her voice, and all the sisters around ululated with her. On that day, there was great joy.[8] Now Walatta Petros sent a message with the good news to all the [Lake Tana] islands, and everyone rejoiced. They beat the drum and sang, “We praise God the praiseworthy to whom praise is due!”[9] Also the king rejoiced, together with his court.[10]

[1] J, CR: *anə-ssä* (lit., I [emph.]); BD: *anä* (I).

[2] BJ: *ənzä halläwa kəlʾehon əntä baḥtiton wəstä bet* (while the two of them . . . were alone in the house); D: *ənzä halläwa kəlʾehon baḥtiton wəstä bet* [substandard through omission of *əntä*, but identical in meaning]; CR: *ənzä halläwa kəlʾehon anəst baḥtiton wəstä bet* (while the two women . . . were alone in the house).

[3] Lit., *ṣäbḫ zä-ḥaml* (vegetable stew), in Amharic *atkəlt wäṭ*. Ethiopian cuisine is rich in vegan dishes, made with onions, garlic, lentils, chickpeas, mustard greens, and other local plants.

[4] DJ: *akosäto lä-wəʾətu ḥaml* (stirred the vegetables); B, CR: *akʷäsäto lä-wəʾətu ḥaml* [identical meaning, but with the substandard scriptorial variant *akʷäsä* for the verb, thereby suggesting a root *ʾ-kʷ-s* instead of the actual root *k-w-s*].

[5] BDJ: *haymanotəki qəddus* [masc.] (your holy [masc.] faith); CR: *haymanotəki qəddəst* [fem.] (your holy [fem.] faith). The BDJ text rhymes, and is in gender agreement, with preceding *haymanotä afrənǧ rəkus* (the filthy faith of the Europeans), where the adjective also appears in the masculine. Rhymes are common in the text; we note them only rarely.

[6] BDJ: *täfäśśəḥi* (rejoice); CR: *wä-täfäśśəḥi* (therefore rejoice).

[7] This is a celebratory sound made by women in particular, a kind of trilling of the voice at a high pitch and without words. It is common in Ethiopia, North Africa, India, and the Middle East.

[8] BDJ: *wä-konä ʿabiy fəśśəḥa* [nom.] (there was great joy); CR: *wä-konä ʿabiyä fəśśəḥa* [with an optional acc. after *konä* (to be); identical translation].

[9] Exodus 15:2, as it appears in the first biblical canticle (First Song of Moses) in the Gəʿəz Psalter. See also Psalm 68[69]:30–31. It also appears in Deuteronomy 3:52, which is not in the Protestant or Catholic Bibles, which have only twenty-nine verses in chapter 3.

[10] Lit., *məslä särawitu* (together with his troops). Perhaps the king was on campaign, and

As the Gospel says, “If a woman has ten coins and one gets lost,[1] will she not light a lamp,[2] rummage through everything in her house, and diligently search until she finds it? And as soon as she has found it, she will call her friends and neighbors and say to these women, 'Rejoice for me because I have found my coin that had gotten lost!' I say to you: In the same way, there will be joy before God's angels[3] because of a single sinner who repents.”[4] So behold the fruit of humility, which springs forth from our Lord and was given to us, as he himself said, “Learn from me because I am gentle, and my heart humble. Then you will find rest for your soul.”[5]

Many theologians, who interpret the books of the Old and of the New Testament, toiled[6] and exhausted themselves for many years but were unable to convert Walatta Giyorgis. By contrast, our holy mother Walatta Petro humbled herself and thereby became a broom for the filth of apostasy, converting Walatta Giyorgis back in a blink.[7] She [re]introduced Walatta Giyorgis to the true faith, just as our Lord,
humbling himself and taking on the appearance of a servant, had returned man[8] to **91**
his [spiritual] inheritance of old.

Chapter 72: Envious Monks Attack Our Mother's Authority

After that, our holy mother Walatta Petros returned to Afer Faras [from Sadachilla] and lived together with her entire community in one and the same place.

Some resentful theologians arose, however,[9] giving vent to their resentment against our holy mother Walatta Petros with satanic zeal[10] when they saw that all

---

not in Gondär, and thus celebrated only with his army, but we chose to regard *särawit* as a synecdoche, with the army rhetorically standing in for the entire court.

[1] Lit., *tägädfäta* (gets lost to her). The same construction is found in the next sentence.

[2] BDJ: *akko-nu täḫattu* [*sic*: substandard orthography for *taḫattu*] *maḫtotä* (will she not light a lamp); CR: *akko-nu täḫattu maḫtot* (will not a lamp be lit). BDJ is in agreement with the Greek original of the biblical verse.

[3] BDJ: *bä-qədmä mäla*ʾ*əktä əgzi*ʾ*abḥer* (before God's angels); CR: *bä-qədmä əgzi*ʾ*abḥer* (before God). MS B originally had the CR variant too, but then was changed and made to agree with the longer DJ variant.

[4] Luke 15:8–10.

[5] Matthew 11:29.

[6] BDJ: *ṣamäwu* ([they] toiled); CR: *ṣämäwu* [substandard orthography, but identical meaning].

[7] Rhyme marks elevated speech and this sentence could be an aphorism in WP's community because, in Gəʿəz, “the filth of apostasy” and “in a blink” rhyme.

[8] Lit., *Addam* (Adam), standing in for all humanity.

[9] BDJ: *wä-bo əllä tänśə*ʾ*u əmənnä mämhəran mängʷärgʷəran* (lit., but there were those who arose from among the resentful teachers); CR: *wä-bo*ʾ*u əllä tänśə*ʾ*u əmənnä mämhəran mängʷäragʷəran* [*sic*] (but then came forth those who had risen up from among the resentful teachers).

[10] BDJ: *bä-qən*ʾ*at säyṭanawi* (with satanic zeal); Abb. 88: *wä-qən*ʾ*atä säyṭan* (and Satan's

the world followed her, that she was greater[1] than and superior to them, and that they ranked below her.[2]

Therefore, they said to her, "Is there a verse in the scriptures that [states that] a woman, even though she is a woman, can be a religious leader and teacher?[3] This is something that scripture forbids to a woman when it says to her,[4] 'Regarding a woman, we do not allow her to teach. She may not exercise authority over a man.' "[5] With this argument, they wanted to make Walatta Petros quit—but they did not succeed.[6]

At that point, *Abba* Fatla Sillasé, the teacher of the entire world, said to them, "Did God not raise her up for our chastisement because we have become corrupt,[7] so that God appointed her and gave our leadership role to her, while dismissing us? For this reason, you will not be able to make her quit. It is just as Gamaliel[8] said in Acts, 'Leave these men alone and do not harm them.[9] If[10] what they put forward is

---

zeal), which does not fit in syntactically and which CR therefore altered to *wä-qän'u qən'atä säyṭan* (being envious [of her] with devilish envy).

[1] D: *kämä ʿabyät* (that she was greater); BJ, CR: *ʿabäyät* [a substandard vocalization variant, but identical in meaning]. Yet because *ዐ ʿa* and *አ ʾa* could be exchanged almost freely in postmedieval Gəʿəz orthography since the historically different sounds they once had represented had been merged, substandard *ʿabäyät* opened up the possibility of being interpreted as an orthographical variant of the different verb *ʾabäyät* (she refused/disobeyed/was recalcitrant). This, in fact, was the meaning Ricci translated.

[2] Part of the reason the male religious leaders were so angry is that WP was not an older woman. While older women often became nuns, and such matriarchs might be seen as types of leaders, it would have been extremely rare for a woman to lead in her thirties and forties as WP did.

[3] BDJ: *liqtä wä-mämhərtä* [twice fem.] (a religious leader and teacher); CR: *liqä wä-mämhərä* [twice masc., but otherwise identical in meaning].

[4] BDJ: *zä-käl'a* [written as ከልአ] *mäṣḥaf wä-yəbela* (lit., which scripture forbids to her. It says to her); Abb. 88: *zä-käl'a* [written as ከለአ, with substandard orthography] *mäṣḥaf wä-yəbela* (which scripture forbids. It says to her). CR took the substandard ከለአ not to be a variant of ከልአ, but as a genuine form not containing the object suffix *to her*. On this basis, he then altered Abb. 88 to drop the object suffix in the verb *to say*, arriving at *zä-käl'a* [ከለአ] *mäṣḥaf wä-yəbe* (which scripture forbids. It says).

[5] 1 Timothy 2:12. The Greek original is in the first-person singular.

[6] BDJ: *fäqädu yaḫdəgəwwa wä-baḥtu i-kəhlu aḫdəgota* (lit., they wanted to make her quit. However, they could not make her quit); CR: *fäqädu yäḫaddəgəwwa* [*sic*: ind.] *wä-baḥtu i-kəhlu ḫədgäta* (they wanted to leave her. However, they could not leave her).

[7] Lit., *mädälləwan* (tippers of the scale), that is, those who are corrupt because they use their positions to misuse the scales of justice in favor of the powerful at the expense of the weak.

[8] *Gämaləyal* was a respected Jewish teacher of Saint Paul. Here, he is a scholar who spoke up against killing the apostles.

[9] BDJ: *wä-i-təsḥaṭəwwomu* (and do not harm them); CR: *wä-i-təssäḥaṭəwwomu* [*sic*] (and do not be harmed [by] them).

[10] BDJ, Abb. 88: *lä-əmmä-hu*, a rare extension of the basic conditional conjunction *lä-əmmä* (if); CR mistook *lä-əmmä-hu* for a corruption and reduced it to *lä-əmmä*.

of man, it will pass and come to naught. But if instead it is from[1] God, you will not be able to make them quit.[2] Do not be like people who quarrel with God.' "[3]

In the same way also, the resentful theologians were unable[4] to make our holy mother Walatta Petros quit because God had authorized her. If her teaching had not been from God, her community would not have held up until now, but would quickly have disappeared. Through its continued existence,[5] it is evident that her community is from God.

Chapter 73: Our Mother Provides the Miracle of Flour

Afterward, our blessed mother Walatta Petros lived with this community of hers in love and in peace. Even when they were afflicted and hungry, they did not think about nourishment for the body and did not say, "What shall we eat and what shall we drink?" but rather thought about spiritual nourishment, namely, fasting, prayer, love, humility, and other such things. 92

One day,[6] a Friday, the food came to an end; there was none left at all. Even when they sought to borrow some,[7] none could be found. When, as a result, Eheta Kristos—for she[8] was full of mercy and compassion for everyone—had lost all hope, she went to our holy mother Walatta Petros, stood before her full of sorrow, and said to her, "What will I do[9] on the Sabbaths [of Saturday and Sunday]?[10] Our sick will be dying of hunger, and I have absolutely no grain whatsoever in the storehouse.[11] I have tried to borrow some by touring the region, but I was unsuccessful. Even if

[1] BDJ: *wä-lä-əmmä əm-ḫabä* (lit., but if from); CR: *wä-lä-əm-ḫabä* [*sic*: contextually nonsensical].

[2] Lit., *i-təkəlu aḫdəgotomu* (you will not be able to make them quit).

[3] Acts 5:38–39.

[4] B, CR: *i-kəhlu* ([they] were unable); D: *i-yəkəlu* ([they] will be unable); J: *i-təkəlu* [*sic*] (you [2nd-ps. pl.] will be unable).

[5] Lit., *bä-zəntu* (through this).

[6] BDJ: *wä-bä-aḥatti ʿəlät əmənnä ʿəlätat* (lit., on one day from among the days); Abb. 88 with nonsensical: *ʿəlätat* (days) only, which CR sensibly altered to *wä-bä-1 əm-ʿəlätat* (on one from among the days).

[7] BDJ: *ləqqaha* (lit., a loan); Abb. 88 with nonexistent *ləqḥa*, which CR correctly altered to *ləqqaḥa*.

[8] BDJ: *əsmä yəʾəti* (for she); CR: *əntä* (who).

[9] BDJ: *əfo əgäbbər* (lit., how will I do); CR: *əfo əgbär* (how shall I do).

[10] Lit., *bä-əllon sänbätat* (on these Sabbaths), that is, the two Sabbaths of the Täwaḥədo Church, which traditionally has revered the original Jewish Saturday Sabbath as well as the historically Christian Sunday Sabbath. Ricci here unspecifically translates as *in quei giorni festivi* (on these holidays).

[11] BDJ: *wəstä bet* (lit., in the house); CR: *wəstä betəyä* (in my house). This anecdote demonstrates that Ǝḫətä Krəstos was the day-to-day manager of the community, with WP serving more as a spiritual leader.

some grain arrives tomorrow, can it be ground on the Sabbaths, or will our sick have to die of hunger?"[1]

Our holy mother Walatta Petros replied, "O you of little faith! Are you not thinking these thoughts due to your hungry stomach?[2] Tomorrow, though, you will witness God's power." Now Eheta Kristos felt comforted and was full of faith.[3]

Therefore, Eheta Kristos then went to the kitchen building and ordered the women to prepare for the various cooking tasks.[4] They were bewildered and said among themselves, "Where did she get the grain so that she can order us to get ready?"

Also, Eheta Kristos sent the same orders to the monks.[5] On the next day, then, men arrived from afar, bringing with them flour of various cereals, on nine donkeys.[6] They handed the flour over to our holy mother Walatta Petros.

So she called Eheta Kristos and said to her, "Take this which God has given us. Rejoice today, since you were worried yesterday!"

Now Eheta Kristos praised God, took the flour, and gave it to the women who cooked. Likewise, she gave flour to the monks. Thus, they all had food to eat on the Sabbaths.

On another day, food was once again lacking in the same way.[7] So Eheta Kristos, who lent her services in the kitchen, asked Walatta Petros,[8] "What shall we eat for dinner[9] tonight? Look, the grain[10] has come to an end!"

Walatta Petros asked, "We have no flour at all?"

[1] One could do basic cooking on the Sabbath, but not plow, wash clothes, gather wood, or grind grain. Whatever food came would have to be ready to cook. For instance, it could not be grain but would have to be flour.

[2] Lit., *bä-kämä ṣəbbätä kärśəki* (lit., according to the tightness of your stomach). Ricci here incorrectly translates as *secondo l'angustia del suo sentire* (according to the narrowness of her [your] thinking).

[3] D: *wä-sobeha tänazäzät wä-mälʾat haymanotä* (lit., now she felt comforted and was full of faith); BJ: *wä-sobeha nazäzät wä-mälʾat haymanotä* (now she comforted [her] and filled [her] with faith); CR: *wä-sobeha nazäzäta wä-mälʾat lati haymanotä wəstä ləbba* (now she comforted her and, for her benefit, filled her heart with faith).

[4] BJ: *kämä yastädalləwa tägbaratä bä-bä-ṣotahon* (lit., that they prepare the works in their various kinds); D: *kämä yastädalləwa tägbarä* [*sic*] *bä-bä-ṣotahon* (that they prepare the work [*sic*] in their various kinds); CR: *kämä yastädalləwa tägbaratä bä-bäynatihon* (that they prepare the works among themselves).

[5] The men cooked for the men, but Ǝḫətä Krəstos was still their manager.

[6] BJ: *ənzä yəṣəʿənu ḥariṣä əkl zä-zä-ziʾahu bä-9 aʾdug* (lit., having loaded grain flour of various kinds, on nine donkeys); D: *ənzä yəṣəʿənu ḥariṣä əkl bä-zä-zä-ziʾahu bä-9 aʾdug* (having loaded grain flour, in its various kinds, on nine donkeys); CR: *ənzä yəṣəʿənu ḥariṣä əkl zä-ziʾahu 9 aʾdug* (having loaded grain flour, which amounted to [the loads of] nine donkeys).

[7] BDJ: *kämahu* (in the same way); CR omits.

[8] BDJ, Abb. 88: *wä-təbela lä-Ǝḫətä Krəstos* (lit., so she [namely, WP] . . . said to Ǝḫətä Krəstos), with a reversal of speaker and addressee, which does not make sense in the context. Our translation therefore follows Conti Rossini's alteration of Abb. 88 to *wä-təbela Ǝḫətä Krəstos* (so Ǝḫətä Krəstos said to her [viz., to WP]).

[9] BDJ: *məntä-nu nəddärrär* (what shall we eat for dinner); CR: *məntä-nu nədderrär* (what will we eat for dinner).

[10] CR adds *bä-betä tägbar* (in the kitchen).

Eheta Kristos replied, "There is just one *éf* measure of flour."[1]

So Walatta Petros ordered Eheta Kristos to put that flour into the leather bag to make it ferment.[2]

But Eheta Kristos replied, "I won't put it into the [large] leather bag but rather into a small clay jar."[3]

Yet Walatta Petros said to her,[4] "Don't be distressed; put it into the usual leather bag."

Eheta Kristos obeyed, put the flour into the leather bag, and let it ferment. When
the time came for baking, she thought that with so little flour she would only be
able to bake [enough] for the few community members who were sick. Yet when 93
she opened the leather bag she found it full. So Eheta Kristos went ahead and baked
the dough, and it turned out as much as always. It sufficed for the daily meal for the
entire community.

Chapter 74: King Fasiladas Enables Our Mother to Complete the Church on Réma Island

When, then, the reconstruction of the church on Réma Island was finished, our holy mother Walatta Petros sent the good news to King Fasiladas. In turn, he sent her fat cows, honey, clothing, curtains,[5] and carpets.[6] After that, following church law, she introduced the consecrated tabot.[7] In so doing, she made the people of Réma Monastery happy, as well as the others who had come[8] from all the [neighboring] churches. This took place on the fifth of the month of Hamlé.[9]

[1] BDJ: *wä-yəʾəti-ni təbela hallo mäṭänä if ḥariṣ* (lit., she said to her: there is the quantity of an *éf* of flour); CR omits.

[2] The dough for *ənǧära* bread is made by mixing flour with water and setting it aside for two days to ferment, like sourdough.

[3] BDJ: *wəstä nəstit ləḥəkʷt* (into a small clay jar); CR: *wəstä nəstitä ləḥkʷ* [*sic*; *ləḥkʷ* is a nonexistent lexeme, and *nəstitä* cannot function as an adjective]. That is, Əḫətä Krəstos wanted to put the flour in a small vessel because there was only a little flour, but WP told her to put it in the large vessel they usually used in making food for so many, knowing that it would expand.

[4] BDJ, Abb. 88: *wä-təbela Əḫətä Krəstos* (lit., Əḫətä Krəstos said to her [viz., to WP]), which does not make sense in the context. Our translation therefore follows Conti Rossini's change of Abb. 88 to *wä-təbela lä-Əḫətä Krəstos* (lit., she [viz., to WP] said to Əḫətä Krəstos).

[5] BDJ: *mänṭäwaləʿatä* (curtains); CR: *mänṭäwaləʿa* [variant, with identical meaning]. Curtains are used within Täwaḥədo churches to separate out sacred spaces, especially the sanctuary and altar.

[6] This is an example of emperors as patrons of and donors to churches. King Fasilädäs actively supported Orthodox reconstruction (physically and metaphorically) after the contrasting policies of his father Susənyos.

[7] BDJ: *agbəʾat tabotä* (lit., she introduced the tabot); CR: *agbəʾat tabota* (she introduced its tabot).

[8] BDJ: *wä-lä-kaləʾan-hi säbʾ əllä mäṣʾu* (as well as the others who had come); CR: *wä-lä-kaləʾan-hi əllä mäṣʾu säbʾ* [identical meaning, but with Amharicizing syntax].

[9] BDJ: *amä 5 lä-wärḫa ḥamle* (on the fifth of the month of Ḥamle); CR: *amä 5 lä-ḥamle* (on the fifth of Hamlé).

Afterward, Walatta Petros dispatched people to the province of Tigré so that they would transport her brother Yohannes's remains and bring them to her.[1] They did as she had ordered and brought the body to her. She received it and wept over it,[2] then took it to the church on Réma Island and placed it in a coffin. Now our holy mother Walatta Petros said, "Last night my brother Yohannes came to me [in a dream] and said to me, 'Do not keep weeping over me and bothering me! Come and see my dwelling place in heaven: my lot is with the martyrs!'[3] Then he took me and showed me around. Thus, my heart was comforted, and I was happy."

Chapter 75: Our Mother Sees an Angel in Zhan Feqera

In those days, our holy and blessed mother Walatta Petros, together with a few from her community, set out for [the town of] Zhan Feqera[4] and [the house of] *Woyzaro* Walatta Kristos[5] to inspect an unsettled area[6] well suited for living.[7] Eheta Kristos remained behind at Afer Faras. After reaching Zhan Feqera,[8] Walatta Petros went to *Woyzaro* Walatta Kristos's house and stayed with her. She there observed the Fast of Lent.[9]

During that period, Maqdasa Maryam[10] fell ill. So our holy mother Walatta Petros went to visit her in the house in which she lay bedridden. While she was with Maq-

[1] Yoḥannəs had died on 1 Mäskäräm (in the second week of September, in a year in the mid-to-late 1630s) and she sent for his body about ten months later, after 5 Ḥamle (in the second week of next year's July). People preferred that loved ones be buried close by. Further, saints' bodies were sometimes moved from one place to another after death because blessings emanated from his or her tomb.

[2] BDJ: *wä-bäkäyäto* (and wept over it); CR: *wä-bäkäyät* (and wept).

[3] Regarding martyrdom, it is unlikely that Yoḥannəs was killed by unbelievers; it is more likely that he died of an epidemic and thus is counted among the martyrs, as the *Gädlä Täklä Haymanot* promised.

[4] *Žan Fäqära* is a town about twenty miles directly north of Gondär and thus more than a hundred miles from Qʷäraṣa and Rema. Since most of the places in which WP considered starting communities were in southeastern Lake Ṭana, this site is unusual. Perhaps she was thinking about moving closer to the court, as events that happen while she is at Žan Fäqära involve several court members.

[5] *Wälättä Krəstos* (Daughter of Christ) is, here, a noblewoman living near the court, not the nun who assists WP earlier in the text.

[6] Lit., *gädäm*, here used with its basic meaning of "wilderness" not "monastic settlement."

[7] Although these members of her community did live in Žan Fäqära for a time, it did not become WP's seventh community, after Afär Färäs.

[8] BDJ: *ḥabä wəʾətu hagär* (lit., that town); CR: *ḥabä wəʾətu mäkan* (that place).

[9] Lit., *ṣomä 40 mäwaʿəl* (the Fast of Forty Days). The Täwaḥədo Church season of Lent is fifty-five days long, but it is divided into parts, and the main part of it, *Ṣomä Arbəʿa* (the Fast of Forty), is the forty days leading up to Palm Sunday. Thus, this is about six months after she buried her brother.

[10] *Mäqdäsä Maryam* ([Saint] Mary's Sanctuary).

dasa Maryam, the third hour came [i.e., 9:00 AM]. Thus, our blessed mother Walatta Petros covered her face with a cloth and began the prayer of the third hour.[1] As for Maqdasa Maryam, she turned her face toward the west.[2]

At that moment, Layika Masqal[3] all of a sudden entered the house—without
[first] having made his voice heard—because he was in service that month.[4] Immediately, the Angel of God who was with our holy and blessed mother Walatta Pet- 94
ros drew his sword to strike him down because he had entered suddenly and dis-
turbed her.[5]

When the sick Maqdasa Maryam noticed [what was happening], she was upset and turned toward Layika Masqal to rebuke him, "How dare you barge in at such an inappropriate time? Had it not been for Walatta Petros, who saved you, a great tragedy would have happened to you. You only narrowly escaped death!"

Now our holy mother Walatta Petros removed the cloth with which she had covered her face and asked Maqdasa Maryam, "What[6] are you saying? What[7] has upset you?"

Maqdasa Maryam dissimulated, however, and responded, "But I didn't say anything."

Our holy mother Walatta Petros retorted, however, "Tell me the truth and don't hide anything from me!"

[1] She covered her face in the presence of God out of reverence, like the seraphim in Isaiah 6:2. Monastic prayers are held seven times a day, at 6:00 AM (*nägh*), 9:00 AM (*śäläst*), noon (*qätr*), 3:00 PM (*təsʿat*), 6:00 PM (*särk*), 9:00 PM (*säʿatä nəwam*), and midnight (*mänfäqä lelit*). The third hour of the evening, or 9:00 PM, is when Christ himself prayed. Monks pray for the Täwaḥədo Church, the country, the dead, and all human beings.

[2] B: *mängälä ʿaräb* (toward the west); DJ: *mängälä aräft* (toward the wall); CR: *mängälä ʿarat* (toward the bed). Among the manuscripts' radically different variants, "toward the west" seems to make the most sense contextually. If Mäqdäsä Maryam had turned toward the "wall" or the "bed," perhaps to give WP privacy while she prayed, it would have been difficult for her to see anyone enter. The suggestion may have been that WP and Mäqdäsä Maryam were facing each other, since people turn to the east to pray, and thus WP was looking east while Mäqdäsä Maryam was looking West. Nuns' huts were often very small, only large enough for a few people to fit.

[3] *Laʾəkä Mäsqäl* (Servant of the cross).

[4] He was in service, meaning that he was probably a deacon (usually a teenager). Deacons have chores that rotate by the month; one month one might carry the host, the next month take care of the ill, and so on. Even so, it is not proper for someone to go straight into a house. Rather, one must do the equivalent of knocking (calling out and announcing one's presence outside a house and then waiting to be called in). This is especially true of a monastic cell, into which many never went, although they might converse with the person inside through the door.

[5] Although WP later asks Mäqdäsä Maryam what happened, as if she was too deep in prayer to have noticed what was happening, she is, as usual, pretending not to know something in order to learn how a person replies.

[6] BDJ: *məntä* [acc.] (what); Abb. 88: *mənt* [nom.] (what), which CR correctly altered to *məntä*.

[7] CR: *mənt* [nom.] (what); BDJ: *məntä* [acc.] (what). The CR variant here is superior.

So Maqdasa Maryam told her, "I saw the angel drawing his sword and getting ready to strike Layika Masqal. But the angel then spared him on account of you."[1]

This story became known throughout Walatta Petros's entire community. The sick woman Maqdasa Maryam [ultimately] died of that illness and was buried at Zhan Feqera.

Chapter 76: Our Mother and the Miracle of Butter and Cheese

In the same month, [*Woyzaro*] Walatta Kristos[2] of Furé[3] also fell ill. So she said to our holy mother Walatta Petros, "Bring me sour curd cheese[4] because my illness has made me crave it." At that time, it was Passion Week.[5]

Therefore, Walatta Petros now dispatched messengers to the ladies and lords of the court [at Gondar] so that they would send her the cheese. Everybody [there] searched for it, but they found none, so the messengers returned and told Walatta Petros this. Also, *Woyzaro* Walatta Kristos herself[6] had searched for curd cheese but found none. Now our holy mother Walatta Petros was distressed because she had not been able to find what the sick Walatta Kristos craved.

[1] We do not see WP do anything specific to save La'əkä Mäsqäl, and if WP had not been there, the angel would not have been there either to endanger the servant.

[2] *Wälättä Krəstos* (Daughter of Christ). This likely is a different Wälättä Krəstos than the woman much earlier in the text who flees when WP was banished to Žäbäy. However, it is probably the same woman as the friend *Wäyzäro* Wälättä Krəstos with whom WP was currently staying in Žan Fäqära, although that honorific doesn't appear here but rather her place of origin. However, the text often omits honorifics in later instances. Furthermore, this sick Wälättä Krəstos unabashedly orders WP around, just as a *wäyzäro* might do; WP dispatches messengers to the court to indulge her whimsical dietary wishes, as one would do for an aristocrat; everyone at court responds to the call, as if they knew the woman; and a *Wäyzäro* Wälättä Krəstos appears just six lines later, looking for cheese "herself." Finally, the ill were not required to fast, but the ascetic members of WP's community would most likely have kept to the fast of Lent, reinforcing the idea that this is a *wäyzäro* not a nun.

[3] BDJ: *zä-Fure* (of Furé); Abb. 88: *zä-Fare* (of Faré). CR accepted this as a legitimate variant of *Fure*, and Ricci accordingly has *Fārīē* in his translation. However, since the fidäl symbols ፉ *fu* and ፋ *fa* are extremely similar, *Fare* is easily recognizable as a scribal error or imprecision.

[4] BDJ: *gəbnätä mäṣiṣä* (lit., sour cheese), CR: *gəbnätä mäṣaṣa* (cheese of vinegar). This milk product is probably something like curd cheese, farmer's cheese, paneer, or Queso blanco, which are all made by combining milk with vinegar, and is common in Ethiopia (called *ayb* in Amharic).

[5] During the week before Easter, the last week of Lent, after more than a month of fasting from animal products, any cheese would have been difficult to find. Easter would generally have fallen in April.

[6] BDJ: *wä-nägärəwwa. Wä-wäyzäro Wälättä Krəstos-ni* (lit., and told her [viz., WP]. Also *Wäyzäro* Wälättä Krəstos herself); CR: *wä-nägärəwwa lä-wäyzäro Wälättä Krəstos-ni* (and told this to *Wäyzäro* Wälättä Krəstos herself).

Meanwhile, there was butter, not yet cooked or purified, in a big pot[1] that had been sent by *Woyzaro* Kristosaweet.[2] On the evening before Easter,[3] a sister dipped out a jar of that butter and purified it.[4] With her was another sister who watched. The first sister then again dipped [butter] from the big pot[5] and purified it. Then, upon the third [hour],[6] that purified butter was found to have turned into curd cheese!

The first sister took some of it, looked at it, smelled it, and found its smell most pleasant, much better than the smell of [ordinary] curd cheese. So she said to her companion, “Listen, this butter has turned into curd cheese!”

The other sister replied to her, however, “Why are you lying and saying things that aren't so?”

The first sister retorted, “But I'm not lying, I'm telling the truth! If you don't 95
believe me, take [some of it] yourself, look at it with your own eyes, and smell it with your own nose!”

Now her companion took a little of it, looked at it, smelled it, and it was just as the first sister had said. The two of them marveled at this, but left the curd cheese alone until morning.[7] When the [Easter] fast was then broken and the time of the Eucharist had come, those two sisters prepared the food [customarily] required[8] for that day and served our holy mother Walatta Petros some of that curd cheese.[9]

When our holy mother Walatta Petros saw it, she said to the first sister, “Where did this curd cheese arrive from today, the cheese that for so many days we looked for but could not find?”

So that sister approached her and whispered in her ear, “The butter that was in the pot: half of it remained butter and half of it has become curd cheese!”

[1] BDJ: *bä-ʿabiy qäśut* (in a big pot); CR: *bä-wəʿuy qäśut* (in a hot pot).

[2] *Krəstosawit* (She of Christ). This might possibly be Susənyos's fifth daughter, also named Krəstosawit.

[3] BDJ: *wä-bä-ʿəlätä mäḫatəwä fasika* (lit., on Easter eve); CR: *wä-bä-ʿəlät bäṣḥa fasika* (then one day Easter came).

[4] Plain butter is made by shaking or churning milk. When the butter is removed, it leaves behind a by-product called whey that is used in making cheese. Thus, it is not possible to make cheese from butter. Ethiopians do not use plain butter in cooking, but rather render it, making a clarified butter (called *qəbe*), by first filtering it and then cooking it with spices over low heat.

[5] BD: *əmənnehu* (lit., from it); J, CR omit.

[6] BDJ: *wä-bä-śaləs* [masc.] (lit., then on the third); CR: *wä-bä-śaləst* [fem.] *ʿəlät* (then on the third day). Since purifying butter only takes minutes, not days, we assume that “on the third” here means “at the third hour,” that is, at 9:00 PM on the night before Easter.

[7] D, CR: *əskä yəṣäbbəḥ gize* (lit., until the time was morning); BJ: *əskä yəbäṣṣəḥ gize* (until the [appropriate] time had come).

[8] BDJ: *zä-yətfäqqäd* (lit., which is required); CR: *zä-yəfäqqəd* (that requires).

[9] The Easter meal is lavish with the animal products that people have avoided for the past two months, including curd cheese, which is eaten with several meat dishes. Yogurt is also traditional on Easter because people have fasted for a long time and the stomach is not prepared for uncultured milk products.

Now our holy mother Walatta Petros raised her eyes to the sky, marveling and awestruck. She remained like this for a long time, praising God. Then she [went and] said to the sick Walatta Kristos, "Get up and eat: what you craved has been found for you!"

Walatta Kristos said to her, "Where did you find it?"[1]

Our holy mother Walatta Petros replied, "God brought it to me because he saw my sadness and distress."

So Walatta Kristos got up and ate [that curd cheese]. Our holy mother Walatta Petros also ate some of it and marveled at its fine taste and delicious smell.

At that time, elder monks[2] from her community were there in that town [of Zhan Feqera], as well as other monks who served under them.[3] Walatta Petros [by way of that first sister] sent the elder monks three bowls of that curd cheese, separately, and the same quantity also to the younger ones,[4] separately, in their respective dining halls. Then that sister wanted to set out a second time to bring the monks some of the curd cheese but found that the rest had turned back into butter, reverting to its earlier condition.

When the sister saw this, she marveled and was awestruck. She then reported this miracle to our holy mother Walatta Petros, that the curd cheese had become butter [again] and reverted to its original state. When our blessed mother Walatta Petros heard about this miracle, she marveled at God's glorious deeds.[5]

She then ordered that sister to go to the monks' dining hall[6] and bring back the
96 curd cheese that she had sent to the young monks[7] so that it would be available for the sick Walatta Kristos the next day and the day after. The sister set out immediately, hurrying at a run. She arrived at the monks' dining hall and [impolitely] opened their door with her own hand. She entered and found the bowls covered. She removed the bowls' covers, looked, and found them full, just as she had delivered them. She took two [of three] bowls and left and hurried back as she had come. She had not said anything, neither upon entering nor upon leaving.[8]

When the [younger] monks later noticed [the missing bowls], they were bewildered and said among themselves, "What is the secret behind this?" They did not know about the miraculous events that had taken place, neither about the earlier

[1] BDJ: *ǝm-ayte räkäbki* (lit., from where did you find); CR: *ǝm-ayte räkäbki zä-fätäwku* (from where did you find what I desired).

[2] BDJ: *aʾrug mänäkosat* (elder monks); CR:*aʾrug wä-mänäkosat* (elders and monks).

[3] BDJ: *ǝllä ǝm-taḥtehomu* (lit., who were under them [masc.]); CR: *ǝllä ǝm-taḥtehon* [*sic*] (who were under them [fem.]).

[4] Lit., *lä-ḥǝṣanat-hi* (also to the children *or* adolescents).

[5] Lit., *ʿǝbäyat* (greatnesses).

[6] Lit., *betä mänäkosat* (the monks' house), here and below.

[7] BDJ: *lä-ḥǝṣanat mänäkosat* (to the young monks); CR: *lä-ḥǝṣanat wä-lä-mänäkosat* (to the young monks [lit., young ones] and to the [older] monks).

[8] BDJ: *bä-bäʾata-hi wä-bä-ṣ́äʾata-hi* (lit., neither upon her entering nor upon her leaving); CR: *bä-bäʾata-hi wä-bä-ṣ́äʾata* (neither upon her entering and upon her leaving). Her silence would seem to suggest that the elder monks were at home and she wished to escape their notice.

one nor about the later one. Those elder [monks] ate the [three bowls of] curd cheese that the sister had left them and marveled at its fine taste and delicious smell. For the younger ones, Walatta Petros substituted another dish and sent it to them.

Later, this miracle[1] was [widely] related[2] and became common knowledge in Walatta Petros's entire community. Those who ate from that curd cheese are still alive today. They are witnesses, and their testimony is true and no lie.[3]

How plentiful and abundant are the stories about the miracles of our holy mother Walatta Petros! Behold, they cover the skies and fill the earth: nobody can conceal them. Can smoke be concealed if they lock it into a house trying to hide it? Does it not waft out to be seen everywhere? Can [even] a small amount of olive oil be hidden if it is poured into the bottom of a jar? Even if lots of water is poured on top of it, in an attempt to conceal it, does the olive oil not rise to the top and gleam on the water?[4] Likewise, we are unable to conceal the story of our holy mother Walatta Petros. Truly, it has spread over the length and breadth of all the lands!

Chapter 77: Why Our Mother Loved to Move Every Year

When King Fasiladas then heard that our holy mother Walatta Petros had gone [to Zhan Feqera], and that[5] *Woyzaro* Walatta Kristos had taken her in, he was profoundly indignant and distraught. He said [to himself], "Is Walatta Kristos better than me that she makes Walatta Petros forsake my company [for hers]?"[6]

However, our holy mother Walatta Petros[7] had not gone looking for a [different] place on a whim but because her community [in Afer Faras] had compelled her, saying to her, "Let us travel to another place where we can till the land and produce
food for our sustenance," since sustaining themselves at Afer Faras was difficult.[8] 97
Walatta Petros herself did not want to stay in a single place [either] but liked to move each year from one place to another,[9] like Abraham, Isaac, and Jacob who had

[1] BDJ: *tä'amər* (miracle); CR: *nägär* (story).

[2] Lit., *täsämʿa* (was heard).

[3] BDJ, Abb. 88: *wä-i-konä ḥassät* [nom.] (lit., and is no lie); CR altered to *wä-i-konä ḥassätä* [acc.] [grammatical variant, but no translation difference].

[4] BDJ: *mälʿəltä may* (on the water); CR: *mälʿəltä sämay* (on the sky). Ricci pointed to the likelihood of such a copyist's error, but nonetheless translated *nell'aria* (in the air).

[5] BDJ: *wä-kämä* (and that); CR: *wä-bä-kämä* (and how).

[6] While there has been no mention of WP going to court or to Gondär to visit King Fasilädäs, Gondär lay directly between Lake Ṭana and Žan Fäqära, so WP would have passed through it on her way north.

[7] BDJ: *Wälättä Peṭros*; CR omits.

[8] Although Saint Mary had enjoined WP to stay at Afär Färäs, *kəfləki* (your [divinely assigned] lot), it seems that food shortages were a legitimate reason to leave.

[9] D, CR: *əm-mäkan ḫabä kalə' mäkan* (lit., from [one] place to another place); BJ: *əm-mäkan ḫabä mäkan* (from place to place).

lived in tents.[1] Our holy mother Walatta Petros did likewise and lived moving from one place to the next.[2]

When people would inquire of her—"What is it with you, that you don't like to live[3] in one place? All the saints like to fix a place [for themselves]! The Desert Fathers said,[4] 'He who [constantly] moves from one place to the next is no [real] monk. He will not produce the fruit of good works; he resembles a tree [constantly] transplanted from one place to another[5] so that it does not grow or produce fruit'"[6]—our holy mother Walatta Petros would say to them in response, "I, too, am well aware that staying in one place is better than moving around. However, I do it for a particular reason. If I settled my sons and daughters in one place, they would [there] build a church, as well as houses for themselves. Then they would find rest from toil and labor, but through rest, the flesh flourishes, and from the flourishing of the flesh springs natural desire, and then Satan will assail them. If, however, I have them move [constantly] from place to place, and if they toil, and their bodies become tired and weak[7] through hard labor and thinking of work, they will never give any thought to sin. When evening falls they will say, 'When will it be morning?'[8] and when morning comes they will wish that the day was twice as long[9] so that they can finish their work [in greater leisure]. So, that's why I do not like to remain in one place."

[1] See Genesis, chapters 12–37. WP was also familiar with itinerant living because she was a noblewoman and presumably grew up in the tents of the itinerant royal court, or *kätäma*.

[2] BDJ: *əm-mäkan ḫabä mäkan* (lit., from place to place); CR: *əm-mäkan ḫabä kalə*ʾ (from [one] place to another).

[3] BDJ: *zä-i-tafäqqəri näbirä* (lit., that you don't like living); CR: *ḫabä* [*sic*] *i-tafäqqəri tənbäri* (where you don't like to live).

[4] Lit., *yəbelu* (lit. they said).

[5] BDJ: *əm-mäkan ḫabä mäkan* (lit., from place to place); CR: *əm-mäkan ḫabä kalə*ʾ *mäkan* (from [one] place to another place).

[6] The quote is from the *Sayings of the Desert Fathers*, "In the same way that a frequently transplanted tree is incapable of bearing fruit, so neither will a monk who moves from place to place bear fruit" (Anonymous 2012). In Western monasticism, Saint Benedict developed his maxim about *stabilitas loci* from this injunction. It seems to exist precisely because of monks' tendency to be itinerant, perhaps due to the rigors of communal and ascetic life.

[7] BDJ: *wä-yədäkkəmu wä-yəmäṣällu śəgahomu* (and their bodies become tired and weak); CR: *wä-yədäkkəmu wä-yamäṣällu śegahomu* (and they become tired, and weaken their bodies).

[8] This question is probably best understood as indirectly articulating the wish that morning might not come too soon so that they can find sufficient rest during an adequately long night.

[9] BDJ: *kämä yətmäkäʿab lomu nuḫa mäʿalt* (lit., that the length of the day would double for them); CR: *kämä yətmäkʿab lomu nuḫa mäʿalt* (so that the length of the day would double for them).

Chapter 78: Our Mother Goes to the Royal Capital and Falls Ill

After that, our holy mother Walatta Petros left Zhan Feqera and returned to Gondar. She stayed there for a short time, and found favor with King Fasiladas. Each day he would pay her a visit, for he cherished her and revered her as a great lady.[1] When he went to see her, he would gird up his clothes like one of his soldiers.[2] The ladies and lords [of the court] also would be submissive to Walatta Petros with the utmost reverence.[3]

While living in Gondar in this way, our blessed mother Walatta Petros became so sick from a violent illness that she was close to death. Consequently, the king, as well as all the noblewomen, were greatly alarmed. However, when Walatta Petros was given water to drink from the washing of Jesus Christ's cross,[4] she recuperated and promptly became healthy, on that very day.

Chapter 79: Our Mother's Friendship with Walatta Maryam

Afterward,[5] Walatta Petros remained [in Gondar] for quite some time, such that the 98
community grumbled against her. They said to Walatta Maryam, "Was it not you who gave [her] this advice because you like to live at court?" With such talk, they aggrieved Walatta Maryam, and she thought about splitting away [from the community] and returning to her home.

Then, when God's will allowed it, Walatta Petros took her leave from the king. On that occasion, he gave her the district of Lag[6] [as a land grant] and bade her farewell with great honor.[7]

[1] Lit., *əgzəʾt* (lady). This is the title of Saint Mary as well: *əgzəʾtənä Maryam* (our Lady Mary).

[2] When a man visits a superior, whether an officer, bishop, or king, he wraps his upper clothing around his waist rather than his shoulders. Thus, the monarch lowers his status by coming to WP in the dress of a subordinate soldier reporting to his commanding superior. Her father did this as well.

[3] Lit., *ənzä yərəʿədu* (while trembling).

[4] BJ: *ḫəṣṣabä mäsqälu lä-Iyäsus Krəstos* (the washing of Jesus Christ's cross); D: *məḫṣabä mäsqälu lä-Iyäsus Krəstos* (the basin of Jesus Christ's cross); CR: *ḫaṣabä mäsqälu* [*sic*: nom.] *lä-Iyäsus Krəstos* (he washed Jesus Christ's cross). When the processional crosses used in the church ceremony were washed with water to clean them, that dusty water was used as holy water to heal the faithful.

[5] BJ: *wä-əmdəḫrehu-ni* (afterward); D: *wä-əmdəḫrehu* [variant form, identical translation]; CR: *wä-əmdəḫrä-ni* [variant form, identical translation].

[6] *Läg* is a region along the southwest shore of Lake Ṭana, where the Gəlgäl Abbay empties into Lake Ṭana, near Ačäfär and Zäge.

[7] Lit., *bä-ʿabiy mogäs* (with great favor).

Our holy mother Walatta Petros then departed from court [with Walatta Maryam] and reached Fintiro.[1] Having arrived there, Walatta Maryam took her leave from our holy mother Walatta Petros, saying to her, "As for me, I won't go [farther] with you, for the community has grumbled against me because I offended them.[2] How can we—they and I—be at peace with each other[3] in such a situation? Therefore, I prefer[4] to live in my home town."

Our holy mother Walatta Petros replied to her as follows,[5] "How can you leave me in this town [of Fintiro] and separate from me? Let's take our leave from each other after we have reached Qirinya.[6] I will go on [from there], while you can return home [then]."

Walatta Maryam said, "Very well," and went on[7] with Walatta Petros by tankwa.

Walatta Maryam then arrived at Qirinya and [there] spent the night together with Walatta Petros. Our holy mother Walatta Petros then once again asked her to keep going with her and accompany her[8] to Fogera.[9] She persuaded Walatta Maryam to do so,[10] and they arrived at Fogera together. There, the two took leave of each other in tears. Our holy mother Walatta Petros knew that Walatta Maryam would return[11] that very day, however.[12]

But for now, they kissed each other good-bye and separated, climbing into their respective tankwas. Our holy mother Walatta Petros there covered her face with a cloth[13] and continued her journey. Walatta Maryam turned toward her [own] journey as well. But our holy mother Walatta Petros then began[14] to pray to God that he would make Walatta Maryam return.

1 BDJ: *Fənṭəro*; CR: *Fänṭär*. Fənṭəro is a town about twenty-five miles due south of Gondär and two miles north of Lake Ṭana.

2 BDJ: *aḥzänkəwwomu* (lit., I gave them cause for distress); CR: *ḥazänkəwwomu* [ungrammatical, since it combines intransitive *ḥazänä* (to be distressed) with a direct object suffix].

3 Lit., *əfo nəṣäddəq anä-hi wä-əmantu-hi* (lit., how can we be righteous, I on the one hand and they on the other).

4 Lit., *yəḫeyyəsäni* (it is better for me). The Gəˁəz construction is parallel to, and likely modeled upon, Amharic impersonal *täšalä* (to be better) plus dative suffix, with the resulting meaning "to prefer."

5 BDJ: *wä-təbela* (lit., and said to her); CR omits.

6 *Qərəñña* is a town on the northeastern shore of Lake Ṭana, about twenty miles south of Fənṭəro and five miles due west of Ṭeza Amba Maryam.

7 BDJ: *wä-ḥorät* (and went on); CR: *ḥorät* (she went on).

8 BDJ: *kämä . . . tabṣəḥa* [subj.] (lit., to take her); CR: *kämä . . . tabäṣṣəḥa* [*sic*: ind.; no translation difference].

9 *Fogära* is a flat, marshy region to the east of Lake Ṭana (across from Ṣana Qirqos Island) and a town near the shore (about twenty-five miles south of Qərəñña and ten miles north of Afär Färäs).

10 Lit., *wä-abäläta oho* (she made her say yes).

11 BDJ: *kämä tətmäyyäṭ wä-təgäbbəʾ* (lit., that she would come back and return); CR: *kämä tətmäyyäṭ wä-tənbär* [*sic*: subj.] (that she would come back and stay).

12 BDJ: *wä-əmənnä-ssä qəddəst* (lit., but our holy mother); CR: *wä-əmənnä qəddəst* (our holy mother).

13 Covering the face is a sign of mourning.

14 BDJ: *wä-tämäyṭät mängälä fənota. Wä-yəʾəti-ni meṭät gäṣṣa mängälä fənota. Wä-aḫazät*

After Walatta Maryam had traveled a little [down the shore],[1] fear and terror, agitation and despair suddenly gripped her heart, and the lake became agitated as well. Now she said to the boatmen, "For my good, take me back!" Having received her orders, the boatmen turned around and poled back. As for our holy mother[2] Walatta Petros, she reached Damboza and spent the night there.[3]

Walatta Maryam passed by, for she did not know that Walatta Petros had arrived at Damboza; rather, Walatta Maryam went on and reached Afer Faras.[4] Our holy mother Walatta Petros arrived [at Afer Faras] the next day. When she saw Walatta Maryam, she laughed and was exceedingly happy.

Thereafter, Walatta Maryam lived together with our holy mother Walatta Petros **99**
and did not separate from her until she died.[5] All this happened due to the prayers of our holy mother Walatta Petros, for she did not want anybody to separate from her for forever.

Chapter 80: Praise for Our Mother's Humility

Once again, it behooves us to recall our holy mother Walatta Petros's humility. For she used to minister in the community when it was her turn, just like an ordinary sister.[6] [For instance,] she would pour water for the washing of hands.[7] At mealtime, she would have the sisters sit, but herself remain standing and serve them; she would not sit down before the prayer of thanksgiving[8] was finished. In addition, she would go into the kitchen, bake bread, and sweep up the ashes and rubbish,[9] which she would carry [in a basket] on her head to throw away outside.

əmmənä qəddəst Wälättä P̣eṭros (lit., and returned toward her path. Also she [namely, Wälättä Maryam] turned her face toward her path. But our holy mother WP then began); CR omits.

[1] BDJ: *wä-əmdəḫrä rəḥqät nəstitä Wälättä Maryam* (lit., after Walatta Maryam had moved away a little); CR omits.

[2] BDJ: *wä-əmənnä-ssä qəddəst* (as for our holy mother); CR: *wä-əmənnä burəkt* (our blessed mother).

[3] That is, she had traveled fifteen miles or so south of where she had last seen Walatta Maryam at Qərəñña.

[4] BDJ: *kämä atäwät Dämboza. Wä-ḫorät wä-bäṣḥat Afär Färäs* (lit., that she [viz., WP] had come to Dämboza. Therefore she [viz., Wälättä Maryam] went on and arrived at Afär Färäs); CR: *kämä Dämboza ḫorät wä-bäṣḥat Afär Färäs* (lit., that she [viz., WP] had gone to Dämboza. Therefore she [viz., Wälättä Maryam] arrived at Afär Färäs).

[5] It is unclear whether this "she" means Walatta Maryam or WP.

[6] BDJ: *kämä aḥatti əmənnehon* [fem.] (lit., like one of them [fem.]); CR: *kämä lä-aḥatti əmənnehon* (like for one of them).

[7] This refers to the Ethiopian practice of hand washing before a meal, since meals were eaten with hands rather than utensils. The lower-status person pours water from a jar over the hands of higher-ranking people at the table, collecting it in a small basin held underneath. Thus, WP's behavior demonstrates her Christian humility.

[8] *Ṣälotä akʷätet* is a set prayer. Servants were not supposed to eat until after this prayer was said at the end of the meal.

[9] BDJ: *gʷədfä* [acc.] (rubbish); CR: *əddawä* [acc.] (filth).

Furthermore, she would brew[1] ale,[2] carry out the dregs,[3] and pour them out at the usual place for such.[4] There was no gate of humility through which our holy mother Walatta Petros would not pass; she could be found in every one. While she was a free woman, she became a maidservant. It was just as Paul says, "While I am free[5] of all this,[6] I have subjected myself to everyone."[7]

One day—it was the Feast of Our Lady Mary's Assumption[8]—Walatta Petros held a great banquet and prepared many tables with all kinds of dishes and drinks. She then assembled all the sisters, adults and youths,[9] seating each one at her place. Our holy mother Walatta Petros remained standing and ministered to them, pouring water for [them to wash] their hands, and making them happy. After the sisters had eaten their fill, she served them beverages, giving appropriate amounts to the adults and youths.

On that day she performed every work of humility, just as our Lord did at the Last Supper,[10] when he washed[11] his disciples' feet and said to them, "Do you understand what I have done for you?[12] While you call me 'Our Master' and 'Our Lord'—and you speak rightly because I am indeed your master and your Lord—I have just washed your feet. Therefore, it likewise is right and behooves you, too,[13] to wash your companions' feet. For I have given you my example[14] so that you too

[1] BDJ: *täʿaṣṣər* (she would brew); CR: *təbäwwəʾ* (she would enter [*sic*]). The Gəʿəz dictionaries do not document *ʿaṣärä* with the meaning "to brew," but only as "to squeeze." However, in Amharic *ṭämmäqä* means "to squeeze" as well as "to brew."

[2] *Säwa* is a smoky low-alcohol beer or ale that is a common drink in Ethiopia, called *ṭälla* in Amharic, and prepared for holidays and saints' feast days. It takes six or seven days to make.

[3] Lit., *ḥaśär* (chaff). However, in Amharic *ḫaśär* can also mean dregs.

[4] BDJ: *wä-təkəʿu ḫabä məkʿaw zä-təkat* (lit., and pour out at the pouring place of old); CR: *wä-təkəʿu ḫabä məkʿaw zä-kʷästärät* (and pour out at the pouring place what she had swept up).

[5] CR adds contextually nonsensical *əsmä* (because *or* truly).

[6] In contrast to the Greek original, which has "being free from all people," the Gəʿəz here has *əm-zəntu kʷəllu* "being free from all this."

[7] BDJ: *aqnäyku rəʾsəyä lä-kʷəllu* (lit., I have subjected myself to all *or* to everything); CR: *ətqännäy rəʾsəyä lä-kʷəllu* (I myself work for all *or* for everything). 1 Corinthians 9:19.

[8] Lit., *bäʿalä fəlsäta lä-əgzəʾtənä Maryam* (the Feast of Our Lady Mary's Departure), which takes place on 16 Näḥase (22 August) after a two-week fast.

[9] BDJ: *nəʾusat* (lit., the young ones [fem.]); CR: *nəhusat* [not meaningful]. Alternatively, *lä-ləhiqat wä-lä-nəʾusat* could be translated as "senior and junior," here and at the end of the paragraph.

[10] Lit., *bä-ṣälotä ḫamus* (lit., at the Thursday Prayer); that is, on Holy Thursday or Maundy Thursday.

[11] BDJ: *amä ḫaṣäbä* (when he washed); CR: *amä ḫaṣäbä əgziʾənä* (when our Lord washed).

[12] BDJ: *aʾmärkəmu-nu zä-gäbärku läkəmu* (do you understand what I have done for you); CR: *aʾmärkəmu-nu* (do you understand).

[13] BDJ: *antəmu-ni . . . yədälləwäkəmu* (it behooves you too); CR: *antəmu . . . yədälləwäkəmu* (it behooves you).

[14] BDJ: *arʾayayä* (my example); CR: *arʾaya* (an example).

will do[1] as I have done to you."[2] Our holy mother Walatta Petros did the same and 100
led the sisters toward the path of humility. As for them, they followed her[3] and emulated her. If they transgressed the [monastic] order that she had established for them, be it in deed or in thought, this transgression lay open and was visible to Walatta Petros, just like a small straw that has fallen into[4] pure milk.[5] Like a water torrent that streams down from a rooftop [after a heavy rain], so the thinking of the entire community was visible to her. Our holy mother Walatta Petros[6] said so [herself], and many from among the sisters [who can testify to this] are still alive today. We know them personally.[7]

Regarding the sisters, our holy mother Walatta Petros also prophesied that in later days tribulations and downfall would afflict every single one of them.[8] Unfortunately for them, the prophecy was fulfilled, and things happened as she had told the sisters. The sisters will testify to this as well.

There also were some from among the brothers and sisters about whom Walatta Petros prophesied[9] that they would leave and split away from the community. This was fulfilled [as well]; things happened as she had said.

Chapter 81: Our Mother Longs to Become a Hermit But Is Told to Stay

While our holy mother Walatta Petros lived in Afer Faras under such circumstances,[10] a troubling thought assailed her, namely, that she had been deprived of the gifts of grace that she had been given[11] in Waldeba, while living [there] as a hermit. There-

[1] BDJ: *kämä təgbäru antəmu-ni* (so that you too will do); CR: *kämä təgbäru antəmu* (so that you will do).

[2] John 13:12–15.

[3] BDJ: *kona yətälləwa kiyaha* (they . . . followed her); CR: *kona däläwa* [*sic*] *kiyaha* (they were appropriate [*sic*] her). This CR variant is evidence for at least occasional dictation in the manuscript reproduction process, as *yətälləwa* and *däläwa* are close in sound, but quite different orthographically.

[4] BDJ, Abb. 88: *əm-wəstä* (from). CR altered this to *bä-wəstä* (into), and we follow him in our translation.

[5] BDJ: *ḥalib ṣəruy* (pure milk); CR: *ḥalib ʿəruy* (still milk).

[6] CR omits *Wälättä Ṗeṭros.*

[7] BDJ: *wä-nəḥnä näʾamməron* [substandard orthography for *naʾamməron*] (we know them personally); CR: *wä-nəḥnä näʾamməro* [substandard orthography for *naʾamməro*] (we know this [to be true]).

[8] BDJ: *lä-lä-aḥatti aḥatti* (every single one of them); CR: *lä-aḥatti* (for one of them [*sic*]).

[9] D: *zä-tänäbbäyät bäʾəntiʾahomu* [masc. pl.] (lit., about whom [masc. pl.] she prophesied); BJ, CR: *zä-tänäbbäyät bäʾəntiʾahon* (about whom [fem. pl.] she prophesied). Since the phrase addresses a mixed-gender group, the masculine plural suffix is required.

[10] BDJ: *bä-zä-kämä-ze gəbr* (under such circumstances); CR: *bä-kämä-zə* (like this).

[11] BDJ: *zä-täwəhbä lati* (that she had been given); CR: *zä-täwəhba lati* (that she had been given [emph.]).

fore, our holy mother Walatta Petros resolved to go to the island of Narga[1] and live[2] [there] alone.

To this end, she came up with a pretext, saying, "Behold, many people have gathered around me, but I don't have anything at hand, neither clothes nor food.[3] Furthermore,[4] I cannot put up with the commotion created by so many people.[5] Therefore, I will go to Narga[6] because I want to live [there]: Get a tankwa ready for me! As for Afer Faras, Eheta Kristos shall remain here[7] because she has the capacity to put up with the commotion created by so many people[8] and to live in such circumstances."

When our holy mother Walatta Petros spoke like this,[9] Silla Kristos[10] responded, "Please don't act rashly! Let us pray first; let us pray for a week."

Our blessed mother Walatta Petros replied, "Very well."

The two of them then prayed for a week. Afterward, Silla Kristos said to Walatta Petros, "Please, tell me[11] what you have discovered."

Our holy mother Walatta Petros replied,[12] "Me? I have not discovered anything."

So Silla Kristos said to her, "Let us pray for another week," to which she [again] said "Very well."

[1] BDJ: *Narga*; CR: *Angära.* Narga is a tiny island connected by a short stone causeway to the western part of Däq Island, the largest island in Lake Ṭana. Queen Məntəwwab built a significant church there a hundred years later.

[2] BDJ: *wä-tənbär* [subj.] (lit., and to live); CR: *wä-tənäbbər* [*sic*: ind.; no translation difference].

[3] BDJ: *wä-albo mənt-ni* [nom.] *wəstä ədeya əmmä-ni ləbs* [nom.] *wä-əmmä-ni sisay* [nom.] (lit., and there is nothing in my hands, neither clothing nor food); CR: *wä-albo məntä-ni* [acc.] *wəstä ədeya əmmä-ni ləbsä* [acc.] *wä-əmmä-ni sisayä* [acc.] [three case differences, but identical translation].

[4] BDJ: *kaʿəbä-ni* (furthermore); CR: *kaʿəbä* [less emphatic, but identical translation].

[5] The author Gälawdewos claims that this is a pretext, but it may be that the burden of being responsible for so many is starting to wear. Earlier in her life, WP confidently said, "If the community grew in number from its current size and increased twofold, my heart would be able to carry it fully through the power of God, my Lord, because I have been given the gift of patient endurance."

[6] BDJ: *Narga*; CR: *Angära.*

[7] BDJ: *zəyyä-ssä tənbär Ǝḫətä Krəstos* (lit., as for here, Ǝḫətä Krəstos shall remain); CR: *zəyyä-ssä tənäbbər Ǝḫətä Krəstos* (as for here, Eheta Kristos will remain).

[8] BDJ: *əsmä təkəl ṣäwirä hukätä bəzuḫ säbʾ* (lit., because she has the capacity of bearing the commotion of many people); CR: *əsmä təkəl ṣäwirä hukät lä-bəzuḫ säbʾ* [not fully grammatical, but identical in meaning].

[9] BDJ: *təbe kämä-zə* (spoke like this); CR: *təbe kämä təgbär* (said that she would do [this]).

[10] This is probably the Śəʿəlä Krəstos whom WP had raised from the dead and who had had a vision.

[11] BDJ: *nəgərəni* [substandard orthography for *nəgərini*: imper. 2nd sg. fem.] (tell me); Abb. 88 *nəgəruni* [imper. 2nd pl. masc.] (tell me), which CR altered (also employing substandard orthography) to the required *nəgərə-ni.*

[12] BDJ: *wä-təbelo əmmənä qəddəst* [B adds: *wä-burəkt*] *Wälättä Ṗeṭros* (lit., our holy [B adds: and blessed] mother WP said to him); CR: *wä-təbelo* (she said to him).

So they prayed a second time like before, [for a week]. Then Silla Kristos a second time asked Walatta Petros,[1] "Please, tell me what you have seen!" 101

Our holy mother Walatta Petros hid and concealed it from him, however. She said to him, "I have seen nothing whatsoever."

Silla Kristos then said to her, "If you hide and conceal it from me, I will report it to you."

In response, our holy mother Walatta Petros said to him, "Go ahead then and report it to me!"

So now Silla Kristos disclosed her secrets to her, according to what the Holy Spirit, the revealer of secrets, unexpectedly had given him to understand.[2] He said to her, "The [gifts of] grace that are conferred when one lives in solitude as a hermit[3] are different from the [gifts of] grace conferred in a community. To the hermit, all the varied gifts of grace are revealed, so that he finds comfort in them and does not stir[4] from his place. By contrast, a community behaves according to its number,[5] form,[6] and shape.[7] If you can put up with and patiently endure the behavior of an entire community, this is equivalent to the hermit's diverse gifts of grace."[8]

Our holy mother Walatta Petros said to him, "You have spoken truly: it's because of this that I was restless.[9] Now, however, our Lord has come and said to me[10] three times, 'Tend my rams and my ewes,[11] and don't be restless in the least! Did I not also say this to Peter before?[12] Now I say the same thing to you as well.' Therefore, from now on I will not be restless."

[1] BDJ: *wä-täsäʾala dagəmä* (lit., he then asked her again); CR: *wä-täsäʾalä dagəmä* (he then asked again).

[2] BDJ: *bä-kämä aläbbäwo gəbtä mänfäs qəddus* (according to what the Holy Spirit . . . unexpectedly had given him to understand); CR: *bä-kämä aläbbäwo gəbrä mänfäs qəddus* (according to what the working of the Holy Spirit . . . had given him to understand).

[3] BDJ: *bä-zämänä bəḥtawe* (lit., in the time of a hermit's solitude); CR: *bä-zämänä baḥtawi* (in the time of a hermit).

[4] BDJ: *kämä . . . i-yanqälqəl* [subj.] (so that he . . . does not stir); CR: *kämä . . . i-yanqäläqqəl* [*sic*: ind.; no translation difference].

[5] BDJ: *ḫʷəllaqʷe* (number); CR: *ḫʷellaqʷe* [faulty spelling, resulting in a nonexistent lexeme].

[6] BDJ: *wä-bä-kämä mälkəʾu* (lit., and according to its form); CR: *wä-kämä mälkəʾu* (and like its form).

[7] Lit., *wä-akalä qomu* (and its body stature).

[8] BDJ: *zä-zä-ziʾahu ṣägga wəʾətu* (lit., it is various graces); CR: *zä-ziʾahu ṣägga wəʾətu* (it is a grace in its own right).

[9] BDJ: *tähawäkku* (I was restless); Abb. 88: *tähawkä* (he was restless), which CR altered to *tähawəkku*: a faulty form, but clearly intended as a first-person singular.

[10] BDJ: *wä-yəbeläni* (and said to me); CR: *wä-yəbe* (and said).

[11] BDJ: *abagəʿəyä wä-abagəʿtəyä* (my rams and my ewes); CR: *abagəʿəyä wä-baggəʿtəyä* (my rams and my ewe). In the Greek biblical passage alluded to, there are only gender neutral plurals: *arnía* (lambs) and *próbata* (sheep).

[12] BDJ: *lä-Ṗeṭros-ni qädimu* (also . . . to Peter before); CR: *lä-Ṗeṭros qädimu* (to Peter before). On the night that he was betrayed, Christ instructed Peter thrice to feed his lambs and sheep (John 21:15–17).

Our holy mother Walatta Petros said this to Silla Kristos, he then told it to us, and we have written it down.

Furthermore, when *Abba* Za-Sillasé said to our holy mother Walatta Petros, “Bless my clothes for me,” she blessed them for him with the following words, “May God bless them for you, and may he make them [like] leather for you.” Thus, they were blessed for him, and lasted for many years.[1]

Chapter 82: Our Mother Survives Drowning

During the great famine in the year of the locusts,[2] Abaala Kristos[3] gave Walatta Petros[4] a large amount of grain from Guna.[5] Then, our holy mother Walatta Petros sent some of the community away [to Guna] so that they might find sustenance there during the months of the rainy season.[6] The others stayed behind[7] at Afer Faras together with our holy mother Walatta Petros. Later, she again sent away[8] a few, from among those who had remained with her [at Afer Faras], to live in Zambowl[9] and sustain themselves on grain from Lag.[10] Our holy mother Walatta Petros kept going back and forth: sometimes she was at Afer Faras, at other times at
102 Zambowl.

One day, while[11] Walatta Petros was returning from Zambowl by tankwa, it capsized when she had almost reached Zagé.[12] Our holy mother Walatta Petros fell and sank into the deep [water]. There she lay, having wrapped herself in her atsf

[1] The poor still wore animal skins during this period, according to the Jesuits, and many monks wore leather tunics, but it seems this monk wore cotton clothing, which had been made in Ethiopia since the thirteenth century.

[2] Great famines due to locusts are recorded in Ethiopia during WP’s lifetime, but the recorded years do not match this period, which had to be between 1636 and 1642. The closest would be locust plagues in 1633 or 1647.

[3] *Abalä Krəstos* (Limb of Christ).

[4] D: *wähaba* (lit., gave her); BJ: *wähabä* (gave); CR: *wähabo* (gave him *or* gave it [namely, the community]).

[5] *Gʷəna* or *Guna* is a mountain fifty miles east of Qʷäraṣa and the origin of the Rəbb River, so perhaps fertile.

[6] The rainy season is also known as the hungry season, since the crops are growing, too immature to have fruit yet, and the grain from the last season is sometimes exhausted.

[7] BDJ: *tärfu* [masc. pl.] ([they] stayed behind); CR: *tärfä* [masc. sg.] (it [namely, the other part of the community] stayed behind), by way of correction of an alleged *tärfa* [fem. pl.] (they [fem.] stayed behind) in Abb. 88, but probably misreading an orthographically very similar *tärfu.*

[8] BDJ: *fännäwät* (sent away); CR: *fännäwäto* (sent him away).

[9] BDJ: *Zämbol*; CR: *Zäbol*; thus also subsequently unless otherwise indicated. Zämbol is on Lake Ṭana in the district of Läg and thus near Zäge and the Gəlgäl Abbay River.

[10] BDJ: *əklä əmənnä Läg* (grain from Lag); CR: *əklä Läg* (the grain of Lag).

[11] BDJ: *ənzä* (while); CR: *əntä* (on which).

[12] BDJ: *Zäge*; CR: *ḥayq* (the shore).

vestment.[1] She remained [there] for quite some time, praying the *Salama Malaak* and the Lord's Prayer.[2]

Those who had fallen [into the water] together with her quickly got out, but our holy mother Walatta Petros remained missing.[3] Everybody was shocked and thought that she had died.[4] When she had finished her prayers, however, she stirred in the deep, and then the lake's waters carried her and tossed her on the shore: She emerged safe and sound. Neither did [her] books perish; rather they emerged unscathed as well.[5]

Thus, Satan was put to shame, who had wanted to endanger her[6] and put her to the test. It was as Paul says, "I was in danger in the sea."[7] After this, Walatta Petros climbed into that same tankwa again and reached Afer Faras. There she lived for as long as it pleased God.[8]

Chapter 83: Our Mother Establishes Her Seventh Community, at Zambowl

Later, our holy mother Walatta Petros left [Afer Faras], and the entire community left with her, all of those who had remained in Afer Faras. Those who had gone to Guna, returned. They all met at Zambowl and lived together in one and the same place,[9] brothers and sisters, in their respective shelters and houses, and according to their respective monastic rules, [one for each gender]. This was the seventh community.

Walatta Petros then reformed the monastic rule [for monks]: for meals and sleeping, she united the monks, youths and adults,[10] in one building. Except for a few elder ones, nobody was allowed to keep separate for any reason.[11] By the will of

[1] BDJ: *ʿaṣfa* (her *ʿaṣf*-vestment); CR: *ʿaṣf* (a *ʿaṣf*-vestment).

[2] Lit., *abunä zä-bä-sämayat* (the Our Father in Heaven).

[3] BDJ: *täḫaṭʾat* (remained missing); CR: *wä-täḫaṭʾat* (and remained missing).

[4] BDJ: *wä-mäsälomu zä-motät* (lit., and it appeared to them that she had died); CR: *wä-mäsälomu kämä zä-motät* (lit., and it appeared to them as if she had died).

[5] Religious people often carried an edifying book with them, if they could afford it, most often the Psalter. WP's piety (and wealth) enabled her to carry several books with her.

[6] BDJ: *zä-fäqädä yamändəba* [subj.] (who had wanted to endanger her); CR: *zä-fäqädä yamänäddəba* [*sic*: ind.; no translation difference].

[7] 2 Corinthians 11:26. The author Gälawdewos has truncated the biblical quote. There is an echo here from the *Kəbrä Nägäśt*, of a passage where the Queen of Sheba talks about "going to sleep in the depths of the sea" (Budge 1922, 131).

[8] Lit., *əskä yəbäṣṣəḥ fäqadä əgziʾabḥer* (until the will of God arrived [for her to go somewhere else]).

[9] BDJ, Abb. 88: *aḥattäne* (lit., in one place); CR for no clear reason omitted *aḥattäne* despite its being extant in Abb. 88.

[10] Lit., *nəʾus wä-ʿabiy* (small and big *or* juniors or seniors).

[11] That is, she is moving her community from a tendency toward idiorhythmic monasticism (where members live separately in separate huts and act independently of one another)

God, she further chose *Abba* Za-Hawaryaat from among them and made him their superior.[1] In addition, she set apart those men who did manual work,[2] in their own huts.[3] She ordered them not to enter into the hut of any other[4] for whatever reason. If they had any task that would take[5] them [there], they should stand outside and announce their business.[6]

As for the sisters, she set them up in groups of fifty,[7] and for each [group of that] number, each in its own house, there was one head woman.[8] With these rules, the brothers and the sisters lived in love and in peace.

Chapter 84: Our Mother and the Miracle of the Candle

In those days, our holy mother Walatta Petros left [Zambowl] one Sunday night,[9]
103 and, with one sister, went to the church of Furé. She stayed in that monastery[10] at
that time. When our holy mother Walatta Petros wanted to read the Gospel of John
during that night, while it was still dark, she sent the young woman[11] to fetch her a
[lit] candle. The young woman went to fetch it, but kept searching for a long time
for a fire because they had all gone out.

---

toward cenobitic monasticism (where members live together in a community). Living more closely together and depending on one another more required better organization. WP also appears to be more strictly segregating the sexes.

[1] Lit., *abä k^{w}əllu* (the father of all). The *Short History of WP's Community* says that she made him abbot in the month of Miyazya before her death, so she appointed him in April–May 1642.

[2] Lit., *əllä yətgebbäru* (those who work). This might also mean, with men being the subject, "those who tilled the land." (If women are the subject, the same verb regularly means "to do kitchenwork.") These men may be lay brothers who did manual labor in order to free up the time of monks. As part of better organizing the community, WP is instituting strict rules regarding tasks, not allowing people to act as they please when they please.

[3] BDJ: *bä-bä-abyatihomu* (lit., in their respective houses); CR: *bä-abyatihomu* (in their houses).

[4] BDJ: *1 wəstä betä 1* (lit., one into the house of one); CR: *1 wəstä 1 bet* (one into one house).

[5] BDJ, Abb. 88: *zä-yəwässəd* (lit., that would take), which CR needlessly altered to *zä-yawässəd* (lit., that would cause [them] to take).

[6] The command not to enter another's house is emphatic; perhaps she intended to prevent sexual activity as well.

[7] BDJ: *wä-lä-aḥat-əssä śärʿaton bä-bä-50* (as for the sisters, she set them up in groups of fifty); CR: *wä-ḥaddäsät śərʿatomu* [*sic*: masc. pl.] *bä-bä-50* (she reformed their [masc. pl.] order according to fifty each).

[8] BDJ: *aḥatti rəʾs* (one head woman); CR: *aḥatti rəʾsa* (one her [*sic*] head woman). Pace Conti Rossini's conjecture, no passage on a reform of monks' rules was missing here: BDJ have no extra text here beyond Abb. 88.

[9] BDJ: *lelitä . . . bä-ʿəlätä əḥud* (lit., at night . . . on a Sunday); CR: *bä-lelit . . . bä-ʿəlätä əḥud* [different construction, but identical meaning].

[10] *Mənet*, which is another word for monastery used only a few times in the text.

[11] Lit., *wälätt* (daughter).

Meanwhile, a [burning] white wax candle[1] descended from heaven to our holy mother Walatta Petros, and she began to read. After quite some time,[2] the sister came back with a light, but found our holy mother Walatta Petros with a light[3] [already], and reading the Gospel.

So, the young woman inquired of our holy mother Walatta Petros, "I have been delayed by going around from house to house searching for fire. Who brought you this light?"

Our holy mother Walatta Petros looked at her indignantly, so the young woman immediately became quiet and did not repeat her inquiry. She now understood that the light had come down for Walatta Petros[4] from heaven.

Chapter 85: Our Mother and the Death of Amata Dinghil's Son

Later, when our holy mother Walatta Petros [again] was at Zambowl[5] with her original community,[6] it grew there too: they became nine hundred. Then a violent illness rose up and struck against the sisters. It made them fall ill and killed many of them. Each day,[7] two or three, or even more, were buried[8] in a single grave.[9]

Subsequently that illness reached the monks as well and began to kill them. Among the brothers there was a young man in the flower of his years whose name was Béza Masqal,[10] the son of our mother Amata Dinghil.[11] That young man had a handsome appearance; therefore, every time our holy mother Walatta Petros[12] saw

[1] BDJ: *maḫtotä säm*ʿ *ṣäʿada* (a white wax candle); CR: *maḫtotä səm*ʿ *ṣäʿada* (a white light of testimony *or* witness).

[2] BDJ: *wä-əmdəḫrä gʷənduy* (after quite some time); CR: *wä-əmdəḫrä gʷənduy mäwaʿəl* (after many days).

[3] Our translation assumes an original *ənzä täḫattu maḫtot* (lit., while a light was burning), whereas BJ, CR have *ənzä täḫattu maḫtotä*. Yet, intransitive *ənzä täḫattu* (while burning) does not go together with accusative *maḫtotä*. D resolved this inconsistency by making the verb transitive: *ənzä taḫattu maḫtotä* (having lit a light), but semantically this does not fit the context.

[4] BDJ: *lati* (lit., for her); CR omits.

[5] BDJ, CR: *Zämbol* (whereas CR otherwise mostly writes Zäbol).

[6] Lit., *məslä əllu maḫbär zä-qädami* (with these community members of before).

[7] BDJ: *bä-bä-ʿəlätu* (each day); CR: *bä-bä-ʿəlät* [variant form with identical meaning]

[8] BDJ: *kona yətqäbbära* [fem. pl.] ([they] were buried); CR: *konä* [*sic*: masc. sg.] *yətqäbbära* [fem. pl.: the two verb forms do not match].

[9] BDJ: *wəstä 1 mäqabər* (in a single grave); CR: *wəstä mäqabər* (in a grave).

[10] *Beza Mäsqäl* (Redemption through the cross).

[11] *Amätä Dəngəl* (Maidservant of the [Holy] Virgin) was the third abbess of the community, after WP and Ǝḫətä Krəstos, and the abbess when the *WP gädl* was written, as the reference to her here as "our mother" confirms. She may be one of the head women recently assigned to lead a group of fifty nuns.

[12] CR omits *Wälättä Ṗeṭros.*

him, she wished for his death and implored God to receive him soon.[1] Also, his mother kept praying for him likewise.

When forty days had passed since he had become a monk, Béza Masqal spent Sunday not resting[2] but girding his loins and, as it was his turn, serving the community at the midday meal. After he had finished his service, he fell ill on that very
104 day and died on the third day [after]. The entire community was shocked.

Our holy mother Walatta Petros received a message informing her that Béza Masqal had died. Before hearing[3] about his falling ill, however, she had already learned about his death. Thus, when our holy mother Walatta Petros heard [this news], she was very[4] happy and praised God.

She then sent for Béza Masqal's mother, summoning her. As for Amata Dinghil,[5] she did not yet know what had happened. She came before our holy mother Walatta Petros, who spoke to her in parables, saying, "When one obtains[6] what one has wished and hoped for, must one be happy[7] or sad?"

Béza Masqal's mother responded, "One must be happy."[8]

Our holy mother Walatta Petros replied, "You have judged well. Now, you too be happy and rejoice: Behold, your son, the heavenly groom, has found [eternal] rest."

Béza Masqal's mother then said, "Who is this son of mine who has found rest?"[9]

Our holy mother Walatta Petros replied to her, "Your son Béza Masqal has found rest."

His mother asked, "When did he fall sick, and when did he die?"[10] But then she sank to the ground in shock, losing her self-control,[11] and wept for a time.

[1] WP may have been worried that he was too good-looking to avoid sexual temptation or to avoid tempting the community members. That is, his death is necessary to safeguard him as well as to protect the community.

[2] Lit., *wäʿalä bä-ʿəlätä əḥud ənzä yəqäwwəm* (he spent Sunday standing).

[3] BDJ: *əm-qədmä təsmaʿ* [subj.] (lit., before she heard); CR: *əm-qədmä təsämməʿ* [*sic*: ind.; no translation difference].

[4] BDJ: *fädfadä* (very); CR omits.

[5] BDJ: *yəʾəti-ssä* (lit., she for her part); CR: *wä-yəʾəti* (but she).

[6] BDJ: *kʷəllu säbʾ sobä räkäbä* (lit., each person, when he obtains); Abb. 88 with changed word order: *kʷəllu sobä räkäbä säbʾ*, which CR needlessly altered to *kʷəllo sobä räkäbä säbʾ* (when a person finds all).

[7] BDJ: *yədälləwo-nu yətfäśśaḥ* [subj.] (must one be happy); CR: *yədälləwo-nu yətfeśśaḥ* [*sic*: ind.; no translation difference]. With following "be sad," CR also has the required subjunctive (*yəḥzən*).

[8] BDJ: *yədälləwo yətfäśśaḥ* [subj.] (one must be happy); CR: *yədälləwo yətfeśśaḥ* [*sic*: ind.; no translation difference]. The recurrence of this mistake points toward reading-based copying of Abb. 88 (in this section at least) because the the acoustic distance between *yətfeśśaḥ* and *yətfäśśaḥ* is rather noticable, whereas their optical differerence in fidäl is small, smaller even than in transcription.

[9] Amätä Dəngəl may be assuming that WP is using the term "son" metaphorically, meaning a male member of her community.

[10] B, CR: *wä-maʾəze motä* (and when did he die); DJ: *wä-motä* (and die).

[11] Lit., *ənzä i-täʾammər* [*sic*: substandard orthography for *i-taʾammər*] (while not knowing). Here our translation differs substantively from Ricci's, who has *ignorando la cosa* (not knowing the matter).

But our holy mother Walatta Petros scolded her and made her stop crying,[1] saying to her, "Didn't you keep wishing to see his death? How can you now be sad? How can you change your mind[2] and [thus] have lied to God? However, if you so desire, I will resurrect[3] [him] for you."

Béza Masqal's mother replied, "What has happened has happened. [But] allow me to go see him one more time."

In reply, our holy mother Walatta Petros said to her, "No, I won't send you. If you go, you will [only] cry there."

Amata Dinghil replied, "No, definitely, I won't cry. Just send me for a short time so that I can see his face [one last time] before he is buried."

Walatta Petros replied, "Very well, I allow you to go. But don't cry."[4]

Now Amata Dinghil left; the sisters who were her companions followed her, in tears, up to the gate of the wall[5] [of the monks' compound where Béza Masqal had been laid out]. When our holy mother Walatta Petros heard the sound of the sisters' crying, she became very angry and ordered that Amata Dinghil be brought back.

Amata Dinghil obeyed, returned, and said, "As for me, I didn't cry! Here, see whether there are tears in my eyes."

So Walatta Petros sent her[6] [again], but had ten elderwomen from among her fellow sisters[7] accompany her. Now Amata Dinghil went[8] to her son's dead body. She looked at him, hugged him, and kissed him. When the brothers saw her,[9] they wept. After this, they took Béza Masqal's dead body to the church with hymns and
songs. Then, they read the *Book of the Dead*[10] over him and buried him. 105

I ask you, my loved ones,[11] if our holy mother Walatta Petros has ordered people not to weep over the dead like this,[12] as you are witnesses, on what grounds do we have all this crying, this loud mourning, and these lamentations [when commu-

[1] BDJ: *wä-aḫdägäta bəkayä* (and made her stop crying); Abb. 88: *wä-ḫadägät bəkayä* (and she stopped crying), which CR sensibly altered to *wä-aḫdägät bəkayä* (and made [her] stop crying).

[2] BJ: *təwelləṭi* [ind.] *qaläki* (lit., change your word); D, CR: *təwälləṭi* [*sic*: subj.] *qaläki* [no translation difference].

[3] BDJ: *əm-anśaʾku* (I will resurrect); CR: *kämä anśaʾku* [*sic*] (that I resurrect).

[4] Perhaps WP thought that Amätä Dəngəl had to be tougher than others as a future leader of the community.

[5] BDJ: *qəṣr* (wall, fence; fortress); CR: *ṣərḥ* (chamber).

[6] BDJ: *fännäwäta* ([she] sent her); CR: *fätäwäta* ([she] desired her).

[7] BDJ: *əmənnä abyaṣiha aḫat* (from among her fellow sisters); CR omits.

[8] BDJ: *ḥorät wä-bäṣḥat* (lit., went and came to); CR: *ḥorät wä-boʾat* (went and proceeded).

[9] BDJ: *wä-sobä näṣṣärəwwa aḫaw* (when the brothers saw her); CR: *wä-sobä näṣṣäru aḫaw* (when the brothers saw).

[10] *Mäṣḥafä Məwətan* (Book of the Dead). Ricci speculates that this book is the one usually called *Mäṣḥafä Gənzät* (The Book of the [Corpse's] Shrouding), which is a collection of rites for funeral services. However, another book that is sometimes called *Mäṣḥafä Məwətan* is the *Ləfafä Ṣədq* (Bandlet of Righteousness), which is popular among monks (Budge 1929).

[11] BDJ: *o-fəquranəyä* (lit., o my loved ones): CR: *o-aḫaw fəquranəyä* (o my beloved brothers).

[12] BDJ: *kämä-zə* (lit., like this); CR omits.

nity members die]? Do we want to defy our mother? Yet if we defy our holy mother Walatta Petros, we will defy Christ, according to what he himself said to the apostles, "He who disobeys you[1] disobeys me, and he who disobeys me disobeys him who has sent me."[2] Therefore, I, for one, believe it is incumbent upon us[3] to observe the commands of our mother; for without such, we have no salvation. Also, Paul says, "We want you to know, concerning those who[4] have fallen asleep [forever], that you do not need to grieve over them like the other people who have no hope."[5]

Chapter 86: Our Mother Sees Nuns Lusting after Each Other

On that day, after Béza Masqal had been buried, *Abba* Za-Hawaryaat went to our holy mother Walatta Petros and said to her, "How can we remain calm[6] in the face of this deadly scourge that kills [people] out of the blue[7] and gets worse every day? I, for one, think it would be best for us to conduct prayers and supplications with the *Praise of the Beloved*[8] so that God might take this scourge away from us and show[9] us mercy and clemency."

Our holy mother Walatta Petros replied to *Abba* Za-Hawaryaat, "Don't worry! These deaths are no scourge, but rather God's mercy."

Abba Za-Hawaryaat responded, "As for me, I know of no such 'mercy of God.' Truly this is a scourge!"

Our holy mother Walatta Petros again replied to him, "But I tell you that this is God's mercy! It is not a scourge. How can you now contradict me and say, 'This is a scourge'?"

In reaction *Abba* Za-Hawaryaat said to her, "So then, tell me about it and explain this secret to me so that I can believe[10] your words."

[1] BDJ: *zä-läkəmu abäyä* (he who disobeys you); CR: *zä-läkəmu ʿaläwä wä-abäyä* (he who rises up against and disobeys you).

[2] Luke 10:16.

[3] BDJ: *yədälləwänä* (it is incumbent upon us); CR: *yəḫeyyəsänä yədälləwänä* (it is better for us [and] incumbent upon us).

[4] BJ: *əllä* (those who); D, CR omit.

[5] 1 Thessalonians 4:13.

[6] BDJ: *əfo narämməm* [ind.] (how can we remain calm); CR: *əfo narməm* [*sic*: subj.; no translation difference].

[7] Lit., *gəbtä* (suddenly).

[8] The *Səbḥatä fəqur* is a communal daily office of the Täwaḥədo Church; that is, an official set of fixed prayers, often used during a period of spiritual retreat. The supplication is addressed to God through the intercession of the saints, who presumably each constitute the singular "beloved" of the title.

[9] BDJ: *yəfännu* [subj.] (lit., send); CR: *yəfennu* [*sic*: ind.; no translation difference].

[10] BDJ: *kämä əʾmän* [subj.] (so that I can believe); CR: *kämä aʾammən* [*sic*: ind.; no translation difference].

But our holy mother Walatta Petros replied to him, "No, I will not tell you. Rather in your heart realize and believe that this is God's mercy."

Abba Za-Hawaryaat responded, "No, I will not believe it unless you clearly explain it to me. I implore you by God to tell me!"

Now our holy mother Walatta Petros revealed [the secret] to him, "Since you
compel me, listen up and let me tell you. It was evening and I was sitting in the
house, facing the gate, when I saw some young nuns pressing against each other 106
and being lustful with each other,[1] each with a female companion. Therefore, my
heart caught fire and I began to argue with God, saying to him, 'Did you put me[2]
[here] to show me this?[3] I now pray and beg you to relieve me of the goods that you
have entrusted to me. Or else take my life![4] I prefer perishing to seeing these [sinful] daughters of mine perish [for eternity].'[5]

"Instantly, God came to me and comforted me with the following words, 'Don't be afraid! I have heard your prayers and will fulfill your wish.'[6] With him were seven[7] black maidservants, namely,[8] six strong young women in their prime and

[1] BCDEFGIJK: *ənzä . . . yətmarrəʿa bä-bäynatihon* (being lustful with each other); H, CR: *ənzä . . . yətmarrəḥa bä-bäynatihon* (leading each other around); A omits *yətmarrəʿa*. (We here checked all available manuscripts due to the phrase's significance.) While the roots of both verbs, namely, *m-r-ʿ* and *m-r-ḥ*, are well attested, the standard dictionaries do not document the specific derived reciprocal stems *tämarəʿa* and *tämarəḥa* that are used here. The verb in MS H and CR obscured the point of the anecdote. Our translation thus differs radically from Ricci's, who had *che spingendosi procedevano tutte insieme, l'una con l'altra* (who, surging against each other, all proceeded together, one with the other). The MS H, CR verb may be an attempt to sanitize the original text about same-sex desire, by suggesting that the women were merely playing children's games; MS A sanitizes through omission. It seems unlikely that the crucial one-letter change, from *ʿa* to *ḥa*, is an accidental corruption.

[2] BDJ: *bo-nu anbärkäni litä* (lit., did you put me *or* did you make me live); CR: *bo-nu agäbbärkäni litä* (did you force me).

[3] Ḥaylä Ṣəyon, a scholar of Gəʿəz literature who grew up in the Täwaḥədo Church and was a monk in it, says this sentence is a *säm-ənna wärq* line (see the glossary for definition). On the surface, it expresses her anger against God for showing her this scene, but the words chosen also suggest that she is angry because she felt desire upon looking at the scene. That the Amharic translation of the *WP gädl* omits this sentence suggests this interpretation has merit.

[4] Lit., *näfsəyä* (my soul).

[5] WP seems to be asking for a redemptive Christlike death, taking their sins upon herself. The disease is a test that brings blessings. Nuns and monks were supposed to abstain from all sexual activity, whether with those of the same sex or the opposite sex. Previously, WP expressed the desire to run through with a spear a monk and a nun flirting with each other.

[6] It seems that Christ fulfills both wishes, that the sisters be removed as burdens and that WP die on their behalf.

[7] BDJ: *wä-halläwa məslehu 7* [number spelled out in J, illegible in B] (with him were seven); CR: *wä-yənbära məsleki 6-tu* (with you [viz., WP] shall stay six).

[8] Lit., *wä-* [unspecific connector particle; most common translation "and," but with a wide range of other possibilities].

one elder woman.[1] Then, he said to me, 'Take these maidservants[2] so that they may carry out[3] your wishes. Assign the six to the sisters' houses,[4] one to each [house].[5] But the elder woman shall stay with you.' Then, everything happened to me as he had told me [it would], and this is why I say to you: This is God's mercy. Won't you say likewise?"

Now *Abba* Za-Hawaryaat agreed, "It is indeed God's mercy."

In those days, 137[6] from among the brothers and sisters died. They traveled from toil to rest, from distress to happiness. May their prayers and blessings be with __________[7] for eternity, amen.

A question [came up]: her followers asked our holy mother Walatta Petros, regarding the brothers and sisters who had died, whether they were saved or damned. They said to her, "Please, tell us[8] whether our hearts can be comforted and we need not doubt. All those who have [recently] died, are all of them counted among the righteous? Or are [only] some of them considered righteous, and others of them have been damned?"[9]

Our holy mother Walatta Petros replied to them, "Nobody from among them will be condemned, nor anyone [from my community] before them or after them.[10]

[1] The emphasis on the fact that the maidservants were black (*ṣällimat*) could indicate that these women were slaves from outside of the Ethiopian highlands, sent to somehow serve the sisters. But since the maidservants are part of a vision, it seems more likely that they are metaphors for death, come to fulfill WP's wishes. That is, the six strong young women have come to take the young women who have become a burden, and the elder woman has come to take WP.

[2] BDJ, Abb. 88: *əllantu aʾmat* [nom.] (these maidservants); CR altered this to the contextually required accusative *əllantä aʾmatä.*

[3] BDJ: *yəfäṣṣəma* (so that they may carry out); CR: *wä-yəfäṣṣəma* (and may they carry out).

[4] BDJ: *bä-bä-abyatihon lä-aḫat* (to the sisters' houses); CR: *bä-bä-abyaṣihon lä-aḫat* (to their respective companions, the sisters).

[5] Since each "house" had fifty sisters, this suggests that three hundred of the nine hundred members of WP's community at Zäbol before the deadly illness were nuns or that only six of the houses would have deaths.

[6] BDJ: *137*; CR: *136*. That is, about one out of six died.

[7] B: *fəquromu Agnaṭəyos* (their beloved Ignatius); D: *fəquromu* [name erased] (their beloved [name erased]); J: *fəqərtomu* [fem.] *Amätä Dəngəl wä-məslä fəquromu Zä-Ḥawaryat* (their beloved [fem.] Amätä Dəngəl and with their beloved Zä-Ḥawaryat); Abb. 88: *fəquromu* [name erased] (their beloved [name erased]), which CR altered to [*məsle*]*nä* ([with] us). The mention in MS J of Amätä Dəngəl and Zä-Ḥawaryat together—who were the abbess and abbot when the author Gälawdewos was writing—may suggest it is the urtext.

[8] BDJ: *nəgərənä* [substandard orthography for *nəgərinä*] (tell us); CR: *nəgərəni* [substandard orthography for *nəgərini*] (tell me).

[9] BDJ: *wä-mimmä mänfäqomu yəṣäddəqu wä-mänfäqomu yəthaggʷälu* (lit., or is one part of them righteous, and the other part of them has perished); CR: *wä-mimmä mänfäqomu yəthaggʷälu* (or has one part of them perished).

[10] BDJ: *männu-hi i-əmqədmehomu wä-i-əmdəḫrehomu* (lit., not anyone, neither before them nor after them); CR: *männu-hi əmqədmehomu wä-əmdəḫrehomu* (not anyone, either before them or after them).

Furthermore, not only the community members[1] who are in my care,[2] but also those in the four corners of the world who invoke my name will be saved and not damned. But this, that which I say to you, does not happen due to my righteousness but due to God's mercy."

Chapter 87: Our Mother and the Restless Nun

In those days, a sister named Fiqirta Kristos,[3] wife[4] of Kifla Maryam, became restless and decided[5] to return home. Kifla Maryam could not convince her to change 107
her mind,[6] neither through advice nor through admonition. He then told our holy mother Walatta Petros that Fiqirta Kristos had become restless; he was distressed and wept because of her.

But our holy mother Walatta Petros consoled him, saying, "Don't be afraid and don't be distressed! Don't think she'll go away."

After Kifla Maryam had heard this, he left [Walatta Petros] a happy man. Then, through the prayers of our holy beatified mother Walatta Petros, Fiqirta Kristos fell ill and passed away and found rest.

Chapter 88: Our Mother Falls Ill and Is Visited by Angels and Demons

Afterward, on the twenty-fourth of Nahaasé,[7] our holy mother Walatta Petros [herself] fell seriously ill.[8] When the disease began to affect her badly,[9] she was moved to the monks' quarters.

[1] BDJ: *əllu maḫbär* (lit., these community [members]); CR: *əm-zəntu maḫbär* [*sic*] (from this community).

[2] Lit., *wəstä ḥəṣnəyä* (in my bosom).

[3] *Fəqərtä Krəstos* (Beloved of Christ). She might possibly be Fəḫərtä Krəstos, given the similarity of their stories, which appear separated by just 30 pages. If so, this is further evidence that the stories collected in this text were told to the author Gälawdewos by different members of the community, members who remembered the details slightly differently.

[4] It is unclear whether the word "wife" (*bəʾəsit*) here indicates Fəqərtä Krəstos's current status or is used merely as an identifier. They might be living as a married couple in the community; they might have become a nun and a monk together; or Kəflä Maryam might have given her permission to become a nun.

[5] Lit., *ḫalläyät* ([she] pondered *or* [she] decided). Because the next sentence says she had made up her mind, here we translate as "to decide," whereas Ricci has *meditò* (she pondered).

[6] BJ: *wä-səʾnä mäyyəṭotä ləbba* (lit., he could not turn around her heart); CR: *wä-səʾnu mäyyəṭotä ləbba* (they could not turn around her heart).

[7] BDJ: *lä-Näḥase* (of Näḥase); CR: *lä-wärḫa Näḥase* (of the month of Näḥase). That is, on 27 August 1642.

[8] WP seems to contract the illness that had already killed so many in her community.

[9] Lit., *wä-sobä ṣänʿa laʿleha ḥəmam* (when the disease grew strong against her), here and

While she was bedridden there, angels came to visit her, bringing with them floral perfume from paradise that they drizzled into her nose. Then, when Silla Kristos visited Walatta Petros, he found her happy thanks to the [heavenly] fragrance. He asked her, "What is making you so happy?" In response, she told him that which[1] we have just related.

Then they moved Walatta Petros again, taking her [from Zambowl] to the church of Furé[2] and laying her down on a sick bed in the hut of a nun. While Walatta Petros was there, her illness became [even] worse, and she almost died. So the community began to chant the *Praise of the Beloved* at the seven [prayer] times of the day.[3] The entire community, brothers and sisters, cried out in woe and threw themselves down to thrash upon the ground.[4]

One of the old men [later] related, "While we were chanting[5] at the seventh hour,[6] I saw the icon of our Lady Mary looking like a grieving woman. When the chanting was over, I went to our holy mother Walatta Petros but found her with a radiant face, happy and rejoicing."[7]

Furthermore, Silla Kristos reported, "After the third hour [i.e., 9:00 AM] had passed, I paid a visit to our holy mother Walatta Petros. While the two of us were talking[8] among ourselves, she said to me: 'Today Satan came to me and tried to deceive me.' So I asked her: 'In what mode did he come to you?'

"Our holy mother Walatta Petros replied to me [CR omits the following]:[9] 'He came to me in the guise of a luminous man, having split the house's roof to descend.[10] In his hand, he held a censer, and from it wafted incense smoke as white as

---

(without *wä-sobä*, "when") seven sentences below, where we translate it as "her illness became [even] worse."

1 BDJ: *bä-kämä* (lit., as); CR: *zä-kämä* (what).

2 BDJ: *Fure* [ፉሬ]; CR: *Fare* [ፋሬ]. However, we suspect that Conti Rossini misread an actual *Fure* in Abb. 88.

3 BDJ: *bä-7 gizeyatä mäʿalt* (at the seven times of the day); Abb. 88: *bä-gize 7 gizeyat mäʿalt* (at the time of seven times, day [*sic*]), which CR altered to *bä-gize 7 gizeyatä mäʿalt* (at the time of seven, [from] the times of the day).

4 Lit., *angärgäru dibä mədr* (they rolled on the ground). It is traditional for family members, upon learning of a death, to hurl themselves to the ground. This was part of the reason why people were not told about a death while working or riding an animal.

5 BJ: *ənzä nətmäḥalläl* (while we were chanting); D: *ənzä yətmäḥalläl* (while he was chanting); CR: *ənzä yətmäḥallälu* (while they were chanting).

6 Either the seventh hour of the day or of the night (at 1:00 PM or 1:00 AM, respectively) or at the seventh time of prayer, in the late evening.

7 Due to Saint Mary's grieving countenance, the monk apparently had suspected that WP had passed away.

8 CR adds *rəʾinä* (we saw), which is contextually nonsensical.

9 Here CR omits about two manuscript pages of material that is not only in BDJ but also in all the other manuscripts at our disposal. Since the missing material is a folio's worth, and resumes halfway through an anecdote midsentence, we assume that either a folio got lost from Abb. 88 or that the scribe of Abb. 88 inadvertently skipped one folio while copying. We have provided the English translation in the text here, but no transliteration in the notes, since we have placed the Gəʿəz original in the appendix.

10 BJ: *mäṣʾa ḫabeyä . . . wä-wärädä śäṭiqo . . .* (lit., he came to me . . . and descended having

snow.[1] It filled my mouth and poured down into my belly. That incense's scent was such that it robbed one of clear thinking. After him came a small child with a face radiant like the sun. In his hands, the child firmly held a cross of light. He approached me to bless me,[2] but I withheld my face from him and threw myself down upon the ground. Yet there also I saw him.[3] When I turned around, there he was as well.[4] I turned right and left, but he was everywhere. Then he gave me a powerful blessing. But I asked him, "Who are you to bless me even though I don't want it?"[5] The child replied, "I am the Son of God, and the one with the censer is a [fallen] angel." ' "[6]

Others further relate that our holy mother Walatta Petros reported, "Our Lady Mary came to me and said to me, 'I would have liked to give you rest from the toil of this world [earlier], but the daily pleas of your sons and daughters roused my compassion. Therefore I let you stay [in this world] for a while [longer], for their sake.' "

When our holy mother Walatta Petros knew that the time for her passing away had drawn near, she decided that she wanted to go to Réma Island so as to be buried there.[7] So she said to the brothers, "Get a tankwa ready for me to go to Réma."[8] They[9] did as she had ordered them, and on the twenty-third of the month of Maskaram, [about a month after she had fallen ill,] she took her leave of the brothers

---

split . . .); D: *mäṣʾa . . . wä-wärädä ḫabeyä śäṭiqo* . . . (he came . . . and descended to me having split . . .).

[1] The use of a *maʿṭänt,* a metal vessel that holds hot charcoal to burn incense, is a part of most rituals of the Täwaḥədo Church. The censer represents Mary's body, the smoke Christ's sacrifice. For Satan to use this symbol was particularly terrifying.

[2] BD: *kämä yəbarəkäni* (lit., in order to bless me); J: *kämä yəbarəkänä* (in order to bless us).

[3] BJ: *wä-bä-həyyä-ni räkäbkəwwo* (yet also there I met him); D: *wä-bä-həyyä räkäbkəwwo* (yet there I met him).

[4] BJ: *bä-həyyä-ni* (there . . . as well); D: *bä-həyyä* (there).

[5] BJ: *ənzä anä i-yəfäqqəd* (lit., even though I don't want); D: *ənzä i-yəfäqqəd anä* [different word order, but identical meaning].

[6] WP tells Śəʿəlä Krəstos about her vision of the fallen angel Satan, depicted as the "luminous" Lucifer of Isaiah 14:12: "How he is fallen from heaven the Day Star, which used to rise early in the morning! He has been crushed into the earth who used to send light to all the nations!" Also, see Ezekiel 8, in which the "Son of Man" takes Ezekiel on a vision journey of the world's lawlessness, including that in the temple: "vain abominations . . . were portrayed all around. . . . And each had his censer in his hand, and the vapor of the incense was ascending." Saints are supposed to have unusual powers in detecting demons; here Christ helps her to detect Satan.

[7] DJ: *ḫalläyät təḥor Rema kämä tətqäbär wəstetu* [masc.] (lit., she decided to go to Rema so as to be buried on it [Gəʿəz: masc.]); B: *ḫalläyät təbaʾ däsetä Rema qəddəst kämä tətqäbär wəsteta* [fem.] (lit., she decided to proceed to the holy island of Rema so as to be buried on it [Gəʿəz: fem.]). MS B, written and archived at Rema Monastery, expands the plain mention of Rema Island with the praise term "holy" here and in the next sentence.

[8] DJ: *astädaləwu litä tankʷa zä-aḥawwər botu Rema* (lit., get a tankwa ready for me with which I go to Rema); B: *astädaləwu litä tankʷa zä-əbäwwəʾ botu däsetä Rema qəddəst* (lit., get a tankwa ready for me with which I proceed to the holy island of Réma).

[9] BJ: *wəʾətomu-ni* (they [emph.]); D: *wəʾətomu* (they).

and sisters, saying to them, "My illness has become grave indeed. Stay here,[1] while I go to Réma. [Farewell] until we meet again, by the will of God!"

At that time, *Abba* Za-Sillasé said to our holy mother Walatta Petros, "Behold, my knees have become weak from standing [in prayer], my throat coarse from chanting,[2] and my eyes dim from the nights and days of incense smoke,[3] [which I have suffered continuously] from when I began [in the Church][4] until now. I have no rest.[5] Since those who see and hear loathe us,[6] let it be done and enough! May we be spared[7] this death [of slow decay]!"[8]

Our holy mother Walatta Petros replied to him [CR resumes], "Do you want death to come [now]?"[9]

108 *Abba* Za-Sillasé responded,[10] "Yes, I do."[11]

So our holy mother Walatta Petros said to him,[12] "If you want it, then let it be as you have said," and right away death struck,[13] just as she had commanded it.

Chapter 89: Our Mother Prepares for Her Death

After that, Walatta Petros was lifted into a tankwa and taken [from Furé] to Réma Island because she wished to die there and to be buried in the tomb of her father and her mother, just as[14] Jacob had said to his sons when he was in Egypt, "Bury me in the tomb of my fathers."[15] Also, Joseph had said as follows to his sons, "When

1 BJ: *antəmu nəbäru* [imper.] *zəyyä* (lit., you, stay here); D: *nəbäru zəyyä antəmu* [different word order, but identical meaning].

2 Lit., *kəlaḥ* (shouting). This might refer to singing and chanting, but also to preaching and reading aloud.

3 BD: *ṭisä ʿəṭan* (incense smoke); J: *ṭis ʿəṭan* [*sic*: ungrammatical].

4 D: *əm-amä täwäṭnä* (lit., from when it began); BJ: *əm-amä täwäṭnä mot* (from when death began [*sic*]).

5 Lit., *ḫaṭaʾku ʿəräftä* (I lack rest). Also, *ʿəräft* (rest) is a euphemism for "death."

6 BJ: *asqorärunä* (loathe us); D: *asqoräruni* (loathe me). The monk was talking about "I" but switches to "we" for unclear reasons here and in the next sentence. Perhaps "us" is just a modest way of saying "me," as the MS D variant suggests.

7 Lit., *wä-yəʾtət əmənnenä* (may be taken away from us).

8 This sentence echoes Christ's prayer in Luke 22:42 and Matthew 26:39, 42. It is unclear who loathes *Abba* Zä-Śəllase.

9 Lit., *bo-nu təfäqqəd antä kämä yəqum* (do you want it [namely, death] to stand up *or* to take effect; *or*, do you want it [namely, life] to stop).

10 BDJ, Abb. 88: *wä-yəbela* (lit., and he said to her); CR altered this to *wä-əbela* (and I said to her) because WP's account of the Christ-child and Satan visiting her was missing in Abb. 88, and therefore CR here still had to assume Śəʿəlä Krəstos to be the speaker.

11 Lit., *əwwä əfäqqəd* (yes, I want).

12 BDJ, Abb. 88: *wä-təbelo* (so she said to him); CR altered this to *wä-təbeläni* (so she said to me) because, due to the missing text in Abb. 88, he had to assume Śəʿəlä Krəstos as the speaker.

13 Lit., *wä-sobeha qomä* (so right away it [namely, death] stood up *or* took effect; *or*, so right away it [namely, life] stopped).

14 BDJ: *bä-kämä* (just as); CR: *wä-kämä* (and that *or* and how).

15 Genesis 49:29. The Hebrew biblical passage references a cave not a tomb.

God will come to look after you,[1] take my bones with you [out of this place]."[2] For this reason, our blessed mother Walatta Petros said, "Take me to Réma." Having transferred her there, they lodged her in the house of one of the monks.[3]

Thereafter, she forbade people to come see her, everybody except the priests *Abba* Za-Mikaél[4] and *Abba* Silla Kristos. With her stayed [the woman] Falaseeta Kristos,[5] who read the Psalms of David [to her] at night and the Gospels during the day. After the third hour [i.e., 9:00 AM], *Abba* Silla Kristos would always pay Walatta Petros a visit to comfort her. On Thursday, the fourteenth of the month of Hidaar,[6] four days before her passing away, Silla Kristos paid her a visit, as was his custom, after the third hour had passed. He entered her room[7] and sat down before her.

Our blessed mother Walatta Petros then asked him, "Do you know who has been with me right now?"[8]

He replied to her, "How can I know? But tell me what happened!"

So our holy mother Walatta Petros[9] replied, "In this past hour,[10] the 144,000 Children of Bethlehem whom Herod killed came to me and have been playing and enjoying themselves before me![11] But just now, when you arrived, they departed from me and left."

In addition, on that day, she summoned the abbot of Réma Monastery, *Abba* Za-

[1] D: *amä ḥawwəṣo yəḥewwəṣäkəmu* [emph. construction] *əgziʾabḥer* (lit., when God will indeed come to look after you); BJ, CR: *amä ḥawwäṣä* [*sic*] *yəḥewwəṣäkəmu əgziʾabḥer* [through *ḥawwäṣa*, lit. "he looked after you," instead of emphasizing *ḥawwəṣo* added to *yəḥewwəṣäkəmu* (he will come to look after you), the entire construction becomes ungrammatical]. Already Ricci had speculated that *ḥawwäṣä* might be corrupted from an original *ḥawwəṣo*.

[2] Genesis 50:25.

[3] BDJ: *wəstä betä 1 əm-mänäkosat* (in the house of one of the monks); Abb. 88: *wəstä 1 mänäkos* (in one monk [*sic*]), which CR sensibly altered to *wəstä betä 1 mänäkos* (in the house of a monk).

[4] *Zä-Mikaʾel* (He of [the Archangel] Michael).

[5] ABCDJ: *Fälasitä Krəstos* (Pilgrim [fem.] of Christ). In the Gəʿəz, the name is gendered and immediately recognizable as feminine; the masculine equivalent would be Fälase Krəstos. The caption in MS A (see plate 19), however, says that the reading woman is not "Fälasitä Krəstos" but "Əḫətä Krəstos." Although Əḫətä Krəstos would make much more sense as WP's final female companion, perhaps she had to stay behind to minister to the community.

[6] BDJ: *10 wä-4 lä-ḫədar* (lit., the tenth and fourth of Ḫədar); CR: *8* [*sic*] *wä-4 lä-ḫədar* (the eighth and fourth of Ḫədar). The corruption in Abb. 88 is explicable as due to a two-step process: First, Gəʿəz "ten" (*ʿaśru*) likely was misheard as "twenty" (*ʿəśra*), and thereafter "twenty" (symbol: ፳) misread as "eight" (pronounced as *sämantu*, but written as ፰). This case demonstrates the role of both dictation and silent one-person copying in the manuscript reproduction process. The date of 14 Ḫədar corresponds to 20 November. WP thus had spent close to two months on her sickbed on Rema Island.

[7] BDJ: *boʾa ḫabeha* (lit., he entered toward her); CR: *boʾa* (he entered).

[8] BDJ: *yəʾəze* (right now); CR: *zä-yəbe yəʾəze* (who said [*sic*] right now).

[9] CR omits *Wälättä Ṗeṭros*.

[10] Lit., *bä-zati säʿat* (at this hour).

[11] The Täwaḥədo Church believes that the number of children Herod killed in Bethlehem is the number of the innocent mentioned in Revelation 7:3 and 14:1–4: 144,000.

Plate 19. "How the [144,000] children [of Bethlehem] came to pay her [i.e., Walatta Petros] a visit [on her deathbed], how our mother [Walatta Petros] suffered" (top), "how Eheta Kristos [sic] repeatedly read the book to our mother" (the text states that the reading woman is not Ǝḫ̮ətä Krəstos but Fälasitä Krəstos) and how *Abba* Silla Kristos came to visit her (bottom) (MS A, f. 152v © SLUB Mscr.Dresd. Eb.415.e,2).

Maryam,[1] as well as *Abba* Kifla Samaat of Gond,[2] and also all the brothers and sisters who were there. Our holy mother Walatta Petros then ordered that the *Comprehensive Book*, the *Rules for the Monks*,[3] and other books be brought,[4] and said to them, "Read!" So they read aloud all the books,[5] chapter by chapter, where the rules for monks are written down.

After this reading from the books was finished, our holy mother Walatta Petros 109
said to them, "I am clean of the blood of any person.[6] Now, behold, I'm about to go to my Lord. Everybody who wants to follow the commands of these books should do so. But he who does not take heed: his sins shall be on himself! They will be none of my concern."[7] After she had said this, she dismissed them, and they went back to their respective houses.

Chapter 90: Our Mother Is Visited by Christ and Made Archdeaconess

On the next day, Friday, *Abba* Silla Kristos again paid Walatta Petros a visit, as was his custom. He entered[8] and sat down before her. Our holy mother Walatta Petros then said to him, "Listen, let me tell you something: Today my Lord Jesus Christ came to me, wearing priestly vestments[9] and shod with shoes of gold.[10] His virgin[11] mother came with him: she sat down before me, directly opposite from me. As for

[1] BDJ: *lä-mämhər zä-Rema abba Zä-Maryam* (lit., the abbot of Rema, *Abba* Zä-Maryam); CR: *lä-mämhəran zä-Rema abba Zä-Maryam wä-lä-abba Kəflä Maryam* (the abbots of Rema, *Abba* Zä-Maryam and *Abba* Kəflä Maryam).

[2] BDJ: *wä-lä-abba Kəflä Sämaʿt zä-Gond* (as well as *Abba* Kəfla Sämaʿt of Gond); CR: *wä-lä-abba Sämaʿt zä-Gonǧi* (as well as *Abba* Sämaʿt of Gonǧi). *Kəflä Sämaʿt* (Dedicated to the Martyrs) is a senior monk from Gond, a monastery about ten miles north and five miles east of Lake Ṭana.

[3] BDJ: *mänäkosat* (monks); CR: *mänäkos* (monk).

[4] DJ: *kämä yamṣəʾu . . . wä-kaləʾanä-hi mäṣaḥəftä* [acc.] (lit., that they bring . . . and other books); B inadequately has the direct object in the nominative: *kämä yamṣəʾu . . . wä-kaləʾan-hi* [nom.] *mäṣaḥəft* [nom.]; CR with hybrid *kämä yamṣəʾu . . . wä-kaləʾan-hi* [nom.] *mäṣaḥəftä* [acc.].

[5] BDJ, Abb. 88: *kʷəllo mäṣaḥəftä* (all the books); CR expanded to *kʷəllomu mäṣaḥəftä* [identical translation], in which *kʷəllomu* now is not only semantically but also formally plural.

[6] BDJ: *nəṣəḥt anä əm-dämä kʷəllu säbʾ* (lit., I am clean from the blood of all people); CR: *ḫərit anä əm-dämä kʷəllu säbʾ* (I am chosen from the blood of all people). The Apostle Paul says the same in Acts 20:26, "I am innocent of the blood of all men." The statement in both cases is a bit puzzling since both Paul and WP had blood on their hands: WP sent more than one of her followers to their death and Paul persecuted Christians before he became a Christian himself.

[7] BDJ: *wä-albotu tälḥaf* (J: *tälḥafä* [acc.]) *əmənneyä* (lit., there is no concern from me); CR: *wä-albotu ḫaläfä əmənneyä* (they will not have come [lit., passed] from me).

[8] BDJ: *wä-boʾa ḫabeha* (lit., he entered toward her); CR: *wä-boʾa sobeha* (he entered immediately).

[9] BDJ: *ənzä yəläbbəs ləbsä mändil* (wearing priestly vestments); CR: *ənzä yəläbbəs ləbsä mängəśt* (wearing the garments of the Kingdom [of Heaven] *or* of kingship).

[10] Compare with Revelation 1:12–16.

[11] BDJ: *dəngəl* (virgin); CR omits.

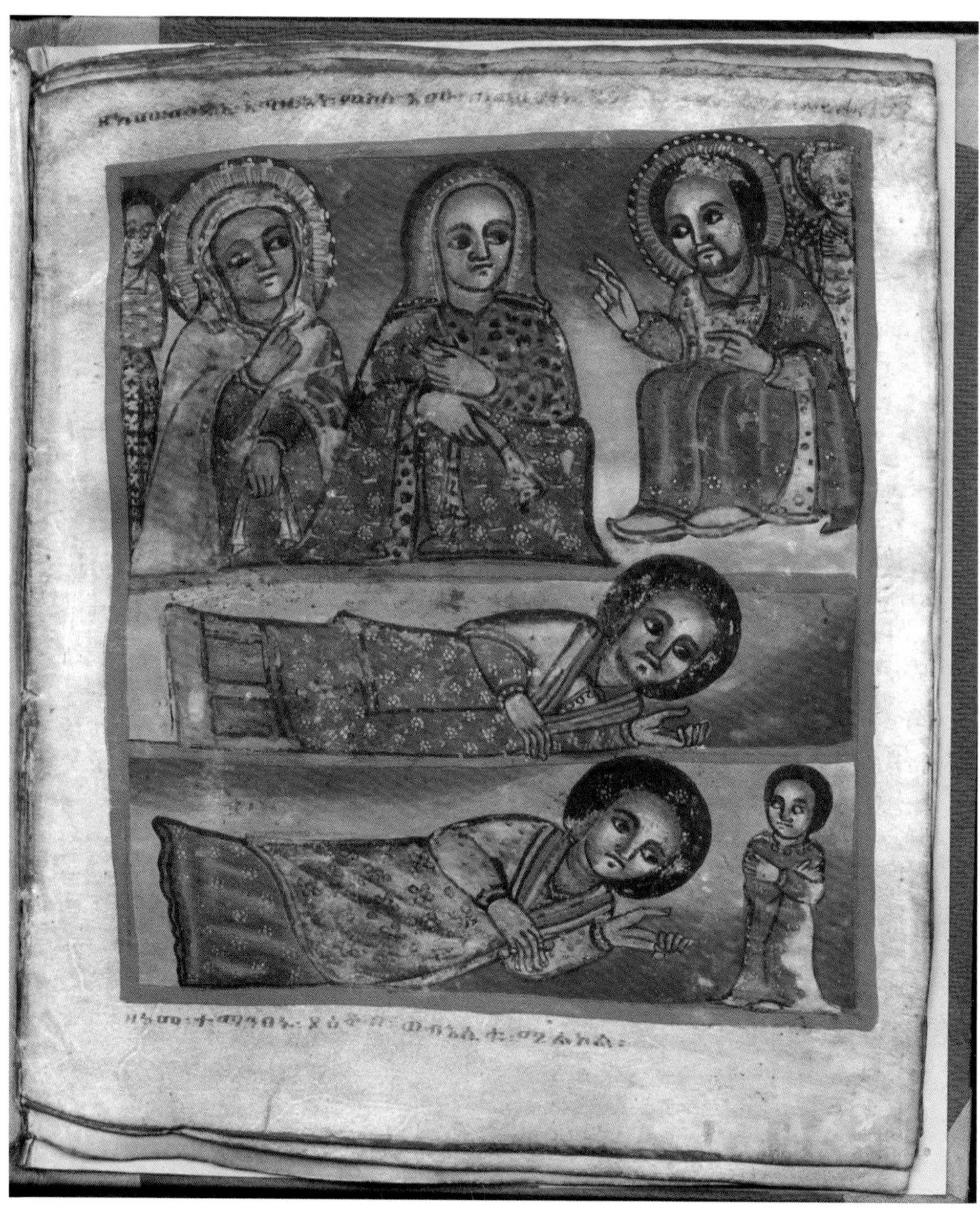

Plate 20. "How our Lord together with his mother [Mary] came" to our mother and blessed her (top) and "how Yacob [middle] and his wife Melkol [bottom] entrusted themselves" to our mother. The small figure standing to the right may be the scribe (MS A, f. 153r © SLUB Mscr.Dresd.Eb.415.e,2).

Plate 21. "How our Lord conferred on our mother Walatta Petros the rank of archdeaconess" and "Falaseeta Kristos" (*labeled in the margin*) is a witness (top). "*Abba* Silla Kristos" (*labeled in the margin*) visits with her on her deathbed (bottom) (MS D, f. 111r [109r]). Photo by Claire Bosc-Tiessé, 1997.

him, Christ leaned upon my bed and said to me three times: 'He who has toiled and endured hardship in this world will be refreshed and live forever [in the next]. Truly, he will not see perdition!' In addition, our Lord breathed on my face and blessed me.[1] So, I said to him: 'What is the meaning of this breathing [on] and blessing [of me]?' He replied to me: 'I have conferred upon you the rank of archdeaconess.' "[2]

"This is what I have heard from her," said Silla Kristos.

Chapter 91: Our Mother Appoints Eheta Kristos Her Successor

Then, on Saturday, when our holy mother Walatta Petros's illness became [still more] grave,[3] everyone gathered in the church, and made prayers and supplications.[4] Great sadness reigned on that day. Also, at the ninth hour of that day [i.e., 3:00 PM], *Abba* Za-Maryam, *Abba* Kifla Samaat, *Abba* Za-Mikaél, and *Abba* Silla Kristos assembled around Walatta Petros, and said to her, "When Moses passed away, he left Joshua in his place, who then watched over Israel.[5] Also, Elijah left behind Elisha [as his successor],[6] and so did all [great spiritual leaders] in their respective times. Therefore, you too should now tell us,[7] who will be mother in your stead and watch over your community?"

Our holy mother Walatta Petros replied to them, "In fact, I have ruled over them for many years. Didn't I time and again tell them: 'Serve!'?[8] From now on, however, they shall be free, live as they see fit, and watch over themselves. Who is the brother

[1] See John 20:22; also see Genesis 2:7; Ezekiel 37:5.

[2] BDJ, Abb. 88: *śemkuki liqä diyaqonawit*, which is grammatically problematic: while *liqä* is masculine and in the accusative, adjectival *diyaqonawit* is feminine and in the nominative. Therefore, CR altered to *śemkuki liqä diyaqonat* (I have named you head of the [male] deacons) and Ricci followed him and translated it as *ti ho conferito il grado di capo dei diaconi* (I have appointed you to the rank of the head of the deacons). Meanwhile, the caption of the relevant image in D has *liqtä diyaqonawitä* (head [fem.] deaconess [fem.]), which is grammatically correct, and which we have assumed in our translation. For a full discussion of WP's title, see "Täwaḥədo Church Monasticism" under "The Text's Religious Context."

[3] BDJ: *sobä ṣänʿa ḥəmam laʿlä əmmənä qəddəst* [B adds: *wä-burəkt*] *Wälättä Peṭros* (lit., when the illness became strong against our holy mother WP); CR: *sobä ṣänʿa ḥəmam laʿleha lä-əmmənä qəddəst Wälättä Peṭros* [different construction, but identical translation].

[4] BDJ: *ṣälotä wä-məḥəlla* (prayers and supplications); CR: *ṣälotä məḥəlla* (prayers of supplication).

[5] Deuteronomy 34:9.

[6] 1 Kings 19:19–21 and 2 Kings 2.

[7] J, CR (through emendation of Abb. 88): *nəgərənä* [substandard orthography for *nəgərinä*] (tell us); BD, Abb. 88: *nəgərəni* [substandard orthography for *nəgərini*] (tell me).

[8] In the Gəʿəz, the two verbs that we render here as "I have ruled over them" and "Serve!," namely, *qänäykəwwomu* and *täqänäyu*, are both derived from the same root *q-n-y*; *qänäykəwwomu* is in an active, *täqänäyu* (which could also be translated as "Submit!" or "Worship!") in a passive stem. The speaker Walatta Petros or the author Gälawdewos, through the use of two root-identical verbs, display stylistic skill.

or sister whom I have not personally admonished[1] and taught? Therefore, all of them are well taught and[2] competent to take care of themselves.

"I say to you, however, that I entrust Eheta Kristos to all of you.[3] Behold, I am **110**
going and leaving her, while she[4] remains behind alone. She will be disconsolate;[5] she has no other hope than me!"[6] Walatta Petros said this to them three times.[7] After she had said these things, she dismissed them. In this veiled manner, she had thus indicated to them that they should appoint Eheta Kristos [as abbess].[8]

Chapter 92: Our Mother Departs to Eternal Life

After this,[9] the suffering of our holy mother Walatta Petros became intense, and she was no longer able to speak. So, the door [to her house] was closed and nobody was allowed to enter. Everybody[10] gathered in the church in the evening, staying into the night[11] to chant supplications and say prayers.

Then, when it was midnight on the turn to Sunday, the seventeenth of the month of Hidaar,[12] Walatta Petros's soul left her body and she passed away in peace when she was fifty years old, [of which she had spent] twenty-four before her repudiation [of the world] and twenty-six after it.[13] On that day,[14] a column of light was planted that appeared to all the world.[15]

[1] BDJ: *zä-i-mäʿadkəwwomu* (whom I have not . . . admonished); CR: *zä-i-ammärkəwwomu* (whom I have not . . . instructed).

[2] CR adds *kʷəllomu* (all of them).

[3] DJ: *amaḥaṣṣənäkəmu lä-kʷəlləkəmu* (I entrust . . . to all of you]); B: *amaḥaṣänkəmu* [*sic*: ungrammatical] *lä-kʷəlləkəmu*; CR: *amaḥṣänkukəmu lä-kʷəlləkəmu* (I hereby entrust . . . to all of you]).

[4] BDJ: *wä-yəʾəti* (while she); CR: *wä-yəʾəti-ni* (but she).

[5] BDJ: *ʿənbəztä* [acc.] (disconsolate); CR: *ḥəzəntä* [acc.] (sad).

[6] See 1 Corinthians 15:19.

[7] BDJ: *wä-təbelomu kämä-zə 3 gize* (lit., she said like this to them three times); CR: *wä-təbelomu anə-ssä qänäykəwwomu kämä-zə 3 gize* (she said to them, "I have ruled over them," like this, three times).

[8] CR adds *əm-dəḫreha* (after her).

[9] BDJ: *wä-əm-dəḫrehu* (after this); CR omits, but has similar *əm-dəḫreha* (after her) at the end of the preceding paragraph.

[10] BDJ: *kʷəllu säbʾ* (everybody); CR omits.

[11] Lit., *bä-gize särk wä-bä-gize nəwam* (in the evening and at the time of sleep).

[12] CR proceeds differently from here, rearranging and adding text, which additions now appear below in the "Alternate Ending of the *Gädlä Wälättä Peṭros*."

[13] ABCDEFGHIJK, CR are in complete agreement about the date and day of her death, her age at death, and her years before and after becoming a nun, although none state an exact year of birth or death. She was twenty-four when she became a nun and then she lived for twenty-six years as a nun. She died on a Sunday on 24 November at the age of fifty, three months after she first fell ill.

[14] BDJ: *wä-bä-yəʾəti ʿəlät* (on that day); CR omits (see below, "Alternate Ending of the *Gädlä Wälättä Peṭros*").

[15] BDJ: *tätäklä . . . wä-astärʾayä wəstä kʷəllu ʿaläm* (lit., was planted . . . and appeared in

All the people from all the [Lake Tana] islands and from all the [neighboring] regions now assembled,[1] because Walatta Petros had been a mother to them in many ways. To him who had looked for instruction, she had given food and cloth-
111 ing[2] and assigned him to a teacher. The assembled wept over her[3] and wailed over her,[4] intensely and loudly, just as the children of Jacob had wept and wailed over him.[5] O such weeping and wailing![6] O such cries of woe and shouts [of pain]![7] [On that day,] nobody looked at his neighbor,[8] everybody was so grief-stricken that none could console.[9] On that day, the monks could not be distinguished from the laypeople because their monks' caps had been cast from their heads [by rolling about in grief].

After this, during the singing of psalms and hymns, Walatta Petros was shrouded in an atsf vestment, according to the rules of monastic life, and buried[10] near the church entrance; she was put in the ground without a coffin.[11]

May her intercession be with ________, with the sinful scribe, and with all of her sons and daughters who have longed for and been anxious for this *Life and Struggles* to be written down. For eternity, amen.[12]

---

all the world); CR: *tätäklä . . . wä-astärʾayä wəstä ʿaläm* (lit., was planted . . . and appeared in the world).

[1] BDJ: *wä-tägabəʾu* (now assembled); CR: *tägabəʾu* (assembled).

[2] BDJ: *sisayä wä-ləbsä* (food and clothing); CR: *sisayo wä-ləbso* (his food and his clothing).

[3] BDJ: *bäkäyəwwa* (wept over her); CR: *bäkäyu* (wept).

[4] BDJ: *wä-laḥawəwwa* (and wailed over her); CR: *wä-laḥawu* (and wailed).

[5] Genesis 50:7–11.

[6] BDJ: *o-zä-ameha bəkay wä-laḥ* (lit., o the weeping of wailing of that time); CR omits.

[7] CR adds *zä-i-konä gəmura* ([the likes of] which had never been).

[8] BDJ: *i-yəneṣṣəro 1 lä-kaləʾu* (nobody looked at his neighbor); CR: *i-yəneṣṣəro 1 lä-1* (nobody looked at anyone).

[9] BDJ: *wä-albo zä-yənazzəz* (lit., and there was none who could console); CR: *wä-albo zä-yətnazzäz* (and there was none who could find consolation).

[10] BDJ: *wä-qäbärəwwa* (lit., and they buried her); CR: *wä-wäsädəwwa wä-qäbärəwwa* (and they took her and buried her).

[11] People were buried in a coffin unless they were poor. That WP sought to be buried without one shows her humility, even in death. Although all Christians were buried near a church, or inside the church fence, only persons of great stature were buried near the church entrance, as WP was.

[12] At the end of each manuscript of the *WP gädl* (after the words "without a coffin") and before the täʾamər (miracles), scribes added a paragraph calling for blessings on particular people (for example, the scribe and commissioner) and included information about the creation of the particular manuscript. Since these paragraphs are so different, the paragraph we have translated here is just an example of how these invocations read, taken from BJ. Meanwhile, the Abb. 88 scribe went further and actually altered and added to the report on her death, including a different paragraph documented in CR (p. 110, lines 11–18), and reproduced below (up to "without a coffin"). Thus, all eleven manuscripts we checked were in agreement among themselves at the end, but differed considerably from CR.

Plate 22. How the community grieved when our mother died (MS F, photo 64, no caption).

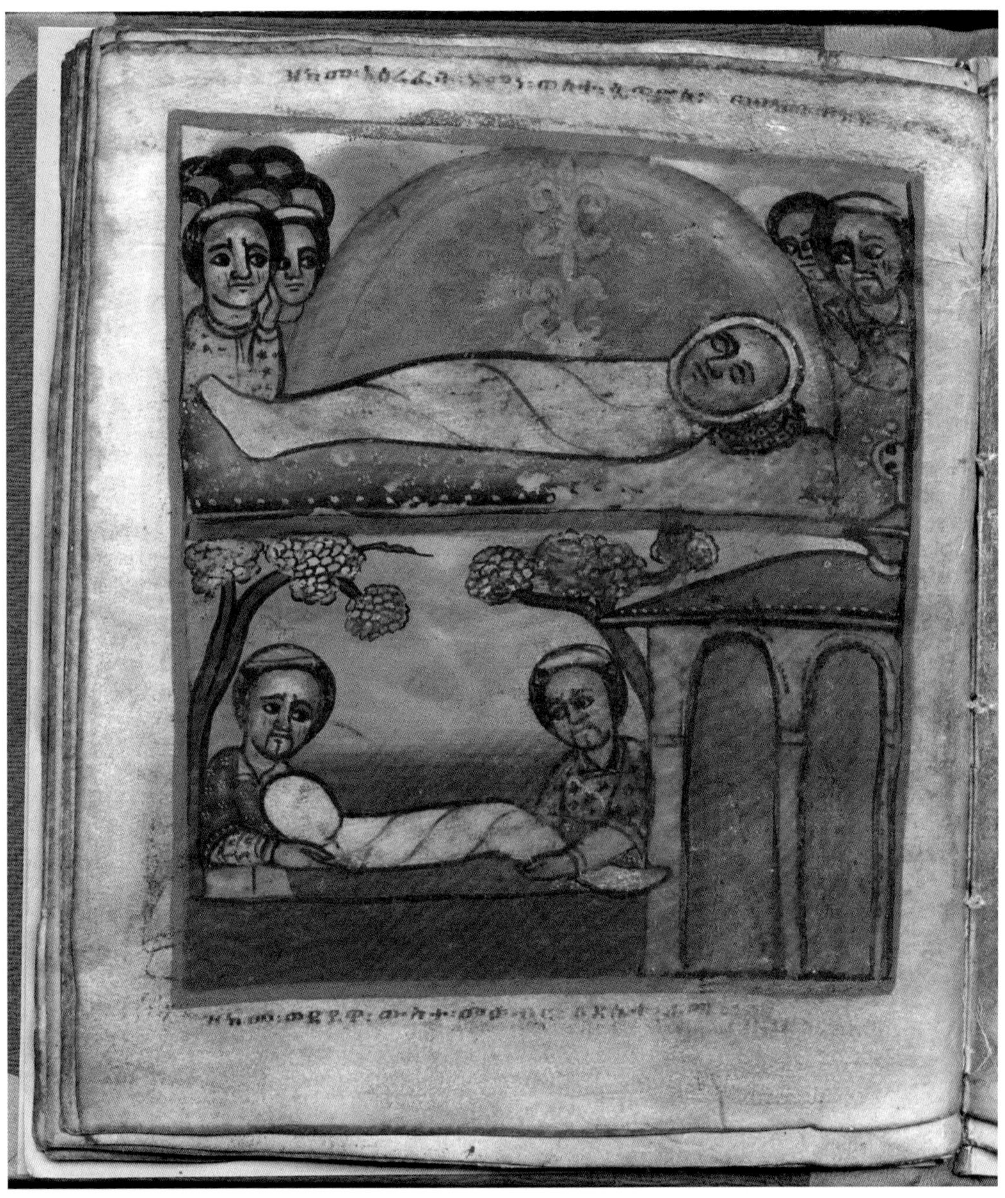

Plate 23. "How our mother Walatta Petros passed away [second part of caption illegible]," was shrouded by the grieving community (top), and "how they put her into the grave on the island of Réma" (bottom) (MS A, f. 153v © SLUB Mscr.Dresd.Eb.415.e,2).

Alternate Ending of the *Gädlä Wälättä Ṗeṭros*

Above, Abb. 88/CR inserts sentences into and alters as follows the fourth paragraph back that starts "Then when it was midnight on the turn to Sunday, the seventeenth of the month of Hidaar":

Then when it was midnight on the turn to Sunday, the seventeenth of the month of Hidaar, our Lord Jesus Christ again came [to Walatta Petros], together with his mother, our Lady Mary. Also, all the angels came, and all the prophets, and Peter and Paul and all the apostles. Furthermore, [Saint] Stephen,[1] [Saint] George,[2] [Saint] Fasiladas, and all the martyrs came;[3] and the 144,000 Children [of Bethlehem] whom Herod had killed; and all the righteous ones led by their father [Saint] Anthony. After all of them had come, Walatta Petros's soul left her body and she passed away in peace. Then a column of light was planted and appeared in the world, and she was taken away to eternal life.

As for me, her sinful servant [name erased]: Do not separate my soul from her soul![4] I implore you, [Christ], through your holy mother Mary. [Thus,] in eternity, amen.

My beatified mother Walatta Petros, I hereby entrust myself to your kidaan [with God] and to your holy prayers for your servant's soul. I implore you, [Walatta Petros,] through our Lady Mary: Do not separate my soul from yours. [Thus,] in eternity, amen, and amen. May it be thus, may it be thus.

Above, Abb. 88/CR further inserts an invocation after the last paragraph of the biography, which ends "she was put in the ground without a coffin":

She was put in the ground without a coffin. May the blessing of her assistance, the power of her holy prayer, and the mediation of her intercession for her servant [name erased] save him[5] from bitter [eternal] death and from the punishment of damnation. [Thus,] in eternity, amen.

[1] *Əsṭifanos* was a first-century deacon and the first martyr of the early Christian church. See Acts 6 and 7.

[2] *Giyorgis* is one of the most revered foreign saints in Ethiopia, celebrated on the twenty-third of every month. It is reputed that this third-century saint George of Lydda saved a young woman from a dragon, and he is usually depicted in this act.

[3] These might be the martyrs specifically associated with Saint Fasilädäs or all the Christian martyrs generally.

[4] We translate this paragraph and the next two quite differently from Ricci. Here, for instance, Ricci makes WP the sentence's agent and endows her with the power to establish the abode of the author's soul after his death: *per me, peccatore servo di lei, ella non disgiunga la mia anima dall'anima di lei: l'ho affidata a Te in nome della tua madre santa Maria* (As for me, her sinful servant, may she not separate my soul from her soul. I have entrusted it to you in the name of your holy mother Mary). The negative imperative *i-tələləya* (do not separate it [namely, my soul]) allows an interpretation as a masculine or a feminine singular, even though its reading as a masculine singular—the choice we made—is more grammatically standard.

[5] Abb. 88: *yətbezäwäwo* [*sic*: adding a 3rd-ps. masc. sg. object suffix to a passive voice verb, with incorrect morphophonology to boot] (may it be saved him [*sic*]); CR altered to

May the Lord have mercy on all of Walatta Petros's [spiritual] sons and daughters, together with [mercy on] all of us. May God jointly admit [all of] us into the Kingdom of Heaven: he who wrote this manuscript, he who commissioned it, he who reads it, he who interprets it, and he who listens to its word. [Thus,] in eternity, amen.

I have commissioned the copying of this book of your *Life and Struggles*, [Walatta Petros,] so that you may admit me to[1] your community [and] each month come to me on the day of your tazkaar with your assistance.[2]

---

yətbezäwänä, putting a first-person plural object suffix instead, but still combining a passive voice verb with an object suffix (may it be saved us [*sic*]). Our translation assumes an original *yəbezəwo* (may [it] . . . save him).

[1] CR: *əm-* (from), which does not make sense contextually.

[2] The commissioner, rather than the author Gälawdewos, speaks here, asking to participate in WP's kidan and be honored by her assistance when he holds her täzkar.

The Translation of the *Miracles of Walatta Petros* (*Täʾamərä Wälättä Ṗeṭros*)

In the name of the Father, the Son, and the Holy Spirit, one eternal God![1] We will now continue by writing down the miracles that our holy mother Walatta Petros performed; may her intercession[2] be with ______[3] for eternity, amen. 112

Listen and let us tell you about the powerful miracles[4] that happened after our holy mother Walatta Petros had passed away. We have heard them and seen them! Many took place[5] on the days of her tazkaar, from the thirtieth-day [tazkaar] until [that of] the end of the year, when[6] God's blessings descended on all the tazkaar works.[7]

On those occasions, many people would gather, in countless numbers,[8] from the islands and the monasteries,[9] from the churches and the monastic settlements,[10] from all the provinces. Among them were abbots, priests, deacons, and monks, with incense burners and crosses; there were the poor and the wretched, and the blind and the lame, because Walatta Petros's fame had spread[11] to the ends of the world.

[1] What follows are the täʾamər (miracles) that appear in ABCDEFGIJK. The täʾamər of BDJ are written in the same hand as the gädl. MS H has an entirely different set of eight miracles. MS I is unique in that it not only has the standard set of miracles but first expands this with five further miracles (written in the same hand as the standard set), then goes on to add the MS H miracles (written now in a different hand), and finally provides three further miracles in this second hand. All these extra miracles are summarized in the next section, and are not translated in this section.

[2] BDJ: *tənbələnnaha* (her intercession); CR: *ṣälota wä-bäräkätä rädʾeta* (her prayer and the blessing of her assistance).

[3] B: *fəqura Agnaṭəyos* (her beloved Ignatius); D: *fəqura* [masc.] *Ḫirutä Śəllase* (her beloved [masc.] *Ḫirutä Śəllase* [the Benevolence of the Trinity]); J: *fəqərta* [fem.] *Akrosəya* (her beloved [fem.] Akrosia); Abb. 88: [*məslä*] *gäbra* [name erased] ([with] her servant [name erased]), which CR altered to [*məsle*]*nä* ([with] us).

[4] Lit, *ḫaylä täʾamər* (the power of the miracles).

[5] Lit., *zä-yətgäbbär* (which took place [sg.]).

[6] B: *amä* (when); DJ, CR: *kämä* (so that).

[7] Lit., *laʿlä kʷəllu zä-konä gəbrä täzkar zä-yətgäbbär* (on every täzkar work that was done [and] that was performed).

[8] BDJ: *əllä albomu ḫʷəlqʷ* (lit., who had no number); CR omits here, but has this phrase at the end of the sentence, after "provinces."

[9] BDJ: *əm-däsäyat wä-əm-adbarat* (from the islands and the monasteries); CR: *əm-məśraq wä-əm-məʿrab əm-adbar* (from east and west, from the monasteries).

[10] Lit., *əm-mäkanat wä-əm-gädamat* (from parish churches and monastic settlements).

[11] BDJ: *əsmä səmuʿ wəʾətu* [D omits *wəʾətu*] *zenaha* (lit., because her story had been heard); CR: *əsmä täsämʿa zenaha* [different construction, but identical meaning].

They [all] were given plenty of food and drink, according to their ranks and needs,[1] until they were so sated that they left some of it untouched.

The First Miracle: How Our Mother Replenished the Batter

The first miracle that happened at the time [of a tazkaar]:

People relate that, in a big jar, there was a little bit of leavened batter[2]—enough for only one *enjera* bread[3]—that was left over from the tazkaar. But then that batter boiled up and filled [the jar] to its brim, spilling over. When they then poured it out, the batter did not decrease or diminish. On the contrary, it increased [anew] each day, and the jar was always full again.[4] As for the sisters who knew about the batter's secret, they kept quiet and did not speak [about it]; rather, they marveled at the great power of our holy mother Walatta Petros.

But then one of the [other] sisters,[5] who habitually spoke rashly, came and looked at the boiling up batter, shouting out, "Look at how this batter boils up!" Immediately,[6] it quieted and ceased to boil up. Then, when the sister cooking scooped some batter out, the remaining batter began to shrink and diminish[7] from its [former] abundance.[8]

Also, the sisters' small quantity of flour increased likewise, so much so that they
113 could take many measures from it, just as the prophet Elijah had done at Sarepta.[9]

[1] Lit., *bä-bä-mäṭänomu* (by their respective measures). Our translation differs here from Ricci, who translated it as *secondo il grado e l'autorità di ciascuno* (according to the degree and the authority of each).

[2] BDJ: *bəḥuʾ* (leavened batter); Abb. 88: *ḫəbuʾ* (hidden [*sic*]), which CR sensibly altered to *bəḥuʾ*.

[3] Lit., *ḫəbəst* (bread). Although there are different types of bread, only *ənǧära* has a liquid batter (rather than dough) that would likely boil over (see continuation of the text).

[4] Lit., *wä-yəträkkäb məluʾa kämahu* (and was found full, in the same manner). This miracle is reminiscent of one that WP performed while alive (making enough bread to feed everyone from a small amount of flour), and also of Christ's feeding of the multitude, a miracle that is related in Matthew 14:13–21, Mark 6:31–44, Luke 9:10–17, and John 6:5–15. In it, Christ feeds the many who have come to hear him preach with just five small barley loaves and two small fish.

[5] BDJ: *aḥatti əm-aḥat* (one of the sisters); Abb. 88: *aḫat əm-aḫat* (sisters from among the sisters), which CR sensibly altered to *əḫət əm-aḫat* (a sister from among the sisters).

[6] BDJ: *wä-bä-gizeha* (immediately); CR: *wä-wəʾətä gize* (at that moment).

[7] BDJ: *aḫazä . . . yəntəg* [subj.] (began to . . . diminish); CR: *aḫazä . . . yənättəg* [*sic*: ind. (unlike in preceding parallel "to shrink"); no translation difference].

[8] BDJ: *məlʾatu* (lit., its fullness); CR: *mələʿtu* [*sic*: an ungrammatical and contextually meaningless form].

[9] BDJ: *Säraṗta*; CR: *ʿƎraṗta* [*sic*]. Säraṗta is the city in which the Old Testament prophet Elijah received the hospitality of a poor widow whose small supply of food God kept miraculously replenishing to feed her, her son, and Elijah. 1 Kings 17:8–24.

Plate 24. Miracle 1: "How they held her tazkaar" after her death (top) and "how the batter boiled up and they scooped it up" (bottom) (MS A, f. 154r © SLUB Mscr.Dresd.Eb.415.e,2).

Plate 25. Miracle 1: "How the batter boiled up and filled up a big jar on our holy mother Walatta Petros's tazkaar day on the fortieth day after the anniversary" of her death (MS D, f. 112v [110v]). Photo by Claire Bosc-Tiessé, 1997.

But when[1] another sister spoke up too, the flour diminished likewise.[2] Truly, he who is rash to speak drives God's blessings away![3]

Regarding this, the Apostle [James] says, "Each man should be quick to listen and slow to speak."[4] In addition, the Spiritual Elder says, "The Creator keeps his distance from him who is rash to speak." Furthermore, it is said,[5] "A small load of wood is more than enough to bake a great deal of bread between evening and morning."[6]

Regarding the further blessings that happened to the bread, the stew, and the ale [at each tazkaar], they are innumerable:[7] I don't know[8] [them all]—but God knows.

[1] BDJ: *wä-sobä* (but when); CR: *wä-kaʿəbä* (then also).

[2] BDJ: *kämahu* (likewise); CR: *əmənnehu* (from him *or* from it).

[3] BDJ: *yəsäddəd* (drives . . . away); CR: *yəssäddäd* (is driven away).

[4] James 1:19.

[5] BDJ: *yəbelu* (lit., they say); CR: *yəbelo* (he says to him).

[6] BDJ: *ṣorä ʿəṣ́ nəstit fädfädät wä-akälät lä-ḫabizä ḫəbəst bəzuḫ əm-məset əskä ṣəbaḥ* (lit., a small load of wood is plentiful and sufficient for baking a lot of bread from evening to morning); CR: *ṣorä ʿəṣ́ nəstit wä-akälät lä-ḥəzb ḫəbəst bəzuḫ əm-məset əskä ṣəbaḥ* (a small load of wood, and it is enough for the people: much bread from evening till morning).

[7] BDJ: *i-yətʾammär ḫʷəllaqʷehu* (lit., their number is not known); CR: *i-yətʾemmär ḫʷəllaqʷehu* (their number is not indicated).

[8] Here our translation varies substantively from Ricci's, who translates *əndaʿi* (I don't know) as *forse* (perhaps) and connects rather than contrasts it with what follows: *forse, lo conosce il Signore* (perhaps the Lord knows it). In Täwaḥədo Church theology, however, this is unacceptable: God always knows.

All this happened through the power of our mother Walatta Petros. May her prayers and her blessing be with ________[1] for eternity, amen.

The Second Miracle: How Our Mother Healed a Monk of Paralysis

The second miracle[2] that our holy mother Walatta Petros performed; may her prayers and her blessing be with ________[3] for eternity, amen.

In Woybina,[4] there was a monk by the name of Atsqa Maryam,[5] curator of the treasury[6] of [the church of] Our Lady Mary's Resting Place.[7]

This monk[8] was afflicted by so grave and violent an illness that he became paralyzed.[9] He could not stand on his feet anymore but became bedridden, as is the rule with paralyzed people,[10] and the herbal doctors[11] could not cure him.[12] He then reflected in his heart and said [to himself], "If I went to Tsana Island, I might be cured of this grave disease and get healthy again through the help of Saint Cyriacus the Martyr."[13]

[1] B: *gäbra Agnaṭəyos* (her servant Ignatius); D: *fəqura Ḫirutä Śəllase* (her beloved Ḫirutä Śəllase); J: [*məsle*]*nä* ([with] us); Abb. 88: *gäbra* [name erased] (her servant [name erased]), which CR altered to [*məsle*]*nä* ([with] us).

[2] BDJ: *kalə˒ tä˒amər* (the second miracle); CR: *tä˒amər* (a miracle).

[3] B: *fəqura Agnaṭəyos* (her beloved Ignatius); D: *fəqura Ḫirutä Śəllase* (her beloved Ḫirutä Śəllase); J: *fəqərta* [fem.] *Akrosəya* (her beloved [fem.] Akrosia); Abb. 88: *gäbra* [name erased] (her servant [name erased]), which CR altered to [*məsle*]*nä* ([with] us).

[4] *Wäybəna* is a town near or on Lake Ṭana, not too far from Ṣana Qirqos; perhaps what is now known as Wäyna on northern Lake Ṭana. Wäybəna may be a variant spelling of the town Wäybəla mentioned in the later recorded miracles of MS I.

[5] BDJ: *˓Aṣqä Maryam* (Branch of Mary); CR: *Anqäṣä Maryam* (Gateway to Mary).

[6] Church treasuries did not hold currency but rather valuable artifacts (some associated with related saints) and manuscripts.

[7] BDJ: *zä-Mə˓rafä Əgzə˒tənä Maryam* (of [the church of] Our Lady Mary's Resting Place); CR: *zä-əm-Mə˓rafä Əgzə˒tənä Maryam* (of from [*sic*] [the church of] Our Lady Mary's Resting Place). This is further evidence for the role of dictation in the manuscript copying process: the copyist appears to have heard the initial *m* sound of *mə˓rafä* twice.

[8] BDJ: *wä-wə˒ətu mänäkos* (lit., that monk); CR: *wä-wə˒ətu mänäkos-əssä* (as for that monk, he).

[9] BDJ: *mäṣagʷə˓a* [acc.] (paralyzed); CR: *ṣənu˓a mäṣagʷə˓a* (strongly paralyzed).

[10] Lit., *kämä mäṣagʷə˓* (like a paralyzed person).

[11] Lit., *˓aqabəyanä śəray* (the custodians of the charms *or* medicines).

[12] He may have contracted poliomyelitis, or polio, a viral disease that affects the spinal cord, most commonly paralyzing the legs only. However, the illustrations of MSS A and D (see plates 26 and 27) do not show any sign that a leg has atrophied.

[13] *Qirqos* is the fourth-century Roman saint martyred at the age of three. He and his mother appear frequently in Ethiopian paintings and texts, and many Täwaḥədo churches are dedicated to him, the most famous of which was this Ṣana Qirqos on Ṣana Island.

Now he begged his fellow monks,[1] "Take me to Tsana! Perhaps I can find healing and restored health [there]. But if I die, let me be buried there."

They replied, "Very well, let your wish be fulfilled."

So they picked him up, carried him, and brought him to Tsana. There he stayed for quite a while, but did not find healing nor see his health restored. Rather, his illness got worse from day to day; he was on the verge of dying and had lost all hope of recovery.[2]

So, he again became restless and wanted to leave that place,[3] saying, "Take me home! I now understand that I will not be healed. If I die and am buried here, it will make it difficult for you to hold the tazkaar.[4] But if I die and am buried at [the Woybina church of] Our Lady Mary's Resting Place, all the tasks involved will be easy for you to do."[5]

114 When the other monks heard his request, they replied, "Very well."

So they carried him down to the lakeshore and put him in a tankwa. With him were two men who poled it. When they passed by Réma Island, the sick monk remembered that the tomb of our holy mother Walatta Petros was there. As a result, a thought crossed his mind,[6] "If you go and take refuge at the tomb of Walatta Petros, you will recover from your illness and be healed of your suffering!"[7] For this reason, he requested of the boatmen, "I pray you,[8] drop me on Réma Island so that I may visit and kiss[9] the tomb of our holy mother Walatta Petros."

"Very well," they replied, and landed their tankwa on the island shore. Then the boatmen picked him up, carried him on their shoulders to the tomb of our holy mother Walatta Petros, put him down, and withdrew from him.

[1] BDJ: *wä-sobeha säʾalomu lä-säbʾu wä-yəbelomu* (lit., now he begged his people and said to them); CR: *wä-sobeha säʾalomu wä-yəbelomu lä-säbʾu* [different word order, but identical meaning].

[2] BDJ: *täsfa ḥayw* (hope of recovery); CR: *täsfa ḥaywät* (hope of life).

[3] Lit., *wä-əm-həyyä-ni* [CR: *wä-əm-həyyä*] *kaʿəbä tähawkä* (and from there too [CR without "too"] he again became restless).

[4] BDJ: *gäbirä täzkar* (to hold the täzkar); CR: *gäbirä täzkarəyä* (to hold my täzkar).

[5] BDJ: *yəqälləl läkəmu k^{w}əllu gəbr* (lit., all the tasks will be easy for you); CR: *yəqälləl läkəmu gəbr* (the task will be easy for you).

[6] BDJ: *wä-mäṣʾa laʿlehu ḫəllinna zä-yəbəl* (lit., so on his mind came a thought which says); CR: *wä-mäṣʾa laʿlehu ḫəllinna* (so on his mind came a thought).

[7] BDJ: *lä-əmmä ḥorkä wä-tämaḥṣänkä bä-mäqabəriha lä-Wälättä Ṗeṭros täḥayyu əm-däwekä wä-tətfewwäs əm-ḥəmamakä* (if you go and take refuge at the tomb of WP, you will recover from your illness and be healed of your suffering); CR with first-person forms throughout: *lä-əmmä ḥorku wä-tämaḥṣänku bä-mäqabəriha lä-Wälättä Ṗeṭros aḥayyu əm-däweyä wä-ətfewwäs əm-ḥəmaməyä* (if I go and take refuge at the tomb of WP, I will recover from my illness and be healed of my suffering).

[8] BDJ: *əsəʾəläkəmu bəq^{w}əʿuni* (lit., I ask you, pray); CR: *əsəʾəläkəmu bəquhuni* [*sic*; a meaningless expression, which Ricci already assumed to be a corruption of *bəq^{w}əʿuni*].

[9] Lit., *kämä əsʿam* (that I may kiss) only, but with the connotation of visiting a religious site and showing one's devotion by kissing it.

Plate 26. Miracle 2: How the monk with paralysis was taken to Réma Island to be healed (MS D, f. 114r [112r]). Photo by Claire Bosc-Tiessé, 1997.

Thus, the sick man[1] remained behind alone. He kissed Walatta Petros's tomb,[2] rolled around on it, and began to implore our holy mother Walatta Petros with a steadfast heart and a strong faith, "My mother, help me and have mercy on me! I, for one, believe and trust: if you are a righteous woman, you can heal me because God will listen to your entreaty on my behalf. As the Apostle [James] says, 'The prayer of a righteous person is powerful and effective.'[3] Therefore, if your prayer is not effective, you cannot be considered a righteous woman."[4] Pleading thus, he remained there for many hours.[5]

[1] BDJ: *wəʾətu dəwəy* (lit., that sick one); CR: *dəwəy* (the sick one).

[2] B, CR: *mäqabəriha* (lit., her tomb); DJ: *mäqabərä* (the tomb).

[3] James 5:16.

[4] BDJ: *wä-əmmä akko-ssä i-konki ṣadəqtä* (lit., otherwise you are not a righteous woman); CR: *wä-əmmä akko-ssä i-konku ṣadəqä* (otherwise I am not a righteous man).

[5] BDJ: *näwwaḫa säʿatä* (lit., long hours); CR: *säʿatä* (an hour).

Plate 27. Miracle 2: "How she [i.e., our mother] healed the sick man who had sought refuge at her grave" (MS A, f. 154v © SLUB Mscr.Dresd.Eb.415.e,2).

Plate 28. Miracle 2: "How our mother Walatta Petros healed *Abba* Atsqa Maryam" (MS D, f. 115v [113v]). Photo by Claire Bosc-Tiessé, 1997.

Then our holy mother Walatta Petros accepted his prayer and promptly healed him; it was as if no illness had ever touched him.[1] Immediately, he got up and stood on his feet. After this, the boatmen[2] arrived to carry him [back]: they did not know[3] that he had become healthy again, and been cured of his illness.

He said to them, however, "Don't carry me! From now on I will walk on my own feet because my mother Walatta Petros has healed me."

When they heard his words, they marveled. But then the monk went down to the lake[shore] on his own feet, climbed into the tankwa, and [soon] arrived at the mainland. From there, he went forth carrying a big sack filled with grain, just as the paralyzed man [in the Gospel] who had carried his bed away.[4] He returned home,
praising God who had worked a miracle due to the name of our holy mother 115
Walatta Petros.

[1] "The second miracle asserts the superiority of Wälättä Ṗeṭros over Qirqos, patron saint of the famous neighbouring convent of Ṣana Qirqos. In this way, Wälättä Ṗeṭros's community asserts its independence from this monastery, whose leaders had patronized Wälättä Ṗeṭros and also had earlier rights to Qʷäraṣa" (Bosc-Tiessé 2003, 413). WP imitates Christ; see the many biblical passages, such as John 5:1–15, in which Christ heals the lame.

[2] BDJ: *əllu notəyat* (the boatmen); CR: *notəyat* (boatmen).

[3] BDJ: *i-ya'märu* (they did not know); CR: *i-ya'märəwwo* (they did not know him).

[4] See Matthew 9:1–8, in which Jesus crosses the Sea of Galilee by boat to go to another town, where men bring him a paralyzed man, lying on a mat. Christ forgives his sins, commands him to get up, take up his mat, and go home. He does so.

Plate 29. Miracle 2: "How she had healed him [i.e., the sick man] so that he could carry grain in a sack and go home" (MS A, f. 155r © SLUB Mscr.Dresd.Eb.415.e,2).

That man is still alive today and is a witness for Walatta Petros; he tells everyone about her miracles and wonders,[1] from the beginning to the end. Truly, Walatta Petros listens to him who implores her, and saves him who entrusts himself to her; may her intercession be with ________[2] for eternity, amen.

The Third Miracle: How Our Mother Protected the Fields from Locusts

The third miracle[3] that our holy mother Walatta Petros performed; may her intercession be with ________[4] for eternity, amen.

There was a man in one of the districts of Tigré, that of Tsellemt.[5] That man used to give a tenth of his grain to the monks of Waldeba, and in return, they regularly

[1] CR omits *wä-mänkəratiha* (and her wonders).

[2] B: *fəqura Agnaṭəyos wä-məslä gäbra Ḥawarya Mäsqäl* (her beloved Ignatius, and with her servant Ḥawarya Mäsqäl [the scribe of MS B]); D: *fəqura Ḫirutä Śəllase* (her beloved Ḫirutä Śəllase); J: *fəqərta Akrosəya* (her beloved Akrosia); Abb. 88: *fəqura* [name erased] (her beloved [name erased]), which CR altered to [*məsle*]*nä* ([with] us).

[3] BDJ: *śaləs tä'amər* (the third miracle); CR: *tä'amər* (a miracle).

[4] B: *fəqura Agnaṭəyos* (her beloved Ignatius); D: *fəqura Ḫirutä Śəllase* (her beloved Ḫirutä Śəllase); J: *fəqərta Akrosəya* (her beloved Akrosia); Abb. 88: *fəqura* [name erased] (her beloved [name erased]), which CR altered to [*məsle*]*nä* ([with] us).

[5] *Ṣällämt* was the same region in which WP first taught the Gospel, after leaving Waldəbba.

Plate 30. Miracle 3: How the monks advised the farmer to call on our mother (MS D, f. 117r [115r]). Photo by Claire Bosc-Tiessé, 1997.

came to see him on visiting days, according to the monastic settlement's rule. While this was the relationship between him and them, locusts swarmed over the entire province [of Tigré] and ate up all the grain that was in the fields; they left nothing untouched, neither grain nor grass.[1] As a result, a great famine arose in the entire[2] province. Many people died of hunger, and those who survived were compelled to seek refuge elsewhere.

When the monks [of Waldeba], following their established practice, came to see this man at that time, they found him deeply afflicted and near desperate because of his grain on the fields:[3] the locusts [already] surrounded them from all sides. The monks then tried to console him, saying to him, "Don't be distressed! If you listen to our counsel and accept our advice, you will have the good fortune of having your grain fields preserved and saved from the locusts."

The man replied, "Please then, [dear] monks, my fathers,[4] tell me! I will certainly do everything you command me to do.[5] I will not disobey your words."

So they advised him[6] as follows, "Consecrate your grain fields to our holy mother Walatta Petros, perform her tazkaar, have trust in her prayers, and cast your worries[7] upon her. Then she will protect your fields for you and prevent the locusts from coming and devouring any of your grain."

"Yes!" the man[8] replied, "I will do everything[9] that you have commanded me, for your advice seems right to me." He then made a vow before them that he would

[1] BDJ: *wä-i-yaträfä mantä-ni i-aklä wä-i-śäʿrä* (they left nothing untouched, neither grain nor grass); CR: *wä-i-yaträfä mantä-ni aklä wä-i-śäʿrä* (they left no grain untouched, nor the grass).

[2] BDJ: *kʷallu* (entire); CR omits.

[3] BDJ: *aklu zä-gäraht* (lit., his grain of the fields); CR: *allu zä-gäraht* (these of the fields).

[4] BDJ: *o-abäwayä mänäkosat* (lit., o my fathers, monks); CR: *abäwayä mänäkosat* (my fathers, monks).

[5] BDJ: *kʷallo gabrä zä-taʾezzazuni* (lit., every deed that you command me); Abb. 88: *kʷallo gabrä zä-azzäzäkamu* (every deed that he commanded you), which CR sensibly altered to *kʷallo gabrä zä-azzäzkamu* (every deed that you commanded).

[6] BDJ: *wä-amkärawwo* (so they advised him); CR: *wä-amäkkärawwo* (so they put him to the test).

[7] Lit., *ḫallinna* (thoughts).

[8] BDJ: *waʾatu baʾasi* (lit., that man); CR: *waʾatu* (that one).

[9] BDJ: *kʷallo* (everything); CR omits.

Plate 31. Miracle 3: "How the man [i.e., farmer] made a vow and the locusts did not approach his fields" (MS A, f. 155r © SLUB Mscr.Dresd.Eb.415.e,2).

perform the tazkaar of our holy mother Walatta Petros,[1] and set aside one of his fields for her, calling it "the field of Walatta Petros."

116 After this, the monks returned to their monastic settlement, but that man remained behind, trusting in her prayers and putting his faith in the assistance of our holy mother Walatta Petros, without entertaining even the slightest doubts. Thus, when the locusts would swarm, he would not [even] leave his house and go to his fields. Since that day on which he had made the vow, the locusts would not approach his fields but rather would fly over them because he had shielded them with the veil of our holy mother Walatta Petros's assistance. Instead, the locusts would descend onto his neighbors' fields and eat up their grain until they had devoured it all. As for his neighbors, they tried hard and ran about their fields yelling, believing that they could [thus] protect their grain and keep back the locusts—but to no avail. No one among all the inhabitants of the district [of Tsellemt] in that year harvested any grain except for that man who had put his trust in the prayers of[2] our holy mother Walatta Petros.

He alone harvested his grain, and therefore began to perform each month the tazkaar of our holy and blessed mother Walatta Petros. Furthermore, on the day on which she had passed away, on[3] the seventeenth of the month of Hidaar, he would

[1] CR omits *Wälättä Ṗeṭros.*

[2] BDJ: *zä-tä*ʾ*amänä bä-ṣälota lä-* (who had put his trust in the prayers of); CR: *bä-ṣälota lä-* (through the prayers of).

[3] BDJ: *amä* (on); CR: *əm-* (from), which already Ricci assumed to result from the corruption of an original *amä.*

Plate 32. Miracle 3: "How our mother Walatta Petros, in the land of Tsellemt, saved from locusts the fields of a man who celebrated her tazkaar" (MS D, f. 117r [115r]). Photo by Claire Bosc-Tiessé, 1997.

assemble the poor and wretched. He would have them sit down at his table, slaughter a sheep for them and give them[1] food and drink, feeding them until they were sated and happy. From that time onward, that man loved our holy mother Walatta Petros, always celebrating her tazkaar and never ceasing to speak her name;[2] may her intercession be with __________[3] for eternity, amen.

The Fourth Miracle: How Our Mother Healed the Boy and Replenished the Ale

The fourth miracle[4] that was performed by our holy mother Walatta Petros; may her intercession[5] be with ________[6] for eternity, amen.

[1] BDJ: *wä-yəhubomu* (and give them); Abb. 88: *wähabomu* (he gave them), which CR expanded to *wä-wähabomu* (and he gave them).

[2] Lit., *wä-i-yaṣärrəʿ əm-afuhu zäkkərotä səma* (and not abandoning from his mouth the mentioning of her name).

[3] B: *gäbra Agnaṭəyos* (her servant Ignatius); D: *fəqura Ḫirutä Śəllase* (her beloved Ḫirutä Śəllase); J: [*məsle*]*nä* ([with] us); Abb. 88: *fəqura* [name erased] (her beloved [name erased]), which CR altered to [*məsle*]*nä* ([with] us).

[4] BDJ: *rabəʿ täʾamər* (the fourth miracle); CR: *täʾamər* (a miracle).

[5] DJ: *tənbələnnaha* (her intercession); B: *ṣälota wä-bäräkäta* (her prayer and her blessing); Abb. 88 omits, which made CR insert *ṣälota* (her prayer).

[6] B: *fəqura Agnaṭəyos* (her beloved Ignatius); D: *fəqura Ḫirutä Śəllase* (her beloved Ḫirutä

In the land of Daq Island,[1] there was a woman who loved our holy mother Walatta Petros and [privately] performed her tazkaar [every month]. Now, when that woman's son, a small boy, became so gravely ill that he was close to death, she became grief-stricken, but could do nothing. So she collected herself and with a steadfast heart and a strong faith appealed to our holy mother Walatta Petros, mak-
117 ing a vow, "My holy mother Walatta Petros, if you relieve me of my sadness by healing this son of mine from his illness and saving him from death, I will become your maidservant. Every year I will [publicly] perform your tazkaar, as best my means allow."[2] When our holy mother Walatta Petros saw the strength of the woman's faith, as well her great sadness and the sorrow of her heart, Walatta Petros had pity on her, accepted her prayer, and healed her son from his illness.

From that time on, that woman began to host with great joy an [annual] tazkaar feast for our holy mother Walatta Petros, praising our mother's abundant goodness,[3] because she had performed a great miracle for her, saving her son from death. Every year, when the day of our holy mother Walatta Petros's feast approached, the woman did as follows:[4] Inside her house she stored one jar filled with ale, only one; there was no other except it. Her intention was to distribute the ale to the poor in honor of our holy mother Walatta Petros's name.

Now, also on that day, the abbot of Daga Monastery arrived [at Daq] from the royal court, after [a stay there of] quite some time.[5] He stopped over near that woman's house, with a neighbor of hers,[6] because that neighbor was the chief of

---

Śəllase); J: *fəqərta Akrosəya* (her beloved Akrosia); Abb. 88: *fəqura* [name erased] (her beloved [name erased]), which CR altered to [*məsle*]*nä* ([with] us).

[1] Lit., *wəstä bəḥerä Däq* (in the country of Däq). Däq is the largest island in Lake Ṭana (ten square miles), with several villages.

[2] Monthly celebrations of WP's täzkar were small individual or domestic events, while the annual täzkar was a large public occasion with a feast. As part of honoring her, devotees would not go to work on the seventeenth day of any month.

[3] BDJ: *ənzä täʾakkʷət* [substandard orthography for *taʾakkʷət*] *śənnä ḫiruta lä-əmmənä* (praising our mother's abundant goodness); CR: *ənzä täʾakkʷəto* [substandard orthography for *taʾakkʷəto*] *śənnä ḫiruta lä-əmmənä qəddəst* [ungrammatical through the -*o* object suffix on *ənzä täʾakkwət*, "praising"].

[4] CR: *wä-ənzä kämä-zə təgäbbər yəʾəti bəʾəsit sobä alṣäqä wä-qärbä ʿəlätä bäʿala lä-əmmənä qəddəst Wälättä Peṭros zä-ʿamät əm-ʿamät* (lit., the woman doing like this, when the day of our holy mother WP's feast approached and came near, from year to year); BDJ: *wä-ənzä kämä-zə təgäbbər yəʾəti bəʾəsit sobä alṣäqä wä-qärbä ʿəlätä bäʿala lä-əmmənä qəddəst Wälättä Peṭros. Bä-1 ʿamät əm-ʿamätat* (the woman doing like this, when the day of our holy mother WP's feast approached and came near. In one year among the years). The CR variant is semantically and syntactically superior here: in BDJ the final temporal subordinate clause is never completed with a main clause.

[5] BDJ: *əmdəḫrä gʷənduy mäwaʿel* (after quite some time); CR: *wä-əmdəḫrä gʷənduy mäwaʿel* [through the initial *wä*-, the otherwise identical CR text creates a different syntactic division, starting a new sentence, "After quite some time, he stopped over"]. One has social obligations toward those who have been away for some time. Daga and Däq are islands less than half a mile apart, but Däq is large, while Daga is very small.

[6] BDJ: *wəstä gorä beta* (lit., with a neighbor to her house); CR: *wəstä betä goräbet* [Amharicizing] (in the house of a neighbor).

Plate 33. Miracle 4: "How our mother Walatta Petros healed the son of the woman who trusted in her prayer" (MS D, f. 118r [116r]). Photo by Claire Bosc-Tiessé, 1997.

that town. The woman then went to pay the abbot her respects. When she returned home, she began to worry,[1] anxious[2] that she did not have any ale to offer him except that single jar she had set aside for the tazkaar of our holy mother Walatta Petros. For long hours, she tried to come to a decision in her mind about which of

[1] BJ: *wä-əmdəḫrä-zə tämäyṭät wəstä beta wä-aḫazät tətäkkəz* (lit., thereafter she returned home and began to worry); D, CR: *wä-əmdəḫrä tämäyṭät wəstä beta wä-aḫazät tətäkkəz* (after she had returned home she began to worry).

[2] BDJ: *bä-ʿabiy astäḥaməmo* (lit., with great concern); CR: *bä-ʿabiy astäḥamimo* [*sic*: converb instead of verbal noun].

Plate 34. Miracle 4: "How our holy mother Walatta Petros turned one jar of ale into two jars of ale" (MS D, f. 119v [117v]). Photo by Claire Bosc-Tiessé, 1997.

the two things was right for her to do, whether to give the jar[1] to the abbot or to the poor in honor of the name of our holy mother Walatta Petros.[2]

She reasoned as follows, "If I give this ale [jar] to the poor and withhold it from the abbot,[3] he will be unhappy with me. However, if I give it to the abbot and[4] withhold it from the poor, my holy mother Walatta Petros will be unhappy with me: I will have failed to perform[5] her tazkaar and to observe the vow that I made to her."

[1] BDJ: *əm-wəhib* (lit., whether to give); CR: *wä-əm-wəhib* (namely, whether to give).

[2] There were no prohibitions forbidding monks from drinking alcohol.

[3] BDJ: *wä-käla'kəwwo lä-mämhər* (lit., and withhold from the abbot); CR: *wä-käla'ku lä-mämhərəyä* [*sic*] (and withhold from my abbot).

[4] BDJ: *wähabku lä-mämhər wä-* (I give to the abbot and); CR omits.

[5] BDJ: *aṣraʿku* (I will have failed to perform); CR: *asraʿku* [*sic*], from an undocumented verb *asrəʿa*. This variant is evidence for the role of dictation in the process of manuscript

She did not know which of these two courses of action[1] to choose. As the two
thoughts competed and fought with each other in her heart, the one that said "Give
it to the abbot" prevailed for two reasons. One was his lordly status,[2] the other was 118
that he was a traveler [to whom hospitality was due].

Now the woman summoned her maidservant, ordering her to fetch[3] the ale [jar] from the pantry[4] and take it to the abbot. But when the maidservant entered [the pantry], she found two jars full of ale.[5]

So she left[6] [the pantry] and returned to her mistress, asking her, "Which one of the two jars do you want me[7] to take?"

Her mistress replied, "Where would a second jar have come from? I certainly put [only] one [there.] Are you telling the truth[8] or just making fun of me?"[9]

The maidservant replied, "I am telling the truth, I am not making fun of you![10] Order me to bring whichever of the two that you want."

So the lady of the house indignantly arose, went to the pantry[11]—and found two jars, just as the maidservant had said. She now marveled at the great power of our holy mother Walatta Petros, who had performed a prodigious miracle for her, relieving her of her distress. She then took one jar of ale and gave it to the abbot, while she gave the other one to the poor in honor of the name of our holy mother Walatta Petros.

Do you see the great power of our holy mother Walatta Petros, who worked this miracle,[12] the like of which had never been before and shall never be again? She caused another jar to be born[13] from the first one, complete with the ale, just as Eve was born from the side of Adam, complete with soul and body.[14] How many mira-

---

reproduction since the acoustic difference between *aṣraʿku* and *asraʿku* is comparatively small, whereas ፀ *ṣ* and ሰ *s* are quite different optically in fidäl.

1 BDJ: *2 gəbr* (lit., two deeds); CR: *2 nägär* (two things).

2 BDJ: *1 bäʾəntä əgziʾənnahu* (lit., one, because of his lordly status); CR omits.

3 BDJ: *kämä tamṣəʾ* (lit., that she bring); CR: *kämä tawṣəʾ* (that she bring out).

4 Lit., *əm-wəsaṭe bet* (from the inner part of the house). Wealthier homes had a section behind an inner wall where utensils, grain, and other provisions were stored and some cooking happened.

5 BDJ: *zä-məluʾ wəsteton* [fem. pl.] *säwa* (lit., into which [fem. pl.] säwa had been filled); CR: *zä-məluʾ wəstetu* [*sic*: masc. sg.] *säwa.*

6 BDJ: *wäṣʾat* (left); CR: *mäṣʾat* (came).

7 Lit., *azzäzkəni* [substandard orthography for *azzäzkini*] (did you order me).

8 CR adds *həyyä* (there).

9 BDJ: *wä-mimmä təssalläqəni-nu* [substandard orthography for *təssalläqini-nu*] *anti* (lit., or are you making fun of me); CR: *wä-mimmä təssalläqi-nu. Ayte hallo* (or are you being funny? Which one [lit., where] is it).

10 BDJ: *i-yəssalläqäki* (I am not making fun of you); Abb. 88: *i-yəssalläkki* [ungrammatical], which CR altered to *i-yəssalläqqi* [still ungrammatical].

11 Lit., *wəsaṭe bet* (the inner part of the house).

12 BDJ: *zäntä täʾamərä* (this miracle); CR: *täʾamərä* (a miracle).

13 BDJ: *awlädät qäśutä* [B omits *qäśutä* (jar)] (lit., she let a jar be born); Abb. 88: *äw wälädät qäśut* [*sic*: nom.] (or did she give birth to a jar), which CR altered to *äw täwäldät qäśutä* [*sic*: acc.] (or was another jar born).

14 See Genesis 2:20–24.

Plate 35. Miracle 4: "How a woman's son fell sick, [she pledged] to celebrate her tazkaar, and how our mother Walatta Petros healed him," and how "there was one jar of ale for our mother Walatta Petros's tazkaar in the house of a certain woman; a guest arrived; she was distressed: she lacked [ale] to give him but [then] found a second jar" (MS A, f. 155v © SLUB Mscr.Dresd.Eb.415.e,2).

cles of our holy mother Walatta Petros we can narrate! May her prayers and her blessing be with __________[1] for eternity, amen.

The Fifth Miracle: How Our Mother Recovered the Lost Candles

The fifth miracle[2] that our holy mother Walatta Petros performed; may her intercession be with ________[3] for eternity, amen.

A woman came from a faraway region, carrying[4] wax candles to present as an offering[5] to the church [of Walatta Petros's community], in honor of the name of our holy mother Walatta Petros on the day of her feast,[6] on the seventeenth of the month of Hidaar. While that woman was on her way, she rested in the shade of a tree, exhausted by travel and the heat of the day.[7] But then she forgot the candles
under the tree where she had rested, setting out[8] from there and continuing on her 119
way. Later, on the road, when her clear thinking returned and her absentmindedness left her, she remembered the candles. So, the woman turned back, distressed and worried, and came to the tree where she had rested before. She looked for the candles[9] but could not find them.

Now she began to argue with our holy mother Walatta Petros, "Why are you treating me like this and humiliating me? Why have you converted my joy into worry and distress?[10] Are you saying: 'My head shall not be anointed with the ointment of sinners, and I will not receive[11] an offering from the hands of a sinful woman'?[12] But does not your Lord[13] say: 'I have not come to call the righteous, but

[1] B: *fəqura Agnaṭəyos* (her beloved Ignatius); D: *fəqura Ḫirutä Śəllase* (her beloved Ḫirutä Śəllase); J: *fəqərta Akrosəya* (her beloved Akrosia); Abb. 88: *fəqura* [name erased] (her beloved [name erased]), which CR altered to [*məsle*]*nä* ([with] us).

[2] BDJ: *ḫaməs täʾamər* (the fifth miracle); CR: *täʾamər* (a miracle).

[3] B: *gäbra Agnaṭəyos* (her servant Ignatius); D: *fəqura Ḫirutä Śəllase* (her beloved Ḫirutä Śəllase); J: *fəqərta Akrosəya* (her beloved Akrosia); Abb. 88: *fəqura* [name erased] (her beloved [name erased]), which CR altered to [*məsle*]*nä* ([with] us).

[4] BDJ: *ənzä təṣäwwər* (carrying); CR: *əntä təṣäwwər* (who carried).

[5] BDJ: *kämä tähab* [subj.] *amməḫa* [D omits *amməḫa*] (lit., in order to give as an offering); CR: *kämä təhub* [*sic*: ind.] (in order to give).

[6] BDJ: *bä-ʿəlätä bäʿala* (on the day of her feast); CR: *bä-ʿəlätä täzkara* (on the day of her täzkar).

[7] BDJ: *waʿyä mäʿalt* (the heat of the day); CR: *waʿyä ṣ́äḥay* (the heat of the sun).

[8] BDJ: *wä-əmzə tänśəʾat* (lit., then she set out); Abb. 88: *wä-əm-zəntu tänśəʾat* (from this [place] she set out), which CR altered to *wä-əmdəḫrä zəntu tänśəʾat* (after this she set out).

[9] BDJ: *ḫaśäśäsäto lä-wəʾətu maḫtot* (she looked for the candles); CR: *ḫaśäśäsäto lä-wəʾətu* (she looked for them).

[10] BDJ: *ḥazän wä-təkkaz* (worry and distress); CR: *təkkaz* (distress).

[11] BDJ: *wä-i-yətwekkäf* (and I will not receive); CR: *wä-i-yətwäkkäf* (and I may not receive).

[12] This is not a direct biblical quote, but a reference to Luke 7:36–50, regarding the hostile attitude of the Pharisees toward the sinful woman who anoints Christ with perfume.

[13] Lit., *amlakəki* (your Lord). As the woman doesn't say "our Lord," perhaps she is not a Christian, but from one of the local ethnic groups that had not been Christianized, like the

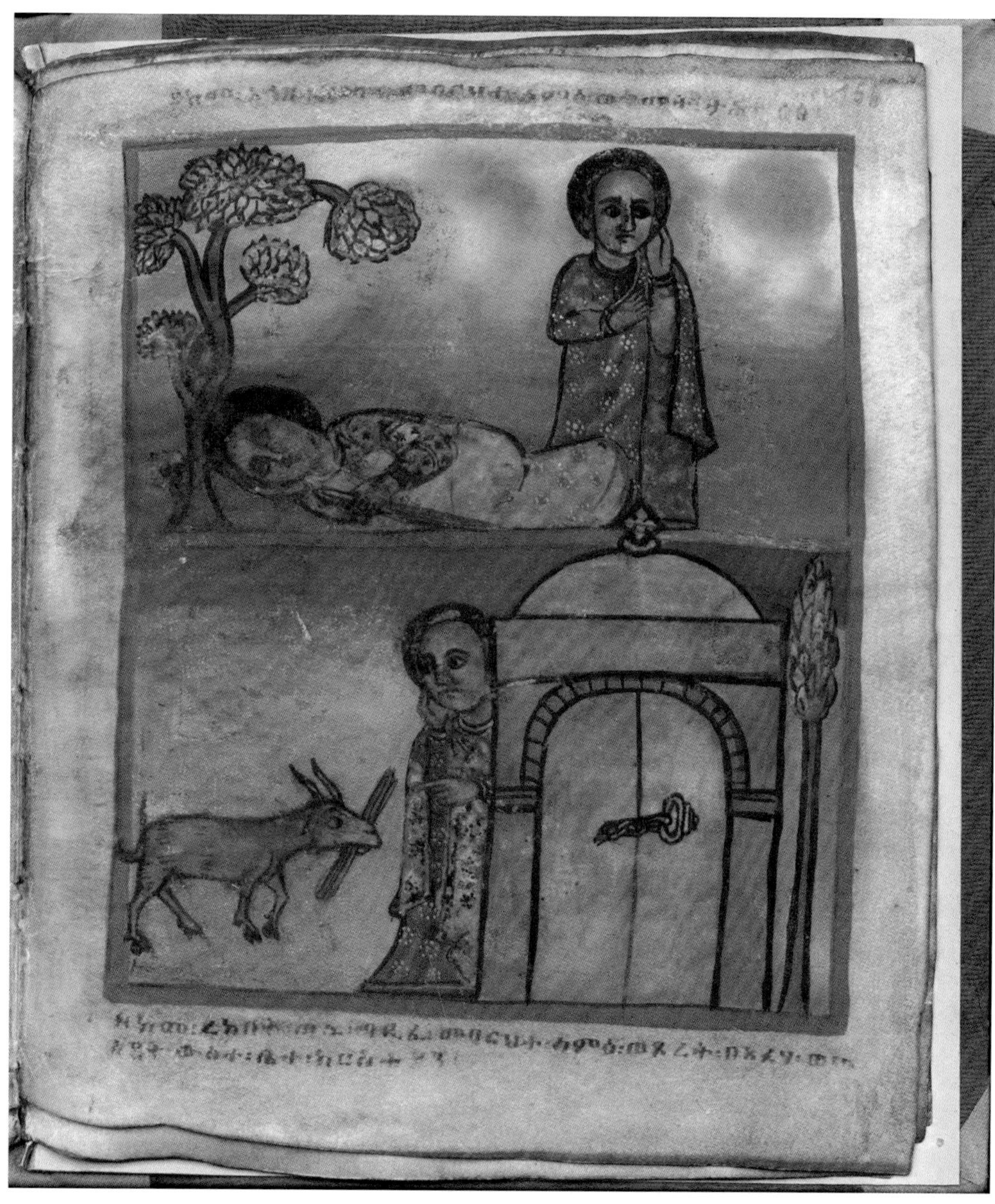

Plate 36. Miracle 5: "How she brought an offering of wax candles but then fell asleep under a tree" (top) and "how a goat found the left-behind wax candles, carried them in her mouth, and brought them to the church" (bottom) (MS A, f. 156r © SLUB Mscr.Dresd.Eb.415.e,2).

Plate 37. Miracle 5: "How a goat brought wax candles" (MS D, f. 121r [119r]). Photo by Claire Bosc-Tiessé, 1997.

the sinners'?"[1] Having said this, the woman turned back on her journey, [heading home,] but now traveling with a divided heart.

Then, once again, she rested under a tree when she was unable to continue traveling because she was feeling dejected.

Meanwhile, our holy and blessed mother Walatta Petros had ordered a nanny goat to pick up the candles that had gone missing and to go give them to the sad woman. So the goat went to the woman, carrying the candles in its mouth. It came to where the woman was and handed the candles over to her, just like a person handing [something] over to another! Then the goat trotted back the way it had come, straying neither to the right nor to the left. As for the woman, she now was incredibly happy,[2] praising God and glorifying our holy mother Walatta Petros,

Wäyṭo. Powerful saints might be appealed to regardless of faith. Or, she is reminding WP of her obligation to follow in the footsteps of the God to whom she is devoted.

[1] Luke 5:32.

[2] BDJ: *täfäśśəḥat ʿabiyä fəśśəḥa* (lit., she was happy with great happiness); CR: *täfäśśəḥat ʿabiyä* (she was greatly happy).

the wonder-worker.[1] The woman rose up, set out [again], and arrived at the church of [Walatta Petros's] community. There she offered the candles and told this miracle to everybody.

As the Psalter says, "I have announced your righteousness to a large community."[2] Therefore, come, all you assembled, let us celebrate and proclaim our admiration for our holy and beatified mother Walatta Petros, so that she may intercede on our behalf with him who loves all human beings, Jesus Christ, so that he may grant us the grace of his clemency and mercy, due to the abundance of his goodness and the prayers of our Lady Mary, his mother. May her[3] intercession be with __________[4] for eternity, amen.

The Sixth Miracle: How Our Mother Rescued the Singing Monk from the Storm

120 The sixth miracle[5] that our holy mother Walatta Petros performed; may her intercession be with __________[6] for eternity, amen.

When Yamaana Kristos, the abbot, had passed away, a monk came from Ghirarya[7] to inform Walatta Petros's community about the abbot's death. When the monk arrived at the community, he informed them of the news, and they wept over Yamaana Kristos's death and lamented him.[8] The monk then continued on his way

[1] BDJ: *gäbaritä täʾamər* (the wonder-worker); CR omits.

[2] BDJ: *bä-kämä yəbe zenoku ṣədqäkä lä-maḫbär ʿabiy* (lit., as it said, "I have announced your righteousness to a large community"); CR: *bä-kämä yəbe Enok ṣədqəkä lä-maḫbär ʿabiy* (as Enoch said, "Your righteousness is for a large community"). Psalm 40:9–10. The later scribe attributes the quote to Enoch, even though the quote appears in Psalms and does not appear in any known Enoch text, thereby revealing the esteem in which Enoch was held. The *Mäṣḥafä Henok* (Book of Enoch) is a pre-Christian Jewish apocalyptic text that survived as a whole only in the Gəʿəz translation. Cited in the New Testament, it was thought lost until James Bruce brought it back from Ethiopia in the late 1770s. It played an important role in Täwaḥədo Church thought.

[3] Grammatically, it is unclear whether the "her" interceding is the Holy Virgin or WP. But since WP has customarily appeared in such miracle final requests for intercession, the reference is probably to WP.

[4] B: *fəqura Agnaṭəyos wä-məslä gäbra Ḥawarya Mäsqäl* (her beloved Ignatius and her servant Ḥawarya Mäsqäl); D: *fəqura Ḫirutä Śəllase* (her beloved Ḫirutä Śəllase); J: *fəqərtu* [*sic*] *Akrosəya* (his [*sic*] beloved Akrosia); Abb. 88: *fəqura* [name erased] (her beloved [name erased]), which CR altered to [*məsle*]*nä* ([with] us).

[5] BDJ: *sadəs täʾamər* (the sixth miracle); CR: *täʾamər* (a miracle).

[6] B: *fəqura Agnaṭəyos* (her beloved Ignatius); D: *fəqura Ḫirutä Śəllase* (her beloved Ḫirutä Śəllase); J: *fəqərta Akrosəya* (her beloved Akrosia); Abb. 88: *fəqura* [name erased] (her beloved [name erased]), which CR altered to [*məsle*]*nä* ([with] us).

[7] *Gərarya* is a monastery established by Täklä Haymanot around 1284, according to tradition, about thirty miles due east of Ṣana Qirqos.

[8] BDJ: *wä-laḥawəwwo* (and [they] lamented him); Abb. 88: *wä-halläwəwwo* [*sic*; *halläwä* means "to be," but here carries an object suffix as if it were transitive]; CR sensibly emended to *wä-lähawəwwo* [with twice substandard orthography, though].

and went to Gazhigé.[1] He circulated among all the monastic settlements [in the southern Lake Tana area], informing them of Yamaana Kristos's death, and then turned back [to Ghirarya].

While he was on his way back, he came to Furé. There he set out onto the lake in a small tankwa. With him was a man who sat at the bow and poled it for him. As for the monk, he[2] was not used to the lake and had no understanding of the behavior of a tankwa. Therefore, he was scared and trembled; he believed that he would drown due to the tankwa's tiny size.

The man who poled it[3] tried to encourage him, saying, "Don't be afraid!" Meanwhile, he did not have another pole[4] with him, only the one that he used.

Traveling on the tankwa like this, they left Zagé [Peninsula] some distance behind. But then they had the misfortune of a strong wind coming up, one that blew toward Abbabeet, and thus turned the tankwa in another direction. Now the monk was afraid and trembled; he almost fainted[5] and expected to meet death in the depths of the lake. He clutched the tankwa with both his hands.[6]

Suddenly, the fierce wind[7] tore the pole from the boatman's hands. So, he exclaimed to the monk, "Now we are lost! Look! The wind has ripped away the pole, and I don't have another one with which to steer."

So the monk burst into cries of woe and shouted out, "Lord of Walatta Petros, help me and have mercy on me!" In addition, with a loud voice he began singing the [Salam] hymn dedicated to her:

> Hail to you, Walatta Petros, Garden [of Paradise]! Enclosed by sweet fragrance,
> you are the doves' shady shelter[8] from the burning heat of affliction
> that rules[9] in the world.[10]

and so on until the [hymn's] end.

[1] BJ: *Gažəge*; CR: *Gažäge*; D: *Gažän* is an area about twenty miles to the west of mid–Lake Ṭana. It is north of Zäge and Fure and somewhere near Abbabit. The Gəlgäl Abbay River is its southern boundary and Ḫirutä Amlak, follower of Saint Iyäsus Moʾa, proselytized there in the thirteenth century.

[2] BDJ: *wä-wəʾətu-ssä bəʾəsi mänäkos* (lit., that monk-man for his part); CR: *wä-wəʾətu bəʾəsi mänäkos* (that monk-man).

[3] CR adds *lä-mänäkos* (for the monk).

[4] *Tərkəza*, variants *tərkəza* and *tərəkkəza* (oar or punting pole), is an Amharic loanword.

[5] Lit., *wä-qärbät näfsu lä-wäṣiʾ* (his soul came close to leaving).

[6] BDJ: *wä-aḫazo lä-tankʷa bä-kəlʾehon ədäwihu* (he clutched the tankwa with both his hands); CR: *wä-aḫazä* [*sic*] *lä-tankʷa bä-kəlʾe* [*sic*] *ədäwihu* [ungrammatical and substandard, respectively, but no translation difference].

[7] BDJ: *wä-wəʾətu-ssä näfas ḫayyal* (lit., then the powerful wind); CR: *wä-wəʾətä gize tänśəʾa näfas ḫayyal* (at that moment a powerful gust blew). In addition, Conti Rossini inserted a *wä-* (and) after this phrase to connect his text properly with what follows.

[8] When Christ grants WP her kidan, he tells her that "many people will gather around you, from east and west. They will be pure doves, and they will benefit [from you] for the salvation of their souls."

[9] DJ: *zä-säfänä* [masc.] (that rules); CR: *zä-säfänät* [fem., with identical translation; also in the full poem (documented in CEFJ) we find both the masc. and the fem. verb forms, with J there again having masc. *säfänä*]; B omits this entire line.

[10] See the full sälam hymn under "The Translation of the Poem *Hail to Walatta Petros* (*Sälamta Wälättä Peṭros*)" in this volume.

Before he had even finished his prayer, the wind calmed and the lake's waves subsided[1] because our holy mother Walatta Petros had right away admonished them when that monk had prayed that hymn dedicated to her, singing it with great
121 harmony. As for the tankwa, it spontaneously returned [to its original course], without anyone steering it or actively returning it. [Indeed,] it followed a better course than before, gliding along on the water without anyone poling, and quickly, in the blink of an eye, brought them to their desired landing place.

After they had disembarked onto the shore, the monk praised God and gave thanks to our holy mother Walatta Petros, who[2] had saved him from drowning and delivered him from death. Then, he said in his heart, "Behold,[3] I had abandoned my remaining years at the gates of the realm of the dead[4] and [was sure that I] would not see any of my relatives again!"

After his escape from the lake, the monk returned to the community of our holy mother Walatta Petros and told them[5] this miracle, from beginning to end. When they heard it, they declared that our holy mother Walatta Petros was truly blessed and addressed her as follows, "Great is the honor that you have been given,[6] our holy mother Walatta Petros! For in the water as well as on dry land you have the power to save the soul that cries out to you!"[7]

Then they turned [their attention] back to that monk and asked him, "Please tell us [again] how you were saved and escaped from drowning!"

The monk replied, "While I was utterly terrified, I remembered our holy mother Walatta Petros and with a loud voice began to sing the hymn dedicated to her. Immediately, the wind abated[8] and the lake calmed."

They said to him, "Please, sing[9] for us in the same way that you sang on the lake!"

He replied "Very well," and sang before them in a harmonious voice. Then the

[1] BDJ: *hadʾa* (subsided); CR: *ahdəʾa* (it [namely, the wind] made subside).

[2] BDJ: *zä-* (who); CR: *wä-* (and), which Ricci had already assumed to result from corruption of an original *zä-*.

[3] B: *yəbe bä-ləbbu nahu* (he said in his heart, "Behold"); DJ, CR: *yəbe bä-ləbbunnahu* (he said in his reasoning). The minority MS B is qualitatively superior, and is either the text's original reading or an improvement of it.

[4] Lit., *siʾol*, originally from Hebrew *šəʾol*, meaning realm of the dead or hell.

[5] BDJ: *wä-nägäromu* (and told them); *wä-nägäro* (and told it [viz., the community]).

[6] BDJ: *zä-täwəhbä läki* (lit., that has been given to you); CR: *zä-täwəhbä laki* [*sic*: *laki* is a nonexistent form].

[7] BDJ: *lä-zä-təṣewwəʿaki näfs* (the soul that cries out to you); CR: *lä-zä-ṣäwwəʿatäki näfs* (the soul that cried out to you).

[8] BDJ: *hadʾa* (abated); CR: *ahdəʾa* (it made abate) [but with nom. *näfas* (wind) instead of acc. *näfasä*, so not a viable alternative].

[9] DJ: *ḥəli* (sing); B, CR: *ḥalli* [*sic*:, as if the verbal stem were *ḥalläyä*, and not, as is correct, *ḥaläyä*].

Plate 38. Miracle 6: "How the monk was overtaken [by a storm on the lake]" and "how our holy mother Walatta Petros saved him and returned him [to shore] from amid the lake" (MS A, f. 156v © SLUB Mscr. Dresd.Eb.415.e,2).

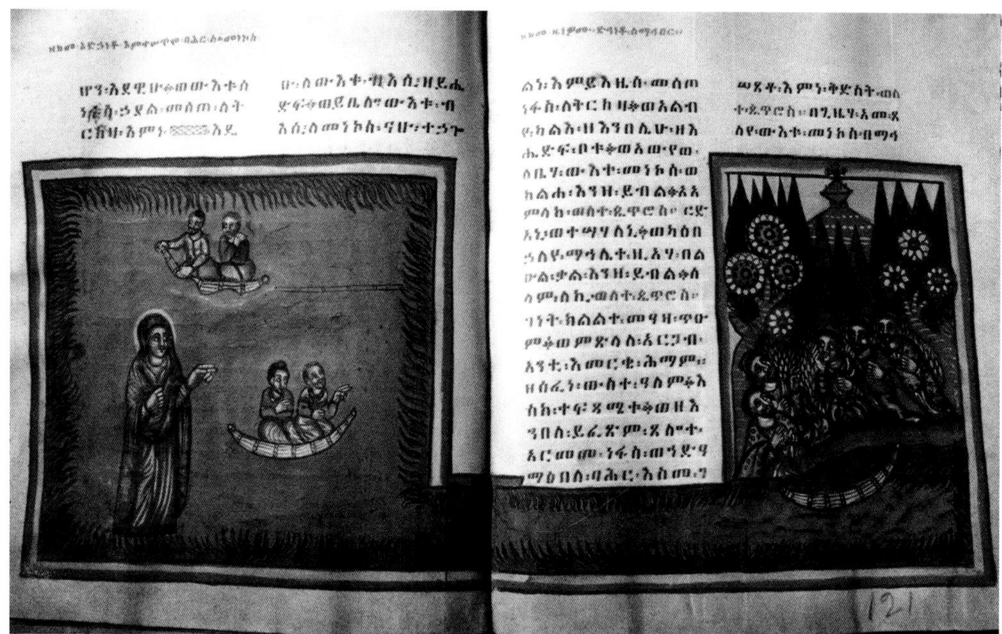

Plate 39. Miracle 6: "How she saved a monk from drowning in the big lake" and "how he told the community about his rescue" (MS D, f. 122v–123r [120v–121r]). Photo by Claire Bosc-Tiessé, 1997.

Plate 40. Miracle 6: "How he told the community about his rescue" (MS D, f. 123r [121r]). Photo by Claire Bosc-Tiessé, 1997.

monk left them, marveling at the great power of our holy mother Walatta Petros;[1] may her intercession be with __________[2] for eternity, amen.

The Seventh Miracle: How Our Mother Recovered the Stolen Book of Poems from the Fisherman

The seventh miracle[3] that our mother Walatta Petros performed;[4] may her intercession be with ________[5] for eternity, amen.

One of the sisters from the community owned a copy of the *Malkih*[6] poem in honor of our holy mother Walatta Petros; it had been copied [onto parchment,] together with the *Golgotha* prayer.[7] She always wore the book around her neck[8] and prayed its text all day long, without ceasing.

One day that sister went down to the lake in order to wash her clothes, with the 122
book containing the *Malkih* poem in honor of our holy mother Walatta Petros dangling from her neck. When she reached the lake at the washing place for clothes, she took the book from her neck and put it on a stone near her so that she could wash her clothes. Then, when she had finished washing the clothes,[9] she left the washing place and went home, forgetting and leaving the book behind[10] where she had put it.

[1] CR omits *Wälättä Ṗeṭros.*

[2] B: *fəqura Agnaṭəyos* (her beloved Ignatius); D: *fəqura Ḫirutä Śəllase* (her beloved Ḫirutä Śəllase); J: *fəqərta Akrosəya wä-məslä kʷəllənä wəluda wä-awalədiha* (her beloved Akrosia, and with all of us, her [viz., WP's] sons and daughters); Abb. 88: *fəqura* [name erased] (her beloved [name erased]), which CR altered to [*məsle*]*nä* ([with] us).

[3] BDJ: *sabəʿ täʾamər* (the seventh miracle); CR: *täʾamər* (a miracle).

[4] BDJ: *zä-gäbrät əmmənä* [B adds: *qəddəst wä-burəkt*] *Wälättä Ṗeṭros* (that our [B adds: holy and blessed] mother WP performed); Abb. 88 *zä-gäbrät* (which she performed), which CR expanded to *zä-gäbrät əmmənä qəddəst Wälättä Ṗeṭros* (which our holy mother WP performed).

[5] B: *fəqura Agnaṭəyos* (her beloved Ignatius); D: *fəqura Ḫirutä Śəllase* (her beloved Ḫirutä Śəllase); J: *fəqərta Akrosəya* (her beloved Akrosia). CR omits the entire call for intercession.

[6] *Mälkəʾ* (lit., portrait) is a genre of Gəʿəz poetry written in honor of holy figures, praising the saint from head to toe, using the saint's body parts to create an allegory of the saint's virtues and life.

[7] *Golgota* is a well-known magical prayer frequently used or worn as a textual amulet, based on the prayer the Virgin Mary is thought to have said at Golgotha when Christ was crucified.

[8] This would be a small prayer book of poems, ten to fifteen pages, and two or three inches by two or three inches, not a scroll. It would have a leather case and a leather strap like all Gəʿəz books, so it could easily be carried, hung on a wall, and protected from the elements.

[9] BDJ: *wä-sobä fäṣṣämät ḫaṣibä albas* (then, when she had finished washing the clothes); Abb. 88 omits; CR filled the obvious gap by inserting *wä-əmdəḫrä ḫaṣäbät* (after she had washed).

[10] Lit., *wä-mäṣḥaf-əssä täräsʿa wä-täḫadgä* (but the book was forgotten and left behind).

Plate 41. Miracle 7: "How a woman forgot the book containing our mother Walatta Petros's malkih" (MS D, f. 124v [122v]). Photo by Claire Bosc-Tiessé, 1997.

Later, by chance, a fisherman[1] came by. He found the book lying on the stone, picked it up, and took it away, without anyone knowing.[2]

When[3] the sister remembered the book, she became extremely alarmed and hurried down to the lake in order to look for it in the place where she had previously put it. However, when she arrived there and looked for it, she could not find it; so she became incredibly distraught.[4] She returned home despondent and

[1] BDJ: *mäśäggər[ä ʿaśa]* (fisherman); CR with the substandard variant *mäśagər[ä ʿaśa]*, here and throughout.

[2] BJ: *ənbälä yaʾməro* [subj.] *männu-hi* (lit., without anybody knowing it); D, CR: *ənbälä yaʾamməro* [*sic*: ind.] *männu-hi* [no translation difference].

[3] BDJ: *sobä* (when); CR omits.

[4] Such a sacred book was precious for a variety of reasons, including the expense of creating one.

Plate 42. Miracle 7: How the fisherman tried to sell the book (top) and "how in a dream she spoke to the man who had taken away the book" (bottom) (MS D, f. 125r [123r]). Photo by Claire Bosc-Tiessé, 1997.

weeping. Then, she kept imploring and praying to our holy mother Walatta Petros to reveal to her where the book was. In addition, she appealed to the entire community, brothers and sisters, to not forget her in their prayers.[1] She threw herself at their feet each day, during the saying of grace before the meal,[2] as well as during [the reading of] the *Praise of the Beloved*, without desisting even for a single hour.

Meanwhile, the fisherman who had taken away the book with the *Malkih* poem in honor of our holy mother Walatta Petros went around with it, to the towns and among the houses, trying to sell it.

But when the people of any town saw the book,[3] they would ask the man,

[1] BDJ: *kämä i-yərsəʿəwwa bä-gize ṣälot* (lit., to not forget her at prayer time); CR: *kämä yərdəʾəwwa bä-gize ṣälot* (to help her at prayer time).

[2] The *Ṣälotä Maʾədd* (lit., table prayer) is a prayer recited at mealtimes, from the *Śərʿatä Maḫbär* (Rules of the Community).

[3] BDJ: *wä-rəʾiyomu säbʾa hagär wəʾətä mäṣḥafä* (lit., the people of a town having seen the book); CR: *wä-rəʾiyomu säbʾa hagär lä-wəʾətu mäṣḥaf* [*sic*; ungrammatical, but no translation difference].

Plate 43. Miracle 7: "How our mother appeared to the fisherman a second and third time" (top) and "how he returned the book" (bottom) (MS D, f. 126v [124v]). Photo by Claire Bosc-Tiessé, 1997.

"Where did you get that book?[1] Doesn't it belong to Walatta Petros's community? Did you yourself steal it and bring it,[2] or has another thief given it to you? Certainly, we won't buy a stolen book from you, a book that has a sign.[3] We won't take part in another person's sin: he who associates with a thief is a thief himself!"

[1] Abb. 88 adds *yəbeləwwo* (they said to him), which CR expanded to *wä-yəbeləwwo* (they further said to him).

[2] BDJ: *bo-nu antä säräqqä wä-amṣaʾkä* (lit, did you yourself steal and bring); CR: *bo-nu antä amṣaʾkä* (did you yourself bring).

[3] Lit., *zä-botu təʾəmərt* [thus BDJ; CR with the optional acc. *təʾəmərtä*] (on which there is a sign *or* mark). It is not clear what this sign is. Most Gəʿəz books are Psalters or Gospels; a book of poems with the name of a recent female saint on every page would be quite rare and

When no one who would buy it from him, the fisherman took the book back[1] to his house and deposited it there.

Later, he again resolved to go to another district to try to sell the book.[2] Upon this resolution, he said to his wife, "I could not find anyone here who would buy
this book from me. They [even] said to me: 'You are a thief!' But prepare provisions 123
for me: I want to go to a distant district to try to sell the book [there]."

"Very well," his wife[3] replied.

Now, while this was what the man had resolved to do, our holy mother Walatta Petros appeared to him in a dream, at night while he was sleeping, and said to him, "Don't do what you have planned; don't sell the book with my *Malkih* poem!"

The man then awoke from his sleep, but did not believe the dream's message; rather, he considered it a deceptive dream.[4] He fell asleep again [and slept] like before, and Walatta Petros again appeared to him, like before. She said to him, "Watch yourself and don't do what you have planned!" Again, he considered it a [mere] dream,[5] and slept on, as before.

Then our holy mother Walatta Petros appeared to him for a third time, in great majesty and irate with him. She said to him,[6] "Behold, I have appeared to you three times now and said to you, 'Watch yourself and don't do what you have planned![7] Don't sell that book!' But you don't listen to my words and treat them[8] as if they had no weight whatsoever.[9] Now, however, I tell you: Return the book to the

---

thus might have been owned only by those of her community. Or, most texts name the commissioner of the text (in the blessings or a colophon), and that name might not match that of the fisherman. Or, many books include an ending section that anathematizes anyone who steals the text. Even if the townspeople had not opened the book or could not read, they might have invoked the possibility of the text having such an anathema because they suspected the man was a thief.

[1] BDJ: *agbəʾo lä-wəʾətu mäṣḥaf* (lit., he took the book back); CR: *agbəʾa lä-wəʾətu mäṣḥaf* [*sic*; ungrammatical, but no translation difference].

[2] BDJ: *kämä . . . yəśiṭo* (lit., to . . . sell it); CR: *kämä . . . yəśäyyəṭo* [*sic*: an ungrammatical verb form].

[3] BDJ: *bəʾəsitu* (his wife); CR: *bəʾəsit* (the wife).

[4] Lit., *ḥəlmä ḥassät* (a dream of the lie).

[5] BDJ, CR: *ḥəlmä* (dream), although one would expect to find here *ḥəlmä ḥassät* (dream of the lie), as above.

[6] D: *wä-təbelo* (she said to him); BJ, Abb. 88 omit; CR added *wä-təbelo*, as in D.

[7] BDJ: *wä-əbeläkä ʿuq i-təgbär zä-ḫalläykä* (lit., and I said to you, "Take care not to do what you have planned!"); CR omits.

[8] BDJ: *antä-ssä i-sämaʿkä qaləyä wä-rässäyko* (but you don't listen to my words and treat them); CR: *antä-ssä sämaʿkä qaləyä wä-rässäyko* (but you listen to my words, but [then] treat them).

[9] BJ, Abb. 88: *kämä wä-i-mənt-ni lä-nägärəyä* (lit., as if there was nothing whatsoever to my statements); CR unnecessarily altered Abb. 88 to *kämä wä-i-məntä-ni* [acc.] *lä-nägärəyä* [identical translation]; D: *kämä wä-i-mənt lä-nägärəyä* (as if there was nothing to my statements).

community![1] Hand the book over to the abbess,[2] and tell [her] how I appeared to you and how I spoke to you. But if you are afraid, tell that man, you know which one, to go with you. That man can then speak on your behalf,[3] hand over the book, and win you peace and reconciliation. If, however, you refuse to heed my words[4] and disobey what I have told you, I will take my revenge upon you, a real revenge, and bring down a harsh punishment on you." After she had said this, our holy mother Walatta Petros vanished.

The fisherman then woke up fearful and trembling due to the awe-inspiring words of our holy mother Walatta Petros. When morning came, he took the book and went to that man whom our holy mother Walatta Petros had pointed out to him. When the fisherman arrived at that man's place, he informed the man about the entire affair, from beginning to end: how Walatta Petros had appeared to him, and how[5] she had ordered him to go [to the community] in the man's company to give the book back to the abbess.

After having heard this story, the middleman[6] went to the community, taking the fisherman along. The middleman then went to the abbess [alone] and said to her, "My mother, if I find favor with you, for my sake have mercy on a man[7] who has committed a sin [against the community]."

She replied, "Who is it who has sinned [against the community]? I am not aware of any man who is burdened with [such a] sin."

The middleman replied, "There is a man[8] who, without realizing what he did,[9]
124 took a book from where it had been left behind. He is now standing outside."

The abbess replied, "So then, summon him! Let him come himself[10] and tell me what he has done."

[1] BDJ: *wəstä maḫbär* (to the community); CR: *wəstä maḫbär əgälit* (to any community *or* to any woman from among the community members).

[2] BDJ: *hab lä-əmmä maḫbär əgälit* (lit., give to that certain mother of the community); CR omits. We have consistently translated the term for a female religious leader, *əmmä maḫbär*, as "abbess." This woman is not named, but it must be either Əḫətä Krəstos or Amätä Dəngəl, the only two abbesses of the community before the writing of the *WP gädl.*

[3] BDJ: *wä-yətnagär bä'ənti'akä* (lit., he may then speak on your behalf); CR omits.

[4] BDJ: *sämiʿotä qaləyä* (lit., listening to my words); CR: *sämiʿa qaləyä* [different form, identical translation].

[5] BDJ: *wä-zä-kämä* (and how); CR omits.

[6] Lit., *wə'ətu bə'əsi* (that man). But to clarify the story, we have called him the "middleman."

[7] BDJ: *mäḥari litä bə'əse* (for my sake have mercy on a man); Abb. 88 with contextually nonsensical *wä-ḥorä we'ətu bə'əsi* (and that man went), which CR altered to *mäḥari lä-wə'ətu bə'əsi* (have mercy on this man). The corruption in Abb. 88 is evidence for the role of silent copying in manuscript reproduction since *wä-ḥorä* and *mäḥari* sound very different but look similar in fidäl (ወሖረ and መሐሪ).

[8] BDJ: *hallo bə'əsi* (there is a man); CR: *hallo* (there is someone).

[9] Lit., *bä-i-ya'əmro* (in ignorance).

[10] BDJ: *lälihu* (himself); Abb. 88: *laʿlehu* (on him), evidently a corruption of an original *lälihu*; CR altered the *laʿlehu* of Abb. 88 to *məslekä* (with you).

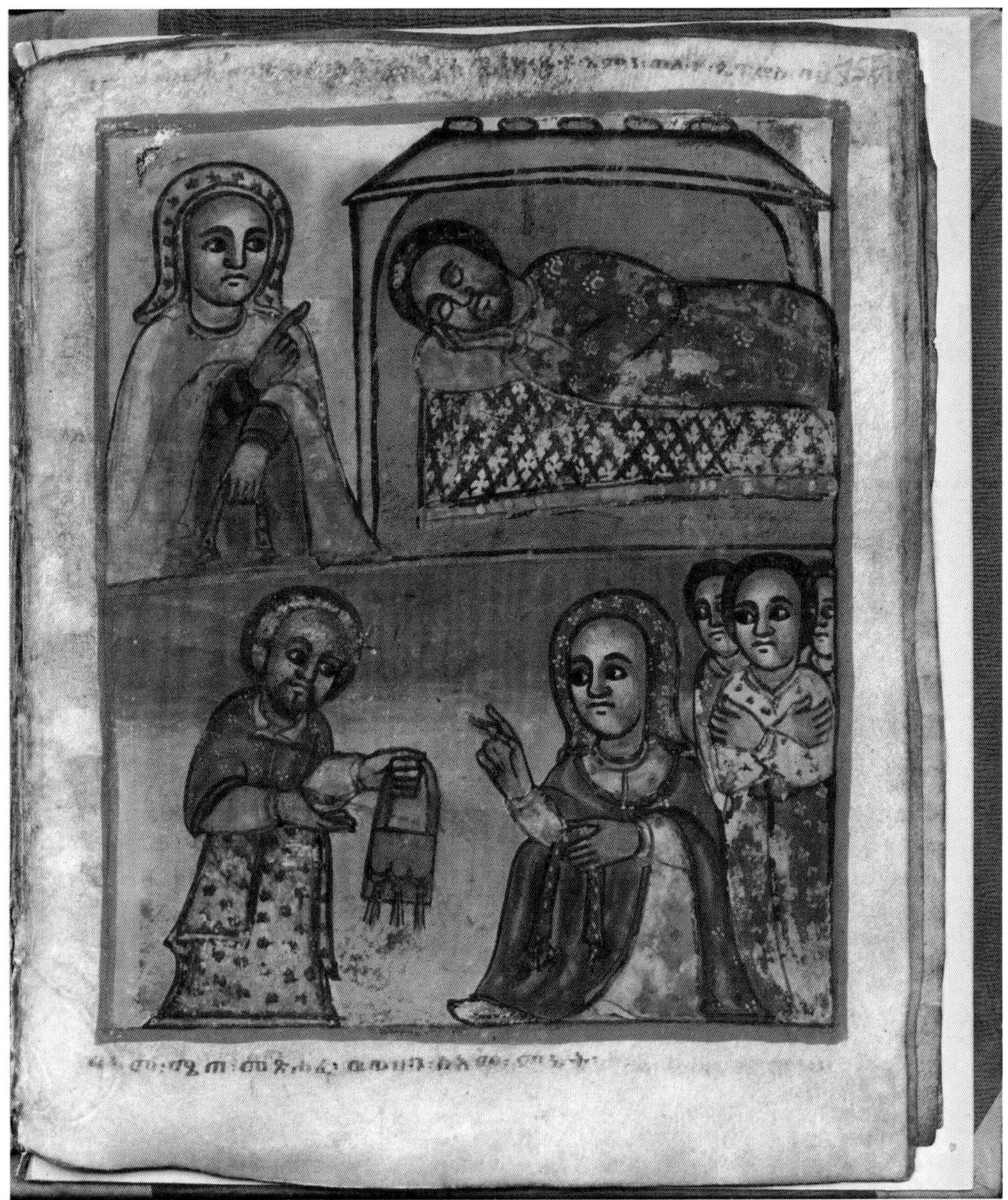

Plate 44. Miracle 7: "How our holy mother admonished him [i.e., the thieving fisherman] in a dream" (top) and "how he returned the book and gave it to the abbess" (bottom) (MS A, f. 157r © SLUB Mscr. Dresd.Eb.415.e,2).

So the middleman summoned the fisherman. The latter entered and, in fear and trembling, related the entire story which we have just told.[1] He then handed that book over to the abbess.

She now asked the fisherman, "What was Walatta Petros's likeness when you saw her, what did she look like?" So he explained to her in what likeness he had seen her.[2] The abbess then absolved him, and he went home.

As for the book, it was restored to the sister who had owned it before. She was delighted and praised our holy mother Walatta Petros. May Walatta Petros's intercession be with _______[3] for eternity, amen.

The Eighth Miracle: How Our Mother Recovered the Stolen Book of Poems from the Convert

The eighth miracle[4] that our holy mother Walatta Petros performed. May her blessing be with[5] _______[6] for eternity, amen.

Furthermore, there was a woman in the town of Zira.[7] An elder woman from Walatta Petros's community had converted her to Christianity.[8] For this reason, the

[1] BDJ: *kʷəllo nägärä zä-aqdämnä nägirä* (lit., the entire story which we have previously told); CR: *kʷəllo zä-aqdämnä* [*sic*: incomplete] (everything which we have previously).

[2] BDJ: *zä-kämä rəʾyä amsaliha* (lit., how he had seen her likeness); CR: *zä-kämä rəʾya amsaliha* (how he had seen her, her likeness). The question may be a test of whether the fisherman had truly seen WP in his vision, because both Əḫətä Krəstos and Amätä Dəngəl had known WP personally and knew what she looked like.

[3] B: *gäbra Agnaṭəyos* (her servant Ignatius); D: *fəqura Ḫirutä Śəllase* (her beloved Ḫirutä Śəllase); J: *fəqərta Akrosəya* (her beloved Akrosia); Abb. 88: *fəqura* [name erased] (her beloved [name erased]), which CR altered to [*məsle*]*nä* ([with] us).

[4] BDJ: *samən täʾamər* (the eighth miracle); CR: *täʾamər* (a miracle).

[5] D: *bäräkäta yähallu məslä* (may her blessing be with); B: *ṣälota wä-bäräkäta yähallu məslä* (may her prayers and blessing be with); J, CR omit.

[6] B: *fəqura Agnaṭəyos* (her beloved Ignatius); D: *fəqura Ḫirutä Śəllase* (her beloved Ḫirutä Śəllase); J, CR omit.

[7] DJ: *bä-wəstä hagär əntä səma Zəra* (lit., in the town whose name was Zira); B: *bä-wəstä hagär əntä təssämmäy Zəra* (in the town that was called Zira); CR: *bä-wəstä hagärä Səma Zəra* (in the town of Sima Zira). Zəra was a town near Lake Ṭana, either east of southern Lake Ṭana or twenty-five miles south of it.

[8] Lit., *abəʾata krəstənna* (had induced her into Christianity), which could mean the elder woman had converted her but could also mean that she was her godmother, that is, the person who stood up for her when she was baptized. Ricci follows the second meaning and has *aveva tenuto a battesimo* (had held [her] in baptism). However, the next sentence then uses a different expression to state unequivocally that the elder woman had received her in baptism, namely, *täwäkfäta bä-ṭəmqät*. Therefore, *abəʾata krəstənna* indicates that the elder woman persuaded the younger one to embrace Christianity when the latter was already an adult (as also suggested by plates 45–46); at her baptism, she then became the younger woman's godmother. Although Christianity was widespread among the Amhara around Lake Ṭana at this time, there were non-Christians among immigrants to the area and other ethnic groups, like the Kəmant. Regarding the rules of baptism, see Zärʾa Yaʿəqob (2013).

younger woman used to go to the elder woman every day, [to] her [god]mother who had received her in baptism. Her [god]mother, the elder woman, then asked her to live with her in Walatta Petros's community, studying scripture, spinning, and sewing.[1] But the younger woman refused and did not accept her [god]mother's suggestion; she continued to live in town.

The young woman then illicitly had sex,[2] illegitimately became pregnant, and gave birth. After that, she paid [her godmother] a visit. She came to the community carrying her child on her back, and as usual[3] went to the elder woman's house. In the house lived a sister who possessed[4] a copy of our holy mother Walatta Petros's *Malkih* poem. The visiting woman stole that book, concealed it [on herself], and left the house[5] to return to her town with the book.

As for the sister[6] who was the book's rightful owner, she looked for it but could not find it. She questioned all her sisters, asking them to tell her whether they had taken it.

But they said to her, "We certainly haven't taken it, and we don't know who has taken it either." However, they also said to her, "But go to that [visiting] woman and ask her whether she has taken it. The power of our holy mother Walatta Petros will reveal[7] [the truth] to you!"

So that sister set out, followed the visiting woman, and came to the market site 125
of Cherr Takkal.[8] There she found her and politely asked her, "Please tell me, my dear sister,[9] whether it was you who took the book."

[1] BDJ: *kämä tənbär məsleha . . . wä-təftəl wä-təsfi* [twice subj.] (lit., to live with her . . . so as to spin and to sew); CR: *kämä tənbär məsleha . . . wä-təfättəl wä-təsäffi* [*sic*: twice ind.; no translation difference]. Most Ethiopian clothes of this time were made with cotton (which was cultivated and woven in Ethiopia by the thirteenth century). Women cleaned and spun it into thread; men wove it. Women then sewed and embroidered the final product. All the ordinary tasks of a household still had to be accomplished in a monastery.

[2] BDJ: *zämmäwät* (lit., fornicated); CR omits. See chapter 86 for another place where CR omits a word regarding sex.

[3] J, CR: *kämä ləmada* (lit., as was her custom); BD: *bä-kämä ləmada* (according to her custom).

[4] BDJ: *wä-halläwät wəstä yəʾəti bet aḥatti əḫət əntä-ba* (lit., in that house there was a sister who possessed); CR: *wä-halläwät wəstä betä aḥatti əḫət əntä baḥtita* (there was in the house of a sister who lived alone *or* she was alone in the house of one sister).

[5] DJ: *wä-wäṣ́ʾat əm-wəʾətu* [masc.] bet (lit., and left from that house); B: *wä-wäṣ́ʾat əm-yəʾəti* [fem.] *bet* [identical translation, but fem. demonstrative]; CR: *wä-wäṣ́ʾat əm-wəstä bet* (and left from inside the house).

[6] BD: *wä-yəʾəti-ssä əḫət* (as for the sister); J, CR: *wä-yəʾəti əḫət* (the sister).

[7] DJ: *yəkäśśət* (will reveal); B, CR: *yəkśət* (may [the power of our holy mother WP] reveal).

[8] BDJ: *Čärr Täkkäl* (Goodness Planted [Amharic]); CR writes the toponym in one word, as *Čär(r)täk(k)äl*, thereby obscuring its composition and meaning. Čärr Täkkäl is an unidentified market site near Zəra, perhaps in the region of Čärä, which was a stronghold of the Agäw, who were not primarily Christian at the time, about fifty miles southwest of Lake Ṭana.

[9] BDJ: *o-əḫətəyä fəqərtəyä* (my dear sister); CR: *o-əḫətəyä wä-fəqərtəyä* (my sister and my friend).

Plate 45. Miracle 8: How the convert stole the book of poems (top) and "how she brazenly swore by the name of our mother Walatta Petros" (bottom) (MS A, f. 157v © SLUB Mscr.Dresd.Eb.415.e,2).

Plate 46. Miracle 8: "How a woman stole the nun's book" (MS D, f. 128r [126r]). Photo by Claire Bosc-Tiessé, 1997.

But the woman replied to her,[1] "My sister, far be it from me! I haven't done what you say."[2] Then she swore with these words, "May the God of Walatta Petros display his wonder-working powers[3] on me and give my body over to the birds of the sky [if I have lied]!"

When the sister heard the woman swearing such a solemn oath,[4] she withdrew and left her alone. Soon thereafter, however,[5] the sister returned and again asked

[1] BDJ: *wä-awśəʾata yəʾəti bəʾəsit wä-təbela* (lit., but that woman replied to her and said to her); CR: *wä-awśəʾata yəʾəti əḫət bəʾəsit wä-təbela* (but that sister woman replied to her and said to her).

[2] BDJ: *zäntä zä-təbəli* (lit., that which you say); CR: *zäntä zä-təbeli* (that which you said).

[3] Lit., *täʾamərihu* (his miracles), here and below.

[4] BDJ: *zä-mäḥalät mäḥala ʿabiyä* (lit., that she swore a big oath *or* the big oath that she swore); CR: *zä-mäḥalät mäḥala* (that she swore an oath *or* the oath that she swore).

[5] BJ: *wä-əmdəḫrä ḥəqqä* (soon thereafter, however); D, CR: *wä-əmdəḫrä ḥəqq* (after a short while, however).

the woman the same thing because she knew that the latter had sworn falsely. Yet the woman again swore, with these words, "May the God of Walatta Petros reveal his wonder-working powers on me and give my body over to the hyenas [if I have lied]!"

After this, the sister said [before everyone],[1] "What [more] can I say now, what [else] can I do?[2] Rather, I will cast my burden upon my holy mother Walatta Petros: Truly, she will return the book to me. However, if she does not return it to me, I will never again invoke her name nor remain in the community, but rather will go to another town."[3] She swore in these terms before everyone. Then she returned to the community to find out what would happen and to see how the affair would end, spending every day worried and distressed.

Meanwhile, the thieving woman entered the town [of Cherr Takkal] and sold the book for two *amole* bars.[4] But when the man who had bought it read it,[5] he found the name of our holy[6] mother Walatta Petros written in it. Immediately, he realized that the book belonged to her community.[7] Therefore, he became afraid and said to that woman, "Give me back my money and take your book! I am afraid: I will not buy it from you lest it bring guilt down upon me.[8] Look, Walatta Petros's name is written in it!"

So the woman took the book back from him and went on to the island of Gwangoot in order to sell it. But [there,] people also read it and found[9] Walatta Petros's

[1] BDJ: *wä-əmdəḫrä zəntu təbe yəʾəti əḫət* (lit., after this, that sister said); Abb. 88: *wä-əmdəḫrä təbe əḫət* (after the sister had said), which CR sensibly altered to *wä-əmdəḫrä-zə təbe əḫət* (after this, the sister said).

[2] BDJ: *məntä əbəl wä-məntä əgäbbər əm-yəʾəze* (lit., what do I say and what do I do from now on); Abb. 88: *məntä əkhal wä-məntä əgäbbər. Əm-yəʾəze-ssä* (of what may I be capable, and what will I do? From now on . . .), which CR altered to *məntä əkhal wä-məntä əgbär. Əm-yəʾəze-ssä* (of what may I be capable, and what may I do? From now on . . .).

[3] BDJ: *wä-i-yənäbbər wəstä maḫbär alla aḥawwər wəstä kaləʾ hagär* (nor remain in the community, but rather will go to another town); CR: *wä-i-yənäbbər wəstä maḫbära alla aḥawwər wəstä maḫbär wəstä kaləʾ hagär* (nor remain in her community, but rather go to a community in a different district).

[4] BDJ: *lä-2 amole* (for two *amole*); CR: *bä-2 amole* [different construction, but identical translation]. Salt bars of standardized size, called *amole*, were used in highland Ethiopia and other parts of the Horn of Africa for many centuries as currency. At this time, according to the Jesuits, two amole would have been worth about a gram of gold.

[5] BDJ: *wä-sobä anbäbo zä-täśayäṭo bəʾəsi* (but when the man who had bought it read it); CR: *wä-sobä anbäbä zä-täśayäṭä bəʾəsi* (but when the man who had bought, read).

[6] BDJ: *qəddəst* (holy); CR omits.

[7] BDJ: *kämä wəʾətu mäṣḥafä maḫbär* (lit., that it was a book of the community); CR: *kämä wəʾətu mäṣḥaf zä-maḫbär* (that that book was of the community). The name of WP appears on every page of the poems, so it is odd that the buyer discovered the name only after buying the text. Perhaps he had not read the text at all before buying it, suggesting that he bought it as a textual amulet for its protective properties rather than its contents, and/or he did not read and some unmentioned person read it to him.

[8] BDJ: *kämä i-yamṣəʾ laʿleyä ʿəda* (lest it bring guilt down upon me); CR: *kämä i-yəmṣaʾ laʿleyä ʿəda* (lest guilt come down upon me).

[9] BDJ: *anbäbəwwo wä-räkäbu* (read it and found); CR: *anbäbəwwa wä-räkäbəwwa* (read her and found her).

Plate 47. Miracle 8: "How she sold the book for two amole [salt bars]" (MS D, f. 129r [127r]). Photo by Claire Bosc-Tiessé, 1997.

Plate 48. Miracle 8: "How a hyena bit her after she swore an oath falsely" using the name of Walatta Petros (MS D, f. 130r [128r]). Photo by Claire Bosc-Tiessé, 1997.

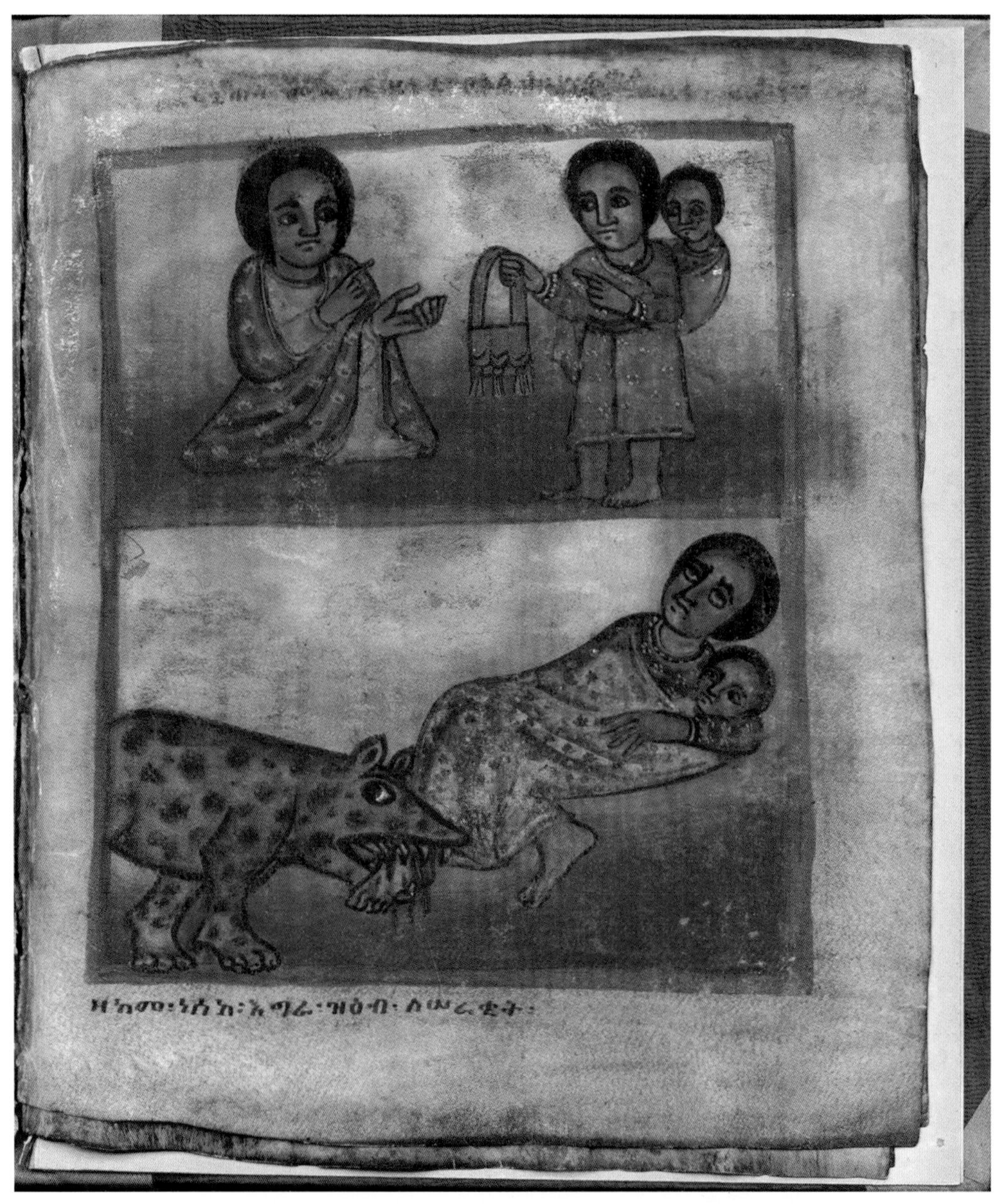

Plate 49. Miracle 8: How the woman returned the book (top) and "how a hyena bit into the thieving woman's foot" (bottom) (MS A, f. 158r © SLUB Mscr.Dresd.Eb.415.e,2).

name written in it, so they too became afraid and said to her, "We won't buy it from
you: it's a book that belongs to Walatta Petros's community!" **126**

When the woman could not find anybody who would buy the book, allowing her to profit, she left the island and went around to many towns, but [still] could not find anyone who would buy it[1] from her. Therefore, she now resolved to return the book to its owner. So, she sent it to the sister with these words, "Take back your book, and do not harbor ill will against me because I took it without realizing what I did.[2] I tried to sell it once or twice, but Walatta Petros's power prevented it and thwarted my plans."[3] Consequently, that sister was incredibly happy and took the book back, praising our holy mother Walatta Petros.

Later, a hyena came to the place where the [thieving] woman slept, bit into her,[4] and ripped her feet[5] because[6] the woman had sworn so brazenly. [In this way,] our holy mother Walatta Petros demonstrated her power[7] over her. May Walatta Petros's most welcome intercession and her abundant help[8] be with __________[9] for eternity, amen.

The Ninth Miracle: How Our Mother Repaired the Broken Jar and Healed the Boy

The ninth miracle[10] that our holy mother Walatta Petros performed; may her intercession be[11] with ________[12] for eternity, amen.

[1] BDJ: *wäṣʾat əm-wəʾətu däset wä-ʿodät wəstä ahgur bəzuḫ wä-i-räkäbät zä-yəśśayyäṭ* (lit., she left that island and went around in many towns, but did not find anybody who would buy); CR omits.

[2] Lit., *bä-i-yaʾəmro* (in ignorance).

[3] BDJ: *wä-baḥtu ḫaylä Wälättä Ṗeṭros kälʾani wä-aʿqäfäni* (lit., but WP's power prevented me and thwarted me); CR: *wä-baḥtu ḫayyälätäni Wälättä Ṗeṭros. Kälʾatäni wä-aʿqäfätäni* (but WP was stronger than me. She prevented and thwarted me).

[4] BDJ: *näsäka* (bit into her); CR: *näkäsa* (bit into her). Both *näsäkä* and *näkäsä* mean "to bite, to bite into."

[5] BDJ: *wä-gämädä säkʷäna əgäriha* (lit., and ripped into pieces the soles of her feet); CR: *wä-gämäṣa* [*sic*] *säkʷäna əgäriha* (and tore her [*sic*] off the soles of her feet).

[6] BDJ: *əsmä* (because); CR: *kämä* (as).

[7] BDJ: *ḫayla* (her power); CR: *ḫaylä* (power).

[8] BDJ: *tənbələnnaha wəkuf wä-rädʾeta təruf* (lit., her most welcome intercession and her abundant help); CR: *tənbələnnaha* (her intercession).

[9] B: *fəqura Agnaṭəyos* (her beloved Ignatius); D: *Ḫirutä Śəllase*; J: *ṣäḥafihu Gälawdewos* (the scribe Gälawdewos); Abb. 88: *fəqura* [name erased] (her beloved [name erased]), which CR altered to [*məsle*]*nä* ([with] us). The mention of the author, "the scribe Gälawdewos," in MS J suggests that MS J may be the urtext.

[10] BJ: *tasəʿ täʾamər* (the ninth miracle); D: *tasəʿ täʾaməriha* (the ninth of her miracles); CR: *täʾamər* (a miracle).

[11] BDJ: *tənbələnnaha yähallu* (may her intercession be); CR omits.

[12] B: *məslä fəqura Agnaṭəyos* (with her beloved Ignatius); D: *məslä fəqura Ḫirutä Śəllase* (with her beloved Ḫirutä Śəllase); J: *məslenä* (with us); CR omits.

Plate 50. Miracle 9: "How the big jar broke and how the ale became visible [through the cracks] but not even a single drop spilled out" (MS A, f. 158v © SLUB Mscr.Dresd.Eb.415.e,2).

Plate 51. Miracle 9: "How the big jar split but no ale spilled out due to the power of our mother Walatta Petros" (MS D, f. 131r [129r]). Photo by Claire Bosc-Tiessé, 1997.

Six months[1] after our holy mother Walatta Petros had passed away, some sisters were at[2] her burial site on Réma Island to perform[3] her tazkaar feast. Now, one sister among them was charged with brewing the ale. She filled[4] a large jar[5] with

[1] Lit., *wä-bä-sadəs wärḫ* (in the sixth month).

[2] BDJ: *halläwa . . . wəstä* (were at); CR: *täfännäwa . . . wəstä* (were sent to).

[3] BDJ: *kämä yəgbära* [3rd-ps. fem. pl.] (lit., so that they would perform); Abb. 88: *käma yəgbär* (so that he would perform), which CR altered to *kämä yətgäbär* (so that it would be performed).

[4] BDJ: *wä-mälʾat* (she filled); Abb. 88: *wä-mäʿalt* (during daytime), which CR altered to *amləʾat* (she made [someone] fill).

[5] Lit., *gan*, an Amharic loanword meaning a large clay container used for storing water or for brewing ale (plates 6, 24, 25, 34, 35, 50, 51, 52, 53, 61). The related Gəʿəz word is *gänʿ* (big

ale[1] and put it down [on the ground], but the jar cracked and broke, splitting into two, so that[2] the ale became visible.[3]

Upon that, one of the sisters working there[4] seized it up with her hands[5] and exclaimed, “My holy mother Walatta Petros, help me!” The ale then kept its shape in the jar,[6] while the sister who had been brewing it went running to another house and fetched some jars. She scooped the ale [into them], without one single drop of it spilling or the [hot] ashes underneath the jar getting wet.[7] After this, the sisters took the jar outside—it had broken into two halves[8]—and threw it away there. The preservation of the ale happened through the power of our holy mother Walatta Petros.

On that very day, a woman arrived [at the community on the shore] carrying a little boy who was blind and paralyzed. She wanted to go to Réma Island to entrust
127 her son to the tomb of our holy mother Walatta Petros. She could not find a tankwa though, and so she searched [on the mainland] for earth from our holy mother Walatta Petros's tomb in order to rub it on her son. But she could not find any of that either, and so she sat down outside[9] [the community's church], with the poor.[10]

People gave her some bread and some ale, which she ate and drank. Then, she rubbed that son of hers,[11] whose eyes were blind and whose back was paralyzed,[12] with some of that ale, trusting in the power of our holy mother Walatta Petros's assistance—and immediately the boy's eyes opened and his back straightened![13] All

---

jar, cauldron). Here our translation differs substantively from Ricci's, who has *otre* (skin for liquids).

[1] DJ: *səte säwa* (lit., the drink of sawa); B, CR: *säwa.*

[2] BDJ: *əskä* (so that); CR: *ənzä* (while).

[3] Lit., *yastärəʾi* (appeared).

[4] BDJ: *əllä halläwa həyyä yətläʾaka* (lit., who were present there serving); CR: *ənzä halläwät həyyä zä-tətläʾak* (while she was there, who served [*sic*]).

[5] CR: *bä-ədäwiha* (with her hands); BDJ: *bä-ədeha* (lit., with her hand or hands).

[6] Lit., *wä-qomä wəʾətu säwa maʾkälä gan* (the ale then stopped in the middle of the jar).

[7] BDJ: *wä-i-rəḥsä* (lit., and [it] did not get wet); CR: *wä-i-tärəḥsä* [different verbal stem, but identical meaning]. Since ale (säwa) involves a process of brewing rather than cooking, the filled jar was not over any ashes. However, before being filled, the gan-jar was often set over a smoky fire to give the ale a smoky flavor, and the grains used in making ale were toasted over a fire first.

[8] Lit., *käwino 2 kəflä gälʿa* (it having become two pieces of fragments).

[9] BDJ: *bä-afʾa* (lit., on the outside); CR: *afʾa* (outside).

[10] The needy often set themselves up near a church or within a churchyard's walls in hope of assistance or alms.

[11] BDJ: *wä-qäbʾato . . . lä-wəʾətu wälda* (she rubbed that son of hers); CR: *wä-qäbʾato . . . lä-wälda* (she rubbed her son).

[12] BDJ: [*lä-wəʾətu wälda,*] *ʿəwwər wä-mäṣ́agʷəʿ ʿayno wä-zäbano* (lit., [that son of hers,] blind and paralyzed, of eye and of back); CR: [*lä-wälda,*] *ʿəwwər ʿayno wä-mäṣ́agwəʿ zäbano* ([her son,] blind of eye and paralyzed of back).

[13] It is not clear why the woman thought she would find earth from WP's tomb on the mainland. Nor is it clear if the miraculous ale got from Rema, where it was brewed, to Qʷäraṣa, or if a different ale was used to heal.

Plate 52. Miracle 9: How a woman brought "her blind boy to the tazkaar of our mother Walatta Petros" (top) and "how our mother Walatta Petros healed the eye of the woman's son" (bottom) (MS A, f. 159r © SLUB Mscr.Dresd.Eb.415.e,2).

Plate 53. Miracle 9: "How the eye of the blind boy became light again when his mother rubbed it with ale from our mother Walatta Petros's tazkaar" (MS D, f. 131v [129v]). Photo by Claire Bosc-Tiessé, 1997.

who saw this miracle marveled at it and praised our holy mother Walatta Petros; may her intercession be with __________[1] for eternity, amen.

The Tenth Miracle: The Vision of the Making of This Book

The tenth miracle[2] that our holy mother Walatta Petros performed; may the blessing of her prayers[3] be with ________[4] for eternity, amen.

There was a monk who was also a priest[5] and whose name was Mazgaba Haymanot.[6] He had been raised and grown up in the community of our holy mother Walatta Petros; in fact, he had entered [the community] together with his mother when he was still a baby nursing at her breast. In the community, he had been instructed in the [sacred] books. He was humble, gentle, good, and loved God. So he became a monk [and lived] in chastity.[7]

[1] B: *gäbra Agnaṭəyos* (her servant Ignatius); D: *fəqura Ḫirutä Śəllase* (her beloved Ḫirutä Śəllase); J: *fəqərta Akrosəya* (her beloved Akrosia); Abb. 88: *fəqura* [name erased] (her beloved [name erased]), which CR altered to [*məsle*]*nä* ([with] us).

[2] BDJ: *ʿaśər täʾamər* (the tenth miracle); CR: *täʾamər* (a miracle).

[3] DJ: *bäräkätä ṣälota* (lit., the blessing of her prayer); B: *bäräkäta* (her blessing); CR: *ṣälota wä-bäräkäta* (her prayer and her blessing).

[4] B: *fəqura Agnaṭəyos* (her beloved Ignatius); D: *fəqura Ḫirutä Śəllase* (her beloved Ḫirutä Śəllase); J: [*məsle*]*nä* ([with] us); Abb. 88: *fəqura* [name erased] (her beloved [name erased]), which CR altered to [*məsle*]*nä* ([with] us).

[5] Most priests were not monks and most monks were not priests. Unlike monks, priests could marry; unlike priests, mere monks were not ordained and thus could not conduct the Liturgy or administer the Eucharist. Only those who were priests and monks could be bishops.

[6] *Mäzgäbä Haymanot* (Treasure-house of the Faith).

[7] Lit., *mänkʷäsä bä-dəngələnna* (he became a monk in chastity *or* in virginity). So another possible interpretation is that Mäzgäbä Haymanot went straight into monkdom as a young,

However, then he fell sick with a severe illness and suffered greatly. His skin became scaly, and for many years he remained bedridden.[1] One night though, while he was asleep, he saw a vision of what would come to pass,[2] in due time.[3] After Mazgaba Haymanot had woken up from his sleep, he summoned me to [ask me to] write this book.[4]

So I went to him and asked him, "Why have you summoned me?"

He replied, "Listen and let me tell you what I saw in my dream just last night: You, yes you, have been ordered[5] to write down our holy mother Walatta Petros's struggles and miracles. In addition, in the blink[6] [of an eye], I have seen you write to the end an important book, elegantly worded and in beautiful handwriting.[7] Furthermore, I heard the book being read aloud amidst a large gathering.[8] What do you think of this dream? Is it true or false? Will you receive[9] this gift from God, him

---

still virginal man. Since most monks and nuns were older widows, his pure status might be relevant to the special vision he has.

[1] It is unclear what this disease is. Leprosy typically has skin areas with marked depigmentation and numbness, but is not characterized by dry skin. Hypothyroidism is marked by dry skin but often progresses to marked confusion and dullness, which the monk does not appear to have. Thus, he may have had one of several infectious diseases, was incapacitated for some time, and thus developed contractures that kept him bedridden. The dry skin may be a mark of poor nutrition.

[2] BDJ: *raʿyä zä-yəkäwwən wä-yətfeṣṣäm* [twice ind.] (lit., a vision of what would be and come to pass); CR: *raʿyä zä-yəkäwwən wä-yətfäṣṣäm* [*sic*: 2nd verb subj.; no translation difference].

[3] Lit., *bä-ʿədmehu* (lit., in its time *or* in his time). Here our translation differs from Ricci's. We assume the idiomatic impersonal use of *bä-ʿədmehu*, in the sense of "in due time," while Ricci took the suffix *-hu* to have a personal reference, namely, Mäzgäbä Haymanot, and therefore translated *nel tempo a lui prefissato* (in the time set for him), even though the text was not written during Mäzgäbä Haymanot's lifetime.

[4] At the beginning of this gädl, the author said that he had been moved to write it by the young nun Qəddəstä Krəstos. Toward the end of the current episode, the author explains that for many years he did not heed Mäzgäbä Haymanot's injunction to write. Only after Mäzgäbä Haymanot's death, when Qəddəstä Krəstos independently approached the author with the same request and ensured that the monastic superiors condoned (or even ordered) the project, did he embark on writing.

[5] BDJ: *azzäzukä läkä* (lit., they have ordered you, you in particular); CR: *azzäzukä* (they have ordered you).

[6] Here our translation differs from Ricci's, who connects *bä-qəṣbät* (in a blink) with what follows rather than with what precedes it: *in un attimo tu avevi scritto* (in a flash you had written). Both translations are grammatically possible.

[7] Since humility demanded that an author not praise himself, the author Gälawdewos may here have put words of praise for himself into the mouth of Mäzgäbä Haymanot, who died about seven years before the author finally took up the task.

[8] Saints' books were read aloud to the faithful who congregated on the saint's feast day.

[9] BDJ: *bo-nu yətwähab läkä* (lit., will be given to you); CR: *bo-nu yətwähabäkä* (will you be given).

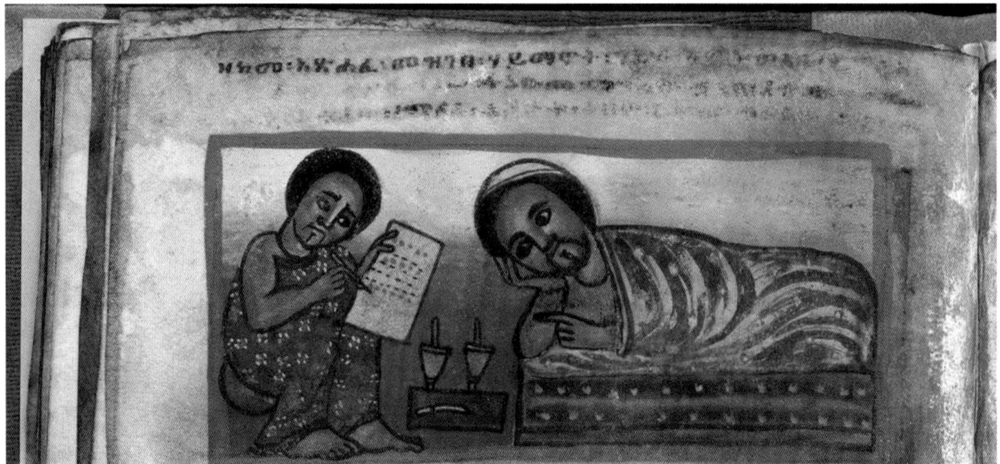

Plate 54. Miracle 10: "How Mazgaba Haymanot had [Galawdewos] write the gädl of our mother Walatta Petros [two more lines of caption text illegible]" (MS A, f. 159v © SLUB Mscr.Dresd.Eb.415.e,2).

128 from whom every good gift and perfect talent comes?"[1] Finally, he said to me, "Were this to happen, would you be capable of writing?"

I replied, "How could *I* be capable of writing?![2] But then again,[3] nothing is impossible for God."

Mazgaba Haymanot then said to me, "As for me, if it were God's will, I would want[4] you to write."

Now[5] I replied, "How could I, of my own volition, go ahead and write what my superiors[6] haven't ordered me [to write]? In addition, how can I know the struggles of our holy mother Walatta Petros? Am I not a new plant[7] who was not even around back then? Yet, if the elders who preceded me told me [about Walatta Petros], I would write."

Mazgaba Haymanot replied, "If you don't write now, you will [just] have

[1] BDJ: *zä-əm-ḫabehu kʷəllu habt śännay wä-kʷəllu fətt fəṣṣum* (lit., he from him every good gift and every perfect talent comes); CR: *zä-əm-ḫabehu kʷəllu habt fəṣṣum wä-kʷəllu habt śännay* (he from him every perfect gift and every good gift comes). James 1:17.

[2] Lit., *əfo əkəl əgbär zäntä* (lit., how would I be capable of doing this).

[3] CR adds *əsmä* (truly).

[4] BDJ: *əm-fäqädku anə-ssä* (lit., I for one would want); CR: *əmmä fäqädku anə-ssä* (if I for one wanted).

[5] BDJ: *kaʿebä* (lit., again); CR omits.

[6] Lit., *abäwəyä* (my fathers). Here and below.

[7] In the *WP gädl*, Ǝḫətä Krəstos early on also describes herself and WP as *ḥaddis täkl* (new plant, neophyte). That is, they are new to monastic life. The author might also be young, but the emphasis is on his few years as a monk.

to write later. Don't imagine that this dream was a deceptive one![1] Preserve it in your heart!"[2]

After Mazgaba Haymanot had let me know about this message, he lived with this illness for another four or five years.[3] Then he passed away in peace; may God give his soul rest[4] in the Kingdom of Heaven, amen.

But then this matter was forgotten, nobody brought it up. Yet, three years after Mazgaba Haymanot had passed away, it again pleased God to stir up a sister, [Qiddista Kristos,] who then made me—yes, me[5]—write [this account].

I told her, "Mazgaba Haymanot witnessed this same message[6] before and told me [to write]. Yet, I ignored it because my superiors hadn't ordered me [to do it]."

Then *she* told the superiors and the abbess [about the need] to write up Walatta Petros's *Life and Struggles*. They then decreed a rite of prayer to last seven days[7] [and afterward ordered me to write this book]. Therefore, I have written it according to God's will and with our holy mother Walatta Petros's assistance; may her intercession be with ________[8] for eternity, amen.

1 BDJ: *i-yəmsälkä zəntu ḥəlm ḥəlmä ḥassät* (lit., this dream should not appear to you as a dream of lie); Abb. 88: *i-yəmsälkä zəntu ḥəlmä ḥassät* (this should not appear to you as a dream of lie), which CR needlessly changed to *i-yəmsälkä zəntu ḥəlm ḥassätä* (this dream should not appear to you as a lie).

2 BDJ: *ʿəqäbo bä-ləbbəkä* (preserve it in your heart); CR: *təʿqäbo bä-ləbbəkä* (may you preserve it in your heart). This is reminiscent of Luke 2:19, in which the Virgin Mary, upon an angel envisioning her newborn son's future, "treasured up all these things and pondered them in her heart."

3 BDJ: *mäṭänä 4 ʿamät aw 5* (lit., for the length of four years, or five); CR: *mäṭänä 4 ʿamät wä-5 awraḫ* (for the length of four years and five months). Mäzgäbä Haymanot thus died around 1664–65, twenty-two years after WP had died in 1642.

4 BDJ: *wä-əmzə aʿräfä bä-sälam. Əgziʾabḥer yaʿrəf näfso* (he then passed away in peace: May God give his soul rest); CR: *wä-əmzə aʿräfä bä-sälamä əgziʾabḥer. Yaʿrəf näfso* (he then passed away in the peace of God. May he [= God] give his soul rest). In both variants *aʿräfä* is used intransitively (to pass away [lit., to find rest]) as well as transitively (to give rest); the latter use is rare.

5 DJ: *wä-agbärätäni litä* (lit., and made me, specifically me); B, CR: *wä-agäbbärätäni litä* (and she compelled or urged me, specifically me).

6 BDJ: *zäntä-ssä nägärä* (this same message); CR: *zäntä nägärä* (this message).

7 A seven-day period of prayer for determining the will of God and the right path happens several times in the *WP gädl*. WP's father had a vision about her destiny and then told her mother, "Come, let us hold a vigil and pray with great penitence for seven days so that God may reveal to us and make us certain that this thing is true." WP prays for a week to determine if she should rebuild the church on Rema Island, and Śəʿəlä Krəstos and WP pray for seven days to determine if she should leave the community and become a hermit. Since writing a gädl is the main part of elevating a local person to sainthood, the week of prayer may have also been for the elders to determine if they should take the step of making her a saint. There is no synod for determining sainthood; the community discusses whether she is worthy, fasts and prays, and most likely presented the *WP gädl* to the king when it was done.

8 B: *gäbra Agnaṭəyos* (her servant Ignatius); D: *fəqura Ḫirutä Śəllase* (her beloved Ḫirutä Śəllase); J: *əmmənä Amätä Dəngəl* (our mother Amätä Dəngəl); Abb. 88: *fəqura* [name erased] (her beloved [name erased]), which CR altered to [*məsle*]*nä* ([with] us).

Plate 55. Miracle 10: "How Mazgaba Haymanot saw in a vision that our mother Walatta Petros's *Life and Struggles* would be written down" (MS D, f. 132v [130v]). Photo by Claire Bosc-Tiessé, 1997.

The Eleventh Miracle: How Our Mother Stopped the Sun, Rain, and Ale

The eleventh miracle[1] that our holy mother Walatta Petros performed; may her intercession be with _________[2] for eternity, amen.

Beyond the Ribb River,[3] there lived a woman who loved our holy mother Walatta Petros and performed her [monthly] tazkaar. One day, while the woman was walk-

[1] BDJ: *täʾamər 11* (miracle eleven); CR: *täʾamər* (a miracle).

[2] B: *fəqura Agnaṭəyos* (her beloved Ignatius); D: *fəqura Ḫirutä Śəllase* (her beloved Ḫirutä Śəllase); J: *fəqərta Akrosəya* (her beloved Akrosia); CR: [*məsle*]*nä* ([with] us).

[3] The *Rəbb* is a river that empties into Lake Ṭana midway up its eastern shore in the region of Fogära, about fifteen miles north of Qʷäraṣa.

Plate 56. Miracle 11: "How the woman implored the sun to stop in the name of our mother Walatta Petros and how the sun stood still while the woman was on her way" (MS A, f. 159v © SLUB Mscr.Dresd. Eb.415.e,2).

ing on the road after she had been to church, she suffered the bad luck of having evening fall while she was still far away from her home. The sun began to sink and was close to setting. 129

Given this situation, the woman said to the sun, "I implore you, in the name of holy Walatta Petros, to stop where you are for my sake! Or, if you set, to [immediately] rise again."[1]

Accordingly, the sun rose high[2] and stood still until the woman had returned home. Then the woman told it, "You have done enough now. Continue on your natural course!"[3] Only then did the sun set.

At another time, while the woman was out on the road together with many people, a great rainstorm arose, with hail, thunder, lightning, and terrible thunderbolts. Now the woman said to the people who were with her, "If you survive this

[1] This is the second episode where the sun is stopped in its tracks. In the earlier part of the *WP gädl*, Ilarya stopped the sun by invoking the Lord of Saint Fasilädäs. Here, a woman stops it by invoking WP herself.

[2] BDJ: *tälәʿlä* (rose up high); CR: *täläʿalä* [variant verb form, but identical meaning].

[3] Lit., *ḥur ḫabä tәʾzazәkä* (go to where your order is).

Plate 57. Miracle 11: "How the sun stood still for a woman when she implored it in the name of our holy mother Walatta Petros" (MS D, f. 134r [132r]). Photo by Claire Bosc-Tiessé, 1997.

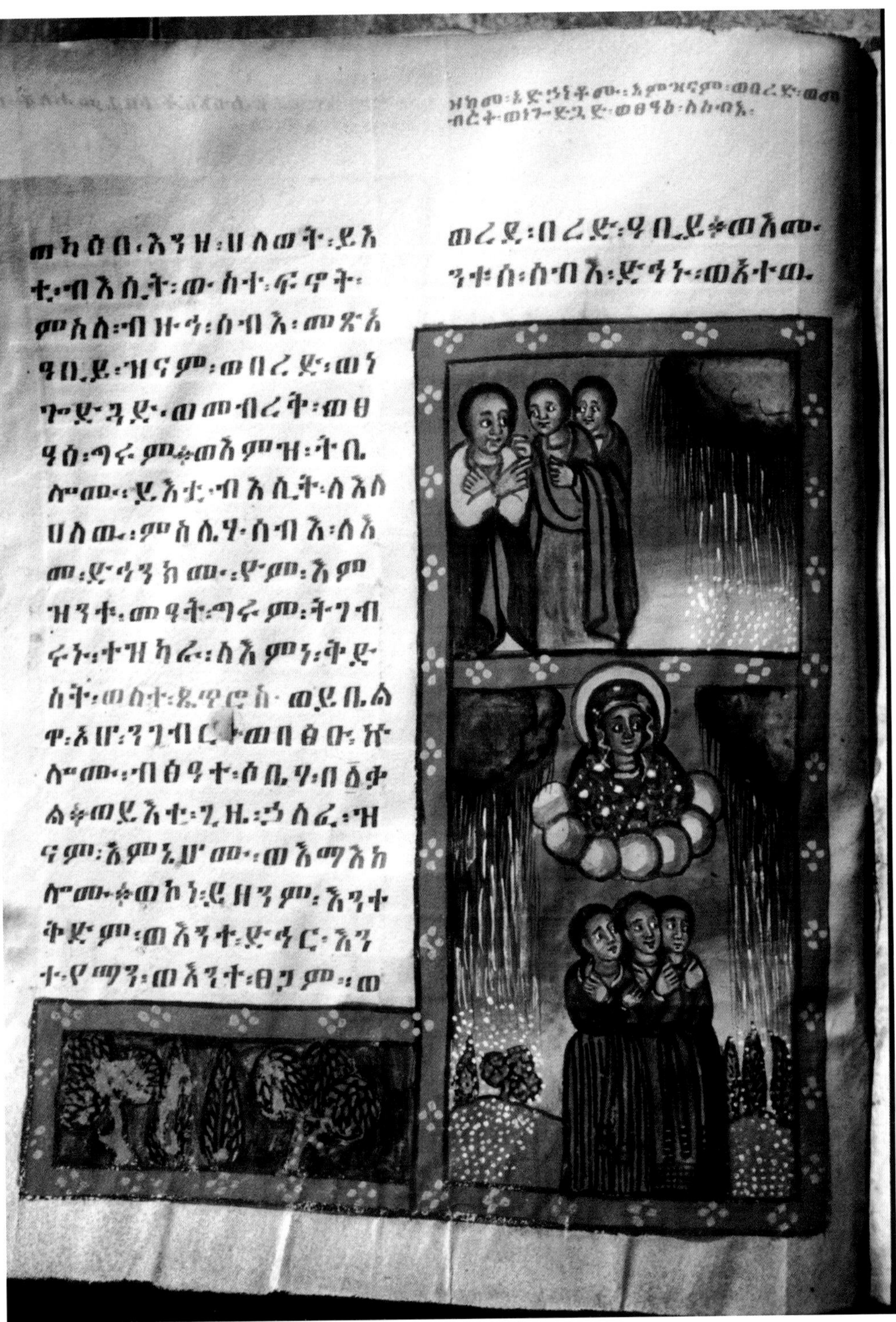

Plate 58. Miracle 11: "How she saved the people from rain, hail, lightning, thunder, and thunderbolts" (MS D, f. 134v [132v]). Photo by Claire Bosc-Tiessé, 1997.

Plate 59. Miracle 11: "How hail, rain, [lightning,] and thunder came down on the people, how they made a vow that they would celebrate the tazkaar of our mother, and how she saved them." Bottom caption illegible. (MS A, f. 160r © SLUB Mscr.Dresd.Eb.415.e,2).

terrible scourge today, will you perform[1] the tazkaar of our holy mother Walatta Petros?"

They replied, "Yes, we will!" and all of them[2] unanimously vowed to do so. At that instant, the rain departed from the very spot where they were standing,[3] but kept falling in front and behind them,[4] to the right and to the left, with big hailstones even. So those people remained unharmed and returned to their homes, without any rain falling on them, not even a single drop.[5] This happened through the prayers of our holy mother Walatta Petros.

A third miracle that happened to that woman: One day,[6] a number of sisters from the community of our holy mother Walatta Petros came to visit her. The woman welcomed them and served them[7] some bread. Now, there was only a single [jar of] ale[8] in her house, no second one. Therefore, thinking that guests that were more important might come tomorrow, the woman was stingy[9] and did not serve it to them.[10] Instead, she gave them *nug* seed[11] water to drink.[12]

The next day, after the sisters had left, the woman's servants brought that jar[13] so that the household could drink its ale. The jar was still sealed, but after they had opened it with some difficulty, they found that the jar was empty and dry,[14] as if ale[15] had never touched it. It was a mystery where the ale[16] had gone.

The woman then declared, "This is an act of power[17] by our holy mother Walatta Petros!" For when she had inspected the jar from top to bottom, it had not shown

[1] BDJ: *təgäbbəru-nu* (will you perform); CR: *təgäbbəru* (you will perform).

[2] BDJ: *kʷəllomu* (all of them); CR omits.

[3] BDJ: *əmənnehomu wä-əm-maʾkälomu* (lit., from them and from among them); CR: *əmənnehomu wä-maʾkälomu* (from them and among them).

[4] BDJ: *əntä qədm wä-əntä dəḫr* (lit., in front and behind); CR: *əntä dəḫr wä-əntä qədm* (behind and in front).

[5] BDJ: *wä-i-näṭäbä gəmura* (lit., not a drop at all); CR: *wä-i-näṭäbä zənam gəmura* (not a drop of rain at all).

[6] BDJ: *wä-bä-1 əm-mäwaʿəl* (lit., on one from among the days); CR: *wä-bä-1 mäwaʿəl* (on one days [*sic*]).

[7] BDJ: *aśbäṭäton* (served them); CR: *abləʿaton* (fed them).

[8] CR, B: *säwa*; DJ: *ṣälla* [the Amharic term for the same beverage].

[9] BDJ: *qeqäyäton* (lit., was stingy toward them); CR: *kälʾaton* (withheld from them).

[10] This is the second episode where a woman has to make a choice between saving her ale for important guests or serving it to poor guests.

[11] *Nug* (*Guizotia abyssinica*) is an herb cultivated in the Ethiopian highlands; its seeds are ground and mostly used for oil.

[12] BDJ: *wä-astäyäton mayä nug* (lit., instead, she gave them nug water to drink); Abb. 88: *wä-astäyäton mayä nəḫdəg* [*sic*] (instead she gave them water to drink; let us abandon); CR altered this by omitting contextually nonsensical *nəḫdəg*, obviously a corruption of *nug*: *wä-astäyäton mayä* (instead she gave them water to drink),

[13] Lit., *wä-bä-sanita . . . aqräbəwwo* (the next day . . . they [masc. pl.] brought it).

[14] BD: *yəbusä* [acc., as required for the predicative complement for *täräkbä* (was found)] (dry); CR, J: *yəbus* [nom.] (dry).

[15] B, CR: *säwa*; DJ: *ṣälla* [the Amharic term for the same beverage].

[16] B: *säwa*; DJ: *ṣälla*; CR: *məzər* (beer).

[17] Lit., *zəntu ḫayl . . . wəʾətu* (this is a power). This also underlies "act of power" about thirty-five words below.

Plate 60. Miracle 11: "How the woman's ale dried up when she was miserly with the sisters" (MS D, f. 135r [133r]). Photo by Claire Bosc-Tiessé, 1997.

Plate 61. Miracle 11: "How the sisters came as guests to the house of a woman. She received them, gave them supper, and *nug* seed water even though there was ale" (top) and "the next day, after the sisters had left, the woman was brought the jar so that they could drink from it but the jar was found empty" (bottom) (MS A, f. 160v © SLUB Mscr.Dresd.Eb.415.e,2).

any crack.[1] This is why she realized that it had been an act of power by our holy
130 mother Walatta Petros. She openly confessed, "Because I have wronged those sisters, daughters of Walatta Petros, this miracle has been visited upon me."[2]

O this marvelous and astonishing[3] power of our holy mother Walatta Petros's miracles![4] May her intercession be with ________,[5] for eternity, amen.[6]

Ending and Colophon of the Conti Rossini Print Edition

After the above, and before the poems, Abb. 88/CR adds:

We who have commissioned the writing of these struggles and miracles of our blessed mother Walatta Petros,[7] and we who have come and assembled on this day to listen to them: may God have mercy on us through the kidaan that he granted her, amen. May he assign us to stand at his right, may he count us among his sheep, amen. May he join us in eternity with those to whom he says, "Come, blessed ones of our Father," amen and amen. May it be thus, may it be thus!

May the blessings of the Ninety-Nine Angelic Orders,[8] of the [heavenly] multitudes, myriads, and multitudes of myriads, be with us, amen. May the blessings of the patriarchs[9] be with us, amen. May the blessings of the Fifteen Prophets[10] be upon

[1] Lit., *i-täśäṭqä məntä-ni* (it had not [been] split at all).

[2] BDJ: *laʿleyä* (upon me); CR: *laʿleha* (upon her).

[3] BDJ: *o-zə-mänkər wä-ʿəṣub* (o this marvelous and astonishing); Abb. 88: *o-zä-mänkər o-ʿəṣub* (o marvelous, o astonishing), which CR altered to structurally more parallel *o-zä-mänkər o-zä-ʿəṣub* (o marvelous, o astonishing).

[4] BDJ: *täʾamər* (miracles *or* miracle); CR: *täʾamərat* (miracles).

[5] B: *fəqura Agnaṭəyos wä-məslä gäbra Ḥawarya Mäsqäl wä-məslä kʷəllomu däqiqa wä-awalədiha wä-məslä əllä ṣahqu wä-astäḥamämu lä-ṣəḥifä zəntu mäṣḥaf* (her beloved Ignatius, and with her servant Ḥawarya Mäsqäl, and with all her sons and daughters, as well as with those who longed and were anxious for the writing of this book); D: [leaves a blank]; J: [*məsle*]*nä* ([with] us); Abb. 88: *gäbra* [name erased] *wä-məslä däqiqa wä-awalədiha wä-məslä kʷəllənä wəludä ṭəmqät* (her servant [name erased], and with her sons and daughters, and with all of us Children of Baptism); CR altered the initial *gäbra* [name erased] of Abb. 88 to [*məsle*]*nä* ([with] us), but otherwise here faithfully reproduced Abb. 88.

[6] DJ: *amen* (amen); B, CR: *amen wä-amen. Lä-yəkun lä-yəkun* (amen and amen. May it be [thus], may it be [thus]). After the täʾamər (miracles) section of each manuscript, mälkəʾ and sälamta poems may appear or information about the creation of the täʾamər and the commissioners.

[7] That is, the writing of this particular manuscript, Abb. 88, in 1714–15, copied from an earlier manuscript.

[8] According to the Täwaḥədo Church, God created one hundred tribes or orders of angels, but one of those orders fell (due to the angel Satan), and so one makes vows by the Ninety-Nine Angelic Orders only.

[9] Lit., *abäw qädämt* (the forefathers). That is, the Old Testament figures Abraham, Isaac, and Jacob.

[10] The fifteen Old Testament prophets are the three major prophets (with long books in the Tanakh) Isaiah, Jeremiah, and Ezekiel, and the twelve minor prophets (with short books in

Plate 62. "Our holy mother Walatta Petros" above the top panel. "My mother Walatta Petros, to you I entrust my soul and flesh, your maidservant" above the bottom panel of an unnamed prostrated woman. Perhaps she is the wife of the manuscript's patron Hiruta Sillasé, or perhaps she is Qiddista Kristos, who urged the making of the book (MS D, f. 136v [134v]). Photo by Claire Bosc-Tiessé, 1997.

us, amen. May the blessings of the 144,000[1] Holy Children [of Bethlehem] whom Herod killed be upon us, amen. May the blessings of the Twelve Apostles[2] be upon

the Tanakh) Hosea, Amos, Micah, Joel, Obadiah, Jonah, Nahum, Habakkuk, Zephaniah, Haggai, Zechariah, and Malachi.

[1] CR: 104,000, which is a corruption of 144,000, since this correct traditional number is given twice earlier.

[2] Matthew 10:2–4, "These are the names of the twelve apostles [of Christ]: first, Simon (who is called Peter) and his brother Andrew; James son of Zebedee, and his brother John;

us, amen. May the blessings of the Seventy-Two Disciples[1] be upon us, amen. May the blessings of [Saint] Stephen, [Saint] George, [Saint] Fasiladas, and of all the martyrs be upon us, amen. May the blessings of the 318 [Bishops] and of all the Orthodox teachers[2] [of the Church] be upon us, amen. May the blessings of [Saint] Anthony, of [Saint] Macarius, and of all the Righteous Ones[3] be upon us, amen. May the blessings of the Thirty-Six[4] Holy Women be upon us, [amen]. May the blessings of the three women—that is, the blessings of Amata Kristos [and her two handmaidens][5]—as well as the blessings of the virgins and nuns be upon us, amen. May the blessing of our holy, beatified, and blessed mother Walatta Petros, who is surrounded by majesty and grace, who reconciles all who quarrel, who is the joy of the body and the soul, be upon us, amen. May the blessings of our mother Eheta Kristos, of Amata Dinghil, of Nazraweet,[6] and of all[7] the holy women [of the com-
131 munity] be upon us, amen and amen. May it be thus, may it be thus!

May God accept these benedictions[8] through the Twelve Apostles. May these benedictions be [upon us] who are in the [Orthodox] faith, asserting that Christ in his essence became God's son[9] through the unction of the Holy Spirit,[10] [as] we learn[11] from the Old and the New Testaments. Amen and amen.

Philip and Bartholomew; Thomas and Matthew the tax collector; James son of Alphaeus, and Thaddaeus; Simon the Zealot and Judas Iscariot, who betrayed him."

[1] Luke 10:1–24, "After this the Lord appointed seventy-two others and sent them two by two ahead of him to every town and place where he was about to go."

[2] Lit., *liqawənt* (teachers), not the usual *mämhəran.*

[3] *Ṣadəqan* (righteous ones) are various groups of anonymous Täwaḥədo Church saints, starting with foreign monks who came to evangelize in Ethiopia in the fifth century.

[4] Lit., *30 wä-7* (37), which we assume is a CR reading mistake of *30 wä-6*: first, because the fidäl symbols for 6 ፮ and 7 ፯ are extremely similar, and second, because the Täwaḥədo Church believes that thirty-six women followed Christ, as well as the apostles and disciples; see Matthew 27:55–56; Mark 15:40–41; Acts 1:12–15.

[5] According to the *Sənkəssar*, a twelve-year-old widow of the city of Constantinople, named Amätä Krəstos, fled with her two handmaidens into the desert to escape a rapist. They lived in a cave for twelve years, bearing the hardships of the desert naked and being fed by birds that brought them fruit. The three women are commemorated in the *Sənkəssar* on 8 Yäkkatit (Budge 1928, 346–47).

[6] *Nazrawit* is listed last in this lineage of Qʷäraṣa's abbesses. Ǝḫətä Krəstos was WP's successor and thus the second *əmmä maḫbär* of WP's community. Amätä Dəngəl was Ǝḫətä Krəstos's successor. So Nazrawit must have been the fourth *əmmä maḫbär* of WP's community, from the 1680s through this date of 1714.

[7] Abb. 88: *kʷəllomu* [masc.] (all), which CR sensibly altered to *kʷəllon* [fem.] (all).

[8] Lit., *lä-zəntu burake yətwäkäf əgzi'abḥer* (may God accept this benediction), which is slightly ungrammatical and which we (and Ricci) therefore assume to be a corruption of *lä-zəntu burake yətwäkäfo əgzi'abḥer.*

[9] Lit., *ənzä nəbəl konä wäldä zä-baḥrəy* (saying: he became the Son by essence).

[10] Through this formula, the Abb. 88 scribe aligns the community with the Unctionists or Qəbat side of the period's doctrinal debates, associated with Saint Ewosṭatewos. "The Father was the anointer, the son was the anointed, and the Holy Spirit was the ointment" (Täklä Śəllase [Ṭinno] 1900, 182).

[11] Lit., *rə'inä* (we see).

Plate 63. An unnamed prostrated woman in an extremely elaborate, full-page illustration. A label (of two lines, with two words each followed by a period) has been erased from the middle of the painting. Perhaps this label identified the woman as Eheta Kristos? It cannot be the queen, because the King Dawit named in the text had no wife, having died in his midtwenties (MS D, f. 137r [135r]). Photo by Claire Bosc-Tiessé, 1997.

The copying of this *Life and Struggles* was begun in the Year of Mercy 7206,[1] in a year of Mark [the Evangelist],[2] on the twenty-fourth of the month of Tiqimt, a Wednesday, in the fourteenth epact [and] in the sixteenth[3] matqi[4] [i.e., 1 November 1714]. It was completed in the month of Yekkateet, [about four months later], on a Wednesday, at the ninth hour [i.e., 3:00 PM].[5]

He who steals, robs, or erases this manuscript shall be cursed and anathematized through the power of the Twelve Apostles and the word of the 318 [Bishops].

I, the sinner Wolde Giyorgis,[6] entrust myself to our mother Walatta Petros, "Do not separate my soul from yours in eternity, amen!" May it be thus, may it be thus!

[In Amharic:] This manuscript was copied for an ounce [of gold] and[7] five [bars] of salt.[8]

[1] Lit., *70 [×] 100 wä-2 [×] 100 əm-*[*sic*] *27* (70 [times] 100 and 2 [times] 100 from 27), in which we assume contextually nonsensical *əm-* (from) is a mistake for *wä-* (and). In addition, we regard extant 7207 as a CR reading mistake of 7206 due to the similarity of the fidäl symbols for 6 and 7. The year of the Mark the Evangelist is 7206, and the year in which 24 Ṭəqəmt falls on a Wednesday is 7206.

[2] Lit., *bä-zämänä Marqos* (in a year of Mark). Here our translation varies substantively from Ricci's, who has *nell' . . . epoca di Marco evangelista* (in an . . . era of Mark the Evangelist).

[3] Lit., *17*, which we assume is a CR reading mistake due to the similarity of the fidäl symbols for 6 and 7. Mäṭqəʿ in 7206 is 16 (not 17). Additionally, the *abäqte* and *mäṭqəʿ* must add up to 30, and the manuscript's 14 plus 17 is 31.

[4] According to a CR note, Abb. 88 here has eight blank, erased lines. These lines must have been an addition to the text, as the other manuscripts do not have any lines here that are missing in CR.

[5] Since the exact day of the month is not being provided, we can only say that Abb. 88 was finished on a Wednesday in February or early March 1714; 7, 14, 21, 28 February and 7 March were Wednesdays that year.

[6] Lit., *Wäldä Geworgis*, which is an uncommon variant of the common name Wäldä Giyorgis.

[7] Lit., *ta-*, which we assume to be a corruption of *tä-*.

[8] That is, amole. Note that the book of WP poems sold for two amole. Gold and amole were the two main forms of local currency at this time.

Summaries of Additional *Miracles of Walatta Petros* (*Täʾamərä Wälättä Ṗeṭros*)

The miracles below are not translations, but summaries of miracles that appear in MSS H and/or I only, written after 1770. MS I includes the most complete set of miracles of any manuscript, with miracles one through twenty-seven. MS H has only miracles seventeen through twenty-four. MS I was written in two hands, one for the beginning of the book through miracle sixteen and a different one for miracles seventeen through twenty-seven. Digital copies of MSS H and I are available through the Hill Museum and Manuscript Library's online archive (under the catalog numbers EMIP 2138 and 2139, respectively).

The Twelfth Miracle Summarized: How Our Mother Healed the Man's Swollen Leg (in MS I only)

The right leg of a man named Petros, from Woybila,[1] became badly swollen after he intentionally stepped in dry blood while going down to the river to wash his clothes. A monk called Talaawé Kristos,[2] having heard about Petros's suffering, paid him a visit and told him that he too had once had a sick leg, with pus flowing from it. Recalling the healing power of our holy mother Walatta Petros's intercessory prayer, however, he had called upon her, pledging to honor her on her annual tazkaar, and so she promptly healed him. When Petros heeded Talaawé Kristos's advice to do the same, Walatta Petros also promptly healed Petros. The two men resolved to make a copy of the book about our mother.[3] They carried out their plan, and their *Life and Struggles* now is the one regularly read aloud in the Saint Mary Church of Woybila.

[1] *Wäybəla* is a town less than five miles northeast of Qʷäraṣa. *Wäybəla* could easily be a variant spelling of *Wäybəna*, a town mentioned in the second standard miracle.

[2] *Tälawe Krəstos* (Follower of Christ).

[3] Lit., *tämakäru kəlʾehomu kämä yəṣḥafu gädla lä-əmmənä qəddəst wä-burəkt Wälättä Ṗeṭros* (they decided together to write a gädl about our holy and blessed mother WP). It is unclear if they commissioned a copy of the standard gädl or if they wrote a *WP gädl* of their own, different from the standard one. The wording here—it speaks of their writing (*yəṣḥafu*, from *ṣäḥafä*, "to write"), not of their commissioning (*yaṣḥəfu*, from *aṣḥafä*, "to make write" or "to commission")—is suggestive of the latter but extremely unlikely.

The Thirteenth Miracle Summarized: How Our Mother Saved the Sick Baby (in MS I only)

That same man, Petros, had a sister who gave birth to quite a few children, all of whom died soon after. When she became pregnant again, she went to her parents' house to give birth to a beautiful little daughter. The little girl became severely ill at two months old, however, with death looming. The whole extended family came together, very distressed and uncertain what to do. Petros then advised his sister to call out to Walatta Petros for help, as he himself had done when his leg had swollen up. He told her to pledge to hold Walatta Petros's annual tazkaar and to name her daughter after Walatta Petros if the saint healed the little girl. The sister did as her brother told her and the daughter immediately was healthy again, on the eve of Walatta Petros's annual tazkaar.

The Fourteenth Miracle Summarized: How Our Mother Restored the Stolen Jar (in MS I only)

A nun from Qoratsa prepared some brewing yeast[1] for our mother's upcoming tazkaar and put it in a sealed jar. A woman from Wonchet who regularly helped the nuns with kitchen work stole that jar, thinking that it contained honey or butter, and took it to the market at Cherr Takkal to sell it. A prospective buyer asked her to open the jar so he could check if the honey was of good quality, but when the thieving woman tried to break the seal, she failed. The prospective buyer then tried himself, but also failed. He went away, marveling at the strange jar of honey. That evening, the woman took the jar back to her house and Walatta Petros appeared to her in a dream, in all her majesty, but without saying anything. In the morning, the frightened woman set out for Qoratsa to return the jar, carrying it on her back, but on the way, robbers assaulted her, beat her up, and stole the jar from her, also believing that it contained honey or butter. The woman returned home in tears. As for the robbers, when they tried to open the jar, they too failed. They then realized that the jar must belong to Walatta Petros's community. So they returned it to Qoratsa for the sisters to use it in brewing ale for Walatta Petros's tazkaar. Then, a monk in a distant region heard about this event and sent a message to Qoratsa, "Let me have some of that blessed ale so that I can use it to cure our sick." So the Qoratsa community dispatched some to him. When the monk tried it, he was surprised at how tasty it was. He then administered it to the sick who came to his monastery, and many were healed by this ale infused with Walatta Petros's healing powers.

[1] Lit., *bəḥuʾ* (leaven *or* yeast).

The Fifteenth Miracle Summarized: How Our Mother Saved People from Fire and with Earth (in MS I only)

One day a devastating fire broke out in Fintiro town in the Dembiya region. The fire came so close to Walatta Petros's house[1] that it was in danger of burning down. The people appealed to Walatta Petros to save it, and she did so. Later, another fire broke out, the people again appealed to Walatta Petros, and she again saved the house. Yet again a fire broke out, this time very fierce, and people gave up all hope that Walatta Petros's house could be saved from the flames. But Walatta Petros then appeared in person, sitting on her house's roof and covering it with her cloak, thereby protecting it. A man sitting on the bank of the Gibaza[2] River saw this from afar. People praised the Lord, as well as Walatta Petros through whom he works wonders.

Another miracle involving Walatta Petros's house: A woman from Dembiya had difficulty giving birth. She asked those of Walatta Petros's house to send her some earth on which our holy mother had walked. However, the community could not locate any. The woman then asked for earth on which the community members, Walatta Petros's children, had walked. When they sent her this, she smeared it on her body, and then was able to give birth easily.

The Sixteenth Miracle Summarized: How Our Mother Healed a Paralyzed Man (in MS I only)

This miracle happened during the reign of King Bakaffa:[3] A man so paralyzed that he had to drag himself on the ground like a snake attended Walatta Petros's tazkaar in search of healing. As he listened to her *Life and Struggles* being read out aloud, Walatta Petros cured him, enabling him to stand on his feet again. When the multitude attending the tazkaar witnessed this miracle, they became so elated that they danced in Lake Tana. The priests in their joy did not finish reading out Walatta Petros's *Life and Struggles*, but took the healed man to the church to administer the Eucharist to him. He received it and returned home, praising Walatta Petros. Thus, all should be mindful of Walatta Petros's legacy and observe her instructions.

[1] It is unclear if the house and the fire were in Fənṭəro or whether the fire started in Fənṭəro and burned all the way down to WP's community in Qʷäraṣa, forty miles south. Since the miraculous appearance of WP on top of her house can be seen from the Gəbaza River, which is almost fifty miles south of Qʷäraṣa and thus ninety miles south of Fənṭəro, the house may be in Qʷäraṣa.

[2] The *Gəbaza* is probably the modern Gäbäzä Maryam River, about forty miles south of Lake Ṭana. This distance suggests that he saw WP's figure in the tower of smoke.

[3] *Bäkaffa* was king of Ethiopia from 1721 to 1730, so this miracle happened about seventy years after WP's death.

The Seventeenth Miracle Summarized: How Our Mother Protected the Rebels against King Bakaffa (in MSS H and I only)

In those days, [i.e., in the late 1720s], a conflict broke out between King Bakaffa and Kucho[1] when Kucho increased his troops, thus conspiring against the kingdom. So King Bakaffa went and killed Kucho in the middle of Kucho's camp.[2] Bakaffa told his herald to announce among his soldiers that they could take Kucho's possessions but not his head, which the king wanted for himself. When Kucho's soldiers heard this pronouncement, they concluded that only Walatta Petros could save them from certain death. Therefore, 2,030 of Kucho's soldiers sought refuge at her monastery at Qoratsa.[3] When Bakaffa learned of this, he dispatched a large body of troops to Qoratsa, with orders to kill everybody there, including the monks and nuns. An enraged Walatta Petros then appeared to Bakaffa in a dream, demanding that the king reverse his orders. Bakaffa became frightened and woke up, but then fell asleep again. Two more times, Walatta Petros delivered the same dream message to him.[4] Finally, in the last dream, she cast him from his throne and set it on fire over him. The terrified Bakaffa then began to suspect that Walatta Petros was actually speaking to him. To find out whether this was the case, he summoned the nun Malakotaweet,[5] who lived at his court. In her youth, Malakotaweet had met Walatta Petros personally and so she knew what Walatta Petros looked like. When the emperor described the appearance of the woman in his dream, Malakotaweet confirmed that it was indeed Walatta Petros warning him. So, Bakaffa sent a swift-running messenger after his army, with orders to tell them to turn back instantly. The messenger arrived, delivered his message, the army turned back, and so Kucho's soldiers at Walatta Petros's monastery were saved. When the monks and nuns later learned about the fate that had awaited them, and which they had been spared thanks to Walatta Petros's intervention,

[1] *Kuččo* was a high-ranking member of the early eighteenth-century court who fell in and out of favor with more than one king, as described in several historical sources. He was executed by Bäkaffa in 1727.

[2] The story here varies slightly from that in the *Short Chronicles* and Bäkaffa's royal chronicle, which state that the king ordered Kuččo's execution.

[3] Qʷäraṣa was long known as a sanctuary for those seeking to avoid the wrath of the king (Bosc-Tiessé 2003). The so-called *Short Chronicles* do not record the troops going to Qʷäraṣa, but only the king telling them to leave Gondär.

[4] In the standard set of miracles, WP also appeared three times in a dream to warn a thief in miracle 7. In the additional miracles, the same happens to *Ras* Mika᾽el in miracle 22.

[5] *Mäläkotawit* (She who belongs to the Godhead) cannot be the important historical figure of the same name who was the concubine of King Iyasu I and who was later made empress by her son, because that woman was hung for treason in 1708 and these events happened in 1727. However, any person who remembered in 1727 what WP looked like would be in their nineties (since WP died eighty-four years earlier), about the right age for the executed Mäläkotawit, so perhaps the oral tradition has inserted her into the story.

they told everyone, and everyone praised the Lord and marveled at Walatta Petros's great power.

The Eighteenth Miracle Summarized: How Our Mother Took Vengeance on King Iyasu II for Pillaging Her Monastery (in MSS H and I only)

During Iyasu II's reign,[1] [around 1730,] a great lord called Biyadgo Yohannes,[2] a rich and arrogant man, hated the king and showed it. When Iyasu learned of this, he set out with the intention of killing Biyadgo Yohannes, who immediately sought refuge at Qoratsa. After living there for a while, he asked the monks and nuns to seek a pardon for him from the king, despite being insincere in his wish for reconciliation. In any case, a delegation from Qoratsa went to see Iyasu and begged his pardon for Biyadgo Yohannes, invoking Walatta Petros's legacy and kidaan. Iyasu granted the pardon, and the monks and nuns made him confirm it in Walatta Petros's name. Then they returned to Qoratsa and told Biyadgo Yoḥannəs, but he was not convinced that he was safe. After a while, he asked the monks and nuns to go to Iyasu again for confirmation, and they did so. When they returned to Qoratsa, they told Biyadgo Yohannes that the king had again confirmed his vow. Still, Biyadgo Yohannes did not leave Qoratsa, and now the monks and nuns started rebuking him, saying that if he did not reconcile with the king, the monarch would wonder whether they had been sincere with him. They told Biyadgo Yohannes that his continued presence at Qoratsa was embarrassing.

Now Biyadgo Yohannes became angry with the monks and nuns, scaring them. Instead of going to see the emperor, he began to assemble a new army. Enraged, Iyasu began assembling a large army himself and told them to capture Biyadgo Yohannes. The king's orders were that, should they happen to find him at Qoratsa, they should pillage and burn down the monastery, kill all the monks and nuns, and lay waste to the surrounding countryside. As Iyasu's armies approached, Biyadgo Yohannes, together with his wife, children, and all his treasures, boarded a tankwa on the shore opposite of Réma Island. Once out on Lake Tana, however, the tankwa stopped due to the intervention of Walatta Petros.

Meanwhile, Iyasu's armies arrived, pillaged the monastery, killed many monks, and took others captive. (With a number of biblical quotes, the text likens the pillaging of Qoratsa to the sacking of Jerusalem/Zion.) While the victorious army and its officers prepared for a victory banquet, feasting on the supplies of Qoratsa, God sent a messenger disguised as one from the king, telling them to refrain from feast-

[1] *Iyasu* (Joshua) II (r. 1730–55) was Bäkaffa's son and his immediate successor as king. Although the text says only "Iyasu," this cannot be Iyasu I (r. 1682–1706), Bäkaffa's father, because the story is about events and people associated with Iyasu II.

[2] *Biyadgo Yoḥannəs* was a rebel against Iyasu II, and his failed escape onto Lake Ṭana near Rema is recorded in Iyasu II's royal chronicle (Anonymous 1912, 37). No mention is made of WP or her monastery in his chronicle, however.

ing and to turn back. They obeyed—but while they left by one route, another army arrived by a different route and pillaged Qoratsa again. Neither army found Biyadgo Yohannes at Qoratsa, but they soon discovered him on his immobilized tankwa, captured him, and took him to Iyasu. He was condemned to exile in the inhospitable region of Wolqait.[1]

Then, because the injustice done to her monastery still had not been remedied and the army still feasted on Qoratsa's stolen cattle, Walatta Petros caused mayhem in the king's camp. She made people draw their knives and cut into other people to eat their flesh, made cattle bite into other cattle, and horses into other horses. King Iyasu was terrified and bewildered, but had only a vague idea of why it was happening. Then, after a few days, the Qoratsa monks who had been able to escape alive arrived at court and complained about the injustice that had been done to them. When Iyasu realized what had happened, he asked them for forgiveness, compensated them liberally, and dispatched them honorably to Qoratsa.

The Nineteenth Miracle Summarized: How Our Mother Saved the Celebration Provisions (in MSS H and I only)

After Walatta Petros's burial on Réma Island, the monks and nuns of Qoratsa held her tazkaar there every year, feeding the poor and wretched. Most years, they took the required provisions to Réma the night before, but one year there was strife in the monastery and they only loaded the tankwa on the day of the tazkaar itself. Then, while the two boatmen were punting to the island, a strong wind came up and capsized the tankwa, with all the provisions—bread and ale—sinking underwater. When the two boatmen cried out to Walatta Petros for help, however, everything rose safe and sound: the bread was dry and the ale had not spilled. Only one jar of ale remained missing; it had sunk to the lake floor. Six months later, when the water was low, this jar was recovered unbroken, without any leaks or any alteration in the taste of its ale. Everyone marveled at this new miracle worked by Walatta Petros.

The Twentieth Miracle Summarized: How Our Mother Took Vengeance on King Iyoas for Pillaging Her Monastery (in MSS H and I only)

In the twelfth year of King Iyoas I[2] [i.e., 1767–68], the noblewoman Walatta Takla Haymanot,[3] the daughter of former king Bakaffa, celebrated Walatta Petros's taz-

[1] *Wälqayt* is a province in northern Ethiopia (directly northwest of Waldəbba) regularly used by kings in the eighteenth century to exile enemies.

[2] *Iyoʾas* (Joas) I (r. 1755–69) was Iyasu II's son and his immediate successor as king. Although the text says only "Iyoʾas," it cannot mean Iyoʾas II (r. 1818–21) because the miracle's central figure, the noblewoman Wälättä Täklä Haymanot, is identified as a daughter of King Bäkaffa (and even if he had conceived her the year he died, in 1730, she would unlikely to be taking long journeys ninety years later).

[3] *Wälättä Täklä Haymanot* (Daughter of [Saint] Täklä Haymanot) was the eldest

kaar at Qoratsa, giving alms to the poor. Soon she quarreled with the king, with Queen Walatta Giyorgis,[1] and with two powerful generals, Awsebiyos[2] and Eshete,[3] who all wanted her to return to the court. But Walatta Takla Haymanot insisted on staying at Walatta Petros's monastery, which she preferred to living with sinners; that is, people at court. Therefore, the court dispatched the officer Wolde Nagodgwaad[4] to Qoratsa with five hundred troops to fetch her by force.

When Walatta Takla Haymanot learned they were coming, she put her husband Finhas[5] in a tankwa with boatmen and sent him to Tsana Island. Once on the open water, however, Finhas's tankwa stopped moving forward. Finhas understood that Walatta Petros did not want him to go to Tsana so he ordered the boatmen to turn back. Without even punting, they returned in a flash, despite not having been able to move in the other direction for many hours. Finhas went into his house and prayed. Now Wolde Nagodgwaad arrived with his soldiers, bound him, and sought to take him away.[6] Walatta Takla Haymanot wailed loudly, and the monks and nuns of Qoratsa heard this and came to hinder Wolde Nagodgwaad. They told him that Finhas had taken refuge in their monastery so that they could not allow him to be taken away. But Wolde Nagodgwaad did not listen to their entreaties and took Finhas away.

Meanwhile, a young soldier stole the clothes of one of the monks. The monks followed the troops to Fogera, where everybody rested for the night. There, the thievish soldier fell ill and died because the day before he had sworn a false oath in Walatta Petros's name.[7] The next day, on the way through the Mitsraaha region,[8] another young soldier tried to mount a mule taken from Qoratsa, but the mule threw him and killed him.[9] All of this was Walatta Petros's work; Wolde Nagodgwaad and his soldiers became afraid of Walatta Petros's power.

---

daughter of King Bäkaffa and Queen Wälättä Giyorgis, and thus the younger sister of King Iyasu II as well as the aunt of the ruling monarch Iyoʾas.

[1] *Wälättä Giyorgis* (Daughter of [Saint] George) is the Christian name of the famous eighteenth-century queen, Bərhan Mogäsa (Məntəwwab), who was the grandmother of and regent for Iyoʾas I, as well as Wälättä Täklä Haymanot's mother.

[2] *Awsäbəyos* (Eusebios) was an important eighteenth-century military commander, significant during the reigns of Iyasu II and Iyoʾas, and the brother of Əšäte. He appears frequently in the time's royal chronicles.

[3] *Əšäte* (My ripe grain), brother of Awsäbəyos, was a military commander who appears frequently in the time's royal chronicles.

[4] *Wäldä Nägwädgwad* (Son of the thunder) was another important eighteenth-century historical figure frequently discussed in the time's royal chronicles.

[5] *Finḥas* must be a later husband as her husband mentioned in the time's royal chronicles, *Ras* Elyas, was killed in 1733.

[6] It is unclear why the main character of the story switches from Wälättä Täklä Haymanot, who troops are sent to fetch, to her husband Finḥas, who is fetched and returned to court without her. Perhaps he was considered a dangerous opposition figure. Alternatively, the story may be experiencing interference from the Biyadgo Yoḥannəs on Lake Ṭana story.

[7] This is the reason the text gives for his death, not his theft.

[8] *Məṣraḥa* is a famous island on eastern Lake Ṭana frequented by kings.

[9] Lit., *bälʿato* (ate him).

Eventually, they all reached Gondar, including many monks, even though travel was difficult because it was the rainy season.[1] When Finhas was brought before King Iyoas, Queen Walatta Giyorgis, and the great lords, he told about the miracles that Walatta Petros had worked on the road back to Gondar. The king, queen, and lords became afraid. When the monks entered, they asked the king's pardon, in the name of Walatta Petros, for their unsolicited appearance. The king granted them pardon and dispatched them home in peace. Then, when Wolde Nagodgwaad fell severely ill and was close to death, he confessed his wrongdoing and asked Walatta Petros's forgiveness and healing, both of which she granted.[2]

The Twenty-First Miracle Summarized: How Our Mother Saved a Man from Woodage Asahél (in MSS H and I only)

A man named Asahél Ayikal,[3] full of faith in Walatta Petros's protective powers, sought refuge at Qoratsa from his powerful enemy Woodage Asahél,[4] who was looking for an excuse to kill him.

Woodage Asahél consulted with his two counselors and then dispatched them to Qoratsa to seize Asahél Ayikal. They did so, and brought Asahél Ayikal back to their master. Woodage Asahél now accused Asahél Ayikal of wrongdoing and had him taken to the bath.[5] Asahél Ayikal survived the punishment through the power of the Lord and Walatta Petros, however. As a result, Woodage Asahél became convinced of Walatta Petros's powers and humbly and sincerely made a pilgrim's trip to Qoratsa.

Then, due to their enemies, adversity fell upon each of Woodage Asahél's two counselors. In their distress, they called upon Walatta Petros for assistance and narrowly survived due to her intervention. Now they became convinced of Walatta Petros's powers as well. The second former counselor even joined the Qoratsa community as a monk, becoming reconciled with the community there, although he soon died. He was buried in the church at Qoratsa.

[1] Thus, since WP's tazkar would be held every November, this happened some time in June through September 1768.

[2] We never learn what became of Finḥas or Wälättä Täklä Haymanot.

[3] *Asahel Ayəkkäl* is an unidentified contemporary person with the name of the biblical character Asahel, King David's nephew.

[4] *Wədağ* [*sic*] *Asahel* (Friend of Asahel [one of King David's mightiest warriors in the Bible]) was a famous eighteenth-century Oromo military leader, frequently described by James Bruce. He died around 1770.

[5] Lit., *betä bəläne* (bathhouse). It is unclear what was done to the prisoner or exactly where it was done, since a bathhouse seems an unlikely place to torture or execute prisoners.

The Twenty-Second Miracle Summarized: How Our Mother Protected Her People from *Ras* Mikaél (in MSS H and I only)

Dejjazmatch Mikaél[1] marched from Tigré to Gondar [around 1767], laying waste and plundering many monasteries and homesteads on his way. In Gondar, he assumed the position of highest authority. When he learned that the Qoratsa Monastery alone had not been devastated, and that many people had sought refuge there, he dispatched an army to it with orders to lay waste to it and pillage everything. The army set out and reached a place called Firqa.[2]

Meanwhile, in Gondar, Walatta Petros appeared to *Dejjazmatch* Mikaél in a dream and told him to call off his army. She appeared twice more to him before he began to understand what was happening. He called his confidant *Dejjazmatch* Binyam,[3] told him about his dreams, and asked Binyam's opinion. The latter believed that the dreams were indeed interventions from Walatta Petros. Therefore, *Dejjazmatch* Mikaél became afraid and sent out a messenger to call off the army. When the messenger reached the soldiers at Firqa, he found them quarreling among themselves, also as a result of Walatta Petros's intervention. They readily obeyed Mikaél's order to return.

After a while, however, *Ras* Mikaél again thought about pillaging Qoratsa because, as he saw it, all his enemies had found refuge there. At first Walatta Petros made him forget about this scheme, but then it occurred to him again, so he sent a message to his enemies sheltering at Qoratsa, telling them to leave because he planned to search for them there.

The refugees were afraid, but did not leave Qoratsa, saying that they were ready to meet their death there. This angered *Ras* Mikaél, and now he himself, at the head of an army, set out against Qoratsa. He laid waste everything along the way, including churches, and reached the region of Dera [in which Qoratsa was situated]. All the people of Dera, as well as all the monks and nuns who were there, wanted to flee from *Ras* Mikaél, but did not know where to go since *Ras* Mikaél, as they saw it, controlled the whole country. Still they ran, carrying with them an icon of Walatta Petros.

But *Ras* Mikaél met them on the way to Fisa[4] and he took them to Geldi.[5] Surprisingly though, he did not harm them, but rather asked the monks to pray for him to Walatta Petros. He even gave Walatta Petros[6] his own gold-embroidered tunic as a gift and took up her veneration.

[1] *Mikaʾel "Səḥul"* (Michael the Astute, 1691–1777) was a powerful prince and kingmaker, one of the most famous figures of eighteenth-century Ethiopia. His title is *Däǧǧazmač* at first and later *Ras*.

[2] *Fərqa* here is probably the town near northeastern Lake Ṭana also called Fərqabärr.

[3] *Bənyam* (Benjamin) is a minor eighteenth-century figure.

[4] *Fisa* is a town about ten miles north of Qʷäraṣa.

[5] *Gäldi* is probably the river Gälda just south of Qʷäraṣa, on eastern Lake Ṭana, or a settlement nearby. The suggestion is that he returned them home.

[6] Presumably, to her followers or her establishment at Qʷäraṣa.

The Twenty-Third Miracle Summarized: How Our Mother Saved a Lying Fisherman (in MSS H and I only)

A fisherman on Lake Tana habitually cheated his master, who gave him compensation and clothing for his labor each year.[1] The fisherman went out fishing every day but sold some on the side. One day his master urgently needed some fish because he expected an important guest, but the fisherman claimed not to have caught anything. He then even went so far as to swear to his boss using the name of Walatta Petros, saying that she should throw him to the hippos if he lied. Soon thereafter, the fisherman was attacked by a hippo when he was out on the lake. The hippo bit him, but then tossed him ashore still alive. While lying on his sickbed recovering, the fisherman repented and asked Walatta Petros for forgiveness. She heard his plea and healed him. He told everyone what happened, and people marveled at Walatta Petros's workings.

The Twenty-Fourth Miracle Summarized: How Our Mother Cured a Lame Man (in MSS H and I only)

A lame man with crippled legs heard about Walatta Petros and her healing powers.[2] Therefore, he asked his relatives to take him to Qoratsa, hoping to be cured there. They agreed and carried him there, arriving at Qoratsa on the eve of Walatta Petros's tazkaar. The lame man then prayed for Walatta Petros's help and promised not to return to his region and family, but to serve Walatta Petros his whole life if she cured him.

The next day, the lame man dragged himself on all fours to the place where Walatta Petros's *Life and Struggles* was being read aloud to the assembled crowd. While he listened to the *Life and Struggles* full of faith, Walatta Petros appeared to him and told him to stand up. So he did. The assembled multitude marveled at this miracle and said that now they had seen what they had only heard of before.

The former cripple then ran to the church and, before the icon of Walatta Petros, thanked the Lord for having created Walatta Petros, as a cure for all the world. After staying at Qoratsa for some time, he returned to his region, praising the Lord all along the way and telling people about Walatta Petros's great powers and deeds.

[1] It seems that this fisherman was working for hire, suggesting the existence of a wage economy and the late date of this miracle. The word we have translated as "master," *əgzi'*, can also be translated as "lord" or "owner." The text states that the fisherman received *ʿasbä ṣamahu wä-ləbso bä-bä-ʿamät* (wages *or* compensation *or* payment for his toil, as well as his clothing, each year).

[2] This miracle is quite similar to the sixteenth miracle.

The Twenty-Fifth Miracle Summarized: How Our Mother Retrieved Her Stolen Book (in MS I only)

A wealthy, hospitable, and pious man, *Naggad-ras* Kasagn,[1] whose Christian name was Gabra Maryam,[2] venerated Walatta Petros very much.

Kasagn celebrated Walatta Petros's tazkaar every nineteenth day of the month of Maskaram, as if it was the day of her departure.[3] Why did he celebrate on that day and not on the actual day she died? One year on that day there was a huge thunderstorm, during which lightning struck the church on Réma Island so that half of its roof burned up. The half that was oriented toward Walatta Petros's tomb remained intact, however, thanks to her protective power. For this reason, her community at Qoratsa also commemorated Walatta Petros on that day, and Kasagn joined them on the occasion.

One year Kasagn sent some of his servants to Zagé to buy *gésho*[4] leaves for Walatta Petros's tazkaar. They did, and loaded the gésho on a tankwa on a Saturday. Then they slept on the lakeshore, near the tankwa. During the night, Walatta Petros intervened and transported the tankwa to Qoratsa, in a flash. When the servants woke up the next morning, they searched for the missing tankwa along the southern lakeshore, all the way from Bahir Dar[5] to Dabra Maryam[6] to Emabra. On Monday, they finally reached Qoratsa—and there found the tankwa and its cargo safe and sound. They told Kasagn, and he marveled at Walatta Petros's deeds and praised her.

A second miracle involving Kasagn: When *Dejjazmatch* Goshu[7] pillaged the Qoratsa Monastery, Walatta Petros's *Life and Struggles* book was also stolen. It found its way to the region of Gojjam, where it remained for a time. But then,

[1] *Kasäññ* (Amharic, "He [i.e., God] has compensated me"; parents normally give this secular name to a boy born after the loss of an earlier child). *Näggadras* (Head of the merchants) was a title for the customs collector during this period, a lucrative position.

[2] *Gäbrä Maryam* (Servant of Mary) is the name of one of MS I's patrons; that is, of the man in the married couple—the wife is Wälättä Maryam—on whom WP's blessing is consistently called in MS I's second set of miracles. A wealthy and pious *näggadras* would be a likely candidate for patron, since he would have the means, as well as the motivation, to have this second set of WP's miracles written down.

[3] Lit., *fəlsäta* (her departure *or* assumption). WP's feast day (the day of her death or departure) is not 19 Mäskäräm (29 September currently) but 17 Ḫədar (26 November currently). The day of Saint Mary's assumption is 16 Näḥase (22 August).

[4] *Gešo* (*rhamnus prinioides*) is an indigenous plant that serves as a type of hops for brewing *ṭälla* beer.

[5] *Baḥər Dar* (Lakeshore) is a town on Lake Ṭana about seven miles southeast of Zäge. The servants are making their way from southwestern Lake Ṭana to southeastern Lake Ṭana.

[6] *Däbrä Maryam* (Monastery of [Saint] Mary) is an island and monastery about one mile northeast of Baḥər Dar.

[7] *Goššu* (The buffalo) was a famous eighteenth-century figure, one of the pillars of the rule of Iyoʾas I. Governor of Goǧǧam and enemy of *Ras* Mikaʾel, Goššu died around 1786.

through Walatta Petros's intervention, *Naggad-ras* Kasagn miraculously found it there, brought it back, and returned it to Walatta Petros's community.

How could Qoratsa be pillaged in the first place? It was not because Walatta Petros had withdrawn her protection from it, but because the evil deeds of its inhabitants made God allow the ravaging to happen [biblical verses are here used to bolster this point].

The Twenty-Sixth Miracle Summarized: How Our Mother Healed Another Lame Man and a Sick Woman (in MS I only)

Relatives brought a man who could not stand on his legs to Qoratsa from a great distance because word about Walatta Petros's healing powers had spread far and wide. At Qoratsa, the lame man always listened when Walatta Petros's *Life and Struggles* was being read out aloud.

One Sunday, while the man and a multitude of people were once again listening to the reading of Walatta Petros's *Life and Struggles*, God decided to manifest Walatta Petros's powers through him. So he let her lift the lame man up and cure his legs, making them as strong as if they had never been touched by any illness. The multitude witnessed that miracle and can testify to it. Everybody praised the Lord and eulogized Walatta Petros for what they both had done.

Another miraculous episode: An elderly nun named Walatta Sillasé[1] lived in the sisters' house at Qoratsa. She loved Walatta Petros dearly and celebrated her tazkaar on the seventeenth of each month as well as on nineteenth day of the month of Maskaram. On those occasions, she always put aside some washing water and then trusted in Walatta Petros's assistance.[2]

Later a woman contracted the *himama eda seb* illness[3] and was close to death. She was then given and drank from the washing water that Walatta Sillasé had conserved from Walatta Petros's tazkaar. Thereupon the ill woman first roared like a wild animal, but then quickly became healthy again. The people who witnessed this praised the Lord who works great wonders through his saints.

[1] *Wälättä Śəllase* (Daughter of the Trinity).

[2] Presumably, the water from washing the cross.

[3] *Ḥəmamä ədä säbʾ* (The illness of the hand[s] of people) is a very serious folk illness caused and cured by folk medicine, something like the evil eye. If someone is doing well, others may become jealous and put a magical potion or poison in his or her food, which causes such symptoms as mental illness, stomach pain, or loss of talent. This illness is considered largely fatal.

The Twenty-Seventh Miracle Summarized: How Our Mother Protected Her Community during the Years of Kings Yohannes, Takla Giyorgis, and Tewodros (in MS I only)

During the reign of King Yohannes II [i.e., in 1769],[1] evil neighbors from the Qoratsa area harassed Walatta Petros's community and ultimately wanted to destroy it, even though the community members did well by them. But the neighbors were bad people, and so they laid a sort of siege on the community, forbidding them to go out to do the necessary labor on the surrounding land, which the evil neighbors claimed was their land. The community members were dejected and wept.

Their weeping reached Walatta Petros, who stirred up King Yohannes, whose name means "Joy" or "Happiness."[2] Indeed, he was a joy to the world because he made a covenant with God, led many peoples to believe, and killed the godless. He was a most righteous Christian ruler.

Yohannes held Walatta Petros very dear and even paid a visit to Qoratsa, thereby making the community and the associated laypeople very happy. In addition, Yohannes gave the community gifts—carpets and some richly ornamented garments—and granted them land rights in the vicinity, making those evil neighbors (who had first claimed the land as theirs and had harassed the community) the community's servants and tributaries.

Walatta Petros did not perform miracles only at and for Qoratsa, but everywhere where people believed in her and called out her name. A miracle she did in the Gondar region: When King Takla Giyorgis I[3] once fought in Madab,[4] he seized a

[1] *Yoḥannəs* (John) II was Bäkaffa's brother and Iyasu II's immediate successor as king. He sat on the throne for only seven months in 1769 and was entirely a creature of *Ras* Mika'el Səḥul, so it is somewhat surprising that so much is said about him here. The text does not specify which King Yoḥannəs this is, but it must be Yoḥannəs II, because the order of the miracles is of exactly consecutive kings: Bäkaffa (1721–30), Iyasu II (1730–55), Iyo'as I (r. 1755–69), and Yoḥannəs II (1769). It is unlikely to be Yoḥannəs I (r. 1667–82), under whom the *WP gädl* was first written, for the story could then have been expected to appear in the first set of miracles. Given the chronological order of kings and the subsequent references to later kings, it is also unlikely to be Yoḥannəs III (r. 1840–41, 1845, 1850–51), a puppet monarch of the late *zämänä mäsafənt* (Era of the Princes, 1769–1855), or Yoḥannəs IV (r. 1872–89). However, the author may have confused the character of Yoḥannəs I with the short-lived Yoḥannəs II, since the first Yoḥannəs had the reputation of someone who conquered and converted many, while being personally very pious (Berry 2014).

[2] This is a folk etymology; Yoḥannəs ultimately goes back to Hebrew *Yochanan*, meaning "God is gracious."

[3] *Täklä Giyorgis I* (Plant of [Saint] George) was Yoḥannəs II's son and a later successor as king. He ruled briefly but repeatedly (six times) between 1779 and 1800. The text does not specify which King Täklä Giyorgis this is, but it must be Täklä Giyorgis I because he founded Däbrä Məṭmaq Maryam and because Täklä Giyorgis II (r. 1869–71) ruled after Tewodros and so could not have seized a cannon that Tewodros later found.

[4] *Mädäb* was a town east of Lake Ṭana, near Däbrä Tabor.

cannon, which he then donated to the monastery and church of Dabra Mitmaaq,[1] which he sponsored. The tabot at the Dabra Mitmaaq church was consecrated in the name of Walatta Petros, and a copy of her *Life and Struggles* was also kept there.[2] Therefore, Walatta Petros's tazkaar was also celebrated there.

The cannon remained at Dabra Mitmaaq for a long time, until the western Tewodros[3] became king. Tewodros then issued a decree that those found to possess cannons or firearms should have their houses pillaged and their possessions confiscated. Due to malicious informants, the cannon at Dabra Mitmaaq was found and confiscated, the priests were taken into custody, and Walatta Petros's tazkaar was stopped there. But when the cannon arrived at court, it broke down and fell apart, due to the intervention of Walatta Petros. Then Tewodros realized what was going on and set the priests of Dabra Mitmaaq free: the plot of those who had denounced them failed. In just this manner, Walatta Petros works miracles and wonders up to our own days.

[1] *Däbrä Mətmaq Maryam* (Mount of the Baptistery of [Saint] Mary) is the church in Gondär just south of the royal castles that was built by Täklä Giyorgis I in 1782–83. MS I only mentions "Däbrä Mətmaq" not "Däbrä Mətmaq Maryam." Either there were two churches at the monastery of Däbrä Mətmaq in Gondär (one dedicated to Saint Mary and the other to WP) or the story conflates the Gondärine Däbrä Mətmaq Maryam church, associated with Täklä Giyorgis I, with a putative WP church at the Däbrä Mətmaq monastery in Shoa.

[2] Although the time's royal chronicles mention the church's tabot, they don't mention that it is dedicated to WP (Blundell 1922, 269).

[3] *Tewodros məʿrabawi* (the western Tewodros) must be King Tewodros II (r. 1855–68), who did much to acquire modern military arms and who is famously associated with cannons in particular. He may have been called "western Tewodros" because he hailed from the Qʷara region west of Lake Ṭana.

Summary of the *Short History of Walatta Petros's Community* (in MSS I and J only)

The texts below are not always direct translations but often paraphrases of material that appears at the end of MSS I and/or J only. These two manuscripts are unusual in having detailed historical information about the community (summarized in "Chronology"). Included is a text we are calling the Short History of Walatta Petros's Community *(1734–35), plus various notes that provide information on the history of the community.*

[*MS J only. This note—written in Amharic, in another hand than the rest of the manuscript, and at the end of an empty column—could have been added at any time:*] In a Matthew the Evangelist year, in the month of Miyazya,[1] and in the time when *Emmahoy* Wubeet (*Woyzaro* Walatta Takla Haymanot) was abbess[2] and *Emmahoy* Walatta Maseeh was prioress.[3] *Dejjazmatch* Iyasu and *Naggad-ras* Asahél, with 8 ounces [of gold], bought this manuscript from *Woyzaro* Walatta Takla Haymanot,[4] the senior Wubeet, and *Woyzaro* Birhan Madhaneetu,[5] the junior Wubeet.

[*MS J only. This note was written in Gəʿəz, in an again different hand, and on a new folio:*] We here write down the number of years of our holy mother Walatta Petros and our blessed mother Eheta Kristos. It has been thirty-nine years since our holy mother Walatta Petros passed away and thirty-three years since Eheta Kristos passed away.[6] At that time, it was the thirteenth year of the rule of King Yohannes [i.e., 1680–81].[7]

[1] *Miyazya* is the eighth month of the year in the Ethiopian calendar (EC; see "Calendar" in the glossary), now extending from 9 April to 8 May in the modern Western calendar.

[2] Lit., *bä-əmmahoy Wəbit ənnatənnät* (when *əmmahoy* Wəbit was mother [Gəʿəz and Amharic mixed]). *Ǝmmahoy* is a respectful title of address for a nun. The secular name Wəbit means "The beautiful one." Her full Christian name is Wälättä Täklä Haymanot; she is also the senior Wəbit listed below.

[3] Lit., *bä-əmmahoy Wälättä Mäsih* [*sic*, for *Mäsiḥ*] *liqä rädənnät* (when *əmmahoy* Wälättä Mäsiḥ held the office of *liq*[*t*]*ä ardəʾt* [female head of the disciples], or prioress [Gəʿəz and Amharic mixed]). The name Wälättä Mäsiḥ means "Daughter of the Messiah."

[4] *Wälättä Täklä Haymanot* (Daughter of Takla Haymanot). She is the elder sister or mother of the junior Wəbit: the two women were mother and daughter or two sisters. This *Wäyzäro* Wälättä Täklä Haymanot may be the noblewoman of the same name who appears in the twentieth miracle: the daughter of King Bäkaffa devoted to Qʷäraṣa in 1767–68. That a princess was the abbess of Qʷäraṣa has been recorded nowhere else, however.

[5] *Bərhan Mädḫanitu* ([Heavenly] light [is] the deliverance).

[6] That is, 1681–82 (EC 1674), because WP died 23 November 1642 (EC 1635) and Ǝḫətä Krəstos died 2 April 1649 (EC 1641).

[7] The thirteenth year of Yoḥannəs I's reign is 1680–81 (EC 1673), since he is reported to

[*MS J. The following history was written in Gəʿəz, in the same hand as the previous note, and in a new column. This history also appears in MS I, written in Gəʿəz, in the same hand as the last miracles, and continuous with them, not in a new column:*] Behold, we have written a history of the events that happened at various times. We wrote this in the fifth year of our King Iyasu II [i.e., 1734–35],[1] son of Bakaffa, when Haykaliya Mammo[2] was Qoratsa's abbot, when Iyoel[3] was its prior, when Mazmura Dinghil[4] was the archpriest, when Ainiya Mammeet[5] was its abbess, and when Haymanotaweet[6] was its prioress. The author of this history is Ba-Haila Maryam.[7]

On the seventeenth of the month of Hidaar, in the tenth year of the rule of King Fasiladas, our holy mother Walatta Petros's soul left her body.[8] She passed away in peace when she was fifty years old, of which she had spent twenty-four before her repudiation of the world and twenty-six after it.

In the month of Miyazya before her death in the month of Hidaar,[9] when they were still living at Zambowl,[10] Walatta Petros appointed *Abba* Za-Hawaryaat as the abbot.

have begun his rule mid-September 1667 (EC 1660). Thus, there appears to be a one-year discrepancy with the figure in the previous sentence.

[1] The fifth year of Iyasu II's reign is 1734–35 (EC 1727).

[2] J: *Haykäləyä Mammo* (The boy "My sanctuary"); I: *Haykäl Mammo* (The boy "Sanctuary"). He is described as the *abä mənet* (father of the monastery [that is, abbot]).

[3] *Iyoʾel* (Joel) was the *liqä ardəʾt* (Male head of the [male] disciples [that is, prior]).

[4] *Mäzmurä Dəngəl* (Hymn of *or* to the Virgin [Mary]) was the *liqä kahənat* (head of the priests, archpriest).

[5] J: *ʿAynəyä Mammit*; I: *ʿAynəyä Mammite*. She is described as the *əmmä mənet* (abbess).

[6] *Haymanotawit* (She who belongs to the faith).

[7] J: *Bä-Ḫaylä Maryam* (Through the power of [Saint] Mary); I: *Ḫaylä Maryam* (The power of [Saint] Mary). He was the author of this history. The scribe of MS I was Kidanä Maryam (Covenant of [Saint] Mary).

[8] This information does not appear in the *WP gädl* but further confirms that the year of her death was 1642; Fasilädäs came to power in June 1632 (EC 1624); she died in November 1642 (EC 1635). The misalignment of years between the Ethiopian and Western system makes calculating dates difficult, however. Fasilädäs came to power on 25 June 1632, about two months before the end of the Ethiopian year. Therefore, the first year of his reign theoretically could be counted from when he came to power, June 1632, and then comprise the twelve months until June 1633 (EC 1624–25); or it could start with the new year after he came to power, September 1632 through August 1633 (EC 1625); or it could be very short, the two months until the end of the year, from 25 June 1632 to 7 September 1632 (EC 1624). In practice, the date given for WP's death shows that the years of Fasilädäs's reign were counted from the new year after he came to power (that is, from September 1632), since the tenth year of his reign was EC 1635 (September 1642 to August 1643, which includes the month of WP's death, November 1642). This short text consistently refers to King Fasilädäs with his regnal name, ʿAläm Säggäd (The world submits [to him]), but we use the king's baptismal name.

[9] That is, between between 6 April and 5 May of 1642 (EC 1634). Although the author later says that *Abba* Zä-Ḥawaryat died forty-one years after being appointed, suggesting he was appointed two years before WP's death (April–May 1640 [EC 1632]), the events of the *WP gädl* suggest it was the year of her death.

[10] J: *Zämbol*; I: *Zäbol*.

During her terminal illness, the community asked Walatta Petros, "Who will watch over your daughters after you pass away?"[1]

She replied, "I have ruled over them for many years. Didn't I time and again tell them: 'Serve!'? I say to you, however, that I entrust Eheta Kristos to all of you because she will be disconsolate upon my death." By saying this, she indicated that they should appoint her after her death, and they did so.

The community then stayed at Afer Faras for seven[2] more years, with Za-Hawaryaat and Eheta Kristos in charge.

Then Eheta Kristos passed away on the twenty-seventh day of the month of Maggabeet[3] in the sixteenth year of Fasiladas's reign.[4] So, the community appointed as her successor a nun named Anjato,[5] whose baptismal name was Amata Dinghil.

After Amata Dinghil took over, the community moved to Qoratsa. For two years, they lived there beyond the river Yimera.[6] Then King Fasiladas granted the community the land of four Oromo officers, for which the latter were compensated with other lands in Fogera. So in the seventeenth year of Fasiladas's reign,[7] the community became fully established at Qoratsa, where *Abba* Za-Hawaryaat and *Emmahoy* Amata Dinghil were in charge.

Decades later, *Abba* Za-Hawaryaat then passed away on 26 Nahaasé, in the fourteenth year of the rule of King Yohannes I.[8] This was forty-one years after he had been appointed at Zambowl.[9] *Abba* Za-Hawaryaat spent seven[10] years of his tenure at Afer Faras, and thirty-seven[11] at Qoratsa. Before his demise, *Abba* Za-Hawaryaat

[1] The author here repeats the story told in the *WP gädl*.

[2] J: *7*; I: *6*. Seven is probably the correct number of years. WP died in November 1642 (EC 1635), so seven years later is 1649 (EC 1642).

[3] Mäggabit is the seventh month of the year in the Ethiopian calendar, now extending from 10 March to 8 April in the modern Western calendar.

[4] That is, Ǝḫətä Krəstos died on 2 April 1649. The sixteenth year of Fasilädäs's reign is September 1648 to August 1649. Ǝḫətä Krəstos's synaxarium entry in Vatican manuscript Eth. No. 112 says she died on a Wednesday, but 27 Mäggabit this year is a Friday. Nollet (1930) mistakenly translated that entry's 27 Mäggabit as 26 Mäggabit. That entry says that Ǝḫətä Krəstos lived thirty-two years as a nun, so she became a nun in 1617, the same year as WP.

[5] *Anǧäto* (One who is dear to me). Through her baptismal name of Amätä Dəngəl, we learn that she is the mother of Beza Mäsqäl, whose story is told at length earlier in the *WP gädl*.

[6] *Yəmära* must be a river or stream very near Qʷäraṣa.

[7] That is, probably around early September 1650 (late EC 1642), since the seventeenth year of his reign is 1649–50, but it has been two years since the death of Ǝḫətä Krəstos in April 1649 (mid-EC 1641).

[8] J: 26 *Näḥase*; I: 27 *Näḥase*. It is unclear which date is right. The date of 26 Näḥase of the fourteenth year of A'laf Säggäd (regnal name of Yoḥannəs I, r. 1667–82) would be 29 August 1681 (EC 1673).

[9] Forty-one years before 29 August 1681 (EC 1673) would be April/May 1640 (EC 1632), but he was most likely appointed in 1642 (EC 1634).

[10] J: *7*; I: *6*. It is most likely seven years.

[11] J: *37*; I: *33*. MS I's numbers total thirty-nine years, MS J's numbers total forty-four years,

designated *Abba* Za-Maryam Esaat Ba-Afu[1] as his successor. The abbess Amata Dinghil passed away on the seventeenth of the month of Ginbowt.[2]

[*MS I only, continued from the above:*] The years from when our holy mother Walatta Petros passed away until now are as follows: it has been ninety-four years since this monastery was established;[3] it has been eighty-eight years since *Abba* Za-Hawaryaat passed away;[4] it has been fifty-four years since the "Rules for the House of Our Holy Mother Walatta Petros,"[5] ordained by *Abuna* Za-Iyasus,[6] were written down.

[*MS I only. This note appears in Amharic, in the same hand, in a new column:*] This note includes a list of donkey loads assigned to various individuals, institutions, or purposes associated with Qoratsa, including an unnamed official, the sick, and housekeepers at the Dembiya, Gondar, and Damboza houses. It was written down when Bitsa Giyorgis[7] was abbot and Gabra Mikaél[8] the prior. It states that whosoever steals or erases the manuscript shall be cursed through the power of Saint Peter, as well as through the word of our teacher Zafara Mikaél.[9]

[*MS I only. This note appears in Amharic, in a different hand, in a half-column:*] This note includes a list of dignitaries who at the time held monastic offices at Qoratsa, including the abbot Gabra Amlak,[10] as of the first day of the month of Tiqimt, in the year of Luke the Evangelist, Year of Mercy 1806 [i.e., 10 October 1813].[11]

---

so in neither manuscript do they add up to the forty-one years of tenure given before. By our calculations, *Abba* Zä-Ḥawaryat served as abbot for thirty-nine years (1642–81 [EC 1634–73]).

1 I: *Zä-Maryam Ǝsat Bä-Afu* (He of [Saint] Mary—In his mouth is fire [Gəʿəz and Amharic mixed]); J: *Zä-Maryam Ǝsat Bä-Afa* (He of [Saint] Mary—In her mouth is fire [Gəʿəz and Amharic mixed]).

2 MS I omits this sentence. She may have died in the same year as Zä-Ḥawaryat.

3 That is, it is now 1744 (EC 1736) because the community at Qʷäraṣa, where MS I still resides, was established in September 1650 (late EC 1642). This is a new section, so it was written later than the section before it, dating to 1735. However, none of the dates in this paragraph tallies with the others.

4 That is, it is now 1769 (EC 1761), because he died on 30 August 1681. However, the author stated earlier that the abbot spent thirty-three years at Qʷäraṣa and forty-one years as an abbott, and the difference between ninety-four and eighty-eight implies he was the abbot for only six years. So it is probably not correct.

5 *Mäṣḥafä śərʿatä beta lä-əmmənä qəddəst Wälättä Ṗeṭros* was written in 1690, assuming this section was written in 1744.

6 *Abunä* Zä-Iyäsus is probably the important seventeenth-century Unctionist (Qəbat) cleric known as Zä-Iyäsus the Blind, who died in 1687.

7 *Bəṣʿa Giyorgis* ([Saint] George's beatitude).

8 *Gäbrä Mikaʾel* (Servant of [Saint] Michael).

9 *Zäfärä Mi[ka]ʾel* (Hem of [Saint] Michael['s garment]).

10 *Gäbrä Amlak* (Servant of the Lord).

11 Lit., *1800-ku [sic] 6 ʿamätä məḥrät.*

The Translation of the Poem *Portrait of Walatta Petros* (*Mälkəʾa Wälättä Ṗeṭros*)

A mälkəʾ is a genre of Gəʿəz poetry in which the poet praises the saint from head to toe, using the saint's body parts to create an allegory of the saint's virtues and life. Thus, many stanzas allude to some episode in the saint's life. Typical mälkəʾ poems have between twenty and fifty stanzas and mention the saint's name in every stanza, generally on the third line. The genre has five rhymed lines per stanza with the rhyme scheme AAAAA, BBBBB, and so on. Generally, the lines rhyme only the last syllable of the line (i.e., the last fidäl character), which always ends in a vowel. Even if it looks like the rhyme is slant (i.e., sharing just a consonant sound), in traditional recitation the singer adds a schwa sound to any sixth-form syllable at the end of a line (e.g., singing amlak *as* amlakə*). To listen to the poem being recited in the original, please go to wendybelcher.com. To aid the scholar or student who does not read Gəʿəz but is interested in understanding the skill and elegance of the original as well as possible, we have provided the poem in fidäl below, in transliteration, and in word-for-word English translation. On the facing page is the poetic English translation by Derek Gideon. Those wishing to read or assign Gideon's translation on its own (in an easy-to-read version properly spaced and without the facing pages of fidäl, transliteration, or word-for-word translation), can find it as a PDF at wendybelcher.com. In the word-for-word translation, we have made sure that the nouns, verbs, and adjectives are all exactly what is there and in the right order, but we have sometimes added articles (since Gəʿəz has none) and dropped relatives for clarity.*

[1] In the name of God, who was when time was not,
(no moment before him, no wink of an eye):
Walatta Petros, may the priest Shenoute[1]
brighten my heart with some small insight, that I
might voice for you these strings in holy song.

[2] Hail to your name's memory, which wears a crown[2] of grace,
and to your hair, poured over with the oil of Mass.[3]
Walatta Petros, our mother, we desire your help
to save us from the rise of the Enemies Three:[4]
for they are most bitter, most bitter indeed.

[3] Hail to your head and your face, that command

[1] *Sinoda* (Shenoute of Atripe) was a fifth-century Egyptian monk. He is a famous figure of Coptic monasticism and considered the greatest author of Coptic literature. He is venerated as an important saint in the Täwaḥədo Church, too. His commemoration takes place on the same day as WP's, 17 Ḫədar.

[2] *Qäṣäla* also means the silk head covering fringed in gold with which Täwaḥədo Church priests cover their heads during the Liturgy, and thus may be a reference to WP's quasi-priestly status.

[3] *Qəddase* (holiness, sanctification) also became the technical term for the Divine Liturgy; the use of this term here implicitly elevates WP to priestly status.

[4] It is unclear who or what the three enemies are; perhaps, as in other Christian traditions, they are the world, the flesh, and the devil. Alternately, perhaps they are bad thoughts, bad speech, and bad actions or anger, arrogance, and lust.

[1] በስመ፡እግዚአብሔር፡ዘሀሎ፡አመ፡ኢሀሎ፡ዘመን። **132**
Bä-səmä əgziʾabḥer zä-hallo amä i-hallo zämän
In the name of | God, | who was | when | not was | time,[1]
ወኢቀደሞ፡ሰዓት፡መጠነ፡ቅጽበታ፡ለዓይን።
wä-i-qädämo säʿat mäṭänä qəṣbäta lä-ʿayn
and not preceded him | a moment, | by the measure of | a blink of it, | of an eye.
እሰንቁ፡ለኪ፡አውታረ፡ነባቢ፡ድርሳን።
Əsänqu läki awtarä näbabi[2] *dərsan*
So that I may play/sound | for you [fem. sg.] | the strings of | a speaking | hymn/composition/poem,
ያብርህ፡ውስተ፡ልብየ፡ወለተ፡ጴጥሮስ፡ምእመን።
yabrəh wəstä ləbbəya Wälättä Ṗeṭros[3] *məʾmän*
may let shine | in | my heart, | Walatta | Petros | faithful,
ጸዳለ፡አእምሮ፡ንስቲተ፡ሲኖዳ፡ካህን።
ṣädalä aʾməro nəstitä[4] *Sinoda kahən*
the gleam of | understanding | a little | Shenoute | the Priest.

[2] ሰላም፡ለዝክረ፡ስምኪ፡ዘቀጸላ፡ሞገስ፡ትርሲቱ።
Sälam lä-zəkrä səməki[5] *zä-qäṣäla mogäs*[6] *tərsitu*
Peace | to the memory of | your name, | a crown of | grace | its adornment/glory,
ወለሥዕርትኪ፡ስውጥ፡ዘቅብአ፡ቅዳሴ፡ውስቴቱ።
wä-lä-śəʿərtəki səwəṭ zä-qəbʾa qəddase wəstetu
and to your hair, | poured | the oil/ointment of | holiness | [is] into it.
ወለተ፡ጴጥሮስ፡እምነ፡ትንብልናኪ፡ንፈቱ።
Wälättä Ṗeṭros əmmənä tənbələnnaki nəfättu
Walatta | Petros | our mother, | your intercession | we crave
ከመ፡ያድኅነነ፡እምትንሣኤ፡አፅራር፡፫ቱ።
kämä yadḫənänä əm-tənśaʾe aṣrar śälästu[7]
so that | it may save us | from the rising of | the enemies | three,
እስመ፡መሪራን፡ፈድፋደ፡እሙንቱ።
əsmä märiran fädfadä əmuntu
for/indeed | bitter/ferocious | very, | they [are].

[3] ሰላም፡ለርእስኪ፡ወለገጽኪ፡ስቡሕ።
Sälam lä-rəʾsəki wä-lä-gäṣṣəki səbbuḥa[8]
Peace | to your head | and to your face, | praiseworthy

[1] Since BDJ do not have the mälkəʾ, we have checked CR against CEF, the only manuscripts providing the mälkəʾ.
[2] CE: *näbabi* [masc.] (speaking); F: *näbabit* [fem.] (speaking); CR: *näbabe* [masc., genitive] (speaking of).
[3] CR needlessly altered to *lä-Wälättä Ṗeṭros* (for Walatta Petros).
[4] CR: *ṣädalä aʾməro nəstit* [nom.] (the gleam of a little understanding).
[5] CR: *səməkä* (your [masc.] name).
[6] CR: *mogäsä* (grace of).
[7] C: *śälästu*; EF: *3tu*; CR: *3*.
[8] CR: *bəzuḫa* (by far).

more praise than ethereal lights.

Saint Peter's Daughter,[1] adorned in faith's garment:

at dusk and at dawn raise up our entreaties

to your Lord, who has freed us from Satan's shackles.

[4] Hail to your eyelashes, and the tears they have suffered,

and to eyes that have seen the beauty of the mother of God.

Walatta Petros, from the chains of sin set me free.

Direct my feet along repentance's path

before cruel-faced death appears to me.

[5] Hail to your ears, which heard the Good News,

and your cheeks, which felt the blows the Lord felt.

Walatta Petros, come to us when we cry out

and on the warring demons and spirits, make war

[1] The first of several plays in the poem on the meaning of WP's name, Daughter of Saint Peter. In these cases, we translate it as Peter's Daughter, to communicate the double function, descriptive as well as appellative.

እምብርሃናቲሁ፡ለሰማይ፡ዘአስተርአየ፡ብዙኅ።
əm-bərhanatihu lä-sämay zä-astärʾayä bəzuḫa[1]
more than its lights, | the sky's, | they appear | by far.
ስርጉተ፡ኵለንታ፡ለጴጥሮስ፡ወለቱ፡ዘሃይማኖት፡እልታኃ።
Sərgutä kʷəllänta lä-Ṗeṭros wälättu zä-haymanot əltaḫa
Adorned | all over, | of Peter | his Daughter, | for whom faith | her cloak:
አዕርጊ፡ስእለተነ፡ሰርከ፡ወነግሀ።
aʿrəgi səʾlätänä särkä wä-nägha
raise | our pleas | at dusk | and at dawn
ኀበ፡አምላክኪ፡ማእሰሮ፡ለሰይጣን፡ዘፈትሐ።
ḫabä amlakəki maʾsäro lä-säyṭan zä-fätḥa
to | your Lord, | his shackles, | namely Satan's, | who has untied.

[4] ሰላም፡ለቀራንብትኪ፡ሕማማተ፡አንብዕ፡እለ፡ጾሩ።
Sälam lä-qäranəbtəki ḥəmamatä anbəʿ əllä ṣoru
Peace | to your eyelashes/eyelids, | sufferings of | tears | which | have borne,
ወለአዕይንትኪ፡ሥነ፡እንተ፡እመ፡አምላክ፡ነጸሩ።
wä-lä-aʿyəntəki śənnä əntä əmmä amlak[2] *näṣṣäru*
and to your eyes: | the beauty | of | the mother of | the Lord | they have contemplated.
ወለተ፡ጴጥሮስ፡ፍትሕኒ፡ለጌጋይ፡እማእሰሩ።
Wälättä Ṗeṭros fətəḥəni lä-gegay əm-maʾsäru
Walatta | Petros, | release me, | of transgression, | from its shackles,
ወአርትዒ፡አእጋርየ፡ፍኖተ፡ንስሓ፡ይሑሩ።
wä-ärtəʿi aʾgarəyä fənotä nəssəḥa yəḥuru
and direct | my feet, | the path of | repentance | so that they may walk
ቅድመ፡ይዳደቀኒ፡ሞት፡ዘፀዋግ፡ሕብሩ።
qədmä yəddadäqäni mot zä-ṣ́äwwag ḥəbru
before | befalls me | death, | cruel | its color/countenance.

[5] ሰላም፡ለአእዛንኪ፡ሰማዕያተ፡ዜና፡በቋዒ።
Sälam lä-aʾzanəki sämaʿəyatä zena bäqʷaʿi
Peace | to your ears, | the hearers of | the story | beneficial,
ወለመላትሒኪ፡ሱቱፍ[3]፡ጽፍዓተ፡አምላክ፡ተሰባኢ።
Wä-lä-mälatəḥəki sutuf ṣəfʿatä amlak täsäbaʾi
and to your cheeks, | partakers of | the slaps to the face of | the Lord | incarnate.
ወለተ፡ጴጥሮስ፡ኀቤነ፡ሶበ፡ንጼውዓኪ፡ንዒ።
Wälättä Ṗeṭros ḫabenä sobä nəṣewwəʿaki nəʿi
Walatta | Petros, | to us | when | we cry out for you, | come,
አጋንንተ፡ወመናፍስተ፡ኢይጽብኡነ፡ትጽብኢ።
aganəntä wä-mänafəstä i-yəṣbəʾunä təṣbəʾi
the demons | and spirits, | so that they not attack us, | to attack

[1] CR: *səbbuḥa* (praiseworthy).
[2] CR: *śənnä əntä ḫabä amlak* (the beauty that is with the Lord).
[3] CEF, CR: *sutuf* [sg., nom.], which we regard as standing in for *sutufatä* [pl., *status constructus*].

with the sword of your mouth, a seraph's slaughter.

[6] Hail to your nostrils, the houses of marvelous scents,
and to lips that provide your power of eloquence.
Daughter of Peter—that Peter whom John overtook on the path,[1]
from you to me may understanding pass—
my own lies buried beneath my foolishness.

[7] Hail to your mouth, which advanced a new order,
and your teeth, which deflected the laughs of those who scorn.
Your voice brings more joy than the wine of Cana.[2]
On the death-day decreed for the Daughter of Peter, John's son,[3]
the whole Church wrapped itself in mourning.

[1] John 20:4 has Saint Peter being outraced in running toward Christ's tomb by "that other disciple, whom Jesus had loved." Traditionally, that disciple has been identified with Saint John the Evangelist.

[2] John 2:1–12. An allusion to the first miracle of Christ, which was changing the water into wine at the wedding of Cana.

[3] Matthew 16:17; John 1:42.

በሰይፈ፡አፉኪ፡ሱራፌል፡ሠዋዒ።
bä-säyfä afuki surafel śäwaʿi
with the sword of | your mouth, | [you] seraph | sacrificing/priestly.

[6] ሰላም፡ለአእናፍኪ፡አብያተ፡ቅታሬ፡ዘአንክሮ።
Sälam lä-aʾnafəki abyatä qəttare zä-änkəro
Peace | to your nostrils, | houses of | the fragrance | of [inducing] marveling,
ወለከናፍርኪ፡ዓቅመ፡እለ፡ሠርዑ፡ለተናግሮ።
wä-lä-känafərəki ʿaqmä əllä śärʿu lä-tänagəro
and to your lips, | the means [acc.], | that | ordained/provide | for speaking.
ወለተ፡ጴጥሮስ፡በረዊጽ፡ዮሐንስ፡ዘበደሮ።
Wälättä Ṗeṭros bä-räwiṣ Yoḥannəs zä-bädäro
Daughter of | Peter, | in running | John | beat him [namely, Peter],
ይትፋለስ፡መንገሌየ፡እመንገሌኪ፡አእምሮ።
yətfaläs mängäleyä əm-mängäleki aʾməro
may pass | to me | from you | understanding.
ለአእምሮትየሰ፡ዝንጋዔ፡ሰወሮ።
Lä-aʾmərotəyä-ssä[1] *zəngaʿe säwwäro*
My understanding, by contrast, | foolishness[2] | has hidden it.

[7] ሰላም፡ለአፉኪ፡መፈክረ፡ሐዲስ፡ቀኖና። 133
Sälam lä-afuki mäfäkkərä ḥaddis qänona
Peace | to your mouth, | expounder of | a new | order/canon,
ወለአስናንኪ፡ሠሐቀ፡ዘመስተሳልቃን፡መነና።
wä-lä-asnanəki śäḥaqä zä-mästäsaləqan männäna
and to your teeth, | the laughter | of the mockers' | they have repulsed/ repudiated.
መስተፍሥሔ፡አልባብ፡ድምፅኪ፡ፈድፋደ፡እምወይነ፡ቃና።
Mästäfśəḥe albab dəmṣəki fädfadä əm-wäynä Qana
Joy-bringing to | the hearts | [is] your voice, | much more | than the wine of | Cana.
ሶበ፡ተኅትመ፡ጊዜ፡ሞት፡ወለተ፡ጴጥሮስ፡ዘዮና።
Sobä täḫatmä gize mot Wälättä Ṗeṭros zä-Yona
When | was sealed/decreed | the time of | death | [for] the Daughter of | Peter, | [the son] of John[3]
ቤተ፡ክርስቲያን፡በልብሰ፡ላሕ፡ገልበበት፡ኀሊና።
betä krəstiyan bä-ləbsä laḥ gälbäbät ḫəllinna
the House of | the Christians, [the Church,] | in the garment of | mourning | wrapped | the mind.

[1] EF: *wä-lä-aʾmərotəyä-ssä* (but my understanding, by contrast).

[2] Ricci translates *zəngaʿe* as *dimenticanza* (forgetfulness), probably misled by Amharic *zänägga* (to forget, be absentminded).

[3] Lit., *zä-Yona* (of John). In Gəʿəz, the standard equivalent of John would be *Yoḥannəs*, not *Yona*, which normally is the equivalent of Jonah. In using Yona as a short form for Yoḥannəs, the author here takes some poetic license so as to arrive at the required rhyme syllable *-na*.

[8] Hail to your tongue, which has never ceased praying,

and your honey-sweet words, harp of praise and thanksgiving.

Walatta Petros, following Christ, Calvary's sacrifice,

you acquired no gold and pursued no silver,

and so the seducing servant fell sick with terror.[1]

[9] Hail to your breath, its fragrance incense,

and your throat, untouched by water or wine.

Walatta Petros, heaven's highest say of you:

"How excellent your blessedness, our sister,

and your reward unseen by mortal eye."

[10] Hail to your neck, which humility's leash dragged down,

and to shoulders that carried tribulation's yoke.

[1] This is another *säm-ənna wärq* line that can be understood in two ways. *Mäsḥati mälʾak* can mean "seducing servant" or "deceitful angel." On the surface level (wax), the line alludes to WP's jailor in Žäbäy, who made sexual advances toward her until he saw her being defended by an angel and fell down in shock. At a deeper level (gold), it alludes to the archseducer Satan, the one driving WP's jailor to behave improperly.

[8] ሰላም፡ለልሳንኪ፡ዘኢያንተገ፡ጸልዮ።
Sälam lä-ləsanəki zä-i-yantägä ṣälləyo
Peace | to your tongue, | which never ceased | praying,
ወለመዓርዒር፡ቃልኪ፡አርጋኖን፡ስብሐት፡ወተጋንዮ።
Wä-lä-mäʿarʿir qaləki arganonä səbḥat wä-täganəyo
and to honey-sweet | your words, | a harp of | praise | and thanksgiving.
በእንተ፡ኢየሱስ፡ክርስቶስ፡ዘተሠዓ፡በቀራንዮ።
Bäʾəntä Iyäsus Krəstos zä-täśoʿa bä-Qäranəyo
On account of | Jesus | Christ, | who was sacrificed | at Calvary,
ኢኀሠሥኪ፡ወርቀ፡ወብሩረ፡ወለተ፡ጴጥሮስ፡አጥርዮ።
i-ḫaśäśki wärqä wä-bərurä Wälättä Ṗeṭros aṭrəyo
you did not seek | gold | or silver, | Walatta | Petros, | to acquire,
እስከ፡ለመስሐቲ፡መልአክ፡ድንጋጼ፡አድወዮ።
əskä lä-mäsḥati mälʾak dəngaṣe adwäyo
so much so that | the seducing/deceiving | servant/angel, | shock | made him fall sick.

[9] ሰላም፡ለእስትንፋስኪ፡ዘመዓዛሁ፡ስኂን።
Sälam lä-əstənfasəki zä-mäʿazahu səḫin
Peace | to your breath, | whose fragrance | [is] incense,
ወለጕርዔኪ፡ዘየብሰ፡እምአጥልሎተ፡ማይ፡ወወይን።
wä-lä-gʷərʿeki zä-yäbsä əm-aṭləlotä may wä-wäyn
and to your throat, | which remained dry | from the moistening of | water | or wine.
ወለተ፡ጴጥሮስ፡ይብሉኪ፡መላእክተ፡ሰማይ፡ኄራን።
Wälättä Ṗeṭros yəbəluki mälaʾəktä sämay ḫeran
Walatta | Petros, | they say to you, | the angels of | heaven, | noble:
ሚይሤኒ፡እኅትነ፡ዘተውህበኪ፡ብጽዓን።
Mi-yəśenni əḫətənä zä-täwəhbäki bəṣʿan
"How beautiful/excellent, | our sister, | [is] that which has been given to you | beatitude,
ወዕሴትኒ፡ዘኢርእየ፡ዓይን።
wä-ʿəsset-ni zä-i-rəʾyä ʿayn
and the [heavenly] reward also, | which never saw | an eye!"

[10] ሰላም፡ለከሳድኪ፡በሐብለ፡ትሕትና፡ዘተስሕበ።
Sälam lä-kəsadəki bä-ḥablä təḥtənna zä-täsəḥbä
Peace | to your neck, | by the leash of | humility | it has been dragged,
ወለመታከፍትኪ፡ዘጾረ፡አርዑተ፡ምንዳቤ፡ዕጹበ።
wä-lä-mätakəftəki zä-ṣorä[1] *arʿutä məndabe ʿəṣubä*
and to your shoulders, | which have carried | the yoke of | tribulation | severe.[2]

[1] CEF: *zä-ṣorä* [sg.] (which have carried); CR: *zä-ṣora* [pl.; identical meaning].
[2] The adjective refers to yoke, not tribulation, as the Gəʿəz makes clear through its case endings.

Walatta Petros, fill my heart with wisdom:

For if, lacking wisdom, I am like a pigeon,

your Lord will permit me no treasure in heaven.

[11] Hail to your back, which cast off luxurious cloaks,

and to your chest, a banquet-table for the wretched.

Walatta Petros, our mother, lover of fasting and prayer,

request forgiveness for our sins before the Lord:

Thus we implore you, we who are yours.

[12] Hail to your bosom, rich embrace of monastic life,

and your hands, outstretched with mercy for the stranger.

Walatta Petros, crown of the True Church,

the myriad hosts of heaven and earth praise you

with one voice of song and delightful hymns.

ወለተ፡ጴጥሮስ፡ምልኢ፡ውስተ፡ልብየ፡ጥበበ።
Wälättä Ṗeṭros mələʾi wəstä ləbbəyä ṭəbäbä
Walatta | Petros, | pour | into | my heart | wisdom:
እንበለ፡ጥበብሰ፡ሶበ፡ተመሰልኩ፡ርግበ።
ənbälä ṭəbäb-əssä sobä tämässälku rəgbä
without | wisdom, specifically, | when | I resemble | a[n ignorant] dove,
ኢያበውሐኒ፡አምላክኪ፡እትዋረስ፡መዝገበ።
i-yabäwwəḥani amlakəki ətwaräs mäzgäbä
he will not permit me, | your Lord, | that I inherit | the [heavenly] treasure.

[11] ሰላም፡ለዘባንኪ፡መዋጥሐ፡ትፍግዕት፡ዘመነነ።
Sälam lä-zäbanəki mäwaṭəḥa təfgəʿt zä-männänä
Peace | to your back, | the cloaks of | luxury | it rejected,
ወለእንግድአኪ፡ምርፋቀ፡ለምስኪናን፡ዘኮነ።
wä-lä-əngədʾaki mərfaqä[1] *lä-məskinan zä-konä*
and to your chest, | a seat/banquet/table | for the wretched | it became.
መፍቀሪተ፡ጸሎት፡ወጾም፡ወለተ፡ጴጥሮስ፡እምነ።
Mäfqäritä ṣälot wä-ṣom Wälättä Ṗeṭros əmmənä
Lover of | prayer | and fasting, | Walatta | Petros, | our mother,
ትተንበሊ፡ቅድመ፡አምላክ፡ስርየተ፡ኀጢአት፡ለነ።
tətänbəli qədmä amlak səryätä ḫaṭiʾat länä
may you request | before | the Lord | forgiveness of | sins | for us:
ናስተበቍዓኪ፡እሊአኪ፡ንሕነ።
nastäbäqqʷəʿaki əlliʾaki nəḥnä
We implore you, | who are yours, | we.

[12] ሰላም፡ለሕፅንኪ፡ሕፅነ፡ምንኵስና፡ክቡር።
Sälam lä-ḥəṣ́nəki ḥəṣ́nä mənkʷəsənna kəbur
Peace | to your bosom/lap, | the bosom/lap of | monasticism | glorious/precious,
ወለአእዳውኪ፡ዘሰፍሑ፡ለምሒረ፡ኵሉ፡ግዩር።
wä-lä-aʾdawəki zä-säfḥu[2] *lä-məḥirä kʷəllu gəyyur*
and to your hands, | which are stretched out | to show mercy toward | every | stranger.
ወለተ፡ጴጥሮስ፡አክሊላ፡ለያዕቆባዊት፡ማኅበር።
Wälättä Ṗeṭros aklila lä-yaʿqobawit maḫbär
Walatta | Petros, | its crown, | of the Jacobite | community,
ይዌድሱኪ፡አእላፍ፡ተዓይነ፡ሰማይ፡ወምድር።
yəweddəsuki aʾlaf täʿayənä sämay wä-mədr
they praise you, | the myriad | hosts of | heaven | and earth
በድምፀ፡ማሕሌት፡ሠናይ፡ወሐዋዝ፡መዝሙር።
bä-dəmṣ́ä maḥlet śännay wä-ḥawwaz mäzmur
with the voice of | song | beautiful | and delightful | hymn.

[1] C, Abb. 88: *mərfaq* [nom.] (banquet), which CR altered to *mərfaqä* [acc.], as is required due to subsequent *konä.*

[2] EF: *zä-säfḥu* [masc. pl.] (which are stretched out); CR: *zä-säfḥa* [fem. pl.; identical meaning]; C omits.

[13] Hail to your arms and your elbows, those buttresses[1]

that have never been captured by fetters of sin.

Walatta Petros, like Martha who loved Christ,[2]

you shrouded in a garment of shame that angel

who made Adam fall from God's high dwelling.[3]

[14] Hail to your forearms, full of strength for works of right,

and your palms, surpassing sun and moon as they shine bright.

Walatta Petros, plead with Saint Mary, Galilee's dove,[4]

to ask her child, Savior of the World,

to keep us safe from Marcian the wolf.[5]

[1] Lit., *məsmak*. Figuratively, the term also refers to the biblical passages read during the service before the reading from the Gospels, usually Psalms. Both WP's arms and these readings are types of supports for the sacred.

[2] Martha is a woman in the New Testament who hosted Christ in her home, witnessed his resurrection of her brother, and acknowledged Christ as the Messiah (John 11).

[3] That is, Satan. Ricci says this alludes to a story told in the *Aksimaros* (the Greek *Hexaemeron*) and in the *Mäṣaḥəftä Mänäkosat* (Books of the Monks). An Ethiopian gädlat topos is the background of these two lines, as many gädlat claim that their subject, a particular saint, could reverse, in their monastic communities, the corruption caused by the fall of the first human beings.

[4] This appositive, "dove of Galilee," appears to be from the *Sənkəssar* (Budge 1928, 1:xliii; 4:1200).

[5] Lit., *Märqəyan*. The fifth-century Eastern Roman emperor Marcian approved the ecclesiastical condemnation of the non-Chalcedonian hero Dioscorus and had him exiled after the Council of Chalcedon in 451.

[13] ሰላም፡ለመዛርዕኪ፡ወለኵርናዕኪ፡ምስማክ። **134**
Sälam lä-mäzarəʿəki wä-lä-kʷərnaʿəki məsmak
Peace | to your arms | and to your elbows, | buttresses/supports
ዘኢተአኀዙ፡ፍጹመ፡በማእሰረ፡ጌጋይ፡ድሩክ።
zä-i-täʾəḫzu fəṣṣumä bä-maʾsärä gegay dəruk
which have not been captured | ever | by the fetters of | transgression | savage.
ወለተ፡ጴጥሮስ፡ማርታ፡መፍቀሪተ፡ክርስቶስ፡አምላክ።
Wälättä Peṭros Marta mäfqäritä Krəstos amlak
Walatta | Petros, | [a] Martha, | a lover of | Christ | the Lord:
ተከድነ፡ልብሰ፡ኀፍረት፡በእብሬትኪ፡መልአክ።
täkädnä ləbsä ḫafrät bä-əbretəki mälʾak
he was covered with | the garment of | shame | through you, | that angel, [Satan,]
ለአዳም፡ዘአውደቆ፡እምሣልስ፡ፈለክ።
lä-Addam zä-awdäqo əm-śaləs fäläk
him, Adam, | who made him fall | from the Third | Heaven.

[14] ሰላም፡ለእመታትኪ፡ለተገብሮ፡ጽድቅ፡ዘተኃየላ።
Sälam lä-əmätatəki lä-tägäbbəro ṣədq zä-täḫayyäla
Peace | to your forearms, | for the work of | righteousness, | which were strong,
ወለእራሕኪ፡ብሩህ፡እምሥነ፡አርያሬስ፡ወእብላ።
wä-lä-əraḥəki bəruh əm-śənnä aryares wä-əbla
and to your palms, | brighter | than the beauty of | the sun | and the moon.[1]
ወለተ፡ጴጥሮስ፡ተንበሊ፡ኀበ፡ማርያም፡ርግበ፡ገሊላ።
Wälättä Peṭros tänbəli ḫabä Maryam rəgbä Gälila
Walatta | Petros, | intercede [for us] | before | Mary, | the dove of | Galilee,
ትተንበል፡በእንቲአነ፡መድኀኔ፡ዓለም፡እጓላ።
tətänbəl bäʾəntiʾanä mädḫane[2] *ʿaläm əgʷala*[3]
that she may beseech, | on our behalf, | the Savior of | the World, | her child,
ከመ፡ይዕቀበነ፡እመርቅያን፡ተኵላ።
kämä yəʿqäbänä əm-Märqəyan täkʷəla
so that | he may save us | from Marcian | the wolf.

[1] The terms for sun and moon employed here, *aryares* and *əbla*, are rarely used loanwords, both of which may first occur in the book of Enoch, traditionally regarded in Ethiopia as part of the biblical canon. In addition, these terms also occur in the *Sənkəssar* entry for 17 Näḥase and in a sälam poem to a saintly Anṭawos, according to Dillmann (1865, col. 744, 756). For the sake of the rhyme, *əbla* here is to be pronounced as *əbəla*. The standard Gəʿəz terms for the sun and the moon are *śäḥay* and *wärḫ*, respectively.

[2] E, CR: *əm-mädḫane* (from the Savior of).

[3] CEF: *əgʷala* (her child); CR: *əgʷla* (different term, but identical meaning).

[15] Hail to your fingers, branches of their trunk, the hand,

and their tips, your nails, their color is snow and hail.

Walatta Petros, oh, you topaz and emerald stone,

your rebuke has given wisdom to the fool

and to many the gift of a return from heresy.

[16] Hail to your breasts, which gave forth the milk of grace:

their fullness for mercy has never diminished.

Daughter of the judge Saint Peter, when you,

our lamp, lay hidden in the basket that was death,

darkness then ruled on our right and our left.[1]

[17] Hail to your sides, adorned with verdant gold,

[1] Matthew 5:15, "Nor do people light a lamp and put it under a basket." This is one of the most common New Testament quotations in Gəʿəz hagiobiographies, whose authors deployed the metaphor with tremendous skill. Here, the death of WP is compared to a basket that covers a shining lamp, which causes darkness to descend.

[15] ሰላም፡ለአጻብዕኪ፡አዕጹቀ፡ተቅዋም፡እድ።
Sälam lä-aṣabəʿəki[1] *aʿṣuqä täqwam əd*
Peace | to your fingers, | branches of | the base, | the hand,
ወለአርእስቲሆን፡አጽፋር፡ዘሕብረ፡እማንቱ፡በረድ።
wä-lä-arʾəstihon aṣfar zä-ḥəbrä əmantu bäräd
and to their heads, | the nails, | the color of | them | snow/ice.
ወለተ፡ጴጥሮስ፡ወራውሬ፡ወእብነ፡መረግድ።
Wälättä Ṗeṭros wärawre wä-əbnä märägd
Walatta | Petros, | [you] topaz | and stone of | emerald,
ጥበበ፡እምተግሣጽኪ፡አጥረየ፡አብድ።
ṭəbäbä əm-tägśaṣəki aṭräyä abd
wisdom | through your rebuke/instruction | acquired | the fool,
ወሀብተ፡ሚጠት፡ብዙኃን፡እምካሕድ።
wä-häbtä miṭät bəzuḫan əm-kaḥd
and the gift of | turning away, | many, | from heresy.

[16] ሰላም፡ለአጥባትኪ፡ዘሐሊበ፡ጸጋ፡አንቅዓት።
Sälam lä-aṭbatəki zä-ḥalibä ṣägga anqəʿat
Peace | to your breasts, | which the milk of | grace | poured forth,
ወኢይውኅዶን፡ምሕረት።
wä-i-yəwəḫədon məḥrät
and never decreased on them | mercy.
ወለተ፡መበይን፡ጴጥሮስ፡በከፈረ፡ሞት።
Wälättä mäbäyyən Ṗeṭros[2] *bä-käfärä mot*[3]
Daughter of | the judge | [Saint] Peter, | with the basket of | death
ጊዜ፡ተሰወርኪ፡ማኅቶትነ፡ብርህት።
gize täsäwwärki maḫtotənä bərəht[4]
when | you were hidden,| our lamp | shining,
ውስተ፡ገጸ፡የማን፡ወፀጋም፡ሰፈነ፡ጽልመት።
wəstä gäṣṣä yäman wä-ṣ́ägam säfänä ṣəlmät
on | the side of | right | and left | ruled/prevailed | darkness.

[17] ሰላም፡ለገቦኪ፡ስርግው፡ዘወርቅ፡ሐመልማል።
Sälam lä-gäboki sərgəw zä-wärq ḥamälmal[5]
Peace | to your flanks/ribs | adorned | with gold | green/verdant,

[1] CR: *lä-lä-aṣabəʿəki* (to each of your fingers).

[2] CEF: *Wälättä mäbäyyən Ṗeṭros* (daughter of the judge Peter); CR: *Wälättä Ṗeṭros mäbäyyən* (WP, judge).

[3] *Bä-käfärä mot* (with the basket of death) where Ricci expected *bä-känfärä mot* (with the lips of death) and translated accordingly (*con le labbra della morte*). However, CEF confirm CR, with the biblical allusion clearly being to the "basket" of Matthew 5:15.

[4] CR: *mäbrəht* (illuminating).

[5] CEF: *ḥamälmal* [fem.] (green); CR: *ḥamälmil* [masc.; identical meaning]. See Psalm 68:13.

and your belly, treasury of the Gospel's pearl.[1]

Walatta Petros, loftier in your struggles than Sarah,

may your wings shade me, just as in the wilderness

God's cloud gave shade to the Tent of the Testimony.[2]

[18] Hail to your heart and your kidneys. Every moment,

they let sprout no iniquity and harbored no deceit.

Walatta Petros, break me blessing's bread

and I will give you the fruit of my lips,

a hymn to your boundless glory.

[19] Hail to your mind, which dwelt on the Crucifixion,

and your bowels, never knotted with even the least evil.

Walatta Petros, while my people listen, say to me:

[1] *Baḥrəyä wängel* (Pearl or essence of the Gospel) is a common metaphor in the Täwaḥədo Church for Christ, symbolizing a pure seed passed down through human bodies since Adam. See also Matthew 13:45–46.

[2] The Tent of the Testimony was part of the temporary building that the Israelites set up for worship in the wilderness while on their way from Egypt to the Promised Land. It contained the Ark of the Covenant and the Ten Commandments, which is why it was also called the Place of the Testimony or of the Law. Regarding the cloud covering it, see Numbers 9:15 and Jubilees 1:2. God lifted the cloud over the Tent of the Testimony when it was time to move on, and lowered it when the Israelites had reached the next camp spot, so it was a visible sign of God's presence and protection.

ወለከርሥኪ፡መዝገቡ፡ለባሕርየ፡ወንጌል።
wä-lä-kärśəki mäzgäbu lä-baḥrəyä wängel
and to your belly/interior, | a store/treasury | for the pearl/essence of | the Gospel, [Christ].
ወለተ፡ጴጥሮስ፡እምሳራ፡ልዕልተ፡ዝክር፡ወገድል።
Wälättä Ṗeṭros əm-Sara ləʿəltä zəkr wä-gädl[1]
Walatta | Petros, | than Sarah | loftier in | memory/fame | and struggle,
ይጸልላኒ፡አክናፍኪ፡ከመ፡ጸለላ፡በሐቅል።
yəṣälləlani aknafəki[2] *kämä ṣälläla bä-ḥaql*[3]
may shade me | your wings, | like | it [the cloud] shaded it | in the wilderness,
ለደብተራ፡ስምዕ፡ደመና፡ቀሊል።
lä-däbtära səmʿ dämmäna qälil
namely, the Tent of | the Testimony,[4] | a cloud | light.

[18] ሰላም፡ለልብኪ፡ወለኵልያትኪ፡ንስቲተ።
Sälam lä-ləbbəki wä-lä-kʷələyatəki nəstitä
Peace | to your heart | and to your kidneys, | for even a moment
ዘኢያሥረጹ፡ዓመፃ፡ወኢዘገቡ፡ጽልሑተ።
zä-i-yaśräṣu ʿammäṣ́a wä-i-zägäbu ṣəlḥutä
they did not let sprout | inquity | and they did not harbor | deceit/falsehood.
ወለተ፡ጴጥሮስ፡ፈትቲ፡ኅብስተ፡በረከት፡ሊተ።
Wälättä Ṗeṭros fättəti ḫəbəstä bäräkät litä
Walatta | Petros, | break | the bread of | blessing | for me:
ህየንተ፡አቅረብኩ፡ፍሬ፡ከናፍር፡ማሕሌተ።
həyyäntä aqräbku fəre känafər maḥletä
in exchange, | hereby I offer | the fruit of | lips, | a hymn
ለዕበይኪ፡ዘአልቦ፡መስፈርተ።
lä-ʿəbäyəki zä-albo mäsfärtä
to your greatness/magnificence, | which does not have | a measure/limit.

[19] ሰላም፡ለኀሊናኪ፡ስቅለተ፡ፈጣሪ፡ዘኀለየ። **135**
Sälam lä-ḫəllinnaki səqlätä fäṭari zä-ḫälläyä
Peace | to your mind, | the crucifixion of | the creator | it pondered,
ወለአማዑትኪ፡ሐቀ፡ዘኢቈጸረ፡እከየ።
wä-lä-amaʿutəki ḥəqqä zä-i-qʷäṣärä əkäyä
and to your bowels, | even a little | they did not knot/hatch evil.
ወለተ፡ጴጥሮስ፡በልኒ፡እንዘ፡ይሰምዑ፡ሕዝብየ።
Wälättä Ṗeṭros bäləni ənzä yəsämməʿu ḥəzbəyä
Walatta | Petros, | say to me | while | they listen, | my people:

[1] *Gädl* for the sake of the rhyme here is to be pronounced as *gädəl.*

[2] CR: *yaṣälləlani* [*sic*] *aknafəki* [the verbal stem to be reconstructed from *yaṣälləlani,* namely, *aṣällälä,* is not attested].

[3] *Ḥaql* for the sake of the rhyme here is to be pronounced as *ḥaqəl.*

[4] *Däbtära səmʿ* is not, pace Ricci's *arca della testimonianza,* an ark.

"Truly, I have prepared a home for you in heaven
where we shall be together. Do not worry, my son."

[20] Hail and hail again to your organs within,
and your navel without, the seal that stamps them.
Walatta Petros, like Elizabeth, the Baptist's mother,[1]
all the orders of the angels and of humankind,
fashioned of all four elements,[2] proclaim you blessed.

[21] Hail to your womb, like a grape-bearing vine,
which has brought forth fruits of holiness and Law.
Daughter of Peter, that leader of leaders,
together with Shenoute and the Martyrs of Waseef,[3]

[1] That is, Elizabeth the mother of John the Baptist, who heralded the coming of Christ in the New Testament.

[2] Likely a reference to the four elements of Greek medicine: melancholic (bile, autumn, earth), choleric (bile, summer, fire), phlegmatic (phlegm, winter, water), and sanguine (blood, spring, air). Alternatively, it might be two elements for the angels (fire and air) and two for humans (earth and water), perhaps from such original Gəʿəz works as *Sennä Fəṭrät* (Beauty of Creation).

[3] WP shares her saint's day with the two invoked here: the fifth-century Coptic saint Shenoute of Atripe and a group of Egyptian martyrs about whom very little is known, the *Ṣadəqanä Wäṣif* (Righteous Ones of Waseef).

ማኅደረ፡በሰማያት፡ከመ፡ተሀሉ፡ምስሌየ።
Maḫdärä bä-sämayat kämä tähallu məsleyä
"An abode | in the heavens, | so that | you will be | with me,
እስመ፡አስተዳለውኩ፡ለከ፡ኢትሕዝን፡ወልድየ።
əsmä astädaläwku läkä i-təḥzən wäldəyä
truly | I have prepared | for you: | do not worry, | my son!"

[20] ሰላም፡ሰላም፡ለንዋየ፡ውስጥኪ፡ኅቡእ።
Sälam sälam lä-nəwayä wəsṭəki ḫəbuʾ
Peace, | peace | to the vessels/organs of | your interior, | hidden,
ወለሕንብርትኪ፡ዘአፍአ፡ከመ፡ዓይነ፡ማኅተም፡ልኩእ።
wä-lä-ḥənbərtəki zä-afʾa kämä ʿaynä maḫtäm ləkuʾ
and to your navel | of outside, | like | the eye of | a seal | stamped/impressed.
ወለተ፡ጴጥሮስ፡ኤልሳቤጥ፡ወላዲተ፡መጥምቅ፡ብጹዕ።
Wälättä Ṗeṭros Elsabeṭ wäladitä mäṭməq bəṣuʿ
Walatta | Petros, | [you are like] Elizabeth, | the mother of | the Baptist | blessed:
ያስተበጽዑኪ፡ነገደ፡መላእክት፡ወሰብእ።
yastäbäṣṣəʿuki nägädä mälaʾəkt wä-säbʾ[1]
they proclaim you blessed, | the order of | angels | and humans
እለ፡ሡሩራን፡እምጾታ፡አርባዕ።
əllä śururan əm-[2]*ṣota arbaʿ*
who | are made | of the elements[3] | four.

[21] ሰላም፡ለማሕፀንኪ፡ከመ፡አስካለ፡ወይን፡ዘሐረግ።
Sälam lä-maḥṣänəki kämä askalä wäyn zä-ḥaräg
Peace | to your womb, | like | a bunch of | grapes | on the vine
ዘፈረየ፡ፍሬ፡እንተ፡ቅድስና፡ወሕግ።
zä-färäyä fəre əntä qəddəsənna wä-ḥəgg
it has brought forth | [numerous] fruits | of | holiness | and the Law.
ለርእሰ፡ርኡሳን፡ጴጥሮስ፡ወለቱ፡እንበለ፡ነቲግ።
Lä-rəʾsä[4] *rəʾusan Ṗeṭros wälättu ənbälä nätig*
Of the head of | the leaders, | Peter, | his daughter: | without | ceasing
አንቲ፡ወሲኖዳ፡ወጻድቃነ፡ወጺፍ፡አእሩግ።
anti wä-Sinoda wä-ṣadəqanä Wäṣif aʾrug
you | and Shenoute | and the Righteous Ones of | Waseef, | the elders,

[1] *Säbʾ* for the sake of the rhyme here is to be pronounced as *säbəʾ*.

[2] C, CR: *əllä śururan əm-* (which are made of); EF: *əllä səruran əm-* (which are higher up than).

[3] Ricci translates *ṣota*, which normally means "order, class, kind, gender," as *elementi*, explaining in a note that here he regards it as equivalent with *ṭäbayəʿ*. Dillmann defines *ṭäbayəʿ* as (the four) elements (of traditional cosmology), (the four) human types (of traditional psychology) (1865, col. 1233). Since the conventional meanings of *ṣota* do not yield a contextually convincing translation, we have followed Ricci.

[4] CR: *lä-rəʾusä* (of the leader of).

pour the saffron of your blessing on us.

[22] Hail to your hips, grown thin through much fasting,

and your legs, paired pillars with a sturdy stance.

Walatta Petros, enlighten my heart's dim eye,

so I can see you standing there together

with the Firstborn's[1] joyful community of Law.

[23] Hail to your knees, always bent in genuflection,

and your feet, ever-swift on the ministry's path.[2]

Walatta Petros, protect your children from disorder.

And as for Satan, who hates camaraderie and love,

tear his snares apart and uproot his thorn.

[24] Hail to your soles and the ground where they stood,

[1] In the Bible, the firstborn son is consecrated to God and firstborn animals are used in holy sacrifice; see Deuteronomy 12:6. Regarding Christ as the firstborn, see Colossians 1:18.

[2] This is another *säm-ənna wärq* line that can be understood in two ways. What here appears as "and your feet, ever-swift on ministry's path" could also be translated as "and to the Apostles, [that is,] your feet on mission's path."

መጽርየ፡በረከት፡ላዕሌነ፡ነስንሱ፡በደርግ።
mäṣrəyä bäräkät laʿəlenä näsnəsu bä-därg
the saffron of | blessing | upon us | sprinkle, | [you] jointly.

[22] ሰላም፡ለሐቌኪ፡በአብዝኆ፡ጸዊም፡ዘደግደገ።
Sälam lä-ḥaqʷeki bä-äbzəḫo ṣäwim zä-dägdägä
Peace | to your hips, | through the multiplying of | fasting | they have become emaciated,
ወለአቍያጽኪ፡አዕማድ፡እለ፡ይትሌለያ፡ዘውገ።
wä-lä-aqʷyaṣəki aʿmad əllä yətlelläya zäwgä
and to your legs/thighs, | columns | that are | separate, | a pair of.
ወለተ፡ጴጥሮስ፡አብርሂ፡ዓይነ፡ልብየ፡ሕሙገ።
Wälättä Ṗeṭros abrəhi ʿaynä ləbbəyä ḥəmugä[1]
Walatta | Petros, | enlighten | the eye of | my heart/mind | dim,[2]
ከመ፡እነጽርኪ፡እንዘ፡ትቀውሚ፡ደርገ።
kämä ənäṣṣərki ənzä təqäwwəmi därgä
so that | I can see you | while | you are standing | together
ምስለ፡ማኅበረ፡በኵር፡ፍሡሓን፡ዘሰለጡ፡ሕገ።
məslä maḫbärä bäkʷr fəśśuḥan zä-sälläṭu ḥəggä
with | the community of | the Firstborn, [Christ,] | the happy ones, | who have observed/fulfilled | the Law.

[23] ሰላም፡ለአብራክኪ፡እለ፡አዝለፉ፡አስተብርኮ።
Sälam lä-äbrakəki əllä azläfa astäbrəko
Peace | to your knees, | which | continuously did | genuflecting,
ወለሐዋርያት፡ሰላም፡አእጋርኪ፡ፍና፡ተልእኮ።
wä-lä-ḥawarəyat sälam aʾgarəki fənna täləʾəko
and to the ever-moving/the apostle-like, | peace [upon them], | your feet, | on the path of | service/ministry/mission.
ወለተ፡ጴጥሮስ፡ዕቀቢ፡ማኅበረ፡ደቂቅኪ፡እምተሀውኮ።
Wälättä Ṗeṭros ʿəqäbi maḫbärä däqiqəki əm-tähawko
Walatta | Petros, | preserve | the community of | your children | from turmoil.
ለሰይጣንሰ፡ዘኢያፈቅር፡ተዓርኮ።
Lä-säyṭan-əssä zä-i-yafäqqər täʿarəko
As for Satan, in particular, | who does not like | harmony:
መሣግሪሁ፡ብትኪ፡ወስብሪ፡ሦኮ።
mäśagərihu bətəki wä-səbəri śoko
his snares | tear apart | and break | his thorn.

[24] ሰላም፡ለሰኳንውኪ፡ምስለ፡መከየድ፡ዘቆሙ።
Sälam lä-säkʷanəwəki məslä mäkäyäd zä-qomu
Peace | to the soles of your feet, | together with | the ground | on which they stood,

[1] CR: *ʿaynä ləbbunnayä ḥəmugä* (the dim eye of my reason).

[2] The adjective refers to eye, not heart/mind, as the Gəʿəz makes clear through its case endings.

never nourished by rest's loaf that feeds the weary.

Walatta Petros, sound the prayer bell of our plea

for the Jacobites, believers in his name:

May Christ our sins through His blood redeem.

[25] Hail to your toes, twice five in their number,

and your ten toenails, that sit well there together.

Daughter of Peter our elder,[1] from your distance

draw near to the griever and fill his longing;

and consecrate the righteous for their righteousness.

[26] Hail to your stature, beautiful as choice cedar,

and hail to your figure, a sun that inspires joy.

Walatta Petros, instead of riches, give me

[1] See 1 Peter 5:1.

ኅብስተ፡አዕርፎ፡እምጻማ፡እንዘ፡ይጸውሙ።
ḫəbəstä aʿrəfo əm-ṣama ənzä yəṣäwwəmu
the bread of | rest | from toil, | while | abstaining from [it].
ወለተ፡ጴጥሮስ፡ጥቅዒ፡መጥቅዓ፡ስእለት፡ለለጌሰሙ።
Wälättä Ṗeṭros ṭəqəʿi mäṭqəʿa səʾlät lä-lä-gesämu
Walatta | Petros, | blow/sound | the trumpet/church bell | of pleading | each new morning,
ለእለ፡አመነ፡ያዕቆባውያን፡በስሙ።
lä-əllä amännä yaʿqobawəyan bä-səmu
for us who | believe, | the Jacobites, | in his name:
ቤዛ፡ኀጣውኢነ፡ይኩን፡ለክርስቶስ፡በደሙ።
beza ḫaṭawəʾinä yəkun lä-Krəstos bä-dämu
the redemption | of our sins, | may it happen | [by] Christ's, | by his blood.

[25] ሰላም፡ለአጻብዓ፡እግርኪ፡ኀምስ፡ክዑባት፡በኍልቆ። **136**
Sälam lä-aṣabəʿa əgrəki ḫams kəʿubat bä-ḫʷälqo[1]
Peace | to the fingers of | your feet, | five | doubled | in their number,
ወለአጽፋርኪ፡ዓሥር፡እለ፡ይነብራ፡በተላጽቆ።
wä-lä-aṣfarəki ʿaśər[2] *əllä yənäbbəra bä-tälaṣəqo*
and to your [toe]nails | ten, | which | sit | neatly side by side.[3]
ወለተ፡አረጋይ፡ጴጥሮስ፡ቅረቢ፡እምተራሕቆ።
Wälättä arägay Ṗeṭros qəräbi əm-tärahəqo
Daughter of | the elder, | Peter, | draw near | from being distant
ለትኩዝ፡ብእሲ፡ከመ፡ትፈጽሚ፡ጻህቆ።
Lä-təkkuz bəʾəsi kämä təfäṣṣəmi ṣahqo
to the grieving | man, | so that | you fulfill | his longing,
ወለጻድቅ፡ትባርኪ፡ጽድቆ።
wä-lä-ṣadəq təbarəki ṣədqo
and to the righteous one, | so that you bless/consecrate | his righteousness.

[26] ሰላም፡ለቆምኪ፡ሥነ፡ቄድሮስ፡ኅሩይ።
Sälam lä-qoməki śənnä qedros ḫəruy
Peace | to your stature, | of the beauty of | a cedar | chosen,
ወለመልክእኪ፡ሰላም፡ወላዴ፡ፍሥሓ፡ፀሓይ።
wä-lä-mälkəʾəki sälam wälade fəśśəḥa śäḥay
and to your figure/face/aspect, | peace: | [it is] a procreator | of happiness, | a sun.
ወለተ፡ጴጥሮስ፡ሀብኒ፡ተውላጠ፡ንዋይ።
Wälättä Ṗeṭros habəni täwlaṭä nəway[4]
Walatta | Petros, | give me, | in exchange for | wealth/possessions,

[1] Lit., *bä-ḫʷälqo* (in its number), rather than the more grammatically correct *bä-ḫʷälqon* (in their [fem. pl.] number). The author takes some poetic license to make sure this stanza's lines all end in *-qo*.

[2] Standard form *ʿaśru*; the author has altered the form for poetic purposes.

[3] Our translation here differs from Ricci's, who has *che vi si trovano per attaccatura* (which find themselves attached there [i.e., the nails to the toes]).

[4] CR: *täwlaṭä zəntu nəway* (in exchange for these possessions).

a morsel of blessing before the Great Gathering,[1]

a taste of your blessing that is ever so sweet.

[27] Hail to your soul's departure, sung on its way by our hymns,

and the corpse of your flesh, more radiant than pearl.

Walatta Petros, so wise and upright, our morning star,

when your memory's rays shine forth,

worry vanishes from troubled hearts.

[28] Hail to your shroud, its glory beyond all glory,

and your tomb, a refuge for all who seek it there.

Walatta Petros, crystal vessel, bowl for faith's ointment,

pour clemency's fountain that your sheep may drink

when the heat of hellfire blazes near.

[1] See 1 Thessalonians 4:13–18, regarding the reunion of all believers (living and dead) upon the Second Coming of Christ.

ፍተ፡በረከት፡በቅድመ፡ጉባኤ፡ዓባይ።
fəttä bäräkät bä-qədmä gubaʾe ʿabbay
a morsel of | blessing | before | the Gathering/Reunion | Great,
እምበረከትኪ፡ዘጥቀ፡ሠናይ።
əm-bäräkätəki zä-ṭəqqä śännay
from your blessing | that is so | good.

[27] ሰላም፡ለፀአተ፡ነፍስኪ፡በጣዕመ፡ዝማሬ፡ሐዋዝ።
Sälam lä-ṣ́äʾatä näfsəki bä-ṭaʿmä zəmmare ḥawwaz
Peace | to the departure of | your soul, | under the delight of | singing of hymns | sweet,
ወለበድነ፡ሥጋኪ፡ጽዱል፡እምጸዳለ፡ባሕርይ፡ዕንቡዝ።
wä-lä-bädnä śəgaki ṣədul əm-[1]*ṣädalä baḥrəy ʿənbuz*
and to the corpse of | your flesh, | radiant/splendid | more than the radiance/splendor of | a pearl | stupefying.[2]
ወለተ፡ጴጥሮስ፡ጠባብ፡ወሠናይተ፡ግዕዝ።
Wälättä Ṗeṭros ṭäbbab wä-śännaytä gəʿz
Walatta | Petros, | wise | and fine of | character,
ለለይሠርቁ፡ምዕዛራተ፡ዝክርኪ፡ቤዝ።
lä-lä-yəśärrəqu məʿzaratä zəkrəki bez
each time when shine | the rays of | your memory, | [you] morning star,
እምልበ፡ብእሲ፡ሐዙን፡ይትረሳዕ፡ትካዝ።
əm-ləbbä bəʾəsi ḥəzun yəträssaʿ təkkaz
from the heart/mind of | a man | troubled | is forgotten | worry.

[28] ሰላም፡ለግንዘተ፡ሥጋኪ፡ዘትሩፈ፡ትሩፍ፡ዕበዩ።
Sälam lä-gənzätä śəgaki zä-tərufä təruf ʿəbäyu
Peace | to the shrouding of | your flesh, | eminent of | eminent | its glory,
ወለመቃብርኪ፡ምስካይ፡ለእለ፡ቦቱ፡ሰከዩ።
wä-lä-mäqabərəki məskay lä-əllä botu säkäyu
and to your tomb, | a refuge | for those who | at it | seek refuge.
ወለተ፡ጴጥሮስ፡ቢረሌ፡ለዕፍረተ፡አሚን፡ሙዳዩ።
Wälättä Ṗeṭros birälle lä-ʿəfrätä amin mudayu
Walatta | Petros, | crystal vessel, | for the perfume of | faith | its vase,
ቅድሒ፡ፈልፈለ፡ሣህል፡አባግዕኪ፡ይርወዩ።
qədəḥi fälfälä śahl abagəʿəki yərwäyu
pour | the fountain of | mercy/clemency | for your sheep, | that they may drink
ጊዜ፡አንበልበለ፡ለመርቄ፡ዋዕዩ።
gize anbälbälä[3] *lä-märqe waʿyu*
when | blazes, | of the burning [of hell], | its heat.

[1] C, CR: *ṣədul əm-* (more radiant than); EF: *ṣəruy əm-* (purer than).

[2] Gəʿəz *ʿənbuz* means being fainthearted, downcast, senseless, foolish, or bewildered, which does not immediately make sense.

[3] CR: *anbälbäla* [*sic*: fem. pl.] (blaze).

[29] To your cowl—like the thorns on Christ's brow

when the Jews crucified him that he might redeem the world—

and to your cloak woven of purity,

and to your habit, your belt, and your gown,

I say "Hail, hail." My poem I close with a seal.

[30] Praise unto Him, Lord of Lords, God of gods,

His essence a light that shines above all lights.

He has saved even me from the Entangler's snares

and has let your child finish, Walatta Petros,

the song in your memory I began for you.

[29] ለቆብዕኪ፡አክሊለ፡ሦክ፡ዲበ፡ርእሰ፡ክርስቶስ፡ዘተሠይመ፡፡
Lä-qobʿəki aklilä śok dibä rəʾsä Krəstos zä-täśäymä
To your monastic cap, | [like] the crown of | thorns | upon | the head of | Christ
| that was set/who was appointed,[1]
አመ፡ሰቀልዎ፡አይሁድ፡ከመ፡ይቤዙ፡ዓለመ፡፡
amä säqäləwwo ayhud kämä yəbezu ʿalämä
when | crucified him | the Jews, | so that | he might redeem | the world;
ወዓጽፈ፡ንጽሕና፡ዓጽፍኪ፡ወአስኬማኪ፡ቅድመ፡፡
wä-ʿaṣfä nəṣḥənna ʿaṣfəki wä-askemaki qədmä
and [to] the *atsf*-vestment | of purity, | your *atsf*-vestment, | and [to] your
askema-vestment, | first,
ለቅናትኒ፡ወቀሚስ፡ወለተ፡ጴጥሮስ፡ዳግመ፡፡
lä-qənat-ni wä-qämis Wälättä Ṗeṭros dagəmä
[and] to the belt/sash also, | and [to] the gown/shirt, | Walatta | Petros, | second:
ሰላም፡ሰላም፡እንዘ፡እብል፡ረሰይኩ፡ማኅተመ፡፡
Sälam sälam ənzä əbəl rässäyku maḫtämä
"Peace, | peace" | while | saying, | I hereby put | the [closing] seal.

[30] ይትባረክ፡እግዚአብሔር፡አምላከ፡አማልክት፡መላኪ፡፡
Yətbaräk əgziʾabḥer amlakä amaləkt mälaki
Praised be | God, | the Lord of/over | the lords/idols, | the Ruler,
ዘባሕርይሁ፡ብርሃን፡ዘመልዕልተ፡ብርሃናት፡ያዋኪ፡፡
zä-baḥrəyhu bərhan zä-mälʿəltä bərhanat yawakki
whose essence | a light | that above | [all] lights | shines.
እስመ፡ዓቀበኒ፡ሊተ፡እመሥገርተ፡ሰይጣን፡ሀዋኪ፡፡
Əsmä ʿaqäbäni litä əm-mäśgärtä säyṭan hawaki
Truly, | he has saved me, | [yes,] me, | from the snares of | Satan, | the Subverter
ወአፈጸመኒ፡ወለተ፡ጴጥሮስ፡ወልድኪ፡፡
wä-äfäṣṣämäni Wälättä Ṗeṭros wäldəki
and has let me finish/accomplish, | Walatta | Petros, | your child,
ማሕሌተ፡ዝክርኪ፡ዘወጠንኩ፡ለኪ፡፡
maḥletä zəkrəki zä-wäṭänku läki
the song in | your memory | that I began | for you.

[1] This is another *säm-ənna wärq* line that can be understood in two ways: the relative *zä-* can refer to the crown or to Christ, and the semantic range of the verb *täśäymä* is such that, depending on which *zä*-reference one favors, it takes on the meaning of "was set" or "was appointed."

The Translation of the Poem *Hail to Walatta Petros* (*Sälamta Wälättä Ṗeṭros*)

A sälam or sälamta is a short poem or hymn in Gəʿəz that focuses on a leader's or saint's good deeds or spiritual essence and begins each stanza with the words sälam lä- *(peace upon,* or *hail to). Sälamat (plural) generally have between six and twelve stanzas, with only three lines per stanza, with a long first line and two shorter lines of three to four words each following it, and a final four-line stanza. To aid the scholar or student who does not read Gəʿəz but is interested in understanding the skill and elegance of the original, we have below provided the poem in fidäl, in transliteration, and in word-for-word English translation. On the facing page is the poetic English translation, by Kristin Fogdall. Those wishing to read or assign Fogdall's translation on its own (in an easy-to-read version properly spaced and without the facing pages of fidäl, transliteration, or word-for-word translation), can find it as a PDF at wendybelcher .com.*

[1] Hail to you, Walatta Petros, a garden! Wrapped in heavenly scent,
you are shade for the doves,[1] from the heat of misery
that fills our world.

[2] Hail to you, Walatta Petros, a mirror! You reveal the Trinity
in its holiness to everyone, high and low:
now the faithful sit safe on dry ground.[2]

[3] Hail to you, Walatta Petros, a light! Your preaching split the darkness
and the foolish friends of this world
ran eagerly toward repentance.

[1] When Christ grants WP her kidan, he says, "many people will gather around you, from east and west. They will be pure doves, and they will benefit [from you] for the salvation of their souls." The doves are a metaphor here for WP's disciples.

[2] The author appears to allude to the episode when water suddenly rushed down the dry riverbed where WP and her followers had camped. Alternately, it is a reference to God creating dry ground for his people to cross dangerous seas or rivers; for example, Exodus 14:22 and Joshua 4:23.

[1] ሰላም፡ለኪ፡ወለተ፡ጴጥሮስ፡ገነት፡ክልልተ፡መዓዛ፡ጥዑም። **137**
Sälam läki Wälättä Ṗeṭros gännät kəlləltä mäʿaza ṭəʿum
Peace/hail | to you | Walatta | Petros, | a garden/Eden | enclosed/protected by | fragrance | sweet/delicious,[1]
ወምጽላለ፡አርጋብ፡አንቲ፡እምርቄ፡ሕማም።
wä-məṣlalä argab anti əm-märqe ḥəmam
and a shade/refuge for | the doves | you [are], | from the burning of | affliction
ዘሰፈነት፡ውስተ፡ዓለም።
zä-säfänät[2] *wəstä ʿaläm*
that rules | in | the world.

[2] ሰላም፡ለኪ፡ወለተ፡ጴጥሮስ፡መጽሔት፡ሃይማኖተ፡ሥሉስ፡ቅዱስ።
Sälam läki Wälättä Ṗeṭros mäṣḥet haymanotä śəllus qəddus
Peace/hail | to you | Walatta | Petros, | a mirror. | The faith in | the Trinity | holy
ዘተከሥተ፡ብኪ፡ለዘነብ፡ወርእስ።
zä-täkäśtä bəki[3] *lä-zänäb wä-rəʾs*
has been revealed | through you | to tail | and head:[4]
ኅዱራን፡መልዕልተ፡የብስ።
ḫəduran mälʿəltä yäbs
they sit/dwell | on | dry ground.

[3] ሰላም፡ለኪ፡ወለተ፡ጴጥሮስ፡ብርሃን፡ስብከትኪ፡አመ፡ውስተ፡ጽልመት፡አብርሀ።
Sälam läki[5] *Wälättä Ṗeṭros bərhan səbkätəki amä wəstä ṣəlmät abrəha*
Peace/hail | to you | Walatta | Petros, | a light. | Your preaching, | when | into | darkness | it brought light,
ለመክፈልተ፡አብዳን፡ዓለም፡አዕርክቲሃ።
lä-mäkfältä abdan ʿaläm aʿrəktiha
of the share of | fools, | the world, | its friends
ተባደሩ፡ኀበ፡ንስሓ።
täbadäru ḫabä nəssəḥa
ran eagerly | toward | repentance.

[1] Since BD do not have the sälam, we have checked its CR text against CEFJ, the only manuscripts providing it. Note that in MS J, the sälam appears before the miracles, not after them.

[2] FJ: *zä-säfänä* [masc., as opposed to fem. *zä-säfänät*; no translation difference].

[3] CR: *läki* (to you).

[4] "Tail and head" is probably a metaphor for "everyone," like "young and old" or "high and low," as in Isaiah 19:15.

[5] Abb. 88: *sälaməki* (your peace), which CR sensibly altered to *sälam läki*.

[4] Peace upon you! What no eye has seen nor ear ever heard,[1]

that mystery you chose as your wedding finery,

refusing a life of luxury.[2]

[5] Hail to you, Walatta Petros, our mother! Strength of will carried you

through the narrow gate[3]—like thousands of martyrs before

and the righteous monks of Waseef.

[6] Peace upon you and your forebear Shenoute, arrayed in the armor of chastity!

Come, comfort our distress and woe;

guard us while the whirlwind rages.[4]

[1] Regarding God promising as a heavenly reward what no eye has seen nor ear heard, see 1 Corinthians 2:9.

[2] This is an allusion to WP leaving a wealthy man and her life as a pampered wife to become the bride of Christ as an ascetic nun.

[3] See Matthew 7:13–14; Luke 13:24.

[4] See Proverbs 1:27–28.

[4] ሰላም፡ለኪ፡ዘዓይን፡ኢርእየ፡ወእዝነ፡መዋቲ፡ኢሰምዓ።
Sälam läki zä-ʿayn i-rəʾyä wä-əznä mäwati[1] *i-sämʿa*
Peace/hail | to you. | What an eye | has not seen | and ear of | mortal | has not heard,
ከመ፡ትትረሰዪ፡ትርሲተ፡መርዓ።
kämä təträssäyi[2] *tərsitä märʿa*
so as to | adorn yourself [with that], | as the adornment of | a [heavenly] wedding,
ገደፍኪ፡ ሰርጐ፡ፍግዓ።
gädäfki[3] *särgʷä*[4] *fəgʿa*
you rejected | the trappings of | a life of pleasure.

[5] ሰላም፡ለኪ፡ወለተ፡ጴጥሮስ፡እምነ፡ተኀየልኪ፡ለበዊአ፡ጸባብ፡ምኅላፍ።
Sälam läki Wälättä Ṗeṭros əmmənä täḫayyälki lä-bäwiʾa ṣäbbab məḫlaf[5]
Peace/hail | to you, | Walatta | Petros, | our mother. | You had the strength | to enter through | the narrow | gate,
ከመ፡ተኀየሉ፡ቅድመ፡ሰማዕታት፡አእላፍ።
kämä täḫayyälu qədmä sämaʿtat aʾlaf
like | they had the strength | before, | martyrs | thousands,
ወጻድቃን፡እለ፡ወጺፍ።
wä-ṣadəqan əllä Wäṣif
and the Righteous Ones | of | Waseef.

[6] ሰላም፡ለኪ፡ምስለ፡ሲኖዳ፡አቡኪ፡ስርግወ፡ሎግዮ፡ድንጋሌ።
Sälam läki məslä Sinoda abuki sərgəwä logyo[6] *dəngale*
Peace/hail | to you | together with | Shenoute, | your father, | adorned with | the priestly armor of | chastity.
ለናዝዞትነ፡ንዒ፡እምሐዘን፡ወወይሌ።
Lä-nazəzotənä nəʿi əm-ḥazän wä-wäyle[7]
To our comforting | come, | from distress | and woe
ወሐውጺ፡አመ፡ውልዋሌ።
wä-ḥawwəṣi amä[8] *wəlwale*[9]
and watch over [us] | at the time of | agitation/whirlwind.

[1] F: *wä-əzn mäwati* (and a mortal ear); CR: *wä-əzn* (and an ear).

[2] FJ: *kämä təträssäyə* [substandard orthography, but identical meaning]; CR: *kämä tərässəyi* (so that you adorn [trans.]).

[3] CE: *zä-gädäfki* (it is that you have rejected).

[4] In Amharic, the similar word *särg* means "wedding" or "wedding celebration." Therefore Gəʿəz *särgʷ*, despite its different meaning, here amplifies the stanza's wedding imagery for the poem's monastic audiences, who would have known both Gəʿəz and Amharic.

[5] CR has stanzas 5 and 6 in the opposite order.

[6] CR: *logyon* [orthographic variant].

[7] E, CR: *əm-ḥazän wäyle* (from distress, woe).

[8] CEFJ, CR: *kämä* (like), which makes little sense contextually. We assume that ከመ *kämä* is a corruption of optically and acoustically similar አመ *amä*.

[9] CR: *wəlawle* [scribal error, producing a nonexistent lexeme]. See Proverbs 1:27–28.

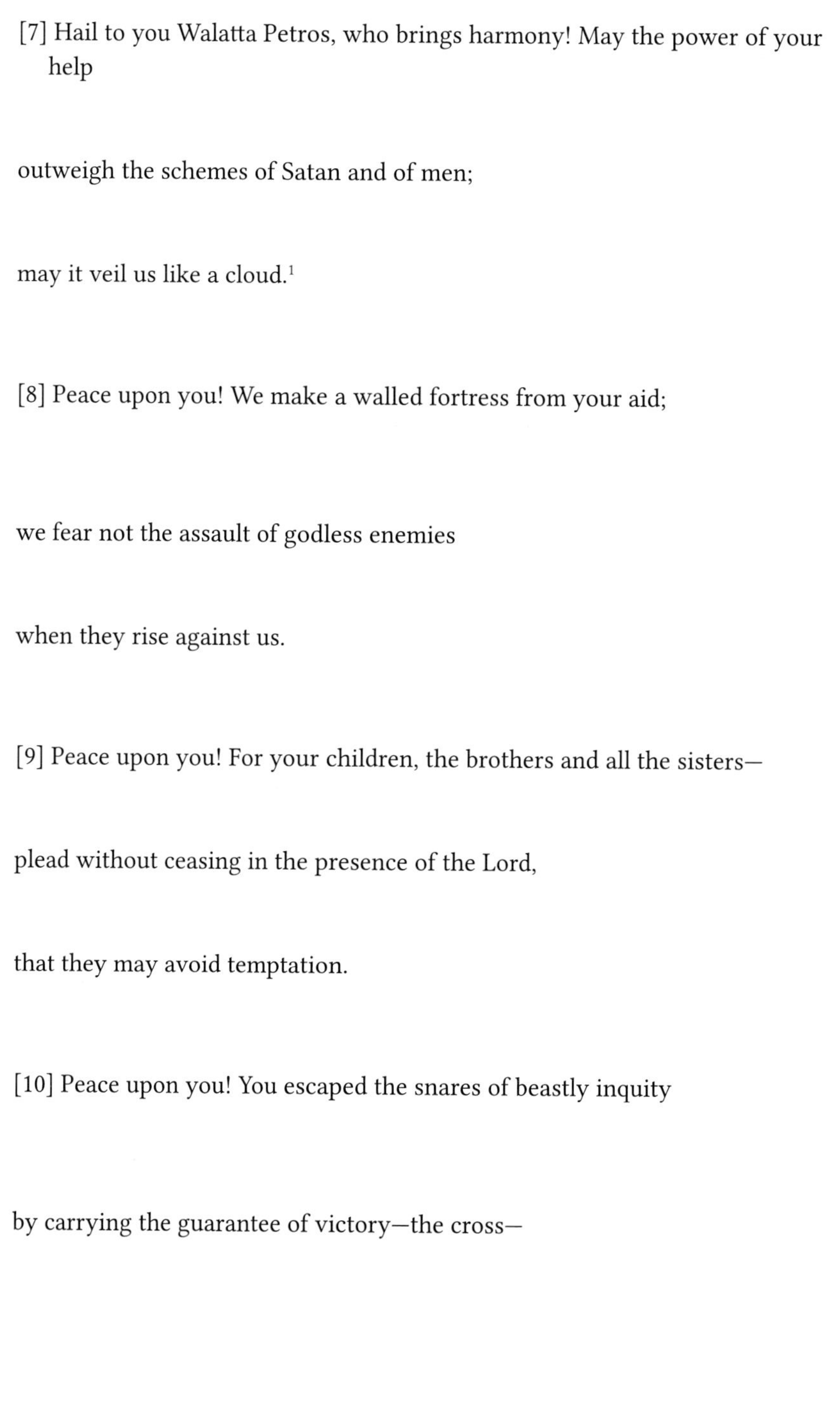

[7] Hail to you Walatta Petros, who brings harmony! May the power of your help

outweigh the schemes of Satan and of men;

may it veil us like a cloud.[1]

[8] Peace upon you! We make a walled fortress from your aid;

we fear not the assault of godless enemies

when they rise against us.

[9] Peace upon you! For your children, the brothers and all the sisters—

plead without ceasing in the presence of the Lord,

that they may avoid temptation.

[10] Peace upon you! You escaped the snares of beastly inquity

by carrying the guarantee of victory—the cross—

[1] For references to God as a protective cloud, see, for example, Mark 9:7 and Matthew 17:5.

[7] ሰላም፡ለኪ፡ሞገሰ፡ረድኤትኪ፡ኀይል፡ወለተ፡ጴጥሮስ፡ሱላሜ።
Sälam läki mogäsä räd'etəki ḫayl[1] *Wälättä Ṗeṭros sulame*
Peace/hail | to you. | The favor of | your assistance | [is] a force, | Walatta | Petros, | [embodiment of] harmony.
እመከራ፡ሰይጣን፡ወሰብእ፡በኢፍጻሜ።
Əm-mäkära säyṭan wä-säb' bä-i-fəṣṣame
From the temptations/plots of | Satan | and men | without end
ይክድነነ፡አምሳለ፡ጊሜ።
yəkdənänä[2] *amsalä gime*
may it [your assistance] veil/protect us | like a | mist.

[8] ሰላም፡ለኪ፡ለረድኤትኪ፡ጸወን፡እንዘ፡ንሬስዮ፡አረፍተ።
Sälam läki lä-räd'etəki[3] *ṣäwän ənzä nəressəyo aräftä*
Peace/hail | to you. | Your assistance: | a fortress, | by | making it [i.e., your assistance] into | the walls of [that fortress],
መራደ፡ረሲዓን፡አፅራር፡ኢንፈርህ፡ምንተ።
märadä räsiʿan aṣrar[4] *i-nəfärrəh məntä*
the attack of | godless | enemies | we do not fear | at all
ጊዜ፡ሠርዑ፡ተቃውሞተ።
gize śärʿu täqawəmotä
at the time when | they plot | rising up.

[9] ሰላም፡ለኪ፡ለደቂቅኪ፡አኀው፡ወለኵሎን፡አኃት። 138
Sälam läki lä-däqiqəki aḫaw wä-lä-kʷəllon aḫat
Peace/hail | to you. | For your sons, | the brothers, | and for all | the sisters,
ቅድመ፡ገጸ፡አምላክ፡ተንብሊ፡እንበለ፡ፅርዓት።
qədmä gäṣṣä amlak tänbəli ənbälä ṣərʿat
before | the countenance of | the Lord | plead | without ceasing
ኢይባኡ፡ውስተ፡መንሱት።
i-yəba'u wəstä mänsut
so that they may not enter | into | perdition/temptation.

[10] ሰላም፡ለኪ፡እመሣግሪሁ፡አምሠጥኪ፡ለአርዌ፡ዓመፃ፡መሥገሪ።
Sälam läki əm-mäśagərihu amśäṭki lä-ärwe ʿammäṣa mäśgäri
Peace/hail | to you. | From its snares | you escaped, | [the snares] of the beast of | wickedness, | the ensnaring one, [Satan,]
አረቦነ፡መዊእ፡መስቀለ፡እንዘ፡ትጸውሪ።
aräbonä mäwi' mäsqälä ənzä təṣäwwəri
the collateral of | victory, | the cross, | by | carrying,

[1] CR: *mogäsä räd'etəki ḫayyal* (the favor of your powerful assistance).
[2] CR: *yəkdänäni* (may it protect me).
[3] CEFJ: *lä-räd'etəki* (lit., regarding your assistance); CR: *räd'etəki* (your assistance).
[4] CR: *märaʿəyä räsiʿan aṣrar* (the flocks of the godless enemies).

as did the disciples of Saint Macarius.

[11] Hail to you, Walatta Petros! From the Four Creatures of Heaven[1]

to where the Holy Trinity is worshipped,

raise the incense of our song—

with a censer wrought of light!

[1] This refers to the four living creatures of Revelation 4:6–8: the lion, the calf, a humanlike creature, and the eagle, each of which has six wings and praises God saying, "Holy, holy, holy."

ዘጸርዎ፡እለ፡መቃሪ።
zä-ṣorəwwo əllä Mäqari
that which [also] had carried | those of | Macarius.[1]

[11] ሰላም፡ለኪ፡ወለተ፡ጴጥሮስ፡አዕርጊ፡ዕጣነ፡ማሕሌትነ፡ዝንቱ።
Sälam läki Wälättä Peṭros aʿrəgi ʿəṭanä maḫletənä zəntu
Peace/hail | to you, | Walatta | Petros. | Make rise | the incense | of our song/
hymn/poem | this,
እምእንስሳ፡ሰማይ፡አርባዕቱ።
əm-ənsəsa sämay arbaʿtu[2]
from the Creatures of | Heaven | Four
ኀበ፡ይትቄደሱ፡አካላት፡ሠለስቱ።
ḫabä yətqeddäsu akalat śälästu[3]
to where | are revered | the Persons | Three [of the Trinity],
በማዕጠንት፡ዘብርሃን፡ግብረቱ።
bä-maʿṭänt zä-bərhan gəbrätu.
with an incense censer: | of light | its making.

[1] For the purposes of the end rhyme, the poet has shortened Saint Macarius's name from Mäqarəyos to Mäqari.
[2] C, CR: *arbaʿtu* (four); EFJ: ፬ (4).
[3] CE, CR: *śälästu* (three); FJ: ፫ (3).

Colophons

MSS C and E have no colophons after the sälam because they continue with the miracles. MS F has no colophon and terminates with the sälam. MS J puts the sälam before the miracles. After the sälam, Abb. 88/CR has the following:

I, the sinner Wolde Giyorgis,[1] entrust myself to our mother Walatta Petros, "Do not separate my soul from yours!"

[1] This same name also appears at the end of the miracles in CR, but not at the end of the *WP gädl*. Here, as at the end of miracles, the name does not appear in its normal form, as Wäldä Giyorgis, but with the very unusual variant spelling of Wäldä Geworgis.

APPENDIX: MANUSCRIPT FOLIO MISSING FROM THE CONTI ROSSINI PRINT EDITION (FROM MS J)

Manuscript comparison revealed that the Conti Rossini print edition was missing the equivalent of an entire folio, material that would have been between lines 31 and 32 on page 107 of his edition. We have provided the missing material below, but as it appeared in our MS J, images 114 and 115, not MS Abb. 88. Black arrows indicate the beginning and end of the missing material.

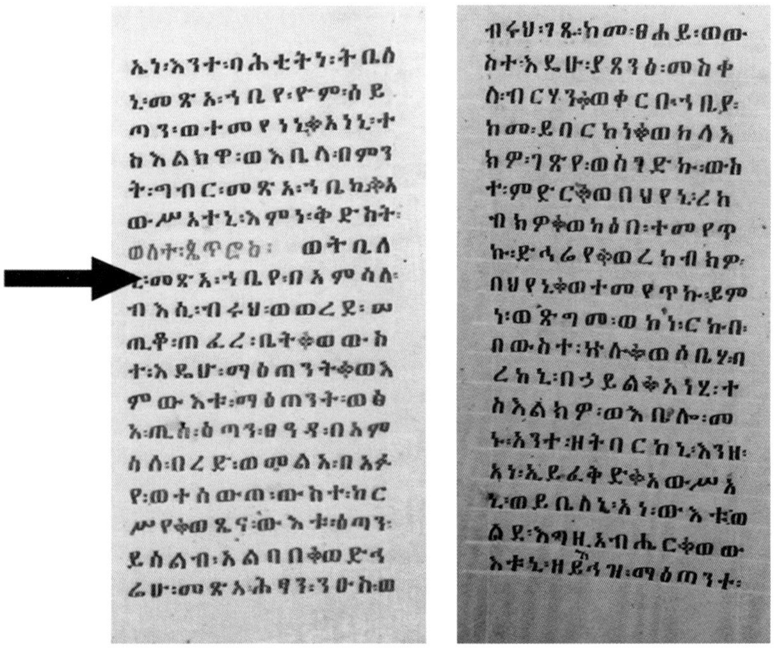

Plate 64. Manuscript folios missing from the Conti Rossini print edition (from MS J, parts of images 114 and 115).

መልአክ፡ውእቱ። ወካዕበ፡
ይቤሎ፡ክልአን፡ትቤ፡እምነ፡
ቅድስት፡ወለተ፡ጴጥሮስ፡መ
ጽአት፡ኀቤየ፡እግዝእትነ፡ማ
ርያም፡ ወትቤለኒ፡እምፈቀ
ድኩ፡አንሰ፡አዕርፍኪ፡እም
ፃማ፡ዝንቱ፡ዓለም። ባሕቱ፡
አሕዘንኒ፡ብካዮሙ፡ዘዮ
ም፡ለደቂቅኪ፡ወለአዋል
ድኪ። ወበእንተዝ፡ኀደጉኪ፡
ትንበሪ፡ሎሙ፡ሓዳጠ። ወ
እምዝ፡ሰበ፡አእመረት፡እም
ነ፡ቅድስት፡ወለተ፡ጴጥሮስ፡
ከመ፡ቀርበ፡ጊዜ፡ዕረፍታ፡ሐ
ለየት፡ትሕር፡ሬማ፡ከመ፡ት
ትቀበር፡ውስቴቱ። ወትቤሎ
ሙ፡ለአኃው። አከተዳልው፡
ሊተ፡ታንኳ፡ዘአሖውር፡በቱ፡

ሬማ። ውእቱ፡ሙኒ፡ገብሩ፡በ
ከመ፡አዘዞሙ። ወአመጽ
ወጽሎ፡ወርኃ፡መስከረም፡ተ
ሰነዓለቶሙ፡ወትቤሎሙ።
ለአኃው፡ወለአኃት። ናሁ፡ጸ
ንዓ፡ለዕሌየ፡ሕማም። አንት
ሙ፡ኅበሩ፡ኀዘየ፡ወአነ፡አሐው
ር፡ሬሚ። አስከ፡ትትሬከብ፡በ
ፈቃደ፡እግዚአብሔር። ወበ
ይአቲ፡ሰዓት፡ይቤላ፡አባ፡ዘ
ሥላሴ፡ለእምነ፡ቅድስት፡
ወለተ፡ጴጥሮስ፡ ናሁ፡ይክ
ማ፡አብራኪየ፡በቀዊም። ወ
ስሕከ፡ጕርዔየ፡በክላሕ። ወ
ለከዋ፡አዕይንትየ፡እምጢ
ስ፡ዕጣን፡ዘሌሊት፡ወዘመዓ
ልት። እምአመ፡ተወጥነ፡ሞ
ት፡እስከ፡ይእዜ። ወኀጣእኩ፡

ዕረፍተ። ወእለሂ፡ይሬእዩ፡
ወይሰምዑ፡አስቆረሩኒ። እ
ምይእዜሰ፡ከነ፡ወአክለ።
ወይእቲ፡እምነኒ፡ዝንቱ፡
ሞት። አውሥአቶ፡እምነ፡ቅ
ድስት፡ወለተ፡ጴጥሮስ፡ወ
ትቤሎ፡[illegible]
ከመ፡ይቁም። ወይቤላ፡እ
ወ፡እፌቅድ። ወትቤሎ፡እ
ምነ፡ቅድስት፡ወለተ፡ጴጥሮ
ስ፡ እመሰ፡ፈቀድከ፡ይኩ
ን፡በከመ፡ትቤ። ወሰቤሃ፡ቆ
መ፡በከመ፡አዘዛ። ወእ
ምዝ፡አዕረግዋ፡ለታንኳ፡ወ
ወሰድዋ፡ሬማ፡እኩመ፡ይእ
ቲ፡ሠምረት፡ከመ፡ትሙት፡
ህየ፡ወትትቀበር፡ውስቴታ
ቀብረ፡አቡሃ፡ወእማ። በከ

GLOSSARY: PEOPLE, PLACES, AND TERMS IN THE TEXT

Wendy Laura Belcher

Substantive notes within the translation are, by necessity, short. Further, explanatory notes appear only on a term's first appearance in the translation and never thereafter. Therefore, below is fuller information on the people, places, events, plants, foods, and so on in the *Gädlä Wälättä Ṗeṭros.*

Words are alphabetized according to their simplified spelling in the *Gädlä Wälättä Ṗeṭros* translation, then provided in the original fidäl and *Encyclopedia Aethiopica* transliteration. If the entry headword is not simplified, this means it does not appear in the translation itself but only in the front matter, back matter, or notes.

To ensure no confusion about proper names, we italicize all Gəʿəz titles.

The *Encyclopedia Aethiopica* (2003–14), edited by Siegbert Uhlig, was our most frequent source, always cited below when consulted. Common sources for geographical information were Huntingford's *Historical Geography of Ethiopia*, Cheesman's *Lake Tana and the Blue Nile*, and Lindahl's *Local History in Ethiopia.* We have chosen to use the term "Ethiopia" for the region, since this is what the text itself uses.

The categories are *historical person* (a person who appears in this text as well as the Ethiopian royal chronicles of the period, usually members of royalty or military leaders), *local person* (a person whom Walatta Petros knew or who appears in the miracles after her death), *modern person* (a twentieth-century person with some role related to the text), *biblical figure* (someone who appears in the Bible, like King David), *religious figure* (a famous religious leader, including saints), *folkloric figure* (legendary person or creature); *local place* (a place in Ethiopia) and *biblical place* (a place mentioned in the Bible, like Sodom); *ethnic term* (names of ethnic groups), *religious term, temporal term* (names of months and times of prayer), and *medical term* (diseases); *religious occasion* and *cultural practice*; and *food, plant, animal, text, title* (honorifics), *unit of measurement*, and *object* (like boats or buildings).

Latitude and longitude of places are represented using Google Earth format for coordinates and signaled with "LatLon." The exact location of a place was not always easy to identify, but the general location could sometimes be estimated. For instance, if Walatta Petros was traveling south from Gondär and went through a now-unknown town on the way to Qʷäraṣa, we know it is located around northern or eastern Lake Ṭana. All places in the glossary appear on the maps at the beginning of this volume.

15 Prophets. *See* Fifteen Prophets.

36 Holy Women. *See* Thirty-Six Holy Women.

72 Disciples. *See* Seventy-Two Disciples.

99 Angelic Orders. *See* Ninety-Nine Angelic Orders.

318 Bishops. Also, 318 Nicene Fathers. Religious figure. The number of bishops said to have attended the Council of Nicaea in 325, the first ecumenical council of the church. Nicaea's main achievement was the rejection of the Arian heresy, which denied the presence of a fully divine nature in Christ. In addition, the Council of Nicaea decreed a number of ecclesiastical statutes, and later other apocryphal ones were ascribed to it due to its prestige.

144,000 Children. Biblical figure. The Täwaḥədo Church believes that the number of children Herod killed in Bethlehem in trying to prevent the Christ-child from later becoming the king of the Jews is the number of the innocent discussed in Revelation 7:3 and 14:1–4; namely, 144,000.

Abb. 88. *See* d'Abbadie.

Abaala Kristos. አባለ:ክርስቶስ Abalä Krəstos. "Limb of Christ." Local person. A man of some means who sent much grain from Guna to WP's community in Afär Färäs. We have not found this person in the historical or encyclopedic sources, except for an "Abala Krestos" discussed in Susənyos's royal chronicle, as killed and avenged.

Abbabeet. አባቢት Abbabit. Local place. A place on the southwestern side of Lake Ṭana above the Zäge Peninsula, according to locals. WP went there for a few days to escape the wrath of *Ras* Śəʿəlä Krəstos, traveling to it from Zäge by *tankʷa*. Later, she escaped a hippopotamus near there. Also, the place appeared in the sixth miracle as a place toward which the wind blows near Zäge. Probably within ten miles of LatLon: 11.772251, 37.314449.

Abba. አባ Abba. From Greek. "Father." Title. Title used in addressing the clergy of the church, including monks, abbots, bishops, and the supreme head of the church, the patriarch. *See* Kaplan (2003a).

Abbay. አባይ "The Great One." Local place. The river that provides the majority of Egypt's water. Known in the West as the Blue Nile, this river flows out of southern Lake Ṭana and curves in a great arc around the region of Goǧǧam.

Abbess. እመ:ማኅበር Əmmä maḫbär. "The community's mother." Title. Title used in the *WP gädl* to address the female leader of WP's religious community. The title usually used in Ethiopia for an abbess is *əmmä mənet* (mother of the monastery) or *əmmahoy* (revered mother) and sometimes *mämhərt* (female teacher). An *əmmä mənet* had absolute authority over the day-to-day lives of women in a monastery, but the abbot usually presided over large religious matters like repentance, death, or theological debates. The term *əmmä maḫbär* does not appear in any of the standard reference works, so it may be a term used only in WP's community, which was a different type of monastic community. It seems that the *əmmä maḫbär* was responsible for leading both men and women. In the additional later texts of MSS I and J, an *əmmä mənet* and two *əmmahoy* appear.

Abbot. መምህር Mämhər. "Teacher." TITLE. Common title for the head of a monastery. *Mämhər* could also mean teacher, leader, or theologian. In other texts, an abbot is sometimes called *abä mənet* (father of the monastery), *abbahoy* (revered father), or *mäggabi* (steward). In the additional later texts of MSS I and J, an *abä mənet* appears. *See* Kaplan (2003a, 2007).

Abimelech. አቤሜሌክ Abemelek. From Hebrew. "My father is king." BIBLICAL FIGURE. The king of the Philistines, of the region Gerar, who tries to take Abraham's wife Sarah when Abraham claims she is his sister (Genesis 20 and 26).

Absaadi. አብሳዲ Absadi. RELIGIOUS FIGURE. A monk about whom WP had a vision; also called Absadi of Azäzo (Azäzo was an important town north of Lake Ṭana and about eight miles southwest of Gondär). He was associated with Mägʷəna Monastery, near Gondär and Azäzo. There is a *Gädlä Absadi*, but since it is unpublished, scholars do not know much about him or even when he lived. He is better known as the founder of the nearby Zoz Amba Monastery in the district of Sälaša, Bägemdər. He was not the fourteenth-century saint, also named Absadi, who founded Däbrä Maryam, a monastery in Təgray (sometimes called Absadi Monastery), and was the chief disciple of and a leader in the monastic movement following Saint Ewosṭatewos. The Mägʷəna Monastery was of the house of Täklä Haymanot, not Ewosṭatewos, and was Unionist, not Unctionist (Qəbat). He is also not Bishop *Abba* Absadi of Upper Egypt or the martyred *Abba* Absadi celebrated on 29 Säne, both of whom appear in the *Sənkəssar*. *See* Lusini (2003a, 2003b); Abbadie (1890, 468).

Abuna. አቡነ Abunä. "Our father." TITLE. A title used in addressing leading members of the clergy. In contrast to *abba*, which can be used to address any clergy member, *abunä* is usually reserved for saints, heads of monasteries, and the patriarch. It most often refers to the patriarch, the Egyptian metropolitan assigned as head of the Täwaḥədo Church. Since the patriarch came from another country and did not speak the language, he was often isolated on matters of local church politics and doctrine. *See* Nosnitsin (2003a).

Achan. አካን Akan. From Hebrew. BIBLICAL FIGURE. An Israelite, the son of Carmi, who steals precious objects after Joshua conquers Jericho. God punishes the Israelites by allowing them to be defeated; they in turn stone to death Achan and his family. Appears in Joshua 7.

Afer Faras. አፈር፡ፈረስ Afär Färäs. "Horse's soil." LOCAL PLACE. A place on the southeastern shore of Lake Ṭana, extremely close to Rema Island and about seven miles north of Qʷäraṣa. It was the seat of the sixth of the religious communities that WP founded. There WP built a residence, saw a vision, was attacked by theologians, and contemplated becoming a hermit. When Rema became too crowded, WP was given this plot of land on the lakeshore just opposite Rema Island and near a cliff. It was close enough for WP to commute to Rema from Afär Färäs every day and for people in both places to see her boat when a storm whipped up. LatLon: approximately 11.833414, 37.476756. Transcribed elsewhere as Afar Faras, Afer Feres. *See* Bosc-Tiessé (2008, 69–70).

Afonsu. አፎንሱ Afonsu. In Portuguese: Afonso Mendes (or Alfonso or Alphonso Mendez). HISTORICAL PERSON. The Portuguese Jesuit Afonso Mendes (1579–1656) was appointed as the Catholic patriarch of Ethiopia in 1622 by the pope and served in Ethiopia as a missionary from 1625 to 1634. He arrived from Portugal after the conversion of King Susənyos from the Täwaḥədo Church to Roman Catholicism in 1624 but was then important in increasing Susənyos's pro-Catholic policies and officially establishing Roman Catholicism as the state religion in 1626. Because Mendes was stricter than Páez, many scholars attribute the failure of Roman Catholicism in Ethiopia to him. Mendes forbid many cherished Ethiopian cultural practices, such as male circumcision, Saturday Sabbaths, and some fasting. In particular, Mendes worked one-on-one to convert the women of the royal court, as the Jesuit accounts attest. According to the *WP gädl*, one of these women was WP, whom he was not able to persuade. By 1630, Catholicism was on the wane, and when Susənyos stepped down from the throne in 1632, his heir, Fasilädäs, asserted his commitment to the Täwaḥədo Church. It quickly became difficult to be Roman Catholic in Ethiopia, and in 1634 Fasilädäs expelled the Jesuits. Mendes spent the next two decades at the Jesuit mission in Goa, India. While in Ethiopia, Mendes lived on the shore of northern Lake Ṭana, near the Jesuit residence at Gorgora and the royal court at Dänqäz. Mendes was well educated, gaining a doctorate and teaching at two universities in Portugal, which may explain why he wrote entirely in Latin, unlike the other Portuguese Jesuits. He wrote many annual reports and letters (edited in Beccari [1910]) and an important book on the Jesuit mission in Ethiopia (edited in Mendes [1908]). *See also* Cohen (2007). His name sometimes appears in Gəʿəz texts as Awfänyos.

Afqaranna Egzee. አፍቀረነ፡እግዚእ Afqärännä Ǝgziʾ. "The Lord has loved us." RELIGIOUS FIGURE. A venerated fourteenth-century Ethiopian saint, usually spelled Yafqərännä Ǝgziʾ. According to his hagiography, he was born in Təgray in approximately 1309 and joined the Lake Ṭana monastery of Ṭana Qirqos as a young man at the beginning of the reign of ʿAmdä Ṣəyon I (r. 1314–44). He was a disciple of the fourteenth-century saint Mädḫaninä Ǝgziʾ, who was a disciple of perhaps the most revered Ethiopian saint, Täklä Haymanot. Afqärännä Ǝgziʾ is said to be the founder of the monasteries on Lake Ṭana at Məṣəlle and Gʷəgʷəben. The former also became the seat of WP's third community. The hagiobiography of his life, *Gädlä Yafqərännä Ǝgziʾ*, is an important source on Christianity and monasticism in Lake Ṭana. Although the author of the *WP gädl* claims that the *Gädlä Yafqərännä Ǝgziʾ* forbids women from his monastery, the editor of that gädl shows that it contains no such prohibition on female creatures (Wajnberg 1917, 11). In the *WP gädl*, the first element of the saint's name, Afqärännä, differs from that in most texts, which have Yafqərännä Ǝgziʾ, meaning "May the Lord love us." *See* Kaplan (2014b).

Agag. አጋግ Agag. From Hebrew. BIBLICAL FIGURE. Saul defeated and then spared the life of this king of the Amalekites. Samuel rebuked Saul for this unsanctioned mercy and then killed Agag himself. Appears in 1 Samuel 15.

Ainiya Mammeet. ዓይንየ፡ማሚት ʿAynəyä Mammit. "The girl 'My eye.'" Local person. The *əmmä mənet* (abbess) of WP's Qʷäraṣa community in 1735, the fifth year of Iyasu II's reign. Spelled ʿAynəyä Mammite (The servant woman "My eye") in MS I. Mentioned in the extra texts of MSS I and J only.

Ale. ሰዋ Säwa. Food. Säwa is an indigenous low-alcohol beer made from grain, usually barley, but sometimes also *ṭef* (an annual grass with a small grain that was domesticated in the Ethiopian highlands eight thousand years ago), maize, millet, or sorghum. A common drink in Ethiopia (called *ṭälla* in Amharic and *səwa* or *säwa* in Tigrinya), when it is blessed by priests, it is called "holy water" and is used in feasts for saints and church meetings. It takes six days to make, has a smoky flavor, and is dark brown in color. The name *säwa* comes from an alternative word for one of its ingredients, the indigenous plant *gešo* (*Rhamnus prinoides*), which, when boiled, serves as a type of hops in making fermented drinks. It is a very ancient drink, with the word *səw[w]a* appearing in King ʿEzana's fourth-century inscriptions. In Gəʿəz manuscript texts, by contrast, it is found only rarely (one other appearance being in the *Gädlä Täklä Haymanot*). The drink is so common that it is used in metaphorical expressions, such as "I will drink your *säwa*," which means "I will take up your burdens." Transcribed elsewhere as *sewa* or *śəwa*. *See* Pankhurst (2005c); Amborn (2010).

Alexandrian Church. *See* Coptic Orthodox Church of Alexandria.

Amata Dinghil. አመተ፡ድንግል Amätä Dəngəl. "Maidservant of the [Holy] Virgin." Local person. Əḫətä Krəstos's successor as leader of the entire community and thus its third abbess or *əmmä maḫbär*. Her name was invoked alongside that of the abbess Əḫətä Krəstos in the concluding blessings and she was the one upon whom prayers and blessings are consistently called in MS J, along with two other figures in the community: the abbot Zä-Ḥawaryat and the scribe Gälawdewos. The author calls her "our mother," confirming that she was abbess when the *WP gädl* was written. She and WP pray for the death of Amätä Dəngəl's son Beza Mäsqäl because he was handsome, and therefore perhaps open to the temptations of the flesh. When Beza Mäsqäl dies, Amätä Dəngəl begs WP to be allowed to go see him. She was granted her wish on the condition that she not weep, which she succeeds in doing. She seems to be one of the head women who WP assigned at Zämbol to lead a group of fifty nuns. The *Short History of WP's Community* says that her everyday name was Anǧäto (One who is dear to me). The name is derived from Amharic *anǧät* (entrails), a metaphor for that which is closest and dearest to a person.

Amata Kristos. አመተ፡ክርስቶስ Amätä Krəstos. "Maidservant of Christ." Historical person. King Susənyos's cousin, being the daughter of his mother Ḥamälmal Wärq's brother. She was also the stepmother of Mälkəʾa Krəstos, WP's husband, and the mother of Wälättä Giyorgis, whom WP worked so hard to convert back from Catholicism, "the faith of the Europeans." Amätä Krəstos was a great favorite of the king for her prudence and good counsel, once warning him of assassins. It was said that she was the wealthiest woman in the kingdom. She married twice. According to the Jesuits, she only appeared to convert to Roman Catholicism, but in fact was against it and gave her land to monks to shelter anti-Catholic resistors. She was addressed with the honorific *Yəte* (Her Majesty) in the *WP gädl* but was not an official queen. In the *WP gädl,* Ǝḫ̮ətä Krəstos begged Amätä Krəstos to plead with Mälkəʾa Krəstos to ask the king to allow Ǝḫ̮ətä Krəstos to join WP in exile, since she missed her so much. Amätä Krəstos was moved and did so. For more information, *see* Täklä Śəllase ([Ṭinno] 1900, 78, 374n; 1892, ix n); Tellez (1710); Páez (2011, 2:350). Transcribed elsewhere as Amata Krestos.

Amata Kristos. አመተ:ክርስቶስ Amätä Krəstos. "Maidservant of Christ." LOCAL PERSON. A beautiful young woman, a nun in WP's community, who bragged and argued with others. WP challenged her devotion to her lush body, scolded her severely, and soon after the young woman fell ill and became emaciated and paralyzed.

Amata Kristos. አመተ:ክርስቶስ Amätä Krəstos. "Maidservant of Christ." RELIGIOUS FIGURE. According to the *Sənkəssar,* a Greek female saint. The twelve-year-old widow of the city of Constantinople fled with her two handmaidens to a cave under a hill in order to escape a rapist. They lived there for twelve years, bearing the hardships of the mountains naked and being fed by birds that brought them fruit. The three women are commemorated in the *Sənkəssar* on 8 Yäkkatit (Budge 1928, 604–5); transcribed elsewhere as Ammata Krestos.

Amata Petros. አመተ:ጴጥሮስ Amätä Ṗeṭros. "Maidservant of [Saint] Peter." LOCAL PERSON. An older nun who hid WP in Wänčät when WP was first leaving her husband.

Amba Maryam. አምባ:ማርያም Amba Maryam. "The Mountain of [the Virgin] Mary." LOCAL PLACE. A place that WP visited that is probably what is now known as Ṭeza Amba Maryam (Dew of Mount Mary), a church on the eastern side of Lake Ṭana, about twenty miles north of Qʷäraṣa, between the Rəbb and Sabän Rivers that empty into Lake Ṭana and half a mile inland; LatLon:12.007001, 37.607475. WP took some of her community members there while others remained nearby at Afär Färäs. While WP was there, the icon of the Virgin Mary took hold of WP's clothes and demanded that she stay through the rainy season with her. This church was famous as one of the places where the Ark of the Covenant and the Virgin Mary stopped on her way to Ṭana Qirqos by *tankʷa* (Cheesman 1936, 187; Bosc-Tiessé 2008, 242–43). Transcribed elsewhere as Teza Amba Maryam.

Amba Maryam. አምባ:ማርያም Amba Maryam. "The Mountain of [the Virgin] Mary." LOCAL PLACE. Many places are called Amba Maryam, so it is not clear where this place is or whether it is the same place as above. It may be the monastery of this name in Ǝnfraz, just south of Qorada, about ten miles due east of the top northern part of Lake Ṭana. One of WP's disciples came from this Amba Maryam; another of WP's disciples was exiled from this Amba Maryam. *See* Täklä Śəllase ([Ṭinno] 1900, 92). *Also see* Huntingford (1989, 162); Abbadie (1890, 236–38). LatLon: 12.344026, 37.712367.

Amba-Ras. አምባራስ Ambaras. "Head of a Mountain." Title. Middle-rank title given to the commander, or *ras*, in charge of guarding a fortification, or *amba*. The name probably came about because an *amba*, or flat-topped mountain, is typical of the Ethiopian highlands and formed a natural fortress. Over time, these positions became civil, with the title being used for small local governors. Also seen as Balambaras, under which, *see* Nosnitsin (2003b).

Amole. አሞሌ Amole. Object. A salt bar of standardized size that was used in Ethiopia/Eritrea for many centuries as a currency. Mined in the Afar Depression and transported throughout the Horn of Africa, it would increase in value the farther it was from the mine, so it was quite valuable as far away as Lake Ṭana. In the *WP gädl*, the short book of *mälkəʾ* poems about WP sold for two amole, which in those days, according to the Jesuits, was worth about a gram of gold. *See* Pankhurst (2003); Smidt (2010a); Tsegay B. Gebrelibanos (2009).

Angaraa. አንገራ Angära. Local place. A small island (about 1,300 feet long) in northern Lake Ṭana about 1,500 feet from the shore, just south of Gorgora and east of Susənyos's palace. It is close to Ç̣anqʷa, in the region of Dämbəya. WP fled there with her community when sickness decimated them at Ç̣anqʷa. Its church is called Angära Täklä Haymanot. LatLon: 12.215123, 37.302777. *See* Cheesman (1936, 198); Bosc-Tiessé (2008, 67). Transcribed elsewhere as Angara.

Animals. A multitude of animals appears in the text: mammals, such as dogs, donkeys, leopards, lions, wolves, hyenas, gazelles, stags, antelopes, hippopotamuses, and mice; birds, such as doves, partridges, eagles, and vultures; and fish, snakes, bees, and locusts. In the notes, we have included the scientific name for all flora and fauna where known.

Anjato. *See* Amata Dinghil.

Anthony. እንጦንስ Ǝnṭonəs. Religious figure. Widely considered the first of the Desert Fathers, this saint was an ascetic who lived in fourth-century Egypt and is considered the founder of Christian monasticism. Also known as Anthony the Great, Anthony of Egypt, and Father of All Monks, his hagiobiography, written by Saint Athanasius, is one of the first Christian hagiographies and is believed to be one of the first works translated into Gəʿəz. He is frequently invoked in Täwaḥədo Church hagiographies, usually together with Saint Macarius, his disciple. In the *WP gädl*, the monastic "path of Anthony and Macarius" represents the path that WP will take. Both of Ethiopia's monastic "houses," that of Täklä Haymanot and Ewosṭatewos, claim that their founders trace back to Saint Anthony. *See* Meinardus and Kaplan (2003).

Archdeacon. ሊቀ፡ዲያቆናት Liqä diyaqonat. "Head of the deacons." Title. The archdeacon is found only in important churches and is usually an ordained priest who supervises the deacons and priests involved in the Liturgy. The term *liq* indicates a senior person with authority and is often used in religious titles to mean "arch-" or "chief." *Liqä diyaqonat* is common, dating back to at least the fourteenth century, since it appears in the *Kəbrä Nägäśt*. *See* Heyer (2003) and Nosnitsin (2007b).

Archdeaconess. ሊቅተ፡ዲያቆናዊት Liqtä diyaqonawit *or* ሊቀ፡ዲያቆናዊት Liqä diyaqonawit. "Head deaconess." Title. According to the *WP gädl*, Christ tells WP that she is a *liqä diyaqonawit*. For men, such honorary titles are only given to those recognized as the highest experts in the Old and New Testament, the Liturgy, the *Haymanotä Abäw*, and so on (Sokolinskaia 2007). Thus, it was a distinct honor that Christ gave her this title. Christ appointing the saint to a position in the church hierarchy is a common hagiographical topos; for instance, the saint Täklä Haymanot was appointed *liqä kahənat* (head of the priests). Whether the deacons that WP was in charge of were just women or also men is unclear. Traditionally, there are women who are head deacons of the women and there are men who are head deacons of the men and women. *Liqtä diyaqonawit* is an extremely rare title, perhaps even specifically coined for the *WP gädl*. Just as the word "archdeaconess" in English does not make it clear whether the gender marker "-ess" applies to the official or her followers, the Gəʿəz is also not clear. Most of the WP manuscripts use the grammatically problematic term (due to gender incongruence) *liqä diyaqonawit*, but a caption in MS D has (acc.) *liqtä diyaqonawitä*. Thus, the scribe may have stumbled in formulating a neologism for the feminine equivalent of *liqä diyaqonat* or the more common saintly title *liqä kahenat*, since there was no such thing as a female head of the deacons or priests in the Täwaḥədo Church, and since the Gəʿəz word for a female spiritual leader, *liqt*, is very rare. Since WP was the head of her community, it is not clear why Christ would be needed to give her a special dispensation to be in charge of only the female deaconesses.

Archpriest. ሊቀ፡ካህናት Liqä kahənat. "Head of the priests." Title. The archpriest is found only in important churches. The term *liq* indicates a senior person with authority. This position is sometimes localized (a man who is the head of the priests at a particular church) and sometimes generalized (a man who is the head of the priests in a region). The term is old, dating back to at least the twelfth century. *See* Nosnitsin (2007b). Mentioned in the extra texts of MSS H and I only.

Arganonä Maryam. *See* Lyre of Saint Mary.

Arseesaan. አርሲሳን Arsisan. From Greek. "Heretics." Religious term. The Greek word for "choice" or "sect" is αἵρεσιν (*haíresin*) and it appears as a foreign word for "heretics" in the *Rules for the Monks*, according to the *WP gädl*.

Arsenius. አርሳንዮስ Arsanyos. Religious figure. One of the Desert Fathers, a fourth-century learned Roman deacon and solitary monk. According to the *Sayings of the Fathers*, he frequently stayed up all night praying (Grébaut and Tisserant 1935, 155). The *WP gädl* says that WP was like Arsenius in similarly doing so. According to the *Sənkəssar*, Arsenius was so devoted to asceticism that he even lost his eyelashes and tall stature (Budge 1928, 3:885).

Asahél. አሳሄል Asahel. Local person. A wealthy *näggadras* who, along with *Däğğazmač* Iyasu, bought MS J from *Wäyzäro* Wälättä Täklä Haymanot and *Wäyzäro* Bərhan Mädḫanitu. Mentioned in the extra texts of MS J only.

Asahél Ayikal. አሳሄል፡አይከል Asahel Ayəkkäl. Local person. A person persecuted by the eighteenth-century historical figure Wədağ Asahel in this text. The compound name is unusual: Asahel is a biblical character, a warrior nephew of King David, and the second part of the name may be a shortened form derived from the Amharic verb *täkälla* (be prevented), so the whole name may have a meaning something like "Asahel the warrior, he who will not be prevented from doing what he wants." Transcribed elsewhere as Aykel, Ayekel, and Ayikel. Mentioned in the extra texts of MSS H and I only.

Assumption of Our Lady Mary. *See* Feast of Our Lady Mary's Assumption.

Atinatewos. አትናቴዎስ Atənatewos. From Greek. "Athanasius (The immortal one)." HISTORICAL PERSON. The husband of Wälättä Giyorgis (who was the daughter of King Śärṣä Dəngəl and helped WP reconcile with her husband) and the father of Wälättä Ṗawlos, who became a nun with WP. Atənatewos helped Susənyos come to power and was one of the highest members of his court, a *ras*, but was then sidelined until Susənyos put him on trial and exiled him to Amhara in 1617 (Chernetsov 2003a). His name appears repeatedly in Susənyos's royal chronicle and the Portuguese sources. Transcribed elsewhere as Atenatevos or Athanatêus.

Atsfa Kristos. ዐጽፈ፡ክርስቶስ ʿAṣfä Krəstos. "The mantle of Christ." LOCAL PERSON. The superior of the monastery on Məṣəlle Island. According to the *WP gädl*, during the Susənyos period when Orthodox priests were persecuted, *Abba* ʿAṣfä Krəstos was a captive in the town of Tera. After King Fasilädäs reinstated the Orthodox faith, ʿAṣfä Krəstos returned to his leadership of the Məṣəlle Monastery. WP stayed there for one year after this. Then, as she was leaving, she asked that ʿAṣfä Krəstos pronounce an edict forever forbidding female creatures on Məṣəlle Island, which he did. We have not found this person in the historical or encyclopedic sources.

Atsf. ዐጽፍ. ʿAṣf. "[Sacerdotal] Vestment." OBJECT. A yellowish, knee-length leather tunic of fine and durable quality worn by nuns and monks or students of traditional (religious) schools.

Atsqa Hawaryaat. ዐጽቀ፡ሐዋርያት ʿAṣqä Ḥawaryat. "Branch of the Apostles." LOCAL PERSON. A male disciple of WP. He, along with Täklä Maryam, with whom he is always mentioned, followed her to Žäbäy and from there used to go to WP's mother, brothers, and other relatives to collect goods to bring to the community of Žäbäy exiles.

Atsqa Maryam. ዐጽቀ፡ማርያም ʿAṣqä Maryam. "Branch of Mary." LOCAL PERSON. A paralyzed monk who WP heals in the second posthumous miracle. He was the curator of the treasury at the Ṭana Qirqos Monastery on Tsana Island, which reputedly held the Ark of the Covenant for six hundred years before it was moved to Aksum. This treasury did not hold currency, but rather was filled with valuable artifacts and manuscripts. We have not found a mention of this person in the historical or encyclopedic sources. Name erroneously given as *Anqäṣä Maryam* (Gateway to Mary) in CR.

Awsebiyos. አውሰብዮስ Awsäbəyos. From Greek. "Eusebios." HISTORICAL PERSON.

An important eighteenth-century military commander, significant during the reigns of Iyasu II and Iyoʾas, who appears in this text with his brother Əšäte, another important eighteenth-century military commander. During the reign of Iyasu II (r. 1730–55), Awsäbəyos had several titles (*baša, däǧǧazmač,* and *bäǧərond*) and his military sorties are regularly discussed in Iyasu's royal chronicle (Anonymous 1912, 11, 123, 133, 141, 145, 201, 204, 237, 238). Mentioned in the extra texts of MSS H and I only; sent to recover the royal daughter Wälättä Täklä Haymanot from Qʷäraṣa. Transcribed elsewhere as Awsābyos.

Azezo. አዘዞ Azäzo. LOCAL PLACE. An important town, north of Lake Ṭana but eight miles southwest of Gondär, that served as the de facto capital during the Susənyos period. Susənyos and his court, and therefore the Jesuits, lived there from 1607 until 1632, building castles, palaces, and churches (including their main cathedral, *Gänätä Iyäsus*), and otherwise supporting the arts. It was from this town's church that Catholicism was declared the official state religion and where Susənyos was buried. It was an important religious center, as thousands of monks came there to debate the religious issues inspired by the presence of the Jesuits. It is not surprising then that WP's husband Mälkəʾa Krəstos had a home in this town, and brought her there to be converted by the head Jesuit Afonso Mendes. Gondär only became the capital after Fasilädäs came to power. *See* Mulatu Wubneh (2003). LatLon: 12.584052, 37.4263. Transcribed elsewhere as Azzazo, Assozo, Azoza, Azozo, Azaza, Azazo, and Azezo.

Azmach. አዝማች Azmač. TITLE. Title of a military commander but given as the name of a man under WP's husband Mälkəʾa Krəstos in the Śəlṭan Märʿəd (It makes the [Muslim] sultan shiver) regiment. See Chernetsov (2003b).

Babnooda. ብብኑዳ Bäbnuda. RELIGIOUS FIGURE. In the *Sənkəssar*, *Abba* Bäbnuda is the Egyptian disciple of Saint Macarius, as well as a hermit and a martyr. In certain versions of the *Gädlä Kiros* and the *Sənkəssar*, Bäbnuda (in Greek Paphnutius) was condemned by God to be devoured by a lion for sharing his "heavenly food" with a deceitful monk. However, he was saved from hell because he called on Christ to honor his *kidan* with Kiros. WP's community was visited by a deceitful monk, just as *Abba* Bäbnuda was, says the *WP gädl.* Abb. 88/CR erroneously had this name as *Abba* Ṣəge [Haymanot]. *See* Marrassini (2007).

Ba-Haila Maryam. በኀይለ፡ማርያም Bä-Ḫaylä Maryam. "Through the power of [Saint] Mary." LOCAL PERSON. A captive monk in Žäbäy, whose feet had been put in heavy chains because of his adherence to the Täwaḥədo Church and refusal to convert to Roman Catholicism. He prophesied that God would not have mercy on his soul unless WP buried him. When WP was given the news that the king had commanded the end of her exile in Žäbäy, she delayed her return until the monk had passed away and she could bury him.

Ba-Haila Maryam. በኀይለ፡ማርያም Bä-Ḫaylä Maryam. "Through the power of [Saint] Mary." LOCAL PERSON. The author of the *Short History of WP's Community*, which appears in MSS I and J. He wrote it in 1735, the fifth year of Iyasu II's reign, and about sixty-three years after Gälawdewos had written the *WP gädl.* Shortened to

Ḫaylä Maryam ("The power of [Saint] Mary") in MS I. Mentioned in the extra texts of MSS I and J only.

Bahir Dar. ባሕር፡ዳር Baḥər Dar. "The lake shore." Local place. A town located at the southern tip of Lake Ṭana, previously called Baḥər Giyorgis. A town with either of these names is not mentioned in the main part of the text, suggesting that it came into being after 1673. Today it is one of the largest cities in Ethiopia, capital of the Amhara National State; LatLon: 11.595573, 37.391439. *See* Seltene Seyoum (2003). Mentioned in the extra texts of MS I only.

Bahir Saggad. ባሕር፡ሰገድ Baḥər Säggäd. "The [regions by the] sea submit[s] [to him]." Local person. WP's father. He came from a noble family, called the "house of Däwaro and Fäṭägar." He was married to Krəstos ʿƎbäya and had five sons: P̣awlos, Zä-Mänfäs Qəddus, Ləsanä Krəstos, Zä-Dəngəl, and Yoḥannəs. He is important enough to be discussed in Susənyos's chronicle, which notes that he held the position of *azmač* and was the father of two important men of Susənyos's court: Ləsanä Krəstos and Zä-Mänfäs Qəddus (Täklä Śəllase [Ṭinno] 1900, 40, 47, 64). In the *WP gädl*, he was well known for his devotion, frequently going to Rema Island Monastery to engage in ascetic exercises. He and his wife were later buried at this monastery, where their relics can still be seen. He had a vision that his wife would bear a daughter who would be a saint. From the day of her birth, Baḥər Säggäd was devoted to WP, loving her more than any of his grown sons. Unfortunately, he did not live to see his daughter's adulthood. The *WP gädl* and the royal chronicle refer to him by this secular/military name rather than his (unknown) Christian name. Transcribed elsewhere as Bahir, Baher, or Bahr Sagad. On names, including those with the *Säggäd* formative, *see* Kleiner (2007).

Bakaffa. በካፋ Bäkaffa. Local person. King of Ethiopia from 1721 to 1730, about seventy years after WP's death and forty years after Gälawdewos wrote the original *WP gädl* and its miracles. He founded many churches, including one on a Lake Ṭana island. He appears as an enemy of WP's community, although he later repents. *See* Crummey (2003). Mentioned in the extra texts of MSS H and I only.

Basil the Martyr. *See* Fasiladas.

Basiladas. *See* Fasiladas.

Bərhan Mogäsa. *See* Walatta Giyorgis.

Béta Manzo. ቤተ፡መንዞ Betä Mänzo. Local place. A very small island about a mile out in Lake Ṭana, a bit south of Qʷäraṣa; LatLon: 11.747546, 37.427145. Cone-shaped, it is about three hundred feet in diameter and once had a church dedicated to "the Savior of the World" (Mädḫane ʿAläm). WP regularly spends time at this place. When local leaders refused to allow WP to stay at Zäge, where she set up her fourth community, she went to Betä Mänzo to study and rebuild the church there. Her mother came to visit, then fell ill and died there; WP grieved the death of her mother there. After once leaving, she returned to spend the Feast of the Mount of Olives there. *See* Bosc-Tiessé (2000, 239); Cheesman (1936, 116). Transcribed elsewhere as Bet Manzo.

Béza Masqal. ቤዛ፡መስቀል Beza Mäsqäl. "Redemption through the Cross." Local per-

SON. A handsome young man, a member of the community at Zäbol/Zämbol, the son of Amätä Dəngəl, who dies, and thus goes on to a better life, due to the prayers of WP.

Bible. TEXT. The author(s) have vast biblical knowledge, as revealed in the number of quotes from biblical books, most likely quoted from memory. Almost all the books of the Bible are cited, including Genesis (2 times), Exodus (7 times), Leviticus (1 time), Numbers (2 times), Deuteronomy (6 times), Judges (6 times), 1 Samuel (3 times), 1 Kings (6 times), 2 Kings (1 time), 2 Chronicles (2 times), Jubilees (1 time), Enoch (2 times), Job (2 times), Psalms (54 times), Proverbs (3 times), Song of Songs (1 time), Isaiah (9 times), Jeremiah (2 times), Ezekiel (1 time), Daniel (4 times), Micah (1 time), Habakkuk (1 time), Matthew (43 times), Mark (13 times), Luke (32 times), John (43 times), Acts (10 times), Romans (13 times), 1 Corinthians (11 times), 2 Corinthians (10 times), Galatians (2 times), Ephesians (2 times), Philippians (1 time), Colossians (1 time), 1 Thessalonians (4 times), 1 Timothy (4 times), Hebrews (2 times), 1 Peter (9 times), 2 Peter (1 time), James (5 times), and Revelation (4 times). The following biblical books appear to be absent, but since the author(s) sometimes quoted the Bible silently, without calling attention, we may have missed quotes from the following: Ezra, Ecclesiastes, Lamentations, Judith, Esther, Hosea, Amos, Micah, Joel, Obadiah, Jonah, Nahum, Habakkuk, Zephaniah, Haggai, Zechariah, and Malachi, as well as books found in the Ethiopian Bible: Tobit, Maccabees, and so on.

Bihono. ቢሆኖ Bihono. "If this happens to him." HISTORICAL PERSON. Commander of the anti-Catholic rebel forces fighting to depose Susənyos. He did so for a man who had the same name as WP's husband, Mälkəʾa Krəstos, and who declared himself king and chief defender of the Orthodox faith. Bihono was a brilliant military strategist; among other victories, he defeated *Ras* Śəʿəlä Krəstos. Although his forces were successful in almost reaching the royal court, in June 1632 Susənyos defeated Bihono, who died on the battlefield. *See* Täklä Śəllase ([Ṭinno] 1900, 254, 258, 592); Wudu Tafete Kassu (2003). Yet, within a few months Susənyos died. The closeness of these events may be why the *WP gädl* states that Susənyos vowed that should he be successful in defeating Bihono, he would abandon Roman Catholicism.

Billa Kristos. ብዕለ፡ክርስቶስ Bəʿlä Krəstos. "The abundance of Christ." HISTORICAL PERSON. King Susənyos's cousin and confidant. *Däǧǧazmač* Bəʿlä Krəstos was a great lord who helped to bring Susənyos to power and was a friend of the Jesuits. He had become Roman Catholic and even wrote essays attempting to show that the Täwaḥədo Church had not always been anti-Chalcedonian (Páez 2011, 2:63, 2:301). It is not surprising, then, that WP was made to stay in his house while the court tried to convert her to Roman Catholicism. He also has the title *Abetohun*, used for male members of the Solomonic dynasty (Merid Wolde Aregay 2003a). Appears often in Susənyos's royal chronicle and Portuguese sources, transcribed as Bella Christos, Bêla Christôs, and so on.

Binyam. ብንያም Bənyam. HISTORICAL PERSON. The godfather of *Däǧǧazmač* Ǝšäte's son Ḫaylu (Blundell 1922, 305). *Däǧǧazmač* Bənyam appears in the eighteenth-century royal chronicles once. He was the confidant of *Ras* Mika᾽el in WP's twenty-second miracle. Mentioned in the extra texts of MSS H and I only.

Birhan Madhaneetu. ብርሃን፡መድኃኒቱ፡ Bərhan Mädḫanitu. "[Heavenly] light [is] the deliverance." LOCAL PERSON. The woman who, along with *Wäyzäro* Wälättä Täklä Haymanot, sold MS J to *Däǧǧazmač* Iyasu and *Näggadras* Asahel. Bərhan Mädḫanitu is also called the junior Wəbit (Beautiful One). Mentioned in the extra texts of MS J only.

Bitsa Giyorgis. ብጽዐ፡ጊዮርጊስ Bəṣʿa Giyorgis. "[Saint] George's beatitude." LOCAL PERSON. The abbot of WP's monastery at some unknown time, when it had houses in Dämbəya, Gondär, and Dämboza; thus, probably in the 1700s. Mentioned in the extra texts of MS I only.

Biyadgo Yohannes. ቢያድጎ፡ዮሐንስ Biyadgo Yoḥannəs. "If he grows past him—[son of] Yoḥannəs." HISTORICAL PERSON. A rebel against King Iyasu II (r. 1730–55). His failed escape onto Lake Ṭana near Rema is recorded in Iyasu's royal chronicle (Anonymous 1912, 37). However, no mention is made of WP or her monastery in the chronicle, only of Maḫdärä Səbḥat, an island about one thousand feet from Rema. Both the chronicle and WP's miracles state that he was captured with his wife and children. Mentioned in the extra texts of MSS H and I only.

Bizaaba. ቢዛባ Bizaba. LOCAL PLACE. A place about four miles directly east of and inland from Qʷäraṣa, now known as Bizäb. Some of WP's community stayed there during the rainy season while the rest were at Amba Maryam or Afär Färäs. LatLon: 11.74637, 37.494857.

Blacks. ሻንቅላ Šanqəlla. ETHNIC TERM. A pejorative ethnic term used by highland Ethiopians for various ethnic groups living west of the historical Ethiopian kingdom's border. Such peoples were held in contempt by highland Ethiopians—Christians and Muslims alike—because of their traditional religion, different cultures, Nilo-Saharan rather than Semitic languages, and physical appearance, including a darker complexion. Since the Christian highlanders frequently raided these groups for slaves, the lowlanders' given ethnic name became synonymous with "slave" itself. The highlanders, of which WP was a member, saw themselves as "red" and the Šanqəlla as "black." We have chosen not to use the word Šanqəlla, which is now considered very pejorative, but to use the term "Blacks," which suggests to readers familiar with the American history of slavery that the group was considered lesser and enslavable. In older European texts about Ethiopia, orientalists often glossed the term "Shanqalla" as "Negroid." The term is not to be confused with *barya*, which is a different racialized term for slaves. *See* Smidt (2010b).

Blue Nile. *See* Abbay.

Book of the Dead. መጽሐፈ፡ምውታን Mäṣḥafä Məwətan. TEXT. A book providing instructions for the burial of the dead. Ricci speculates that this book is the one usually called *Mäṣḥafä Gənzät* (Book of the [Corpse's] Shrouding), which is a collection of ritual texts for funeral services. This title sometimes also appears as *Mäṣḥafä Gənzät: Ṣälot laʿlä Məwutan* (Book of the Shrouding: Prayer over the

Dead). *See* Tedros Abraha (2005), where it is called "Book of the [Corpse's] Wrapping." However, *Qäsis* Melaku Terefe points out that another book that is sometimes called the *Mäṣḥafä Məwətan* is the *Ləfafä Ṣədq* (Bandlet of Righteousness), which is popular among monks (Budge 1929).

Books of the Monks. መጻሕፍት፡መነኮሳት Mäṣaḥəftä Mänäkosat. Text. The foundation of spiritual life in Ethiopian monasteries. It comprises three sections or books, *Filkəsyos* (stories of the Egyptian fathers), *Mar Yəsḥaq* (the third treatise on asceticism by Isaac of Nineveh), and *Arägawi Mänfäsawi* (a treatise by John of Saba). The last takes up a significant part of church education, being one of the most important commentaries. *See* Bausi (2007).

Burial. Religious term. People were buried wrapped in a cloth and with a coffin, unless no one could be found to cut down a tree and hollow it out or the person was so poor his or her house did not have wooden doors that could be used for the purpose. Some very religious people also chose to be buried without a coffin because of their humility, or because the coffin was seen as an obstacle to going straight to heaven. Although all Christians were buried near a church, or inside the church compound fence, only persons of great stature were buried near the church entrance, as WP was. *See* Pearce (1831, 2:68); Pankhurst and Aspen (2005).

Č. *See* Ch.

Ç. *See* Ch.

Calendar. Temporal term. Based on the so-called Alexandrian or Egyptian calendar, the Ethiopian calendar (EC) is different from the modern Western calendar and calculates the hour, day, month, and year differently. For instance, 7:00 am on 12 September 2015 is one in the morning on 2 Mäskäräm 2008. Year. The Ethiopian year is seven or eight years behind the Western calendar, depending on the month. The new year starts on 11 September, not 1 January. In other words, 11 September 2016 falls in the Ethiopian calendar year 2009 while 10 September 2016 falls in the Ethiopian calendar year 2008. According to the Täwaḥədo Church, time started when God created the world 5,500 years before the birth of Christ. Rarely, the year will be given in this form and one can arrive at the Ethiopian year by subtracting 5,500 (e.g., if the year is 7207 in the text, subtract 5,500 to get the EC year 1706 and the Western year 1713–14). The number thus arrived at is seven or eight years behind the Western calendar. Traditionally, each year in Christian Ethiopia is assigned the name of one evangelist, in recurring four-year cycles. Month. The year has twelve thirty-day months and one five- or six-day month (depending on leap year). The beginnings of the month are not identical with the Western calendar month, rather, they fall between the third and the eleventh. Particular months and their European equivalents are explained under the Ethiopian month name entries. Season. The windy season is from early September to mid-December; the dry season is from mid-December to early March; the sowing season is from early March to early June; the rainy season is from early June to early September. For an explanation of the many intricacies and holy days of the Ethiopian calendar, *see* Fritsch and Zanetti (2003); Uhlig (2003b).

Name of Ethiopian Month	Date in modern Western calendar on which the month started in 2016–17	Date in modern Western calendar on which the month started in 1632
Mäskäräm	11 September	8 September
Ṭəqəmt	11 October	8 October 8
Ḫədar	10 November	7 November
Taḫśaś	10 December	7 December
Ṭərr	10 January	7 January
Yäkkatit	9 February	6 February
Mäggabit	10 March	7 March
Miyazya	9 April	6 April
Gənbot	9 May	6 May
Säne	8 June	5 June
Ḥamle	8 July	5 July
Näḥase	7 August	4 August
Ṗagʷəmen	6 September	3 September

Calvary. ቀራንዮ Qäranəyo. Biblical place. A sacred site in Christianity, the hill outside Jerusalem where Christ suffered and was crucified, also called Golgotha. The New Testament states in Greek that "They brought Jesus to the place called Golgotha (which means 'the place of the skull')." *Qäranyo* is derived from the Greek *kraníou tópos* (the place of the skull), the translation of Aramaic "Golgotha," in the same way that the English term "Calvary" is derived from the the Latin translation of the same, "calvariæ locus."

Canons of the Apostles. ሥርዓተ፡ሐዋርያት Śərʿatä Ḥawaryat. "Rules of the Apostles." Text. The last chapter of the eighth book of the *Apostolic Constitutions*, a pseudo-apostolic collection of ecclesiastical decrees of the early Christian Church, part of the genre of Ancient Church Orders. It includes eighty-five canons approved in the Eastern Church in 692. Books 1 through 6 of the *Apostolic Constitutions* are what is known in Ethiopia as the *Didəsqəlya* (Teaching [of the Apostles]). They are in the same genre as the *Senodos* (a collection of church orders popular in Ethiopian Christianity). *See* Bausi (1995). WP uses the *Canons of the Apostles* to establish an order of communal life.

Chan. ጫን Č̣an. Unit of measurement. An Amharic word for a particular measurement of grain, literally a "load," and hence the amount of grain a donkey can carry at one time. A typical mule load is approximately sixty pounds.

Chanqwa. ጫንቋ Č̣anqʷa. Local place. A town in the region of Dämbəya, the fertile plain that borders northern Lake Ṭana, and from which it is easy to reach the island Angära. It is probably the town transcribed as Jangua in the translation of Susənyos's chronicle (Täklä Śəllase [Ṭinno] 1900, 127). It is north of Gorgora, on the left bank of the Gälikora River at LatLon: 12.375048, 37.288186, or the current town often transcribed Jangwa, less than a mile away at LatLon: 12.07, 36.59. It was the second of the religious communities that WP founded. They soon left this place, however, when a violent illness broke out and the local people blamed them. Transcribed elsewhere as Žangwa, Jangua, Jangwa, Yangua, Chanchwa, Ch'ank'e, and Chanqe.

Chegwaré Zigba. ጨጓሬ፡ዝግባ Çäggʷarre Zəgba. "Caterpillar Cedar." Local place. A town in the Dära region on the southeastern side of Lake Ṭana, presumably not far south of Wänčät. LatLon: approximately 11.775276, 37.530563. WP hid here from her religious persecutors. "Chaguarit Zegba" appears in Täklä Śəllase ([Ṭinno] 1892, 200) and "Çägwarit Zĕgba" in Huntingford (1989, 176), but not with a pinpointed location.

Cherr Takkal. ቸር፡ተከል Čärr Täkkäl. "Goodness planted." Local place. A marketplace where one thieving woman sold a manuscript of the poems in honor of WP and another thieving woman attempted to sell a jar from WP's community (in MS I miracles only). Perhaps it was in the region of Çara, which was a stronghold of the Agäw, who at the time were not primarily Christian, about fifty miles southwest of Lake Ṭana. There is a town of this name today, Čärä, at LatLon: 11.194026, 36.760334. Or it may be Čärä Čärä, the first cataract on the Abbay (Blue Nile), about a mile south of Lake Ṭana, LatLon: 11.565471, 37.395374.

Community. ማኅበር Maḫbär. Religious term. A *maḫbär*, which we always translate as "community," was the type of institution that WP established. Those people who devoted themselves to a life of spirituality in a *mənet*, or monastery, were sometimes called a *maḫbär*. But lay organizations with such a name also have a long history in Ethiopia and were often established by someone interested in meeting with others who revered a particular saint. One did not need to be a monk or nun to belong to such an association or even start one. They often provided mutual assistance to members (such as rebuilding houses or caring for orphans) and traditionally met monthly at members' homes. In the troubled times of WP, when local churches and monasteries had become tainted by the foreign faith, WP may have borrowed from this particular form of *maḫbär* to establish communities for the Christians who followed her and wanted to live near her to worship in the Orthodox faith. Such a use was without precedent, but, as a woman, WP could not set up churches (*betä krəstiyan*) or monasteries (*gädam* or *däbr*). Later, it seems WP worked to establish her *maḫbär* as a *gädam* with formal monastic rules. Her seven communities were at Žäbäy (a hot lowland place far west of Lake Ṭana); Çanqʷa (along northern Lake Ṭana); Məṣelle, Dämboza, and Afär Färäs (all in southeastern Lake Ṭana); and Zäge and Zäbol/Zämbol (both in southwestern Lake Ṭana). Sometimes transcribed as *mahber, mahbar*. *See* Schaefer (2007).

Conti Rossini, Carlo. Modern person. One of the most important Ethiopianists of the twentieth century and the editor of the print edition of the *WP gädl*, published in 1912. Born in Italy (1872–1949), he served as a civil servant in the Italian administration of Eritrea from 1899 to 1903 and then later held the chair of History and Languages of Abyssinia at the University of Rome. He cataloged Antoine d'Abbadie's collection of Ethiopian manuscripts in Paris, which included the *WP gädl*, inspiring his interest in the text. Throughout the notes, "CR" refers to Conti Rossini's print edition of the *WP gädl*. See Ricci (2003).

Coptic Orthodox Church of Alexandria. Religious term. The Coptic Church dates to the first century and was the home of monasticism. Based in Alexandria, Egypt, it was the head of the non-Chalcedonian African churches until the twentieth century. For instance, the Holy See in Alexandria selected the patriarch of Ethiopia, the head of the Ethiopian Täwaḥədo Orthodox Church, from among the Egyptian monks. As a member of the so-called Oriental Orthodox Churches, the Coptic Church differed from the Roman Catholic Church and the Greek Orthodox Church in doctrine, due to the Council of Chalcedon in 451 CE. While the Ethiopian Täwaḥədo Orthodox Church was, therefore, in effect, a Coptic Church, in fact, its practices were often quite different than in Egypt.

Corpus Scriptorum Christianorum Orientalium (CSCO). Text. This book series, started in 1903, publishes editions and translations of Eastern Christian texts (often in separate volumes), as well as monographs about such texts. Most of the translated texts are from Syriac, but others are from Arabic, Coptic, Armenian, and Georgian, and more than 115 are from Gəʿəz (in the subseries Scriptores Aethiopici), including the *Gädlä Wälättä Ṗeṭros.* The series is currently published by Peeters but was published by Louvain Catholic University in Belgium and the Catholic University of America in Washington, DC. *See* Kleiner (2003).

Covenant with God. *See* kidaan.

CR. *See* **Conti Rossini, Carlo.**

CSCO. *See* Corpus Scriptorum Christianorum Orientalium.

Cyriacus the Martyr. ቂርቆስ Qirqos. Religious figure. A fourth-century Roman saint martyred at the age of three. Saint Qirqos is one of the most highly venerated saints in Ethiopia, and many Täwaḥədo churches are dedicated to him, the most famous of which is Ṭana Qirqos. He and his mother appear frequently in paintings and texts. The paralyzed monk ʿAṣqä Maryam, in the second miracle, went in search of healing to the Ṭana Qirqos church dedicated to this saint. This saint is not to be confused with Cyriacus of Jerusalem (Həryaqos), Cyriacus of Corinth, Cyriacus the Monk, or Cyriacus of Antioch. Transcribed elsewhere as Kirkos, Qurqos, and Quiricus. *See* Balicka-Witakowska (2010); Pisani (2013). For various persons called Cyriacus, *see* Budge (1928, 1:74–75, 1:114–15, 1:205–6).

d'Abbadie, Antoine. Modern person. One of the most important Ethiopianists of the nineteenth century and the collector of the manuscript that served as the base for the Conti Rossini print edition, and thus the Ricci Italian translation of the *WP gädl.* A French-Basque-Irish geographer and linguist (1810–97), d'Abbadie explored the Horn of Africa from 1837 to 1848, along with his brother Arnauld d'Abbadie, and was a founder of Ethiopian studies in France. Throughout the notes, "Abb. 88" refers to the *WP gädl* manuscript that d'Abbadie had copied between 1837 and 1849 and donated, along with many other Ethiopian manuscripts, to the Bibliothèque nationale de France. *See* Zitelman (2003).

Däbr. *See* Monastery.

Dabra Anqo. ደብረ:ዓንቆ Däbrä ʿAnqo. "Monastery of the Jewel." Local place. An unidentified place probably on the southwest side of Lake Ṭana near Zäge. WP took up monastic garments to become a nun here. The term *ʿanqo* is not documented in Gəʿəz dictionaries. However, the term resembles *ʿənqu*, meaning precious stone, pearl, gem, or jewel in Amharic. In Gurage, *anqo* means egg. *ʿAnqo* does appear in other texts, but not with a clear provenance. Cheesman observed a ford across the Abbay River (Blue Nile) called the Dabunko, but it was at least fifty miles southwest of Lake Ṭana, near Zakas Ford (1936, 340).

Dabra Entonyos. ደብረ፡እንጦንዮስ Däbrä Ǝnṭonyos. "Monastery of [Saint] Anthony." LOCAL PLACE. The monastery on Ǝnṭonəs, an island near the shore in southern Lake Ṭana, about one mile north of modern-day Baḥər Dar and three miles southeast from Zäge Peninsula; LatLon: 11.645658, 37.368036. *Ras* Śəʿəlä Krəstos searched for WP from here when she was at Zäge. Däbrä Ǝnṭonyos was important during WP's lifetime, as witnessed by the seventeenth-century patriarch *Abunä* Səməʿon (in office 1607–17) translating from Coptic there. It appears as both Ǝnṭones and Ǝnṭonyos. Sometimes transcribed as Entons. *See* Bosc-Tiessé (2005d); Cheesman (1936, 152).

Dabra Maryam. ደብረ፡ማርያም Däbrä Maryam. "Monastery of [Saint] Mary." LOCAL PLACE. An island with a monastery, about five hundred feet from the southern shore of Lake Ṭana, right above the Abbay (Blue Nile); LatLon: 11.622414, 37.403618. *See* Bosc-Tiessé (2005a). Mentioned in the extra texts of MS I only.

Dabra Mitmaaq. ደብረ፡ምጥማቅ፡ማርያም Däbrä Məṭmaq. "Monastery of the Baptistery." LOCAL PLACE. This is most likely the famous church in Gondär called Däbrä Məṭmaq Maryam, just south of the royal castles, that was built by Täklä Giyorgis I in 1782–83; LatLon: 12.60638, 37.470094. *See* Bosc-Tiessé (2005b). That MS I titles it just "Däbrä Məṭmaq" suggests that either there were two churches at the monastery (one for Mary, one for WP) or the story conflates it with the Däbrä Məṭmaq monastery in Shoa. Täklä Giyorgis donated a cannon to the monastery in the twenty-seventh miracle of the *WP gädl*; mentioned in the extra texts of MS I only.

Daga. ዳጋ Daga. LOCAL PLACE. A small conical island just east of Däq Island, in the center of Lake Ṭana, with a three-hundred-foot-high hill. Daga Island is where the Daga Ǝsṭifanos Monastery is, perhaps the first monastery set up on one of the lake's islands, in the thirteenth century, and still one of the most important. When WP was living with her second community at Č̣anqʷa, she thought about settling on Daga but decided not to. During WP's time, Fasilädäs rebuilt the church of Daga Ǝsṭifanos in 1646, and he was later buried there. *See* Bosc-Tiessé (2005c). LatLon: 11.885325, 37.299442.

Damboza. ደምቦዛ Dämboza. LOCAL PLACE. An island adjacent to Ṣana Island in southeastern Lake Ṭana. WP founded her fifth religious community there, moving with a large community from Zäge after a leopard attack. She housed her nuns at Dämboza and her monks at Ṣana and later left Dämboza when an epidemic broke out. The island no longer has a monastery, but it previously had a church devoted to Saint Mary of Qʷəsqʷam (Bosc-Tiessé 2000, 218). The text says that when WP and her community fled Zäge to Dämboza, they reached it by *tankʷa* and on foot. At some times of the year, if the lake level is low, it is possible to walk from some islands to the shore. *See* Berry and Smith (1979). Transcribed elsewhere as Demboza. LatLon: 11.880076, 37.498632

Daniel. ዳንኤል Danəʾel. BIBLICAL FIGURE. A Jewish noble about whom many stories are told in the biblical book of Daniel and whose experiences are cited in the *WP gädl.* Carried off to Babylon as a young man, he and three other young men, Shadrach, Meshach, and Abednego, were thrown into a fiery furnace for refusing to bow to the Babylonian idols. God saved them from destruction and Daniel became known for his talented interpretation of dreams, a skill that soon elevated him to a prominent position in King Nebuchadnezzar's kingdom. Serving in the Persian Empire under King Darius, Daniel refused to pray to the king and was thrown into the lion's den. The lions did not kill him, however, due to the divine protection he enjoyed. Indeed, he was there long enough that, according to the Apocrypha, he became hungry and an angel transported the prophet Habakkuk from Israel to Babylon to feed Daniel in the lion's den. When Daniel was not killed, the king rescinded the edict commanding everyone pray to the king. Some of the stories about Daniel appear in the apocryphal sections of Daniel, specifically Daniel 3:30–100, and chapters 13 and 14 (which are also called *Bel and the Dragon*).

Daq. ደቅ Däq. LOCAL PLACE. The largest island in Lake Ṭana, about three miles in diameter, with several small villages and churches. Perhaps because it is in the center of the lake and quite large, it was used as a prison, but it also served as a royal mausoleum. It is next to two small islands: Daga Island to the east, which is home to the lake's oldest monastery, Daga Ǝsṭifanos, and Narga Island to the west, with a church built by Queen Wälättä Giyorgis (Məntəwwab). It takes about two and a half hours to reach Däq by *tankʷa* from the shore (Cheesman 1936, 123). In the fourth miracle, WP healed the son of a woman who lived on Däq. *See* Bosc-Tiessé (2005c); transcribed as Dek in Cheesman (1936, 119–37). LatLon: 11.911865, 37.271263.

Dara. *See* Dera.

Dates. *See* Calendar.

David. ዳዊት Dawit. BIBLICAL FIGURE. A famous and powerful king of biblical Israel who was the father of Solomon. David started out as a court musician for King Saul but soon became a successful military commander and then king; he established the new capital of Jerusalem and maintained the Ark of the Covenant there. He is traditionally believed to be the author of the biblical book of Psalms.

Dawaro. ደዋሮ Däwaro. LOCAL PLACE. One of the two historical highland regions in southern Ethiopia from which WP's family hailed. Däwaro was about 450 miles southeast of Lake Ṭana. It was the immediate southeastern neighbor of Fäṭägar, east of the Awash River, more or less coextensive with the twentieth-century imperial province of Arsi. Fäṭägar and Däwaro were southern frontier provinces of the historical Christian Ethiopian Empire (the modern Ethiopian state extends farther south). During WP's time, the late sixteenth and early seventeenth century, the region was not under its effective control anymore. In the early 1530s, the charismatic Islamic leader Aḥmad Grañ (Aḥmad the Left-Handed)—from the eastern sultanate of Adal, centered around the town of Harar—had conquered the two provinces (as well as many others) in a spectacularly successful jihad. Thereafter, the Christian Ethiopian Empire only briefly regained control of them and, weakened by the war, could not withstand the massive migratory pressure of the southern Oromo, a Cushitic-speaking people who began to move into these zones in the 1550s. For more information, see Muth (2005) and Shinn, Ofcansky, and Prouty (2004, 100–11), and the chapters on Däwaro in Pankhurst (1997). For the conquest of the place, see ʿArab Faqīh (2005). Transcribed elsewhere as Dawāro, Dewaro, Dewarro, Dauarro, Davvaro, Dauri, or Dauarri.

Dawit. ዳዊት. "David." HISTORICAL FIGURE. This Ethiopian king Dawit III (r. 1716–1721) is honored in MS D.

Deacon. ዲያቆን Diyaqon. TITLE. The first rank of the clergy. Before becoming a priest, men must serve as a deacon. Many young men and women serve as deacons, whose main task is to participate in the Divine Liturgy (*qəddase*) by reading the Bible aloud, carrying various sacred objects during the Liturgy, preparing the bread and raisin wine for the Eucharist, and even teaching and preaching, as supervised by the archdeacon. Often it is women deacons who prepare the bread and wine. According to the *WP gädl*, without deacons, the Liturgy cannot be celebrated. A deacon cannot lead the service, but the service cannot be held without them. *See* Heyer (2003).

Deaconess. ዲያቆናዊት Diyaqonawit. TITLE. A female deacon. Since women cannot enter the inner sanctum where the *tabot* is kept, the service they give as deacons during the Liturgy is limited. They keep order among the women in church and help the priest with the baptism of baby girls, since the priest must put holy oil on twelve parts of the body, including the genitals, as instructed in the *Didəsqəlya* (Teaching [of the Apostles]) 34. Outside the service, a main task of the deacons is making the bread and wine for the Eucharist, which women deacons mainly do. While a female and male deacon may work together as equal partners, in some areas he is the one who makes decisions. The *Didəsqəlya* also states that a female deacon must accompany a woman who wants to speak to a leading priest (6), and that priests may only send female deacons to a woman's house (34). Female deacons date back to the ancient church (see Romans 16: 1; 1 Timothy 5: 9). Regarding the role of deaconess, *see* Negussie Andre Domnic (2010, 60).

Dejjazmatch. ደጃዝማች Däğğazmač. "He who leads the center column into battle." TITLE. One of the highest, sometimes the highest, military rank, generally below a *ras*. The leader with this title had the duties of being a regional governor, a regional judge, and a regional military commander. WP stayed with a *däğğazmač*, Bəʿlä Krəstos, when the Europeans tried to convert her. *See* Bairu Tafla (2003).

Dembiya. ደምብያ Dämbəya. LOCAL PLACE. The region in which WP set up her second community. Dämbəya is the fertile plain that borders all of northern Lake Ṭana and stretches up to Gondär. Starting in the mid-sixteenth century through the late nineteenth century, it became the political center of the Ethiopian kingdom, especially through its towns of Gorgora, Azäzo, and Gondär. *See* Tsegaye Tegenu et al. (2003). LatLon: 12.413777, 37.290344.

Demons. ሰይጣናት Säyṭanat. RELIGIOUS FIGURE. In the Täwaḥədo Church, demons are evil spirits led by Satan. They lead people astray and even possess them, as they do with the royal woman in chapter 65 of the *WP gädl*: they surrounded "her entire body, like flies and mosquitoes surround a rotting carcass." The ordinary term for demons is *aganənt*, connected with Arabic *ğinn* and Latin *genius*, but in the *WP gädl* they are called *sayṭanat* (satans).

Dera. ደራ Dära. LOCAL PLACE. A region on the southeast side of Lake Ṭana, stretching from where the Abbay (Blue Nile) flows out of the lake in the south and north to Ṭana Qirqos. It was second in importance to the region of Dämbəya, which was along northern Lake Ṭana. During the period of Roman Catholicism, WP moved to this region partly because it was near her brother's land, but also according to the will of God as revealed by the casting of lots. The main settlement in this region is Qʷäraṣa. *See* Kleiner (2005a). In the eighteenth century, *Ras* Mika'el laid waste to this region according to the extra texts of MSS H and I.

Desert Fathers. HISTORICAL PERSON. Famous ascetics who lived in fourth- through sixth-century Egypt and founded Christian monasticism; they are invoked regularly in the *WP gädl*. Among them were the saints Anthony, Arsenius, and Macarius, and the books collecting their thoughts include the *History of the Holy Fathers* and the *Sayings of the Fathers*.

Devil. *See* Satan.

Dinbeets. ድንቢጽ Dənbiṣ. ANIMAL. The name (*dənbiṭ* or *dəmbiṭ* in Amharic) for one of two small Ethiopian birds, either the *Sylvia lugens* (brown warbler) or *Uraeginthus bengalus* (sometimes called the Abyssinian Red-cheeked Cordon-bleu). It appears frequently in proverbs and folklore as an exemplar of smallness (Kane 1990).

Dioscoros. ዲዮስቆሮስ Diyosqoros. HISTORICAL PERSON. A patriarch of the Alexandrian Church in the fifth century who remained so even after he had been deposed by the mainstream Church as a heretic for refusing to agree with the Council of Chalcedon in 451. He was thus later regarded as a hero in the Täwaḥədo Church, and one of its fourteen liturgies is the Anaphora of Saint Dioscorus.

EC. *See* Calendar.

Eda Kristos. እደ፡ክርስቶስ Ǝdä Krəstos. "The hand of Christ." LOCAL PERSON. A priest who joined WP at her fifth community, Dämboza, along with *Abba* Zä-Ḥawaryat.

Éf. ኤፍ Ef. From Hebrew. UNIT OF MEASUREMENT. A measure that frequently appears in the Old Testament, *ʿephah*, most often a dry measure used for grain. Estimates vary as to the exact amount of the biblical measure: it was anywhere from .63 to 1 bushel, 22 to 35 liters, or 6 to 10 gallons. The modern Amharic Bible translation notes that an *ef* is about 40 liters (10.5 gallons) (see Ruth 2:17 and the injunctions in Leviticus regarding measures and fair dealing). Although a delicate noblewoman, WP could grind five *ef* of grain in a day. She would have done this by rolling one stone, shaped something like a rolling pin, against another stone, so this is a significant amount. Also sometimes written as ኢፍ *if*.

Egyptians. ግብጻውያን Gəbṣawəyan. ETHNIC TERM. Although *Gəbṣawəyan* literally means Egyptians, it is often used for foreigners of the Orthodox faith, including Armenians and even the Chalcedonian Greeks (Pankhurst 2005a). In the *WP gädl*, the term is used of a painting, even though it probably had not been done by Egyptians but was only in a foreign, perhaps even Byzantine, style. *See* Heldman (2005b).

Egzi Harayaa. እግዚእ፡ኀረያ Ǝgzi᾽ Ḫaräya. "The Lord has chosen her." RELIGIOUS FIGURE. The mother of Ethiopia's most famous saint, Täklä Haymanot. According to Täklä Haymanot's hagiography, Ǝgzi᾽ Ḫaräya was a noblewoman of Šäwa, married to his father, a priest. The wicked pagan king Motälämi of Damot invaded Šäwa, captured Ǝgzi᾽ Ḫaräya, and sought to marry her, but the Archangel Michael saved her. Soon afterward, she conceived and gave birth to Täklä Haymanot.

Eheta Kristos. እኅተ፡ክርስቶስ Ǝḫətä Krəstos. "Sister of Christ." LOCAL PERSON. A noblewoman who left her husband and daughter to become a nun. She then became WP's long-term companion, served as a leader in her communities, and died on April 2, 1649. A *Sənkəssar* manuscript, Vatican Eth. No. 112, gives a short (one-thousand-word) biography of her life, which has been translated into French (with some errors) (Nollet 1930). Transcribed elsewhere as Ikhta Kristos, Eheta Kristos, and ᾽Eḫta-Krestos. *See* "The Biography of Ǝḫətä Krəstos" in this volume for extensive information about her.

Elijah. ኤልያስ Elyas. BIBLICAL FIGURE. An Old Testament prophet who preached against foreign idols. To escape persecution, Elijah first fled into the wilderness, where God kept him alive by commanding ravens to feed him. Later, in Phoenicia, a poor widow fed him with a small supply of food that God kept miraculously replenishing. His experiences are cited in the *WP gädl.*

Elohé. ኤሎሄ Elohe. "My God." RELIGIOUS TERM. An expression used during intense suffering, based on Christ's cry on the cross, transcribed from the Greek text as "Eli, Eli, lema sabachthani?" (Matthew 27:46), or "Eloi, Eloi, lama sabachthani?" (Mark 15:34), translated in the King James Version as "My God, My God, why hast thou forsaken me?" Christ was quoting from the first line of Psalm 22, which was in Hebrew, but Christ mixes in some Aramaic. In the *WP gädl,* the word may be a hybrid term, using the Hebrew *eloi* and adding the Amharic first-person singular possessive suffix *-e.* According to Ricci, this term also appears in magical prayers to cast out demons.

Emabra. እሙብሬ Ǝmäbra. LOCAL PLACE. An unidentified town probably about two miles due east of Robit, on the southeastern shore of Lake Ṭana, opposite Zäge. Servants traveling northeast through Baḥər Dar and Däbrä Maryam reach it next. Probably LatLon: 11.702669, 37.434437.

Emmahoy and **Ǝmmahoy.** *See* Abbess.

Emma mahber and **Ǝmmä maḫbär.** *See* Abbess.

Enfraaz. እንፍራዝ Ǝnfraz. LOCAL PLACE. A fertile plain that borders the east side of Lake Ṭana, spreading in the Bägemdər region from the Dämbəya district south to the Fogära district. The modern town of Addis Zämän lies at its center. Ǝnfraz was the seat of Orthodoxy and the kingdom in the sixteenth century, and the Jesuits heavily proselytized there in the seventeenth century (Chernetsov and Berry 2005). When a violent illness fell on her second community at Çanqʷa,

WP's brother Zä-Dəngəl urged her to move to his land in Ǝnfraz. Transcribed elsewhere as Infranz, Infrantz, Infraz, and Enfranz.

Enjera. እንጀራ Ǝnğära. FOOD TERM. A spongy flatbread that is a staple in Ethiopia. It is made from the grain *ṭef*, which is combined with water to ferment for several days and then poured onto a large, flat surface to cook. It is the most frequently eaten food in Ethiopia.

Enoch, Book of. መጽሐፈ፡ሄኖክ Mäṣḥafä Henok. TEXT. A pre-Christian Jewish apocalyptic text ascribed to the great-grandfather of the biblical Noah who appears in Genesis 5:18–24. Originally composed partially in Aramaic and partially in Hebrew, it survived as a whole only in the Gəʿəz translation and played an important role in Ethiopian religious thought. It is cited in the New Testament, but was thought lost until James Bruce brought it back from Ethiopia in the late 1770s. *See* Knibb and Ullendorff (1978); Uhlig (2005).

Epact. አበቅቴ Abäqte. From Greek. TEMPORAL TERM. A way of measuring time according to the lunar year. There is an eleven-day difference between the lunar year (354 days) and the solar year (365 days). To make up for this, there is a cycle of nineteen lunar years, with months added to keep it within the framework of the solar years. The lunar year was important for establishing when the movable feasts like Easter should be scheduled. *See* Uhlig (2003a).

Ersinna. ኤርስና Ersənna. RELIGIOUS FIGURE. Probably a local female religious leader, now unknown. When WP and Ǝḫ̮ətä Krəstos were first becoming nuns, *Abba* Ṣəge Haymanot told Ǝḫ̮ətä Krəstos to inform her sister that she wanted to become a disciple of Ersənna and then took WP to see Ersənna. However, there is a remote possibility that this "Ersənna" is another spelling for "Arsima," as she is known in the Täwaḥədo Church, who is the Armenian female martyr "Hripsime" or "Rhipsime," and to whom the Arsima Sämaʿətat Church on Däq Island in Lake Ṭana is dedicated. Arsima is celebrated in the *Sənkəssar* on 29 Mäskäräm. The story of this particular saint, a woman who flees a king, may have inspired the connection. A very beautiful young women, she was a virginal nun in a Roman nunnery when a third-century Roman emperor sought to marry her. She fled to Armenia, where the pagan king Tiridates tried to rape her, but she was able to beat off this warrior. Embarrassed at his defeat by a young woman, he had her and her twenty-six companions brutally killed. He was then possessed and tormented by a demon (Budge 1928, 1:101–3). Her *Gädlä Arsima* is popular in Ethiopia (Krawczuk 2006), and many pilgrims visit her church on Däq. Regarding the paintings of the saint in the Arsima Sämaʿətat Church, *see* Cheesman (1936, 128–29, 161, 162).

Esau. *See* Jacob.

Esheté. እሸቴ Ǝšäte. "My ripe grain." HISTORICAL PERSON. An important eighteenth-century historical figure, a member of the political group called Qʷäräññočč, and a cousin to Queen Məntəwwab, and thus significant during the reign of Iyasu II (r. 1730–55) and Iyoʾas, whom he helped bring to power. He held many titles, including *asallafi*, *balambaras*, and *däğğazmač*, and his actions are frequently discussed in the period's royal chronicles (Anonymous 1912, 11, 121, 161, 165, 172, 177–80, 184, 188–92, 203, 206–7, 231, 234, 236–39, 257). Regarding his affiliation with WP's monastery, *see* Crummey (2005, 137). Mentioned in the extra texts of MSS H and I only; they relate how he was sent to recover the royal daughter Wälättä Täklä Haymanot from Qʷäraṣa. Transcribed elsewhere as Ešaté.

Eskindiraweet. እስክንድራዊት Ǝskəndərawit. "She of Alexander [the Great]." LOCAL PERSON. WP's maidservant, one of three who served her when she was with her husband and who WP took with her when she left him. She was with WP in Zäge and Ṣällämt. In many spheres of Eastern Christianity, Alexander the Great anachronistically acquired the status of a Christian hero, thus her name.

Ethiopian Orthodox Church. *See* Tawahedo Church.

Ewostatéwos. ኤዎስጣቴዎስ Ewosṭatewos. From Greek. "The Strong One." HISTORICAL PERSON. An Ethiopian monk and monastic reform leader (1273–1352), perhaps the most venerated indigenous saint after Täklä Haymanot. According to the *Gädlä Ewosṭatewos*, the important fifteenth-century text about his life, Ewosṭatewos became a monk at the age of fifteen and established his own community in 1300, gathering many followers. He preached the importance of the clergy remaining independent of the state and called for observing not only the Sunday but also the Saturday Sabbath, which arose from ancient Christian practices but was later condemned by both the Egyptian and Roman Catholic churches. Ewosṭatewos suffered a great deal for his views, especially because of his support of a protest movement against the king, and eventually fled into exile in Egypt, then Jerusalem, and then Cyprus and Armenia, where he died. The "house" or order of Ewosṭatewos came to form an independent strain in the Täwaḥədo Church, moving from a repressed minority into an accepted majority in 1450 when their views on the Sabbath were mandated by the throne. Later, those who followed Ewosṭatewos adopted the Unctionist (Qəbat) doctrine, and those who followed Täklä Haymanot adopted the Unionist doctrine. *See* Revol-Tisset and Smidt (2005); Fiaccadori (2005). His commemoration is celebrated on 18 Mäskäräm (28 September). In the *WP gädl*, *Abba* Śəʿəlä Krəstos temporarily passed away on the day of Ewosṭatewos's commemoration and had a vision of *Abba* Ewosṭatewos showing him a beautiful town with large trees without fruit and small trees with fruit, which symbolized arrogant, lazy monks and humble, hardworking monks, respectively. This suggests that WP's community looked to Ewosṭatewos and were Unctionist. Transcribed elsewhere as Ēwōstātēwos.

Faith of the Fathers. ሃይማኖተ፡አበው Haymanotä Abäw. TEXT. A collection of the writings of the early Church Fathers and non-Chalcedonian patriarchs of Egypt, translated from the Arabic into Gəʿəz perhaps just fifty years before WP's birth. In Ethiopia, it is read during the services of Holy Week and the Communion of the clergy. In the anti-Catholic struggles of WP's time, the *Haymanotä Abäw* became the preferred doctrinal reference work of the Orthodox Ethiopians, probably because it provides many defenses of the non-Chalcedonian doctrine about the one nature of Christ. In fact, the Jesuits considered it the most important expression of the Täwaḥədo Church's creed and tried to emend it to be less favorable to the non-Chalcedonian view. *See* Wion and Fritsch (2005). In the *WP gädl*, this book falls into a river. That the author adds that not a single letter in the text was erased must be understood in the context of the Jesuits' attempts at emendation. That is, WP's actions to save the book are "an expression of the holy saint's strength to protect [the book] from any form of alteration or interpolation" (Cohen 2009a, 110n92).

Falaseeta Kristos. ፈላሲተ፡ክርስቶስ Fälasitä Krəstos. "[Female] Pilgrim to Christ." LOCAL PERSON. One of only three people allowed to see WP on her deathbed. Fälasitä Krəstos read to WP from Psalms and the Gospels while she was dying. Being able to read suggests that she might be a noblewoman, since usually they were the only women who learned to read. We could not find any mention of her in the historical or encyclopedic sources.

Fasiladas. ፋሲለደስ Fasilädäs. From Greek. HISTORICAL PERSON. The Ethiopian king who fully restored Ethiopian Orthodoxy after his father, King Susənyos, had converted the country to Roman Catholicism (regnal names Səlṭan Säggäd "The [Ottoman] sultan submits [to him]"or ʿAläm Säggäd "The world submits [to him]"). Fasilädäs was born in 1603, died in 1667, and reigned from 1632 to 1667. Although he officially converted to Roman Catholicism on 11 February 1626, along with most of the rest of the court, he did not long remain a supporter and worked in 1631 and 1632 to restore the Orthodox faith, which was achieved on 25 June 1632. Fasilädäs became king shortly after, although his father was still alive, probably because the latter was incapacitated by a stroke. His castle was in Gondär. *See* van Donzel (2005). In the *WP gädl*, Fasilädäs persuaded his father the king to allow WP to return from exile. Upon becoming king, he consolidated the return to the Orthodox faith. He sent Wälättä Giyorgis, a daughter of the former king Śärṣä Dəngəl (r. 1563–97), who had converted to Catholicism, to WP to be converted back to Orthodoxy. WP later spent several months at the court advising him. Transcribed elsewhere as Fasiledes.

Fasiladas. ፋሲለደስ Fasilädäs. From Greek. RELIGIOUS FIGURE. A third-century Greek Christian martyr and saint popular in Ethiopia. There are a confusing number of saints named Basil, Basilaos, Basilicus, Basilius, Basilides, or Fasilidas. Ten such saints are celebrated in the *Sənkəssar*. The *WP gädl* is clear, however, that its Saint Fasilädäs is a martyr and is celebrated on 11 Mäskäräm. According to the *Sənkəssar*, when the Greek lands were ruled by the idol-worshipping Roman King Diocletian, he tortured and killed Fasilädäs for being a Christian, inspiring many to follow his example and receive crowns of martyrdom (Budge 1928, 2:38–41). In Ethiopia, Fasilädäs is popular as one of the equestrian saints (Balicka-Witakowska 2005a). Military saints were represented as mounted knights in the Täwaḥədo Church tradition and have an apotropaic function, so their portraits were often placed near the entrance of churches. In the *WP gädl*, the Məṣəlle Island Monastery is called Məṣəlle Fasilädäs, and he played a special role for those who stayed on the island: WP made a vow to this saint to stay in Məṣəlle if the Orthodox faith was restored; *Abba* Śəʿəlä Krəstos traveled to Məṣəlle specifically for the feast of this saint; and WP's servant Ilarya developed a strong affection for this saint while staying in Məṣəlle, during which stay he performed several miracles for her. The saint also appeared beside WP's deathbed. This saint is not to be confused with Vassilios/Basilios or the fourth-century saints of Anatolia, including Basil the Elder, Basil of Ancyra or Basil the Martyr, and Basil of Caesarea or Saint Basil the Great, about whom, *see* Witakowski (2003).

Fasting. ጾም Ṣom. Cultural practice. An essential part of Täwaḥədo Church practice. Clergy observe 250 fasting days out of the year, while the ordinary believer observes 180 days a year. Those fasting do not totally abstain from food but eat only one meal a day, generally after 3:00 pm, and do not eat any animal products, avoiding meat, eggs, and milk. The longest fasts are those of Lent and Advent. All fasts are followed by feasts. Fasting was required for the forgiveness of sins and the dampening of physical desires. It may also have served a purpose over time of training people to endure famines.

Fatagar. ፈጠጋር Fäṭägar. Local place. One of the two historical highland regions in south-central Ethiopia from which WP's family hailed. Fäṭägar was in an area east and south of modern Addis Ababa and north of the Awaš River. Until the 1530s, the royal court frequently stayed there. Later in the sixteenth century, Fäṭägar came under the control of the Muslims and then the Oromo. The term is no longer used for this region. *See* Derat (2005); Pankhurst (1997). Transcribed elsewhere as Fatagar, Fatagār, Fetegār, Fäṣägar, and so on. *See also* Dawaaro.

Fatla Sillasé. ፈትለ፡ሥላሴ Fätlä Śəllase. "Cord of the Trinity." Historical person. A high-ranking monk associated with the royal court who appears in Susenyos's chronicle and the *WP gädl.* In the chronicle, he participates near southeastern Lake Ṭana in a famous debate before King Susənyos about the nature of Christ. He is the first of many monks who argued the winning side of the Unctionist (Qəbat) doctrine, which some argue emerged due to a sympathy for some Roman Catholic doctrine. Since *Abba* Fätlä Śəllase is also regularly associated in the *WP gädl* with a converted member of the court, *Wäyzäro* Wälättä Giyorgis (whom WP is later said to have converted back to Orthodoxy), we might conjecture that he was one of the priests who initially embraced Roman Catholicism. At any rate, in the *WP gädl, Abba* Fätlä Śəllase was a special mentor to WP, as well as the "teacher of the entire world." He sent monks to chaperon WP from her husband Mälkəʾa Krəstos's home to Zäge, where she wanted to become a nun. When WP's husband then laid waste to the nearby town, *Abba* Fätlä Śəllase joined with Wälättä Giyorgis to rebuke him and broker peace between him and WP. When WP was reluctant to return to her husband, it was *Abba* Fätlä Śəllase who persuaded her to do so to save others' lives. When her husband subsequently did not live up to his promises, the monk and the princess again confronted him and again reconciled the two. *Abba* Fätlä Śəllase appears a final time in the *WP gädl* when male priests attacked WP's leadership on the grounds that she was female. They then reluctantly admitted to *Abba* Fätlä Śəllase that perhaps God had appointed her to chastise them. That the *WP gädl* speaks approvingly of him suggests that he had abandoned any pro-Catholic stance he might have taken up before but also that WP's community was Unctionist, which, over the long term, was not the winning side.

Feast of the Mount of Olives. ደብረ፡ዘይት Däbrä Zäyt. "Mount of Olives." Religious occasion. A movable feast that honors the prophecies about the Second Coming that Christ delivered to his disciples on the Mount of Olives. It is celebrated on the Sunday midway through the Lenten fast (not before 28 Yäkkatit in early March nor after 2 Miyazya in early April). The faithful spend the day praying that they may be found worthy on the Day of Judgment. The Bible passages read on this occasion address God's judgment: 1 Thessalonians 4:13–18, 2 Peter, 3:7–15, Acts 24:1–22, Psalms 50:3, and Matthew 24:1–36. The Second Coming of Christ is one of the Five Pillars of Mystery in the Täwaḥədo Church. *See* the Church's website at http://www.eotc-mkidusan.org.

Feast of Nahaasé. *See* Feast of Our Lady Mary's Assumption.

Feast of Our Lady Mary's Assumption. በዓለ፡ፍልሰታ፡ለእግዝእትነ፡ማርያም Bäʿalä fəlsäta lä-əgzəʾtənä Maryam. Religious occasion. The most important of the feasts for Saint Mary, which is celebrated in all churches. It marks the day when Saint Mary was believed to have been physically taken up into heaven at the end of her life, according to apocryphal literature. In other traditions, this event is also called her "ascension," but some prefer "assumption" theologically since Christ "ascended" but Mary was drawn up into heaven. Prior to the feast is the *Ṣomä Fəlsäta* (Fast of the Assumption), which lasts from 1 Näḥase to one day before the feast day itself on 16 Näḥase (22 August). A six-day feast follows, until 21 Näḥase. *See* Heldman (2005a). Sometimes called the Feast of Näḥase.

Feast of Peter and Paul. በዓለ፡ጴጥሮስ፡ወጳውሎስ Bäʿalä Ṗeṭros wä-Ṗawlos. Religious occasion. The Feast of Peter and Paul takes place on 5 Ḥamle, in honor of the two most important apostles of Christ. It is at the end of the *Ṣomä Ḥawaryat* (Fast of the Apostles), which lasts from the Monday after Pentecost to this feast.

Feast of Qusqwaam. ቍስቋም Qʷəsqʷam. From Coptic. "Kōskam." Religious occasion. A mountain in central Egypt where the Holy Family stayed during its Egyptian exile, according to tradition, while hiding from Herod's persecution. The Fast of Qʷəsqʷam commemorates this flight of the Holy Family and lasts from 26 Ṭəqəmt until 6 Ḫədar, ten days. It is one of the thirty-three feasts dedicated to the Virgin Mary and is also called the Season of Flowers. The Mountain of Kōskam is near Manfalūt and the famous Dayr al-muḥarraq (Burnt Monastery).

Feast of Tsédénya. ጼዴንያ Ṣedenya. From Arabic. "Ṣaydnāyā." Religious occasion. Celebrated on 10 Mäskäräm (17 September), this is one of the thirty-three feasts devoted to the Virgin Mary. According to the *Sənkəssar*, this feast is in honor of the day that an icon of Mary sweated holy oil in Ṣedenya, Syria, the seat of the patriarch of Antioch and long a holy site due to this famous icon. Among other miracles, this portrait, reputedly painted by Saint Luke, protected a monk named Theodore on his journey home and then became flesh (Budge 1928, 1:34–36). *See* Cerulli (1943, 276–89). Transcribed elsewhere as Saidnaya.

Fifteen Prophets. Biblical figure. The fifteen Old Testament prophets are the three major prophets (with long books in the Bible) Isaiah, Jeremiah, and Ezekiel, and the twelve minor prophets (with short books in the Tanakh) Hosea, Amos, Micah, Joel, Obadiah, Jonah, Nahum, Habakkuk, Zephaniah, Haggai, Zechariah, and Malachi. (Note that in the Hebrew Bible and in the Täwaḥədo Church tradition, Daniel was not considered a major or minor prophet. The book of Daniel was placed among the Writings.)

Fihirta Kristos. ፍኅርተ፡ክርስቶስ Fəḫərtä Krəstos. "Betrothed of Christ." LOCAL PERSON. A woman in the Afär Färäs community who became restless and wanted to return home. WP persuaded her to stay with the community, but not long after Fəhərtä Krəstos died. When the nuns went to Sädäç̣əlla to tell WP the news, WP demonstrated her power by asserting that she already knew this information because she herself had God kill Fəhərtä Krəstos, presumably to hasten her entrance into paradise. She might possibly be Fəqərtä Krəstos, given the similarity of their names and stories.

Filaatawos. ፊላታዎስ Fälatawos. From Greek. "Philotheos (Friend of God)." LOCAL PERSON. Susənyos's military officer in charge of the region of Ṣällämt, to which WP had fled. The king sends *Ambaras* Fälatawos to fetch WP to appear before the court, which he does. He does not seem to appear in Susənyos's royal chronicle. Transcribed elsewhere as Filatewos.

Finhas. ፊንሐስ Finḥas. HISTORICAL PERSON. The husband in 1767–68 of Wälättä Täklä Haymanot, the eldest daughter of King Bäkaffa and Queen Məntəwwab. Wälättä Täklä Haymanot's husband of record, *Ras* Elyas, was killed in 1733, so Finḥas appears to be a later spouse. Mentioned in the extra texts of MSS H and I only.

Fintiro. ፍንጥሮ Fənṭəro. LOCAL PLACE. A town about twenty-five miles due south of Gondär, forty miles north of Qʷäraṣa, and about two miles north of Lake Ṭana at LatLon: 12.320134, 37.430017. WP and Wälättä Maryam passed through this town. A fire later started in this town (in MS I miracles only). Transcribed elsewhere as Fentero, Finterro, and Fintʾiro. It is near the modern town of Fänṭär (which is how the name appears in the Abbadie manuscript), a town about two miles south of Gondär and four miles east of Azäzo, at LatLon: 12.566753, 37.483354.

Fiqirta Kristos. ፍቅርተ፡ክርስቶስ Fəqərtä Krəstos. "Beloved of Christ." LOCAL PERSON. Like Fəḫərtä Krəstos, Fəqərtä Krəstos was a woman who became restless and decided to return home. Her husband, Kəflä Maryam, told WP of his distress about his wife's decision. Thereafter, Fəqərtä Krəstos grew ill and died, through the will of WP. Fəqərtä Krəstos might possibly be Fəhərtä Krəstos, given the similarity of their names and trajectories, with the story of one individual being told by two different members of the community. She is not the saint of *Gädlä Fəqərtä Krəstos,* since her behavior and her husband's name are different. The recent publication of *Gädlä Fəqərtä Krəstos* was based on the extant version of the text, which had recently been copied from an earlier manuscript damaged by fire.

Fiqirta Kristos. ፍቅርተ፡ክርስቶስ Fəqərtä Krəstos. "Beloved of Christ." HISTORICAL PERSON. A noblewoman of WP's period who also became a saint due to refusing to convert to Roman Catholicism, according to her *Gädlä Fəqərtä Krəstos* (Anonymous 2002). In modern Ethiopia, she is also known as *Əmmä Muz* (Perfumed Mother), from her childhood name Muzit or Məʿəzt. She and her husband, Zärʾa Krəstos, who was a military officer, had only one child, a boy who died when he was seven. The two were very pious, refused to convert, and were eventually executed for their resistance. Fəqərtä Krəstos rose from the dead, however, to threaten Susənyos with the relics of her own dead body. He then returned to the Orthodox faith. Subsequently, she moved to Waldəbba, famous for hosting many women during this period of resistance, then to southeastern Lake Ṭana, two places where WP had lived as well. She met and befriended many other nuns. She then traveled to Jerusalem and Armenia, to see the tomb of Ewosṭatewos, and upon returning, she established a monastery in the Wällo region, near Däse. She died on 27 Yäkkatit; her name does not appear in the royal chronicles of the period, and *Sənkəssar* entries have not been found so far. *See* Nosnitsin (2005a; pace, the *WP gädl* does specifically mention Susənyos). It seems clear that the Fəqərtä Krəstos gädl bears some relationship to the *WP gädl*. Whether it was inspired by it during the period or much later is unclear. Hagiographies tended to be produced in clusters and to share themes (Kaplan 2005c).

Firqa. ፍርቃ Fərqa. LOCAL PLACE. *Ras* Mikaʾel's army went there on the way from Gondär to Qʷäraṣa. It may be the district of this name in Bägemdər region, just north of Lake Ṭana, deserted by the nineteenth century, or, perhaps more likely, the town near northeastern Lake Ṭana also called Fərqabärr (transcribed elsewhere as Farqabar, Ferkaber, Fercaber, and Fercaber); LatLon: 12.215878, 37.651412. Mentioned in the extra texts of MSS H and I only.

Fisa. ፊሳ Fisa. LOCAL PLACE. A town about ten miles north of Qʷäraṣa with a church devoted to Saint Michael; LatLon: 11.734227, 37.450026. Mentioned in the extra texts of MSS H and I only.

Fogera. ፎገራ Fogära. LOCAL PLACE. A flat, marshy region to the east of Lake Ṭana (which included the church of the fifteenth-century female saint Krəstos Śämra and was the land across from Ṭana Qirqos Island) and a town near the shore, about twenty-five miles south of Qərəñña and ten miles north of Afär Färäs; LatLon: 11.950326, 37.583488. WP persuaded Walättä Maryam to travel there with her from Fänṭär and Qərəñña; troops also stopped there, according to the extra texts of MSS H and I. Since the region often floods, many residents move to higher ground during the rainy season. Susənyos camped there twice, once in 1619 and again in 1622, where he hosted a debate on theology. *See* Kleiner (2005b). Transcribed elsewhere as Fogerra, Foghera, and Fogara.

Food. *See* Fasting.

Furé. ፉሬ Fure. LOCAL PLACE. A place on the southwestern shore of Lake Ṭana, probably what is now the town of Furi Maryam, just south of Lake Ṭana's Zäge Peninsula, according to Bosc-Tiessé (2000). It is unlikely that it is the Däbrä Sina on the northern shore of Lake Ṭana, as supposed by Zanetti (2005). In the *WP gädl*, it is where Läbasitä Krəstos, *Abba* Ṣəge Haymanot, and Əḫətä Krəstos lived at different times. After first meeting WP, Əḫətä Krəstos moved from there to follow WP. Transcribed as Fura, Fure, Furē, Furi, Foura, and Fare. In the *WP gädl*, it appears in most manuscripts as "Fure," but in some as "Fare" (e.g., Abb. 88), probably because the fidäl symbols for *fu* and *fa* are extremely similar. LatLon: 11.686111, 37.316603. *See* Bosc-Tiessé (2008, 67, 72, 172, 372).

Gabra Amlak. ገብረ፡አምላክ Gäbrä Amlak. "Servant of the Lord." LOCAL PERSON. The abbot (*mämhər*) of WP's monastery in October 1813 (EC 1806), according to a note in Amharic. Mentioned in the extra texts of MS I only.

Gabra Maryam. *See* Kasagn.

Gabra Mikaél. ገብረ፡ሚካኤል Gäbrä Mika'el. "Servant of [Saint] Michael." LOCAL PERSON. The prior of WP's monastery at some unknown time, when it had houses in Dämbəya, Gondär, and Damboza; thus, probably in the 1700s. Mentioned in the extra texts of MS I only.

Gädam. *See* Monastic settlement.

Gädl. ገድል Gädl. "Struggle, contest." TEXT. The Gəʿəz genre of literature depicting the life and spiritual struggles of a saint—a biography of a holy person, also called a hagiography or hagiobiography. The *gädlat* (the plural form of *gädl*) about the lives of non-Ethiopian saints were translated from other languages into Gəʿəz. Then, monks wrote many about indigenous Ethiopian saints, largely founders of monastic communities. The Täwaḥədo Church did not have the extremely formal process of the Roman Catholic Church in establishing saints. Rather, for an Ethiopian to become a saint, a *gädl* has to be written that then is read aloud on their feast day. The *gädl* often has three parts: the tale of the saint's life, followed by tales of the miracles that occurred after his or her death when his or her name was invoked, and a poem of the *mälkəʾ* genre. A *gädl* also has to include the *kidan*, a covenant that Christ makes with the saint to protect anyone who invokes the saint's name. Certain themes recur, including the saint's parents praying desperately for a child, a precocious childhood, a choice to become a monk or nun against the family's wishes, struggles with demons, efforts to convert nonbelievers, and fights with the king. Over two hundred *gädlat* about Ethiopian saints have been cataloged. Few copies of each Ethiopian saint's *gädl* existed, preserved mostly only in the monasteries devoted to that particular saint. When copying a *gädl*, scribes sometimes expanded the text. Most *gädlat* about Ethiopian saints were written between the late fourteenth century and the seventeenth century; WP's is unusual in having been written not long after her death. Few have been published or translated into European languages. *Gädl* is sometimes translated as "vita" or "contendings." *See* Kaplan (2005c).

Galawdeos. ገላውዴዎስ Gälawdewos. From Latin. "Claudius." LOCAL PERSON. The author of the *Gädlä Wälättä Ṗeṭros*. He gives little information about himself, writing only that he is a novice monk and member of WP's monastery at Qʷäraṣa. As a novice, he was probably a young man when he wrote the text in 1672–73, thirty years after WP's death, and so he probably had not known her personally. Rather, as he repeatedly states in the *WP gädl*, he relates stories told to him by community members who did know her.

Gazhigé. ጋዥጌ. Gažəge. LOCAL PLACE. A historically recorded area in the 1600s that now is known as Saba, about twenty miles to the west of mid–Lake Ṭana. A tributary of the Gəlgäl Abbay was the boundary between Gažəge and the historic region of Ačäfär, which ran along southwestern Lake Ṭana and was regularly pillaged by Susənyos (Pankhurst 1997, 361). In WP's days, Gažəge may have had a monastery, since the monk reporting Yämanä Krəstos's death went there in the *WP gädl*. Also, Ḫirutä Amlak, follower of Saint Iyäsus Moʾa, proselytized there in the thirteenth century (Kur 1965, 28; Tadesse Tamrat 1991). The hunter Powell Cotton camped there in April 1900 and mentions a "Wogadar Maryam" Church (1902, 267–68). Spelled Gažäge in CR. Transcribed elsewhere as Gāžgē, Gazgé, Gazge, and Gajghe.

Geldi. ገልዲ Gäldi. LOCAL PLACE. Probably the river Gälda (Gelda) just south of Qʷäraṣa; LatLon: 11.724174, 37.436577. It is probably not Geldi, two hundred miles directly east of Lake Ṭana, at LatLon: 11.501557, 40.55809. Mentioned in the extra texts of MSS H and I only.

Gəlgäl Abbay. ግልገል፡አባይ "Cub Big One." LOCAL PLACE. A river with many tributaries that empties into southern Lake Ṭana about ten miles northwest of Zäge. It contributes the largest flow of water into the lake. As the name "cub" suggests, this river has long been seen as the source of the Abbay River (Blue Nile), which flows out of Lake Ṭana to the southeast. LatLon: 11.804977, 37.125929. Transcribed elsewhere as Gilgel Abbay, Gilgel Abay, Lesser Abay, or Small Abay.

George. ጊዮርጊስ Giyorgis. RELIGIOUS FIGURE. George of Lydda, in Palestine, is one of the most revered foreign saints in Ethiopia. This third-century saint, who is also the patron saint of England, is so important in Ethiopia that he is celebrated on the twenty-third of every month and has many churches devoted to him. His hagiobiography is a common manuscript. Along with other saints, he appears to WP on her deathbed to escort her to heaven. His hagiobiography was translated from the original Greek into Arabic in the fifteenth century and subsequently into Gəʿəz (Pasicrates and Theodosius 1930). It states that he was born in Anatolia and served a king, but then decided to give away his belongings to serve Christ. He was martyred three times and rose to life each time, until he was beheaded. During the Crusades, a story arose about him saving a young woman from a dragon. This resulted in him usually being depicted astride a horse and spearing a dragon with a young woman nearby; that is, as one of the equestrian saints. *See* Raineri (2005); Balicka-Witakowska (2005b).

Gésho. ጌሾ Gešo. PLANT. An indigenous plant, scientific name *Rhamnus prinoides*, which when boiled serves as a type of hops in making fermented drinks, especially a common alcoholic drink in Ethiopia, an ale called *ṭälla* in Amharic and *səwa* or *säwa* in Tigrinya. *See* Pankhurst (2005c); Amborn (2010). Mentioned in the extra texts of MS I only.

Ghirarya. ግራርያ Gərarya. LOCAL PLACE. The place where *Abba* Yämanä Krəstos died in the sixth miracle. It is most likely the monastery Gərarya established by Täklä Haymanot in approximately 1284 (Nosnitsin 2010f), about thirty miles due east of Ṭana Qirqos, near Däbrä Tabor; LatLon: approximately 11.879278, 37.97868. Transcribed elsewhere as Grarya, Gerarya, Grariya, and Graria. Alternatively, it may be Gərarya Giyorgis, a place also called Amba Maryam, on Lake Ṭana.

Ghirmana. ግርማና Gərmana. Local person. A nun and companion of WP who was with her in Waldəbba. Gərmana asked WP about her visions of Christ and thus was a witness of WP's report that she had a vision in which Christ commanded her to take care of his flock and found communities.

Gibaza River. ግበዛ Gəbaza. Local place. This may be the Gäbäzä Maryam River forty miles south of Lake Ṭana; LatLon: 10.993772, 37.431938. One can see the top of WP's community house in Fənṭəro from this river, according to the fifteenth miracle of the *WP gädl*; mentioned in the extra texts of MS I only.

Ginbowt. ግንቦት Gənbot. Temporal term. The ninth month of the year in the Ethiopian calendar, now extending from 9 May to 7 June in the modern Western calendar. It falls during the sowing season, called *Ṣädäy*, sometimes called the hungry season because food supplies can run out before the next harvest. A number of feasts fall during this month, including Pentecost, the Feast of Mary's Birth (1 Gənbot), the Feast of Christ's Ascension (8 Gənbot), the Feast of Mary's Apparition (21 Gənbot), and the Feast of Christ's Entry into Egypt (24 Gənbot). *See* Fritsch and Zanetti (2003).

Gojjam. ጎጃም Goǧǧam. Local place. One of the major regions of Ethiopia, just south of Lake Ṭana, spreading west and north of the Abbay River (Blue Nile), which almost encircles it. On the boundary of the highland Christian kingdom, Goǧǧam was evangelized in the fourteenth century by monks from Lake Ṭana monasteries and became a stronghold of the Unctionist (Qəbat) doctrine in the seventeenth century (Nosnitsin 2005b). Mentioned in the extra texts of MS I only.

Golgotha. ጎልጎታ Golgota. Text. A well-known prayer frequently used, and even worn as a textual amulet, based on the prayer of the Virgin Mary at Calvary. It is bound together with a poem for WP in one of the miracles. *See* Burtea (2007); Basset (1895). For the text, *see* Budge (1929, 112–27).

Gond. ጎንድ Gond. Local place. A monastery about fifteen miles north and a bit east of Lake Ṭana; LatLon: 37.683178. In most of the *WP gädl* manuscripts, Gond is the place from which *Abba* Kəflä Sämaʿt came (Abb. 88 has Gonǧi).

Gondar. ጎንደር Gondär. Local place. Originally a modest market town thirty miles north of Lake Ṭana until King Fasilädäs established his court there in 1636. It remained Ethiopia's capital and seat of power until the late eighteenth century. It was Ethiopia's first post-Aksumite permanent royal town (*kätäma*, originally meaning encampment). Fasilädäs built a castle there, as did kings and queens after him until 1755, with many nobles and merchants settling there as well. *See* Berry (2005). Gondär only appears in the *WP gädl* after the death of Susənyos and only in connection with Fasilädäs. WP visited Fasilädäs there, was healed of a sickness she contracted there, and then stayed so long that her community began to grumble. Some speculate that the name of Gondor, the capital of the realm of the humans of Middle Earth in Tolkien's *Lord of the Rings*, was inspired by the name of Ethiopian Gondär. LatLon: 12.602313, 37.466984.

Gonji. ጎንጂ Gonǧi. Local place. Probably the monastery of Gonǧ Tewodros Däbrä Ṭəbäb, about thirty miles south of Lake Ṭana; LatLon: 11.217806, 37.666916. *Abba* Kəflä Sämaʿt, who visited WP on her deathbed, is said to have come from this monastery in MS Abb. 88, with other manuscripts having the variant Gond. Perhaps the copyist of MS Abb. 88 upgraded the monk's origin from the unspectacular Gond to the renowned monastery of Gonǧi. In 1620, Gonǧi's leader Ləbso or Ləbsä Krəstos argued the Unctionist (Qəbat) side in the theological debate before Susənyos. He was ordained as a Catholic priest by the Jesuits and led Gonǧi as a Catholic monastery until approximately 1636 when Fasilädäs executed him for deserting the Orthodox faith. After the return to Orthodoxy, Fasilädäs sent many gifts to this monastery. *See* Wion (2005); Bosc-Tiessé (2008, 167, 239–42, 244–45). Transcribed elsewhere as Gonǧ, Gonj, Genj, Gonǧ, and Gʷanǧ.

Goshu. ጎሹ Goššu. "The buffalo." Historical person. An eighteenth-century aristocrat, great-grandson of King Susənyos, and one of the pillars of the rule of Iyoʾas I (1755–69). He was governor of Goǧǧam. *Ras* Mikaʾel gave orders for *Däǧǧazmač* Goššu to be strangled in 1769, but he lived until approximately 1786. *See* Chernetsov (2005c). Transcribed elsewhere as Gosho. The extra miracles say he pillaged Qʷäraṣa and took the *WP gädl* to Goǧǧam. Mentioned in the extra texts of MS I only.

Grace. ጸሎተ፡ማእድ Ṣälotä maʾədd. "The table prayer." Text. A prayer recited at mealtime, from the *Rules of Pachomius*, titled *Śərʿatä Maḫbär* (Rules of the Community) in Ethiopia. For the text of the prayer, *see* Dillmann (1866, 61).

Guna. ጐና Gʷəna. Local place. A mountain fifty miles directly east of Qʷäraṣa, near the city of Däbrä Tabor, visible from some parts of Lake Ṭana. More than 13,000 feet tall, it is the origin of the Rəbb River, which flows into Lake Ṭana. Grain was sent to the community from here. LatLon: 11.716116, 38.234375. Written as both Guna and Gʷəna in the *WP gädl.* Transcribed elsewhere as Gouna.

Gwangoot. ጓንጉት Gʷangʷət. Local place. The place on the southeastern shore of Lake Ṭana, about ten miles north of Qʷäraṣa, now most closely associated with Krəstos Śämra, Ethiopia's most venerated indigenous female saint. Her monastery is located where the Gumära River empties into Lake Ṭana, on a rocky outcrop surrounded by wetlands. It is a popular pilgrimage site, and worshippers travel long distances to celebrate her feast day there. A nearby island is now called Ç̣əqla Mänzo. WP's community went to Gʷangʷət to escape illness in Zäge, and a thieving woman went there in one of the miracles. LatLon: 11.896593, 37.506718. Transcribed elsewhere as Guangot, Guangut, Gʷangut, and Gʷāngut. *See* Bosc-Tiessé (2000, 222).

Habakkuk. ዕንባቆም ʿƎnbaqom. Biblical figure. A Jewish prophet, considered the author of the biblical book of Habakkuk. According to the Apocrypha, Habakkuk is transported by an angel from Israel to Babylon to feed Daniel in the lion's den (Daniel 14:31–42). This story appears in the *WP gädl,* inspired by "Now the prophet Habakkuk was in Judea; he had made a stew and crumbled bread into the bowl, and he was on the way to his field, carrying it to the reapers, when an angel of the Lord said, 'Habakkuk, carry the meal you have with you to Babylon, for Daniel, who is in the lion-pit' " (Daniel 14:33).

Habesha. ሐበሻ Ḥabäša. ETHNIC TERM. The comprehensive name that the various Christian and Semitic-speaking peoples of the Ethiopian and Eritrean highlands use for themselves. Ḥabäša in Amharic; Ḥabäśa in Gəʿəz; Habesha in online references. For an explanation of the term, *see* Müller (2005). For an explanation of the choice to use it sometimes rather than "Ethiopians," *see* Belcher (2012). WP and the author Gälawdewos were Ḥabäša.

Hail Mary. *See* Salama Malaak.

Hamlé. ሐምሌ Ḥamle. TEMPORAL TERM. The eleventh month of the year in the Ethiopian calendar, now extending from 8 July to 6 August. It falls during the rainy season, *kərämt. See* Fritsch and Zanetti (2003).

Hatsanaa. ሐፀና Ḥaṣ́äna. CULTURAL PRACTICE. Some kind of grooming or beautifying activity, perhaps manicuring or hennaing the hands. This uncommon term does not appear in any of the standard dictionaries, but the root *ḥ-ṣ́-n* denotes the semantic field of caretaking. In Tigrinya, *ḥəṣ́ənot* means what the bride does to prepare to welcome the bridegroom, which includes putting oil in one's hair, brightening one's face, putting on woody perfumes, and making one's palms black. Some of WP's nuns repented of doing *ḥaṣ́äna* instead of working.

Haykaliya Mammo. ሃይካልየ፡ማሞ Haykäləyä Mammo. "The boy 'My sanctuary.' " LOCAL PERSON. The abbot (*abä mənet*) of Qʷäraṣa in 1735, the fifth year of Iyasu II's reign. Appears with the name variant Haykäl Mammo (The boy "Sanctuary") in MS I. Mentioned in the extra texts of MSS I and J only.

Haymanotaweet. ሃይማኖታዊት Haymanotawit. "She who belongs to the Faith." LOCAL PERSON. The prioress (*liqtä ardəʾt*) of Qʷäraṣa in 1735, the fifth year of Iyasu II's reign. Mentioned in the extra texts of MSS I and J only.

Haymanotä Abäw. *See* Faith of the Fathers.

Henok. *See* Enoch.

Hezekiah. ሕዝቅያስ Ḥəzqəyas. BIBLICAL FIGURE. As the Old Testament relates, this righteous king of Judah fell ill and was close to dying, but when he repented of his sins and prayed to God for healing, it was granted. Upon his recovery, he composed a poem. *See* 2 Kings 20:1; 2 Chronicles 32:24; Isaiah 38:1–14. According to the *WP gädl*, WP suffers like Hezekiah.

Hidaar. ኅዳር Ḫədar. TEMPORAL TERM. The third month of the year in the Ethiopian calendar, now extending from 10 November to 9 December in the modern Western calendar. It falls during the windy season, *mäṣäw*. Feasts of Saint Mary are held on 6 and 21 Ḫədar; Advent starts during this month. *See* Fritsch and Zanetti (2003).

Himama eda seb. ሕማመ፡እደ፡ሰብእ Ḥəmamä Ǝdä Säbʾ. "The illness of the hand[s] of people." MEDICAL TERM. A serious folk illness caused and cured by folk medicine, something like the evil eye. If someone is doing well, others may become jealous and put a magical potion or poison in his or her food, which causes such symptoms as mental illness, stomach pain, or loss of talent. This illness is considered largely fatal. A woman in the twenty-sixth miracle experienced this illness. Mentioned in the extra texts of MS I only.

Hintsiwaal. ሕንጽዋል Ḫənṣəwal. PLANT. A type of oat (*Avena abyssinica*) used as horse fodder. It was not cultivated on purpose but allowed to grow wild in planted barley fields and therefore came to mean thorns, thistles, and weeds. WP used it as a metaphor for what Satan sows.

History of the Holy Fathers. ዜናተ:አበው:ክቡራን Zenatä abäw kəburan. "Stories about the venerable fathers." TEXT. A collection of anecdotes about and sayings by the Egyptian Desert Fathers who founded monasticism in the fourth and fifth century. Part of the patristic literature, it is based on *Apophthegmata Patrum Aegyptiorum* (Sayings of the Egyptian Fathers), but with hagiographical accounts added. It was translated into Gəʿəz in the thirteenth century at the latest. It is also called *Zena Abäw* (Stories about the Fathers), *Zena Abäw Kəburan* (Stories about the Venerable Fathers), or *Zena Abäw Qəddusan* (Stories about the Holy Fathers), which is a capacious name for collections of different sayings and anecdotes. In the *WP gädl*, it appears with the rare plural *zenat* (stories). *See* Bausi (2007).

Hours. TEMPORAL TERM. Ethiopians count the hours as is done in the Bible (and also generally in East Africa), from sunrise, with the first hour of the day ending at 7:00 AM. Thus 7:00 AM in Western time is one in the morning in Ethiopian time and 1:00 PM in Western time is the seventh hour, or seven in the afternoon in Ethiopian time. The Ethiopian eleventh hour ends at the Western 5:00 PM. This system may have developed in East Africa and the Middle East due to their closeness to the equator, where the hours of daybreak and nightfall are fairly steady.

Icon. ሥዕል Śəʿəl. OBJECT. Painting on wood of a saint, which in Ethiopia dates to the fifteenth century. Depictions of the saints were meant not simply to educate but also to protect the faithful. Mary was a popular subject, particularly depictions of her miracles, especially after the fifteenth-century Ethiopian emperor Zärʾa Yaʿqob mandated their display in every church during the Liturgy. WP speaks to icons of Saint Mary at Ṣana, Məṣəlle, Rema, and Amba Maryam. *See* Heldman (2010).

Ilarya. ኢላርያ Ilarya. From Greek. "Hillary (the cheerful one)." LOCAL PERSON. A maidservant of WP's mother, Krəstos ʿƎbäya, sent to serve WP in Žäbäy and who then stayed with her many years. She is called "saintly" in the *WP gädl* and, in a miracle of her own, successfully stopped the sun. Ilarya is an elegant Latin name and thus typical for a servant or slave. Just as in the United States, where slaves were often called names like "Caesar" or "Prince," slaves in Ethiopia, coming from far places with other languages, were regularly given new, often elegant names. Thus, she was likely a slave originally from what is modern southern or western Ethiopia. In the *Sənkəssar*, the daughter of the late-fifth-century Greek emperor Zeno had a daughter, Hilaria, who longed to become a monk, so she dressed in a man's garments and, acting like a man, joined a monastery. The monks did not suspect anything, but because she did not grow facial hair, they called her Hilarion the Eunuch. She lived a long life as a monk.

Isaac. *See* Jacob.

Iyasu. ኢያሱ Iyasu. "Joshua." LOCAL PERSON. A wealthy man and *däǧǧazmač* who, along with *Näggadras* Asahel, buys MS J from two important women: Wälättä Täklä Haymanot and Bərhan Mädḫanitu. Mentioned in the extra texts of MS J only.

Iyasu II. ኢያሱ Iyasu. "Joshua." HISTORICAL PERSON. King Iyasu II (r. 1730–55), throne name ʿAläm Säggäd (The world submits [to him]), was born in 1723 to King Bäkaffa and Queen Wälättä Giyorgis (Məntəwwab). He ascended the throne at the approximate age of seven, with his mother as regent. It was a time of peace and the building of churches and castles in Gondär, but of declining royal power. The religious party of the Unctionist (Qəbat) doctrine was dominant. He died during an epidemic at the age of thirty-two and his son by his second wife Wəbit, Iyoʾas I, ascended the throne. *See* Chernetsov and Nosnitsin (2007). Mentioned in the extra texts of MSS H and I only.

Iyoas I. ኢዮአስ Iyoʾas. "Joas." HISTORICAL PERSON. King Iyoʾas I (r. 1755–69), throne name Adyam Säggäd (The provinces submit [to him]), was born in approximately 1749 to King Iyasu II and Wəbit (who was the daughter of an Oromo chief). His grandmother Wälättä Giyorgis (Məntəwwab) was regent for him, as she had been for his father, when he came to power at the approximate age of six; Iyoʾas never became a strong king. *See* Natsoulas and Nosnitsin (2007). Mentioned in the extra texts of MSS H and I only.

Iyoel. ኢዮኤል Iyoʾel. "Joel." LOCAL PERSON. The prior (*liqä ardəʾt*) of Qʷäraṣa in 1735, the fifth year of Iyasu II's reign. Mentioned in the extra texts of MSS I and J only.

Iyopraxia. ኢዮጰራቅስያ Iyop̣äraqsəya. From Greek. "Eupraxia (good conduct)." LOCAL PERSON. WP's maidservant, one of three who served her when she first left her husband. She was named after a saint commemorated in the *Sənkəssar* on 26 Mäggabit (4 April): A fifth-century Roman girl who went to live an ascetic life in an Egyptian monastery, never eating meat, drinking wine, or eating anything cooked during Lent. She loved to sing, was very obedient to her abbess, and was much loved by all the other nuns. It has been a tradition, since the Romans, to name servants after the great men and women of old, and thus to surround yourself with the furniture of your illustrious heritage, the signs of your own greatness.

Jacob. ያዕቆብ Yaʿqob. BIBLICAL FIGURE. In the book of Genesis, Jacob and Esau were twins born to Rebecca and Isaac, the only son of Abraham and Sarah. The twins quarreled their whole lives and the firstborn Esau foolishly sold his birthright to Jacob for a bowl of lentils. Esau was his father's favorite, and Jacob was his mother's favorite but tricked his father into making him his heir. Jacob wrestled with an angel of the Lord and was renamed Israel. Then Jacob fell in love with a beautiful woman named Rachel, and worked for her father Laban for seven years to gain her, but was tricked into marrying her plain sister Leah. He then had to work another seven years to gain Rachel as a second wife. At first, his favorite wife Rachel was barren, but she later gave birth to Joseph and Benjamin. Joseph was his father's favorite, which made his brothers jealous so that they stealthily sold him into slavery in Egypt. But Joseph rose to second-in-command there and saved his brothers during a famine. When his father followed him to Egypt, he asked to be buried at home in Israel.

Jacobites. ያዕቆባውያን Yaʿqobawəyan. RELIGIOUS FIGURE. Another name for the believers of the various non-Chalcedonian churches of which the Täwaḥədo Church is one. A sixth-century bishop of Edessa in northern Syria/southeastern Anatolia, Jacob Baradaeus, was one of the main organizers of this church, especially in Syria, during its most difficult period, thus the name Jacobites.

James. ያዕቆብ Yaʿqob. "Jacob." BIBLICAL FIGURE. Following the Greeks, the Gəʿəz text refers to the Apostle James, one of Christ's Twelve Apostles, as Jacob. The author of the *WP gädl* cites the Apostle James's Epistle several times.

John, Gospel of. ወንጌል፡ዘዮሐንስ Wängel zä-Yoḥannəs. TEXT. The Gospel traditionally thought to have been written by Saint John. In general, the reading of the Gospel of John is favored by Ḫabäša monks and is an important feature of monastic life. According to Denis Nosnitsin, it was the only Gospel copied separately in pocket format, which indicates that it was often used for private devotion and meditation, not just in a monastic context or in church services. Some priests say Christ's words come through most clearly in this Gospel. It is also the Gospel in which WP's namesake, Saint Peter, is mentioned most. As a priest early in her monastic life told her to, WP often read from the Gospel of John.

John Saba. አረጋዊ፡መንፈሳዊ Arägawi Mänfäsawi. "The spiritual[ly gifted] elder." HISTORICAL PERSON. Known by his title *Arägawi Mänfäsawi* (Spiritual Elder) in Ethiopia, John Saba was a Christian ascetic from eighth-century Syria whose writings were translated into Gəʿəz in the sixteenth century. He wrote more than two dozen homilies and more than fifty letters, the eponymous anthology of which is called *Arägawi Mänfäsawi* in Ethiopia. It is one of the three parts of the *Mäṣaḥəftä Mänäkosat* (Books of the Monks), which is the foundational work of Ethiopian monasticism. It was translated into Gəʿəz from Arabic in the sixteenth century. John Saba's story appears in the *Sənkəssar*. *See* Lucchesi (2003). Sometimes called John of Dalyatha elsewhere.

John the Short. ዮሐንስ፡ሐጺር Yoḥannəs Ḫaṣir. HISTORICAL PERSON. An Egyptian Coptic saint, much venerated in the Täwaḥədo Church, who was treated harshly by his mentor, an old man named *Abba* Bamoy, which aided John greatly on his way to sainthood. WP is said to have emulated him. His story is told in the *Sənkəssar* for 20 Ṭəqəmt (30 October), including such comments as "*Abba* Bamoy fell sick of a very severe sickness, and he continued to suffer from this sickness for eighteen years, and though *Abba* John ministered unto him [all this time] he never once said unto him, 'Thou hast done well,' for the old man *Abba* Bamoy had grown very old, and he used to try him exceedingly" (Budge 1928, 172).

Joseph. *See* Jacob.

Kasagn. ካሳኝ Kasäññ. "He [i.e., God] has compensated me." LOCAL PERSON. *Näggadras* Kasäññ, whose Christian name was Gäbrä Maryam (Servant of [Saint]

Mary), experienced several miracles and appears to be the patron of their addition to MS I. Kasäññ is a name that parents normally give to a boy born after the loss of an earlier child. Mentioned in the extra texts of MS I only.

Kəbrä Nägäśt. ክብረ፡ነገሥት. "The Glory of the Kings." TEXT. Medieval Ethiopian retelling of biblical story of Solomon and Sheba.

Kidaan. ኪዳን Kidan. "Covenant." RELIGIOUS TERM. A pact or covenant made by Christ with a particularly holy person during a visitation. This is an important concept in the Täwaḥədo Church and a vital part of any of its hagiographies: Christ promises that anyone who follows that saint will find favor with God. After the saint's death, if a Christian asks the saint to intercede with Christ on the Christian's behalf, Christ will honor the request. The *kidan* appears in every Gəʿəz hagiography, but was not common in the Egyptian hagiographies that otherwise served as models for Gəʿəz hagiographies. In other traditions, such pacts were usually only made with Saint Mary. Saints typically receive their *kidan* toward the end of their lives, even on their deathbeds, but Christ granted WP a *kidan* as a young woman, when he pleaded with her at the holy place of Waldəbba to give up seclusion and become the leader of seven spiritual communities. *See* Kur and Nosnitsin (2007).

Kifla Maryam. ክፍለ፡ማርያም Kəflä Maryam. "Dedicated to [Saint] Mary." LOCAL PERSON. A boat owner who helped WP when she was first leaving her husband. He later suffered at the hands of her husband and appears to have married a woman named Fəqərtä Krəstos, who much later tried to leave the community.

Kifla Samaat. ክፍለ፡ሰማዕት Kəflä Sämaʿt. "Dedicated to the Martyrs." LOCAL PERSON. A priest from Gond (or Gonǧi) Monastery summoned by WP on her deathbed.

Kristos Ebayaa. ክርስቶስ፡ዕበያ Krəstos ʿƎbäya. "In Christ lies her greatness." LOCAL PERSON. WP's mother. She was married to Baḥər Säggäd, gave birth to at least five sons and WP (the only known daughter), sent food to WP while she was in Waldəbba, and sent her a servant when she was in Zäbol/Zämbol. She then went to visit WP in Betä Mänzo, fell ill, and was sent to Rema, where she died and was buried. Transcribed elsewhere as Krestos Ebaya.

Kristos Sinnaa. ክርስቶስ፡ሥና Krəstos Śənna. "In Christ lies her beauty." LOCAL PERSON. The unnamed father of this woman brought the plague to Zäge; she was a member of the community presumably.

Kristosaweet. ክርስቶሳዊት Krəstosawit. "She of Christ." A CONTEMPORARY PERSON. A noblewoman from Gondär who sent a large gift of uncooked butter to WP at Fure to heal Wälättä Krəstos. She might possibly be Susənyos's fifth daughter (by a concubine) because that woman was also named *Wäyzäro* Krəstosawit and was alive at the time.

Kucho. ኩቾ Kuččo. HISTORICAL PERSON. A high-ranking member of the eighteenth-century court who fell in and out of favor with more than one king, as described in several historical sources. The so-called *Short Chronicles* state that King Dawit (r. 1716–21) appointed Kuččo *bäǧər wänd* (keeper of the crown), an important royal position. In 1721, Kuččo killed two men he suspected of poisoning and killing Dawit. The next year, the new king, Bäkaffa, arrested Kuččo and exiled him to

Wälqayt. In 1727, upon hearing rumors that Bäkaffa, who had not left his palace in Gondär for some time, had fallen ill and died, a *Blattengeta* Kuččo told his troops to get ready (despite the title change, it is most probably the same man, returned from exile and promoted). When Bäkaffa emerged from his palace in full health and went to Däbrä Bərhan, however, he accused Kuččo of treason. Kuččo tried to justifiy the mobilization of his troops by saying that he had heard of a conspiracy by two high dignitaries to take Bäkaffa captive. The king did not believe him and ordered Kuččo's execution; soon after, Kuččo's soldiers pleaded with Bäkaffa to give them a new commander. Instead, the enraged king told them to evacuate Gondär. *See* the *Short Chronicles* (Anonymous 1983, B: 264, 269, 275, 285–86). According to Bäkaffa's own chronicle, *Blattengeta* Kuččo was condemned and executed (Anonymous 1903b, 320, 324). *See also* Munro-Hay (2002, 86, 91, 126). Note that the story in this text varies slightly from that in the chronicles. Also spelled Kʷəččo. Mentioned in the extra texts of MSS H and I only.

Laban. *See* Jacob.

Lag. ለግ Läg. Local place. A historical region just southwest of Lake Ṭana, where the Gəlgäl Abbay empties into Lake Ṭana, near Ačäfär and Zäge. Susənyos had recently conquered it, Fasilädäs gave it to WP as a fief, and she later sustained her followers in Zäbol/Zämbol on grain grown in Läg. *See* Berry (2003a, 153, 160); Huntingford (1989). LatLon: 12.182321, 37.595901. It is not the place now called Layge, Lage, or Lege, on the northeastern shore of Lake Ṭana, LatLon: 12.11 37.36.

Lasta. ላስታ Lasta. Local place. A historical province in a rugged region about 100 miles east of Lake Ṭana, in what was later commonly known as Wällo Province. Its population long retained a separate Agäw identity even after having converted to Christianity and having been incorporated politically into the Amhara-dominated Ethiopian Christian kingdom. Inaccessibility and a separate ethnocultural identity made Lasta a hotbed and refuge for rebels against the central authority and the monarch. One of these was the seventeenth-century rebel Mälkəʾa Krəstos, sometimes called "the restorer of the faith." The medieval Zagʷe Dynasty, famous for the rock-hewn churches created during their rule in the Lasta town of Lalibäla, also came from this region. LatLon: 12.189704, 38.589048. *See* Wudu Tafete Kassu (2007a).

Layika Masqal. ላእከ፡መስቀል Laʾəkä Mäsqäl. "Servant of the Cross." Local person. A male deacon (probably a teenager) providing service in Žan Fäqära. He narrowly avoids being killed by an angel when he enters Mäqdäsä Maryam's cell without first announcing himself. Deacons have chores that rotate by the month.

Leah. *See* Jacob.

Lebaseeta Kristos. ለባሲተ፡ክርስቶስ Läbasitä Krəstos. "She who wears Christ as her garment." Local person. A wealthy woman who sent one of her servants (possibly a slave) to help WP. Läbasitä Krəstos would appear to have been a part of WP's life for a long time, since her servant helped WP when she first became a nun and was still with WP at least three years later, after they returned from Žäbäy.

Leo. ልዮን Ləyon. Religious figure. A mid-fifth-century bishop of Rome. Pope Leo I wrote a theological treatise, important to the Council of Chalcedon, that approved the doctrine of the dual nature of Christ (fully human and fully divine), which became Catholic doctrine. The Täwaḥədo Church rejected this council and saw Leo as emblematic of the heresy of Christ being split rather than unified. Therefore, his name was regularly reviled by the Täwaḥədo Church and used as a sort of shorthand denunciation of Catholic Christology altogether. *See* Bandrés and Zanetti (2003).

Lisaana Kristos. ልሳነ፡ክርስቶስ Ləsanä Krəstos. "Tongue of Christ." Historical person. WP's third brother. He was a member of the royal court, listed in Susənyos's royal chronicle as participating in the Easter feast with Susənyos. Transcribed elsewhere as Lisana Kristos.

Lives of the Saints. ስንክሳር Sənkəssar. From Greek. "Collection." Text. A large collection of short accounts of saints' and martyrs' lives organized by date, called the *Synaxarium* in Latin. Each day has readings for the foreign and indigenous saints who are said to have died on that day. Through its wide circulation in Ethiopia and the integration of readings from it into the Liturgy, over the centuries this particular set of hagiographies deeply shaped Ethiopian Christian culture and piety. Almost every church has a *Sənkəssar*, which is traditionally read right before the closing words of the service. The first version was translated in the fourteenth century from Arabic, with only foreign saints, but the text was significantly expanded in Ethiopia, particularly between 1563 and 1581, not long before WP's birth. Thus, the *Sənkəssar* is quite different than the *Synaxarium* known in other churches. Some manuscripts include additional stories for local saints; for instance, a short account about Əḫətä Krəstos is found in some Lake Ṭana monasteries' *Sənkəssar* manuscripts. *See* Colin and Bausi (2010).

Lyre of Saint Mary. አርጋኖነ፡ማርያም Arganonä Maryam. Text. This massive volume is perhaps the most rapturous text in praise of the Virgin Mary ever written. It is one of the great works of original Gəʿəz literature, written by Giyorgis of Sägla, widely acknowledged as the most exemplary Gəʿəz author. It dates to the fifteenth century. Also known as the *Arganonä Wəddase* (Lyre of Praise). *See* Getatchew Haile (2003).

Maateb. ማዕተብ Maʿtäb. "Seal." Religious term. The term most often refers to a cord, either simple or appended with a cross, that Orthodox Christians, especially women, traditionally wear around the neck or the wrist. It can also sometimes refer to a cross tattooed on the arm or the forehead, which, for its bearer, becomes an indelible marker—a final seal—of adherence to the Täwaḥədo Church, and thus prevents one from giving in to the temptation to deny one's faith in times of persecution (which historically confronted Täwaḥədo Church Christians mostly from Muslims).

Macarius. መቃርዮስ From Greek. Mäqarəyos. Religious figure. One of the Egyptian Desert Fathers, ascetics who lived in the fourth and fifth centuries and founded Christian monasticism. He was Saint Anthony's disciple and is often invoked in Ethiopian hagiographies together with him. Not to be confused with Märqorewos (Mercurius).

Madab. መደብ Mädäb. LOCAL PLACE. A town east of Lake Ṭana, near Däbrä Tabor, thus near LatLon: 11.856935, 38.008865. *Ras* Mikaʾel's son and successor Wäldä Gäbrəʾel died there during a battle against *Ras* Ali Gʷangul in the 1780s (Parkyns 1853, 109). Transcribed elsewhere as Medeb or Meddeb. King Täklä Giyorgis I once fought and seized a cannon there, according to the twenty-seventh miracle of the *WP gädl*; mentioned in the extra texts of MS I only.

Maggabeet. መጋቢት Mäggabit. TEMPORAL TERM. The seventh month of the year in the Ethiopian calendar, now extending from 10 March to 8 April in the modern Western calendar. It falls during the dry season, *ḥagay.*

Maguna. መጕና Mägʷəna. LOCAL PLACE. An ancient monastery north of Lake Ṭana and directly west of Gondär about thirty miles. King Fasilädäs is said to have looted it in 1657 and killed two of its priests, probably because it was a Unionist (and thus anti-Qəbat) center. It was rebuilt sometime between 1667 to 1682 and was a stronghold of Unionist sentiment well into the next century. *Abba* Absadi was associated with the Mägʷəna Monastery. Little is known about him, although he has a gädl. Transcribed elsewhere as Magwena, Magwina, Magwenā, and Mägʷina. LatLon: approximately 12.513436, 36.978895. *See* Wion (2007a).

Maḫbär. *See* Community.

Mahdere Sibhat. ማኅደረ፡ስብሐት Maḫdärä Səbḥat. "Residence of Praise [of God]." LOCAL PLACE. A Lake Ṭana island about 1,000 feet from Rema Island and 1,000 feet from the shore of Lake Ṭana, about 350 feet in diameter. Now abandoned, there once was a Saint Mary of Qʷəsqʷam Church on it, founded during the late-sixteenth-century reign of Śärṣä Dəngəl by one of the king's nobles (Cheesman 1936, 167–68). *See also* Bosc-Tiessé (2000, 233). Transcribed elsewhere as Mahdera Sibhat, Maḫdara Sebḥat. LatLon: 11.833876, 37.468222.

Malakotaweet. መለኮታዊት Mäläkotawit. "She who belongs to the Godhead." LOCAL PERSON. A nun at Bäkaffa's court in 1727 who had met WP, according to the seventeenth miracle. It is unlikely that she is actually the woman of the same name who was the concubine of Bäkaffa's father, Iyasu I (1682–1706), the mother of Bäkaffa's older half brother Täklä Haymanot (r. 1706–8), and the sister of the Ṗawlos who took refuge at Qʷäraṣa after rising up against Iyasu I. Although she lived at court, King Tewoflos (r. 1708–11) had her and Ṗawlos hung for treason in 1708, twenty years before the events in the WP miracle. However, any person in 1727 who remembered what WP looked like would be in their nineties at least (since WP had died eighty-four years earlier), about the right age for Mäläkotawit, so perhaps the oral tradition has inserted her into the WP miracles in the figure of this nun. *See* Chernetsov (2007b). Transcribed elsewhere as Malakotwit or Malākotwit. Mentioned in the extra texts of MSS H and I only.

Malkih. መልክእ Mälkəʾ. "Image, portrait." TEXT. A genre of Gəʿəz poetry written in honor of holy figures, listing and eulogizing the spiritual powers of the various body parts of the saint, from head to toe. The *Mälkəʾa Wälättä Ṗeṭros*, a poem in honor of WP, is included in this volume. *See* Habtemichael Kidane (2007a) and "The Text's Genres" in this volume.

Malkiya Kristos. መልክአ፡ክርስቶስ Mälkəʾa Krəstos. "Image of Christ." HISTORICAL PERSON. WP's husband and the chief adviser of King Susənyos. A wealthy man, he went on many military campaigns with the king and received several titles. As the king's main advisor, Mälkəʾa Krəstos was involved in supporting "the faith of the Europeans," that is, Roman Catholicism, and repressing the indigenous Täwaḥədo Church. Although he and WP did not have any living children (three children died in infancy), it seems unlikely that he divorced WP and married another woman for this reason. He is not recorded as having married anyone else, and the *WP gädl* insists on his continued support and affection for WP even after their separation. Historical records show that he did have three sons, but two of them were governors in the 1620s, suggesting that they were born long before his marriage to WP and were of an age with her. His mother was *Wäyzäro* Mäsqäl ʿƎbäya (In the Cross lies her greatness) (Täklä Śəllase [Ṭinno] 1900, 235). Transcribed elsewhere as Malki'a Kristos, Malkia Kristos. *See* Nosnitsin (2007c).

Malkiya Kristos. መልክአ፡ክርስቶስ Mälkəʾa Krəstos. "Image of Christ." HISTORICAL PERSON. A noble who claimed to be the rightful king between 1629 and 1635 because Susənyos had converted to Roman Catholicism. He was from Lasta, a rugged region east of Lake Ṭana and including the famous town of Lalibäla. In 1632, Susənyos tried several times to suppress his rebellion and was successful at the battle of Wäyna Däga, even though Mälkəʾa Krəstos escaped. Since Susənyos restored the Orthodox faith not long after his battles with Mälkəʾa Krəstos, Mälkəʾa Krəstos is sometimes called "the restorer of the faith" or "king of the faith." A few years later, Susənyos's son and successor, Fasilädäs, killed him in battle. While this rebel shares his name with WP's husband, he is not the same person. Many famous men had this name at the time; the index to the seventeenth-century texts that the Jesuits wrote lists fourteen men with the name Mälkəʾa Krəstos. *See* Wudu Tafete Kassu (2007b).

Malkiya Kristos. መልክአ፡ክርስቶስ Mälkəʾa Krəstos. "Image of Christ." LOCAL PERSON. A monk who lived in Waldəbba with WP and had the same name as her husband. He predicted that WP would found seven communities.

Mankir. መንክር Mänkər. "The miraculous one." LOCAL PERSON. A monk who came from Wänčät, due east of Qʷäraṣa a couple of miles, and advised WP regarding the Zäge male leaders who worked against her.

Maqdas. መቅደስ Mäqdäs. RELIGIOUS TERM. The holy innermost part of a Täwaḥədo Church, where only priests can go, that holds the object that makes a church a church, the *tabot*. *See* Fritsch (2007).

Maqdasa Maryam. መቅደሰ፡ማርያም Mäqdäsä Maryam "[Saint] Mary's sanctuary." LOCAL PERSON. A woman who fell ill while WP was in Žan Fäqära and who died there. She saw WP prevent an angel from killing a man.

Maqwé. ማጔ Maqʷe. MEDICAL TERM. An illness, probably with a fever, that a person was likely to catch in lowland areas, so perhaps malaria. The term arises from the root *m-w-q* "to be warm, hot," suggesting that the main symptom is a fever or that one caught it in hot areas. This is not a Gəʿəz word but an Amharic one. *Maqʷe* was generally thought to arise from proximity to *buda-* or *zar*-spirits (Kane 1990, 233). *See* Strelcyn (1955). A monk in the *WP gädl* predicted that WP would catch it in the lowlands, and her husband hoped her companion Ǝḫ̮ətä Krəstos would catch it there.

Marcian. መርቅያን Märqəyan. RELIGIOUS FIGURE. The fifth-century Byzantine emperor (in Latin called Flavius Marcianus Augustus) who approved the ecclesiastical condemnation of the anti-Chalcedonian hero and Alexandrian patriarch Dioscorus and had him exiled after the Council of Chalcedon in 451. Thus, he is considered an enemy of the faith by the Täwaḥədo Church. He is described in the *sälamta* poem in honor of WP as "Marcian the Wolf."

Marqoréwos. መርቆሬዎስ Märqorewos. From Greek. "Merkourios (Mercurius or Mercury)." LOCAL PERSON. A monk at Məṣəlle Island who was said to fly. He appears only once. Not to be confused with Mäqarəyos (Macarius).

Marqos. ማርቆስ Marqos. "Mark." HISTORICAL PERSON. The Egyptian patriarch of the Täwaḥədo Church from 1636 to 1647. According to protocol, *Abunä* Marqos III had been assigned by the head church in Alexandria. He was the first to fill the office again after a vacancy during the Catholic interlude, that is, after *Abunä* Səmʿon had been killed in 1617 and after Roman Catholicism had been forced out again in 1632. WP went to greet him not long after he arrived, and he asked her if she was the woman whose fame had reached them even in Egypt. He then blessed her for her righteous defense of the Orthodox faith, while she asked him for advice: Should she stay to lead her community when she really wanted to just be a hermit? He told her that God would strengthen her for the task and then conferred the priesthood on the men with her. Since the position of patriarch had been vacant since at least 1632, when the Roman Catholic patriarch Afonso Mendes left, but really since 1617, when the last Orthodox patriarch had been killed, this was probably the first opportunity that members of WP's community had to become priests. *See* Wion (2007b).

Martha. ማርታ Marta. BIBLICAL FIGURE. A woman in the New Testament who, along with her older brother Lazarus and her younger sister Mary, followed Christ, hosting him in her home and witnessing his resurrection of her brother (John, chapter 11). She enthusiastically acknowledged Jesus as the Messiah (John 11:27). WP is compared favorably to her in the *mälkəʾ* poem.

Martha. ማርታ Marta. RELIGIOUS FIGURE. A woman who appears in the *Sənkəssar* or *Täʾamərä Maryam* and is probably the subject of the allusion to Martha's prayer in the *WP gädl*. The Martha of the Bible had nothing to do with children or barrenness while the Martha cited in the *WP gädl* is barren. There are two childless Marthas in the *Sənkəssar* who pray for children: one is the mother of Saint Vincent, celebrated on 5 Taḫ̮śaś, the other is the grandmother of *Abba* Simon of the monastery of Antioch, celebrated on 29 Gənbot. However, this specific prayer is not discussed in the *Sənkəssar*, so it is not clear where the quote in the *WP gädl* comes from. A *Täʾamərä Maryam* manuscript kept at today's Protestant Mekane

Yesus Seminary in Addis Ababa includes a miracle about how the Virgin Mary gave a child to a certain woman named Martha from a royal family in the East and how the Virgin Mary raised the child from the dead when the wife of the Roman emperor Diocletian (r. 284–305) threw the child to the floor out of jealousy (EMIP 601, Mekane Yesus Seminary 1, 190rv).

Mary. ማርያም Maryam. Biblical figure. The mother of Christ, also called Saint Mary, the Virgin Mary, and Our Lady Mary. She is a figure of great reverence in the Täwaḥədo Church, almost a co-redeemer with Christ and the main object of prayer. WP spoke only twice with Christ but multiple times with Saint Mary through her icon, and Saint Mary regularly advised WP.

Maryam Sinnaa. ማርያም፡ሥና Maryam Śənna. "In [Saint] Mary lies her beauty." Local person. A nun who was with WP in the region of Ṣällämt and went with her when she was called before the king's court the second time.

Maryamaweet. ማርያማዊት Maryamawit. "She of [Saint] Mary." Local person. WP's maidservant, one of three who served her when she first left her husband. She lived with WP in Zäge, when she first went there, and was with her in Ṣällämt, so she was probably with her in Waldəbba as well.

Mäṣḥafä Məwətan. See *Book of the Dead.*

Maskaram. መስከረም Mäskäräm. Temporal term. The first month of the year in the Ethiopian calendar, now extending from 11 September to 10 October in the modern Western calendar. It includes the end of the rainy season and the beginning of the dry season.

Matqi. መጥቅዕ Mäṭqəʿ. Temporal term. Part of a complicated formula for calculating the dates on which certain holidays (i.e., the movable feasts of the Täwaḥədo Church) should fall each year, since they are supposed to follow the lunar not the solar calendar. Meshing the lunar and solar calendar depends on the following: the lunar and solar calendar match only once every nineteen years. There are 235 lunar months for every 19 solar years; thus, after a period of 19 solar years the new moons occur again on the same days of the solar year. The calculations named *abäqte* (or epact) and *mäṭqəʿ* are used to determine the lunar and solar calendar by varying individually but always adding up to thirty. *Mäṭqəʿ* is the number of days left in the lunar month on the first of the year; *abäqte* is the number of days into the lunar cycle on the first of the year. The year this text was written had an *abäqte* of eleven, meaning that there was an ecclesiastical new moon on the eleventh of the month during this year.

Matsehafa Hawi. መጽሐፈ፡ሐዊ Mäṣḥafä Ḥawi. From Arabic. "Comprehensive Book." Text. A collection of rules of moral theology used to teach church dogma and history, translated into Gəʿəz in 1582 from the Arabic, which was itself translated from a Greek original (allegedly written in the eleventh century, but perhaps dating to as early as the seventh century). It includes detailed instructions regarding monks and nuns. The Arabic title, *Al-kitāb al-ḥāwī*, means "Comprehensive Book" (with *ḥāwī* [comprehensive] just being transcribed in Gəʿəz, but not translated), which harks back to the meaning of the original Greek title. *See* Ezra Gebremedhin (2005).

Mazgaba Haymanot. መዝገበ፡ሃይማኖት Mäzgäbä Haymanot. "Treasure-house of Faith." Local person. A monk who was also a priest and had the vision that the scribe Gälawdewos would write the *Gädlä Wälättä Ṗeṭros* and urged him to do so. He had grown up in WP's community, had been instructed in the sacred books, and was a humble, gentle monk who lived in chastity. He died about seven years before the book was written down.

Mazmura Dinghil. መዝሙረ፡ድንግል Mäzmurä Dəngəl. "Song of the Virgin [Mary]." Local person. The archpriest (*liqä kahənat*) at Qʷäraṣa in 1735, the fifth year of Iyasu II's reign. Mentioned in the extra texts of MSS I and J only.

Mendes, Alfonso. *See* Afonsu.

Mənet. *See* Community.

Məntəwwab. *See* Walatta Giyorgis.

Metropolitan. *See* Patriarch.

Mezraata Kristos. መዝራዕተ፡ክርስቶስ Mäzraʿtä Krəstos. "Strong arm of/for Christ." Local person. A functionary of the royal court who delivered a written authorization from King Susənyos to the Lake Ṭana region, while WP's community was at Məṣelle, that all those who remained loyal to the Täwaḥədo Church would be taken captive. This was probably not the Mäzraʿtä Krəstos who was related to WP and is a saint in the Täwaḥədo Church for founding a monastery (Raineri 2007).

Mihillaa. ምሕላ Məḥəlla. "Supplication." Religious term. A special, often daylong service of the Täwaḥədo Church. *Məḥəlla* is the name of a day of entreaty held on ten fixed dates throughout the year, but they are also held as the need arises, when priests pray intensely for guidance on a particular matter, such as the election of a patriarch, to end a drought, or to gain victory in war. It includes singing psalms and hymns, sacred dancing, readings from sacred books, and entreaties to God for blessings. Such a service happens in Waldəbba, where most practices are done more intensely, as it seems this supplication lasted for much longer than a day in the *WP gädl*. *See* Habtemichael Kidane (2007b).

Mikaél. ሚካኤል Mikaʾel. "Michael." Historical person. A noble originating from the province of Təgray who was a dominant figure of the early *zämänä mäsafənt* (Era of the Princes, 1769–1855). *Ras* Mikaʾel "Səḥul" (Mikaʾel the Clever One, 1691–1777) was so powerful he had the kings Iyoʾas I and Yoḥannəs II killed, installed another as his puppet (Täklä Hamanot II), and commissioned a chronicle devoted to himself, something that was normally the prerogative of the monarchs. The Scottish author James Bruce wrote about *Ras* Mikaʾel frequently, describing him as astute and ruthless. The royal chronicles described him as a military commander so cool that during battles he "played at chess," a habit "that burnt like fire the hearts of the enemy; for the soul of Ras Mikaʾel was not moved in the moment of great slaughter" (Blundell 1922, 207–8). He killed so many enemies in 1770 that the streets of Gondär were strewn with body parts. He was not known as a religious man. *See* Abbink (2007). Mentioned in the extra texts of MSS H and I only.

Miraafa Egzitina Maryam. *See* Our Lady Mary's Resting Place.

Miracles. ተአምር Täʾamər. Text. The narration of the miracles performed by a saint after his or her death that forms part of the composite text that is the saint's hagiography. The *tä'amər* normally appear after the biography and before the poems in honor of the saint. They are part of the distinctive genre of indigenous Ethiopian saints' lives, a genre innovated in the fourteenth century and that flourished for the next five centuries. The *Tä'amərä Wälättä Ṗeṭros* are quite extensive, with almost thirty posthumous miracles recorded.

Mitsillé. ምጽሌ Məṣəlle. LOCAL PLACE. An island with a monastery about half a mile south of Ṭana Qirqos Island in Lake Ṭana and maybe two miles north of Rema Island. WP founded the third of her seven religious communities there. Formerly it had been the residence of the famous saint Afqärännä Ǝgzi'. The monastery there was dedicated to Saint Fasilädäs, so it is often called Məṣəlle Fasilädäs (which is also the name of the region on the east side of Lake Ṭana near it). It is about half a mile long and at one time had three churches dedicated to Saint Fasilädäs and his two sons. *See* Di Salvo, Chojnacki, and Raineri (1999, 43). LatLon: 11.865075, 37.490914. MS Abb. 88 lists Məṣraḥ rather than Məṣəlle as the place of WP's third community. Transcribed elsewhere as Meṣlé, Məṣəl, Meselé, Mesle, and Misilai.

Mitsraaha. ምጽራሐ Məṣraḥa. LOCAL PLACE. A famous island in eastern Lake Ṭana, about thirty miles north of Qʷäraṣa, with monasteries founded by kings and graves where kings were buried (thus appearing often in the royal chronciles). LatLon: 12.187292, 37.56442. *See* Cheesman (1936, 189–93). Soldiers pass this place in the twentieth miracle. Possibly related to the substitution of Məṣelle Island with Məṣraḥ in MS Abb. 88. Transcribed elsewhere as Mesraha, Meṣraha, and Meṣrāhā, and as Mitraha Mariam in Cheesman. Mentioned in the extra texts of MSS H and I only.

Miyazya. ሚያዝያ Miyazya. TEMPORAL TERM. The eighth month of the year in the Ethiopian calendar, now extending from 9 April to 8 May in the modern Western calendar. It falls during the sowing season, sometimes called the hungry season because supplies run out while waiting for the harvest, and often includes Palm Sunday, Good Friday, and Easter Sunday.

Monastery. ደብር Däbr. "Mount, Mountain." RELIGIOUS TERM. Throughout, we have translated *däbr* as "monastery," with the understanding that the term was not used for small churches but for substantial institutions that had at least three priests, often royal patronage, and that served as centers of education. By contrast, we have translated *gädam* as "monastic settlement" and *maḫbär* as "community." A *däbr* had different types of clergy, including priests who were not monks, who performed all the services and ceremonies. In modern use, *däbr* can also mean an important church without a monastery, but this did not seem to be the case when Gälawdewos composed the *WP gädl*, so we have always translated it as "monastery" and never as just "church." As the literary critic Northrop Frye long ago noted, there are four key spaces in the Bible—the mountain, the garden, the cave, and the furnace. In the ancient world generally, high places were frequently sacred places. Thus, the term "mountain" came to be used in Egypt and

Ethiopia to designate also a monastery, which often was located on elevated ground or a mountaintop. There are at least eight hundred monasteries of all types in Ethiopia, most established after the fourteenth century and most built in remote or difficult-to-access sites. New monasteries were set up as daughter monasteries or by a religious leader moving on his or her own into a new area and attracting a community of like-minded people, as WP did. Those who established new monastic communities often disagreed with established monasteries. Part of establishing a monastery was to consecrate a *tabot* and ordain ministers. Monasteries often hold the relics of the founding saint or other holy people. Some monasteries are cenobitic (*andənnät*), in which the members live in community, living and eating together, while others are idiorythmic (*qʷərit*), in which members live autonomous lives and are often called hermits. Every monastery has a church, a cemetery, and huts for the monks. Almost all monasteries have libraries of manuscripts. The *WP gädl* uses the term *mənet* only three or four times, and we also translate it as "monastery." *See* Kaplan (2005a, 2007), and also http://www.monasticlife.org/MonasticLife.html.

Monastic settlement. ገዳም Gädam. "Wilderness." RELIGIOUS TERM. Throughout, we have translated *gädam* (and only *gädam*) as "monastic settlement," with the understanding that the term was not used for a church or a wealthy, established monastery (which was called a *däbr* or a *mənet*), but often for a more autonomous or less settled community of monks without a permanent location, and who appointed their own leaders and did not have connections to the court. A *gädam* was a place of seclusion, a dedicated monastery, having only monks and nuns and no priests who were not also monks. A *gädam* has a *mämhər* (lit., teacher, but the title of the head of a large church, an abbot), while a *däbr* does not. In the *WP gädl*, Rema Island Monastery is called a *däbr*, while Qʷäraṣa and Waldəbba are called *gädam*. Monasticism began in the Egyptian desert, with monks living in individual isolation rather than as one group in a building as part of an institution. Perhaps for this reason, the term "wilderness" came to be used in Ethiopia to designate a certain type of monastic community. *See* Kaplan (2005b, 2007). Regarding Ethiopian monasticism generally, *see* Getatchew Haile (2000).

Monk. መነኮስ Mänäkos. TITLE. A man who makes a commitment to live a spiritual life of renunciation, including celibacy, fasting, and prayer.

Monophysitism. *See* Tewahedo Church.

Months. *See* Calendar.

Mount of Olives. *See* Feast of the Mount of Olives.

Motalami. ሞተለሚ Motälämi. "King of cows." FOLKLORIC FIGURE. An evil heathen king in folklore who is said to have abducted Ǝgziʾ Ḫaräya, the mother of Ethiopia's most famous saint, Täklä Haymanot, and plotted to marry her against her will but was stopped by an angel who saved her. WP invoked Ǝgziʾ Ḫaräya, along with the biblical Sarah and the apocryphal Susanna, as examples of women who were saved from evil men, as WP hoped to be saved from her husband. Also appears as as Mätälomi or Motälami. The first part of the name is derived from a Cushitic language, perhaps Oromo (in which *mootii* means "king, ruler") and the second part from Amharic (in which *lam* means "cow").

Naggad-ras. ነጋድራስ Näggadras. "Head of the merchants." TITLE. A title first used of those who ran long-distance caravans but then used after the eighteenth century for customs collectors, who were appointed by local aristocrats. These were lucrative positions. *See* Garretson (2007). Mentioned in the extra texts of MSS I and J only.

Nahaasé. ነሐሴ Näḥase. TEMPORAL TERM. The twelfth and thereby second-to-last month in the Ethiopian thirteen-month solar calendar, now extending from 7 August to 5 September in the modern Western calendar. Transcribed elsewhere as Nahase or Nahāsē.

Narga. ናርጋ Narga. LOCAL PLACE. A tiny island connected by a short stone causeway to the western part of Däq Island in Lake Ṭana; LatLon: 11.915728, 37.244541. It later became the home of the famous church of Narga Śəllase, established by Queen Wälättä Giyorgis (Məntəwwab) in 1737. WP occasionally retreated there from the community at Afär Färäs.

Nazraweet. ናዝራዊት Nazrawit. "The Nazarene woman." LOCAL PERSON. The fourth abbess (*əmmä maḫbär*) of WP's community. In the *WP gädl*, she is blessed once alongside Əḫətä Krəstos and Amätä Dəngəl, who were previous abbesses of WP's community, so we conclude Nazrawit was the community's fourth abbess.

Ninety-Nine Angelic Orders. BIBLICAL FIGURE. According to the Täwaḥədo Church, God created one hundred tribes or orders of angels, but one of those orders fell (due to the angel Satan), and so one makes vows by the Ninety-Nine Angelic Orders only.

Non-Chalcedonian Church. *See* Tewahedo Church.

Nug. ኑግ. PLANT. *Guizotia abyssinica* is an herb cultivated in the Ethiopian highlands; its seeds are ground and mostly used for oil.

Nun. መነኮሳይት Mänäkosayt or መነኮሳዊት Mänäkosawit. TITLE. A woman who makes a commitment to live a spiritual life of renunciation, including celibacy, fasting, and prayer. The Ethiopian process of becoming a nun was described in the various works of *Śərʿatä Mənkʷəsənna* (Rules of the Monks) (Grébaut 1940, 237–38). A nun marks her intention by shaving her head (being tonsured) and putting on the monastic *qobʿ* (cap). There is then usually a three-year novitiate, although this varies (Chaillot 2002, 154). Two stages characterize the process of becoming a monk or nun. In the *rädʾ* (or first) level, they receive the *qobʿ* and are trying out the life. They are free to travel, for instance. Novices and young monks are supposed to do the manual labor around the monastery and take care of sick or elderly monks. In the *ärdəʾt* (or second) level, they receive the mantle, sash, and belt, and thereby become full members. Most commonly, it was older women, often widows, who became nuns. Thus, in this text, it seems that older nuns were called *əḫət* (sister) and young nuns were called *dəngəl* (virgin). We have treated the two terms as a reference to monastic commitment along with age, not sexual status. It's possible that the "sisters" in the *WP gädl* were just members of WP's community during troubled times, not actual nuns, but a married woman who was still actively married would probably not be called an *əḫət*. Likewise, a *dəngəl* might be a young girl, but was most likely a nun. A monastery of only women, a nunnery or convent, was called *beta dänagəl* (house of virgins). Many monasteries did not allow women, but those that did often practiced strict separation of men and women. Nuns are more likely to live idiorythmic (*qʷərit*) instead of communal religious lives, often living at home rather than in religious communities. Marta Camilla Wright argues that part of being a nun is to efface the female body's natural impurities by deliberately moving toward a more traditionally masculine identity and thus achieving gender neutrality, or what she calls a "holy gender." *See* Fluche and Persoon (2007), Wright (2001), Kaplan (2007), and Nosnitsin (2010d).

Orit. ኦሪት Orit. From Aramaic. "Law." TEXT. In Gəʿəz texts, a reference to the Old Testament (Tanakh) as a whole, but it can also mean just the Octateuch, the first eight books of the Bible, including the Pentateuch (consisting of Genesis, Exodus, Leviticus, Numbers, and Deuteronomy), as well as the next three books (Joshua, Judges, and Ruth). Together they are known as the Book of Law, thus the term Orit. *See* Pietruschka (2010).

Our Lady Mary of the Presentation. *See* the Presentation of Our Lady Mary.

Our Lady Mary's Resting Place. ምዕራፈ፡እግዝእትነ፡ማርያም Məʿrafä Əgzəʾtənä Maryam. LOCAL PLACE. Apparently a church near or in Wäybəna at which ʿAṣqä Maryam served as the custodian of the treasury. It may have something to do with Ṭana Qirqos, ʿOf Goǧǧo, or Amba Maryam, where it is believed that Saint Mary and the Ark of the Covenant stopped on their way through Ethiopia (as the name of the place states). It cannot be the church on Ṭana Island itself, however, where the Ark of the Covenant is reputed to have stayed for six hundred years, because that church has another name, and ʿAṣqä Maryam said that he would be far from this church if he was buried on Ṭana.

Owf Gojjo. ዖፍ፡ጎጆ ʿOf Goǧǧo. "Bird's nest." LOCAL PLACE. A very small island in Lake Ṭana, about two miles north of Qʷäraṣa. Approximately 150 feet in diameter, it was one of the places where the Holy Family and the Ark of the Covenant were believed to have stopped on the way to Ṭana Qirqos. Transcribed elsewhere as Oaf Goja Tsiyon, Oafgogia Sion, Woffa Gojjo, and Wef Gojo. LatLon: 11.793666, 37.450215. *See* Cheesman (1936, 167); Bosc-Tiessé (2008, 67–68).

Papyrus boat. *See* Tankʷa.

Patriarch. ጳጳስ P̣ap̣pas. TITLE. The head of the Täwaḥədo Church who was always assigned to Ethiopia by the Egyptian Church. During the 1610s and 1620s, there were two patriarchs, Səmʿon, who was murdered by pro-Roman Catholic forces, and Marqos. The patriarch from Egypt alone had the authority to ordain new priests and deacons. An *abunä* is not necessarily the patriarch: he can also be a high-ranking or particularly venerated priest or monk; the terms are used interchangeably in some texts. *See* Abuna.

Paul. ጳውሎስ P̣awlos. BIBLICAL FIGURE. A famous first-century missionary, theologian, and author—about half of the New Testament is attributed to him. Although

Saint Paul is an apostle, he is not one of the Twelve Apostles (he never met Christ in person). He is quoted more than thirty times in the *WP gädl.* Before his conversion from Judaism to Christianity on the road to Damascus, he persecuted Christians. Afterward, he suffered greatly while supporting the growing Christian community.

Pawlos. ጳውሎስ P̣awlos. "Paul." Local person. The first of WP's brothers. Nothing further is said about him in the *WP gädl.* Transcribed elsewhere as Paulos.

Peter. ጴጥሮስ P̣eṭros. "Peter." Biblical figure. One of Christ's Twelve Apostles. The word "pétra" in Greek means "rock," and so Saint Peter is called "the rock" on which Christ built his church. As the *WP gädl* states, WP resembled her namesake in also being the founder of a religious community, preaching the Gospel, enduring persecution for the faith, being put in prison, having the keys to heaven, pastoring her flock in their spiritual struggles, being the head of all religious teachers, and having the power to kill and resurrect.

Petros. ጴጥሮስ P̣eṭros. Local person. A monk whom WP heals of a swollen leg. Mentioned in the extra texts of MS I only.

Phinehas. ፊንሐስ Finḥas. Biblical figure. A Jewish high priest who stopped the plague, which God had brought upon the Israelites for worshipping idols, by going in search of the Israelite Zimri (in Gəʿəz, Zänbäri) and a Midianite woman—who were having sex in view of the temple—and driving a spear through both of them with righteous zeal.

Praise of Our Lady Mary. ውዳሴ፡ማርያም Wəddase Maryam. Text. A lectionary or divine office containing prayers in praise of the Holy Virgin to be recited each day of the week. Each day has two to five pages praising Mary and requesting her intercession. It is one of the most beloved texts in the Täwaḥədo Church.

Praise of the Beloved. ስብሐተ፡ፍቁር Səbḥatä Fəqur. Text. A communal daily office of the Täwaḥədo Church; that is, an official set of fixed prayers to be said at certain times of the day or during certain services, also called the Divine Office or the Liturgy of Hours. The *Səbḥatä fəqur* could be used in the daily service or on feast days, sung during a procession, but had a particular use during a period of spiritual retreat. The supplication is addressed to God through the intercession of the prophets, patriarchs, apostles, Saint George, and the three most important Ethiopian male saints, who each constitute the "beloved" of the title. *See* Habtemichael Kidane (2010).

Presentation of Our Lady Mary. እግዝእትነ፡ማርያም፡ዘበአታ Ǝgzəʾtənä Maryam Zä-Bäʾata. "Our Lady Mary of the Presentation." Local place. The name of the church in Robit where WP spent a week after leaving her brother's home. The name of the church is based on a second-century apocryphal story about the Virgin Mary's early life, about which the Bible is silent. According to the story, Mary's parents, Joachim and Anna/Hannah, took their daughter to the Temple in Jerusalem and offered her up to God, just as the prophet Samuel's parents and Christ's parents had offered each of them up for holy service. This date is celebrated in the Orthodox and Roman Catholic churches. In the Ethiopian Täwaḥədo Orthodox Church, it is celebrated on 29 November, one of thirty-three feasts in honor of the Virgin Mary. Although *bäʾata* in Gəʿəz literally means "her entry [into the Jerusalem temple]," in the West the established term for the event is generally "presentation."

Prior. ሊቀ:አርድእት. Liqä ardəʾt. "Male head of the [male] disciples." TITLE. A monastic leadership position below the abbot. Mentioned in the extra texts of MS I only.

Prioress. ሊቅት:አርድእት Liqtä ardəʾt. "Female head of the [female] disciples." TITLE. A female monastic leadership position below the abbess. The office is called *liqä rädʾənnät.* Mentioned in the extra texts of MS I only.

Psalms. ዳዊት Dawit. TEXT. Along with many other early Christians, the Ethiopians considered King David the author of the Psalms and therefore often start a quote from Psalms with the phrase "as David says." The number and numbering of Psalms differs depending on whether the translation was originally made from Hebrew (Masoretic) or Greek (Septuagint) manuscripts. Protestant tradition follows the Hebrew numbering; Catholic, Eastern Orthodox, and Täwaḥədo Church traditions follow the Greek numbering. The numbering of the Psalms is the same in both traditions until Psalm 9, when the Greek tradition collapses Psalms 9 and 10 into one Psalm 9. *See* Stoffregen-Pedersen (1995, 10). The numbering differentiates as follows:

Hebrew (Masoretic) Psalms	Greek (Septuagint) Psalms (Ethiopic)
Pss. 1–8	1–8
9–10	9
11–113	10–112
114–15	113
116	114–15
117–46	116–45
147	146–47
148–50	148–50
	151

Qäsis. ቀሲስ. "Elder." TITLE. A church leader equivalent to a reverend. Today, a *qäsis* is a married priest, not a celibate monk priest; his duties may include preaching, leading worship, and celebrating the Liturgy and other rituals. Before becoming a *qäsis*, a man is a *diyaqon* (deacon).

Qəbat. *See* Unctionist.

Qiddista Kristos. ቅድስተ:ክርስቶስ Qəddəstä Krəstos. "She who is sanctified by Christ." LOCAL PERSON. A young woman who urged the writing of the *WP gädl* and whom the author repeatedly praised. Although, according to the author, she had not known WP personally, she urged the writing when WP's living disciples had not.

Qirinya. ቀርኛ Qərəñña. LOCAL PLACE. A town on the northeastern shore of Lake Ṭana, about twenty miles south of Fənṭəro and five miles due west of Ṭeza Amba Maryam. It is on a promontory on the shore of Lake Ṭana, with a church called Qərəñña Maryam (Cheesman 1936, 188). LatLon: 12.100004, 37.700045. Transcribed elsewhere as Karania, Keranya, and Qiranya (perhaps also Karanio, Keranyo, Keraniyo, and Qaranyo).

Qirqos. *See* Cyriacus the Martyr.

Qoratsa. ቈራጻ Q^{w}äraṣa; but today Q^{w}äraṭa. Local place. A town and monastery on the eastern shore of Lake Ṭana, in the region of Dära, about ten miles north of Baḥər Dar. It has now been the home of WP's main monastery and community for more than 350 years, although the place became associated with WP only after her death, when her community moved there in 1649. Several of WP's communities were within ten miles of Q^{w}äraṣa on the lower southeastern end of Lake Ṭana, but Q^{w}äraṣa is mentioned only twice in the *WP gädl*: *Abba* Ṣäware Mäsqäl stated that WP could live in Q^{w}äraṣa if the leaders at Zäge cast her out and the author wrote that they were living in Q^{w}äraṣa in 1672. According to the *Short History of WP's Community*, they became fully established at Q^{w}äraṣa in the seventeenth year of Fasilädäs's reign (1650) when Fasilädäs granted them land. Fasilädäs is reputed to have built a church there for WP. Since the restricted size of the monastic islands did not encourage large communities, much less two different communities, WP's growing community may have moved to the shore because it was easier to expand there and be independent of established monasteries with strong identities. *See* Bosc-Tiessé (2000); Cheesman (1936, 19, 20, 167, 169, 216). Transcribed elsewhere as Q^{w}äraṣ́a, Qoräta, Qwärät'a, Qorata, Qawarata, Quorata, Quorta, Quarata, Querata, Koratsa, Kiratza, Koreta, Kwarata, Korata, Koreta, Kiratza, or Wärota; it is also called Gädamä Wälättä Ṗeṭros or Q^{w}äraṣa Wälättä Ṗeṭros. Some speculate that the term may come from *qorräṭä*, meaning "to cut" or "to trim" in Amharic; from *qoräta*, meaning a siege style of warfare in Tigrinya; or perhaps from *k^{w}ərʿatä rəʾsu* (striking of his head/spitting image), a way of referring to the Crown of Thorns of Jesus (Lindahl 2008). LatLon: 11.753434, 37.44692.

Qusqwaam. *See* Feast of Qusqwaam.

Q^{w}äraṭa. *See* Qoratsa.

Qulqwaas. ቍልቋስ Q^{w}əlq^{w}as. Plant. A treelike cactus endemic to the Horn of Africa. It is used for building poles, as firewood, and as living fences, as well as for traditional medicine, dyes, and fishing poison. It appears commonly in proverbs and is often present on sacred ground, whether a burial ground or a church compound (therefore, it is sometimes used by archaeologists to identify places to dig). It belongs to the vast *Euphorbia* genus of plants, mostly succulents, and its scientific name is *Euphorbia candelabrum*, after its distinctive upright branches. *See* Revol-Tisset and Smidt (2005). Transcribed elsewhere as kulkwas or qwolqwal (from Amharic *qulq^{w}al*).

Qwarf. ቋርፍ Q^{w}arf. Food. A dish of bitter roots, eaten by monks and nuns at Waldəbba only. The bitter roots are local plants called *ṣable*, *gämälo*, and *sadda*, which are rendered edible only with much labor and preparation. They are supposed to have been discovered by Christ as a child when the Holy Family traveled through Ethiopia, according to local tradition. Eating grains such as wheat, barley, or corn is forbidden in Waldəbba, and *qʷarf* is a sign of the extreme asceticism of the place. *See* Persoon (2010).

Racha. ረቻ Räča. LOCAL PLACE. A town about fifteen miles south of Lake Ṭana, approximately halfway between Səmada and the Zäge Peninsula, near Ṭisəsat Falls. The town and its church are still important. LatLon: 11.419372, 37.580095, according to Täklä Śəllase ([Ṭinno] 1900, 202, 539).

Rachel. *See* Jacob.

Rainy season. ክረምት Kərämt. TEMPORAL TERM. The rainy season lasts from about mid-June to the end of September. Traveling during this season in the seventeenth century was not only cumbersome due to poor road conditions but also posed serious health risks due to the cold, wetness, swollen rivers, and lack of adequate shelter along the road. If they could afford it, people often moved temporarily to a drier location during *kərämt.* People of the court often returned to their homes right before this season started, so the population of the court during this period was often halved.

Ranch. ረንጭ Ränč̣. PLANT. An indigenous Ethiopian edible plant or herb: *Caylusea abyssinica.* Monks and nuns especially devoted to asceticism would eat only greens; according to tradition, the Ethiopian saint Täklä Haymanot ate bitter leaves during Lent. *Ränč̣* grows like a weed, is very bitter, and is also used as fodder, so only the ascetic would eat it. Transcribed elsewhere as *renč* (Amharic) or *renči* (Oromo).

Ras. ራስ Ras. "Head." TITLE. The title of a male noble, with a rank roughly equivalent to a duke. It is the second-highest title in the traditional system of aristocratic hierarchy and the highest one attainable for those not in the royal family. Susənyos changed its duties, elevating its importance. *See* Nosnitsin (2010a).

Réma. ሬማ Rema. LOCAL PLACE. A famous island and monastery in Lake Ṭana about six miles north of Qʷäraṣa, a fifteen-minute row from shore, and nine hundred feet in diameter. Its church is dedicated to Christ, Savior of the World (*Mädḫane ʿAläm*). Rema plays a vital role in the *WP gädl,* being one of the places most frequently mentioned: WP's father used to fast there, and WP was brought out of her husband's home by monks from there, unsuccessfully sent her mother to be healed there, raised a man from the dead there, repaired the church there, founded her sixth community on the shore opposite, buried her brother there, chose to die there, and performed several posthumous miracles there. The present-day monastery includes a grave for WP, a coffin with her parents' skeletons, and several hanging stones that she reputedly used as a boat. Nuns still live there. The monastery houses many valuable manuscripts (including a *Gädlä Wälättä Ṗeṭros*), many of which were microfilmed in the early 1970s (Hammerschmidt 1977b). Transcribed elsewhere as Rēma or Rima. *See* Six (2010a). LatLon 11.838213, 37.47328.

Ribb. ርብ Rəbb. LOCAL PLACE. A river that empties into Lake Ṭana midway up its eastern shore, in the region of Fogära, approximately fifteen miles north of Qʷäraṣa. It was a trade tributary, ferrying salt *amole* to be traded for coffee. A stone bridge with five arches was built over it during the period of the *WP gädl.* Transcribed elsewhere as Reb or Rib. *See* Gascon (2010). LatLon: 12.040431, 37.598128.

Ricci, Lanfranco. MODERN PERSON. One of the most important Ethiopianists of the twentieth century and the translator of the *WP gädl* into Italian, published in 1970. Born in Italy (1916–2007), he studied with the editor of the *WP gädl,* Conti Rossini, and was a civil servant in the Italian administration of Ethiopia from 1938 to 1941, until being captured and held as a prisoner of war by the British for five years. He was then an academic in Ethiopian studies at the University of Rome and the Istituto Universitario Orientale from 1947 to 1991.

Righteous Ones of Waseef. ጻድቃን፡ወጺፍ Ṣadəqanä Wäṣif. RELIGIOUS FIGURE. WP shares her saint's day with the "righteous" men who suffered martyrdom in the Egyptian desert of Wäṣif, according to the *Sənkəssar.* Little is known about these men, *əllä Wäṣif* (the Wäṣifites), who constitute one of the lesser known groups of anonymous Täwahədo Church saints collectively called the *ṣadəqan* (righteous ones) (Brita 2010). *See* Budge (1928, 1:256). *Waṣīf* is a place about ten miles southwest of Port Safaga, which is on the Red Sea in Egypt. Däbrä Wäṣif might be a defunct monastery in Ethiopia.

Robeet. ሮቢት Robit. LOCAL PLACE. A town on southeastern Lake Ṭana about ten miles north of Baḥər Dar, in a region now known as Robit Bata. Robit appears several times in the *WP gädl*: WP first went through this town on her way from Wänčät to Ǝmäbra; her husband then nearly destroyed this town in his pursuit of her; WP searched for her spiritual teacher there; and she lived there with Ǝḫətä Krəstos. According to an English-language pamphlet from the Kəbran Gäbrəʾel Island Monastery, its founder Zä-Yoḥannəs was led to a town called Robit on the lakeshore that is "in front of" the island. Several towns around Lake Ṭana are called Robit, but the *WP gädl* makes clear it is near southern Lake Ṭana. *See* Bosc-Tiessé (2008, 250–51, 254, 256). LatLon: 11.72015, 37.475052.

Roman Catholicism. ሃይማኖተ፡አፍርንጅ Haymanotä Afrənğ. "The Faith of the Europeans." RELIGIOUS TERM. Roman Catholic Jesuit priests arrived in the Ethiopian highlands in the mid-1500s and again in the 1590s. In this second missionary phase, they managed to convert King Susənyos in the early 1600s. His conversion and subsequent edict establishing Roman Catholicism as the state religion triggered a religious civil war that ended in 1632 with Susənyos's proscription of Catholicism and the banishing of all missionaries by the next king, his son Fasilädäs. *See* "The Text's Seventeenth-Century Historical Context" in this volume.

Royal Chronicles. ታሪክ Tarik. TEXT. Beginning with royal inscriptions during the Aksumite period, Ethiopia has had a rich tradition of written historiography. Formal royal chronicles describing the military feats and administrative actions of the king began in the fifteenth century. Each king's chronicle was written during his reign, sometimes by multiple authors. Susənyos's chronicle was written by three authors and is arranged chronologically. The seventeenth and eighteenth century is a period rich in royal chronicles. *See* Chernetsov (2007a).

Rules for the House of Our Mother Walatta Petros. መጽሐፈ፡ሥርዓተ፡ቤታ፡ለእምነ፡ቅድስት፡ወለተ፡ጴጥሮስ Mäṣḥafä śərʿatä beta lä-əmmənä qəddəst Wälättä P̣eṭros. TEXT. A collection of precepts for monastic life in WP's monastery ordained by *Abunä* Zä-Iyäsus and perhaps written down in 1690. Mentioned in the extra texts of MS I only.

Rules for the Monks. ሕንጻ፡መነኮሳት Ḥənṣa Mänäkosat. TEXT. A collection of precepts for monastic life and part of the larger books *Haymanotä Abäw* and *Senodos.* This book is mentioned twice in the *WP gädl,* once as the source of a quotation on not praying with heretics and again when WP calls upon her deathbed for it to be read. Regarding its recensions and different names, *see* Bausi (2007). It is not an alternative title for *Mäṣaḥəftä Mänäkosat* (Books of the Monks).

Ṣ. *See* Ts.

Ṣ́. *See* Ts.

Sadachilla. ሰደጭላ Sädäç̣əlla. LOCAL PLACE. A town on the shore of southeastern Lake Ṭana, just opposite Məṣəlle Island. WP fled from Məṣəlle to this town when King Susənyos authorized the capture of all Orthodox Christians in the region of Därа and later fled from Afär Färäs to this place with Wälättä Giyorgis. *See* Bosc-Tiessé (2008, 67, 183, 423). LatLon: now unknown, but approximately 11.875372, 37.509556. Transcribed elsewhere as Sadaçelā or Sedechila.

Salam. ሰላም Sälam or ሰላምታ Sälamta "Greeting." TEXT. A short poem or hymn in Gəʿəz that focuses on a leader or saint's good deeds or spiritual essence and begins with the words *sälam lä-* (peace upon, or hail to). *Sälamat* (plural) poems generally have between six and twelve stanzas, with three lines per stanza, of which the first is long and the two others much shorter, with often only three to four words; the final stanza regularly has only four lines. *Sälamat* poems in praise of saints are also found in the *Sənkəssar,* following the commemoration of the saint, and sometimes at the end of a saint's hagiography, but those *sälam* variants usually have only one stanza of five lines. A *Sälamta Wälättä P̣eṭros* is included in this volume. *See* Nosnitsin (2010b).

Salama Malaak. ሰላመ፡መልአክ Sälamä Mälʾak. "Hail of the angel." TEXT. The *WP gädl* shows WP silently praying this prayer in three situations of extreme physical distress on Lake Ṭana: when being attacked by a hippo, when a storm blows their boat off course, and when she falls into the water from a *tankʷa.* It may be the *Hail Mary* or *Ave Maria,* based on the words in Luke 1:28 with which the Archangel Gabriel praised the Virgin Mary when telling her that she would give birth to the savior. Getatchew Haile provides a translation of the Täwaḥədo Church version of the *Hail Mary*: "Greeting to you, with the greeting of the angel Saint Gabriel, O My Lady Mary. You are virgin in your mind and virgin in your body. Greeting to you, Mother of God (of) hosts. Blessed are you among women, and blessed is the fruit of your womb. Rejoice, rejoiced one, O full of grace. God is with you. Ask and pray to your beloved Son, Jesus Christ, that he may forgive us our sins." Or it may be from the *Arganonä Maryam* (Lyre of Mary), one of the great works of original Gəʿəz literature, written by the fifteenth-century author Giyorgis of Sägla, which goes by several different names. It describes Mary as "the ark that is not shaken by a wave of flood" and repeatedly states "I have found thee a refuge," from many beasts, including lions, wolves, and panthers, and that "the flooding of the rivers cannot overwhelm him [who prays to Mary], and the violence of the winds cannot cast him down." *See* Getatchew Haile (2003).

Ṣällämt. *See* Tsellemt.

Salome. ሰሎሜ Sälome. BIBLICAL FIGURE. Not the salacious Salome, but Mary Salome who, according to the *Sənkəssar*, was Saint Mary's sister and thus Jesus's aunt. Tradition has it that she was the midwife at the birth of Christ, fled with the Holy Family into Egypt, and was a second mother to Christ throughout his life. Although the *Sənkəssar* does not specify the closeness of Mary and Salome, she spent her whole life with the Holy Family and, according to the *Sənkəssar* reading for 25 Gənbot, "she ministered unto Christ all His days—three and thirty years. On the day of His Passion she was not separated from Him, and she lamented and wept, and on the day of His Resurrection she saw Him before the Apostles saw Him" (Budge 1928, 3:928). She also appears regularly in Budge (1933a). In the Bible, Salome is briefly mentioned in Mark 15:40 and 16:1.

Ṣälotä Maʾədd. *See* Grace.

Säm-ənna wärq. ሰምእና፡ወርቅ "Wax and gold." TEXT. A famous rhetorical device of double meaning common in the Gəʿəz poetic form of *qəne.*

Samson. ሶምሶን Somson. BIBLICAL FIGURE. A great warrior blessed with extraordinary physical strength who slew many of the Israelites' enemies. He once killed a lion with his bare hands and later, finding honey in the carcass of the lion, went to his wedding with a riddle for his in-laws based on this experience. When they were able to figure out the riddle, he knew that he had been betrayed by his future wife, and a cycle of vendettas broke out between her people, the Philistines, and his people, the Israelites.

Ṣana. *See* Tsana.

Saqalaa. ሰቀላ Säqäla. OBJECT. A large rectangular building with a pitched roof. Such buildings often served as dormitories for monks and nuns and were divided into single-room apartments, or, more rarely, as churches. The circular churches so commonly seen now in Ethiopia are a relatively late innovation of the last six hundred years; rectangular stone churches have been built in northern Ethiopia since the first millennium CE (Phillipson 2009). While almost all of the churches in the Lake Ṭana region are round with a conical roof, rectangular church foundations do exist at Ṭana Qirqos and Daga Ǝsṭifanos, two of the earliest monasteries on Lake Ṭana. In the past, the royal encampment had a long tent, called a *säqäla,* which was used as a court of justice.

Sarepta. ዕሬጵታ ʿƎrap̣ta. From Hebrew. BIBLICAL PLACE. A port city sometimes also called Zarephath, on the Phoenician coast north of Tyre, now Sarafand in southern Lebanon. In this city of Phoenicia, the biblical prophet Elijah is said to have received the hospitality of a poor widow and in return increased her grain and raised her son from the dead (1 Kings 17:8–24). Christ mentions this visit in Luke 4:25–27. The place is mentioned in the first miracle, where the text states that the sisters' small quantity of flour increased as it did with the prophet Elijah.

Sartsa Dinghil. ሥርጸ፡ድንግል Śärṣä Dəngəl. "Scion of the Virgin [Mary]." HISTORICAL PERSON. Son of King Minas who was born in 1550 and ruled Ethiopia from 1563 to 1597. He was king when WP was born and the father of one of her supporters, *Wäyzäro* Wälättä Giyorgis. While friendly with the Portuguese, he was an ardent supporter of the Täwaḥədo Church, and during his reign, many churches were established and many important religious texts were translated, like the *Haymanotä Abäw* and the *Mäṣḥafä Ḥawi*. His capital, Guzära/Guba'e, with a castle, overlooked the northeastern shore of Lake Ṭana, and he is reportedly buried on Rema Island. *See* Nosnitsin (2010c).

Satan. ሰይጣን Säyṭan. RELIGIOUS FIGURE. In the theology of the Täwaḥədo Church, Satan, the first angel created by God, fell from heaven due to pride and is forever the adversary of God. He is the head of the demons and the embodiment of evil, often called the Seducer, the Rebel, or the Enemy. He tempted Adam and Eve into sin. Textual amulets often contain prayers to bind Satan and prevent him from harming the owner. The WP *mälkə'* describes WP's triumph over Satan several times. *See* Burtea (2005).

Sawa. *See* Ale.

Sayings of the Fathers. ነገረ፡አበው Nägärä Abäw. TEXT. An alternative title in the *WP gädl* for the *Apophthegmata Patrum Aegyptiorum* (commonly titled *Sayings of the Desert Fathers*), as a Gəʿəz book with this exact title is not known. Alternatively, the phrase in the *WP gädl* may not be a title but a reference to just one of the sayings from the *Haymanotä Abäw*, which is the famous compendium of aphorisms by and anecdotes about the Desert Fathers. *See* Bausi (2007).

Səbḥatä fəqur. See *Praise of the Beloved.*

Sənkəssar. See *Lives of the Saints.*

Seventy-Two Disciples. BIBLICAL FIGURE. The Täwaḥədo Church believes that Christ had seventy-two special disciples in addition to the Twelve Apostles. Luke 10:1–24: "After this the Lord appointed seventy-two others and sent them two by two ahead of him to every town and place where he was about to go."

Šanqəlla. *See* Blacks.

Shenoute. ሲኖዳ Sinoda. RELIGIOUS FIGURE. Shenoute (or Shenouda) of Atripe (a town in Upper Egypt), also known as Shenoute the Archimandrite, was a fifth-century Egyptian monk of the White Monastery of Atripe. He was a foundational figure of Coptic monasticism, and hence is one of the most important saints of the Täwaḥədo Church. As abbot, he oversaw a huge expansion of the White Monastery and was the most admired and prolific author of Coptic literature. His works were not known in the West until the late 1700s and only fully published in 2004. However, the Täwaḥədo Church had several texts about him, by him, or attributed to him in Gəʿəz, including the *Gəbrä Ḥəmamat* (Acts of the Passion) and the *Gädlä Sinoda* (The Life of Shenoute); the latter was translated into Gəʿəz no later than the fourteenth century. Information about him also appears in the *Sənkəssar*, and he is celebrated in the Ethiopian calendar on the same day as WP, 17 Ḫədar, which is part of why he appears in WP's *mälkə'*. He was well known for encouraging literacy and urging monks to write. *See* Buzi and Bausi (2010). Transcribed elsewhere as Šenoute, Sinodyos, Sənudyos, and Sunutuyus.

Shilhoolhoot. ሽልኍልኍት Šəlḫʷəlḫʷət. Folkloric figure. A mythical beast. Šəlḫʷəlḫʷət is not a Gəʿəz term and is not an established Amharic noun either. However, due to several broadly similar vocabulary items in Amharic, Šəlḫʷəlḫʷət evokes slime and filth, crawling and creeping, and pointedness. See such terms as *šäläl* (excrement, filth), *šälala* (lame, crippled), *anšallälä* (to crawl), *šəl* (embryo, fetus; together with related *šəla bäll* [barbaric person who eats the unborn or newborn of cows and sheep]), and finally *šul*, with its reduplicative variant *šulašul* (pointed, sharp). It may be related to the Amharic *wäbbo šämmane*, a cheetah (*Acinonyx jubatus*) that came by night to dig up human graves and feed on the cadavers, and that plagued the monks of Däbrä Zämäddo until they finally hunted it. Alternately, the name may be related to the Amharic word *šuluwliwit*, which Kane translates as "marmoset-like animal (KBT), kind of bird (MH)."

Short Chronicles. Text. In addition to the various royal chronicles, this composite text is an important historical source on Ethiopia's rulers. An alternative approach to Ethiopian historiography, it was written by the clergy and not the court scribes. Each new author edited, erased, and added parts to it, producing many recensions, from the sixteenth century through the eighteenth century. It begins with the legendary geneaology of the Ethiopian kings up to the thirteenth century. Then, starting in the fourteenth century, the authors give brief information on the current kings. Starting with the reign of Ləbnä Dəngəl in the early sixteenth century, it becomes a real source relating events. *See* Anonymous (1983); Basset (1882).

Silla Kristos, *Ras.* ሥዕለ፡ክርስቶስ Śəʿəlä Krəstos. "Image of Christ." Historical person. Susənyos's half brother, an imperial advisor, and a great lord who was a staunch Catholic convert and the head military enforcer of Roman Catholicism. Śəʿəlä Krəstos (ca. 1570–1636) appears throughout Susənyos's chronicle and the Jesuits' accounts, so has been considered, incorrectly, the inspiration of the character Rasselas in Samuel Johnson's *Rasselas* (Belcher 2009). Among other positions, he was the governor of Goǧǧam, the large and wealthy province south of Lake Ṭana. He spied on WP's activities in Zäge by using a soldier who was a son of Ǝḫətä Krəstos's husband. As the text states, Śəʿəlä Krəstos refused to convert back to Orthodoxy and therefore was exiled by Fasilädäs. *See* Cohen (2010a).

Silla Kristos. ሥዕለ፡ክርስቶስ Śəʿəlä Krəstos. Local person. A monk and important confidant of WP. When WP ordered *Abba* Śəʿəlä Krəstos, who was not a priest, to celebrate the Liturgy since no one else was available, he refused, questioning her right to command him, a man. He soon fell sick and died on Rema Island on the feast of *Abba* Ewosṭatewos. When WP told Saint Mary that she didn't want him dead, just punished, Saint Mary allowed WP to resuscitate him, and he became a monk. While dead, he saw a vision of Ewosṭatewos. Later, he advised WP to stay put with her community rather than become a hermit, listened to her tell him about her vision of Christ appointing her archdeaconess, and was one of the few whom she allowed to see her on her deathbed.

Siltaan Marid. ሥልጣን፡መርዐድ፡ Śəlṭan Märʿəd. "It makes the [Muslim] sultan shiver." TITLE. The name of a regiment of soldiers that WP's husband Mälkəʾa Krəstos had set up in Wudo. Mälkəʾa Krəstos used the Śəlṭan Märʿəd regiment to search for WP when she left him, and they laid waste to the town of Robit and terrorized the population. *See* Täklä Śəllase ([Ṭinno] 1900, 127, 452).

Simaada. ስማዳ Səmada. LOCAL PLACE. A town and region about seventy miles southeast of Lake Ṭana, west of where the Bäšəlo River flows into the Abbay (Blue Nile). It is part of a larger region called Gayənt, known for its good farmland and many monasteries. WP lived there with her husband in their castle; presumably, it is where he was a governor and/or where his ancestral lands lay. LatLon: 11.250000, 38.250000. *See* Cheesman (1936, 248, 254, 269). Transcribed elsewhere as Semada, Samada, Simada, and Sāmāda.

Simeon. ስምዖን Səmʿon. "Simon." HISTORICAL PERSON. The Egyptian-born *abunä* (patriarch) of the Täwaḥədo Church under Susənyos, who refused to convert to Roman Catholicism. He arrived in Ethiopia in 1607 and was at first friendly with the Jesuits, but participated in the public debates regarding the faith in 1613 and 1614 and then forbade conversion to Roman Catholicism. He joined forces with the anti-Catholic rebel Yolyos, and after their defeat in battle on 11 May, 1617, he was tortured, killed, left to rot for two days, and then his severed head was delivered to the king. If he was not killed by WP's husband, he was killed by someone who knew her husband well enough to give him the patriarch's garments of office. This shocking event caused WP to leave her husband. *See* Martínez d'Alòs-Moner (2010).

Sitti. ስቲ፡ Sətti. From Sudan Arabic. "My Lady." TITLE. During WP's exile in Žäbay, her guard addressed her with the Sudan Arabic word *Sittī*, using a loanword from a Muslim prestige language to designate his high-ranking Christian Ethiopian prisoner. This further confirms that she had been banished to the west of the Ethiopian highlands, in the border region of today's Ethiopia and Sudan, where the local people were in political, cultural, economic, and linguistic contact with their more powerful eastern and western neighbors.

Sodom and Gomorrah. ሰዶም፡ወገሞራ Sädom wä-Gämora. BIBLICAL PLACE. Cities in Canaan that God destroyed with fire and brimstone because its people were wicked sinners, according to Genesis 13:13. Abraham begged God to spare the city if only ten righteous people could be found therein, but the city was so devoted to cruelty and inhospitality that ten could not be found. The author Gälawdewos wrote that without WP, those in her community would have been "destined for perdition"; if God had not planted her as "a seed, we would have become like Sodom and would have resembled Gomorrah."

Spiritual Elder. አረጋዊ፡መንፈሳዊ Arägawi Mänfäsawi. *See* John Saba.

Stephen. እስጢፋኖስ Ǝsṭifanos. RELIGIOUS FIGURE. A first-century deacon and the first martyr of the early Christian church. *See* Acts 6 and 7. This saint is invoked in the blessings of MS Abb. 88 but not in the other manuscripts.

Stew. *See* Wot.

Susanna. ሶስና Sosənna. BIBLICAL FIGURE. A young Jewish wife whose story appears in the apocryphal chapter 13 of Daniel. Two older men see Susanna in her bath and attempt to blackmail her into having sex with them by threatening her with the false accusation that she had a young lover. She refuses to sleep with them and is about to be executed for adultery, when Daniel demands that the old men be questioned about their account. She is then saved and they are executed. WP invoked her name, along with the biblical Sarah and Ǝgziʾ Ḫaräya, the chaste mother of the great Ethiopian saint Täklä Haymanot, as examples of women who are saved from lustful men, as WP hoped to be saved from her husband.

Susinyos. ሱስንዮስ Susənyos. Historical person. Born in 1572 and king of Ethiopia from 1606 to 7 September 1632. Bearing the throne name Mälʾak Säggäd III (The emissary submits [to him]), he is sometimes labeled *nəguśä nägäśt* (king of kings), but not in the *WP gädl*. Under the influence of Portuguese Jesuit missionaries, he converted from the Täwaḥədo Orthodox Church to Roman Catholicism in 1621. The Portuguese Jesuits had first been allowed into the country in the 1550s, in the wake of, and in gratitude for, their country's aid against Muslim invaders in the early 1540s. Two generations later, their endeavors resulted in the king's conversion and his edict that all Christians had to become Roman Catholic, which triggered a religious civil war. It ended when a disheartened Susənyos rescinded that edict and soon afterward died. His son Fasilädäs then proscribed Catholicism and banished all missionaries. In the *WP gädl*, Susənyos was a mortal enemy of WP, condemning her, calling her before a tribunal, ordering her to undergo reeducation by the Jesuits, exiling her, and only narrowly avoiding killing her. However, when he rescinded the conversion edict, he sent WP a message informing her of this change of heart; thus, the *WP gädl* suggests that he regretted his actions. Transcribed elsewhere as Susenyos, Sissinios, and Sūsinyōs.

Synaxarium. See *Lives of the Saints.*

Tabot. ታቦት Tabot. Religious term. The most sacred object of the Täwaḥədo Church. Every church has a *tabot*, which is a copy of the stone tablets of the Ten Commandments and their wooden container, as it was kept by the Israelites. A *tabot* thus replicates the Ark of the Covenant. The *tabot* can serve as a part of the altar and renders a church a consecrated place. A church is not a church without one.

Tabota Kristos. ታቦተ፡ክርስቶስ Tabotä Krəstos. "Altar of Christ." Local person. A member of the Rema monastic community. The mortally ill monk Śəʿəlä Krəstos was taken to Tabotä Krəstos's house to die.

Takla Giyorgis I. ተክለ፡ጊዮርጊስ Täklä Giyorgis. "Plant of [Saint] George." Historical person. The son of King Yoḥannəs II who ruled briefly but repeatedly (six times) between 1779 and 1800; he was the last of the Gondär kings. His longest stint was the first one, 1779–84, when he was brought from the royal prison to rule. He embarked on many military campaigns but also sponsored many churches, including building Däbrä Məṭmaq Maryam, an important church and monastery in Gondär, as the *WP gädl* mentions. *See* Crummey (2010). Mentioned in the extra texts of MS I only.

Takla Haymanot. ተክለ፡ሃይማኖት Täklä Haymanot. "Plant of the Faith." Religious figure. The most revered indigenous saint in the Täwaḥədo Church, whose veneration has even spread to Egypt. This monk lived in the fourteenth century, founded the Däbrä Libanos Monastery in 1284, was an evangelist in much of central and southern Ethiopia, and died in 1313. His hagiobiography is one of the most widespread manuscript texts in Ethiopia and has many recensions. He is said to have stood praying in one place for so long that one leg fell off. He has three feast days every year and is also celebrated on the twenty-fourth of every month. Transcribed elsewhere as Takla Hāymānōt. Budge translated his hagiobiography, written by Täklä Ṣəyon, into English (Täklä Ṣəyon 1906). *See* Nosnitsin (2010f).

Takla Maryam. ተክለ፡ማርያም Täklä Maryam. "Plant of [the Virgin] Mary." Local person. A disciple of WP's who looked after her and ministered to her, for instance, by bringing her food when she lived in Žäbäy. In Waldəbba he was also a witness of WP's report of her vision of Christ's command to take care of his flock and found communities. In another episode, he slept on a serpent, but was saved due to WP.

Talaawé Kristos. ተላዌ፡ክርስቶስ Tälawe Krəstos. "Follower of Christ." Local person. A monk whom WP posthumously heals of a swollen leg. Mentioned in the extra texts of MS I only.

Ṭälla. *See* Ale.

Tana. ጣና፡ሐይቅ Ṭana Ḥayq (during this period also called ጻና Ṣana). Local place. Lake Ṭana, from which the Abbay (Blue Nile) flows and the largest lake in Ethiopia, is the site of many island monasteries that have been refuges for the persecuted and the nation's archive for many centuries. Lake Ṭana is the center of all the action in the *WP gädl*, together with three important adjacent regions, Bägemdər to the east, Dämbəya to the north, and Goǧǧam to the south. In WP's time, Dämbəya had become the political center of the country, the area where the monarch and his court most frequently sojourned, and the churches of Lake Ṭana took on added significance. Several of the kings built castles in the Lake Ṭana region, including Susənyos. The lake contains several dozen small islands (the largest is about six square miles, whereas some are only several hundred feet across), many of which host monasteries, including Rema, Ǝnṭonəs, Məṣəlle, Kəbran, Däq, and Daga. Important works on the island monasteries include Cheesman (1936), Hammerschmidt (1977b), and Bosc-Tiessé (2000, 2008). The lake is shallow but large enough to have dangerous storms with about forty miles of open water at some points. Transcribed elsewhere as Tsana or Tana. LatLon: 12.157486, 37.379608.

Tana Qirqos. *See* Tsana.

Tankwa. ታንኳ Tank^{w}a. Object. The standard boat in use on Lake Ṭana for many centuries. In the shape of a canoe, it was made of bundles of local papyrus tied with the bark of the local fig tree (*warka*). In mostly shallow Lake Ṭana, it often was propelled by pole not paddle, so boatmen used to punt close to shore and only paddled when they were crossing to an island. They averaged about one mile an hour, and thus it took about two and a half hours to go from the shore to the island of Däq. Since the papyrus grew waterlogged, the *tankʷa* had to be rebuilt after three or four days of heavy use. *Tankʷas* were of different sizes and could be more than thirty feet long, with the largest able to carry fifty mule loads (3,000 pounds) and even entire cows. They are still used by some for the transport of goods and persons on Lake Ṭana, although paddles are now common. A particular ethnic group, the Wäyṭo, made and propelled the *tankʷa*. *See* Cheesman (1936, 90–92).

Täwaḥədo Church. ኦርቶዶክስ፡ተዋሕዶ፡ቤተ፡ክርስቲያን Orthodox Täwaḥədo Church. Religious term. The indigenous name for Ethiopia's and Eritrea's ancient church, whose roots reach back to the fourth century CE. Although others call the church non-Chalcedonian, monophysite, Coptic, Oriental Orthodox, or Ethiopian Orthodox, members themselves prefer the term Täwaḥədo Church, since the word *täwaḥədo* (unified) is a reference to the doctrine of Christ's having one nature, fully human and divine. Now that there is an Ethiopian and an Eritrean branch, as well as various churches in the diaspora, it seems particularly useful not to call it the Ethiopian Orthodox Church. As one of the earliest forms of Christianity still extant and an important form of African Christianity, it has many distinctive practices, including following most of the Old Testament proscriptions (including infant male circumcision), practicing severe fasting, worshipping with a *tabot*, and having a high number of nuns, monks, and monasteries. Its liturgical language is Gəʿəz, and its thousands of churches and monasteries preserve a written Christian tradition dating back to at least the sixth century.

Tazkaar. ተዝካር Täzkar. "Commemoration." Religious term. This major commemorative ritual in the Täwaḥədo Church is a lavish feast held on the fortieth day after a person dies. Daily prayers are held every day for forty days after a person's death while God judges where his or her soul shall spend the time until the Second Coming of Christ. On the fortieth day is God's final decision. A *täzkar* is not a private gesture of filial piety but a public ritual in which the extended family and community participates. For saints, the commemoration happens annually on the day of their death; for major saints it is celebrated each month on that day. *See* Mersha Alehegne (2010).

Tazkaara Dinghil. ተዝካረ፡ድንግል Täzkarä Dəngəl. "Commemoration of the Virgin." Local person. A monk from Lake Ṭana who, along with *Abba* Yämanä Krəstos, met WP when she was still living with her husband and helped her to flee her husband's house and go to Zäge. *Abba* Täzkarä Dəngəl acted as a boatman during this period and was wounded by WP's husband's troops for helping her.

Täʾamər. *See* Miracles.

Téra. ቴራ Tera. Local place. Town where the abbot of Məṣəlle Island Monastery was held captive; may be what is now the Tera Monastery, about ten miles east of Lake Ṭana and about fifty miles north of Qʷäraṣa. As this place is about a mile from what is now the town of Addis Zämän, which grew up recently around the modern highway, it may be the site of the old town of Tera. Or it may be Tera, an area about a hundred miles northeast of Lake Ṭana, in or right above the Səmen

Mountains. LatLon of Tera Gädam: 12.144979, 37.745440. Transcribed elsewhere as Tara or Ṭārā.

Tewodros. ቴዎድሮስ Tewodros. Historical person. One of Ethiopia's most well-known kings. King Tewodros II (r. 1855–68) took a strong interest in modernizing and, in particular, acquiring military technology. In a famous international incident, he prevented missionaries from returning home, demanding that they cast a cannon for him. He is called *Tewodros məʿrabawi* (western Tewodros) in the *WP gädl*, perhaps because he hailed from the Qʷara region west of Lake Ṭana, on the edge of the Christian state geographically and culturally. *See* Crummey, Nosnitsin, and Sokolinskaia (2010). Mentioned in the extra texts of MS I only.

Thirty-Six Holy Women. Biblical figure. The Täwaḥədo Church believes that thirty-six women followed Christ, as well as the apostles and disciples; see Matthew 27:55–56, Mark 15:40–41, and Acts 1:12–15.

Tigré. ትግሬ Təgre. Local place. The Amharic name for a northern region of highland Ethiopia (called Təgray by its inhabitants), at least 150 miles north of Qʷäraṣa and northeast of Gondär. In WP's days, Təgray included parts of what is now Eritrea and was part of the highland Christian empire. The people of Təgray are mostly Təgrəñña speakers and Christian. Its most famous city and spiritual center was Aksum, and its southern boundary was usually the Täkkäze River. WP preaches in Təgray (in Ṣällämt), WP's brother dies in Təgray, and one of WP's miracles happens in Təgray. *See* Smidt (2010c).

Timqat. ጥምቀት Ṭəmqät. "Baptism." Religious occasion. The festival of *ṭəmqät* is one of the most important and unique rituals of the Täwaḥədo Church, in which priests bless all by sprinkling holy water on the faithful or immersing them in it. It is celebrated each year on 11 Ṭərr in commemoration of Christ's baptism in the river Jordan by John the Baptist (see Mark 1:9–13; Luke 3:21–22). Because of *ṭəmqät*'s proximity in time to Epiphany of Western Christian tradition, it is sometimes called that in early Western sources, even though *ṭəmqät* has little to do with it. Equally, *ṭəmqät* was sometimes incorrectly interpreted as an annual rebaptism by earlier Western visitors to Ethiopia, although it is commemorative only.

Tiqimt. ጥቅምት Ṭəqəmt. Temporal term. The second month of the year in the Ethiopian calendar, now extending from 12 October to 10 November in the modern Western calendar.

Tirr. ጥር Ṭərr. Temporal term. The fifth month of the year in the Ethiopian calendar, now extending from 9 January to 7 February in the modern Western calendar. It falls during the end of the windy season and the beginning of the dry season. Epiphany often happens during this month.

Torah. *See* Orit.

Town. ሀገር Hagär. Local place. A generic term that can be translated as town, district, or region. We have most often rendered it as "town," but such should not be understood to be the size of modern towns, but rather, as was typical of early modern settlements anywhere, a place where no more than a couple hundred lived.

Tsana. ጻና Ṣana. LOCAL PLACE. An island very close to shore in southwestern Lake Ṭana (indeed, it connects to the shore during the dry season) and about ten miles north of Qʷäraṣa. It is home to the monastery of Ṭana Qirqos (in this text called Ṣana Qirqos), one of the most important and ancient monasteries on Lake Ṭana, and the church of Məˁrafä Ǝgzəʾtənä Maryam (The Resting Place of Our Lady Mary). Some suggest that the name of the island comes from *ṣäˁana bä-dämmäna* (he put her on a cloud), a reference to the story about the Virgin Mary flying over Ethiopia on a cloud (Six 1999, 55). WP considered living there before deciding in favor of Məṣəlle; *Abba* Ṣäware Mäsqäl comes from Ṣana. *See* Six (2010b); Conti Rossini (1910). LatLon: 11.885577, 37.494106.

Tsana Qirqos. ጻና፡ቂርቆስ Ṣana Qirqos; but today Ṭana Qirqos. LOCAL PLACE. A monastery dedicated to Saint Qirqos on Ṣana Island, on the eastern shore of Lake Ṭana. One of the oldest and most important monasteries on Lake Ṭana and in Ethiopia, it is believed that the Ark of the Covenant rested there for six hundred years before it was moved to Aksum, that Saint Mary stopped there with the Holy Family when fleeing Herod, and that its first abbot was the son of a Jewish high priest from Jerusalem. Saint Qirqos is said to have saved his monastery from Aḥmad Grañ. It was a center for missionary activity in the region for several centuries. It had the status of a royal church, with significant funding from both Susənyos and Fasilädäs. ˁAṣqä Maryam seeks to go to this monastery to be healed by Saint Qirqos. *See* Six (2010b).

Tsawaaré Masqal. ጸዋሬ፡መስቀል Ṣäware Mäsqäl. "He who carries the cross." LOCAL PERSON. The abbot of Ṣana Island Monastery after the return of the Orthodox faith. A supporter of WP, *Abba* Ṣäware Mäsqäl said that he would grant Qʷäraṣa to her.

Tsédénya. *See* Feast of Tsédénya.

Tsegga Kristos. ጸጋ፡ክርስቶስ Ṣägga Krəstos. "The Grace of Christ." LOCAL PERSON. A learned theologian, originating from Amba Maryam, who is said to be competent to interpret the *Mäṣḥafä Ḥawi* (Comprehensive Book). He was probably not the Ṣägga Krəstos who was a well-known church leader and *əč̣č̣äge* (abbot) of Däbrä Libanos Monastery, active in the 1670s through the 1690s, since the *WP gädl* theologian was active in the 1630s.

Tsellemt. ጸለምት Ṣällämt. LOCAL PLACE. A region approximately 150 miles north of Lake Ṭana in what is now Təgray. It is directly east of Waldəbba, stretching from the Səmen Mountains north to the Täkkäze River. It was largely populated by the Betä Ǝsraʾel ethnic and religious group, and in 1623–24 Susənyos suppressed a rebellion there. It was such an important region that the eldest son of the king was generally appointed governor of it. WP went there from Waldəbba to preach, and one of her posthumous miracles happened to a farmer in this region. *See* Quirin (2010). LatLon: approximately 13.666171, 38.166477. Transcribed elsewhere as Salamt.

Tsigé Haymanot. ጽጌ፡ሃይማኖት Ṣəge Haymanot. "Flower of the Faith." LOCAL PERSON. A monk from Fure who went to visit WP in Robit and recommended that she meet Ǝḫətä Krəstos, who also lived in Fure. When the two women agreed to live together, *Abba* Ṣəge Haymanot arranged for Ǝḫ̮ətä Krəstos's sister to let her go and then secretly took WP and Ǝḫ̮ətä Krəstos to Ersənna before they went on to Robit to live there. Later, he joined the two women in Zäge, providing guidance. When WP secretly left for Waldəbba, she chastised him when he pursued her. He does not seem to appear in other historical sources.

Tsiyaat. ጽያት Ṣəyat. LOCAL PLACE. A town approximately one hundred miles east of Lake Ṭana. Although its exact location is not known, King Susənyos passed through it on his way from just south of Lalibela (at LatLon: 11.918416, 39.03437) to Ambassäl (a mountain range to the west of Lake Ḥayq at LatLon: 11.549998, 39.564308) (Täklä Śəllase [Ṭinno] 1900, 190). It was the first place that WP (and Ǝḫ̮ətä Krəstos and Wälättä Ṗawlos) fled to after the king established Roman Catholicism. *See* Huntingford (1989, 175); Merid Wolde Aregay (2003b). The error in CR, spelling the name with a final *n*, lead some scholars to say that WP went to the home of Zion, the Ark of the Covenant, which is Aksum (Cohen 2010b; Chernetsov 2005d), but nothing in the *WP gädl* suggests she went there.

Twelve Apostles. BIBLICAL FIGURE. Christ had twelve disciples of special prominence who were appointed apostles so that they could first be taught by Christ and then be sent by Christ to evangelize after his death. "These are the names of the twelve apostles [of Christ]: first, Simon (who is called Peter) and his brother Andrew; James son of Zebedee, and his brother John; Philip and Bartholomew; Thomas and Matthew the tax collector; James son of Alphaeus, and Thaddaeus; Simon the Zealot and Judas Iscariot, who betrayed him" (Matthew 10:2–4).

Unctionism. ቅባት Qəbat. RELIGIOUS TERM. A religious doctrine that originated during this period and was opposed to the Unionist doctrine. Unctionists (*qəbatočč*) professed that "The Father was the annointer, the son was the anointed, and the Holy Spirit was the ointment" (Täklä Śəllase [Ṭinno] 1900, 182). Regarding this debate, and the doctrine of Unctionism, *see* Tedros Abraha (2010); Getatchew Haile (2007a). The Unctionists were associated with the house of *Abba* Ewosṭatewos, and some argue that Unctionism emerged due to a sympathy for some Roman Catholic doctrine. The doctrine adopted by those in the house of Täklä Haymanot was Unionism (Revol-Tisset and Smidt 2005; Fiaccadori 2005). In the *WP gädl*, *Abba* Śəʿəlä Krəstos has a vision of *Abba* Ewosṭatewos. This, along with the MS Abb. 88 colophon alluding to Unctionism and the presence of the Unctionist *Abba* Fätlä Śəllase, suggests that WP's community leaned toward the House of Ewosṭatewos and were Unctionist.

Unionism. *See* Unctionist.

Walwaj. ዋልዋጅ Walwağ. LOCAL PLACE. A place in the Dämbəya region, north of Lake Ṭana and slightly northeast of Gondär. WP went there to see *Abunä* Marqos, the new patriarch. It was later a *gult* (fief) granted to the Gondär church of Däbrä Bərhan Śəllase by Iyasu I (Crummey 2000, 88–89, 181–82). Transcribed elsewhere as Walwaj, Ualag, Walaj, and Walag. It might be what is now known as Walwach, about five miles from Gondär, LatLon: 12.666802, 37.495394.

Walatta Giyorgis. ወለተ፡ጊዮርጊስ Wälättä Giyorgis. "Daughter of [Saint] George." HISTORICAL PERSON. The daughter of the former king Śärṣä Dəngəl (r. 1563–97) and Queen Maryam Śənna. Wälättä Giyorgis was a princess and a noblewoman of great wealth. She was also the wife of *Ras* Atənatewos, one of the highest members of King Susənyos's court, and the mother of Wälättä P̣awlos, who became a nun with WP. Wälättä Giyorgis and her husband had converted to Roman Catholicism early on. However, Atənatewos was then put on trial and exiled to the Amhara region in 1617 (Chernetsov 2003a). She presumably went with him, having also turned away from Roman Catholicism. Later, Susənyos put her on trial for arguing against Roman Catholicism (Páez 2011, 2:252). Before these events, however, Wälättä Giyorgis negotiated in the *WP gädl* between husband and wife for WP to return to Mälkəʾa Krəstos.

Walatta Giyorgis. ወለተ፡ጊዮርጊስ Wälättä Giyorgis. "Daughter of [Saint] George." HISTORICAL PERSON. The daughter of "Queen" Amätä Krəstos, the cousin of King Fasilädäs (r. 1632–67), and the wife of *Abeto* (Prince) Zä-Iyäsus. According to the *WP gädl*, Fasilädäs sent her to WP to be converted back to Orthodoxy from Catholicism, but it was not until after the death of Susənyos that Wälättä Giyorgis was converted back to Orthodoxy. However, as Ricci points out, some Jesuits report that Wälättä Giyorgis never reconverted to Orthodoxy but rather died in exile, a Catholic martyr. Almeida says she remained constant in the Catholic faith and was punished by Fasilädäs for it (1908, 209, 450–51), a view supported by others (Beccari 1913, 70–72, 102, 110–11). Mendes says that she was eventually sent to Däq Island to be converted by nuns but refused and so was tortured until she died in 1652 (1909, 335–41). Transcribed elsewhere as Oleta Ghiorghis.

Walatta Giyorgis. ወለተ፡ጊዮርጊስ Wälättä Giyorgis. "Daughter of [Saint] George." HISTORICAL PERSON. Woman mentioned in the twentieth miracle as queen (*nəgəśt*) during the twelfth year of King Iyoʾas I's reign (1767–68) and thus identified as the famous queen Məntəwwab (crown name Bərhan Mogäsa, 1706–73). Wälättä Giyorgis served an important role in Ethiopian leadership for almost fifty years as the mother of Iyasu II and the grandmother and regent for Iyoʾas I. She was the wife of Bäkaffa and the mother of Wälättä Täklä Haymanot, who also figures in the miracle. *See* Berry (2003b). She appears in documents as "Wälättä Giyorgis" or "Bərhan Mogäsa" (Crummey 2000, 94). It cannot be her contemporary, Iyasu I's wife Walatta Giyorgis (Mammit), because that woman died in 1723. Mentioned in the extra texts of MSS H and I only.

Walatta Kristos. ወለተ፡ክርስቶስ Wälättä Krəstos. "Daughter of Christ." LOCAL PERSON. A woman who was with WP when Susənyos sent her to her husband Mälkəʾa Krəstos's house in Azäzo to be converted, but who fled when WP was banished to Žäbäy. She may be the same woman as *Wäyzäro* Wälättä Krəstos, who is also associated in the *WP gädl* with a place near the court in Gondär.

Walatta Kristos. ወለተ፡ክርስቶስ [*Wäyzäro*] Wälättä Krəstos. "Daughter of Christ." LOCAL PERSON. A noblewoman with whom WP stayed in Žan Fäqära, north of Gondär, when she was looking for a place to set up a monastery. In a later episode, a sick woman named Wälättä Kristos appears, but without the honorific *wäyzäro* and who is said to be from Fure, but she was probably the same woman. The text often omits honorifics in later instances. Further, this sick Wälättä

Krəstos unabashedly ordered WP around, just as a *wäyzäro* might do. WP even dispatched messengers to the court to indulge the sick woman's whimsical dietary wishes, as one would do for an aristocrat. Everyone at court responded to the call, as if they knew the woman, and a *Wäyzäro* Wälättä Krəstos appeared looking for the dietary object "herself." Finally, while ill people were not required to fast, the ascetic members of WP's community would most likely have kept to the fast of Lent, reinforcing the idea that this woman was a *wäyzäro* and not a nun. Thus, she was probably a different Wälättä Krəstos than the woman much earlier in the *WP gädl* who fled when WP was banished to Žäbäy.

Walatta Maryam. ወለተ:ማርያም Wälättä Maryam. "Daughter of [Saint] Mary." Local person. A woman in WP's community at Afär Färäs who was a close friend. After parting once, the *WP gädl* says that the two did not separate from each other until they died. It was Wälättä Maryam whom WP thought she was talking to when she saw a vision while living at Afer Faras; whom God caused to refuse to eat so he could reveal his power through the servant Ilarya; who witnessed, in Sädäçəlla, WP's advance knowledge of death; who was attacked for causing WP to remain at court; and who was reunited with her forever when WP prayed that they not be parted.

Walatta Maseeh. ወለተ:መሲሕ Wälättä Mäsiḥ. "Daughter of the Messiah." Local person. A woman who was the prioress (*liqä räd'ənnät*) of the Qʷäraṣa Monastery at some point after 1681. Mentioned in the extra texts of MS J only.

Walatta Pawlos. ወለተ:ጳውሎስ Wälättä P̣awlos. "Daughter of [Saint] Paul." Local person. The daughter of *Ras* Atənatewos and *Wäyzäro* Wälättä Giyorgis. Atənatewos helped Susənyos come to power but was then sidelined and eventually even put on trial by the monarch and exiled to the Amhara region in 1617 (Chernetsov 2003a). Wälättä P̣awlos's mother, Wälättä Giyorgis, was the daughter of King Śärṣä Dəngəl, which would make Wälättä P̣awlos the granddaughter of a king and a high-ranking noblewoman. Wälättä P̣awlos became a nun at approximately the time that WP and Ǝḫətä Krəstos did, in 1617, perhaps partly because her father and mother had just been exiled from the court. She was with WP when she entered Zäge.

Walatta Petros. ወለተ:ጴጥሮስ Wälättä P̣eṭros. "Daughter of [Saint] Peter." Historical person. An important female saint of the Täwaḥədo Church and the subject of the *WP gädl.* She was born in 1592 to Baḥər Säggäd and Krəstos ʿƎbäya; she died on Sunday, 24 November 1642 CE (17 Ḫədar 1634 EC) at the age of fifty. She was married to Mälkəʾa Krəstos and gave birth to three children (*wəlud,* which might mean just sons or sons and daughters) who died in infancy. She refused to convert to Roman Catholicism and inspired many to do the same. She set up seven religious communities, in this order: Žäbäy, Ç̣anqʷa, Məṣelle, Zäge, Dämboza, Afär Färäs, and Zäbol/Zämbol. Her gädl was completed in 1672–73. Transcribed elsewhere as Wälätä, Wallatta, Walatta, Wallata, Walata, Walete, Waleta, Walleta, Waletta, Welete, Wolata plus Pétros, P̣əṭros, Pietros, and Petrus. *See* the "Introduction to the Text" in this volume for extensive information about the saint.

Walatta Sillasé. ወለተ:ሥላሴ Wälättä Śəllase. "Daughter of the Trinity." Local person. An elderly nun especially devoted to WP at Qʷäraṣa. Mentioned in the extra texts of MS I only.

Walatta Takla Haymanot. ወለተ፡ተክለ፡ሃይማኖት Wälättä Täklä Haymanot. "Daughter of [Saint] Takla Haymanot." Historical person. The eldest daughter of King Bäkaffa and Queen Wälättä Giyorgis (Məntəwwab), and thus a younger sister of King Iyasu II (r. 1730–55). Her marriage to *Ras* Elyas is noted in the royal chronicle of Iyasu II (Anonymous 1912, 35). That husband was killed in 1733, so Finḥas, who appears as her spouse in the context of a WP miracle, presumably was a second husband in the 1760s. Mentioned in the extra texts of MSS H and I only.

Walatta Takla Haymanot. ወለተ፡ተክለ፡ሃይማኖት Wälättä Täklä Haymanot. "Daughter of [Saint] Takla Haymanot." Local person. The abbess of Qʷäraṣa at some point after 1681. At least three abbesses preceded her, since the earliest ones were Ǝḫətä Krəstos, Amätä Dəngəl, and Nazrawit. Since she is called *Wäyzäro* Wälättä Täklä Haymanot and is in possession of a valuable manuscript, she may be the other Wälättä Täklä Haymanot who appears in the miracles, the eldest daughter of King Bäkaffa and Queen Wälättä Giyorgis. She is called the senior Wəbit (Beautiful One), and thus was the mother or older sister to Bərhan Mädḫanitu. *Wäyzäro* Wälättä Täklä Haymanot and *Wäyzäro* Bərhan Mädḫanitu sold MS J to *Däǧǧazmač* Iyasu and *Näggadras* Asahel. Mentioned in the extra texts of MS J only.

Waldeba. ዋልድባ Waldəbba. Local place. A region 150 miles north of Lake Ṭana in a rugged, relatively lowland area between the town of Däbarq and the Täkkäze River. It is famous for its three monasteries, which claim to have hosted the Holy Family on its flight from Herod, and for the extreme asceticism of its monks. According to Kindeneh Endeg Mihretie (2014), "Waldəba is the emblem of monasticism. Its isolation and reputation as the site of the utmost rigorous monastic asceticism has made it the metaphor for the pursuit of spiritual life in the form of extreme self-denial." Waldəbba has two monastic houses: Betä Minas and Betä Ṭama. Its monasteries are idiorythmic (*qʷərit*), in which members live as hermits, dispersed over a large area and with little communal life. As one of the leading monastic centers in the country, Waldəbba was favored as a spiritual retreat by nobles, many of whom are buried there. WP took up her ascetic life there, and several texts have noted that it was a popular retreat for noblewomen (Bruce 1813a, 283; Salt 1967, 293). During WP's period, it was a hotbed of anti-Catholic sentiment (Cohen 2010b). *See* Saporito, Kosinctz, and le Cadre (2012) ; Nosnitsin (2010g). Videos filmed about the place can be found online, such as www.youtube.com/watch?v=jmuXs0qQycw. Transcribed elsewhere as Wäldebba, Waldaba, Waldebba, Waldiba, Waldibba, Weldebba, Woldeba, Woldebba, and Uoldebba. LatLon: 13.628598, 37.792110.

Waseef. ወጺፍ Wäṣif. *See* Righteous Ones of Waseef.

Wəddase Maryam. See *Praise for Our Lady.*

Wolde Giyorgis. ወልደ፡ጊዮርጊስ Wäldä Giyorgis. "Son of [Saint] George." Local person. A scribe of one of the copies of the *WP gädl.* The spelling MS Abb. 88 is quite peculiar, namely, ወልደ፡ጌዎርጊስ Wäldä Geworgis.

Wolde Nagodgwaad. ወልደ:ነጐድጓድ Wäldä Näg^{w}ädg^{w}ad. "Son of the Thunder." HISTORICAL PERSON. An important eighteenth-century historical figure and grandson of *Wäyzäro* Mammit. He is discussed in the royal chronicles (Anonymous 1912, 11, 123, 133, 141, 145, 201, 204, 237, 238). In the *WP gädl*, Wäldä Näg^{w}ädg^{w}ad made his appearance as a military officer who was dispatched by King Iyoʾas I (r. 1755–69), along with five hundred troops, to capture and return Wälättä Täklä Haymanot to the court. Transcribed elsewhere as Walda Naguadguad. Mentioned in the extra texts of MSS H and I only.

Wolqait. ወልቃይት Wälqayt. LOCAL PLACE. A rugged region in northern Ethiopia (directly northwest of Wäldəbba) to which eighteenth-century kings regularly exiled enemies (Nosnitsin 2010h). Transcribed elsewhere as Wälqayit, Walkait, Welkayit, and Wolkayit. LatLon: 13.491928, 37.368611. Mentioned in the extra texts of MSS H and I only.

Wonchet. ወንጬት Wänçät. LOCAL PLACE. A town about five miles directly east of Q^{w}äraṣa, to the east of southern Lake Ṭana. Today it is on Highway 3 about fifteen miles north of Baḥər Dar. WP spends a night in this town upon leaving her husband, and *Abba* Mänkər, as well as a thieving woman (the latter in the MS I miracles only), come from there. LatLon: 11.789391, 37.548523. Transcribed elsewhere as Wanche, Wenchet, Wonchit, Uanche, Uanchet, and Uanchit.

Wondigé. ወንድጌ Wändəge. "Men's land." LOCAL PLACE. A town near the southwestern shore of Lake Ṭana, perhaps five to ten miles west of the Gəlgäl Abbay, that briefly served as an imperial capital for King Zä-Dəngəl in 1603–4 (Pankhurst 1982, 101); thus, near LatLon: 11.667703, 37.003906. WP went there to get wood for building the *säqäla* on Rema Island. Since some palace building went on there (Pankhurst 1992, 105; Munro-Hay 2002, 74), perhaps building materials were still available there after it stopped being a capital. Transcribed elsewhere as Wandge, Wandegé, Wainadga, Wendige, Wendige, Ondega, and Ondegue.

Woodage Asahel. ውዳጅ:አሳሄል Wədağ Asahel. "Friend of Asahel." HISTORICAL PERSON. A famous eighteenth-century Oromo military leader who has been frequently discussed, described, and even drawn by James Bruce (1813c, 100–101). Born in the Damot region of Goğğam Province, he was the bitter enemy of *Ras* Mikaʾel, and so often engaged in horseback upon the field that some claimed they had never seen him walk. He died in battle in approximately 1770. Gəʿəz names often have a possessive construction like this (e.g., "Daughter of Peter," "Servant of Christ," "Plant of the faith"), but this name is unusual not only in using a variant of the Amharic word *wädağ* (friend) but also in displaying imperfect Gəʿəz grammar (the ultimately correct form would have been Wädağä Asahel). Asahel was a biblical character, a nephew of King David and among his mightiest warriors, which perhaps explains the appellation for this military leader. *See* Sokolinskaia (2014). Transcribed elsewhere as Asahel Woodage or Woodaje Asahel. Mentioned in the extra texts of MSS H and I only.

Wot. ወጥ Wäṭ. FOOD. The generic name for the variety of stews that are served with *ənğära* (a flat bread made of *ṭef*) at most Ethiopian meals. On fasting days, it would be a vegetable stew, like *šəro wäṭ* (lentil stew), often with greens. On nonfasting days, if the family was not poor, it might be a meat stew, often spiced with red peppers, such as *doro wäṭ* (chicken stew) or *yä-śəga qäyy wäṭ* (beef with red stew). Another generic name for stew in Gəˁəz is *ṣäbḫ* and in Təgrəñña *ṣäbḥi.*

Woybila. ወይብላ Wäybəla. LOCAL PLACE. A town near Lake Ṭana less than five miles northeast of Qʷäraṣa; LatLon: 11.79709, 37.478506. It is where the lame man Ṗeṭros came from and where there is said to be a copy of the *Gädlä Wälättä Ṗeṭros* in the Saint Mary Church. It is quite possibly the same town as Wäybəna (*see* Woybina), with a linguistic shift from *-bəna* in the earlier recorded miracles to *-bəla* in the later recorded miracles (Cheesman locates this town, which he spells Waibela, south of Lake Ṭana, very near Mota, LatLon: 11.111032, 37.866697, but that is not this place). Mentioned in the extra texts of MS I only.

Woybina. ወይብና Wäybəna. LOCAL PLACE. A town on Lake Ṭana, perhaps five miles from Ṭana Qirqos, according to locals. The monk ˁAṣqä Maryam came from this town when WP performed a miracle of healing for him. It appears to have a church named Məˁrafä Ǝgzəʾtənä Maryam (the Resting Place of Our Lady Mary), which may be a reference to the folklore that the Holy Family, including Mary, traveled through Ethiopia when fleeing Herod. It is quite possibly the same town as Wäybəla (*see* Wäybəla), with a linguistic shift from *-bəna* in the earlier recorded miracles to *-bəla* in the later recorded miracles. It is not the town Weybla, Weyibla, or Wäybəla nor the town on northern Lake Ṭana now known as Wäyna Kidanä Məḥrät (transcribed elsewhere as Waina Kedanemehret or Waina Kidane Mehret) (Cheesman 1936, 195). LatLon: 12.299081, 37.43454.

Woynayat. ወይናያት Wäynayät. LOCAL PLACE. A town that is said to be the home of *Abba* Fätlä Śəllase and Wälättä Giyorgis, two important members of the court. It might be the town now called Wäyna on the northern shore of Lake Ṭana, about thirty miles south of Gondär and ten miles east of Gorgora. LatLon: 12.283168, 37.431514.

Woyzaro. ወይዘሮ Wäyzäro. "Princess, Lady." TITLE. The title for all direct female descendants of kings, even if they were many generations removed. WP and Ǝḫətä Krəstos were both noblewomen but were not called *wäyzäro* in the *WP gädl.* Such wealthy women commanded respect and would have servants. Some of the *wäyzäro* who appear in the *WP gädl* are the king's daughter Wälättä Giyorgis and wealthy WP patrons Wälättä Krəstos and Krəstosawit. Following the typical commonalization pattern of aristocratic titles of address, *wäyzäro* now means "Mrs." Transcribed elsewhere as Woyzero, today commonly abbreviated as W/z. *See* "The Text and Ḥabäša Noblewomen's Anticolonial Role" in this volume.

Wubeet. *See* Birhan Madhaneetu and Walatta Takla Haymanot.

Wudo. ውዶ Wəddo. LOCAL PLACE. A region where WP's husband Mälkəʾa Krəstos set up his regiment, about twenty miles east of Lake Ṭana, near Aringo. LatLon: 11.872055, 37.932774. *See* Bosc-Tiessé (2008, 277, 280, 419). Transcribed elsewhere as Wäddo, Wedo, Weddo, and Uedo.

Yafqərännä Ǝgziʾ. *See* Afqaranna Egzee.

Yamaana Kristos. የማነ፡ክርስቶስ Yämanä Krəstos. "Right Hand of Christ." LOCAL

PERSON. One of the monks from Rema who met with WP while she was still married to help her leave her husband's home and take her to Zäge. *Abba* Yämanä Krəstos also served as her boatman.

Yamaana Kristos. የማነ፡ክርስቶስ Yämanä Krəstos. "Right Hand of Christ." LOCAL PERSON. A Yämanä Krəstos who had just died appeared in the sixth miracle as an abbot of a monastery at Gərarya.

Year. *See* Calendar.

Yekkateet. የካቲት Yäkkatit. TEMPORAL TERM. The sixth month of the Ethiopian calendar, now extending from 8 February to 9 March (in non–leap years) in the modern Western calendar.

Yimera. ይመራ Yəmära. LOCAL PLACE. This must be a stream or creek very near Qʷäraṣa, as the community is said to have lived in Qʷäraṣa "beyond the river Yəmära" from 1650 to 1652. It does not appear in other sources. Qʷäraṣa now lies between two rivers that empty into Lake Ṭana: the Gälda River to the south at LatLon: 11.738563, 37.423667 and the Ǝsure River to the north at LatLon: 11.900387, 37.489348. Mentioned in the extra texts of MSS I and J only.

Yohannes. ዮሐንስ Yoḥannəs. "John." LOCAL PERSON. WP's fifth brother. He beseeched Fasilädäs, son of King Susənyos and heir to the throne, to ask his father to release WP from her exile at Žäbäy. When her brother died in Təgray on Mäskäräm 1, while WP was living at Amba Maryam, WP mourned him greatly, celebrated his *täzkar*, and later sent for his body to be brought back from Təgray to be buried on Rema Island.

Yohannes. *See* Zara Yohannes.

Yohannes I. ዮሐንስ Yoḥannəs. "John." HISTORICAL PERSON. The fourth son of King Fasilädäs and the king of Ethiopia from 1667 to 1682. King Yoḥannəs I's regnal name was Aʾlaf Säggäd (The multitudes submit [to him]). It was in the fifth year of his reign that the *Gädlä Wälättä Ṗeṭros* was written. During his reign, many religious controversies regarding the nature of Christ continued, stirred up in part by the presence of the Jesuits earlier in the century. For instance, Yoḥannəs issued a decree in his first year, 1668, that all remaining Catholics had to leave the kingdom or convert to Orthodoxy, and in 1669 he had them marched out. He was a follower of the Unctionist (Qəbat) doctrine, but in 1680 the Unionist doctrine was affirmed. He made almost constant military campaigns against the peoples south of Lake Ṭana, and religious wars broke out in Təgray. In the early 1670s, he sent the Armenian merchant Murād on a mission to India and Batavia. He is buried on Məṣraḥa Island. *See* Berry (2014).

Yohannes II. ዮሐንስ Yoḥannəs. "John." HISTORICAL PERSON. The son of King Iyasu I, brother of King Bäkaffa and King Täklä Haymanot I, and the father of King Täklä Giyorgis I and King Täklä Haymanot II. He ruled very briefly, only from May to October of 1769, when *Ras* Mikaʾel brought him down from the royal prison to rule. At that time, he was more than seventy years old and not interested in military matters. Although it is often said that *Ras* Mikaʾel had him killed, he died after a long illness (Bekele 2002). *See* Dege (2014). In direct contrast to this reputation, the extra miracles praise him as a righteous ruler who led many to believe and killed the godless, which suggests that the author may have confused the characters of King Yoḥannəs I with King Yoḥannəs II. Mentioned in the extra texts of MS I only.

Yolyos. ዮልዮስ Yolyos. "Julius." Historical person. A nobleman who betrayed Susənyos and supported the Täwaḥədo Church. Yolyos started off as a lowly lieutenant to Susənyos before the latter became king but rose through the ranks. In 1607, Susənyos married him to his daughter Mäläkotawit and made him the governor of Goǧǧam. In 1609, however, Yolyos participated in a plot against Susənyos. Although Susənyos pardoned him, Yolyos embarked on a decadelong conflict with *Ras* Śəʿəlä Krəstos, partly because Susənyos gave *Ras* Śəʿəlä Krəstos lands in Goǧǧam. By 1614, Yolyos was an active enemy of the Catholics, and the emperor executed him for rebellion in 1617. He was a hero to the anti-Catholics. *See* Toubkis (2014).

Ž. *See* Zh.

Zabol. *See* Zambowl.

Zacharias. ዘካርያስ Zäkaryas. Biblical figure. A priest and the father of John the Baptist by Elizabeth, who was a cousin of the Virgin Mary. An angel told Zacharias that his barren wife would conceive a child who would prophesy the coming of the Lord (Luke 1:13). Sometimes also called Zachary or Zechariah, but not to be confused with the Old Testament prophet Zechariah. In chapter 24 of the *Gädlä Wälättä Ṗeṭros*, the scribe invokes him as a good example of someone who did not immediately believe strange messengers.

Za-Dinghil. ዘድንግል Zä-Dəngəl. "He of the Virgin [Mary]." Local person. WP's fourth brother, an important lord of the court. When WP left her husband for the second time, she went to live with this brother. Then she secretly left his house to become a nun. Later, he invited her to live on his land near Ǝnfraz. Not to be confused with the king of the same name who ruled from 1603 to 1604.

Zafara Mikaél. ዘፈረ፡ሚካኤል Zäfärä Mikaʾel. "Hem of [Saint] Michael['s garment]." Local person. A teacher in WP's community at some unknown time, when it had houses in Dämbəya, Gondär, and Dämboza; thus, probably in the 1700s. Mentioned in the extra texts of MS I only.

Zagé. ዘጌ Zäge. Local place. A forested peninsula on the narrow southernmost end of Lake Ṭana, about twelve miles west of Baḥər Dar, and one of the most important monastic centers in seventeenth-century Ethiopia. It is now famous for its seven monasteries (Wərra or Ura Kidanä Məḥrät, Aswa Maryam, Däbrä Śəllase, Bäträ Maryam, Maḥəl Zäge Giyorgis, Fəre Maryam, and Təgända Täklä Haymanot), which house some of the most beautiful church frescoes in Ethiopia. WP founded the fourth of her religious communities at Zäge; later, many people died of the plague in this community. The *WP gädl* appears to imply that there was only one monastery there in the seventeenth century by saying that WP went to "Zäge" rather than naming any particular monastery there. However, this may be due to its plethora of religious communities; in the nineteenth century it had more than two hundred (Balicka-Witakowska 2014). Belcher and Selamawit Mecca digitized one of the manuscripts of the *Gädlä Wälättä Ṗeṭros* used for this volume at the Zäge monastery of Bäträ Maryam. Zäge was also a trading port on Lake Ṭana. LatLon: 11.708384, 37.331886. Transcribed elsewhere as Zage.

Za-Hawaryaat. ዘሐዋርያት Zä-Ḥawaryat. "He of the Apostles." LOCAL PERSON. A monk who joined WP at her fifth community, Dämboza. Later she appointed *Abba* Zä-Ḥawaryat as the superior of the monks in her seventh community, Zäbol/Zämbol, and he served after her death for more than forty years. WP explained to him alone the reason for the plague that killed so many of them. Oral tradition in Qʷäraṣa has it that an *Abba* Zä-Ḥawaryat founded the monastery there during Fasilädäs's reign (1632–67) (Bosc-Tiessé 2000, 237). The *Short History of WP's Community* confirms this, saying that he was appointed in April–May 1642 (Ḫədar 1634 EC), just six months before WP died. He was abbot for many years, dying on 29 August 1681 (26 Näḥase 1673 EC), the fourteenth year of Yoḥannəs I's reign. Blessings are called upon a man with his name in MS J, further confirming that he was the abbot of WP's community when the author wrote the *WP gädl.*

Za-Iyasus. ዘኢየሱስ Zä-Iyäsus. "He of Jesus." HISTORICAL PERSON. Probably the important seventeenth-century cleric known as *Abunä* Zä-Iyäsus ʿƎwwur (Zä-Iyäsus the Blind), who appears in the royal chronicles of Yoḥannəs I and Iyasu I and was repeatedly excommunicated for his Unctionist (Qəbat) views in the 1680s. He became an important figure in Unctionist historiography and is portrayed in the so-called *Short Chronicles* as active during the reign of Fasilädäs, which is unlikely (Wion 2014). In the *Short History of WP's Community,* he is said to have ordained the "Rules for the House of Our Mother Walatta Petros" in the 1680s. He died in 1687. This would further associate her community with Unctionist teaching. Mentioned in the extra texts of MS I only.

Za-Manfas Qidduus. ዘመንፈስ፡ቅዱስ Zä-Mänfäs Qəddus. "He of the Holy Spirit." LOCAL PERSON. WP's second brother. He probably was not the governor of Goǧǧam of the same name who converted to Roman Catholicism in 1613 but then rebelled against King Susənyos and was killed on 1 June 1626. Transcribed elsewhere as Manfas Qaddus, Menfes Kidus (without the initial *zä-* being reflected).

Za-Maryam. ዘማርያም Zä-Maryam. "He of [Saint] Mary." LOCAL PERSON. A priest and the superior of Rema Monastery when WP was living in Dämboza. *Abba* Zä-Maryam asked WP to construct a church building on Rema. Later she summoned him to her deathbed. His name can be added to the incomplete list of abbots of Rema in Hammerschmidt (1977a, 168).

Za-Maryam Esaat Ba-Afu. ዘማርያም፡እሳት፡በአፉ Zä-Maryam Ǝsat Bä-Afu. "He of [Saint] Mary—In his mouth is fire" (Gəʿəz and Amharic mixed). LOCAL PERSON. The second abbot of WP's community, succeeding *Abba* Zä-Ḥawaryat in 1681. In MS J, *Abba* Maryam Ǝsat Bä-Afu's name is spelled *Zä-Maryam Ǝsat Bä-Afa* (He of [Saint] Mary—In her mouth is fire [Gəʿəz and Amharic mixed]).

Zambowl. ዘምቦል Zämbol. LOCAL PLACE. The seventh of WP's religious communities. Zämbol is an unidentified town on Lake Ṭana in the district of Läg and thus near Zäge and the Gəlgäl Abbay River; near LatLon: 11.806468, 37.172926. It can be reached by *tank*^{w}*a* from Afär Färäs, according to the *WP gädl*. It appears to have been her largest community, with nine hundred people. It is not Zebul/Zobil, which is at least one hundred miles east of Lake Ṭana. Zämbol appears mostly as Zäbol in MSS H, I, and Abb. 88. The fact that the name is written differently in different manuscripts suggests that perhaps the place was unknown to later scribes and was a village that disappeared once WP's community left.

Za-Mikaél. ዘሚካኤል Zä-Mika'el. "He of [the Archangel] Michael." Local person. A priest of WP's community whom WP allowed to see her on her deathbed. *Abba* Zä-Mika'el was there at the very end with only three other priests.

Zara Yohannes. ዘርአ፡ዮሐንስ Zär'a Yoḥannəs. "Offspring of [Saint] John." Local person. A monk who died at Amba Maryam, from which (or to which) he had been exiled. WP commemorated his death not long after the restoration of the Orthodox faith. *Abunä Abba* Zär'a Yoḥannəs may have been a high-ranking member of WP's community, but since *abunä abba* can mean patriarch, perhaps he was treated as the Orthodox patriarch for the ten years that Mendes was the official patriarch during the period of Roman Catholicism. He cannot be Patriarch Yoḥannəs who arrived from Egypt in 1650 and who was rejected and exiled to Särka, because WP died in 1642 (Wion 2007b). His name is shortened to Yoḥannəs in MS Abb. 88.

Zarephath. *See* Sarepta.

Za-Sillasé. ዘሥላሴ Zä-Śəllase. "He of the Trinity." Local person. A priest of WP's community who witnessed two of her miracles during her lifetime. When she blessed *Abba* Zä-Śəllase before he went fishing, he caught thirteen fish, which matched the number of the Twelve Apostles plus Christ, and when WP commanded his clothes to be like leather, they indeed lasted for many years.

Zhan Feqera. ዠን፡ፈቀራ Žan Fäqära. Local place. A town about twenty miles directly north of Gondär and south of Dabat. WP considered it as a possible site for one of her communities and saw an angel there. LatLon: 13.000544, 37.764027. Transcribed elsewhere as Janfenkera, Janfenkere, Janifenkera, and Žān Faqarā.

Zhebey. ዠበይ Žäbäy. Local place. WP founded the first of her religious communities in Žäbäy while exiled to and imprisoned there for three years by King Susənyos. In the *WP gädl*, Žäbäy was a hot region where people were familiar with Sudan Arabic. This region was on the border with Sudan, at least one hundred miles west of Lake Ṭana, but its exact latitude is unclear (Lindahl 2008). Although the place appears as "Žäbäy" in most of the WP manuscripts, there are also the variants Žäbäy and Žäbäl in MS Abb. 88, with Žäbäl being dominant. Žäbäl could easily be derived from Arabic *ǧabal* (mountain), and thus appear in the *WP gädl* as a generic name for the border region with Sudan, where the foothills of the mountains of Ethiopia begin. Žäbäl was also likely the original name because an *l* to *y* change (palatization) frequently occurs in Ethio-Semitic languages. Transliterated elsewhere as Gebel, Jabal, Jebel, or Zeba. LatLon: between 13.667338,36.385002 (Žäbäl Nahut, Jabal Nahut) in the north and 9.550000, 34.100278 (Žäbäl Manga, Jabal Manga) in the south.

Zikra Maryam. ዝክረ፡ማርያም Zəkrä Maryam. "Commemoration of [Saint] Mary."

LOCAL PERSON. An *abba* of WP's community at Angära who attacked WP when she asked him to dig graves for those who had died in an epidemic.

Zimri. *See* Phinehas.

Zira. ዝራ Zəra. LOCAL PLACE. One of the miracles posthumously worked by WP happened in this place. Many places have the similar name of Zara, some quite far from Lake Ṭana, but this is probably Zara in southeastern Lake Ṭana; LatLon: 11.817174, 37.598597. Alternatively, this might be Zärʾa Buruk, about twenty-five miles south of Lake Ṭana at LatLon: 11.235317, 37.48275.

WORKS CITED

Abbadie, Antoine d'. 1859. *Catalogue raisonné de manuscrits éthiopiens.* Paris: Editions.

———. 1890. *Géographie de l'Ethiopie: Ce que j'ai entendu, faisant suite à ce que j'ai vu.* Paris: Mesnil.

Abbink, Jon. 2007. "Mika'el 'Səḥul.'" *Encyclopaedia Aethiopica*, ed. Siegbert Uhlig. Vol. 3, *He–N*, 962–64. Wiesbaden: Harrassowitz.

Addis Ababa University Library. 1970. *Annual Report.* Addis Ababa: Addis Ababa University Library.

Admasu Addi. 2003. "Bees and Beekeeping." *Encyclopaedia Aethiopica*, ed. Siegbert Uhlig. Vol. 1, *A–C*, 515–16. Wiesbaden: Harrassowitz.

Almeida, Manoel de. 1908. *Historia Aethiopiae.* Ed. Camillo Beccari. Vol. 7 of Rerum aethiopicarum scriptores occidentales inediti a saeculo XVI ad XIX. Rome: C. de Luigi.

Alvares, Francisco. 1881. *Narrative of the Portuguese Embassy to Abyssinia during the Years 1520–1527.* Ed. Henry Edward John Stanley. London: Hakluyt Society.

Alvarez, Francisco. 1961. *The Prester John of the Indies.* Ed. C. F. Beckingham and George Wynn Brereton Huntingford. Cambridge: University of Cambridge Press.

Amborn, Hermann. 2010. "Ṭälla." *Encyclopaedia Aethiopica*, ed. Siegbert Uhlig. Vol. 4, *O–X*, 848–49. Wiesbaden: Harrassowitz.

Andrzejewski, B. W., Stanislaw Piłaszewicz, and Witold Tyloch. 1985. *Literatures in African Languages: Theoretical Issues and Sample Surveys.* Cambridge: Cambridge University Press.

Anonymous. 1800s. "Walatta Petros (for 17 Ḫədar)." *Synaxarium* (*Ethio-SPaRe MKL-019*), f. 91vc–92vb. Tegray, Ethiopia: Läqay Kidanä Məḥrät Church.

———. 1845. "Berigten." *Algemeene konst-en letterbode voor het jaar 1845* 29, no. 2 (11 July): 15–20.

———. 1898. *The Lives of Maba' Seyon and Gabra Krestos.* Trans. E. A. Wallis Budge. Lady Meux manuscript. Vol. 1. London: W. Griggs.

———. 1900s. "Walatta Petros (for 17 Ḫədar)." *Synaxarium* (*Ethio-SPaRe MKL-003*), f. 91vc–92vb. Tegray, Ethiopia: Medrä Ruba Däbrä Gännät Qəddəst Śəllase Church.

———. 1903a. *Annales Iohannis I, Iyasu I, et Bakaffa: I* [*Iohannis I en Français*]. Trans. Ignatius Guidi. Ed. Ignatius Guidi. Corpus Scriptorum Christianorum Orientalium 23: Scriptores Aethiopici 6. Versio: Series Altra. Paris: E. Typographeo Reipublicae.

———. 1903b. *Annales Iohannis I, Iyasu I, et Bakaffa: III* [*Bakaffa en Français*]. Trans. Ignatius Guidi. Ed. Ignatius Guidi. Corpus Scriptorum Christianorum Orientalium 25: Scriptores Aethiopici 8. Paris: E. Typographeo Reipublicae.

———. 1912. *Annales Regum Iyasu II et Iyo'as* [*en Français*]. Ed. Ignatius Guidi. Corpus Scriptorum Christianorum Orientalium 66: Scriptores Aethiopici 29. Paris, Leipzig: E. Typogropleo Republicae, Otto Harrossowitz.

———. 1983. *Ṭānāsee 106: Eine Chronik der Herrscher Äthiopiens.* Äthiopistische Forschungen 12B. Wiesbaden: Franz Steiner.

———. 1994. *Haymanotä Abäw.* Addis Abba: Tensae Printing Press.

———. 2002. *Gädlä Fəqərtä Krəstos* [*The Life of Fəqərtä Krəstos: In the Original Ge'ez and Translated into Amharic*]. Trans. Mäl'akä Gännät Mənasse Zälläqä. Addis Ababa, Ethiopia: Tənśa'e zä-guba'e.

———. 2012. *The Book of the Elders: Sayings of the Desert Fathers; The Systematic Collection.* Trans. John Wortley. Trappist, KY: Liturgical Press.

———. n.d. [2000s]. "Lä-tabotä ṣəyon maräfiya lä-ḥəggwa lä-śərʿatwa mäfäṣṣämiya mähon [The Ark of the Covenant Came to Rest so that the Law and the Tradition Could Be Fulfilled]." *Yä-Ṭana Qirqos tarikawi-nna ṭəntawi yä-abbatočč-ənna yä-ənnatočč andənnät gädam [The Historical and Ancient Fathers' and Mothers' Coenobitic Monastery of Ṭana Qirqos]*. Gondär, Ethiopia: Saint Gabriel Printing Press.

Appiah, Anthony, and Henry Louis Gates. 2005. "Walatta Petros." *Africana: The Encyclopedia of the African and African American Experience. 2nd ed.*, 336. New York: Basic Books.

ʿArab Faqīh, Šihāb ad-Dīn Aḥmad bin ʿAbd al-Qāder [sic] bin Sālem [sic] bin ʿUṯmān. 2005. *Futūḥ Al-Ḥabaša: The Conquest of Abyssinia (Sixteenth Century).* Trans. Paul Lester Stenhouse. Hollywood, CA: Tsehai Publishers.

Ayele Takla Haymanot. 1982. *The Ethiopian Church and Its Christological Doctrine.* Addis Ababa: Graphic Printers.

Bairu Tafla. 2003. "Däǧǧazmač." *Encyclopaedia Aethiopica*, ed. Siegbert Uhlig. Vol. 1, *A–C*, 62. Wiesbaden: Harrassowitz.

Balicka-Witakowska, Ewa. 2005a. "Equestrian Saints." *Encyclopaedia Aethiopica*, ed. Siegbert Uhlig. Vol. 2, *D–Ha*, 349–51. Wiesbaden: Harrassowitz.

———. 2005b. "George of Lydda: Iconography of St. George in Ethiopia." *Encyclopaedia Aethiopica*, ed. Siegbert Uhlig. Vol. 2, *D–Ha*, 764–66. Wiesbaden: Harrassowitz.

———. 2010. "Qirqos." *Encyclopaedia Aethiopica*, ed. Siegbert Uhlig. Vol. 4, *O–X*, 292–94. Wiesbaden: Harrassowitz.

———. 2014. "Zäge." *Encyclopaedia Aethiopica*, ed. Siegbert Uhlig. Vol. 5, *Y–Z*, 104–6. Wiesbaden: Harrassowitz.

Bandrés, José L., and Ugo Zanetti. 2003. "Christology." *Encyclopaedia Aethiopica*, ed. Siegbert Uhlig. Vol. 1, *A–C*, 728–32. Wiesbaden: Harrassowitz.

Barradas, Manoel. 1906. *Tractatus tres Historico-Geographici.* Ed. Camillo Beccari. Vol. 4 of Rerum aethiopicarum scriptores occidentales inediti a saeculo XVI ad XIX. Rome: Printed for C. de Luigi.

———. 1996. *Do Regno de Tigre e Seus Mandos em Ethiopia: Tractatus Tres historico-geographici; A Seventeenth Century Historical and Geographical Account of Tigray, Ethiopia.* Trans. Elizabet Filleul and Richard Pankhurst. Äthiopistische Forschungen. Wiesbaden: Harrassowitz. Original edition, 1634.

Basset, René-Marie-Joseph. 1882. *Études sur l'histoire d'Ethiopie.* Paris: Imprimerie Nationale.

———. 1895. *Les Prières de la Vierge a Bartos et au Golgotha.* Paris: Bibliothèque de la Haute Science.

Bausi, Alessandro. 1992. "Introduzione." *Il Qalementos etiopico: La rivelazione di Pietro a Clemente; I, libri 3–7.* Napoli: Istituto universitario orientale, dipartimento di studi e ricerche su Africa e paesi arabi.

———. 1995. *Il Senodos etiopico: Canoni pseudoapostolici; Canoni dopo l'Ascensione, Canoni di Simone Cananeo, Canoni Apostolici, Lettera di Pietro.* Corpus Scriptorum Christianorum Orientalium 552/553. Leuven, Belgium: Peeters.

———. 2007. "Monastic Literature." *Encyclopaedia Aethiopica*, ed. Siegbert Uhlig. Vol. 3, *He–N*, 993–99. Wiesbaden: Harrassowitz.

Beccari, Camillo. 1903. *Notizia e saggi di opere e documenti inediti riguardanti la storia di Etiopia durante I secoli XVI, XVII e XVIII.* Vol. 1 of Rerum aethiopicarum scriptores occidentales inediti a saeculo XVI ad XIX. Rome: C. de Luigi.

———. 1910. *Relationes et Epistolae Variorum.* Vol. 10 of Rerum aethiopicarum scriptores occidentales inediti a saeculo XVI ad XIX. Rome: C. de Luigi.

———. 1911. *Relationes et Epistolae Variorum.* Vol. 11 of Rerum aethiopicarum scriptores occidentales inediti a saeculo XVI ad XIX. Rome: C. de Luigi.

———. 1912. *Relationes et Epistolae Variorum.* Vol. 12 of Rerum aethiopicarum scriptores occidentales inediti a saeculo XVI ad XIX. Rome: C. de Luigi.

———. 1913. *Relationes et Epistolae Variorum.* Vol. 13 of Rerum aethiopicarum scriptores occidentales inediti a saeculo XVI ad XIX. Rome: C. de Luigi.

———. 1914. *Relationes et Epistolae Variorum.* Vol. 14 of Rerum aethiopicarum scriptores occidentales inediti a saeculo XVI ad XIX. Rome: C. de Luigi.

Bekele, Shiferaw. 2002. "Yohannes II (r. May 10, 1769–October 15, 1769)." *Aethiopica: International Journal of Ethiopian Studies* 5: 89–111.

Belaynesh, Michael. 1975. "Walata Petros." *The Dictionary of Ethiopian Biography: From Early Times to the End of the Zagwé Dynasty c. 1270 A.D.*, ed. S. Chojnacki and Richard Pankhurst. Addis Ababa: Institute of Ethiopian Studies.

———. 1977a. "Walata Petros." *The Encyclopedia Africana Dictionary of African Biography*, ed. L. H. Ofusu-Appiah, 141–42. New York: Reference Publications.

———. "Walata Petros." *Dictionary of African Christian Biography.* New Haven, CT: Overseas Ministries Study Center 1977b. Available from http://www.dacb.org/stories/ethiopia/walata_petros.html.

Belcher, Wendy Laura. 2005. "Manuscripts in 2,000-year-old Language: Priests Identify UCLA Library's Sacred Treasures." *UCLA Today* (April 12).

———. 2009. "Origin of the Name Rasselas." *Notes and Queries* 56, no. 2 (June): 253–55.

———. 2012. *Abyssinia's Samuel Johnson: Ethiopian Thought in the Making of an English Author.* New York: Oxford University Press.

———. 2013. "Sisters Debating the Jesuits: The Role of African Women in Defeating Portuguese Proto-Colonialism in Seventeenth-Century Abyssinia." *Northeast African Studies* 12 (Spring): 121–66.

———. Forthcoming. "Same-Sex Intimacies in an Early Modern African Text about an Ethiopian Female Saint, *Gädlä Wälättä Ṗeṭros* (1672)." *Research in African Literatures.*

Berry, LaVerle. 2003a. "Ačäfär." *Encyclopaedia Aethiopica*, ed. Siegbert Uhlig. Vol. 1, *A–C*, 67. Wiesbaden: Harrassowitz.

———. 2003b. "Bərhan Mogäsa." *Encyclopaedia Aethiopica*, ed. Siegbert Uhlig. Vol. 1, *A–C*, 534–35. Wiesbaden: Harrassowitz.

———. 2005. "Gondär." *Encyclopaedia Aethiopica*, ed. Siegbert Uhlig. Vol. 2, *D–Ha*, 838–43. Wiesbaden: Harrassowitz.

———. 2009. "Relinquishing the Solomonic Throne: The 'Abdications' of Susenyos (1632) and Iyasu I (1706)." Paper read at the Seventeenth International Conference of Ethiopian Studies, 1–5 November, at Addis Ababa, Ethiopia.

———. 2014. "Yoḥannəs I." *Encyclopaedia Aethiopica*, ed. Siegbert Uhlig. Vol. 5, *Y–Z*, 69–70. Wiesbaden: Harrassowitz.

Berry, LaVerle, and Richard Smith. 1979. "Churches and Monasteries of Lake Tana, Ethiopia, 1972." *Africa: Rivista trimestrale di studi e documentazione dell'Istituto italiano per l'Africa e l'Oriente* 34: 1–34.

Blundell, H. Weld. 1922. *The Royal Chronicle of Abyssinia, 1769–1840.* Cambridge: Cambridge University Press. Original edition, 1851.

Böll, Verena. 2007. "Mälkəʾa Maryam." *Encyclopaedia Aethiopica*, ed. Siegbert Uhlig. Vol. 3, *He–N*, 708–9. Wiesbaden: Harrassowitz.

Bosc-Tiessé, Claire. 2000. "Notes sur l'histoire et l'art des églises du lac Tana: Rapport de mission (27 décembre 1997–28 janvier 1998)." *Annales d'Éthiopie* 16: 207–70.

———. 2003. "Creating an Iconographic Cycle: The Manuscript of the Acts of Wälättä Ṗeṭros and the Emergence of Qʷäraṭa as a Place of Asylum." *Fifteenth International Conference of Ethiopian Studies*, ed. Siegbert Uhlig, 409–16. Wiesbaden: Harrassowitz.

———. 2004 "'How Beautiful She Is!' in Her Mirror: Polysemic Images and Reflections of Power of an Eighteenth-Century Ethiopia Queen." *Journal of Early Modern History* 8, nos. 3–4: 294–318.

———. 2005a. "Däbrä Maryam." *Encyclopaedia Aethiopica*, ed. Siegbert Uhlig. Vol. 2, *D–Ha*, 32–33. Wiesbaden: Harrassowitz.

———. 2005b. "Däbrä Mәṭmaq Maryam." *Encyclopaedia Aethiopica*, ed. Siegbert Uhlig. Vol. 2, *D–Ha*, 35. Wiesbaden: Harrassowitz.

———. 2005c. "Daga Ǝsṭifanos." *Encyclopaedia Aethiopica*, ed. Siegbert Uhlig. Vol. 2, *D–Ha*, 57–59. Wiesbaden: Harrassowitz.

———. 2005d. "Ǝnṭonәs." *Encyclopaedia Aethiopica*, ed. Siegbert Uhlig. Vol. 2, *D–Ha*, 320. Wiesbaden: Harrassowitz.

———. 2008. *Les îles de la mémoire: Fabrique des images et écriture de l'histoire dans les églises du lac Tana.* Paris: Publications de la Sorbonne.

Bremmer, Jan, and Herman Roodenburg. 1993. *A Cultural History of Gesture: From Antiquity to the Present Day.* Cambridge, UK: Polity Press.

Brita, Antonella. 2010. "Ṣadәqan." *Encyclopaedia Aethiopica*, ed. Siegbert Uhlig. Vol. 4, *O–X*, 446–47. Wiesbaden: Harrassowitz.

Bruce, James. 1813a. *Travels to Discover the Source of the Nile: In the Years 1768, 1769, 1770, 1771, 1772, and 1773.* 3rd ed. Vol. 5 of 8 vols. Edinburgh: Printed by George Ramsay and Company.

———. 1813b. *Travels to Discover the Source of the Nile: In the Years 1768, 1769, 1770, 1771, 1772, and 1773.* 3rd ed. Vol. 4 of 8 vols. Edinburgh: Printed by George Ramsay and Company.

———. 1813c. *Travels to Discover the Source of the Nile: In the Years 1768, 1769, 1770, 1771, 1772, and 1773.* 3rd ed. Vol. 6 of 8 vols. Edinburgh: Printed by George Ramsay and Company.

Budge, E. A. Wallis. 1922. *The Queen of Sheba and Her Only Son Menyelek: Being the History of the Departure of God and His Ark of the Covenant from Jerusalem to Ethiopia, and the Establishment of the Religion of the Hebrews and the Solomonic Line of Kings in That Country; A Complete Translation of the Kebra Nagast.* 1st ed. London: Medici Society Limited.

———. 1928. *The Book of the Saints of the Ethiopian Church: A Translation of the Ethiopic Synaxarium; Made from the Manuscripts Oriental 660 and 661 in the British Museum.* 4 vols. Cambridge: Cambridge University Press.

———. 1929. *The Bandlet of Righteousness (Lefafa Sedek): An Ethiopian Book of the Dead.* Vol. 19 of Luzac's Semitic Text and Translation Series. London: Luzac & Co.

———. 1933a. *Legends of Our Lady Mary the Perpetual Virgin and Her Mother Hanna.* London: Oxford University Press, H. Milford.

———. 1933b. *One Hundred and Ten Miracles of Our Lady Mary.* London: Oxford University Press, H. Milford.

Burtea, Bogdan. 2005. "Devil in Religion and Literature." *Encyclopaedia Aethiopica*, ed. Siegbert Uhlig. Vol. 2, *D–Ha*, 147–48. Wiesbaden: Harrassowitz.

———. 2007. "Magic Literature." *Encyclopaedia Aethiopica*, ed. Siegbert Uhlig. Vol. 3, *He–N*, 638–40. Wiesbaden: Harrassowitz.

Buzi, Paola, and Alessandro Bausi. 2010. "Shenoute of Atripe." *Encyclopaedia Aethiopica*, ed. Siegbert Uhlig. Vol. 4, *O–X*, 648–50. Wiesbaden: Harrassowitz.

Castanhoso, Miguel de, Joao Bermudez, and Gaspar Correa. 1902. *The Portuguese Expedition to Abyssinia in 1541–1543 as Narrated by Castanhoso, with Some Contemporary Letters, the Short Account of Bermudez, and Certain Extracts from Correa.* Ed. Richard Stephen Whiteway. Vol. 10. Hakluyt Society. London: Hakluyt Society.

Cerulli, Enrico. 1943. *Il libro etiopico dei Miracoli di Maria e le sue fonti nelle letterature del medio evo latino.* Rome: G. Bardi.

Chaillot, Christine. 2002. *The Ethiopian Orthodox Tewahedo Church Tradition: A Brief Introduction to Its Life and Spirituality*. Paris: Inter-Orthodox Dialogue.
Cheesman, R. E. 1936. *Lake Tana and the Blue Nile*. London: Macmillan.
Chernetsov, Sevir. 2003a. "Atnatewos." *Encyclopaedia Aethiopica*, ed. Siegbert Uhlig. Vol. 1, *A–C*, 394. Wiesbaden: Harrassowitz.
———. 2003b. "Azmač." *Encyclopaedia Aethiopica*, ed. Siegbert Uhlig. Vol. 1, *A–C*, 418–19. Wiesbaden: Harrassowitz.
———. 2005a. "Ǝleni." *Encyclopaedia Aethiopica*, ed. Siegbert Uhlig. Vol. 2, *D–Ha*, 253–54. Wiesbaden: Harrassowitz.
———. 2005b. "Ethiopian Theological Response to European Missionary Proselytizing in the Seventeenth–Nineteenth Centuries." *Ethiopia and the Missions: Historical and Anthropological Insights*, ed. Verena Böll, Steven Kaplan, Andrew Martínez d'Alòs-Moner, and Evgenia Sokolinskaia, 54–62. Münster, Germany: LIT Verlag Münster.
———. 2005c. "Goššu." *Encyclopaedia Aethiopica*, ed. Siegbert Uhlig. Vol. 2, *D-Ha*, 860–61. Wiesbaden: Harrassowitz.
———. 2005d. "A Transgressor of the Norms of Female Behaviour in the Seventeenth-Century Ethiopia: The Heroine of *The Life of Our Mother Walatta Petros*." *Khristianski Vostok* [*Journal of the Christian East*] 10: 48–64.
———. 2007a. "Historiography." *Encyclopaedia Aethiopica*, ed. Siegbert Uhlig. Vol. 3, *He–N*, 40–45. Wiesbaden: Harrassowitz.
———. 2007b. "Mäläkotawit." *Encyclopaedia Aethiopica*, ed. Siegbert Uhlig. Vol. 3, *He–N*, 690–91. Wiesbaden: Harrassowitz.
Chernetsov, Sevir, and LaVerle Berry. 2005. "Ǝnfraz." *Encyclopaedia Aethiopica*, ed. Siegbert Uhlig. Vol. 2, *D–Ha*, 301–2. Wiesbaden: Harrassowitz.
Chernetsov, Sevir, and Denis Nosnitsin. 2007. "Iyasu II." *Encyclopaedia Aethiopica*, ed. Siegbert Uhlig. Vol. 3, *He–N*, 251–52. Wiesbaden: Harrassowitz.
Cohen, Leonardo. 2005. "The Jesuit Missionary as Translator (1603–1632)." *Ethiopia and the Missions: Historical and Anthropological Insights*, ed. Verena Böll, Steven Kaplan, Andreu Martínez d'Alòs-Moner, and Evgenia Sokolinskaia, 7–30. Münster, Germany: LIT Verlag.
———. 2007. "Mendes, Afonso." *Encyclopaedia Aethiopica*, ed. Siegbert Uhlig. Vol. 3, *He–N*, 920–21. Wiesbaden: Harrassowitz.
———. 2009a. *The Missionary Strategies of the Jesuits in Ethiopia (1555–1632)*. Vol. 70 of Äthiopistische Forschungen series. Wiesbaden: Harrassowitz Verlag.
———. 2009b. "Visions and Dreams: An Avenue for Ethiopians' Conversion to Catholicism at the Beginning of the Seventeenth Century." *Journal of Religion in Africa* 39: 4–29.
———. 2010a. "Śəʿəlä Krəstos." *Encyclopaedia Aethiopica*, ed. Siegbert Uhlig. Vol. 4, *O–X*, 591–92. Wiesbaden: Harrassowitz.
———. 2010b. "Wälättä Ṗeṭros." *Encyclopaedia Aethiopica*, ed. Siegbert Uhlig. Vol. 4, *O–X*, 1086–88. Wiesbaden: Harrassowitz.
Colin, Gérard, and Alessandro Bausi. 2010. "Sənkəssar." *Encyclopaedia Aethiopica*, ed. Siegbert Uhlig. Vol. 4, *O–X*, 621–23. Wiesbaden: Harrassowitz.
Conti Rossini, Carlo. 1910. "Il Convento di Tsana in Abissinia e le sue laudi alla Vergine." *Rendiconti della Reale Accademia dei Lincei, Classe di scienze morali, storiche e filologiche*, ser. 5, 19: 581–621.
———. 1912. *Catalogue des manuscrits éthiopiens de la collection Antoine d'Abbadie, Paris*. Paris: Imprimerie nationale.
———. 1946. "Pubblicazioni etiopistiche dal 1936 al 1945." *Rassegna di Studi Etiopici* 4: 1–132.
Conti Rossini, Carlo, and C. Jaeger. 1912. "Praelocutio." *Vitae Sanctorum Indigenarum: I*

Acta S. Walatta Petros, II Miracula S. Zara-Buruk, v–ix. Leuven, Belgium: L. Durbecq. Reprinted 1954.

Crummey, Donald. 2000. *Land and Society in the Christian Kingdom of Ethiopia from the Thirteenth to the Twentieth Century*. Oxford: Oxford University Press.

———. 2003. "Bäkaffa." *Encyclopaedia Aethiopica*, ed. Siegbert Uhlig. Vol. 1, *A–C*, 449–50. Wiesbaden: Harrassowitz.

———. 2005. "Ǝšäte of Qʷara." *Encyclopaedia Aethiopica*, ed. Siegbert Uhlig. Vol. 2, *D–Ha*, 376. Wiesbaden: Harrassowitz.

———. 2010. "Täklä Giyorgis." *Encyclopaedia Aethiopica*, ed. Siegbert Uhlig. Vol. 4, *O–X*, 826–27. Wiesbaden: Harrassowitz.

Crummey, Donald, Denis Nosnitsin, and Evgenia Sokolinskaia. 2010. "Tewodros." *Encyclopaedia Aethiopica*, ed. Siegbert Uhlig. Vol. 4, *O–X*, 930–36. Wiesbaden: Harrassowitz.

Dege, Sophia. 2014. "Yoḥannəs II." *Encyclopaedia Aethiopica*, ed. Siegbert Uhlig. Vol. 5, *Y–Z*, 70–71. Wiesbaden: Harrassowitz.

Delamarter, Stephen. 2010. "Line Length in Ethiopic Psalters: An Example of the Statistical Analysis of Scribal Practice and Developments across Time." Society of Biblical Literature. University of Victoria, Canada.

Derat, Marie-Laure. 2005. "Fäṭägar." *Encyclopaedia Aethiopica*, ed. Siegbert Uhlig. Vol. 2, *D–Ha*, 504–5. Wiesbaden: Harrassowitz.

Di Salvo, Mario, Stanislaw Chojnacki, and Osvaldo Raineri. 1999. *Churches of Ethiopia: The Monastery of Narga Selassie*. Milan: Skira.

Dillmann, August. 1865. *Lexicon Linguae Aethiopicae, cum indice latino*. Leipzig: Weigel.

———. 1866. *Chrestomathia Aethiopica*. Leipzig: Weigel.

Ezra Gebremedhin. 2005. "Ḥawi: Mäṣḥafä ḥawi." *Encyclopaedia Aethiopica*, ed. Siegbert Uhlig. Vol. 2, *D–Ha*, 1052–53. Wiesbaden: Harrassowitz.

Fiaccadori, Gianfranco. 2005. "Ewosṭateans." *Encyclopaedia Aethiopica*, ed. Siegbert Uhlig. Vol. 2, *D–Ha*, 464–69. Wiesbaden: Harrassowitz.

Filəp̣p̣os. 1956. *Atti di Krestos Samra* [Italian translation]. Trans. Enrico Cerulli. Corpus Scriptorum Christianorum Orientalium. Leuven, Belgium: Imprimerie orientaliste L. Durbecq.

Finnegan, Ruth. 1970. *Oral Literature in Africa*. Oxford, UK: Clarendon Press.

Flemming, Johannes. 1890–91. "Hiob Ludolf: Ein Beitrag zur Geschichte der orientalischen Philologie." *Beiträge zur Assyriologie und vergleichenden semitischen Sprachwissenschaft* 1:537–82; 2:63–110.

Fluche, Marina, and Joachim Persoon. 2007. "Nunneries." *Encyclopaedia Aethiopica*, ed. Siegbert Uhlig. Vol. 3, *He–N*, 1206–9. Wiesbaden: Harrassowitz.

Fritsch, Emmanuel. 2007. "Mäqdäs." *Encyclopaedia Aethiopica*, ed. Siegbert Uhlig. Vol. 3, *He–N*, 765–67. Wiesbaden: Harrassowitz.

Fritsch, Emmanuel, and Ugo Zanetti. 2003. "Calendar." *Encyclopaedia Aethiopica*, ed. Siegbert Uhlig. Vol. 1, *A–C*, 668–72. Wiesbaden: Harrassowitz.

Gälawdewos. 1912. *Vitae Sanctorum Indigenarum: I: Acta S. Walatta Petros*. Ed. Carlo Conti Rossini. Corpus Scriptorum Christianorum Orientalium 68; Scriptores Aethiopici 30. Rome, Paris, Leipzig: Karolus de Luigi; Carolus Poussielgue Bibliopola; Otto Harrassowitz. Reprinted 1954 and 1962.

———. 1970. *Vita di Walatta Piētros*. Trans. Lanfranco Ricci. Corpus Scriptorum Christianorum Orientalium 316; Scriptores Aethiopici 61. Leuven, Belgium: Secrétariat du CSCO.

———. 2004. *Gädlä Wälättä Peṭros* [*The Life of Wälättä Peṭros: In the Original Gəʿəz and Translated into Amharic*]. Trans. Mälʾakä Gännät Mənasse Zälläqä. Addis Ababa, Ethiopia: Ethiopian Orthodox Täwaḥədo Church Press.

Garretson, Peter. 2007. "Näggadras." *Encyclopaedia Aethiopica*, ed. Siegbert Uhlig. Vol. 3, *He–N*, 1112–13. Wiesbaden: Harrassowitz.

Gascon, Alain. 2010. "Rəbb." *Encyclopaedia Aethiopica*, ed. Siegbert Uhlig. Vol. 4, *O–X*, 343–44. Wiesbaden: Harrassowitz.

Getatchew Haile. 2000. "Ethiopia." *Encyclopedia of Monasticism: M–Z*, ed. William M. Johnston, 454–60. Chicago: Fitzroy Dearborn.

———. 2003. "Arganonä Maryam." *Encyclopaedia Aethiopica*, ed. Siegbert Uhlig. Vol. 1, *A–C*, 329–30. Wiesbaden: Harrassowitz.

———. 2007a. "Karra." *Encyclopaedia Aethiopica*, ed. Siegbert Uhlig. Vol. 3, *He–N*, 348–49. Wiesbaden: Harrassowitz.

———. 2007b. "Synaxary Entry on Abunä Śärṣä Maryam of Leba Mäṭaya." *Journal of Ethiopian Studies* 40, no. 1/2: 37–43.

Gideon, Derek. 2012. "*Gädlä Wälättä Peṭros*: Unraveling an Image of Animals in Africa." Undergraduate paper, Princeton University.

Gourgouris, Stathis. 2003. *Does Literature Think? Literature as Theory for an Antimythical Era*. Stanford, CA: Stanford University Press.

Grébaut, Sylvain. 1940. *Rituel éthiopien de prise d'habit*. Paris: Firmin-Didot.

Grébaut, Sylvain, and Eugène Tisserant. 1935. *Codices Aethiopici Vaticani et Borgiani*. Rome: Biblioteca Apostolica Vaticana.

Grierson, Roderick. 1993. *African Zion: The Sacred Art of Ethiopia*. New Haven: Yale University Press.

Guidi, Ignazio. 1906. *Le synaxaire éthiopien: Le mois de Sanê*. Trans. Ignazio Guidi. Vol. 1 of 12 vols. Paris: Firmin-Dido.

Gundani, P. H. 2004. "Christian Historiography and the African Woman: A Critical Examination of the Place of Felicity, Walatta Pietros and Kimpa Vita in African Christian Historiography." *Studia Historiae Ecclesiasticae* 30, no. 1: 75–89.

Habtemichael Kidane. 1998. *L'Ufficio divino della chiesa etiopica: Studio storico-critico con particoloare riferimento alle ore cattedrali*. Orientalia Christiana Analecta. Rome: Pontificio istituto orientale.

———. 2003. "Anaphoras." *Encyclopaedia Aethiopica*, ed. Siegbert Uhlig. Vol. 1, *A–C*, 251–53. Wiesbaden: Harrassowitz.

———. 2005. "ʿƎnzirä Səbḥat." *Encyclopaedia Aethiopica*, ed. Siegbert Uhlig. Vol. 2, *D–Ha*, 328. Wiesbaden: Harrassowitz.

———. 2007a. "Mälkəʾ." *Encyclopaedia Aethiopica*, ed. Siegbert Uhlig. Vol. 3, *He–N*, 701–2. Wiesbaden: Harrassowitz.

———. 2007b. "Məḥəlla." *Encyclopaedia Aethiopica*, ed. Siegbert Uhlig. Vol. 3, *He–N*, 912–13. Wiesbaden: Harrassowitz.

———. 2010. "Səbḥatä fəqur." *Encyclopaedia Aethiopica*, ed. Siegbert Uhlig. Vol. 4, *O–X*, 589–90. Wiesbaden: Harrassowitz.

Hammerschmidt, Ernst. 1977a. *Äthiopische Handschriften vom Ṭānāsee 2: Die Handschriften von Dabra Māryām und von Rēmā*. Verzeichnis der orientalischen Handschriften in Deutschland (VOHD) 20, 2. Wiesbaden: Franz Steiner.

———. 1977b. *Illuminierte Handschriften der Staatsbibliothek Preussischer Kulturbesitz und Handschriften vom Ṭānāsee*. Codices Aethiopici. Graz: Verlagsanstalt.

Hammerschmidt, Ernst, and Otto A. Jäger. 1968. *Illuminierte äthiopische Handschriften*. Verzeichnis der orientalischen Handschriften in Deutschland (VOHD) 15. Wiesbaden: Franz Steiner.

Hammerschmidt, Ernst, and Veronika Six. 1983. *Äthiopische Handschriften 1: Die Handschriften der Staatsbibliothek Preussischer Kulturbesitz*. Verzeichnis der orientalischen Handschriften in Deutschland (VOHD) 20, 4. Wiesbaden: Franz Steiner.

Harden, J. M. 1926. *An Introduction to Ethiopic Christian Literature*. London: Macmillan.

Hastings, Adrian. 1994. *The Church in Africa: 1450–1950*. Oxford; New York: Clarendon Press; Oxford University Press.
———. 1997. *The Construction of Nationhood: Ethnicity, Religion and Nationalism*. Cambridge: Cambridge University Press.
Heffernan, Thomas J. 2012. *The Passion of Perpetua and Felicity*. New York: Oxford University Press.
Heldman, Marilyn. 2005a. "Fəlsäta." *Encyclopaedia Aethiopica*, ed. Siegbert Uhlig. Vol. 2, *D–Ha*, 518–20. Wiesbaden: Harrassowitz.
Heldman, Marilyn E. 2005b. "St. Luke as Painter: Post-Byzantine Icons in Early-Sixteenth-Century Ethiopia." *Gesta: International Center of Medieval Art* 44, no. 2: 125–48.
———. 2010. "Painting on Wood." *Encyclopaedia Aethiopica*, ed. Siegbert Uhlig. Vol. 4, *O–X*, 99–101. Wiesbaden: Harrassowitz.
Henze, Paul B. 2000. *Layers of Time: A History of Ethiopia*. London: Hurst & Co.
Heyer, Friedrich. 2003. "Diyaqon." *Encyclopaedia Aethiopica*, ed. Siegbert Uhlig. Vol. 1, *A–C*, 174–75. Wiesbaden: Harrassowitz.
Houchins, Sue. 2007. "Between Hagiography and Slave Narrative: Teresa Chicaba, an African Nun in Eighteenth-Century Spain (Lecture, November 15)." Los Angeles: UCLA Center for the Study of Women.
Houchins, Sue E., and Baltasar Fra-Molinero. 2009. "The Saint's Life of Sister Chicaba, c. 1676–1748: An As-Told-To Slave Narrative." *Afro-Latino Voices: Narratives from the Early Modern Ibero-Atlantic World*, ed. Kathryn Joy McKnight and Leo J. Garofalo, 214–39. Indianapolis, IN: Hackett.
Huntingford, George Wynn Brereton. 1989. *The Historical Geography of Ethiopia: From the First Century AD to 1704*. Oxford: Oxford University Press.
Ibn al-ʿAssāl, aṣ-Ṣafī Abū l-Faḍāʾil. 1968. *Fetha Nagast: The Law of the Kings*. Trans. Paulos Tzadua. Ed. Paulos Tzadua and Peter L. Strauss. Addis Ababa: Faculty of Law, Haile Sellassie I University.
Kane, Thomas Leiper. 1990. *Amharic-English Dictionary*. Wiesbaden: Harrassowitz.
Kaplan, Steven. 1981. "Hagiographies and the History of Medieval Ethiopia." *History in Africa* 8: 107–23.
———. 2003a. "Abba." *Encyclopaedia Aethiopica*, ed. Siegbert Uhlig. Vol. 1, *A–C*, 9. Wiesbaden: Harrassowitz.
———. 2003b. "Birth." *Encyclopaedia Aethiopica*, ed. Siegbert Uhlig. Vol. 1, *A–C*, 589–92. Wiesbaden: Harrassowitz.
———. 2003c. "Däbtära." *Encyclopaedia Aethiopica*, ed. Siegbert Uhlig. Vol. 1, *A–C*, 53–54. Wiesbaden: Harrassowitz.
———. 2005a. "Däbr." *Encyclopaedia Aethiopica*, ed. Siegbert Uhlig. Vol. 2, *D–Ha*, 6–7. Wiesbaden: Harrassowitz.
———. 2005b. "Gädam." *Encyclopaedia Aethiopica*, ed. Siegbert Uhlig. Vol. 2, *D–Ha*, 641–42. Wiesbaden: Harrassowitz.
———. 2005c. "Gädl." *Encyclopaedia Aethiopica*, ed. Siegbert Uhlig. Vol. 2, *D–Ha*, 642–44. Wiesbaden: Harrassowitz.
———. 2007. "Monasticism." *Encyclopaedia Aethiopica*, ed. Siegbert Uhlig. Vol. 3, *He-N*, 987–93. Wiesbaden: Harrassowitz.
———. 2014a. "Monasticism." *Encyclopaedia Aethiopica*, ed. Siegbert Uhlig. Vol. 5, *Y–Z*, 443–45. Wiesbaden: Harrassowitz.
———. 2014b. "Yafqərännä Ǝgziʾ." *Encyclopaedia Aethiopica*, ed. Siegbert Uhlig. Vol. 5, *Y–Z*, 10–11. Wiesbaden: Harrassowitz.
Kendon, Adam. 2004. *Gesture: Visible Action as Utterance*. Cambridge: Cambridge University Press.
Kindeneh Endeg Mihretie. 2014. "Founded by, Dedicated to, and Fighting About the

Holy Savior: Schism in Waldəba, a Microcosm of Factionalism in the Ethiopian Church." *Northeast African Studies* 14, no. 1: 43–66.

Kinefe-Rigb Zelleke. 1975. "Bibliography of the Ethiopic Hagiographic Traditions." *Journal of Ethiopian Studies* 13, no. 2 (July): 57–102.

Kleiner, Michael. 2003. "Corpus Scriptorum Christianorum Orientalium." *Encyclopaedia Aethiopica*, ed. Siegbert Uhlig. Vol. 1, *A–C*, 804. Wiesbaden: Harrassowitz.

———.2005a. "Dära." *Encyclopaedia Aethiopica*, ed. Siegbert Uhlig. Vol. 2, *D–Ha*, 97–98. Wiesbaden: Harrassowitz.

———. 2005b. "Fogära." *Encyclopaedia Aethiopica*, ed. Siegbert Uhlig. Vol. 2, *D–Ha*, 555–56. Wiesbaden: Harrassowitz.

———. 2007. "Name(s): Regnal Names." *Encyclopaedia Aethiopica*, ed. Siegbert Uhlig. Vol. 3, *He–N*, 1122–24. Wiesbaden: Harrassowitz.

———. 2008. "The Ethiopic Life of Daniel: Translation and Commentary." *Witness to Holiness: Abba Daniel of Scetis*, ed. Tim Vivian, 127–80, 343–79. Kalamazoo, MI: Cistercian Publications.

———. 2010. "Säblä Wängel." *Encyclopaedia Aethiopica*, ed. Siegbert Uhlig. Vol. 4, *O–X*, 434–35. Wiesbaden: Harrassowitz.

Knibb, Michael A., and Edward Ullendorff. 1978. *The Ethiopic Book of Enoch: A New Edition in the Light of the Aramaic Dead Sea Fragments*. 2 vols. Oxford: Clarendon Press; New York: Oxford University Press.

Krawczuk, Marcin. 2006. *Ethiopic Life of Rhipsime (Gädlä Arsima): Critical Edition with Polish Translation and Commentary*. Diss., Institute of Oriental Studies, Warsaw University, Poland.

Kur, Stanislas. 1965. *Actes de Iyasus Moʾa, abbé du couvent de St-Etienne de Hayq*. Corpus Scriptorum Christianorum Orientalium; v. 260. Scriptores Aethiopici; t. 49–50. Leuven, Belgium: Secrétariat du CSCO.

Kur, Stanislaw, and Denis Nosnitsin. 2007. "Kidan." *Encyclopaedia Aethiopica*, ed. Siegbert Uhlig. Vol. 3, *He–N*, 394–95. Wiesbaden: Harrassowitz.

Leonessa, Mauro da. 1942. "La Versione etiopica dei canoni apocrifi del concilio di Nicea secondo i codici vaticani ed fiorentino." *Rassegna di Studi Etiopici* 2, no. 1: 29–89.

Leslau, Wolf. 1987. *Comparative Dictionary of Geʾez (Classical Ethiopic): Geʾez-English, English-Geʾez, with an Index of the Semitic Roots*. Wisbaden: Otto Harrassowitz.

Lindahl, Bernhard. 2008. *Local History in Ethiopia*. Uppsala: Nordic Africa Institute.

Lobo, Jerónimo. 1971. *Itinerário e outros escritos inéditos*. Ed. Father M. Goncalves da Costa. Porto: Civilização.

———. 1983. *The Itinerário of Jerónimo Lobo*. Trans. Donald M. Lockhart. Ed. Donald M. Lockhart, Father M. Goncalves da Costa, and C. F. Beckingham. London: Hakluyt Society.

Lobo, Jerónimo, and Joachim Le Grand. 1985. *A Voyage to Abyssinia (Translated from the French)*. Trans. Samuel Johnson. Ed. Joel Gold. Vol. 15 of 23 vols. Yale Edition of the Works of Samuel Johnson. New Haven: Yale University Press. Original edition, 1735.

Lucchesi, Enzo. 2003. "Arägawi Mänfäsawi." *Encyclopaedia Aethiopica*, ed. Siegbert Uhlig. Vol. 1, *A–C*, 309–10. Wiesbaden: Harrassowitz.

Lusini, Gianfrancesco. 2003a. "Absadi of Azäzo." *Encyclopaedia Aethiopica*, ed. Siegbert Uhlig. Vol. 1, *A–C*, 50. Wiesbaden: Harrassowitz Verlag.

———. 2003b. "Absadi of Däbrä Maryam." *Encyclopaedia Aethiopica*, ed. Siegbert Uhlig. Vol. 1, *A–C*, 50. Wiesbaden: Harrassowitz Verlag.

Marcus, Cressida. 2001. "The Production of Patriotic Spirituality: Ethiopian Orthodox Women's Experience of War and Social Crisis." *Northeast African Studies* 8, no. 3: 179–208.

Marcus, Harold G. 2002. *A History of Ethiopia*. Updated ed. Berkeley: University of California Press.

Marrassini, Paolo. 2007. "Kiros." *Encyclopaedia Aethiopica*, ed. Siegbert Uhlig. Vol. 3, *He–N*, 409–11. Wiesbaden: Harrassowitz.

Martínez d'Alòs-Moner, Andreu. 2010. "Səmʿon." *Encyclopaedia Aethiopica*, ed. Siegbert Uhlig. Vol. 4, *O–X*, 618. Wiesbaden: Harrassowitz.

Meinardus, Otto, and Steven Kaplan. 2003. "Anthony, Saint." *Encyclopaedia Aethiopica*, ed. Siegbert Uhlig. Vol. 1, *A–C*, 282–83. Wiesbaden: Harrassowitz.

Mellors, John, and Anne Parsons. 2002. *Ethiopian Bookmaking: Bookmaking in Rural Ethiopia in the Twenty-First Century.* London: New Cross Books.

Mendes, Alfonso. 1692. *Bran-Haymanot Id Est Lux Fidei In Epithalamium Aethiopissae, Sive In Nuptias Uerbiet Ecclesiae.* 3 vols. Cologne, Germany: Coloniae Agrippinae. Original edition, Lisboa, 1642.

Mendes, Alphonso. 1908. *Expeditionis Aethiopicae Liber.* Ed. Camillo Beccari. Vol. 8 of Rerum aethiopicarum scriptores occidentales inediti a saeculo XVI ad XIX. Rome: Printed for C. de Luigi.

———. 1909. *Expeditionis Aethiopicae Liber.* Ed. Camillo Beccari. Vol. 9 of Rerum aethiopicarum scriptores occidentales inediti a saeculo XVI ad XIX. Rome: Printed for C. de Luigi.

Merid Wolde Aregay. 1998. "The Legacy of Jesuit Missionary Activities in Ethiopia." *The Missionary Factor in Ethiopia: Papers from a Symposium on the Impact of European Missions on Ethiopian Society*, ed. Getatchew Haile, Samuel Rubenson, and Aasulv Lande, 31–56. Frankfurt: Verlag.

———. 2003a. "Abetohun." *Encyclopaedia Aethiopica*, ed. Siegbert Uhlig. Vol. 1, *A–C*, 40. Wiesbaden: Harrassowitz.

———. 2003b. "Angot." *Encyclopaedia Aethiopica*, ed. Siegbert Uhlig. Vol. 1, *A–C*, 268. Wiesbaden: Harrassowitz.

Mersha Alehegne. 2010. "Täzkar." *Encyclopaedia Aethiopica*, ed. Siegbert Uhlig. Vol. 4, *O–X*, 881–82. Wiesbaden: Harrassowitz.

———. 2011. *The Ethiopian Commentary on the Book of Genesis: Critical Edition and Translation.* Wiesbaden: Harrassowitz.

Mersha Alehegne, and Denis Nosnitsin. 2005. "Däwäl." *Encyclopaedia Aethiopica*, ed. Siegbert Uhlig. Vol. 2, *D–Ha*, 108–9. Wiesbaden: Harrassowitz.

Morin, Didier. 2004. *Dictionnaire historique afar (1288–1982).* Paris: Karthala Editions.

Mulatu Wubneh. 2003. "Azäzo." *Encyclopaedia Aethiopica*, ed. Siegbert Uhlig. Vol. 1, *A–C*, 415–16. Wiesbaden: Harrassowitz.

Müller, Walter W. 2005. "Ḥabašāt." *Encyclopaedia Aethiopica*, ed. Siegbert Uhlig. Vol. 2, *D–Ha*, 948–49. Wiesbaden: Harrassowitz.

Munro-Hay, Stuart. 2002. *Ethiopia, the Unknown Land: A Cultural and Historical Guide.* London: I. B. Tauris.

Muth, Franz-Christoph. 2005. "Däwaro." *Encyclopaedia Aethiopica*, ed. Siegbert Uhlig. Vol. 2, *D–Ha*, 109–11. Wiesbaden: Harrassowitz.

Nast, Heidi J. 2005. *Concubines and Power: Five Hundred Years in a Northern Nigerian Palace.* Minneapolis: University of Minnesota Press.

Natsoulas, Theodore, and Denis Nosnitsin. 2007. "Iyoʾas I." *Encyclopaedia Aethiopica*, ed. Siegbert Uhlig. Vol. 3, *He–N*, 259–60. Wiesbaden: Harrassowitz.

Negussie Andre Domnic. 2010. *The Fetha Nagast and Its Ecclesiology: Implications in Ethiopian Catholic Church Today.* Bern, Switzerland: Peter Lang.

Nollet, Geneviève. 1930. "La légende de ʾEḫta-Krestos d'après le ms. du Synaxaire Vat. éth. no. 112." *Aethiops* 4: 51–53.

Nosnitsin, Denis. 2003a. "Abunä." *Encyclopaedia Aethiopica*, ed. Siegbert Uhlig. Vol. 1, *A–C*, 56. Wiesbaden: Harrassowitz.

———. 2003b. "Balambaras." *Encyclopaedia Aethiopica*, ed. Siegbert Uhlig. Vol. 1, *A–C*, 452. Wiesbaden: Harrassowitz Verlag.

———. 2005a. "Fəqərtä Krəstos." *Encyclopaedia Aethiopica*, ed. Siegbert Uhlig. Vol. 2, *D–Ha*, 521–22. Wiesbaden: Harrassowitz.
———. 2005b. "Goǧǧam." *Encyclopaedia Aethiopica*, ed. Siegbert Uhlig. Vol. 2, *D–Ha*, 825–28. Wiesbaden: Harrassowitz.
———. 2007a. "The Ethiopic Synaxarion: Text-Critical Observations on Täklä Haymanot's Commemoration (24 Näḥase)." *Orientalia Christiana Periodica* 73, no. 1: 141–83.
———. 2007b. "Liqä Kahənat " *Encyclopaedia Aethiopica*, ed. Siegbert Uhlig. Vol. 3, *He–N*, 578–79. Wiesbaden: Harrassowitz.
———. 2007c. "Mälkəʾa Krəstos." *Encyclopaedia Aethiopica*, ed. Siegbert Uhlig. Vol. 3, *He–N*, 706–7. Wiesbaden: Harrassowitz.
———. 2010a. "Ras." *Encyclopaedia Aethiopica*, ed. Siegbert Uhlig. Vol. 4, *O–X*, 330–31. Wiesbaden: Harrassowitz.
———. 2010b. "Sälam." *Encyclopaedia Aethiopica*, ed. Siegbert Uhlig. Vol. 4, *O–X*, 484. Wiesbaden: Harrassowitz.
———. 2010c. "Śärṣä Dəngəl." *Encyclopaedia Aethiopica*, ed. Siegbert Uhlig. Vol. 4, *O–X*, 544–47. Wiesbaden: Harrassowitz.
———. 2010d. "Śərʿatä Mənkʷəsənna." *Encyclopaedia Aethiopica*, ed. Siegbert Uhlig. Vol. 4, *O–X*, 634–36. Wiesbaden: Harrassowitz.
———. 2010e. "Täʾammər." *Encyclopaedia Aethiopica*, ed. Siegbert Uhlig. Vol. 4, *O–X*, 787–88. Wiesbaden: Harrassowitz.
———. 2010f. "Täklä Haymanot." *Encyclopaedia Aethiopica*, ed. Siegbert Uhlig. Vol. 4, *O–X*, 831–34. Wiesbaden: Harrassowitz.
———. 2010g. "Waldəbba." *Encyclopaedia Aethiopica*, ed. Siegbert Uhlig. Vol. 4, *O–X*, 1112–13. Wiesbaden: Harrassowitz.
———. 2010h. "Wälqayt." *Encyclopaedia Aethiopica*, ed. Siegbert Uhlig. Vol. 4, *O–X*, 1122–23. Wiesbaden: Harrassowitz.
———. 2013. "The Birth of an African Literary Form: The Ethiopian Hagiographical Novel in Comparative Perspective." Paper presented in Los Angeles: UCLA.
Ogot, Bethwell A. 1992. *Africa from the Sixteenth to the Eighteenth Century*. Vol. 5 of General History of Africa. Berkeley: University of California Press.
Paez, Gasparo. 1903. "Lettere annue di Etiopia del 1624, 1625, e 1626." *Notizia e saggi di opere e documenti inediti riguardanti la storia di Etiopia durante I secoli XVI, XVII e XVIII*, ed. Camillo Beccari. Rome: C. de Luigi.
Páez, Pedro. 2011. *Pedro Páez's History of Ethiopia, 1622*. Trans. Christopher J. Tribe. Ed. Isabel Boavida, Hervé Pennec, and Manuel João Ramos. 2 vols. Burlington, VT: Ashgate for the Hakluyt Society.
Pankhurst, Richard. 1982. *History of Ethiopian Towns from the Middle Ages to the Early Nineteenth Century*. Wiesbaden: Steiner.
———. 1992. *A Social History of Ethiopia: The Northern and Central Highlands from Early Medieval Times to the Rise of Emperor Téwodros II*. Lawrenceville, NJ: Red Sea Press.
———. 1997. *The Ethiopian Borderlands: Essays in Regional History from Ancient Times to the End of the Eighteenth Century*. Lawrenceville, NJ: Red Sea Press.
———. 2003. "Amole." *Encyclopaedia Aethiopica*, ed. Siegbert Uhlig. Vol. 1, *A–C*, 248–49. Wiesbaden: Harrassowitz.
———. 2005a. "Färänǧ." *Encyclopaedia Aethiopica*, ed. Siegbert Uhlig. Vol. 2, *D–Ha*, 492–93. Wiesbaden: Harrassowitz.
———. 2005b. "Fire-arms." *Encyclopaedia Aethiopica*, ed. Siegbert Uhlig. Vol. 2, *D–Ha*, 547–49. Wiesbaden: Harrassowitz.
Pankhurst, Richard, and Harald Aspen. 2005. "Grave Culture in Christian Regions." *Encyclopaedia Aethiopica*, ed. Siegbert Uhlig. Vol. 2, *D–Ha*, 873–75. Wiesbaden: Harrassowitz.

Pankhurst, Rita. 2005c. "Gešo." *Encyclopaedia Aethiopica*, ed. Siegbert Uhlig. Vol. 2, *D–Ha*, 773. Wiesbaden: Harrassowitz.

———. 2009. "Ṭaytu's Foremothers: Queen Ǝleni, Queen Säblä Wängel and Bati Dəl Wämbära." *Proceedings of the Sixteenth International Conference of Ethiopian Studies*, ed. Svein Ege, Harald Aspen, Birhanu Teferra, and Shiferaw Bekele, 51–63. Trondheim, Norway: Norwegian University of Science and Technology.

Papi, Maria Rosaria. 1943. "Una santa abissina anticattolica: Walatta-Petros." *Rassegna di Studi Etiopici* 3, no. 1: 87–93.

Parkyns, Mansfield. 1853. *Life in Abyssinia: Being Notes Collected during Three Years' Residence and Travels in that Country*. Vol. 2 of 2 vols. London: John Murray.

Pasicrates, and Theodosius. 1930. *George of Lydda, the Patron Saint of England: A Study of the Cultus of St. George in Ethiopia*. Trans. E. A. Wallis Budge. Vol. 20 of Luzac's Semitic Text and Translation Series. London: Luzac & Co.

Pearce, Nathaniel. 1831. *The Life and Adventures of Nathaniel Pearce, Written by Himself during a Residence in Abyssinia from the Years 1810 to 1819*. Ed. John James Halls. 2 vols. London: Henry Colburn and Richard Bentley.

Pennec, Hervé. 2003. *Des Jésuites au royaume du prêtre Jean (Éthiopie): Stratégies, rencontres et tentatives d'implantation, 1495–1633*. Paris: Fundação Calouste Gulbenkian.

Persoon, Joachim. 2010. "Qʷarf." *Encyclopaedia Aethiopica*, ed. Siegbert Uhlig. Vol. 4, *O–X*, 315. Wiesbaden: Harrassowitz.

Phillipson, David W. 2009. *Ancient Churches of Ethiopia: Fourth–Fourteenth Centuries*. New Haven: Yale University Press.

Pietruschka, Ute. 2010. "Octateuch." *Encyclopaedia Aethiopica*, ed. Siegbert Uhlig. Vol. 4, *O–X*, 6–7. Wiesbaden: Harrassowitz.

Pisani, Vitagrazia. 2013. *Il culto di San Qirqos nell'Etiopia storica: Analisi storico-filologica, con edizione critica della "Passio" (Gädlä Qirqos)*. PhD, African Studies (Curriculum Literatures, Philology and Studies on African Antiquity and Middle Ages), Università degli Studi di Napoli "L'Orientale," Napoli, Italy.

Porcellet, Philippine de, and Kathleen E. Garay. 2001. *The Life of Saint Douceline, a Beguine of Provence*. Trans. Madeleine Jeay. Cambridge: Boydell & Brewer.

Powell-Cotton, Percy Horace Gordon. 1902. *A Sporting Trip through Abyssinia: A Narrative of a Nine Months' Journey from the Plains of the Hawash to the Snows of Simien*. London: R. Ward.

Quirin, James. 2010. "Ṣällämt." *Encyclopaedia Aethiopica*, ed. Siegbert Uhlig. Vol. 4, *O–X*, 495–96. Wiesbaden: Harrassowitz.

Raineri, Osvaldo. 2005. "George of Lydda: Cult and Hagiography of St. George." *Encyclopaedia Aethiopica*, ed. Siegbert Uhlig. Vol. 2, *D–Ha*, 763–64. Wiesbaden: Harrassowitz.

———. 2007. "Mäzraʿətä Krəstos." *Encyclopaedia Aethiopica*, ed. Siegbert Uhlig. Vol. 3, *He–N*, 899–900. Wiesbaden: Harrassowitz.

Revol-Tisset, Meaza Haile, and Wolbert Smidt. 2005. "Euphorbia." *Encyclopaedia Aethiopica*, ed. Siegbert Uhlig. Vol. 2, *D–Ha*, 450–51. Wiesbaden: Harrassowitz.

Reyes, Kathryn Blackmer, and Julia E. Curry Rodríguez. 2012. "Testimonio: Origins, Terms, and Resources." *Equity & Excellence in Education* 45, no. 3 (July 1): 525–38.

Ricci, Lanfranco. 1970. "Premessa." *Vita di Walatta Pieṭros*, v–xii. Leuven, Belgium: Secrétariat du CSCO.

———. 2003. "Conti Rossini, Carlo." *Encyclopaedia Aethiopica*, ed. Siegbert Uhlig. Vol. 2, *A–C*, 791–92. Wiesbaden: Harrassowitz.

Salt, Henry. 1967. *A Voyage to Abyssinia, and Travels into the Interior of that Country, Executed under the Orders of the British Government in the Years 1809 and 1810*. Cass Library of African Studies, Travels and Narratives, no. 16. London: Cass.

Salvadore, Matteo. 2010. "Faith over Color: Ethio-European Encounters and Discourses in the Early-Modern Era." PhD diss., Temple University, Philadelphia, PA.

Saporito, Jean-Louis, Flore Kosinetz, and François le Cadre. 2012. *En Ethiopie, sur les traces des premiers chrétiens.* Documentary film. Produced by ARTE France; TGA production CFRT. France: CNRS.
Schaefer, Charles. 2007. "Maḫbär." *Encyclopaedia Aethiopica,* ed. Siegbert Uhlig. Vol. 3, *He–N,* 649–50. Wiesbaden: Harrassowitz.
Selamawit Mecca. 2006. "Hagiographies of Ethiopian Female Saints: With Special Reference to Gädlä Krestos Sämra and Gädlä Feqertä Krestos." *Journal of African Cultural Studies* 18, no. 2 (December): 153–67.
Seltene Seyoum. 2003. "Baḥər Dar." *Encyclopaedia Aethiopica,* ed. Siegbert Uhlig. Vol. 1, *A–C,* 442–44. Wiesbaden: Harrassowitz.
Shaw, Brent D. 1993. "The Passion of Perpetua." *Past & Present,* no. 139 (May): 3–45.
Shinn, David Hamilton, Thomas P. Ofcansky, and Chris Prouty. 2004. *Historical Dictionary of Ethiopia.* Lanham, MD: Scarecrow Press.
Siebert, Ralph. 2003. "Ç̣ara." *Encyclopaedia Aethiopica,* ed. Siegbert Uhlig. Vol. 1, *A–C,* 683–84. Wiesbaden: Harrassowitz.
Six, Veronika. 1994. *Äthiopische Handschriften 3. Handschriften deutscher Bibliotheken, Museen und aus Privatbesitz.* Verzeichnis der orientalischen Handschriften in Deutschland (VOHD) 20, 6. Stuttgart: Franz Steiner.
———. 1999. *Äthiopische Handschriften vom Ṭānāsee Teil 3: Nebst einem Nachtrag zum Katalog der Äthiopischen Handschriften deutscher Bibliotheken und Museen.* Verzeichnis der orientalischen Handschriften in Deutschland (VOHD) 20, 3. Stuttgart: Franz Steiner.
———. 2010a. "Rema." *Encyclopaedia Aethiopica,* ed. Siegbert Uhlig. Vol. 4, *O–X,* 364. Wiesbaden: Harrassowitz.
———. 2010b. "Ṭana Qirqos." *Encyclopaedia Aethiopica,* ed. Siegbert Uhlig. Vol. 4, *O–X,* 857–58. Wiesbaden: Harrassowitz.
Smidt, Wolbert. 2010a. "Salt." *Encyclopaedia Aethiopica,* ed. Siegbert Uhlig. Vol. 4, *O–X,* 500–503. Wiesbaden: Harrassowitz.
———. 2010b. "Šanqəlla." *Encyclopaedia Aethiopica,* ed. Siegbert Uhlig. Vol. 4, *O–X,* 525–26. Wiesbaden: Harrassowitz.
———. 2010c. "Təgray." *Encyclopaedia Aethiopica,* ed. Siegbert Uhlig. Vol. 4, *O–X,* 888–95. Wiesbaden: Harrassowitz.
Sokolinskaia, Evgenia. 2014. "Wädağğe." *Encyclopaedia Aethiopica,* ed. Siegbert Uhlig. Vol. 5, *Y–Z,* 549–50. Wiesbaden: Harrassowitz.
———. 2007. "Liq." *Encyclopaedia Aethiopica,* ed. Siegbert Uhlig. Vol. 3, *He–N,* 576–78. Wiesbaden: Harrassowitz.
Stoffregen-Pedersen, Kirsten. 1995. *Traditional Ethiopian Exegesis of the Book of Psalms.* Vol. 36 of Äthiopistische Forschungen. Wiesbaden: Otto Harrassowitz.
Störk, Lothar, and Richard Pankhurst. 2007. "Hippopotamus." *Encyclopaedia Aethiopica,* ed. Siegbert Uhlig. Vol. 3, *He–N,* 36–37. Wiesbaden: Harrassowitz.
Strelcyn, Stefan. 1955. *Prières magiques éthiopiennes pour délier les charmes (maftəḥe šərāy).* Vol. 18 of Rocznik Orientalistyczny. Warsaw: Panstwowe Wydawnictwo Naukowe.
Stylianoudi, Lily, and Denis Nosnitsin. 2007. "Kätäma." *Encyclopaedia Aethiopica,* ed. Siegbert Uhlig. Vol. 3, *He–N,* 355–58. Wiesbaden: Harrassowitz.
Tadesse Tamrat. 1991. "An Early Apostle of Matakkal: *Abba* Tatamqa Madhen of Gažge (1616–1678)." *Proceedings of the Eleventh International Conference of Ethiopian Studies,* ed. Bahru Zewde, Richard Pankhurst, and Taddese Beyene. Addis Ababa: Institute of Ethiopian Studies, Addis Ababa University.
Täklä Śəllase [Ṭinno]. 1892. *Chronica de Susenyos: Rei de Ethiopia; Texto Ethiopico.* Ed.

Francisco Maria Esteves Pereira. Vol. 1 of 2 vols. Lisbon: Imprensa Nacional. Reprint, 1982.

———. 1900. *Chronica de Susenyos: Rei de Ethiopia; Traducção e Notas.* Ed. Francisco Maria Esteves Pereira. Vol. 2 of 2 vols. Lisbon: Imprensa Nacional.

Täklä Ṣəyon. 1906. *The Life of Takla Haymanot in the Version of Dabra Libanos and the Miracles of Takla Haymanot in the Version of Dabra Libanos, and the Book of the Riches of Kings.* Trans. E. A. Wallis Budge. Lady Meux. London W. Griggs.

Täwäldä Mädḫən. 2006. *The Gəʿəz Acts of Abba Ǝsṭifanos of Gʷəndagʷənde.* Trans. Getatchew Haile. Ed. Getatchew Haile. 2 vols. Corpus Scriptorum Christianorum Orientalium 620. Leuven, Belgium: Peeters.

Tedros Abraha. 2005. "Gənzät: Mäṣḥafä gənzät." *Encyclopaedia Aethiopica,* ed. Siegbert Uhlig. Vol. 2, *D–Ha,* 748–49. Wiesbaden: Harrassowitz.

———. 2010. "Qəbat." *Encyclopaedia Aethiopica,* ed. Siegbert Uhlig. Vol. 4, *O–X,* 267–70. Wiesbaden: Harrassowitz.

Tellez, Balthazar. 1710. *The Travels of the Jesuits in Ethiopia.* London: James Knapton.

Thornton, John Kelly. 1991. "Legitimacy and Political Power: Queen Njinga, 1624–1663." *Journal of African History* 32, no. 1: 25–40.

———. 1998. *The Kongolese Saint Anthony: Dona Beatriz Kimpa Vita and the Antonian Movement, 1684–1706.* Cambridge: Cambridge University Press.

Toubkis, Dimitri. 2014. "Yolyos." *Encyclopaedia Aethiopica,* ed. Siegbert Uhlig. Vol. 5, *Y–Z,* 89–90. Wiesbaden: Harrassowitz.

Tsegay B. Gebrelibanos. 2009. "The Ethiopian Salt Trading System in the Twentieth Century: A View from Mäqäla, Northern Ethiopia." *Proceedings of the Sixteenth International Conference of Ethiopian Studies,* ed. Svein Ege, Harald Aspen, Birhanu Teferra, and Shiferaw Bekele, 185–201. Trondheim, Norway.

Tsegaye Tegenu, Alain Gascon, Sevir Chernetsov, and Denis Nosnitsin. 2003. "Dämbəya." *Encyclopaedia Aethiopica,* ed. Siegbert Uhlig. Vol. 1, *A–C,* 75–76. Wiesbaden: Harrassowitz.

Turaev, Boris. 1902. *Izsledovaniya v oblasti agiologicheskih istochnikov istorii Etiopii* [*Studies in the Hagiographic Sources on the History of Ethiopia*]. Saint Petersburg: N.p.

Uhlig, Siegbert. 2003a. "Abäqte." *Encyclopaedia Aethiopica,* ed. Siegbert Uhlig. Vol. 1, *A–C,* 6–7. Wiesbaden: Harrassowitz.

———. 2003b. "Chronography." *Encyclopaedia Aethiopica,* ed. Siegbert Uhlig. Vol. 1, *A–C,* 733–37. Wiesbaden: Harrassowitz.

———, ed. 2003–14. *Encyclopaedia Aethiopica.* 5 vols. Wiesbaden: Harrassowitz.

———. 2005. "Enoch, Book of." *Encyclopaedia Aethiopica,* ed. Siegbert Uhlig. Vol. 2, *D–Ha,* 311–13. Wiesbaden: Harrassowitz.

van Donzel, Emeri. 2005. "Fasilädäs." *Encyclopaedia Aethiopica,* ed. Siegbert Uhlig. Vol. 2, *D–Ha,* 499–502. Wiesbaden: Harrassowitz.

Wajnberg, Isaak. 1917. *Gadla Jāfqerana ʾEgzīʾ: Das Leben des hl. Jāfqerana ʾEgzīʾ (Aethiop. Text, Übersetzung und Einleitung).* Weimar: Druck der Hof-Buchdruckerei.

Weninger, Stefan. 2011. *Semitic Languages: An International Handbook.* Berlin: De Gruyter Mouton.

Wion, Anaïs. 2005. "Gonǧ Tewodros." *Encyclopaedia Aethiopica,* ed. Siegbert Uhlig. Vol. 2, *D–Ha,* 848. Wiesbaden: Harrassowitz.

———. 2007a. "Mägʷina." *Encyclopaedia Aethiopica,* ed. Siegbert Uhlig. Vol. 3, *He–N,* 644–45. Wiesbaden: Harrassowitz.

———. 2007b. "Marqos III." *Encyclopaedia Aethiopica,* ed. Siegbert Uhlig. Vol. 3, *He–N,* 790–91. Wiesbaden: Harrassowitz.

———. 2012. "Collecting Manuscripts and Scrolls in Ethiopia: The Missions of Johannes Flemming (1905) and Enno Littmann (1906)." *In kaiserlichem Auftrag: Die Deutsche*

Aksum Expedition 1906 unter Enno Littmann, Band 2; Altertumskundliche Untersuchungen der DAE in Tigray/Äthiopien, ed. Steffan Wenig, 353–62. Wiesbaden: Reichert.

———. 2014. "Zäʾiyäsus." *Encyclopaedia Aethiopica*, ed. Siegbert Uhlig. Vol. 5, *Y–Z*, 115–16. Wiesbaden: Harrassowitz.

Wion, Anaïs, and Emmanuel Fritsch. 2005. "Haymanotä Abäw." *Encyclopaedia Aethiopica*, ed. Siegbert Uhlig. Vol. 2, *D–Ha*, 1073–74. Wiesbaden: Harrassowitz.

Witakowski, Witold. 2003. "Basil the Great." *Encyclopaedia Aethiopica*, ed. Siegbert Uhlig. Vol. 1, *A–C*, 496–98. Wiesbaden: Harrassowitz.

Wright, Marta Camilla. 2001. "The Holy Gender: Becoming Male; The Life of Ethiopian Orthodox Nuns." MA thesis, Department of Cultural Studies, University of Oslo, Norway.

———. 2002. "At the Limits of Sexuality: The Femininity of Ethiopian Orthodox Nuns." *Journal of Ethiopian Studies (Addis Ababa)* 35, no. 1: 27–42.

Wright, William. 1877. *Catalogue of the Ethiopic Manuscripts in the British Museum Acquired since the Year 1847*. London: British Museum.

Wudu Tafete Kassu. 2003. "Bihono." *Encyclopaedia Aethiopica*, ed. Siegbert Uhlig. Vol. 1, *A–C*, 583. Wiesbaden: Harrassowitz.

———. 2007a. "Lasta." *Encyclopaedia Aethiopica*, ed. Siegbert Uhlig. Vol. 3, *He–N*, 505–7. Wiesbaden: Harrassowitz.

———. 2007b. "Mälkəʾa Krəstos." *Encyclopaedia Aethiopica*, ed. Siegbert Uhlig. Vol. 3, *He–N*, 705–6. Wiesbaden: Harrassowitz.

Zanetti, Ugo. 2005. "Ǝḫətä Krəstos." *Encyclopaedia Aethiopica*, ed. Siegbert Uhlig. Vol. 2, *D–Ha*, 249–50. Wiesbaden: Harrassowitz.

Zärʾa Yaʿəqob. 2013. *The Homily of Zärʾa Yaʿəqob's Mäṣḥafä Bərhan on the Rite of Baptism and Religious Instruction*. Trans. Getatchew Haile. Corpus Scriptorum Christianorum Orientalium 653, Scriptores Aethiopici 114. Leuven: Peeters.

Zegeye, Desalegn, Berihun Megabiaw, and Abay Mulu. 2009. "Age at Menarche and the Menstrual Pattern of Secondary School Adolescents in Northwest Ethiopia." *BMC Women's Health* 9, no. 1: 29.

Zemede Asfaw. 2007. "Koso." *Encyclopaedia Aethiopica*, ed. Siegbert Uhlig. Vol. 3, *He–N*, 432–33. Wiesbaden: Harrassowitz.

Zitelmann, Thomas. 2003. "d'Abbadie, Antoine and Arnauld d'." *Encyclopaedia Aethiopica*, ed. Siegbert Uhlig. Vol. 1, *A–C*, 25–26. Wiesbaden: Harrassowitz.

INDEX